Principles of Forensic Toxicology

Fourth Edition

Principles of
Forensic Toxicology

Fourth Edition

Edited by
Barry Levine, Ph.D., DABFT, DABCC-T

900 Seventh Street, NW, Suite 400
Washington, DC, 20001

For additional information on this title and others available through AACC, visit the AACC online store:

www.aacc.org/store/books/8200/principles-of-forensic-toxicology-4th-edition

or contact AACC Customer Service
900 Seventh Street, NW, Suite 400
Washington, DC 20001
Phone: 1.800.892.1400 or 1.202.857.0717, option 2
Email: custserv@aacc.org

Fourth printing 2017 PCP

Printed in the United States of America

Library of Congress Cataloging-in-Publication Data

Principles of forensic toxicology / edited by Barry Levine. — Fourth edition.
      p. ; cm.
Includes bibliographical references and index.
ISBN 978-1-59425-158-0
I. Levine, Barry, editor of compilation. II. American Association for Clinical Chemistry, issuing body.
[DNLM: 1. Forensic Toxicology—methods. 2. Postmortem Changes. 3. Substance Abuse Detection—methods. W 750]

RA1228
614'.1—dc23

                                2013015431

Contents

About the Editor   ix

Contributors   ix

Part I. Introduction

1. Postmortem Forensic Toxicology 3
   Barry Levine

2. Human Performance Toxicology 15
   Gary W. Kunsman

3. Forensic Drug Testing 31
   Amanda J. Jenkins

4. Performance-Enhancing Drug Testing 49
   Dennis J. Crouch and Melinda K. Shelby

5. Drug Testing in Pain Management 61
   Anne Z. DePriest

6. Pharmacokinetics and Pharmacodynamics 77
   Vina Spiehler and Barry Levine

Part II. Methodologies

7. Specimen Preparation 97
   Theodore J. Siek

8. Spectrophotometry 111
   Kenneth Cole and Barry Levine

9. Chromatography 121
   David T. Stafford

10. Immunoassay 149
   Michael L. Smith

11. Mass Spectrometry 171
John Cody and Shawn P. Vorce

12. Method Validation 193
Justin M. Holler and Shawn P. Vorce

Part III. Analytes

13. Alcohol. 205
Barry Levine, Yale H. Caplan, and Alan Wayne Jones

14. Benzodiazepines 237
Rebecca A. Jufer-Phipps and Barry Levine

15. Gamma-Hydroxybutyric Acid (GHB) 253
Marc LeBeau

16. Miscellaneous Central Nervous System Depressants 261
Barry Levine

17. Opioids. 271
Sarah Kerrigan and Bruce A. Goldberger

18. Cocaine 293
Daniel S. Isenschmid

19. Cannabis 317
Marilyn A. Huestis

20. Amphetamines/Sympathomimetic Amines. 353
Michele L. Merves and Karla A. Moore

21. Hallucinogens 371
Amanda J. Jenkins

22. Therapeutic Drugs I: Anticonvulsants and Antiarrhythmics 391
Barry Levine

23. Therapeutic Drugs II: Antidepressants 403
William H. Anderson

24. Therapeutic Drugs III: Neuroleptics (Antipsychotics) 421
Claudine Habib, Monica L. Hollowell, and James H. Nichols

25. Therapeutic Drugs IV: Antihistamines 435
Barry Levine

26. Therapeutic Drugs V: Nonnarcotic Analgesics 441
Barry Levine

27. Carbon Monoxide/Cyanide 447
Gary W. Kunsman and Barry Levine

28. Inhalants 461
Larry A. Broussard

29. Metals 471
Joseph J. Saady

Part IV. Special Topics

30. Stability of Drugs of Abuse in Biological Specimens 487
Barry Levine, Daniel S. Isenschmid, and Michael L. Smith

31. Postmortem Redistribution of Drugs 495
Fred S. Apple

32. Postmortem Clinical Testing 501
Barry Levine

33. Pharmacogenomics 507
Thomas Kupiec

34. Hair 515
Michael Schaffer and Virginia Hill

35. Meconium 525
Teresa Gray

Index 533

About the Editor

Barry Levine, Ph.D., is Director, Forensic Toxicology Laboratory, Armed Forces Medical Examiner, in Dover, Delaware. He was Chief Toxicologist, Office of the Chief Medical Examiner, State of Maryland, from 1992 to 2012. He is also Clinical Associate Professor, Department of Pathology in the School of Medicine at the University of Maryland and an Adjunct Professor in the Forensic Sciences Department at Stevenson University. Dr. Levine is a diplomate of the American Board of Forensic Toxicology and the American Board of Clinical Chemistry—Toxicological Chemistry.

Contributors

William H. Anderson, Ph.D.
National Medical Services, Inc.
Willow Grove, Pennsylvania

Fred S. Apple, Ph.D.
Hennepin County Medical Center
Minneapolis, Minnesota

Larry A. Broussard, Ph.D.
Louisiana State University Health Sciences
    Center
New Orleans, Louisiana

Yale H. Caplan, Ph.D.
National Scientific Services, Inc.
Baltimore, Maryland

John Cody, Ph.D.
Deceased

Kenneth Cole, Ph.D.

Dennis J. Crouch, B.S., M.B.A.
Aegis Laboratories
Nashville, Tennessee

Anne Z. DePriest, Pharm.D.
Aegis Laboratories
Nashville, Tennessee

Teresa Gray, Ph.D.
Bureau of Forensic Sciences
Richmond, Virginia

Bruce A. Goldberger, Ph.D.
University of Florida College of Medicine
Gainesville, Florida

Claudine Habib, M.D.
Northern Westchester Hospital
Mount Kisco, New York

Virginia Hill
Psychemedics Corporation
Culver City, California

Justin M. Holler
Office of the Armed Forces Medical
   Examiner
Dover, Delaware

Monica L. Hollowell, M.D.
Boston Children's Hospital
Boston, Massachusetts

Marilyn A. Huestis, Ph.D.
Division of Intramural Research
National Institute on Drug Abuse
Baltimore, Maryland

Daniel S. Isenschmid, Ph.D.
National Medical Services
Willow Grove, Pennsylvania

Amanda J. Jenkins, Ph.D.
University of Massachusetts Memorial
   Medical Center
Worcester, Massachusetts

Alan Wayne Jones, Ph.D.
Linköping University
Faculty of Health Sciences
Sweden

Rebecca A. Jufer-Phipps, Ph.D.
Office of the Chief Medical Examiner
Baltimore, Maryland

Sarah Kerrigan, Ph.D.
Sam Houston State University
Huntsville, Texas

Gary W. Kunsman, Ph.D.
Oakland County Medical Examiner
Pontiac, Michigan

Thomas Kupiec, Ph.D.
Analytical Research Laboratory
Oklahoma City, Oklahoma

Marc Lebeau, Ph.D.
FBI Laboratory
Quantico, Virginia

Barry Levine, Ph.D.
Office of the Armed Forces Medical
   Examiner
Dover, Delaware

Michele L. Merves, Ph.D.
Pinellas County Forensic Laboratory
Largo, Florida

Karla A. Moore, Ph.D.
Deceased

James H. Nichols, Ph.D.
Vanderbilt University Medical Center
Nashville, Tennessee

Joseph J. Saady, Ph.D.
Richmond, Virginia

Michael Schaffer, Ph.D.
Psychemedics Corporation
Culver City, California

Melinda K. Shelby, Ph.D.
Utah Toxicology–Expert Services, LLC
Sandy, Utah

Theodore J. Siek, Ph.D.

Michael L. Smith, Ph.D.
Fort Meade Forensic Drug Testing
   Laboratory
Fort Meade, Maryland

Vina Spiehler, Ph.D.
Spiehler & Associates
Newport Beach, California

David T. Stafford, Ph.D.
Memphis, Tennessee

Shawn P. Vorce
Office of the Armed Forces Medical
   Examiner
Dover, Delaware

PART I

INTRODUCTION

CHAPTER 1

Postmortem Forensic Toxicology

Barry Levine

Forensic toxicology is defined as the application of toxicology for the purposes of the law. Until the middle of the twentieth century, forensic toxicology was practiced almost exclusively as a result of investigating a fatality. Therefore, analyses were performed on specimens from dead individuals.

HISTORY

Although the study of the science of toxic substances and poisons began in the early 1800s, knowledge of poisons and poisonings has existed for thousands of years. Writings from ancient Egypt and Greece report poisonings due to herbs, plants, and food. For instance, the Greeks used hemlock as a means of state-sponsored execution, Socrates being the most famous case. Poisonings by opium, arsenic, and hydrocyanic acid were also reported throughout Europe during the Middle Ages. It was during this period that Philippus Aureolus Theophrastus Bombastus von Hohenheim—or Paracelsus—observed that any substance could be a poison, depending on its dose (Fig. 1).

In 1814, M. J. B. Orfila, the Chairman of the Legal Medicine Department at the Sorbonne in France, made the first attempt to systematically study and categorize poisons. In his book *Traité des Poisons ou Toxicologie Generale*, he established six classes of poisons, basing the six classes mainly on their toxic effects. He also isolated arsenic from a variety of postmortem specimens, and he was the first to state that poisons must be absorbed, or enter the blood, to manifest their toxic effects.

In 1851, Jean Servais Stas developed the first effective method for extracting alkaloids from biological specimens. Specifically, his method detected nicotine in postmortem specimens obtained from Gustave Fougnies, who was allegedly poisoned by his brother-in-law. The extraction procedure used by Stas was modified several years later by F. J. Otto. This method, which enabled the isolation of purer alkaloid substances, became known as the Stas-Otto method and remains the basis for drug extraction to this day.

Forensic toxicology did not develop in the U.S. until the beginning of the twentieth century. Under Charles Morris, New York City replaced its coroner system with a medical examiner system. The Medical Examiner's Office included a toxicology laboratory directed by Alexander Gettler, the first forensic toxicologist in the U.S. Gettler directed the laboratory for 41 years and trained the first generation of forensic toxicologists in the country.

The ubiquitous use of alcohol drove the development of analytical methods to study alcohol's pharmacokinetics. Maurice Nicloux and Erik Widmark performed detailed pharmacokinetic studies on alcohol, developing a formula relating body weight, amount consumed, and blood alcohol concentration. To address the problem of drinking and driving, Rolla Harger developed an instrument, the Drunkometer, which measured alcohol concentration in breath. Then Robert

4 / CHAPTER 1

> "What is there that is not poison?
>
> All things are poison and nothing without poison.
>
> Solely the dose determines that a thing is not a poison."

Fig. 1. Paracelsus's statement about dose in Paracelsus's *Third Defense*.

Borkenstein developed the Breathalyzer®, which became the standard for breath alcohol testing for many years.

TYPES OF POSTMORTEM FORENSIC TOXICOLOGY CASES

The most obvious use for postmortem forensic toxicologic analyses lies in suspected drug intoxication cases, which are not readily diagnosed at autopsy. In intravenous drug deaths, a recent injection site may be observable, and oral intoxications may be inferred from a large amount of unabsorbed tablet fragments in the stomach. However, the only other anatomic findings indicating drug intoxication are pulmonary congestion and edema. In some cases, investigation at the scene may indicate the causative agent or agents. Nevertheless, a toxicology laboratory analysis is needed to identify and quantify the substances present in the biological specimens in order to determine whether these drugs caused or contributed to death.

Toxicologic investigations are also important in deaths other than drug intoxications, such as homicides and accidental deaths. Many medical examiner or coroner's offices routinely perform drug screens on all homicides, for example, for the following reasons:

- many homicides are drug related;
- the abuse of drugs may provide a motive for homicide; and
- an individual under the pharmacologic effects of drugs has a greater chance of committing or falling victim to homicides.

A drug-of-abuse screen can provide information related to solving a particular homicide case. Often, postmortem carbon monoxide analysis can also be relevant, since arson deaths are considered homicides.

In certain accidental deaths, impairment issues may have significant forensic relevance. Comprehensive testing for both therapeutic drugs and drugs of abuse, such as alcohol, is routinely requested in driver motor vehicle fatalities to ascertain the potential role of drugs in the accident.

Toxicologic analyses may even be important in deaths due to natural causes. For instance, deaths from seizures occur with or without anatomic findings. Being able to quantify blood levels of anticonvulsant drugs, for example, would allow the medical examiner to identify whether the deceased had been undermedicated or noncompliant. Conversely, the presence of anticonvulsant drugs in an individual who had no prior seizure history may require investigation. Patient compliance may also be an issue in deaths of individuals being treated for depression or mental illness.

Investigations of natural deaths may require postmortem clinical chemistry assays, and in these assays, vitreous humor is the specimen of choice. Vitreous urea nitrogen values are useful evidence in determining death from dehydration or renal malfunction. Markedly elevated vitreous glucose concentrations would indicate antemortem hyperglycemia.

DEATH INVESTIGATION

There are two main systems of death investigation in the U.S.: the coroner system and the medical examiner system. Regardless of the type of investigation, the types of cases under their jurisdiction are similar.

In general, any unnatural or suspicious death is subject to investigation: deaths involving trauma or violence, deaths that are potential suicides, or deaths that potentially result from criminal activity. Even apparently natural deaths, if occurring suddenly or unexpectedly, fall under the jurisdiction of the medical examiner or coroner.

Specific governmental subdivisions may also define specific circumstances of death that require an investigation. Each coroner or medical examiner has the authority to conduct investigations, perform autopsies, request toxicologic analysis, or employ the services of any other forensic experts deemed necessary to arrive at the final determination of cause and manner of death.

Though both systems handle similar types of cases, there are some significant differences in how the director of each system is chosen, and in which credentials are required in order to be a director. A coroner is elected by the people or appointed by a governmental authority. A medical examiner is appointed usually by the health department. A coroner is not required to have any particular training or experience in medicine, whereas a medical examiner must be a physician, usually a pathologist, with specific training in forensic medicine.

SPECIMEN ACQUISITION

A critical and often overlooked component of the forensic autopsy is the collection of proper specimens for toxicologic analysis. Since it is difficult, if not impossible, to acquire quality specimens after an autopsy has been completed, the pathologist must ensure that all necessary specimens are made available to the toxicologist.

Blood

The single most important specimen to be collected is blood. Blood should be obtained during all inspections and limited or complete autopsies. Ideally, two blood specimens should be collected, one from the heart (50–100 mL) and the other from a peripheral site, such as the femoral or ileac veins. In certain situations, heart blood can be contaminated either by trauma or from the release of drugs

from tissue sites; in these cases, the alternate blood specimen can be used for analysis. If subdural or epidural clots exist, blood from these sites should also be collected. These specimens could be useful when there is some period between an injury and death.

Vitreous Humor

In addition to blood, vitreous humor should be collected in all postmortem cases. Vitreous humor displays good stability and resides in an anatomically isolated area. Therefore it is more resistant to putrefactive changes than are other specimens. As previously stated, postmortem clinical assays can be performed on vitreous humor. Ethanol analysis in vitreous humor can also help in the interpretation of postmortem blood ethanol concentrations.

Urine

All available urine should be collected in all autopsied cases. The utility of urine in postmortem cases is similar to its uses in other types of drug testing. Many drugs and metabolites are present in higher concentration in urine than in blood. Drugs also remain in the urine for days or longer after use. Some color and immunoassay tests can be performed rapidly without pretreating the specimens.

Bile

In the absence of urine, bile from the gallbladder is a useful specimen. Because bile can concentrate certain drugs such as narcotics and benzodiazepines, all available bile should be collected.

Liver

Drug metabolism occurs in the liver, so parent drugs and their metabolites may be present in higher concentrations in the liver than in the blood, thus making detection easier. Many drugs, like the tricyclic antidepressants, are sequestered in the liver. One drawback to using the liver is that drug detection requires treating the specimen first.

Other Specimens

Lung tissue is frequently collected in cases involving the inhalation of volatile substances. Spleen, being a source of red cells, can be used for carbon monoxide analysis when blood is unavailable or unsuitable for analysis. In overdoses, stomach contents can provide easy identification of the ingested substance or substances if tablets are still intact. A large amount of drug would also be present in the stomach contents, thus facilitating analytical identification. Hair can also be used to identify long-term drug use; moreover, metals such as arsenic can be detected in hair.

SPECIMEN RECEIPT AND ACCESSIONING

Once the pathologist or investigator acquires the specimens, they are transported to the laboratory. Specimens should be enumerated. Each should be individually packaged and labeled with the decedent's name and autopsy or case number, and accompanied by the following documentation:

- relevant demographic information about the deceased (age, sex, and race),
- the name and address of the contributor, and
- a brief history of the case.
  - If the cause of death is known, listing this is usually sufficient.
  - If the cause of death is pending, then a brief summary of the known history suffices.
  - List any suspected drug use or involvement; this directs the laboratory regarding any nonroutine testing that may be required.

- Indicate the types of analyses requested by the contributor. Many coroner or medical examiner offices use a standard request form when submitting specimens for toxicologic analysis (Fig. 2). This form may also serve as the external chain-of-custody form.

Specimens received in the laboratory are then accessioned. All specimens should be checked against the request sheet and the contributor notified of any discrepancies. Each case is then assigned a laboratory number and each specimen is labeled with that number. Choice of specimens for analysis should be made on the basis of laboratory policy or case history. All remaining specimens should then be placed in the freezer for storage or future analysis.

ANALYTICAL PROCESS

The analytical process begins after the accessioning process is complete. The process used on postmortem specimens is both similar to and different from the process used to analyze toxicology specimens from living individuals. For example, commercially available immunoassays can be used to screen postmortem urine specimens; occasionally, postmortem urine specimens require centrifugation prior to immunoassay. Tests designed to detect adulteration, such as pH and specific gravity, need not be performed because the specimen is collected directly from the bladder by the pathologist or autopsy assistant during the autopsy.

Part II of this book will deal with the analytical process in more detail, but the following is a brief overview of the process.

Separation

The initial step in the process for postmortem specimens is analyte separation. Except for some drug classes that can be analyzed directly in urine specimens, the analytes of interest usually require separation from the biological matrix. For example, volatile

OFFICE OF THE CHIEF MEDICAL EXAMINER
REQUEST FOR TOXICOLOGIC ANALYSIS

LABORATORY # _____

NAME _____ *DATE OF REQUEST* _____

MEDICAL EXAMINER _____ *DATE OF DEATH* _____

PATHOLOGIST _____ *AUTOPSY #* _____

_____ *CHECK HERE IF DECOMPOSED* *CLASSIFICATION: Natural* _____ *Other* _____

_____ *CHECK HERE IF SUSPECTED BIOHAZARD* *AGE* _____ *RACE* _____ *SEX* _____

_____ *CHECK HERE IF DRUG DEATH AND DEATH CERTIFICATE SIGNED (non-pending)*

Cause of Death: _____

Brief History: _____

Note Any Drugs Suspected: _____

SAMPLES SUBMITTED:

____ *BLOOD (HEART)* ____	____ *SPLEEN* ____
____ *BLOOD (FEMORAL)* ____	____ *LUNG* ____
____ *BLOOD (SUBCLAVIAN)* ____	____ *BRAIN* ____
____ *BLOOD (PERIPHERAL)* ____	____ *SPINAL FLUID* ____
____ *BLOOD* ____ ____	____ *SWABS* *V_A_O_*
____ *URINE* ____	____ *EVIDENCE*
____ *BILE* ____	____ *HOSP SPEC* *A_B_C_*
____ *VITREOUS HUMOR* ____	*D_E_F_*
____ *LIVER* ____	____ ____ ____
____ *KIDNEY* ____	____ ____ ____
____ *STOMACH CONTENTS* ____	____ ____ ____

ANALYSES REQUESTED:

____ *ALCOHOL* _____ *DRUG TESTING*
____ *CARBON MONOXIDE* _____ *ROUTINE*
_____ *RULE OUT TOXICOLOGY - PENDING*
_____ *DRUG DEATH LIKELY - PENDING*

____ *OTHER* _____

FOR LABORATORY USE ONLY

SAMPLE	ALCOHOL, ETHYL	OTHER VOLATILE	
_____	_____ %	_____ %	**Received:**
_____	_____ %	_____ %	**Date**
_____	_____ %	_____ %	**Time**
_____	_____ %	_____ %	**Initials:**
_____	*CARBON MONOXIDE* _____	*% SATURATED*	**Blood Fluoride**
			Tube Prepared:
			Volume:
			Initials:

Reviewed by: _____

Fig. 2. An example of a toxicology request form.

substances can be separated from an aqueous matrix by heating the specimen in a sealed container at 60–80 °C. The gaseous phase above the matrix layer will contain volatile substances that can be sampled and analyzed.

Protein precipitation is another relatively simple separation technique. Inorganic acids such as tungstic acid and trichloroacetic acid may be used to precipitate protein. Alternatively, organic solvents such as methanol or acetonitrile may be used. Color tests and high-performance liquid chromatography (HPLC) may benefit from this separation method.

The most common separation method used in postmortem forensic toxicology is liquid–liquid extraction. Ionization and solubility characteristics of drugs can affect separation of basic, neutral, and acidic drugs. For instance, a basic drug will be nonionized in an alkaline medium; adjusting the matrix pH to alkaline allows basic drugs to leave the matrix and enter an immiscible organic solvent. Similarly, acidic drugs can be extracted after acidifying the biological matrix. This process allows for the removal of contaminating aqueous components and permits easy concentration of the extract by evaporation.

Solid-phase extraction (SPE) is frequently used in the toxicology laboratory. The general process of SPE involves column conditioning, sample application, column washing, and analyte elution. Solid-phase extraction may not always work on postmortem specimens, especially whole blood and tissues, because they often contain clots or particulate matter that prevent the flow of specimens or solvents through the column.

Identification by Spectrophotometry, Chromatography, and Immunoassay

After separation, toxic substances are identified. Identification techniques in forensic toxicology can be grouped into spectrophotometry, chromatography, and immunoassay techniques.

The simplest example of visible spectrophotometry is color tests. Color tests are easy to use and can be done directly on the specimen or on a protein-free filtrate of the specimen. Color tests are commonly used to screen postmortem specimens for salicylate, acetaminophen, cyanide, ethchlorvynol, and trichloroethanol. Ultraviolet spectrophotometry can be used to screen for certain drug classes, such as antidepressants, barbiturates, and benzodiazepines. The drawback

to spectrophotometric methods in general is their lack of sensitivity in detecting therapeutic concentrations of many drugs encountered today. These methods also lack the specificity to distinguish parent drugs and metabolites. This can be critical if metabolites have varying degrees of pharmacologic activity.

Over the past 40 years, gas chromatography (GC) has become a major component of the postmortem toxicology laboratory in the identification and quantification of drugs. Various components of the chromatographic system can be modified to enhance resolution, sensitivity, and specificity. The stationary phase can be changed to improve resolution of a particular group of substances. Conversely, a general phenylmethylsilicone packing material can be used to identify a large group of substances. Temperature programming of the stationary phase permits the identification of substances with differing volatilities within a single chromatographic run. Mobile phase composition and flow rate can be varied to improve resolution, but this does not happen often. Detector selection can assist various analyses. The flame ionization detector, for example, is a general detector for all compounds containing carbon and hydrogen atoms. The addition of a rubidium bead increases sensitivity to nitrogen-containing compounds. Halogenated compounds such as benzodiazepines can be analyzed at very low detection limits with an electron capture detector.

For polar and thermally labile compounds, high-performance liquid chromatography (HPLC) is a preferred chromatographic technique. A variety of stationary phases and detectors exists, and mobile phase composition can be varied, either between runs or within a run. Within-run mobile phase modification is known as gradient elution and is analogous to temperature programming in GC. Currently, ultraviolet detection dominates, but detectors such as fluorescence, electrochemical, and refractive index are also available.

Immunoassays are based on the competition between a labeled drug and the drug or drug class in the specimen for sites on the antibody to that drug or drug class. A separation step may be required prior to measurement. These assays have several advantages over other techniques. They can be performed directly on urine specimens or on blood or tissue specimens after pretreatment, and they have good sensitivity to a particular drug or drug class. A number of commercially available immunoassays, which differ primarily in the type of drug label used, are in use today. Each has distinct advantages that dictate its particular application.

Confirmation

Each identification technique individually can indicate the presence or absence of a particular analyte. However, for a substance to be reported as positive, at least two different analytical techniques must be used.

The use of a second or confirmatory technique is a fundamental principle in forensic toxicology. Numerous combinations of techniques meet this requirement, e.g., a combination of immunoassay and GC, or color test and HPLC. Two different immunoassays would not be acceptable because of antibody similarity among commercially available immunoassays.

More definitive confirmatory techniques provide structural information about the substance itself. Mass spectrometry (MS), in combination with a separation technique such as GC or HPLC, is currently the benchmark confirmatory technique used in the field. For example, a gas chromatographic retention time plus a full-scan electron ionization mass spectrum can be compared to a standard to provide conclusive identification in most but not all circumstances. For drugs present in lower concentrations, selected ion monitoring of three major ions may be sufficient; HPLC-MS, with a number of ionization techniques, is also commonly used. Gas chromatography/infrared detection (GC/IR) can provide conclusive identification in some situations. However, sensitivity limitations prevent large-scale application of this technique.

Quantification

That a substance is present does not necessarily mean that it was a cause of death. For this determination, the substances in the relevant specimens must be quantified.

Quantification of drugs in blood is most commonly associated with toxicity or lethality. In chromatographic methods, the signal generated by the detector will be proportional to the amount of substance present. By preparing calibrators of known concentration, response factors can be calculated to quantify the analyte in the case specimens.

Enhanced quantitative precision can be achieved by using an internal standard, a compound with extraction and chromatographic characteristics similar to the analyte being measured. The same amount of internal standard is added to each calibrator, control, and case specimen, and quantification is based on the area or height ratio of analyte to internal standard.

In certain circumstances, the quantification of drugs in tissue may have particular utility. When blood specimens are unavailable, liver is usually used as a substitute specimen. Moreover, the amount of drug in liver is often helpful in interpreting postmortem tricyclic antidepressant concentrations.

ANALYTES

Ethanol

Ethanol is the most frequently encountered drug in the postmortem forensic toxicology laboratory. Specimens should be analyzed for ethanol in all postmortem cases.

One approach is to initially analyze the heart blood for ethanol. If it is negative, no further analyses are required. If it is above a predetermined cutoff such as 0.01 or 0.02 g/dL, then peripheral blood, vitreous humor, and urine should also be quantified. There are numerous reasons for this approach. In some cases, such as chest trauma, the heart blood can be contaminated, causing a spuriously high concentration of ethanol. An interpretation based on this single analysis would lead to false conclusions, whereas a peripheral blood sample would give a better indication of antemortem ethanol concentration. In head trauma cases, the analysis of subdural blood can indicate blood ethanol concentration at the time of injury, especially if there is a significant period of time between injury and death.

Quantification of ethanol in urine or vitreous humor is useful for several reasons, such as ascertaining the absorptive status of the individual. Postabsorption, the average vitreous humor:blood ethanol concentration ratio is about 1.18. If an individual was still absorbing ethanol at the time of death, then this ratio would be decreased. This is significant if blood ethanol concentration at a prior event is estimated. The average urine:blood ratio in the postabsorptive state is 1.3, but there are wide variations in this ratio. Therefore both specimens should be analyzed if information about absorptive status is required.

Urine and vitreous humor analysis can also help determine whether a measured blood ethanol concentration resulted from antemortem consumption or from postmortem ethanol formation. A variety of microorganisms can produce ethanol as well as acetaldehyde and n-propanol from various sugars or fatty acids, but urine and vitreous humor are resistant to this process. Therefore, a positive blood ethanol concentration in conjunction with a positive vitreous humor and urine ethanol concentration would suggest antemortem ethanol consumption. Conversely, a negative vitreous humor and urine ethanol concentration would indicate postmortem ethanol formation in the blood.

Methods of Ethanol Analysis

Ethanol analysis on postmortem specimens can be conducted by a variety of methods. Nonspecific chemical methods can be used to identify the presence of volatile substances such as alcohols, ketones, or aldehydes. Potassium permanganate or sodium dichromate will oxidize ethanol to acetaldehyde and acetic acid. As this occurs, these oxidizing agents change colors, which can be observed visually or measured spectrophotometrically.

Enzymatic methods use alcohol dehydrogenase, which converts ethanol to acetaldehyde and NAD to NADH. The increase in absorbance at 340 nm is directly proportional to the amount of ethanol in the specimen. This reversible reaction is shifted toward the production of NADH by adding a trapping agent such as hydrazine or semicarbazide, which reacts with acetaldehyde to produce a stable derivative. Although these assays were designed for serum or plasma specimens, their effectiveness in the analysis of postmortem specimens has been demonstrated.

GC is the preferred analytical technique. Specimens can be analyzed directly after dilution with an aqueous internal standard, or by heating the diluted specimen to 60 °C in a sealed container and sampling the vapor. Analysis of this headspace permits quantification without interference from the biological matrix. It has the sensitivity and precision to quantify ethanol concentrations as low as 0.01 g/dL. Multiple volatile compounds, including other alcohols, acetone, or hydrocarbons, can be separated, identified, and quantified by GC.

Interpretation

The interpretation of blood ethanol concentrations in postmortem specimens, provided that no postmortem ethanol formation occurred, is similar to the interpretation of blood specimens from living individuals. All individuals with a blood alcohol concentration above 0.07 g/dL would be expected to show some impairment due to ethanol. This impairment would manifest itself in reductions in judgment, attention, and abilities in multi-tasking events. As the blood ethanol concentration increases, more overt symptoms of alcohol impairment would be observable. In the absence of other pathological findings, a blood ethanol concentration at or above 0.40 g/dL can be consistent with causing death due to ethanol intoxication.

More details on ethanol will be provided in Chapter 13.

Carbon Monoxide

Carbon monoxide (CO) is produced by the incomplete combustion of organic material. CO is the causative agent in many fire deaths. In general, fire deaths can be explained by thermal injuries, smoke and soot inhalation, or a combination of the two. CO binds with great affinity to hemoglobin (Hb), forming carboxyhemoglobin (COHb) and reducing the blood's oxygen-carrying capabilities. The unit of measurement of CO is "percent saturation" (% sat) and is defined as the percent of total Hb that is COHb.

Methods

CO may be measured in several ways. For instance, CO may be measured directly through microdiffusion or by GC. A microdiffusion screening test uses a Conway cell. The outer well contains the specimen and an agent that releases the CO from Hb. The released CO reduces the palladium chloride in the center well to metallic palladium, producing a black film. Chromatographic methods also require the release of CO from Hb, usually by the addition of potassium ferricyanide to the blood in a sealed container. The released CO can be passed through a molecular sieve gas chromatographic column and measured directly with a thermal conductivity detector or after catalytic reduction to methane using a flame ionization detector. The % sat is obtained either by measuring Hb to correct for the Hb content of the specimen or by analyzing a second aliquot of specimen after saturating with CO. This latter method removes the need to measure Hb because % sat is calculated by dividing the area of the CO peak in the untreated sample by the area generated from the saturated sample and then multiplying by 100.

CO content in a blood specimen can also be measured directly as COHb by spectrophotometry. These methods are based on the difference in absorption spectra between various forms of Hb, and a large number have been published. Certain automated systems can simultaneously measure these Hb species by measuring absorbances at wavelengths where these spectra intersect.

The analysis of postmortem specimens for CO creates numerous problems not encountered in the analysis of clinical specimens. Methemoglobin (MetHb), a form of Hb where the iron is in the $+3$ valence state, can adversely affect spectrophotometric methods. Treating the blood with sodium hydrosulfite reduces MetHb to Hb but does not affect COHb. Therefore all postmortem specimens should be treated prior to spectrophotometric analysis. If blood is unavailable for analysis, a tissue fluid may have sufficient Hb to permit CO quantification; otherwise, spleen is an acceptable specimen.

Interpretation

The interpretation of COHb levels is relatively straightforward. In general, values less than 10% are considered normal and are not associated with significant smoke inhalation. Smokers generally have higher basal CO levels than do nonsmokers. This implies that any fire death with normal % sat occurred prior to or shortly after the start of the fire, assuming that no medical treatment had ensued. Saturation values greater than 50% are consistent with death resulting from smoke and soot inhalation. Lower lethal concentrations can be observed in individuals with anemia or with compromised respiratory systems. Unlike other deaths from gaseous substances, CO can be detected in decomposed bodies because it is bound to Hb.

More details on carbon monoxide will be provided in Chapter 27.

Drugs

The most involved aspect of postmortem forensic toxicology is the analysis of drugs. One difference between the postmortem laboratory and other forensic toxicology laboratories is that postmortem laboratories must have methodologies for therapeutic and abused drugs. Thus, methods should be established for identification, confirmation, and quantification of both types of drugs.

The most common approach is to develop a protocol or a battery of tests to comprehensively screen for drugs. A negative screening test requires no additional analytical work. Once tentative identification of a drug or drugs has occurred, more specialized testing can be performed for confirmation and quantification. No single analytical method is appropriate for all drugs; rather, a combination of methods provides a wide range of testing.

Fig. 3 illustrates one comprehensive approach. Color tests are simple assays that can be done quickly to screen for certain drugs; several color tests can be included in a comprehensive approach. An alkaline extraction followed by GC with nitrogen-phosphorus detection and temperature programming can identify drugs within the following classes: antiarrhythmics, antidepressants, antihistamines, benzodiazepines, narcotics, neuroleptics, and sympathomimetic amines.

Not all drugs within a class can be detected in appropriate concentrations, and the toxicologist must know which drugs will be identified and at which detection limits. A weak acid extraction followed by GC or HPLC can identify acid and neutral drugs such as barbiturates, anticonvulsants, and glutethimide. A variety of commercially available immunoassays can identify amphetamines, barbiturates, benzodiazepines, cannabinoids, cocaine, opiates, and phencyclidine.

The interpretation of drug results can be easy or difficult. The presence of drugs or metabolites in bile or urine will indicate exposure, but assessment of toxicity is usually impossible.

Quantification of drugs in blood, on the other hand, is better correlated with toxicity or fatality, and must be correlated in light of available history. A high concentration of a drug or a group of drugs in the blood of an individual with suicidal ideation, a suicide note, and no anatomic cause of death at autopsy is consistent with a suicidal drug or multiple drug intoxication. The ratio of parent-to-metabolite concentrations may indicate an acute death. A therapeutic postmortem blood concentration in an individual treated in the hospital for several days may indicate much higher concentrations at an earlier time. Often, hospital laboratories perform drug testing on urine specimens without associated blood quantifications. The postmortem

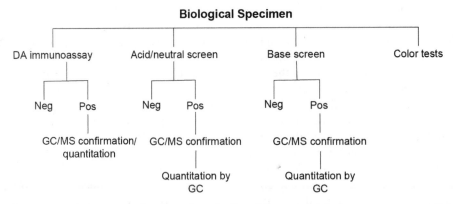

Fig. 3. One approach to comprehensive drug testing. DA = abused drugs; neg = negative; pos = positive; GC/MS = gas chromatography/mass spectrometry; GC = gas chromatography.

laboratory should obtain hospital blood specimens so that toxicity can be assessed. Of course, the clinical picture as documented by the hospital is extremely critical to this overall assessment.

A series of drugs, each present in therapeutic concentrations, may have synergistic effects when present in combination. These synergistic effects may be additive or potentiating, where the overall effect is greater than the sum of the individual effects. For instance, a combination of ethanol and other central nervous system depressants can have potentiating effects and cause death.

A drug need not be present in toxic amounts to play a role in an individual's death. Therapeutic drug use may reduce judgment or performance, leading to an accident. Moreover, certain behavior may be altered by a drug, leading an individual to become a victim of violent activity.

One point that must be emphasized is that a laboratory's routine testing procedures are established to identify a large cross section of therapeutic and abused drugs. Each laboratory must determine the type of testing offered based on available resources. Not every drug available can be detected in a routine testing protocol; even within a drug class, some drugs may be identified and others not. It is crucial for the laboratory director to understand the capabilities of the laboratory's routine testing procedures. These facts reinforce the need for drug history when a case is submitted. If the suspected agent is not identified routinely, then special testing can be done. Alternatively, a specimen can be sent to a reference laboratory for testing.

One complication in the interpretation of postmortem blood drug concentration is whether the measured drug concentration accurately reflects the concentration at death. Some drugs have been shown to redistribute after death, especially those with high volumes of distribution. For instance, tricyclic antidepressants may redistribute into the heart blood from the liver, producing an artificially high blood concentration.

Measurement of these drugs in peripheral blood or tissues can minimize the possibility of misinterpreting results.

It is also possible that drug concentrations decrease during the postmortem interval. Cocaine in blood is hydrolyzed in vitro to ecgonine methyl ester, especially at room temperature and at alkaline pH. The presence of a cholinesterase inhibitor and storage of blood at reduced temperature can reduce this loss once the specimen is collected.

REPORTING

After the analytical work is completed, all data should be submitted for review by the laboratory director or an appropriate designee. This review should include all aspects of the administrative and analytical processes. The results should also be reviewed in the context of the case. Consultation with the pathologist or medical examiner may clarify any unresolved issues. Once this review has been completed, a final report is generated and signed by the laboratory director. This report is then sent to the case contributor for final disposition.

SUGGESTED READING

1. Baselt RC, ed. Analytical procedures for therapeutic drug monitoring and emergency toxicology, 2nd ed. Littleton, MA: PSG Publishing Co., 1987.
2. Baselt RC, ed. Disposition of toxic drugs and chemicals in man, 9th ed. Seal Beach, CA: Biomedical Publications, 2011.
3. Ellenhorn MJ, Schonwald S, Ordog G, Wasserberger J, eds. Ellenhorn's medical toxicology—diagnosis and treatment of human poisoning. Baltimore, MD: Williams and Wilkins Publishing Co., 1997.
4. Garriott J, ed. Medicolegal aspects of alcohol, 5th ed. Tucson, AZ: Lawyers and Judges Publishing, Inc., 2008.
5. Gough T, ed. The analysis of drugs of abuse. Chichester, England: John Wiley & Sons, Ltd., 1991.
6. Moffat AC, Osselton MD, Widdop B, eds. Clarke's analysis of drugs and poisons. London, England: Pharmaceutical Press, 2004.

CHAPTER 2

Human Performance Toxicology

Gary W. Kunsman

The evaluation of human performance, often termed psychomotor performance, is a daily occurrence for most people. Whether the ability to perform routine yet complex psychomotor tasks is determined on the highway or in the workplace, such monitoring occurs frequently. Inability to perform may affect the safety of other persons and have economic and legal implications. Many factors may affect an individual's ability to perform routine tasks such as operating machinery or driving a car, but psychoactive drugs, including alcohol (ethanol), are frequently implicated.

DEFINITION

Human performance toxicology, also referred to as behavioral toxicology, relies on the behavioral toxicologist to elucidate and quantify the dose–effect relationship between drugs that elicit behavioral changes and those changes.

The field of behavioral toxicology combines aspects of psychology, toxicology, and pharmacology. Modern psychology is not a study of the mind, as the term suggests (a combination of the Greek terms *psyche* for mind and *logos* for subject of discourse), but is more accurately defined as the study of behavior. Behavior encompasses the manner of one's conduct and one's response to environmental stimuli; the study of behavior is a science that deals with human action and seeks generalizations of human behavior in society. Performance is defined as the execution of an action, the manner of reacting to stimuli, and the carrying out of an action or behavior. It involves the effective use of higher brain centers in the coordination and control of motor functions resulting in movements appropriate to a given stimulus. Human performance toxicology or behavioral toxicology, then, is the study of the human response to environmental conditions and stimuli under the influence of drugs.

This field of study was originally the realm of psychologists. They were interested in learning how people learn, and they applied both respondent conditioning (classical or Pavlovian) and operant conditioning (Skinner) in an effort to understand the learning process. An offshoot of this research attempted to elucidate the neurochemical basis for responding to external stimuli. Over time, this research led to establishing fields of study such as skills acquisition, human engineering, and motor performance testing, the area of psychology that has most significantly affected human performance toxicology.

Forensic toxicologists have become interested in human performance toxicology because it is a natural extension of their interest in the medicolegal implications of drug use, misuse, and abuse. The effects of drugs on skills acquisition, learning, and performance have broad social and economic implications both on the road and in the workplace. The behavioral toxicologist uses "real life" tests and laboratory-based psychomotor tests to monitor the behavioral effects of drugs.

It is important to note that drugs may alter normal behavior by either enhancing or impairing performance. In behavioral toxicology, the impairing effects of drugs are typically of more interest. In fact, those drugs, such as stimulants, that enhance performance in the short term often impair performance when they are used chronically over an extended period. Therefore, behavioral toxicologists generally speak only of performance decrements when they refer to the behavioral effects of drugs.

APPLICATION

Although it is common to think that forensic toxicology in general and human performance toxicology in particular are interested only in the use of illicit drugs, e.g., heroin, marijuana, and others, therapeutic drugs such as antidepressants and muscle relaxants also have significant behavioral effects. The behavioral toxicologist must focus on both licit and illicit drugs and must evaluate the effects of therapeutic drugs when administered in the prescribed manner for their normal medical applications, as well as when they are incorrectly administered or abused.

A classic example of this type of problem is the study of the benzodiazepines. When these drugs are used appropriately as anxiolytics, they may improve driving behavior. However, they are often used in higher doses and for a longer period of time than prescribed or recommended, or in conjunction with popular drugs of abuse, or to supplement methadone maintenance by heroin addicts. In such cases these drugs may adversely affect driving behavior.

When evaluating the behavioral effects of a drug, it is also important to consider the metabolic profile of that drug. The presence of active metabolites is certainly important in evaluating the behavioral effects of drugs, because they contribute to the parent drug's effect. The presence of inactive metabolites, although exerting no behavioral effects themselves, may provide some information about the approximate time that a drug was used.

The specimen most commonly used for establishing dose and concentration/effect relationships is blood. Because blood is most intimately in contact with the central nervous system (CNS), it provides the best information concerning how a drug, its active metabolites, and their concentrations are related to performance impairment. Alternate specimens such as urine, sweat, and hair are becoming increasingly popular, but it is unlikely that a direct behavioral/concentration relationship can be established using these specimens.

ALCOHOL AND DRIVING

The most commonly studied drug with performance-impairing effects is alcohol, and the most frequently studied task is driving. (Even studies that examine the impairing effects of other drugs typically use alcohol as a standard of comparison.) Perhaps this is so because drinking alcohol and driving is such a common occurrence and has such profound social and economic implications. Epidemiological studies have shown that 40–60% of all fatally injured drivers have a blood alcohol concentration (BAC) $\geq$0.10 g/dL, and 30–40% of those have a BAC >0.15 g/dL. The central issue in the history of the relationship between drinking and driving has been to establish a causal link between alcohol use and driving impairment and automobile accidents, and to use this information to effect societal change.

History

The impairing effects of alcohol have been well known and well documented throughout recorded history. Although its impairing effects have always had significant societal consequences, these consequences probably have even greater significance and cost in our industrial and mechanized society.

The invention of the steam locomotive and the advent of railway transportation in the mid-1800s brought to light the adverse consequences of combining high-speed travel with alcohol. By 1843, the New York Central Railroad prohibited employees from drinking while on duty. Along with the invention of the automobile and its rapid growth in popularity as a means of personal transportation came the problem of drinking and driving. An editorial as early as 1904 made the correlation between drinking before driving and automobile accidents. In 1910, the New York City traffic code noted that the misuse of alcohol was a factor in traffic safety. Even Henry Ford commented that the use of alcohol was incompatible with the speed at which Americans operated their automobiles, their machinery, and their lives in general.

The growth of industry in the U.S. in the early twentieth century was accompanied by an ever-increasing awareness of safety issues, not only in factories but also on the roads and in the home. The safety movement gained impetus in 1912 with the formation of the National Council for Industrial Safety, which became the National Safety Council in 1914. By 1924, the National Safety Council had expanded its interests to include highway safety, and therefore, by implication, the effects of alcohol on driving. The work of this organization has been continued and expanded by the National Highway Traffic Safety Administration (NHTSA).

Despite the awareness of the behavioral effects of alcohol throughout history, scientific documentation and evaluation of these effects did not begin until the early 1900s. Erik Widmark, from the University of Lund in Sweden, was among the first to quantify the amount of alcohol in various body fluids and correlate those concentrations to measures of impairment, and then apply that information to traffic safety issues. By the early 1920s, Widmark had developed a protocol for physicians to follow when evaluating drivers suspected of driving under the influence (DUI) of alcohol. This protocol consisted of behavioral and physiological measures including pupillary reaction to light, signs of ataxia, the Romberg test, finger-to-finger test, odor of alcohol on the breath, and general appearance. The evaluation concluded with drawing blood to analyze for the presence of alcohol.

In the U.S., Herman Heise spurred the interest in alcohol and traffic safety in the early 1930s. From 1935 to 1938, the Evanston study reported on 270 drivers hospitalized after involvement in automobile accidents in Evanston, Illinois. During the same period, the police tested a sample of 1750 drivers for BAC. The Drunkometer, invented by Rolla Harger of Indiana University, was used to evaluate BAC in these drivers by measuring alcohol in the breath. The recent invention of this breath-testing device allowed researchers to overcome the legal and logistical problems associated with collecting blood or urine from these randomly stopped drivers. Richard Holcomb of the Northwestern University Traffic Institute reported the results of this study in 1938. Holcomb found that the chances of having an accident increased geometrically with the presence of any alcohol in the blood to the extent that each 0.02 g/dL rise in BAC doubled the risk of accident.

The first legislation making DUI an offense in the U.S. was passed in Indiana in March 1939 and in Maine in April 1939. These statutes established a three-level offense based on BAC. A BAC of ≤0.05 g/dL was considered presumptive evidence of no guilt; >0.15 g/dL was considered presumptive evidence of guilt; and a BAC between these two concentrations was considered supportive evidence of DUI. This legislation was based on the joint statement issued in 1938 by the Committee to Study Problems of Motor Vehicle Accidents (a special committee of the American Medical Association) and the Committee on Alcohol and Other Drugs (a committee of the National Safety Council). The Committee on Alcohol and Other Drugs (its name later changed to the Committee on Alcohol and Drugs) has remained active in this area since its formation in 1936. The committee makes recommendations toward controlling the problem of drinking and driving, including legislative matters, law enforcement issues, education, chemical testing methods and equipment, and training of personnel. The recommendations of the two committees also formed the basis for the Chemical Tests Section of the Uniform Vehicle Code published by the National Committee on Uniform Traffic Laws and Ordinances in 1946. In 1953, Implied Consent legislation was passed in New York State and was soon included in the Uniform Vehicle Code; implied consent laws have been passed in all 50 states. The implied consent legislation provides that, as a condition precedent to being issued a driver's license, an applicant agrees, by implication, to submit to a chemical test in any case in which he is suspected of DUI. Refusal to submit to the test results in the loss of driving privileges.

In 1958, the Symposium on Alcohol and Road Traffic at Indiana University issued a statement that a BAC of 0.05 g/dL definitely impairs the driving ability of some individuals. As the BAC increases, an increasing proportion of individuals experience impairment, until the BAC reaches 0.10 g/dL, at which point all individuals are definitely impaired. In 1960, the Committee on Alcohol and Drugs released a statement recommending that DUI laws be amended to reflect a 0.10 g/dL BAC as presumptive evidence of guilt. The Uniform Vehicle Code was amended to reflect this recommendation in 1962.

Another study conducted by Indiana University, the Grand Rapids Study, was published in 1964. This study essentially confirmed the results of the Evanston study and also stated that drivers with BAC >0.04 g/dL tend to have more single-vehicle accidents and also more severe accidents than do sober drivers. The study reviewed data collected from drivers stopped at four different locations as well as drivers involved in accidents at those sites. All individuals were interviewed and submitted breath specimens, which were later analyzed using the Breathalyzer®, a breath-testing device developed by Robert Borkenstein of Indiana University in 1954. This study also found that accident-related factors other than alcohol decreased in significance when the driver's BAC was >0.08 g/dL (i.e., at a BAC >0.08 g/dL, alcohol was the most significant risk factor in having an accident) and that accident involvement increased rapidly when the driver's BAC was >0.05 g/dL. The researchers found no evidence that a BAC of 0.01–0.04 g/dL was associated with an elevated risk of accident. Drivers with BAC 0.04–0.08 g/dL had a greater risk of accident, but alcohol was not necessarily more significant than other risk factors. In terms of the relative probability of having an accident, the following statistics were generated:

- Drivers with a BAC of 0.04 g/dL were just as likely to have an accident as sober drivers.
- Drivers with a BAC of 0.06 g/dL were twice as likely as sober drivers to cause an accident.
- Drivers with a BAC of 0.10 g/dL were more than six times as likely as sober drivers to cause an accident.
- Drivers with a BAC of 0.15 g/dL were more than 25 times as likely as sober drivers to cause an accident.

Federal intervention in the drinking and driving problem began in earnest in 1966 with the passage of the National Highway Safety Act. This act required that a report be submitted to Congress detailing how the problem of the drunken driver was being addressed. This report was submitted in 1968 by the NHTSA, a division of the Department of Transportation. Since its inception, the NHTSA has relied heavily on the recommendations of the Committee on Alcohol and Drugs and has enforced its recommendations, proposals, and legislative initiatives in individual states by withholding federal highway funds when states were not in compliance. In 1971, the Committee released a resolution regarding alcohol impairment in which they stated that any individual, regardless of previous experience with alcohol, has impaired driving performance with a BAC ≥0.08 g/dL. During the past four decades, regulations and legislation concerning the drinking and driving problem have continued to proliferate. Although (for most of this time) the legal limit for driving while impaired has remained at 0.10 g/dL BAC, efforts to enforce these DUI laws have been expanded. In recent years, all jurisdictions have lowered this limit to 0.08 g/dL, with some setting even lower limits for individuals younger than the legal drinking age. Law enforcement agencies continue their effort to reduce the number of impaired drivers through increased intervention and education. In the past few decades, laboratory researchers, law enforcement, governmental agencies, and the courts have combined their efforts to address this issue. It is through these efforts that the Standardized Field Sobriety Test and the Drug Evaluation and Classification program have arisen.

Since the 1970s, the NHTSA and/or the Insurance Institute for Highway Safety have conducted four national surveys of drinking and driving in the U.S. The latest of these surveys was conducted in 2007. Data was collected during a two-hour daytime period on a Friday and at four different two-hour evening sessions: from 10:00 p.m. to midnight and 1:00 a.m. to 3:00 a.m. on Friday and Saturday nights. In this study, 2.2% of the drivers on weekend nights had a BAC ≥0.08 g/dL. This represented a significant decline in the number of "legally impaired" drivers from the 1973 study in which 7.5% of the drivers had a BAC ≥0.08 g/dL. A similar decline was observed throughout the range of positive BACs. As expected, the percentage of daytime drivers with a BAC ≥0.08 g/dL was much lower than the nighttime drivers. The percentages with a BAC ≥0.08 g/dL of day, night, and early morning drivers were 0.2%, 1.2%, and 4.8%, respectively.

Standardized Field Sobriety Tests

As police officers patrol traffic, they often encounter impaired drivers. This encounter initiates a three-phase process. Because this process culminates in the officer's decision to either arrest or release the driver, it is called the DUI arrest decision process. The officer proceeds through the three phases collecting information to determine whether the driver is truly impaired and the cause of that impairment:

1. Phase one is the initial observation of the vehicle in motion and how the driver stops the vehicle. The officer first notes poor driving performance such as weaving within a lane, unsignaled lane changes, rapid changes in speed, and other behaviors consistent with impaired driving. The officer gains additional information about the driver's level of impairment by observing how long it takes for the driver to respond to the officer's signal to stop and how the driver stops the vehicle.

2. Phase two of the arrest decision involves the officer's first direct contact with the driver. At this time the officer interviews the driver, who remains in the car, and evaluates the driver's physical appearance and condition. Officers are trained to notice breath odor, eye condition, demeanor, face color, dexterity, speech, and clothing appearance. If the officer's observations warrant it, the driver is asked to step from the car, providing another observation period. For example, if the driver needs help exiting the vehicle or staggers and stumbles when doing so, this further indicates the driver's level of impairment.

3. Phase three begins after the driver has exited the vehicle. At this time the officer administers several psychomotor tests and a preliminary breath test. By this point the officer should have enough information to make a decision about arresting or releasing the driver. If the driver is arrested, an evidential breath test is obtained or specimens (blood and/or urine) are collected for laboratory analysis.

Standardized field sobriety tests were developed in the 1970s with funding by NHTSA. Several tests have been used over the years by officers in various jurisdictions, and three of these psychomotor tests were chosen for general use to provide an objective measure of impairment. Testing and scoring were standardized through laboratory studies and have been subsequently validated in field studies. The three tests that constitute the standardized field sobriety test are the one-leg stand (OLS), the walk and turn (WAT), and horizontal gaze nystagmus (HGN). Their predictive ability to measure impairment at 0.10 g/dL BAC or 0.10 g/210 L of breath is 68% for the WAT (i.e., 68% of those judged impaired as measured by the WAT have a ≥0.10 g/dL BAC), 65% for the OLS, and 77% for the HGN. When the three tests are used in combination, predictive ability increases to 83.3%.

The WAT test is a divided-attention task in two stages: instruction and walking. The officer gives the suspect instructions while requiring him to place one foot in front of the other on a line and maintain his balance throughout the instructions. The suspect must take nine heel-to-toe steps along a straight line, make a six-step turning motion, and then take nine more heel-to-toe steps along the same line. Impairment is measured (scored) by the number of observed clues, i.e., the failure to perform a certain aspect of the task. The WAT includes nine clues:

- Cannot balance during instructions
- Starts before instructions are completed
- Stops while walking
- Does not touch heel to toe
- Steps off the line
- Uses arms to balance
- Loses balance on turns or turns incorrectly
- Takes incorrect number of steps
- Cannot do test (steps off the line three or more times)

If the suspect scores two or more points (clues) on this test or is unable to complete the test, there is a 68% probability that the suspect's BAC is ≥0.10 g/dL (g/210 L).

The OLS is also a divided-attention task in two stages—instruction, and balancing and counting. The officer gives the suspect instructions while requiring him to keep both heels together and his arms down at his side. After the instructions, the suspect is required to raise one leg approximately six inches off the ground and count rapidly from 1001 to 1030. The OLS has five clues that indicate impairment:

- Sways while balancing
- Uses arms to balance
- Hops
- Puts foot down
- Cannot do test (puts foot down three or more times)

If the suspect scores two or more points on this test or is unable to complete the test, there is a 65% predictability that the suspect's BAC is ≥0.10 g/dL (g/210 L). For both the WAT and the OLS, test results may not be valid for individuals over the age of 60 or who are more than 50 pounds overweight; nor may it be valid for individuals who wear high heels or have leg injuries or inner ear disorders.

The HGN test measures CNS motor pathways. Nystagmus is the involuntary jerking of the eyes, and horizontal nystagmus occurs as the eyes gaze toward the side. Nystagmus is a normal phenomenon that is not caused but is enhanced by alcohol. HGN is the most sensitive test in the battery. In this test, the subject is told to keep his head still and follow the stimulus that the officer presents. The stimulus is usually a pen or pencil that the officer holds in front of the subject and moves slowly from a position directly in front of the subject to either the left or right. The officer observes the suspect's eyes for smooth tracking and the onset of nystagmus. Studies have shown that the earlier that nystagmus occurs (the shorter the angle from directly in front of the subject), the greater the BAC. In fact, BAC and the angle of onset of nystagmus seem to have a dose–response relationship. The HGN test offers six clues (three per eye):

- Loss of smooth pursuit (suspect cannot follow a slowly moving object smoothly)
- Pronounced nystagmus at maximum deviation
- Onset of nystagmus before 45°

If the suspect scores four or more points on this test, there is a 77% predictability that the suspect's BAC is ≥0.10 g/dL (g/210 L). The test results may not be valid for individuals with brain tumors, some types of brain disease, or inner ear disorders.

Behavioral Effects of Alcohol

Alcohol exerts a wide variety of behavioral effects, as documented in numerous studies. Alcohol use decreases visual acuity and peripheral vision, and these effects increase significantly as the BAC rises above 0.07 g/dL. A decreased sensitivity to taste and smell at low alcohol doses has also been noted. Individuals under the influence of alcohol also exhibit an altered time sense, typically a slowed sense of the passage of time. With alcohol concentrations of 0.08 g/dL, sensitivity to pain decreases. Choice reaction time is impaired at 0.05 g/dL as measured by an increased latency to respond to the stimulus and a decrease in accuracy. Some studies have noted hand-eye coordination deficits at 0.05 g/dL and impairment in vigilance tasks at 0.06 g/dL, probably as a reflection of drowsiness. Body sway, as measured by the Romberg test and a device called the wobble board, was above normal at 0.05 g/dL; sway degrades to staggering and reeling with increasing BAC. Most tests of driving skill both on the road and in simulators show impairment at 0.05 g/dL. Numerous epidemiological studies also confirm the adverse effects of alcohol on driving performance.

Although individuals may respond differently to different doses of alcohol, behavioral effects tend to fall within BAC ranges. When the blood alcohol reaches 0.05 g/dL, individuals tend to exhibit an increased talkativeness, mild excitement, and a higher-pitched voice. As BAC reaches 0.10–0.15 g/dL, individuals become more talkative, cheerful, loud, boisterous, and then sleepy. When BAC exceeds 0.15 g/dL, the individual experiences nausea, and vomiting may occur, followed by lethargy and then stupor. Subjective tests indicate that as BAC increases, individuals report elation, friendliness, and vigor. As BAC decreases, these same individuals report anger, depression, and fatigue. Behavioral tolerance develops with repeated alcohol use. Those tasks learned under the influence of alcohol are often performed better when repeated at that blood concentration than when no alcohol is present. In general, the more complex the task, the more significant is the impairment at lower BACs. It is important to note, however, that between-study and between-subject variability is large, especially at concentrations below 0.08 g/dL.

Often the results of studies refer only to some of the subjects tested, and the results generally indicate population tendencies and not absolute measures of behavioral effects.

Even at low concentrations, alcohol disrupts performance and can interfere with complex activities such as driving. Alcohol generally causes feelings of happiness and reduces the ability of aversive events to control behavior. Higher doses cause loud, vigorous behavior, and even higher doses cause loss of consciousness and finally death. The effects are generally more pronounced and pleasurable while BAC is rising than when it is falling. Many of the effects of alcohol show tolerance that is a result of both increased metabolism and increased experience.

Specimens

The specimen of choice in DUI alcohol cases is breath. Several devices are available for measuring the amount of alcohol in breath, and they use a number of different analytical methodologies. Law enforcement agents prefer breath as a specimen because its collection is a noninvasive procedure and collection and analysis are typically performed together. Blood specimens, in contrast, must be drawn by a trained healthcare professional, and urine must be obtained under controlled conditions and under direct observation. These specimens must also be forwarded under chain of custody to a laboratory for analysis, and the turn-around time for these analyses may be quite lengthy. Numerous studies have shown that a properly collected breath sample accurately reflects BAC at the time of its collection. Breath samples, therefore, can provide a measure of impairment because the alcohol measured in breath is directly proportional to BAC.

Several key factors in breath alcohol analysis must be considered. The most important is that end-expiratory breath is the only acceptable breath sample. Only the terminal portion of the expired breath is in equilibrium with the arterial blood and therefore reflects BAC. The presence of residual alcohol in the mouth arising from recent ingestion of alcohol, regurgitation of gastric contents, or belching can cause an artificially high alcohol reading on breath-testing devices. Many breath-testing devices report an error when mouth alcohol is detected, thereby negating the breath test. In an effort to avoid contamination by mouth alcohol, a minimum 15-minute waiting period and rinsing the mouth with water before testing are recommended. When alcohol is present in the breath, it is generally the dominant exogenous species present and its concentration is greater than that of any other organic volatile that may be present. Therefore, no other species such as acetone or isopropanol will interfere with alcohol analysis.

DRUGS AND DRIVING

Throughout this century numerous studies have established the correlation between BAC and behavior. At a given BAC, certain behaviors or a range of behavior can be expected without directly observing supporting evidence of impairment in an individual. These studies have permitted legislative bodies and regulatory agencies to enact laws and regulations prohibiting individuals from performing certain activities at or above a specified BAC (e.g., DUI/DWI laws). Unfortunately, this is not the case with other drugs of abuse.

Drug Evaluation and Classification Program*

The need to recognize the role of drugs of abuse in the impaired driver led to the formation of the Drug Evaluation and Classification (DEC) program. The Los Angeles Police Department pioneered the drug recognition procedure to provide a mechanism for obtaining compelling evidence that a driver was impaired at the time s/he was stopped by the police. The DEC program was vali-

*Portions of these sections are adapted from the suggested readings and from Kunsman et al. Phencyclidine blood concentrations in DRE cases. J Anal Toxicol 1997;21:498–502.

dated in 1984 at Johns Hopkins University in a controlled laboratory evaluation jointly sponsored by the NHTSA and the National Institute on Drug Abuse (NIDA), and in a 1985 NHTSA-sponsored field validation study. Using these studies, NHTSA developed a standardized curriculum for training police officers as Drug Recognition Experts (DREs). In 1987, several pilot programs were initiated using this curriculum. Since that time the number of DEC programs has continued to grow and DRE training is available nationwide under the auspices of NHTSA.

The DEC program is based on a cooperative effort between three disciplines: law enforcement, in the person of the DRE who documents impairment; toxicology, in the person of the toxicologist who provides analytical support and expert opinion concerning the effects of drugs on human performance; and prosecution. In the initial step in this program, the DRE administers a series of physiological and psychomotor tests. The DRE's observations are the basis of an opinion concerning impairment resulting from the use of one or more drugs from within seven drug categories: CNS depressants, CNS stimulants, hallucinogens, phencyclidine (PCP), narcotic analgesics, inhalants, and cannabis.

The DEC program uses a standardized, systematic method of examining a person suspected of impaired driving to determine whether the suspect is impaired, whether the impairment is due to drug use or is medically related, and what broad category of drugs might cause the impairment. Blood or urine specimens are collected to corroborate the DRE's opinion. The toxicological analysis provides the scientific and objective support for the subjective report of drug-associated impairment.

Properly trained DREs can correctly predict the presence of certain drug categories in the majority of impaired driving cases. However, the DEC process is not a field test; it is a post-arrest investigative procedure that should be administered in a controlled environment, not at the roadside. Moreover, the DEC program does not determine exactly which drugs are present, but instead narrows the possibilities to broad categories of drugs. The DEC process is thus not a substitute for chemical tests; specimens must be collected for toxicological examination to provide objective support for the subjective opinion of the DRE.

Drug Recognition Evaluation*

The DRE's evaluation has 12 components:

1. *Breath alcohol test.* The breath alcohol test is used to determine if the observed impairment is a result of alcohol consumption and if the degree of impairment is consistent with the concentration of alcohol. A low or negative breath alcohol result may be the DRE's first indication that other impairing drugs are present.
2. *Interview of the arresting officer.* The DRE interviews the arresting officer to develop a fuller understanding of the suspect and to gain important information the suspect may have revealed to the officer at the scene early in the arrest process.
3. *Preliminary examination of the suspect.* This examination is a structured series of questions, specific observations, and simple tests. This is the first opportunity for the DRE to directly examine the suspect and assess the possibility of injury, illness, or some non-drug-related condition as the cause of impairment. This examination is also the beginning of the systematic assessment of the suspect's appearance and behavior for any evidence of drug influence.
4. *Examination of the eyes.* Three tests are used in examining the eyes: HGN, vertical nystagmus, and lack of convergence. Presence or absence of these signs points to different drug categories.
5. *Divided-attention psychophysical tests.* Divided-attention tasks evaluate an individual's ability to perform multiple tasks simultaneously. These tasks, which are particularly sensitive to the impairing effects of drugs, are the WAT, the OLS, the Romberg balance test, and the finger-to-nose test.
6. *Vital signs examination.* Measurements are taken of the suspect's pulse, blood pressure, and body temperature. Certain

drug categories will elevate these vital signs while other categories depress them.

7. *Dark room examination.* The size of the suspect's pupils is evaluated under three lighting conditions: near-total darkness, indirect light, and direct light. Some drug categories affect the pupil size by causing either dilation or constriction.
8. *Examination of muscle tone.* Certain categories of drugs cause muscle rigidity, others cause muscle flaccidity, while some have no effect on muscle tone.
9. *Examination for injection sites.* Some drugs are administered intravenously. Frequent use of such drugs may cause scarring, leaving track marks along the veins of the arms.
10. *Suspect's statements and other observations.* The DRE interviews the suspect concerning his or her drug use. The scope and direction of the interview is based on the DRE's opinion of the suspect's impairment and drug use drawn from the nine preceding steps.
11. *Opinion of the evaluator.* Based on all of the information gathered through the previous 10 steps, the DRE forms an opinion concerning whether the suspect is under the influence of drugs and what drug categories may be responsible for the suspect's impairment.
12. *Toxicological examination.* The evaluation culminates in the collection of blood and/or urine specimens for toxicological analysis to substantiate the DRE's opinion of impairment.

Toxicology*

The opinion of the DRE concerning the suspect's state of impairment and the category of drug responsible for that impairment is a subjective evaluation. The determination of the presence of an impairing drug in the suspect's specimens by the toxicology laboratory provides objective scientific support for the DRE's opinion. The type of specimens submitted to the laboratory for analysis and the type of analyses performed often vary between jurisdictions. Many laboratories screen either blood or urine for drugs of abuse only (e.g., methamphetamine, cocaine metabolite, barbiturates, benzodiazepines, PCP, opiates, and cannabinoids) using an immunoassay system; positive results are typically confirmed by gas chromatography/mass spectrometry. A much smaller number of laboratories perform a more comprehensive analysis to include therapeutic drugs as well as the common drugs of abuse.

In general, blood is considered a more suitable specimen than urine for analysis in DUI/DWI cases. Although urine is an excellent specimen for toxicology screening, no direct relationship exists between impairment and the urine concentration of a drug. The identification of a drug in urine, therefore, only indicates that the suspect has been exposed to that drug. The detection of a drug in blood suggests that the drug is the cause of the suspect's observed impairment. It is important to note, however, that there is no well-established correlation between blood concentration and performance impairment for any drug other than alcohol.

It is the observed impairment, as noted by a DRE, in combination with a confirmed blood concentration of a drug that provides a reasonable scientific certainty that the impairment is related to the use and presence of that drug. The same type of impairment noted by a DRE and a confirmed urine concentration of a drug provide only a reasonable probability that the observed impairment is drug related, because drugs can remain in the urine for several days after use. However, confirming the presence of drugs in blood or urine in and of itself may not be sufficient to establish impairment to the degree that the suspect is incapable of safely operating a motor vehicle. The cooperative effort of the DRE and the toxicology laboratory is essential for the correct evaluation of impairment secondary to drug use.

Drug Class Effects*

The DRE is trained to observe behavior and collect physiologic data in an effort to determine if observed impairment is secondary to drug effects. As a consequence of numerous evaluations, the DRE begins to look for a combination of behaviors and physiological indicators that may suggest that an individual is under the influence of a particular drug or one of the members of a particular class of drugs. Each of the seven categories of drugs is associated with a set of observable and measurable signs. The drug categories used in the DEC program do not directly correspond to traditional drug classes. The drugs are categorized on the basis of the signs they generate during the various examinations of the DEC process and not on their pharmacological properties.

CNS Depressants

Alcohol is the most commonly used CNS depressant and is the prototypical drug in this category. In general, all members of this category produce behavioral and physiological effects similar to alcohol. Other drugs in this category include members of the barbiturate, benzodiazepine, antidepressant, and antipsychotic drug classes as well as many others. Drugs in this category typically result in a dose-related slowing of reflexes, loss of social inhibitions, impaired divided attention, impaired judgment, increased risk-taking behavior, and emotional instability. The following results may be expected during the drug recognition evaluation:

- Pupil size is generally normal, but reaction to light is slowed.
- Horizontal gaze nystagmus is present.
- Vertical gaze nystagmus may be present, depending on the drug dose.
- A lack of smooth convergence is present.
- Pulse rate is elevated after alcohol use, but depressed after use of most other drugs in this category.
- Blood pressure is generally lowered.
- Body temperature is lowered.
- Muscle tone is normal.
- Injection sites are typically not present because most of these drugs are administered orally.

CNS Stimulants

Cocaine and members of the amphetamine class of drugs, especially methamphetamine, are the most commonly used CNS stimulants. Psychomotor stimulants improve mood and cause intense feelings of pleasure ("high") after intravenous, intranasal, and smoked administration. Chronic use causes stereotopy (senseless repetition of a meaningless act to the exclusion of other behaviors) and often leads to paranoid behavior, psychosis (amphetamine psychosis and cocaine-induced psychosis), and violence. Low doses can overcome fatigue effects on cognitive, perceptual, and psychomotor tasks, with improvement measured on some tasks. Retrospective studies suggest that chronic use results in prolonged deficits in motor and cognitive performance. The following results may be expected on the drug recognition evaluation:

- Pupil size is dilated and reaction to light is slowed.
- Horizontal gaze nystagmus is absent.
- Vertical gaze nystagmus is absent.
- Smooth convergence is not affected.
- Pulse rate is elevated.
- Blood pressure is elevated.
- Body temperature is elevated.
- Muscle tone may be rigid.
- Injection sites may be found; cocaine and methamphetamine, the most commonly abused stimulants, may be administered intravenously as well as by smoking or, in the case of cocaine, intranasally.

Hallucinogens

Members of this drug category cause an altered or distorted perception of reality in the user. The most commonly used hallucinogens are LSD, psilocybin (the naturally occurring hallucinogen found in some species of mushrooms), MDA (3,4-methylenedioxyamphetamine), and MDMA (3,4-methylenedioxymethamphetamine). PCP also produces a distorted view of the self and reality but constitutes a category of its own in the DEC program. Marijuana, used at high doses (much greater than typically available in the U.S.), can also act as a hallucinogen, but it also constitutes a category unto itself in the DEC program.

The subjective effects of hallucinogens are difficult to study. In general, the hallucinatory experience starts out with colored visions of tunnel, spiral, and lattice shapes that move. Meaningful images start to become incorporated into these visions and finally there is a rapid succession of meaningful scenes. Apart from the hallucinations, the drug-induced hallucinatory experience often involves feelings of deep insight into oneself and the world, deep religious feelings, and an increase in the ability to enjoy and appreciate art and especially music. Performance is usually impaired by hallucinogens because the user has difficulty remaining motivated and attending to the task. The following results may be expected on the drug recognition evaluation:

- Pupil size is dilated and reaction to light is normal; the hallucinogenic amphetamines (MDMA and MDA) slow the reaction to light.
- Horizontal gaze nystagmus is absent.
- Vertical gaze nystagmus is absent.
- Smooth convergence is not affected.
- Pulse rate is elevated.
- Blood pressure is elevated.
- Body temperature is elevated.
- Muscle tone may be rigid.
- Injection sites are not present.

PCP

This category includes PCP and its structural analogs. In addition to having anesthetic properties and hallucinogenic effects, PCP also acts as an analgesic, a CNS depressant, and a stimulant. It is generally classified as a dissociative anesthetic (produces analgesia and amnesia without respiratory depression, resulting in a state in which the patient appears dissociated from his environment but not necessarily asleep). After high doses or chronic use, an acute psychosis that resembles schizophrenia may develop. Under the influence of PCP, an individual will experience disorientation, slurred speech, agitation, excitement, and an altered perception of self, and will typically be passive with a fixed, blank stare. This constellation of effects makes it difficult to predict or anticipate an individual user's response to PCP. The following results may be expected on the drug recognition evaluation:

- Pupil size and reaction to light are normal.
- Horizontal gaze nystagmus is present, generally with a very early angle of onset.
- Vertical gaze nystagmus is present.
- A lack of smooth convergence is present.
- Pulse rate is elevated.
- Blood pressure is elevated.
- Body temperature is elevated.
- Muscle tone may be rigid.
- Injection sites are typically not present.

Narcotic Analgesics

This category comprises the opiates (natural derivatives of opium such as heroin, morphine, and codeine) and the opioids (synthetic analogs of the opiates such as hydromorphone, hydrocodone, fentanyl, methadone, and others). The first use of opiates causes dysphoria, nausea, and vomiting, but tolerance to these effects develops. Opiates cause a sleepy, dreamy state and when taken intravenously cause "rushes" or feelings of intense pleasure. Chronic opiate use causes constipation and decreases sexual performance, but if doses are not too high, chronic use does not interfere with intellectual or physical abilities. The narcotic analgesic abuser experiences an increased awareness of sights and sounds, altered time sense (slowed for some, hastened for others), and a subjective belief in enhanced creativity. During the period of early analgesic use, the abuser experiences euphoria and relaxation. With continued use there is a shift toward unpleasant mood states and an increase in psychiatric symptoms, with decreased activity, social isolation, and aggression. Low and moderate doses have little performance effect apart from sedation. With higher doses there is a loss of motivation, and drug-seeking behavior will interfere with task performance. Tolerance to most effects of the narcotic analgesics develops rapidly. The following results may be expected on the drug recognition evaluation:

- Pupil size is constricted, but reaction to light is normal.
- Horizontal gaze nystagmus is absent.
- Vertical gaze nystagmus is absent.
- Smooth convergence is not affected.
- Pulse rate is depressed.
- Blood pressure is lowered.
- Body temperature is lowered.
- Muscle tone is normal or flaccid.
- Injection sites may be present in heroin and morphine abusers but not present with abuse of the other narcotic analgesics.

Inhalants

This category comprises the volatile organic solvents (e.g., toluene, gasoline, trichloroethylene), hydrocarbon gases (e.g., butane, freon, propane), anesthetic gases (e.g., halothane, nitrous oxide), nitrites (e.g., isobutyl nitrite, amyl nitrite, and butyl nitrite), and halogenated hydrocarbons (e.g., difluoroethane). Inhalation of the fumes of these substances results in euphoria and a CNS depression similar to that caused by alcohol. Abusers may also experience disorientation, confusion, and a sensation of floating. The following results may be expected on the drug recognition evaluation:

- Pupil size is normal, but reaction to light is slowed; anesthetic gases and nitrites may cause dilation.
- Horizontal gaze nystagmus is present.
- Vertical gaze nystagmus may be present.
- A lack of smooth convergence is present.
- Pulse rate is elevated.
- Blood pressure is lowered with the use of anesthetic gases and nitrites but is elevated with the use of solvents and hydrocarbon gases.

- Body temperature may be elevated, lowered, or unaffected depending on the substance used.
- Muscle tone is normal.
- Injection sites will not be present.

Cannabis

The cannabinoids are a family of compounds, some of which are psychoactive, found in the *Cannabis sativa* plant; over 60 cannabinoids have been identified, but delta-9-tetrahydrocannabinol (THC) is the primary psychoactive agent found in the plant. THC is available as marijuana, hashish, hash oil, and Marinol (a synthetic form of THC used as an antiemetic). At high doses, cannabis acts like a hallucinogen, but at the low doses common in North American use, the drug is reported to cause a pleasurable high that may take several trials to experience and can usually be turned off at will. Systematic measures of mood have indicated that the mood of a user usually reflects the mood of the others who are present. Cannabis causes temporal disintegration, which means that the individual loses the ability to store information in the short term and is easily distracted. Time is usually overestimated. Most performance deficits appear to be due to a lack of motivation and an inability to attend to a task, but impairing effects are measurable. Performance on the standardized field sobriety test is significantly impaired after commonly used doses of marijuana, and in closed-course driving tests subjects' ability to maintain lateral position within the lane is impaired. The following results may be expected on the drug recognition evaluation:

- Pupil size may be normal or slightly dilated with a normal reaction to light.
- Horizontal gaze nystagmus is absent.
- Vertical gaze nystagmus is absent.
- A lack of smooth convergence is present.
- Pulse rate is elevated.
- Blood pressure is elevated.
- Body temperature is normal.
- Muscle tone is normal.
- Injection sites will not be present.

LABORATORY PERFORMANCE TESTING

Workplace and driving performance may be considered to be a series of vigilance and divided-attention tasks. To evaluate the effects of drugs and environmental conditions (e.g., illness, disease, exposure to toxicants in the workplace) on driving and workplace safety and efficiency, a large number of psychomotor tests have been developed. Since laboratory experiments provide a controlled environment, human performance testing most frequently occurs in this setting. The effects of a drug on performance are not typically predictable from a single test, in part because laboratory-based tests do not exactly simulate the performance of interest. Testing batteries, therefore, are believed to more adequately provide predictive value of the effects of drugs on human performance.

Although evaluation of performance on actual tasks (e.g., testing the effects of alcohol on automobile driving using closed-course or on-the-road studies) provides data more directly applicable to understanding and evaluating the behavioral effects of drugs on "real-life" tasks, such studies are not often practical. The high cost and risk associated with such real-life studies is often prohibitive, and researchers turn to laboratory-based studies as an effective alternative. Laboratory studies also allow for subdividing a task into its component parts, which is often not feasible in nonlaboratory studies.

Most tasks, such as automobile driving, may be considered to be routine yet complex psychomotor tasks. This simply means that behaviors such as driving a car may be performed routinely and may seem uncomplicated, but they are in fact a series of small tasks that must be performed simultaneously or in close association with each other to accomplish the larger task. In a field study, it is generally difficult to subdivide tasks into their component parts and measure performance on each aspect of that task. The ability to subdivide tasks in this manner allows the investigator to determine exactly what part of a behavior is impaired and in what way.

For example, it is important to be able to differentiate whether a task is impaired as a result of a loss of visual acuity or due to a reduction in cognitive ability. When assessing a large task as a whole unit, it is generally difficult to determine which portion of the behavior is impaired. In the laboratory study, the investigator is evaluating a number of small tasks that are either a portion of the larger task or that model the types of behaviors used in that larger task in an effort to assess each portion of the whole task.

Although there are many advantages to the laboratory study, some aspects of this type of experimentation are less desirable than the field study. Probably the most significant is directly related to the above discussion. When a task is subdivided into its component parts, it is no longer truly the whole task. It then becomes possible to assess impairment in the real-life task only by association instead of directly, as in the field study. This is frequently a question raised in reference to laboratory studies that attempt to relate impairment to driving. A serious question of validity is raised when a subject's performance is impaired on reaction time tasks or divided-attention tasks and the investigator extrapolates these results to suggest that driving, a task that involves reaction time and divided attention, will also be impaired under the same drug conditions. In addition to validity (i.e., does a task that measures driving ability look like the actual driving task?), there are also issues of learning, training, and practice effects that must be accounted for in the laboratory studies. These effects are minimized when a well-controlled study uses properly validated performance tests. Often, however, the time frame in which subjects learn new performance tests does not compare to the degree of practice and expertise they have developed in the performance of routine yet complex psychomotor tasks such as driving. Highly practiced tasks tend to be more resistant to drug effects than less well-learned tasks; therefore, impairment noted on such laboratory tasks may not reflect the same type or degree of impairment on the real-life task. One way in which laboratory testing is overcoming some of these disadvantages is through the application of increasingly sophisticated and more realistic simulators. For example, current technology has provided automobile and flight simulators that so accurately reflect the real task that they are used for training drivers and pilots. Such simulators overcome the problems of validity and are probably less susceptible to learning and practice effects. The simulator also allows for the measurement of the subtasks that constitute the larger task or behavior.

Various psychomotor tests are available for use in laboratory studies. Despite their differences, they may be grouped into three major categories: perceptual performance tasks, cognitive performance tasks, and motor performance tasks.

Perceptual performance tasks measure the acuity of the senses, especially vision and hearing. The most common task in this category is time estimation, in which the test subject is required to estimate the passage of a fixed time interval, typically 30 seconds. This task evaluates mental acuity. Many drugs alter the subject's ability to estimate the passage of time.

Cognitive performance tests measure intellectual function. Many different types of tasks fall into this category. Vigilance tasks measure the ability to recognize specific information and require the subject to discriminate a specific signal from among a group of choices, e.g., the subject monitors several dials and reports when one varies from the others. These types of tests model many modern workplace tasks as well as aspects of the driving task. Another form of cognitive test uses simple arithmetic problems to evaluate concentration and mental processing time. These tasks include a wide array of mathematical problems such as requiring the subject to perform a series of simple two- or three-digit addition or subtraction problems. One session of these tasks can include a series of 25–50 problems, and answers to each problem are typically required within 5–10 seconds.

Motor performance tests evaluate the integrity and function of motor pathways. This type of testing is also referred to as psycho-motor or sensorimotor testing. The most basic of the motor performance tests is the tapping rate task. This is a test of pure motor speed in which the subject strikes a key or alternate keys on a keypad as rapidly as possible over a short time span. This task has no cognitive component and, therefore, allows for analyzing the motor component of other tasks in a performance test battery.

Among the most popular and frequently used motor tests are the reaction time tests, which evaluate motor response. Reaction time is a basic performance skill that is fundamental to all activity. Although many different variations of these tests are available, the essential element of the task is a button press in response to a critical stimulus. Reaction time tasks may be classified as either simple reaction time or choice reaction time. The simple reaction time tasks evaluate only motor response: how rapidly a response is made after the stimulus is presented. In the choice reaction time tasks, the subject must choose a single stimulus from among a number of alternatives. These tasks evaluate sensorimotor performance in that they have both a motor response component and a recognition time component.

Another popular type of motor performance test is the tracking task. These tests measure visual-motor coordination and contain elements of reaction time, fine and course motor control, and attention. The tracking task also has many variations. These tests are commonly used in behavioral studies because the elements of the tracking tasks are also present in automobile driving.

The motor performance test that provides the most sensitive measure of the impairing effects of drugs is the divided-attention task. This type of test involves the simultaneous performance of two or more subtasks. Many possible combinations of tasks are available, e.g., two tracking tasks or a tracking task and a choice reaction time task. The essential requirement for choosing the best combinations of tasks is that the subject's capacity to absorb and respond to all relevant information be taxed. The information processing demands of the combined tasks must be such that either one or both tasks are performed at a lower performance level than when either task is performed alone. The critical concern in task selection is that the combination of tasks must not overload the subject to such a degree that one of the tasks is neglected. The requirement to share attention is a common feature in everyday tasks such as automobile driving.

Another important aspect of the laboratory-based performance study is the subjective test, in which the subjects self-report their mood, feelings, and impressions using a quantifiable scale. Such self-reporting provides useful information about drug effects and the subject's perceptions regarding impairment.

SUGGESTED READING

1. Center for Studies of Law in Action (Borkenstein RF, Director). Tests for BAC in highway safety programs—supervision and expert testimony (student manual). Bloomington, IN: Indiana University, 1995.
2. Compton R, Berning A. Results of the 2007 national roadside survey of alcohol and drug use by drivers. Washington, DC: NHTSA, 2009.
3. Garriott JC, ed. Garriott's Medicolegal aspects of alcohol, 5th ed. Tucson, AZ: Lawyers and Judges Publishing Co., 2008.
4. McKim WA. Drugs and behavior: an introduction to behavioral pharmacology, 2nd ed. NJ: Prentice Hall, 1991.
5. O'Hanlon JF, deGier JJ, eds. Drugs and driving. Philadelphia, PA: Taylor and Francis, 1986.
6. U.S. Department of Transportation. Drug evaluation and classification program (briefing paper). Washington, DC: NHTSA, March 1990.
7. U.S. Department of Transportation. Drug evaluation and classification training program: The drug recognition school (student manual). Washington, DC: NHTSA, 1993.

CHAPTER 3

Forensic Drug Testing

Amanda J. Jenkins

Drug use has become a significant medical and social problem in the U.S. Resources, both financial and human (i.e., personnel expended to combat this problem), have involved drug interdiction; criminal penalties for cultivation, distribution, possession, and use of illicit drugs; and medical treatment of offenders and drug addicts. Chemical testing of biological specimens from individuals is generally accepted to be the most objective method for determining drug use.

FORENSIC DRUG TESTING IN SOCIETY

The Military

In the U.S., the military establishment was the first to initiate testing of its employees. Testing was motivated by concern about how the use of illegal drugs affected the combat readiness of U.S. Armed Forces. In 1971, Congress directed the Secretary of Defense to devise methods for the identification and treatment of military personnel who abused drugs. Under the 1990 General Military Law 10 U.S.C. 1090, the Secretary of Defense and the Secretary of Transportation (who has responsibility for the Coast Guard), were required to write regulations, implement testing procedures, and provide facilities to identify and treat military personnel who were drug dependent. Such individuals are barred from military service and referred to civilian treatment programs. Furthermore, in 1990, the military instituted a "drug free workplace" policy to preclude the hiring of drug-dependent individuals.

Potential military recruits must undergo drug testing as part of the application process. In addition, drug-dependent individuals already serving in the armed forces who "cannot or will not be rehabilitated" face disciplinary action and/or discharge.

The Criminal Justice System

Drug testing is increasingly used within the criminal justice system to monitor drug use within prison populations. Urinalysis is the method of choice and, under President George Bush's 1991 National Drug Control Strategy, was considered a high priority for its ability to identify and monitor criminal offenders involved with drugs. In addition to a nationwide control strategy, some states mandate that drug-testing programs be initiated at the time of arrest and during pretrial release proceedings, probation, and parole. Several U.S. cities have initiated drug-testing programs for arrestees. Yet in many jurisdictions, drug testing of drug offenders is not mandated.

The Public Sector

In 1983, as a result of a study conducted by the National Transportation Safety Board concerning the involvement of drugs (including alcohol) in train accidents, the Federal Railway Administration and the

National Institute on Drug Abuse (NIDA; U.S. Department of Health and Human Services [DHHS]) began to develop drug-use regulations for the U.S. Department of Transportation (DOT). During this time, national concern about drug abuse was increasing, and many companies in the oil, chemical, transportation, and nuclear industries began implementing their own drug-testing programs. These programs varied in their procedures and standards, which resulted in much controversy and litigation.

In 1986, the executive branch of the federal government became actively involved in developing drug-use regulations when President Reagan issued Executive Order No. 12564 (Federal Register 1986 51:32889, 32890). The order instructed the directors of each federal executive agency to develop testing programs for employees in sensitive positions. The objective of this order was to provide a "drug-free" federal workplace. The Office of Management and Budget estimated the cost of implementing these programs at $18 million per year (although the General Accounting Office was unable to verify this estimate).

A conference convened by NIDA in March 1986 produced a consensus document describing the conditions under which testing could be conducted:

- All individuals must be informed they are subject to testing.
- The confidentiality of the test results must be assured.
- All positive results on the initial screen must be confirmed with alternate methodology.
- Random screening for drug use under a well-defined program is appropriate and legally defensible in certain circumstances.

In 1988, NIDA issued mandatory scientific and technical procedural guidelines (including standards for laboratory accreditation) for federal drug-testing programs (53FR11970–89, April 11, 1988). According to the guidelines, urine would be the testing specimen of choice. The guidelines included specimen collection, procedures for transmitting samples to testing laboratories, assay procedures, evaluation of test results, quality control measures, record-keeping and reporting requirements, and standards and procedures for DHHS accreditation of drug-testing laboratories. The intent of these guidelines was to ensure the accuracy and integrity of the test results and the privacy of the individuals tested. In July of 1988, DHHS/NIDA implemented the National Laboratory Certification Program. The Research Triangle Institute (Research Triangle Park, North Carolina) administered this program under contract and continues administration to this day (2013).

In 1989, the Nuclear Regulatory Commission final rule (54FR24468, June 7, 1989) was published in the *Federal Register*. Implemented on January 3, 1990, the rule incorporated most of the DHHS mandatory guidelines, although the program did permit on-site testing under specific conditions.

The DOT, having published an interim final rule on November 21, 1988, that established drug-testing procedures applicable to transportation employees, released its final rule in 1989 for implementation on January 2, 1990. These regulations covered employees in six transportation industries, namely vehicle, aviation, railroad, mass transit, pipeline, and maritime. Implementation of the program in the Mass Transit Administration was delayed because a federal appellate court overturned the rule, stating that the agency did not have the statutory authority to issue standards requiring drug testing. To remedy this problem, Congress passed the Omnibus Transportation Employee Drug Testing Act of 1991. This act required the DOT to prepare regulations that would expand the existing program to include intrastate operations and the drug ethanol. The final DOT rules were applicable to large and small employers. The legislation was implemented on January 1, 1995, with respect to employers with more than 50 covered employees, and on January 1, 1996, with respect to employers with fewer than 50 employees.

This legislation affects more than 7.4 million transportation workers in the U.S.

These programs have been revised in the last 20 years to include the addition of drugs; changes in cutoff concentrations for testing; addition of specimen validity tests; qualifications, training, and certification of Medical Review Officers (MROs); and the introduction of the instrumented initial testing facility program (DHHS).

Since President Reagan's executive order, states and municipalities have increased employee drug testing. Programs throughout the U.S. differ with regard to policy and testing procedures. Although many states require drug-testing laboratories to be accredited, they may differ as to when an employee may be subject to testing and when and how samples are collected. Today many police, fire, and correctional department personnel across the U.S. are subject to testing.

The Private Sector

Since the mid-1980s, private sector employees have also been subject to drug testing. Surveys have estimated that in 1985, 25% of Fortune 500 companies were screening job applicants for drug use. In 1987, approximately 50% of Fortune 100 companies were conducting pre-employment and for-cause testing. A large proportion of those companies were involved in the manufacturing and utility industries. Today more than 80% of Fortune 500 companies drug test their employees. Although the majority use certified laboratories to conduct the testing, less than 50% use an MRO. Further, not all companies require confirmatory testing of presumptive positive results. Urine is the specimen of choice, but blood and hair are also used.

Other Segments of Society

Drug testing is not limited to the workplace or the criminal justice system. Professional athletes and amateurs who compete at national and Olympic levels may be subject

to such testing (Chapter 4). Testing of high school athletes is controversial, but today parents may privately test their children by collecting samples and sending them to laboratories for anonymous testing. Approximately 47% of students report the use of illicit drugs. In recent years, public secondary schools have been provided with federal money to test students. Random testing, usually for marijuana, stimulants, and opiates, typically involves high school age children. However, some school districts test middle school students. Athletes and those involved in school-related competitive extracurricular activities may be subject to testing. In addition, some districts test students who drive to school and who want to attend the school prom. National estimates indicate that during the 2004–5 school year, 14% of public school districts conducted drug testing in their high schools.

Several politicians have endorsed the concept of drug testing for welfare recipients and possibly using testing results to limit eligibility for these benefits. Additionally, applicants to federal job training programs may also be subject to drug testing in the future. The insurance industry is also currently testing life insurance applicants for illicit drug use. In medicine, hospital emergency rooms, prenatal clinics, and delivery rooms test individuals for illicit drugs as part of diagnostic care. Depending on individual circumstances, these test specimens may or may not become forensic specimens.

STATUS OF FORENSIC DRUG TESTING IN THE UNITED STATES

The economic and social cost to the U.S. due to illicit drug use has been investigated. One study showed that approximately 35% of state prison inmates and 40% of juvenile offenders in long-term correctional facilities admitted to being under the influence of illicit drugs while committing the crime for which they were incarcerated. Drug defendants comprised 33% of defendants in criminal cases filed in federal court in 2006. Approximately

93% were convicted compared with 76% in 1981. During this period the proportion of offenders sentenced to prison and the length of the prison sentence increased. The majority of adult illicit drug users are employed full or part time and although the number of individuals testing positive has declined since the mid-1980s, the positive rate is approximately 5%. The economic impact of such use has been estimated to exceed $150 billion per year. This cost includes lost productivity due to increased sick time, lateness, increased number of workplace accidents, and worker's compensation claims.

An estimated 30 million working Americans are tested for illegal drugs each year. In the forensic arena, the generally accepted objective of drug testing is to detect and deter drug use among individuals subject to the testing. In addition, athletes are tested to determine whether they have used drugs that may improve performance and therefore result in an unfair competitive advantage. In the criminal justice system, prison inmates are tested so that individuals who may benefit from drug rehabilitation programs can be identified.

Employees may be tested in the workplace in several situations: during pre-employment background checks, before promotion, return to duty, at random, for cause, follow up, and post accident. Employers may test job applicants to identify those individuals who may pose a safety risk to themselves or others. Random drug testing of employees may be conducted as a potential deterrent to illicit drug use and consequent safety risks. Companies may drug screen for cause if a supervisor has reasonable suspicion (such as behavior or accident) that the employee is abusing drugs. Post accident drug screening may be conducted in order to include or exclude drug use as a possible cause of the accident.

THE TESTING PROCESS

Testing may be highly regulated with safeguards built into the system to protect the rights of the individual tested, such as the DHHS guidelines for federal employees. Alternatively, drug testing may be conducted informally, with no regulation and few safeguards, as in the case of a high school athlete whose parent collects a specimen. Workplace drug testing is unique in that single test results may be the only piece of evidence involved in the hiring and/or firing of an individual. Therefore, every test result may produce litigation.

The quality of the result is only as good as the quality of the entire process. This process begins at the collection site and continues with the transportation of the specimen to the testing laboratory, the accessioning, testing, data review and report generation, and the transmission of the results to a qualified individual for interpretation. In regulated workplace drug testing, this individual is known as an MRO.

Collection and testing facilities must follow forensic toxicology standards. Instructions for collection facilities cover procedures for collecting the specimens, maintaining specimen integrity, and establishing a chain of custody. Currently in workplace drug testing, urine is the specimen of choice, and the collection may be witnessed. In federally regulated programs this occurs, for example, if a donor's previous drug test was reported by an MRO as positive, adulterated, or substituted. Standards for testing laboratories cover facilities, standard operating procedures, security, chain of custody, testing methods and validation, quality assurance, reporting methods, confidentiality, personnel, and laboratory accreditation.

The testing facility must have the physical capacity to perform the work required. This means adequate space and adequate security that limits access not only to the physical premises but also to data in electronic and paper format. The facility must also have a sufficient number of qualified personnel and appropriate instrumentation to conduct the required tests, including that required for screening and for confirmatory assays.

Collecting the specimen initiates a chain of custody, i.e., procedures that account for the integrity, identification, and security of each specimen by tracking its handling and storage from point of collection to final disposition. The chain of custody is documented on a custody and control form (CCF). The collection site must offer adequate facilities for specimen collection and sufficient numbers of trained personnel.

Documentation of the collection process appears on the CCF, and on the specimen and container. Typically, the donor initials a label on the container, along with the date the specimen was collected. Trained collection personnel also sign the container, and "seals of integrity" are placed on the container to prevent tampering after collection. All federal agency collections utilize a single-use container and the collector, in the presence of the donor, then pours the urine into two specimen bottles, labeled A and B. The specimen is then packaged for transport to the testing facility by courier, express delivery, or U.S. mail. Upon receipt at the laboratory, trained personnel accession the specimen into the laboratory's information management system. The specimen container is examined for evidence of tampering: e.g., breakage of seals and incomplete documentation (such as failure of one party to initial the container). It is also examined to ensure a match between the information on the specimen and that on the accompanying CCF. If there is a mismatch, the submitting agency must be contacted and discrepancies corrected. The laboratory then gives the specimen an accession number, and an internal chain of custody is initiated for specimen testing. The initial screen reflects testing for the classes of drugs identified by the submitting agency. All positive screening results are then confirmed using a second sample aliquot and an alternate technique. Laboratories under federal and military drug-testing programs screen using immunoassay, with confirmation by gas/liquid chromatography/tandem mass spectrometry.

The current mandatory guidelines for federal workplace drug-testing programs, effective in 2010, introduced a new type of testing facility: the instrumented initial testing facility (IITF). These facilities perform initial drug tests and specimen validity tests. They are permitted to report specimens as negative, negative and dilute (creatinine ≥5 and ≤20 mg/dL), or rejected. Specimens must be sent to an HHS-certified laboratory for additional testing if results may be positive, adulterated, substituted, invalid, or dilute with a creatinine ≤5 mg/dL.

TESTING METHODOLOGIES

Initial Test/Screening: Immunoassay

Screening by immunoassay typically involves no extraction, minimal specimen handling, and semiquantitative results. These tests have high sensitivity and moderate specificity. Many of the commercially available immunoassay tests cross-react with multiple drugs within a class, due to the choice of target analyte. (For detailed information about cross-reactivities of individual assays, see Ropero-Miller and Goldberger's *Handbook of Workplace Drug Testing* in "Suggested Reading.") These assays may also be sensitive to interferences from additives that a donor might have used to adulterate the specimen. Such adulterants include bleach, glutaraldehyde, ammonia, soap, nitrite, and vinegar.

Commercial assays are based on radioimmunoassay (RIA), enzyme-multiplied immunoassay (EMIT®), enzyme-linked immunosorbent assay (ELISA), cloned enzyme donor immunoassay (CEDIA), fluorescence polarization immunoassay (FPIA), and kinetic interaction of particles (KIMS). Tests typically screen for the "HHS 5" drug classes that include amphetamines, cannabinoids, cocaine, phencyclidine, and opiates. Recently, a sixth drug has been added, MDMA. Commercial assays developed to measure these drugs target certain analytes within each class. Therefore, for the amphetamine assay, methamphetamine and/or amphetamine may be the target analyte (meaning that during assay development, antibodies are produced to this specific analyte). In the cannabinoid assay, the inactive metabolite of delta-9-tetrahydrocannabinol (THC), delta-9-carboxy-THC, is the target analyte. For the cocaine assay, the target analyte is benzoylecgonine, and for the opiate assay, morphine. The tests are conducted using mandated cutoff concentrations (Table 1). Samples that screen positive by immunoassay are known as presumptive positive specimens. The presence of the specific drug must be confirmed by an alternate analytical technique.

Specimen Validity Tests

In order to verify that the specimen collected is human urine, several validity tests may be performed. In regulated drug testing, specimen validity tests are conducted on each urine sample. These tests include creatinine, pH, and a minimum of one test for oxidizing adulterants. If the creatinine is less than 20 mg/dL, the specific gravity must also be measured. In addition, if the specimen exhibits unusual characteristics such as an abnormal odor or color, or produces reactions that interfere with testing, additional testing may be performed. Oxidizing adulterants include tests for nitrite, chromium VI, halogens, glutaraldehyde, pyridine, and surfactants.

Validity tests utilize methodologies that include pH meter (pH), colorimetry (pH, nitrite, halogen), multiwavelength spectrometry (nitrite, surfactant), ion chromatography (nitrite, chromium VI), capillary electrophoresis (nitrite, halogen), atomic absorption spectrometry (chromium VI), ICP-MS (chromium VI, halogen), aldehyde test (glutaraldehyde), and GC/MS (glutaraldehyde, pyridine).

Urine specimens may be reported as adulterated, dilute, or substituted, as follows:

- Adulterated. A specimen that has been altered by the addition of an exogenous substance or an abnormal concentration of an endogenous substance
  - pH $\leq$3 or $\geq$11
  - Nitrite $\geq$500 mcg/mL
  - Chromium (VI) $\geq$50 mcg/mL
  - Halogen $\geq$LOQ of the test
  - Glutaraldehyde $\geq$LOQ of the test
  - Pyridine $\geq$LOQ of the test
  - Surfactant $\geq$100 mcg/mL dodecylbenzene sulfonate
- Dilute. A specimen in which the creatinine and specific gravity are lower than normal but still physiologically possible for human urine
  - Creatinine $\geq$2 but $\leq$5 mg/dL AND specific gravity >1.0010 but <1.0030
  - Creatinine >5 but <20 mg/dL AND specific gravity $\geq$1.002 but <1.003
- Substituted. A specimen that is not the donor's urine. The specimen may produce validity results outside the physiologically possible range for human urine

Table 1. Cutoff Concentrations and Reporting Requirements DHHS Accredited Laboratories

Drug (Class)	Immunoassay Screening	Confirmation
Amphetamines	500 ng/mL	250 ng/mL amphetamine, 250 ng/mL methamphetamine[a]
Cannabinoids	50 ng/mL	15 ng/mL THCCOOH
Cocaine metabolite	150 ng/mL	100 ng/mL benzoylecgonine
Opiates	2000 ng/mL	2000 ng/mL morphine 2000 ng/mL codeine
6-Acetylmorphine	10 ng/mL	10 ng/mL 6-acetylmorphine
MDMA	500 ng/mL	250 ng/mL MDMA 250 ng/mL MDA 250 ng/mL MDEA
Phencyclidine	25 ng/mL	25 ng/mL phencyclidine

[a]To report methamphetamine, amphetamine must be present $\geq$100 ng/mL.

- Creatinine <2 mg/dL on both initial and confirmatory test on two aliquots AND specific gravity ≤1.0010 but ≥1.0200 on both initial and confirmatory test on two aliquots

Confirmation: Chromatography/ Mass Spectrometry

The initial document and four revisions of the U.S. Mandatory Guidelines for Federal Workplace Drug Testing Programs required the use of gas chromatography/mass spectrometry (GC/MS) for confirmation of presumptive positive urine specimens. The fifth revision of the guidelines, effective May 1, 2010, allows for the use of additional technologies that combine chromatographic separation with mass spectrometric identification. These include LC/MS, LC/MS/MS, and GC/MS/MS. Each assay measures specific drugs and metabolites: amphetamine, methamphetamine, MDMA, MDA, MDEA, delta-9-carboxy-THC (THC-COOH), morphine, codeine, 6-acetylmorphine, benzoylecgonine, and phencyclidine. Assays generally use liquid–liquid or solid-phase extraction, with or without derivatization. The mass spectrometer is operated in the selected ion-monitoring mode. Table 1 lists the current cutoff concentrations for immunoassay and confirmation testing under the federal program, with reporting requirements.

For amphetamines, derivatives such as trifluoroacetyl, trichloroacetyl, and heptaflurobutyryl have been utilized after basic liquid–liquid extraction or solid-phase extraction using modified XAD-2 resin or hydrophobic cation exchange columns. The class of drugs to which the amphetamines belong, namely, sympathomimetic amines, have similar chemical structures. Therefore, when developing an assay for amphetamines it is important to evaluate the assay for interference from similar drugs such as pseudoephedrine, ephedrine, phentermine, and phenylpropanolamine. Potential interference includes co-elution and similar mass ions and ion ratios. Procedures that do not use chiral columns or derivatives will not permit the differentiation between the licit l-isomer, the illicit d-isomer, and racemic mixtures of the parent compound. Chiral derivatizing reagents such as N-trifluoroacetyl-1-prolyl chloride and (–)-menthylchloroformate allow methamphetamine isomers to be distinguished using a nonchiral chromatographic column. False-positive results may occur if extracts are derivatized with 4-carbethoxyhexafluorobutyryl chloride, heptafluorobutyric anhydride, or N-trifluoroacetyl-1-prolyl chloride. In this instance, methamphetamine is formed by thermoconversion of ephedrine or pseudoephedrine. This typically occurs at high GC injection port temperatures and when significant concentrations of pseudoephedrine/ephedrine are present in the specimen.

The major metabolite of tetrahydrocannabinol is the carboxy acid that is present in urine in both free and conjugated forms. This metabolite is typically measured in urine specimens utilizing base hydrolysis followed by acidification and liquid–liquid extraction. Extracts may be derivatized with bis(trimethylsilyl)-trifluroacetamide and 1% trimethylchlorosilane to form the trimethylsilyl derivative. C_{18} bonded phase adsorption columns or basic anion-exchange resin may also be used after base hydrolysis. Trimethylanilinium hydroxide and iodopropane form propyl THC-carboxy acid derivatives.

Positive cocaine samples are confirmed by measuring the presence of the metabolite benzoylecgonine. Benzoylecgonine may be extracted from urine utilizing liquid–liquid or solid-phase procedures. In the latter, Amberlite XAD-2 extraction material has been used in addition to hydrophobic cation exchange columns.

Opiate-positive samples are confirmed by measuring morphine. This metabolite of heroin and codeine is present in the free form that is subsequently conjugated with glucuronic acid. Initial methods developed for opiate analysis utilized liquid–liquid extraction procedures. Samples may be hydrolyzed with acid or with glucuronidase, alkalinized, and extracted with an organic solvent solution such as methylene chloride isobutanol (9:1, v/v). After further acid-base extraction and re-extraction into organic solvent, acetyl derivatives are formed by having the extracts react with acetic anhydride and pyridine. Other procedures have formed perfluoroester derivatives with a solution of pentafluoropropanol and pentafluoropropionic anhydride. More recent GC/MS methods for determination of opiates have utilized copolymeric-bonded phase extraction cartridges such as hydrophobic cation exchange columns.

Opiate assays should be evaluated for potential interference from opiate metabolites and semisynthetic 6-keto-opioids such as hydromorphone, hydrocodone, oxymorphone, and oxycodone. Currently, assays for opiate detection in workplace drug testing also measure 6-acetylmorphine, a metabolite of heroin. In measuring 6-acetylmorphine, techniques should be developed to avoid chemical and enzymatic hydrolysis. The derivatizing reagent used for opiate analysis should be chosen with care since some opiates form similar derivatives. For example, formation of acetyl derivatives will convert both morphine and 6-acetylmorphine to heroin (diacetylmorphine), rendering them indistinguishable. Further, the mass spectrum of the trimethylsilyl derivative of hydromorphone resembles the trimethylsilyl derivative of morphine.

Confirmatory assays for the detection of phencyclidine have utilized liquid–liquid and solid-phase extraction techniques. Samples are alkalinized and extracted with organic solvents such as chloroform:isopropanol. Hydrophobic cation exchange solid-phase methods have also been described.

In many assays deuterated internal standards are used. Additionally, assays that use phenylcyclohexylamine (amphetamines), meclofenamic acid (cannabinoids), ketamine (cocaine metabolite and phencyclidine), nalorphine (opiates), and difluorophencyclidine (phencyclidine) as internal standards have been described.

Benzodiazepines and barbiturates may also be measured in forensic drug testing.

Screening assays are typically immunoassay based but confirmation may utilize GC, HPLC, LC/MS, and GC/MS technology.

QUALITY CONTROL

The validity of testing results is assured by maintaining a laboratory-wide quality assurance program and, specifically, using good quality control. This includes the use of appropriate reference standard materials that are typically purchased from commercial vendors. These materials must be validated before they are put online. In addition, appropriate control materials should be assayed concurrent with client specimens to serve as a check on the assay. Negative and positive control samples should be run with each batch of specimens; control samples may be blind or open but ideally examples of both should be run. Open control samples are those specimens that the analyst knows are controls; the analyst also knows the identity of the drugs present and the concentration. These serve to check that assay parameters are correct. Blind controls are those in which the identity of the control is blinded to the analyst in some way; i.e., the analyst may not know a sample is a control, or may not know the drug involved or its concentration. These samples are added to the run list by the quality assurance officer in the laboratory and are then evaluated by that individual.

Assays used for screening and confirmation must be validated. With commercial immunoassays, the laboratory should still generate validation data, especially if the laboratory does not follow the manufacturer's recommended procedure. Typical modifications include dilution of assay reagents or extension of reagent shelf life in order to decrease costs. For GC/MS and LC/MS assays, sample preparation, extraction, and instrumental analysis must be validated. Therefore, specimen handling, matrix considerations, and optimal extraction conditions should be evaluated. Each assay must be quantitative due to mandated cutoff concentrations.

To validate the assay, four issues must be addressed: method validation, instrument performance, assay calibration, and quality control.

A laboratory must demonstrate that the analytical method is acceptable for the intended purpose and that the assay produces accurate and reliable data. Therefore the laboratory must evaluate basic characteristics such as accuracy, precision, linearity, specificity, sensitivity, carryover potential, and "ruggedness" of the method. Additional parameters include stability of the analyte, recovery from the matrix, use of partial sample volumes, and identification and concentration of internal standard. For LC/MS assays ion suppression and process efficiency should be assessed.

Accuracy and precision determine the error of the method. Accuracy is a measure of the degree to which the experimental mean agrees with the true or theoretical concentration or amount of substance and may be determined by analysis of standard reference materials or comparing laboratory-prepared standards and controls with an established reference method. The generally accepted accuracy range is ±20% in forensic urine drug testing (FUDT). Precision is a measure of reproducibility, or the variability of measurements within a batch or set of samples. Precision may be assessed by testing multiple samples during a single analytical run or batch (within-run precision) and a single measurement over several runs (between-run precision). The result of this testing is expressed as coefficient of variation (CV) and is calculated as follows:

$$\%\,CV = \frac{\text{Standard Deviation}}{\text{Mean}} \times 100$$

CV values <15% are considered acceptable in FUDT.

Linearity is determined by evaluating responses from a series of standards as a function of the concentration of the analyte. The result is evaluated by using a statistical method such as least squares regression analysis. The correlation coefficient (r) provides a measure of the degree of linearity.

A method's linearity may be determined when the correlation coefficient (r) exceeds a defined value such as 0.99 and the quantitative concentration of each point is within ±20% of the target value. The limit of detection (LOD) of a method is the lowest concentration of drug that produces a detectable response. The limit of quantitation (LOQ) is the lowest concentration of analyte that can be accurately and precisely measured. The LOD may be determined by assaying negative or blank samples over time to determine the degree of noise or background in the system. The LOD is then calculated as mean of the signal intensity plus 3 standard deviations (SD). Similarly, the LOQ is the mean plus 10 SDs. Alternatively, blank specimens may be assayed with specimens of low analyte concentration, using a signal-to-noise ratio of 3:1 for LOD and 10:1 for LOQ.

Specificity refers to the ability of the method to measure an analyte in the presence of all potential analytes. Assays should be challenged with endogenous substances in addition to structurally related compounds. For example, an assay for methamphetamine and amphetamine should be challenged with sympathomimetic amines such as pseudoephedrine, phentermine, and phenylpropanolamine. Potential interferents that are not structurally related may include over-the-counter medications.

Carryover refers to the contamination of a sample by the preceding sample. A laboratory should determine the concentration of drug that may result in carryover for each analyte. Drug standards of increasing concentration, over the range that the laboratory may reasonably expect to encounter, are injected with a solvent or reagent blank immediately following each standard.

Each method should be further evaluated to establish criteria to monitor instrument performance. For GC/MS techniques this should include tuning procedures, checking for water and air leaks, and evaluating chromatographic performance, which includes peak shape, resolution, and signal abundance. Calibration curves are typically multi- or single-point or historical. Historical calibration refers to a historical multipoint calibration curve in which the calibration is determined and then the laboratory verifies that the calibration has not changed between batches by assaying positive and negative control samples. One of the control samples must be at the cutoff concentration.

For the federal urine drug testing program, each batch of samples must contain positive and negative quality control specimens. The target concentration of one control must be 125% of the cutoff concentration. Quality control results may be evaluated by utilizing a fixed criterion for the quantitative range, for example, ±20% of target concentration. Alternatively, Westgard quality control rules may be used. In this case, the laboratory establishes out-of-control limits for the assay based on the validated mean and standard deviation for the control in question.

A laboratory must delineate criteria for designating positive results. For screening assays, this should include review of calibration and control data. For mass spectrometric assays, this should include chromatographic criteria, transition ion ratios, mass spectral matches, and determination of the quantitative results. In addition, the laboratory standard operating procedure manual should include details of dilution protocols, reinjection of extracts, and data presentation.

DATA REVIEW

In the testing laboratory, data should be reviewed during each stage of the testing process. This includes review of specimen accessioning, aliquot chain of custody, quality control results, screening data, and confirmation data. Finally, before a report is generated, a senior scientist should review the complete case:

- At the bench, the analyst conducting the assay reviews the data.

- The supervisor of that section in the laboratory may then review the data.
- If the screening result is negative, a negative-certifying scientist will review the data before the results are recorded in a data management system.
- All positive results will also be reviewed and the specimen processed for confirmation. A positive-certifying scientist then reviews the screening and confirmation data.
- At this time the results for each specimen, including chain-of-custody documentation, are reviewed. If the data are valid the result is reported.

REPORTING

Reporting of results should be secure. Reports are typically sent electronically because telephone reporting is prohibited under the federal workplace drug-testing program. Reports utilize standardized forms and provide certified copies. In the federal program, the results are sent only to the MRO.

MRO REVIEW

The MRO is a licensed physician responsible for receiving laboratory results. This physician must have knowledge of substance abuse disorders and the appropriate training and experience to evaluate and interpret an individual's drug-testing results. In addition, they must pass an examination administered by a nationally recognized entity. The donor provides his/her medical records, in addition to relevant medical history, to the MRO. The MRO must give the donor the opportunity to discuss the drug-testing results before making a final determination. If a drug-test result is positive but there is an alternate medical explanation, the MRO will report the result as negative to the employer. If there is no explanation, the result is reported as positive. The MRO also reviews adulterated, substituted, rejected, and invalid test results. The MRO must also review negative results since many results for double-blind performance samples are sent to them. This review permits a continuous quality control program for specimen testing.

PROFICIENCY TESTING

As part of a comprehensive quality assurance program, laboratories must subject their work to independent evaluation. This is most commonly accomplished by enrolling in proficiency programs, which are typically established and administered by independent consultants or accrediting organizations.

On a regular basis, proficiency programs provide participating laboratories with samples that may be fortified with the drugs of interest. The laboratory is required to analyze these samples according to normal routine testing procedures, providing qualitative and quantitative data. The results of the testing must be reported to the accrediting agency within a specified due date.

Proficiency checks test the ability of the laboratory not only to provide accurate results but also to provide accurate data review and reporting procedures, and ensure that the laboratory completes work in a timely manner. The accrediting agency then compares a participant's results with those obtained by other laboratories within the same sample and also with laboratories chosen to act as reference facilities.

Results of proficiency tests may be used to identify strengths and weaknesses in laboratory operations. Resources may then be more effectively utilized, whether in personnel, method development, or instrumentation, etc. Acceptable proficiency testing results increase a laboratory's confidence in its analytical process.

The proficiency testing programs used by a laboratory must reflect the complexity of the work produced by that laboratory. For example, a laboratory that measures only ethanol in blood need only subscribe to a blood alcohol proficiency program.

However, laboratories providing comprehensive services in multiple biological matrices must participate in more rigorous programs and/or several programs, since one program is usually insufficient to test the qualitative and quantitative capabilities of a laboratory that assays multiple drugs in several biological specimens.

ACCREDITATION/CERTIFICATION

Government

As a result of President Reagan's Executive Order 12564, approximately 1.8 million federal employees, 600,000 Nuclear Regulatory Commission licensees, and 7 million DOT industry employees are tested for drugs. Laboratories conducting drug testing for these employees are subject to the Mandatory Guidelines for Federal Workplace Drug Testing Programs published in the *Federal Register*. These guidelines cover requirements for personnel, quality assurance, analytical methodologies, and standard operating procedures for urine drug testing. The technical and scientific requirements detailed in section B of the guidelines form the basis of the National Laboratory Certification Program (NLCP). In December 1988, 10 laboratories were certified under this program; by July, 1997, 69 laboratories had been certified. As of March 2013, 35 laboratories and no instrumented initial testing facilities meet the minimum standards to conduct urine drug testing for federal agencies.

Nongovernment

The College of American Pathologists (CAP) Laboratory Accreditation Program began in the 1960s as an extension of the CAP proficiency program. CAP maintains four accreditation programs and has accredited more than 5,000 laboratories. In the 1980s, the CAP Toxicology Resource Committee, under the chairmanship of the

Toxicology Commissioner, created the Forensic Urine Drug Testing Accreditation Program. Its mission was to oversee workplace drug testing performed by nonfederal employers. This program is intended to improve laboratory testing through peer review of testing practices, with on-site inspections and the use of proficiency testing. In a manner similar to that of the NLCP, accreditation standards cover personnel, quality assurance, resources and facilities, analytical procedures, proficiency testing, and laboratory safety.

ON-SITE TESTING

On-site drug testing is the testing of samples at the specimen collection site or site of current or future employment. Some regulated workplace programs prohibit this practice, but it is increasingly used in the criminal justice system and in the off-shore oil and shipping industries. The advantage of such testing is that results are available within a short period of time. This is important in certain industries when decisions regarding fitness for duty and access to safety-sensitive facilities must be made quickly.

Testing may take several forms. If the company has a large number of employees at one site, the drug testing of an employee's urine may be instrument-based with immunoassay technology. In recent years rapid "quick" tests have been developed. These are usually based on immunoassay technology but are self-contained and require no instrumentation. If the specimen tests negative, no further action may be required. However, if the specimen is positive, the drug-testing program should require that a portion of the specimen be sent to a laboratory for confirmation. (Some programs send a percentage of specimens, regardless of testing status, to a laboratory for confirmation.)

On-site drug-testing programs may limit testing to one or two drugs/drug classes such as opiates and cannabinoids, or may perform more comprehensive screening to include ethanol, amphetamines, cocaine, methadone, barbiturates, and benzodiazepines. When on-site devices were initially marketed, they utilized urine as the testing specimen. However, several devices currently being marketed use saliva to test for ethanol. More sophisticated devices that use a reader are now available to test saliva for cannabinoids, amphetamines, opiates, benzodiazepines, and cocaine use.

The validity of specimen collection, handling, security, chain of custody, quality control, and reporting procedures must be assured when on-site testing is performed. A study of 11 on-site drug-testing facilities funded by NIDA made the following recommendations for ensuring testing quality:

- Establish criteria for training and demonstrating personnel competence.
- Use a standardized custody and control form.
- Establish guidelines that ensure the security of specimens and records.
- Establish minimum standards for quality assurance, quality control, and system supervision.

SPECIMENS

Many biological specimens may be tested for drugs of abuse. The mandatory guidelines for workplace drug testing require the use of urine as the drug-testing matrix. Urine specimens usually have high drug concentrations and typically contain metabolites.

However, alternate specimens provide certain advantages over urine. Blood, breath, saliva, semen, nails, hair, meconium, sweat, breast milk, sebum, earwax, and nasal secretions may all have potential as drug-testing matrices. Blood is a useful matrix if the intent of the testing is to relate drug concentrations to pharmacological effects. Nails and hair can detect long-term or chronic use. In general, the potential advantages of using biological matrices as an alternative to urine include less invasive collection requirements, availability of multiple samples, ability to detect the parent or the pharmacologically active moiety, greater analyte stability, a lower disease risk, and easier shipment and storage.

Urine

Regulated workplace drug testing utilizes urine as the specimen of choice for identifying cocaine metabolite, phencyclidine, opiates, cannabinoids amphetamines, and MDMA. In nonregulated workplace drug testing, urine is also used to test for additional drugs or drug classes such as methadone, benzodiazepines, and ethanol.

More than 90% of U.S. companies select urine as the testing specimen. Advantages include ease of collection, ease of testing, the presence of high concentrations of the parent drug and/or metabolites, and the relative inexpensiveness of testing. The limitations of using urine as a testing matrix include the following: drug concentrations cannot be related to impairment; drugs and/or metabolites may remain in urine for one to seven days, therefore reflecting only recent use; urine collection procedures may be embarrassing or uncomfortable to an individual if the testing procedures mandate witnessing the void; and specimens may be adulterated or tampered with. Such adulteration may include substitution of the specimen, dilution with water, or addition of substances to alter the testing results. Compounds that have been used to adulterate samples include alcohol, ammonia, ascorbic acid, Visine®, lemon juice, salt, peroxide, vinegar, detergent, golden seal root, and bleach. These adulterants may affect urine pH, specific gravity, and chloride levels.

Potentially adulterated specimens may be detected by measuring the above parameters. For instance, diluted samples may be identified by monitoring the specimen's creatinine and specific gravity, though not all possible adulterants may be identified by these procedures. A case in point: detection of glutaraldehyde requires fluorometric determination using an Abbott ADx® analyzer or GC/MS analysis. Potentially adulterated specimens may also be detected by observing sample smell and appearance. Some adulterants, such as salt, may not completely dissolve in the specimen, whereas an adulterant like Drano® produces a green precipitate. Foam may be visible in specimens adulterated with soap or detergent.

Screening procedures are typically more sensitive to the effects of adulterants than confirmation techniques. Since most screening procedures utilize immunoassay technology, a substance that interferes with the antibody will impact the results. Adulterants may also cause absorbance in enzyme and fluorescence immunoassays. The impact of adulterants is also dependent on the drug being assayed. For example THCCOOH assays are especially sensitive to the effects of adulterants. However, the effects may cause a positive or a negative result. Results may also be dependent on the particular immunoassay technology utilized, for example, detergent causes a false-negative EMIT THCCOOH result but causes the RIA to measure THCCOOH at elevated concentrations.

Hair

Hair, comprised of approximately 65–95% protein (keratin, melanin); 1–9% lipid; and trace elements, polysaccharides, and water, is an epidermal outgrowth of the hair follicle. The base of the follicle is a bulb that contains matrix cells for producing the cell matrices present in the shaft, namely the hair cuticle, cortex, and medulla. Drugs enter the hair by several mechanisms: diffusion from the blood supplying the hair follicle; absorption of sebaceous gland secretions; absorption of drugs from sweat deposited on the skin surface; and absorption through the hair shaft of drug particles deposited on the surface by the external environment.

Hair has been used as a testing matrix in forensic toxicology for many years, initially to identify exposure to metals such as arsenic, lead, and mercury. More recently, hair has been utilized to detect drugs of abuse. To date, heroin, 6-acetylmorphine, codeine, morphine, methamphetamine, amphetamine, caffeine, cocaine and metabolites, nicotine and cotinine, delta-9-tetrahydrocannabinol, barbiturates, benzodiazepines, phencyclidine, methadone, and several therapeutic drugs have been measured in hair. In such testing, head hair is typically utilized, although axillae, arm, and beard hair have been used.

Existing analytical methodologies may be used to assay hair for drugs. However, more attention must be given to sample collection, sample preparation, and the method's analytical sensitivity. Head hair samples are usually plucked using tweezers or cut as close to the scalp as possible. Samples may be collected from different scalp areas but the vertex or crown is the most common. Since head hair grows approximately 1 cm per month, segmental analysis may be possible to determine time of use. If this testing is to be done, the head hair should be aligned after collection, to identify the root and tip ends. Approximately 150–200 strands (or 50 mg) are needed. Sample preparation for analysis will include a washing step in which the hair is washed in a buffer, water, or methanol in order to remove potential external contaminants. (However, repeated washings may remove drug from the hair itself.) After washing, the hair may be incubated in buffer or organic solvent for a period of time prior to solid-phase extraction of the supernatant. Alternatively, the hair may be digested by enzyme or acid/base hydrolysis prior to extraction. Some investigators have pulverized the hair, producing a powder for analysis. Most testing methods utilize solid-phase extraction followed by GC/MS or tandem mass spectrometry analysis for the identification and quantitation of drugs in hair.

Advantages of hair as a drug-testing matrix include the ease and noninvasiveness of collection and the ability of the specimen to measure long-term drug use. In addition, hair may be the only sample available for testing under certain circumstances, such as in death investigations of skeletal remains or traumatic injury. Another advantage is the stability of the specimen, permitting hazard-free storage and transportation. Limitations

of hair as a drug-testing matrix include the cost, which is estimated to be at least twice the cost of urinalysis. At the present time, drug concentrations in hair have not been correlated with dose or time of administration. In addition, most investigators consider issues of environmental contamination to be significant; active drug use may not be able to be differentiated from passive exposure. The current state of knowledge about how substances are incorporated into the hair is actually in its infancy. In addition, recent research suggests that there may be a potential for bias regarding race and hair color in hair testing, because drugs may be preferentially bound to pigmented hair.

Sweat

Sweat, or perspiration, is produced as the body's response to exercise or thermal stress. Sweat is produced by eccrine glands located over most of the body surface. Apocrine sweat glands, located in the axillae, pubic, and mammary areas, also produce sweat. In addition, water is lost from the skin by a process known as insensible perspiration. This results from passive diffusion of substances through the dermal and epidermal layers of skin. Although the body excretes drugs in sweat, the mechanism by which drugs are deposited into sweat is ill defined. Transfer from the extensive blood supply throughout the skin is a possible mechanism.

Several devices have been invented to collect sweat to test for drugs of abuse. These collection devices typically consist of a tamper-proof adhesive membrane with an absorbent patch. The individual wears the patch for a period of time, commonly ranging from one day to one week. The patch is then removed and sent to a laboratory for testing. At the laboratory, the absorbent patch or collection pad is soaked and agitated in an aqueous buffer before subjecting the supernatant to testing. Testing procedures developed for the analysis of drugs of abuse in sweat have used solid-phase extraction followed by

GC/MS. Other testing methodologies have utilized ELISA and RIA. To date, the following drugs have been detected in sweat: ethanol, amphetamine, methamphetamine, barbiturates, benzodiazepines, buprenorphine, cocaine, codeine, heroin, methadone, 6-acetylmorphine, phencyclidine, and delta-9-tetrahydrocannabinol. Typically, the parent drug is the principal analyte detected in sweat. Therefore, assays targeted to drug metabolites would not be sufficiently sensitive for this type of testing. The range of drug concentrations found in sweat are as follows: from 2–4000 ng/mL for cocaine; –0.6 g/L for ethanol; to 40–600 ng/patch for methadone.

Sweat collection devices have been approved by the U.S. Food and Drug Administration for clinical and drugs of abuse testing. They are currently used to monitor drug abstinence in criminal justice and drug treatment programs. The advantage of testing for drugs in sweat is the noninvasive collection technique for providing a cumulative specimen. These semiocclusive sweat collection patches are impermeable to environmental contaminants and cannot be replaced after removal. However, adulterants may be injected into the patch and in this way adversely affect subsequent testing. Additional limitations of this matrix include the lack of information regarding drug incorporation into sweat and the paucity of pharmacokinetic data relating dose to drug concentrations. This renders interpretation of results problematic. Drug concentrations may be related to dose if the sweat drug concentrations could be normalized to the volume of sweat collected. Additionally, the minimum dose to produce a positive result and the minimum length of time the patch should be worn to optimize collection are unknown. Testing of the sweat patch costs approximately the same as urinalysis. However, the entire patch is usually consumed in the analysis, preventing further testing. Currently, sweat testing is not utilized in the workplace drug-testing industry and there are no proficiency programs that utilize this specimen.

Saliva or Oral Fluid

Saliva is a colorless fluid secreted by the salivary glands. These are compound racemose glands with many lobes that may be subdivided into major and minor glands. The major glands (parotid, submandibular, and sublingual) are located outside the buccal cavity and contain a long duct system in order to deposit secretions into the mouth. The minor glands (labial, buccal, palatine, and lingual) have short ducts and are located in the walls of the mouth and under the tongue. Drugs may enter the saliva through the processes of passive diffusion, ultrafiltration, and active transport. The partition of drugs between plasma and saliva has been described utilizing the principles of drug transfer across biological membranes.

As a drug-testing matrix, saliva has been useful in therapeutic drug monitoring, the insurance industry (HIV, benzoylecgonine, cotinine), and the transportation industry (ethanol). Specimens may be collected by several techniques: secretions from individual glands may be collected by isolating the gland, followed by cannulation; by tilting the head forward and allowing the saliva to drain freely from the mouth into a container; by expectorating into a container; or by placing a cotton swab or gauze in the mouth and allowing the saliva to be absorbed over a period of time or until saturated. In all cases except the first example, it is more correct to state that oral fluid is being collected. For multiple drug analysis, several milliliters of saliva are necessary. Therefore, collection techniques may incorporate stimulation of saliva flow. This may be achieved by chewing a piece of Teflon® or Parafilm®, or placing citric acid crystals in the mouth. Changes in saliva flow result in alterations in pH that will affect the concentration of drugs in saliva.

Many drugs have been detected in saliva: ethanol, amphetamines, barbiturates, benzodiazepines, caffeine, cocaine, THC, opiates, and phencyclidine. The parent drug is typically the principal analyte. In one study, peak saliva concentrations of cocaine, after intravenous administration of 40 mg to human subjects, ranged from 428–1927 ng/ mL. After smoked administration of a similar dose, peak saliva concentrations ranged from 15,000 to >500,000 ng/mL (high concentrations of drugs after smoking are due to drug contamination of the oral cavity). Drug detection times were slightly longer in saliva than plasma after administration by both routes. However, in both matrices this time was short, approximately 10 h. After smoking cocaine, anhydroecgonine methyl ester (AEME), the pyrolysis product of cocaine, may be detected in saliva. There have been no published clinical reports to date of detection of this analyte in plasma. Similarly, after heroin and marijuana smoking, high concentrations of the parent drug are detected in saliva in the immediate period following drug administration. Since saliva may be considered a filtrate of blood, conventional screening and confirmation methodologies may be utilized to analyze drugs in this matrix. Sample preparation may include cell disruption, centrifugation, and filtration.

The advantages of saliva as a drug-testing matrix include noninvasiveness and relative ease of collection; determination of pharmacokinetic parameters for drug appearance, metabolism, and excretion; possibility of relating drug concentrations to pharmacological effects; detection of unique analytes (e.g., AEME); and little modification of existing analytical methods. The limitations include the lack of data regarding drug deposition in this matrix, relatively short drug detection times, and appearance of the parent drug as a major analyte, thereby limiting the usefulness of assays targeted toward drug metabolites. Further, oral and smoked routes of drug administration will result in contamination of the buccal cavity immediately following drug use, which complicates interpretation of saliva levels. In addition, collection methods will alter the amount of the parent drug and metabolites excreted in saliva. Therefore, if saliva is to be considered in the future as a specimen for workplace drug testing, collection and sample preparation procedures should be standardized.

SUGGESTED READING

1. Armbruster DA, Tillman MD, Hubbs LM. Limit of detection (LOD)/limit of quantitation (LOQ): comparison of the empirical and the statistical methods exemplified with GC–MS assays of abused drugs. Clin Chem 1994;40:1233–8.
2. Cone EJ, Welch MJ, Grigson Babecki MB, eds. Hair testing for drugs of abuse. Rockville, MD: International Research on Standards and Technology, National Institutes of Health, U.S. Department of Health and Human Services, National Institute on Drug Abuse, 1995. NIH Publication No. 95-3727.
3. Department of Health and Human Services Substance Abuse and Mental Health Services Administration Drug Testing Advisory Board. Scientific meeting on drug testing of alternative specimens and technologies, April 28–30, 1997. Rockville, MD: SAMHSA, 1997.
4. Goldberger BA, Cone EJ. Confirmatory tests for drugs in the workplace by gas chromatography-mass spectrometry. J Chromato 1994;A674:73–86.
5. Goldberger BA, Huestis MA, Wilkins DG. Commonly practiced quality control and quality assurance procedures for gas chromatography/mass spectrometry analysis in forensic urine drug-testing laboratories. Forensic Sci Rev 1997;9:59–78.
6. Goldberger BA, Jenkins AJ. Testing of abused drugs in urine by immunological techniques. AACC Therapeutic Drug Monitoring and Toxicology 1992;13(8):7–25.
7. Huestis MA, Mitchell JM, Cone EJ. Lowering the federally mandated cannabinoid immunoassay cut-off increases true-positive results. Clin Chem 1994;40(5):729–33.
8. Jenkins AJ. Detecting drugs of abuse in saliva. AACC Therapeutic Drug Monitoring and Toxicology 1998;19(3):65–74.
9. Jenkins AJ, Goldberger BA, eds. On-site drug testing. Totowa NJ: Humana Press Inc., 2002.
10. Karch SB, ed. Drug abuse handbook. Boca Raton, FL: CRC Press LLC, 1998.
11. Kintz P, ed. Drug testing in hair. Boca Raton, FL: CRC Press LLC, 1996.
12. Liu RH, Goldberger BA, eds. Handbook of workplace drug testing. Washington, DC: AACC Press, 1995.
13. Ropero-Miller JD, Goldberger BA, eds. Handbook of workplace drug testing, 2nd ed. Washington, DC: AACC Press, 2009.
14. Shults TF, ed. Medical review officer handbook, 9th ed. Research Triangle Park, NC: Quadrangle Research, LLC, 2009.

15. Sniegoski L, Welch M. Interlaboratory studies on the analysis of hair for drugs of abuse: results from the fourth exercise. J Anal Toxicol 1996;20:242.

16. Spiehler V. Detecting drugs of abuse in sweat. AACC Therapeutic Drug Monitoring and Toxicology 1997;18(2):37–45.

17. Wong SH, Sunshine I, eds. Handbook of analytical therapeutic drug monitoring and toxicology. Boca Raton, FL: CRC Press LLC, 1997.

18. Wu AHB, Ostheimer D, Cremese M, Forte E, Hill D. Characterization of drug interferences caused by coelution of substances in gas chromatography/mass spectrometry confirmation of targeted drugs in full-scan and selected ion-monitoring modes. Clin Chem 1994;40(2):216–20.

CHAPTER 4

Performance-Enhancing Drug Testing

Dennis J. Crouch and Melinda K. Shelby

The use of performance-enhancing drugs has traditionally been associated with athletes competing or aspiring to compete in the Olympic Games. However, the use of these drugs has escalated dramatically, and today they are a significant problem in middle and high schools, colleges and universities, organized amateur sports, and professional sports. The attributes of performance-enhancing (PE) drugs (whether actual or perceived) such as competitive advantage, muscle development, and improved self-image have contributed to their use even by recreational athletes and in certain workplace settings. Testing for PE drugs is now common at all levels of sport and in safety-sensitive work environments such as the military, police, security officers, and firefighters. Some applications for testing have both sports and workplace implications, such as the testing of professional athletes. Medical examiner investigations of the deaths of high school, amateur, collegiate, professional, and, even, aspiring athletes have exposed the potential toxicity and lethality of PE drugs.

PE drug testing can, in part, be differentiated from the array of forensic drug testing applications by the scope of drugs tested. Testing programs often include tens if not hundreds of drugs and metabolites. Typically, programs include testing for marijuana, common stimulants and opioids, and anabolic-androgenic steroids (AAS). However, as demonstrated in Table 1, programs may also include diuretics, masking agents, glucocorticosteroids, beta-2 agonists, aromatase inhibitors, and other drugs that affect the production and actions of estrogen, peptide hormones, growth factors, alcohol, beta-blockers, and synthetic cannabinoids. Substances may be prohibited in certain sports, during competition, or at all times. The international scope of athletic competitions, the breadth of testing applications, and the number of drugs require that PE drug-testing laboratories possess diverse analytical capabilities and employ a highly trained technical staff.

The ancient Greeks were believed to have used various herbs and mushrooms during sporting competitions to improve performance. In the late 1800s, French athletes reportedly used cocktails of coca leaves and wine to combat fatigue and prolong exercise routines. By the 1950s, stimulant use was reported in the Oslo Winter Olympics and allegations of AAS use by Russian and other Eastern European athletes surfaced. The abuse of PE drugs reached a critical juncture when stimulant use was implicated in the deaths of several cyclists, including a Danish rider, in the 1960 Rome Olympics. Because of mounting evidence of PE use by competitive athletes, the International Olympic Committee (IOC) developed a drug-testing program for the 1968 Olympics and further refined for the 1972 event. Testing for AAS lagged behind stimulant testing until the mid-1970s, when radioimmunoassay (RIA) tests for AAS were introduced. Subsequently, AAS testing using gas chromatograph (GC) mass spectrometry (MS) was developed and the first widespread AAS testing occurred during the 1976 Olympics in Montreal.

Table 1. Performance-Enhancing Drug Testing—Drug Classes and Example Drugs

Drug Class	Sample Drugs
Steroids and anabolics	Endogenous steroids and precursors: androstenedione, androstendiol, dehydroepiandrosterone, testosterone, dihydrotestosterone
	Exogenous: nandrolone, stanazolol, methyltestosterone, oxandrolone, tetrahydrogestrinone, trenbolone, methandienone, boldenone
	Others: clenbuterol, androgen receptor modulators, testosterone/epitestosterone ratio (T/E ratio)
Stimulants	Amphetamine, methamphetamine, methylphenidate, phentermine, methylenedioxyamphetamine, methylenedioxymethamphetamine, cocaine
	Others: ephedrine, pseudoephedrine, methylhexaneamine, modafinil, selegiline
Diuretics and masking agents	Diuretics: furosemide, hydrochlorothiazide, amiloride, canrenone, triamterene, bumetanide
	Others: epitestosterone, probenecid
Opioids	Morphine, codeine, oxycodone, hydrocodone, hydromorphone, fentanyl, meperidine, pentazocine, propoxyphene
Peptide hormones	Human growth hormone (hGH), insulin-like growth factor (IGF-1), human chorionic gonadotropin (hCH), luteninzing hormone (LH), insulin
	Erythropoetin (EPO)
Marijuana and synthetic cannabinoids	THC, THC metabolites, JWH-018, JWH-073, JWH-200, WIN 55211, HU-308, HU-331, CP-4797
Other drugs	Alcohol: ethanol
	Beta-blockers: alprenolol, atenolol, nadolol, pindolol, timolol, propranolol, metaprolol
	Beta-2-agonists: salbutamol, salmeterol, terbutaline, formeterol
	Glucocorticosteroids: budesonide, betamethasone, dexamethasone, methylprednisolone, prednisolone
	Aromatase inhibitors: anasterole, formestane, exemestane
	Selective estrogen receptor modulators and antiestrogens: tamoxifen, raloxifene, clomiphene, fluvestrant
	Misuse of prescription drugs
	"and related substances"
	Gene doping

50

The availability of robust and affordable mass spectrometers has been a significant factor in the development of effective testing methods for PE drugs and in the proliferation of testing programs. Because of the diversity of tested drugs, the consequences of testing, and the sensitivity and specificity needed to detect and confirm the presence of these drugs and their characteristic metabolites, the use of state-of-the-art technologies such as GC/MS, GC-MS/MS, high-performance liquid chromatography (HPLC)/MS, and HPLC-MS/MS continue to increase.

TESTING APPROACH

The details of many PE drug-testing programs are confidential and highly variable in their application, drugs tested, and consequences. The consequences of a first positive test may be a referral to a qualified assessment and treatment specialist or suspension from competition. Penalties for subsequent positive tests range from treatment to suspension to a permanent ban from competition. Because of this variability, it is difficult if not impossible to discuss the nuances of each program. Therefore, presented here are representative antidoping approaches with accompanying discussion of individual variability.

In-competition PE testing under the World Anti-Doping Agency (WADA) is among the most comprehensive (Table 1). Other programs focus testing efforts, in part due to financial considerations. Testing such as that required by the National Collegiate Athletic Association (NCAA), high schools, institutionally by colleges and universities, and professional sports, is usually limited to a subset of the drugs and drug classes shown in Table 1. Because of its mission and international scope, WADA includes numerous drugs in most of the banned drug classes. Alternate programs are often modeled after WADA and its prohibited substances list, but usually do not contain nearly as many drugs/classes. The drugs tested may also vary by reason for testing. For example, under WADA's program, alcohol and beta-blockers are only banned in certain sports. Many programs limit out-of-competition testing to analyses for commonly abused drugs, AAS, masking agents, and perhaps an expanded list of stimulants. For-cause testing may target a single drug such as alcohol or marijuana.

Blood specimens are collected in a limited number of testing programs and for only a very limited number of tests. For example, blood may be used for ethanol testing (blood or breath) and testing for indications of transfusions and other blood-doping activities. Blood testing for reticulocyte counts and hematocrit and hemoglobin concentrations are often performed in cycling and in Olympic endurance events such as cross-country skiing. Urine is by far the predominant specimen collected and analyzed in antidoping programs. Although collection protocols vary, most are witnessed and specimen identification and handling and analysis procedures follow strict chain-of-custody protocols. Most programs specify "split specimen" collections and designate the specimen bottles as "A" and "B"; testing is performed on the A specimen and the B specimen is reserved for retests (see below). Specimen validity criteria are program dependent but frequently include a minimum volume and specific gravity (SG), pH, and/or creatinine measurements. Minimum volumes of 30 mL and 15 mL, respectively, for the A and B bottles are typical. WADA has a unique requirement designed to ensure that specimens are not too dilute: The athlete must provide a specimen with a SG ≥ 1.005 before the athlete is released from the collection site.

Specimen testing follows the common forensic model of screening followed by confirmation of presumptive-positive screen results. Screening and confirmation analyses are performed on urine from the A bottle. The B bottle urine is tested only at the request of the athlete or an authorized representative. In contrast to workplace testing, often both the A and B bottle samples are tested in the same laboratory. One or more approved observers can usually witness B bottle testing. Many antidoping programs specify screen and confirmation cutoff concentrations, and laboratories must show that the detected drugs or metabolites are present at concentrations ≥ cutoff before they can be reported. The WADA program has a decidedly different approach: It specifies Minimum Required Performance Levels (MRPL) for laboratories in its program. For example, the MRPL for most AAS is 10 ng/mL, which means that labs must be capable of detecting *at least* 10 ng/mL of a specified AAS or its metabolite(s). However, the laboratory *may* test to lower concentrations if it has sufficient analytical sensitivity. The WADA program has a limited number of substances termed "threshold substances"; analysis of these substances fit the more traditional cutoff concentration model. For example, the laboratory must demonstrate that marijuana metabolite (THC-COOH), morphine, or ephedrine have been confirmed at concentrations of ≥15 ng/mL, 1,000 ng/mL, or 10,000 ng/mL, respectively, before these drugs can be reported.

Quality control and batch configuration varies. For those programs adhering to the cutoff model, screening and confirmation batches typically include the following: (1) a drug-free urine sample; (2) one or more calibrators; and (3) sufficient quality control samples to ensure discrimination between positive and negative samples when the drug concentration is near the cutoff. For programs not using specified cutoff concentrations, screening and confirmation batches typically include a drug-free urine sample and one or more quality control samples containing the drug.

Because urine is tested in the vast majority of PE programs, drug metabolites are frequently detected. The inclusion of metabolites greatly expands the number of compounds banned in most programs. Inclusion of metabolites also affects extraction protocols, analysis procedures, and data evaluation and interpretation. For example, metabolites of the many AAS, as well as those of opioids and marijuana, must be hydrolyzed before they can be efficiently extracted. Urinary metabolites are often too polar to be analyzed by GC methods without derivatization. Metabolites detected in the urine may not be unique and may result from metabolic pathways shared with other drugs; for example, morphine may be detected as a metabolite of codeine and amphetamine a metabolite of methamphetamine.

Analyzing urine for PE drugs is also challenging because urine volume varies with the athlete's degree of hydration. Following competition or training, the athlete may be dehydrated, resulting in the transient concentration of drugs and drug metabolites in the urine. Concentration increases the likelihood of detection but confounds interpretation. Conversely, overhydration dilutes the urine, decreases the concentration, reduces the likelihood of detection, and also affects interpretation. As a consequence, many programs attempt to "normalize" or "correct" the drug/metabolite (or cutoff) concentration to a predetermined standard such as a creatinine of 20 mg/dL or a SG of 1.020. Normalizing, or correcting, to SG is more widely accepted and more easily defended than normalizing to creatinine.

The following formula may be used to correct a specimen concentration to a SG of 1.020:

Corrected Specimen Concentration = (Measure Drug Concentration in Specimen) × [(1.020 − 1)/(Specimen SG − 1)].

If the measured SG and concentration of the drug in the specimen were 1.010 and 50 ng/mL, respectively, then:

Corrected Specimen Concentration = (50 ng/mL) × (1.020 − 1)/(1.010 − 1).

Corrected Specimen Concentration = 100 ng/mL

Correction of the urinary drug/metabolite concentration for SG provides a valuable interpretative tool, especially when monitoring an athlete for reuse or continued use of a PE drug.

DRUGS AND DRUG CLASSES

Anabolic-Androgenic Steroids and Anabolic Agents

Anabolic agents are among the most used and detected of all PE drugs. AAS and other anabolic agents promote nitrogen retention, protein synthesis, and the development of lean muscle mass. Clinically, AAS may be used in the treatment of metastatic breast cancer, wasting diseases, types of anemia, male hypogonadism, and delayed male puberty. Anecdotally, AAS are reputed to increase strength, conditioning and the duration of workouts, improve recovery after workouts or injury, and promote aggressiveness. Theoretically, the physiological effects of steroids should benefit athletes. However, controlled clinical studies demonstrating the PE benefits of steroids are rare, although there is a general acceptance scientifically that AAS use has a positive effect on muscle development, strength, and endurance.

For the purposes of this discussion, the AAS are divided into two broad classifications: synthetic (exogenous) and endogenous (Table 1). Synthetic steroids are manufactured, have effects similar to testosterone, and include drugs such as nandrolone, stanozolol, trenbolone, methyltestosterone, methandienone, oxandrolone, and boldenone in addition to a continuing onslaught of designer steroids such as tetrahydrogestrinone (THG). Endogenous steroids include testosterone (T), epitestosterone (E), dehydroepiandrosterone (DHEA), dihydrotestosterone (DHT), androstenedione (A-dione), and androstenediol (A-diol) and are produced in the body primarily by the

testis or adrenal glands (Fig. 1). As shown in Table 2, MS is used to both screen and confirm AAS in the urine. Most AAS substances are extensive metabolized and their Phase 1 metabolites are conjugated; therefore, hydrolysis of the urine is required for efficient extraction and detection. Sample preparation for screening usually involves isolation of the free and conjugated metabolites using solid-phase extraction (SPE), enzymatic hydrolysis, liquid:liquid extraction (LLE) of the hydrolysates, and formation of trimethylsilyl derivatives prior to GC/MS analysis. Although HPLC/MS, HPLC-MS/MS, and GC-MS/MS and full scan MS acquisition are sometimes used, selected ion monitoring (SIM) using GC/MS remains the standard screening approach. Confirmation of synthetic AAS presumptively identified during screening may be by any of the MS techniques shown in Table 2. However, there is increasing use of MS/MS analyzers and higher, or high-resolution, instruments such as time of flight (TOF) and Orbitrap mass spectrometers. Sample preparation for confirmation is typically similar to that used for screening. Often certified reference materials are not available for use as standards or to fortify quality control samples. Therefore, urine collected from subjects given the suspected drug in controlled clinical studies is used as an "excretion" control. At a minimum, confirmation batches include a drug-free

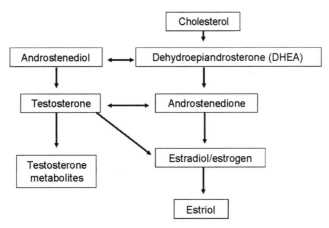

Fig. 1. Abbreviated steroid pathway.

sample, a drug/metabolite-fortified sample or excretion control, and the athlete's sample. For confirmation of drugs/metabolites with a quantitative cutoff or threshold, fortified calibrators are included in each batch. Sample preparation may be very similar to that used for screening. MS or MS/MS analyses often include both full scan and SIM or selected reaction monitoring (SRM) data acquisitions. Data are evaluated by retention time, the presence of characteristic ions, and the absence of interfering chromatographic peaks and extraneous ions. Data evaluation often includes ion ratio calculations and comparisons.

Detection of exogenous use of endogenous steroids, such as T and the examples shown in Table 1 and Fig. 1, is far more challenging than detecting synthetic AAS use. Screening by standard GC/MS, GC-MS/MS, HPLC/MS, or HPLC-MS/MS techniques cannot distinguish steroids produced naturally from those administered exogenously. "Steroid profiling" has been used to identify exogenous administration of a natural steroid. This approach assumes that the athlete's "normal" urinary steroid excretion profile has been characterized and that exogenous administration of a natural steroid produces detectable changes in the normal profile. A variation of this approach has been to establish population-based "normal profiles" to which an individual athlete's profile can be compared. In addition to profiling, the absolute concentrations (or SG-adjusted concentrations) and the ratios of the natural steroids can be monitored as indicators of administration. T/E is the most commonly monitored ratio. The T/E ratio varies somewhat based on factors such as race but is approximately 1 in normal males. The exogenous use of T increases urinary T concentrations, may decrease E concentrations, and results in an increased T/E ratio. Antidoping programs use different T/E ratios (4:1 and 6:1) as evidence of T administration. Although exceeding these ratios may provide suggestive evidence of administration,

Table 2. Performance-Enhancing Drug Testing—Methodologies Used for Different Drug Classes

Drug Class	Screen Techniques	Confirmation Techniques
Steroids and anabolics	GC/MS, GC-MS/MS, HPLC/MS, HPLC-MS/MS	GC/MS, GC-MS/MS, HPLC/MS, HPLC-MS/MS, GC/IR, GC/HRMS, HPLC/HRMS
Stimulants	GC, GC/MS, GC-MS/MS, HPLC, HPLC/MS, HPLC-MS/MS	GC/MS, GC-MS/MS, HPLC/MS, HPLC-MS/MS
Diuretics and masking agents	GC, GC/MS, GC-MS/MS, HPLC, HPLC/MS, HPLC-MS/MS	GC/MS, GC-MS/MS, HPLC/MS, HPLC-MS/MS
Opioids	IA, GC/MS, GC-MS/MS, HPLC/MS, HPLC-MS/MS	GC/MS, GC-MS/MS, HPLC/MS, HPLC-MS/MS
Marijuana	IA, GC/MS	GC/MS
Synthetic cannabinoiods	GC/MS-MSHPLC/MS, HPLC-MS/MS	HPLC/MS, HPLC-MS/MS
Peptide hormones	IA	IA
Alcohol	IA, GC, Breath analyzers	IA, GC, Breath analyzer
Beta-blockers	GC/MS, HPLC/MS, HPLC-MS/MS	GC/MS, HPLC/MS, HPLC-MS/MS
Beta-2-agonists	GC/MS, GC-MS/MS, HPLC/MS, HPLC-MS/MS	GC/MS, GC-MS/MS, HPLC/MS, HPLC-MS/MS
Glucocorticosteroids	HPLC/MS, HPLC-MS/MS	HPLC/MS, HPLC-MS/MS
Aromatase inhibitors	HPLC/MS, HPLC-MS/MS	HPLC/MS, HPLC-MS/MS
Selective estrogen receptor modulators and antiestrogens	HPLC/MS, HPLC-MS/MS	HPLC/MS, HPLC-MS/MS

IA = immunoassay; GC = gas chromatography; HPLC = high-performance liquid chromatography; MS = mass spectrometry; MS/MS = combined mass spectrometry techniques; IR = isotope ratio mass spectrometry; HRMS = high-resolution mass spectrometry.

substantial interindividual variation of T/E ratios exists. As stated, standard MS techniques cannot differentiate exogenous T from that naturally produced by the athlete. However, isotope ratio MS (IRMS) is an evolving and promising technique that is being increasingly used to detect the administration of endogenous steroids such as T. IRMS can distinguish between stable isotope forms such as ^{13}C and ^{12}C. Pharmaceutically prepared T is synthesized from C_3 (soy) plants that incorporate less ^{13}C than C_4 plants. An athlete's normal diet includes both C_3 and C_4 plants. Consequently, steroids such as T produced in the body reflect a diet of both C_3 and C_4 plants and contain more ^{13}C than T produced for pharmaceutical use. When pharmaceutical T is administered, it lowers the $^{13}C/^{12}C$ ratio of the athlete's T and this change can be detected by IRMS. The measured $^{13}C/^{12}C$ of T is then compared to that of an endogenous steroid such as pregnanediol that is not in the anabolic pathway.

Stimulants

Stimulant use was reported in the 1952 Oslo Winter Olympics and has been implicated in the deaths of several cyclists, including a Danish rider in the 1960 Rome Olympics. More recently, the use of stimulants such as ephedrine has been associated with the deaths of high school, college, and professional athletes. Research into the PE effects of stimulants has shown mixed results. Some studies have revealed performance decrements or at best performance-neutral results while others have shown improved body composition (through the loss of fat) as well as improved focus and reaction time, especially in fatigued subjects. The number of banned stimulants in most programs approaches that of AAS and, following the prevalence of AAS, stimulants are among the most frequently detected PE drugs in antidoping programs.

As shown in Table 2, both GC and MS methods are used to screen for stimulants. GC with nitrogen phosphorus detection (NPD)

has been used historically, but this technique is being replaced by GC/MS and HPLC-MS/MS methods. Sample preparation for screening usually involves isolation of the drug or its characteristic metabolites from urine using SPE or LLE. Derivatization may or may not follow extraction depending on the stimulant and the analytical approach preferred by the laboratory. Although GC/NPD, HPLC/MS, HPLC-MS/MS, and GC-MS/MS and full scan MS acquisition may be used, many laboratories use GC/MS with SIM for screening. Confirmation of stimulants presumptively identified during screening may proceed by any of the variety of MS techniques shown in Table 2. There is growing use of MS/MS instrumentation, especially HPLC-MS/MS. Sample preparation for confirmation is typically similar to that used for screening. As with the confirmation of AAS, certified reference materials may not be available for esoteric stimulants that are available only in certain regions or countries, and excretion controls may be used during confirmation. At a minimum, confirmation batches include a drug-free sample, a drug/metabolite-fortified sample, or excretion control in addition to the athlete's sample. MS or MS/MS analyses often include both full scan and SIM or SRM data acquisitions and data are evaluated by retention time, the presence of characteristic ions, ion ratio calculations, and the absence of interfering chromatographic peaks and extraneous ions.

Quantitative cutoffs or threshold concentrations are incorporated into many programs for specified stimulants. Caffeine, ephedrine, pseudoephedrine, methylephedrine, and cathine are among the stimulants often banned only if their concentration exceeds the program's established cutoff. Confirmation of these stimulants requires quality control that ensures the quantitative accuracy of the analysis.

Because of the availability of over-the-counter (OTC) products such as l-methamphetamine, d- and l-stereoisomer determinations may be conducted. These determinations are performed by MS using either a chromatographic column capable of chiral separations or reagents that result in derivatives that can be separated with a standard chromatographic column.

Stimulants such as amphetamine and methylphenidate may used clinically to treat attention deficit disorders. The legitimate therapeutic use of these and other drugs such as opioids, glucocorticoids, certain beta-2-agonists, and, even, T creates a dilemma for sports agencies and antidoping programs. To address this problem, athletes are required to (1) have a clinically valid diagnosis of their disorder; (2) possess a legitimate prescription for the treatment drug; and (3) predisclose their condition. Assuming the diagnosis and therapy are appropriate, athletes are given a therapeutic use exemption (TUE) and can take their prescribed drug without risking disciplinary actions from the governing program. However, the topic of TUEs and the associated requirements of an appropriate clinical diagnosis and drug therapy are often controversial and the subject of substantial programmatic discussion and review.

Diuretics and Masking Agents

Clinically, diuretic drugs are prescribed to increase urine flow and reduce edema associated with conditions such as hypertension and congestive heart failure. Athletes abuse diuretics to reduce body water and "make weight" in sports with weight classifications such as wrestling, boxing, and weight lifting. Diuretics may also be abused to increase urine volume, thereby decreasing urinary drug and metabolite concentrations (see SG discussion above). Decreasing drug and metabolite concentrations reduces the likelihood of detection. It also increases the likelihood that the drug or metabolite concentration may be lower than the program's cutoff or threshold concentration. When abused in sports, diuretic drugs are often referred to as masking agents. Some programs consider E a masking agent because its administration reduces the T/E ratio and can mask exogenous T administration. Probenecid is also considered

a potential masking agent because it can extend the excretion time of some drugs, effectively reducing their urine concentration.

Historically, HPLC, GC, or GC/MS methods have been used to detect diuretics. Sample preparation for screening usually involved LLE of the drug or its characteristic metabolites from the athlete's urine. Derivatization is followed for GC methods but not for HPLC methods. Because the chemical structures and functional groups of the diuretics vary considerably, HPLC/MS or HPLC-MS/MS methods using SRM acquisition are now standard screening approaches. HPLC/MS and HPLC-MS/MS analyses incorporate the formation and monitoring of positive and negative ions or, in some cases, both. Confirmation of diuretics presumptively identified during screening may proceed by any of the variety of MS techniques shown in Table 2. However, there is growing use of HPLC-MS/MS. Sample preparation for confirmation is similar to that used for screening. As with the confirmation of the previously discussed PE drugs, the lack of certified reference materials for esoteric diuretics and their metabolites requires labs to use excretion controls. At a minimum, confirmation batches include a drug-free sample, drug/metabolite-fortified sample or excretion control, and the athlete's sample. MS or MS/MS analyses often include both full scan and SIM or (SRM) data acquisitions and data are evaluated by retention time, the presence of characteristic ions, and the absence of interfering chromatographic peaks and extraneous ions.

Narcotic Analgesics

Antidoping programs ban the nonprescription use of narcotic analgesics. Many laboratories use commercial immunoassay (IA) tests to screen for analgesic drugs such as those listed in Table 1. These compounds may also be detected while screening for AAS via chromatographic techniques. Sample preparation for screening usually involves hydrolysis of the urine and isolation of the free drug and metabolites using SPE or LLE.

Derivatization is needed for GC analyses of most banned analgesics but it is not necessary for the analysis of meperidine, propoxyphene, pentazocine, and methadone. Confirmation of presumptive positive screening results may be by any number of GC/MS, GC-MS/MS, HPLC/MS, or HPLC-MS/MS techniques (Table 2). Confirmation batches minimally include a drug-free sample, drug/metabolite-fortified sample or excretion control, and the athlete's sample. MS or MS/MS analyses often include both full scan and SIM or (SRM) data acquisitions, and data are evaluated by retention time, the presence of characteristic ions, perhaps ion ratio calculations, and the absence of interfering chromatographic peaks and extraneous ions.

Marijuana and Synthetic Cannabinoids

Marijuana (THC) is banned in most antidoping programs because it is illegal and abused. Whether THC has specific PE effects remains a debated question. Since about 2004, synthetic cannabinoids that mimic the effects of THC, such as JWH-018 and JWH-073, have been incorporated into spice products and widely distributed as herbal incense or household aromatics. Spice products were initially available over the counter in the U.S. and other countries. More than 400 synthetic cannabinoids have been synthesized and only a few are currently controlled by drug enforcement agencies. For most synthetic cannabinoids, the absorption, distribution, metabolism, and excretion patterns (especially in humans) have not been studied or reported in the scientific literature. Commercial IA tests can be used to detect marijuana use, and the literature contains numerous GC/MS and HPLC confirmation methods for THC-COOH, the predominate metabolite found in urine. However, synthetic cannabinoids are extensively metabolized and the metabolites can be conjugated. Consequently, sophisticated GC-MS/MS or HPLC-MS/MS procedures are needed to screen for and confirm their use. Hydrolyzed urine samples may be extracted using either LLE or SPE. Because multiple hydroxylated metabolites with similar MS and MS/MS spectra are formed following the use of JWH-018 and JWH-073, chromatographic separation of the metabolites is needed to ensure accurate identification even with MS/MS analyses.

Peptide Hormones

Human chorionic gonadotropin (hCG), luteninzing hormone (LH), erythropoetin (EPO), human growth hormone (hGH), and insulin-like growth factor (IGF-1) are among the peptide hormones banned in PE programs. All are endogenous substances; therefore, the major challenge confronting the laboratory is differentiating an administered peptide from what is naturally produced by the athlete. When exogenous steroids are administered, the body's natural production of T may decrease through normal endocrine feedback, and hCG and LH are used by athletes to stimulate the natural production of T. Commercial IA tests are used to detect hCG and LH administration. Confirmation of elevated concentrations of the peptides found in screening tests is performed with a second immunoassay that uses alternate antibodies, usually from a different commercial source. EPO is secreted by the kidneys and is a major hormone in erythropoiesis (red blood cell production). The PE effects of EPO are related to its stimulation of red cell production and the oxygen-carrying role of the cells. The use of EPO has been extensively chronicled in cycling and other endurance sports such as cross-country skiing. Since the introduction of recombinant EPO in the late 1980s and the subsequent release of similar drugs, various strategies have been advocated for detecting use, including measuring blood markers of EPO. More recently, antidoping scientists have relied on isoelectric focusing coupled with gel electrophoresis to distinguish endogenous EPO from the various exogenous forms that may be abused. There are widespread allegations of Olympic and professional athletes abusing growth factors such as IGF-1 and hGH. Both are naturally occurring and have anabolic effects. Human growth hormone has received the most antidoping attention. Secreted by the pituitary gland, it affects skeletal growth, muscle development, and fat metabolism and is required for normal growth and development. It also promotes vertical growth in individuals who have not yet reached their natural height, increases lean body mass by promoting skeletal muscle growth, and decreases fat mass by causing lipolysis in adipose tissue. Although the performance-enhancing effects of hGH have not been demonstrated scientifically, its metabolic effects have potential benefits for the athlete's image, training, strength, endurance, and performance. During the past decade, antidoping agencies have committed substantial resources to the development of testing strategies for the detection of exogenous hGH use. One strategy relies on monitoring changes in downstream markers of hGH administration such as IGF-1 and pro-collagen type 3 (P-III-P). The second strategy uses an IA testing paradigm to determine the ratio of recombinant hGH (a single epitope–22 kDa) to that of naturally occurring hGH present in multiple forms (22 kDa, 20 kDa, 17 kDa, 5 kDa, etc.). The paradigm detects a change in the ratio of the 22 kDa isoform to that of the other isoforms if the athlete uses recombinant hGH.

The detection and confirmation of exogenous peptide administration through IA tests has raised concerns among many forensic toxicologists and forensic organizations. Most forensic analyses utilize screening and confirmation methods based on differing chemical principles, e.g., IA screen and MS confirmation. Therefore, future research will likely focus on developing effective MS methods to confirm the exogenous administration of PE peptides.

Other Drugs

Alcohol

Alcohol (ethanol) is banned in some sports and competitions. Generally, it is banned only for those not of legal drinking age or if the athlete has a history of alcohol abuse. Programs may require blood, breath, or urine testing. Enzymatic and GC methods are used for blood and urine testing; infrared and electrochemical methods are used for breath testing.

Beta-Blockers

The use of beta-blockers is banned in specific sports and Olympic competitions. These drugs are used to control anxiety and improve performance in competitions such as golf, billiards, shooting, and archery. Historically, urine samples were hydrolyzed, extracted, derivatized, and subjected to GC/MS analyses. Currently, HPLC/MS and HPLC-MS/MS are the methods of choice.

Beta-2-Agonists and Glucocoticosteroids

These two groups of drugs are primarily used therapeutically in sports to treat asthma or as anti-inflammatory agents. Their therapeutic use is not banned in most sports, but abuse can result in sanctions. With the exception of salbutamol, formoterol, and salmeterol, WADA has prohibited the use of beta-2-agonists by inhalation. Salbutamol and formoterol are prohibited if present in urine above specified concentrations that are presumed to show that their use was not therapeutic. Glucocorticosteroids are prohibited when administered by oral, IV, IM, or rectal routes. However, they are not prohibited when inhaled. The challenge to antidoping scientists and programs is to distinguish inhaled use from other routes of administration. The analysis of these drugs has migrated from GC/MS to HPLC/MS and HPLC-MS/MS.

Aromatase Inhibitors (AI), Selective Estrogen Receptor Modulators (SERMS), and other Antiestrogens (AE)

There are shared pathways and intermediates in the endogenous formation of T and estrogens such as estradiol (Fig. 1). Exogenous use of T and its precursors risks decreasing natural T production, increasing estrogen concentrations, and development of unwanted feminine traits such as gynecomastia. In theory, administration of AI, SERMS, or other AE helps avoid development of the unwanted side effects and increases AAS concentrations by reducing conversion of T and its precursors to estrogenic steroids. Specifically, AIs inhibit the enzyme aromatase that converts T to estradiol. SERMS bind to estrogen receptors but have a mixture of agonist and antagonist effects. Administration of some SERMs has been shown to increase pituitary gonadotrophin secretion resulting in T production and increased T concentrations. After LLE or SPE extraction, HPLC/MS and HPLC-MS/MS are the methods of choice for screening and confirmation of AI, SERMS, and AE.

DISCUSSION

Testing for PE drugs is now common at all levels of sport and is increasing in safety-sensitive work environments and death investigations. Regardless of testing indication, almost all PE testing has medico-legal implications. Antidoping programs vary widely in the drugs tested but usually at a minimum include testing for marijuana, common stimulants, narcotics, and AAS. However, programs frequently include exhaustive lists of AAS, stimulants, and narcotics as well as diuretics, masking agents, glucocorticoids, beta-2-agonists, AE, SERMS, peptide hormones, and the catchall phrase "and related substances." The phrase "and related substances" is common in banned substance lists and is used to ensure that drugs of similar chemical structure or with similar effects, but not explicitly listed, are also banned.

Positive test results can have severe consequences for the athlete. A positive test could mean disqualification from competition and a subsequent loss of endorsements. Positive results for college and university athletes may result in suspension from competition, loss

of athletic scholarship, and revoked eligibility. Professional athletes risk disciplinary actions including suspension and expulsion and the accompanying loss of wages. Because of the diversity of drugs and metabolites tested and the consequences of a positive test, sophisticated MS and MS/MS technologies are sometimes used for screening and usually used for confirmation. These technologies including growing use of HPLC-MS/MS, IRMS, and higher-resolution MS instruments. Testing reliability is important because of the forensic nature of PE analyses. Also, most antidoping programs are administered under the concept of strict liability. In essence, this means that athletes are responsible for anything detected in their urine. Unknown or inadvertent ingestion of a banned substance (through supplements or diet) or passive exposure (marijuana smoke) are not viable defenses.

PE drug use by athletes has become increasingly sophisticated as evidenced by the suspected use of hGH and the use of EPO and other peptide hormones. It has also expanded into the use of additional drugs such as synthetic cannabinoids and into potential new avenues of abuse such as gene doping. Therefore, the need to expand testing, update banned substances lists, and improve testing technologies will undoubtedly continue.

SELECTED READINGS

1. Botre F. New and old challenges of sports drug testing. J Mas Spec 2008;43:903–7.
2. Catlin DH, Fitch KD, Ljungqvist A. Medicine and science in the fight against doping in sport. J Internal Medicine 2008;264:99–114.
3. Crouch DJ, Caplan YH, eds. Journal of analytical toxicology special issue on sports drug testing. J Anal Tox 2011;35:9.
4. Heltsley R, Shelby MK, Crouch DJ, Black DL, Robert TA, Marshall L, Bender C, DePriest AZ, Colello MA. Prevalence of synthetic cannabinoids in US athletes: initial findings. J Anal Tox 2012;36:588–93.
5. Karch S, ed. Drug abuse handbook. Sports (Chapter 9). Boca Raton, FL: CRC Press 2007:695–725.

6. Martindale's drugs restricted in sport 2009—pocket companion. Grayslake, IL: Pharmaceutical Press 2009.

7. Robinson N, Saugy M, Mangin P, Veuthey J, Rudaz S, Dvorak J, eds. Fight against doping in 2011. Special Issue. For Sci Int 2011;213:1–114.

8. World Anti-Doping Agency. Prohibited list and related documents. www.wada-ama.org/ (Accessed February 2013).

CHAPTER 5

Drug Testing in Pain Management

Anne Z. DePriest

The art and science of chronic pain management is a complex process that requires continual patient assessment for positive and negative outcomes. The goal of achieving analgesia and improving quality of life must be balanced with the risk of adverse effects and the development of physical dependence or addiction.

Most patients who undergo chronic treatment with opioids, for example, will develop dependence, a physiological adaptation to a medication characterized by a withdrawal syndrome upon abrupt discontinuation. This outcome is expected; however, the development of addiction is not. Hallmarks of addiction include craving, compulsive use of a drug for nonmedical reasons, aberrant behavior, and continued use despite harm. If patients undergoing pain management therapy have an active addiction or substance abuse disorder, prescription of controlled substances may compromise treatment and increase the risk of unintended consequences of drug interactions, overdose, or death. Unfortunately, patients with substance abuse disorders are often difficult to identify. Some addicted patients may appear highly functional and are able to maintain successful careers while projecting the illusion that they are in control of their treatment. While substance abuse is commonly recognized as a health threat, drug misuse may compromise care, as well. Patients who misuse medications are departing from their practitioner's original direction, but such misuse does not always constitute addiction. To illustrate, a patient may make an unsanctioned dose increase for elevated pain without first discussing it with his or her provider. Although the reasons for drug misuse may be fairly benign, outcomes can be severe and healthcare professionals must be diligent in assessing patient compliance.

Patients commonly underreport or deny drug use, but toxicology results provide objective information regarding recent drug exposure. Over the last decade, drug testing has been adopted in clinical practice as an integral piece of the assessment of patient compliance and it is used to determine if patients are taking prescribed or nonprescribed medications. As such, drug test results may identify (but not diagnose) potential substance misuse or abuse. In the clinical setting, testing must be comprehensive and include the breadth of prescription medications and illicit drugs that are encountered in pain management. Unlike federally regulated testing, testing in pain management yields a very high positivity rate and polysubstance use is common. Furthermore, false-negative test results in compliance testing are of heightened concern and can be extremely detrimental to patient care. Testing approaches vary widely in this setting and significant differences from other testing applications exist.

Pain Physiology

Approximately 100 million adults in the U.S. suffer from chronic pain; an estimated one-third of Americans will suffer severe chronic pain at some point in their lifetimes. The physiologic basis of pain may vary depending on the type of pain. Acute and chronic pain are often caused by different mechanisms.

Acute pain is typically caused by nociception and associated with events such as acute illness, trauma, or surgery. Nociceptors are nerve endings found in somatic and visceral tissue; nociceptive pain may therefore be further classified as somatic pain (arising from skin, bone, joint, muscle, or connective tissue) or visceral pain (arising from internal organs such as the intestine). Nociceptors relay information from mechanical, thermal, or chemical impulses. Upon initiation of pain signals, nociceptor activation triggers the release of neurotransmitters such as bradykinins, hydrogen and potassium ions, prostaglandins, histamine, interleukins, tumor necrosis factor alfa, serotonin, and substance P. Nociceptor activation then causes transmission of the pain signal along $A\delta$ and C-afferent nerve fibers, which synapse in the dorsal horn of the spinal cord. At this point, neurotransmitters including glutamate, substance P, and calcitonin-related peptide propagate the signal along the ascending spinal cord pathway to the brain.

Pain signals are modulated by the descending inhibitory pathway through a number of different mechanisms. The endogenous opiate system aids in pain relief and includes enkephalins, dynorphins, and β-endorphins, which bind to delta (δ), kappa (κ), and mu (μ) opioid receptors, respectively. These endogenous opioids are found throughout the central nervous system (CNS). N-methyl-D-aspartate (NMDA) receptors in the dorsal horn of the spinal cord also play a role in signal modification; blockade of NMDA receptors may increase the responsiveness of mu receptors to opiates. Further modulation occurs along the descending pathway by way of neurotransmitters such as serotonin, norepinephrine, and gamma-aminobutyric acid (GABA). The number of complex systems involved in the transmission and perception of pain offers several potential targets for pharmacotherapy beyond the use of traditional pain relievers such as opioids.

Unlike acute pain, chronic pain may persist for months or years, does not serve a useful purpose, and is not always associated with a known pain-producing stimulus. Chronic pain is classified as cancer (sometimes called malignant) pain or noncancer pain. Neuropathic or functional pain syndromes are usually implicated in patients suffering from chronic pain, although nociceptive mechanisms are occasionally present. Neuropathic pain arises from nerve damage and can occur in a variety of chronic conditions such as diabetic neuropathy or postherpetic neuralgia. It may sometimes persist after an injury has healed, as in the case of phantom limb pain. Functional pain syndromes are caused by abnormal operation of the nervous system and may be implicated in fibromyalgia or irritable bowel syndrome. In cases of neuropathic or functional pain, a physical exam may be normal, which complicates the assessment and diagnosis of these pain syndromes. Patients suffering from chronic pain may exhibit anatomical and biochemical changes throughout the nervous system, which can increase pain signal transmission or render receptors less responsive to opioids. Consequently, chronic pain is typically more difficult to treat than acute pain. There is a significant incidence of psychiatric comorbidities such as depression and anxiety disorder in this population, as well. Options for treating chronic pain may therefore be selected to target more than one disorder simultaneously (e.g., antidepressants for neuropathic pain and depression).

Nonpharmacologic and Pharmacologic Treatment

Pain management practitioners will select treatment for chronic pain depending on the etiology. Although treatment with opioids may be necessary, they are not always the first choice for analgesia; for example, pain caused by neuropathic mechanisms may be treated primarily by adjuvant nonopioid medications. Both nonpharmacologic and pharmacologic therapy may be recommended for some types of pain. Nonpharmacologic treatment may include physical manipulation, application of heat or cold, massage, exercise, transcutaneous electrical nerve stimulation (TENS), or psychological interventions such as relaxation, hypnosis, imagery, cognitive behavioral therapy, or biofeedback.

Medications used for pharmacologic treatment vary and may include nonopioid analgesics, adjuvant therapies, and opioids. Nonopioid analgesics are frequently used in combination with opioids according to recommendations by the World Health Organization; these include acetaminophen, nonsteroidal anti-inflammatory drugs or NSAIDs (e.g., ibuprofen, naproxen, celecoxib), and aspirin. These medications can be effective for mild to moderate pain and do not pose a risk for addiction.

Several types of medications are used as adjuvant therapy, particularly for neuropathic or functional pain. These include skeletal muscle relaxants, antidepressants, anticonvulsants, corticosteroids, psychostimulants, capsaicin, local or regional anesthetics, ketamine, clonidine, and ziconotide. Muscle relaxants frequently used for pain management include carisoprodol, cyclobenzaprine, baclofen, methocarbamol, metaxalone, and benzodiazepines. Antidepressants will most commonly be tricyclic antidepressants (TCAs) such as amitriptyline, despiramine, imipramine, and nortriptyline, or serotonin-norepinephrine reuptake inhibitors (SNRIs) such as duloxetine, venlafaxine, desvenlafaxine, and milnacipran. SNRIs are often used preferentially given the anticholinergic side effects of TCAs (e.g., dry mouth, blurred vision, urinary retention), which may be intolerable, particularly in elderly patients. Selective serotonin reuptake inhibitor (SSRI) antidepressants are also frequently used in the pain management population given the high rate of anxiety and depression comorbidities; however, these are thought to be less effective than SNRIs for the treatment of pain. Anticonvulsants may be effective for the amelioration of neuropathic pain symptoms and are staples of chronic

pain treatment. Gabapentin and pregabalin are most often used for this purpose, given the decreased propensity to cause adverse effects and reduced monitoring requirements compared to other drugs in this class. However, other anticonvulsants may be chosen when neuropathic pain is refractory to first-line options. Other anticonvulsants used in the treatment of chronic pain include topiramate, carbamazepine, oxcarbazepine, sodium valproate, tiagabine, levetiracetam, phenytoin, lamotrigine, and zonisamide. Corticosteroids such as dexamethasone and psychostimulants such as dextroamphetamine and methylphenidate may occasionally be prescribed as adjuvants. Topical capsaicin is available over the counter in creams and patches and may provide relief for neuralgia caused by shingles, among other uses. The most commonly used anesthetic is lidocaine, which is available in topical cream and transdermal patch formulations. Ketamine is an NMDA receptor antagonist and a dissociative anesthetic that is sometimes used for pain refractory to other treatment. Of the adjuvants, benzodiazepines are the most commonly detected drug class (presumably prescribed for concurrent anxiety disorders), secondary only to opioids in patients undergoing chronic pain treatment.

Although practitioners are trained to use adjuvants whenever possible, opioid analgesics are frequently the mainstay of treatment for chronic pain. They are the most frequently mentioned drug in office visits, constituting 10% of all drugs prescribed in the U.S. for adults in 2008. Opioids exert their analgesic effects by binding to mu opioid receptors located in the CNS, although some opioids exhibit affinity at kappa and delta opioid receptors. Multiple opioids may be prescribed for patients with chronic pain. Extended-release formulations are prescribed for around-the-clock dosing, with a short-acting immediate-release formulation used for breakthrough pain on a *pro re nata* (PRN), or as needed, basis. Opiates are structurally related to derivatives of the opium plant, limited to the following natural and semisynthetic phenanthrenes: morphine, codeine, hydrocodone, hydromorphone, oxycodone, and oxymorphone. Synthetic opioids include methadone and propoxyphene in the diphenylheptane class, fentanyl analogues and meperidine in the phenylpiperidine class, and novel opioids such as tapentadol and tramadol.

Hydrocodone and oxycodone are the most frequently used drugs in pain management. The U.S. consumes 99% of the world's supply of hydrocodone, which is also the country's most commonly prescribed drug, far exceeding other medications such as antihypertensive or antihyperlipidemic drugs. Hydrocodone is the second most commonly abused prescription drug. A recent amendment to the Food and Drug Administration Safety and Innovation Act is currently under consideration and would reclassify hydrocodone combinations from Schedule III to Schedule II controlled substances. Oxycodone is the most frequently abused medication, according to the Drug Enforcement Administration (DEA). Prevalence data have indicated that oxycodone is the most frequently prescribed drug in pain management. Codeine and meperidine are rarely used for chronic pain given their limited efficacy and, in meperidine's case, potential for neurotoxicity. Use of other opioids such as methadone, fentanyl, oxymorphone, and hydromorphone are significant in the pain management setting.

Tapentadol was first approved in 2008 and is available in immediate- and extended-release forms. In addition to mu opioid activity, tapentadol acts as a norepinephrine reuptake inhibitor, a mechanism considered to be potentially useful for treating neuropathic pain. Tramadol is a weak mu opioid receptor agonist and a norepinephrine and serotonin reuptake inhibitor. Although it is not a controlled substance at the federal level in the U.S., it is subject to abuse and some states have classified it as a Schedule IV controlled substance.

Partial and mixed agonist-antagonists are sometimes encountered in the pain management setting. Buprenorphine is a partial mu opioid receptor agonist, available as a sublingual tablet and film for the treatment of opioid dependence and as a transdermal patch for use as an analgesic. Buprenorphine should not be used in combination with pure mu opioid agonists, as it may precipitate opioid withdrawal. Mixed agonists-antagonists include butorphanol, nalbuphine, and pentazocine. These medications exhibit a ceiling effect for analgesia (e.g., limiting analgesic response when doses are escalated) and carry an increased risk of psychomimetic effects. Their unique pharmacology profile comprises agonism at the kappa receptor and partial agonism or antagonism at the mu receptor, which, similarly to buprenorphine, predisposes patients to opioid withdrawal when given in combination with pure mu opioids. Although use of buprenorphine has increased, especially since the introduction of the transdermal patch in 2010, mixed agonist-antagonists are rarely prescribed for chronic pain.

While the oral route is the most common method of delivery, chronic pain patients may also take opioid medications through other routes, including transdermal, oral transmucosal (sublingual and buccal), rectal, intranasal, intravenous, subcutaneous, intramuscular, and intraspinal (epidural and intrathecal) administration. The parenteral (intravenous, subcutaneous, and intramuscular) routes are not commonly used for most outpatients with chronic pain, except in hospice facilities. Intrathecal pumps may be implanted in the patient via a surgical procedure and periodically refilled with opioids, local anesthetics, baclofen, clonidine (an alpha-2 agonist), or ziconotide (an N-type voltage-gated calcium channel blocker).

Rationale for Drug Testing in Pain Management

Prescription pain reliever use is prevalent in the U.S., with more than 200 million prescriptions dispensed in 2009. While these medications are necessary, they are also subject to abuse. Prescription drug abuse has become an epidemic, with 12 million people reporting nonmedical use of prescription pain relievers in 2010. Drug overdose is listed as the second leading cause of accidental death after motor vehicle accidents. Polysubstance use is widespread, particularly with opioids and benzodiazepines, and 80% of emergency department visits reported by the Drug Abuse Warning Network (DAWN) involved more than one drug.

The prevalence of patients with addiction in pain management and primary care clinics is estimated at 3%–31%. Doctor shopping and drug diversion are significant concerns in the pain management setting, where physicians are charged with the responsibility of monitoring compliance and taking steps to reduce medication misuse and abuse. However, physician training for substance abuse diagnosis and treatment has historically been lacking, and it is impossible to identify all cases of current or potential substance misuse or abuse on the basis of patient demographics or behavioral monitoring. Given these factors, a "universal precautions" approach has been recommended to ensure adequate assessment of pain, treatment, and risk for addictive disorders for all patients. The universal precautions assessment should include drug testing, which is often called "compliance" testing because it is used to determine whether a patient is taking prescribed drugs or other, nonprescribed licit or illicit medications. Frequencies of unexpected toxicology results for chronic pain patients between 45% and 51% have been reported, with a prevalence of illicit drugs between 10.9% and 24%. Although not all patients with unexpected toxicology results will have a substance abuse disorder, these results are concerning because medication noncompliance can significantly reduce treatment efficacy or increase the risk of serious adverse effects, including death.

Systemic literature reviews have not yielded strong support for urine drug-testing programs in pain management; however, implementation has been recommended by numerous organizations, among them the Institute of Medicine (IOM), Drug Enforcement Administration (DEA), American Pain Society (APS), American Academy of Pain Medicine (AAPM), American Society of Interventional Pain Physicians (ASIPP), most state medical boards, and numerous well-known practitioners and prolific authors in pain management. Some proposed state regulations have formally recommended drug testing, most recently in Florida, and further legislation proposals may follow. Finally, guidelines issued by third-party payers also recommend or require drug testing in pain management, such as the Official Disability Guidelines (ODG) for workers' compensation patients.

Implementation of Drug-Testing Programs in Pain Management

Over the last decade, urine drug testing has become an established standard of care in pain clinics. Practitioners specializing in pain management are subjected to increased scrutiny to manage the risk of addiction, thereby improving patient outcomes and reducing their own medicolegal risk. Incorporation of drug testing as part of routine patient assessment remains sporadic in primary care clinics; only 8% of primary care physicians order urine drug tests. This gap in risk assessment continues to be a problem, as the majority of opioid prescriptions are generated in the primary care setting.

Patients undergoing treatment for chronic pain may be asked to sign a treatment agreement during their initial visit that explains the risks of opioid therapy and outlines behavioral boundaries for ongoing treatment. The requirement for submitting to a drug-testing program is divulged in the treatment agreement. Although a free example of such an agreement is available online through the AAPM, practitioners often adapt these to their own practices. Certainly there is no consensus regarding a standard urine drug-testing protocol, as they vary depending on the needs of the patient or prescriber. A drug-testing program may need to adapt to changes in the clinical picture.

Testing frequency depends on physician preference but should be ordered randomly to reduce the opportunity for specimen adulteration or substitution. If an office uses an interview-based screening tool to identify the risk of substance abuse, testing frequency may be based on stratification of risk; however, these are not routinely applied in clinical practice and most providers adopt a general range for testing frequency such as two to four times per year. If patients present with abnormal test results or are diagnosed with a substance abuse disorder, they may be tested more frequently (every month or more).

Patients found to be engaging in substance misuse may be counseled; substance abuse may lead to a referral for addiction treatment, tapering of controlled substances, and/or discharge from care.

Specimen Types

Urine is the gold standard and the most common specimen tested in pain management. Other specimen types may be tested such as blood and oral fluid (saliva), which reflect recent drug use. Hair and sweat testing have not gained traction in this setting, although they may be used occasionally.

Urine testing is preferred because there is a wide body of literature supporting its use and it provides a substantial period of detection for drugs and their metabolites. However, the usefulness of urine testing is sometimes compromised in clinical practice by patient adulteration attempts. Testing of oral fluid and blood both yield shorter detection times; however, this is typically not a problem for most drugs prescribed in pain management, given the chronic nature of medication use. The option of collecting oral fluid or blood is advantageous in cases of shy bladder or suspected specimen tampering. The use of oral fluid in pain management has increased recently due to its ease of collection, limited invasiveness, and relative lack of opportunity for adulteration. The medications of interest in pain management are readily detected in oral fluid.

Blood testing is invasive and costly and is usually not the preferred mode of testing in pain management.

Drugs Included in Testing

Toxicology testing in pain management is challenging given the large number of drugs of interest. Most panels include illicit drugs as well as numerous prescription medications that are either frequently prescribed in pain management or subject to abuse (see Table 1). Metabolites of prescription drugs should be included in urine testing. This is particularly true for opioids and benzodiazepines, which are extensively metabolized. In recent years, evidence regarding the prevalence of opioid normetabolites has been published, indicating that testing for these analytes may avoid the risk of false negatives (see Fig. 1 and Fig. 2 for metabolism pathways for opiates and benzodiazepines).

Many opioid normetabolites are products of cytochrome P450 3A4 (CYP3A4) metabolism, which may be affected by a host of drug-drug interactions. There have been case reports of patients taking CYP3A4-inducing drugs who, upon drug testing, had a normetabolite as the only detectable marker in urine (e.g., noroxycodone only was detected in a patient ingesting extended-release oxycodone and rifampin, an antibiotic with significant CYP3A4- inducing activity). Additionally, other drug markers resulting from CYP2D6 metabolism (e.g., oxymorphone from oxycodone metabolism or morphine from codeine metabolism) may be undetectable if metabolism is impaired by pharmacogenetic poor metabolizer phenotypes or drug-drug interactions with CYP2D6 inhibitors. Finally, normetabolites typically exhibit longer elimination half-lives than their parent drugs and may accumulate with repeated use, exceeding concentrations of parent drug or other metabolites in urine. Inclusion of normetabolites in a test panel may thus increase the detection of ingested drugs and potentially extend the period of detection of drug use. When considering the inclusion

Table 1. Medications Included in Pain Management Testing

Drug Class	Drugs/Metabolites Included in Testing
Amphetamine-like stimulants	Amphetamine Methamphetamine MDMA Phentermine
Barbiturates	Butalbital Phenobarbital

Benzodiazepines	Alprazolam
	  Alpha-hydroxyalprazolam
	Clonazepam
	  7-Aminoclonazepam
	Diazepam/chlordiazepoxide/clorazepate/oxazepam/temazepam
	  Nordiazepam
	  Oxazepam
	  Temazepam
	Flurazepam
	  2-Hydroxy-ethyl-flurazepam
	Lorazepam

Opioids	Buprenorphine / Morphine
	  Norbuprenorphine / Oxycodone
	Codeine / Noroxycodone
	  Morphine / Noroxymorphone[a]
	  Norcodeine / Oxymorphone
	Fentanyl / Oxymorphone
	  Norfentanyl / Propoxyphene[b]
	Hydrocodone / Norpropoxyphene
	  Dihydrocodeine / Tapentadol
	  Hydromorphone / Nortapentadol
	  Norhydrocodone / Tramadol
	Hydromorphone / O-desmethyltramadol
	Meperidine / N-desmethyltramadol
	  Normeperidine
	Methadone
	  EDDP

Illicit drugs	Cocaine / Marijuana (THC)
	  Benzoylecgonine / THCCOOH
	Heroin / Synthetic cannabinoids (Spice/K2)
	  6-Acetylmorphine / Synthetic cathinones (bath salts)
	  6-Acetylcodeine

Others	Carisoprodol / Ethanol
	  Meprobamate / Ethyl glucuronide
	Nicotine / Ethyl sulfate
	  Cotinine / Gabapentin
	Pregabalin

[a]Noroxymorphone testing has not yet become standard in the pain management setting.
[b]The prevalence of propoxyphene has declined (but has not disappeared) since its removal from the U.S. market.

of opiate biomarkers, norcodeine, a metabolite of codeine, may be included but its presence in the absence of codeine or morphine is fairly uncommon. Norhydrocodone- and noroxycodone-only results are more frequently observed. Some pain management specialty laboratories have added some, if not all, of these metabolites to their testing profiles. Many clinical laboratories offering testing in pain management have not yet developed methods for some of the opioid normetabolites, particularly norhydrocodone and noroxycodone.

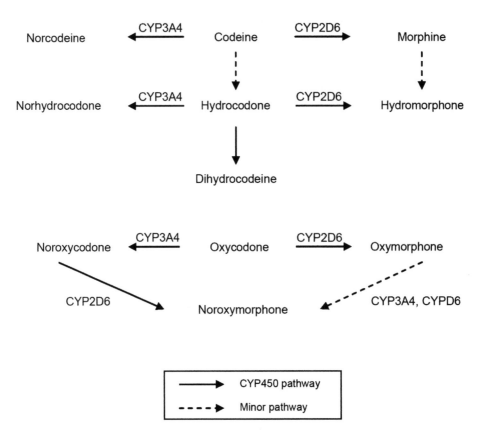

Fig. 1. Opiate metabolism.

Abuse of carisoprodol has increased over the last decade, necessitating its reclassification as a Schedule IV controlled substance in January 2012. Due to its abuse and common use as a muscle relaxant in pain management, it should be included in pain management profiles although it is sometimes omitted. Practitioners may test for nicotine (as cotinine) or alcohol use because addiction to these substances may increase the risk of developing other substance abuse disorders. In addition, alcohol can interact with opioids, particularly some extended-release formulations, exacerbating CNS depression. Provider attitudes toward alcohol use vary: some require their patients to abstain, while others are less concerned with occasional alcohol intake as long as the patient has been stable on chronic opioid therapy for some time. Testing for ethanol or its metabolite ethyl glucuronide is primarily useful for providers who strive to ensure complete abstinence, vs providers who simply wish to assess whether use represents abuse/binge drinking or occasional ingestion.

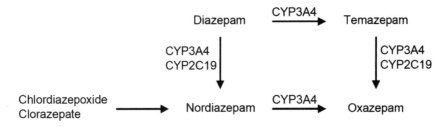

Fig. 2. Benzodiazepine metabolism.

Some practitioners argue against testing for marijuana and may exclude this drug from their testing profile. Studies have indicated a correlation of marijuana use with misuse of opioids or other illicit drugs, and it remains to be seen if exclusion of marijuana from patient assessment increases physician liability from a legal or medical board perspective. Designer drugs, particularly synthetic cannabinoids (marketed as Spice/K2), have emerged as a significant risk in pain management, and tests for these compounds are increasingly requested. Some practices may elect to also test for antidepressants (TCAs, SNRIs, or SSRIs), methylphenidate, or anabolic steroids, although test requests for these drugs are less common. PCP is rarely tested in confirmation testing given its low prevalence.

Drug Concentrations and Testing Thresholds

Urinary concentrations of drugs in pain management occur over a dynamic range. Clinical use of drugs, particularly those administered on a PRN basis, may result in low urine concentrations. In contrast, chronic use can result in drug or metabolite accumulation and impressively high concentrations. Thus, testing methodology should be engineered to measure both very high and very low concentrations, which can be challenging for a laboratory.

Thresholds used in clinical practice must be lower than those established for workplace drug testing, or false negatives may result. This is particularly true for benzodiazepines and opiates, which are often tested to a laboratory 50 or 100 ng/mL threshold in urine. An opiate testing threshold of 2000 ng/mL is not recommended in clinical practice. Variations in laboratory-reported testing thresholds in pain management exist. Some clinicians advocate "zero-threshold" testing at low concentrations; however, this approach may complicate result interpretation. Recently, laboratories have reported increased detection of low concentrations of unexpected opiates, presumably originating from minor metabolism pathways or pharmaceutical impurities. Practitioners are often unaware of these opportunities for detection of incidental exposure, and threshold selection should consider these factors.

Specimen Collection

There are no collection or chain-of-custody requirements governing specimen collection in clinical practice, and medical personnel are not always adequately trained in proper collection procedures. Furthermore, offices may not have staff available to devote to managing a drug-testing program. A laboratory may elect to place collection technicians in clinics to facilitate proper collection procedures and reduce the risk of error, although not all states allow this practice.

Safeguards should be instituted by clinics to prevent sample mix-up at the point of collection (e.g., patient signatures required on the requisition form and/or specimen cup label). The ordering practitioner must either sign the test request form or have a signature on file at the reference laboratory, as the requisition form is treated as a physician's order. Personnel performing specimen collections should be reminded to use a cup with a temperature strip and to observe the visual characteristics of the urine after the patient provides the specimen. The addition of bluing agent to toilets is not a standardized practice and water is not typically turned off in pain clinics, thereby increasing the risk that a patient may adulterate a specimen by adding water. Laboratory measurements of creatinine and specific gravity are imperative to identifying possible occurrences of substitution. As in nonclinical drug testing programs, adulteration attempts may be made to obscure the presence of illicit or nonprescribed licit drugs. However, there is additional risk inherent in pain management testing programs, as patients may adulterate specimens to appear compliant with prescribed treatment. Patients may crush a pill or tablet for addition directly to the urine specimen post collection. Such attempts may result in obvious sediment in a urine specimen, the detection of parent drugs in the absence of metabolites in urine, and/or extremely high concentrations of the parent drug. If adulteration or tampering is suspected, or if the patient has a history of a prior adulteration attempt, an observed collection may be warranted. Some practitioners are uncomfortable with the prospect of observing urine collections and may elect to obtain an alternative specimen type such as blood or oral fluid. If a clinical practice decides to order oral fluid testing, collection practices should be thoroughly explained, as they may affect the validity of results. Dry mouth, or xerostomia, is a side effect of chronic opioid therapy and drugs such as tricyclic antidepressants, tobacco, cannabis, amphetamines, antipsychotics, and antihistamines. If a patient cannot provide an adequate specimen, an alternative specimen type should be considered. Collection devices that contain buffer solution should include a volume adequacy indicator to ensure complete collection; testing of a specimen comprised mostly or entirely of buffer solution will fail to detect drug use. Stimulation of saliva production with gum or candy may increase salivary flow and affect oral fluid pH, thereby reducing drug levels in oral fluid. Medical personnel should be advised to ensure the patient's mouth is clear before a specimen collection.

Specimens collected in pain practices are usually shipped to a laboratory, either by courier or overnight delivery. Clinics that house their own on-site immunoassay screening in a physician's office laboratory (POL) may test the specimen initially before sending it out for confirmation testing, thus delaying shipping to the reference laboratory. Clinics in a network may have one central location in which a benchtop immunochemistry analyzer is housed; for those practices, specimens are first sent to the POL before being routed to the reference laboratory. Although refrigeration is recommended, in reality specimens are sometimes left to sit on the counter for several days before shipping. Noting the date of specimen collection and receipt at the reference laboratory is critical in evaluation of potential impact of drug stability and possible degradation on analytical results, particularly for unstable analytes such as 7-aminoclonazepam or 6-monoacetylmorphine. When confronted with an adamant patient denial of drug use, practitioners may request retesting of specimens. Storage times at the laboratory should be discussed with providers, but typically do not exceed 30 days.

Methodology

There are several similarities between testing in pain management and forensic settings in that a large number of analytes are included. However, there are important differences as well. No specific requirements govern the methods used for drug testing in the clinical setting. Several testing methodologies are used in pain management, with the most common being immunoassay screening and mass spectrometry–based confirmation. Immunoassay testing poses a challenge for the detection of some prescription drugs and their metabolites. In recent years, laboratories providing drug testing in pain management have increasingly departed from immunoassay technology in favor of testing specimens directly by gas chromatography/mass spectrometry (GC/MS) or liquid chromatography/tandem mass spectrometry (LC-MS/MS). Further driving this paradigm shift is the increasing practice of point-of-care testing in pain management clinics, wherein immunoassay screening is performed in the POL.

Testing programs may be set up as follows:

- Immunoassay screening only;
- Immunoassay screening with mass spectrometry confirmation of non-negative or unexpected results;
- Immunoassay screening with mass spectrometry testing for an expanded profile of drugs and metabolites;
- Mass spectrometry testing only for an expanded profile of drugs and metabolites.

Testing programs that rely on immunoassay technology may exhibit an increased risk of false negatives due to reduced identification of specimens that contain only drugs or metabolites that are poorly cross-reactive (e.g., 7-aminoclonazepam, or normetabolites such as norhydrocodone, noroxycodone, or norfentanyl). Because normetabolites are frequently present in the absence of other drug markers (with a prevalence of 2–50%, depending on the opioid), the impaired detection of commonly prescribed drugs may affect the decision to rely on immunoassay as a screening technique. Immunoassay tests yield qualitative results for a drug class that are marginally useful when assessing compliance for specific prescribed drugs. Furthermore, the likelihood that some drug classes such as opioids will be positive in pain management patients may reduce the cost effectiveness of performing immunoassay as an initial screening step. Testing directly by mass spectrometric methods such as gas chromatography/mass spectrometry (GC/MS) or liquid chromatography/tandem mass spectrometry (LC-MS/MS) allows the inclusion of multiple drugs and metabolites that may not be efficiently tested by immunoassay.

The sensitivity of LC-MS/MS and its ability to test small specimen volumes have made this technology a mainstay of oral fluid testing. Drug concentrations in oral fluid are 10- to 100-fold lower than in urine, and testing this matrix necessitates very low testing thresholds. For example, the testing threshold for opiates such as hydrocodone and oxycodone may be 1 ng/mL, whereas THCCOOH may be detected in the pg/mL range.

Quality of testing may vary depending on the laboratory. Most labs that specialize in pain management are more sophisticated than POLs or hospital laboratories. There are no accreditations or certifications designed for pain management specifically, but accreditation through agencies such as the Substance Abuse and Mental Health Services Administration (SAMHSA), the American Society of Crime Lab Directors (ASCLD), and the College of American Pathologists (CAP) may be evaluated as evidence of competence.

Many laboratories rely exclusively on LC-MS/MS technology, with some testing all drugs in the profile in either one or a limited number of LC-MS/MS analyses. This approach can facilitate the rapid turnaround time

sometimes requested by practitioners, but such methods may introduce quality concerns.

Other testing methodologies are occasionally used in pain management, including (but not limited to) time-of-flight mass spectrometry (TOFMS) and laser diode thermal desorption/tandem mass spectrometry (LDTD-MS/MS). The landscape of instrumentation used for drug testing in the clinical setting continues to evolve.

Point-of-Care Testing

Increasingly, practitioners are relying on point-of-care testing (POCT) to provide an immediate result. Rapid test results obtained during the patient's office visit may be used to direct short-term care. A wide variety of profiles and immunoassay tests are employed in pain management clinics, including cups, dipcards, and instrumented testing with small benchtop analyzers. POCT programs vary in their effectiveness and inclusion of drugs and metabolites; many omit common drugs such as fentanyl, carisoprodol, and even oxycodone. There are varying recommendations regarding the decision to send specimens to a laboratory for confirmation. Some practitioners will send only non-negative or unexpected immunoassay results; however, following this recommendation increases the risk of false negatives due to an incomplete assessment of prescription medication use. Testing for an expanded class of prescription drugs and metabolites at a laboratory is warranted and some authors have recommended this step on at least an annual or biannual basis. In addition, identification of illicit drugs such as marijuana and cocaine may be increased at a laboratory using lower thresholds than those employed in POCT programs. The opportunity for false positives and false negatives with POCT is frequently underestimated by practitioners. Most recommendations in pain management advise delaying changes to patient care until a result has been confirmed using a more specific method such as GC/MS or LC-MS/MS.

Clinic personnel involved in POCT programs should be trained in quality control measures and test interpretation, and laboratories may assist with these endeavors. Few practices have attempted POCT with GC/MS or LC-MS/MS, as the expertise needed for method development, quality measures, and result interpretation is challenging, and most clinics do not have experienced or qualified personnel in this specialty. POCT at this time is generally limited to urine testing, since oral fluid devices have not achieved the desired level of sensitivity to monitor compliance with prescription medications.

Interpretation

Practitioners may struggle with how to manage patients with unexpected toxicology results. Frank discussion with the patient and/or laboratory experts is encouraged.

Unexpected positive findings will indicate the need for patient evaluation. Non-negative immunoassay test results should be confirmed by a more specific method such as mass spectrometry. Confirmed positive results should be evaluated for the medication source, keeping in mind metabolism pathways (e.g., hydrocodone metabolism to hydromorphone). Additionally, pharmaceutical impurities pose a risk for unexpected opiate positives in patients on chronic opioid therapy or taking high dosages of medications. The most commonly observed impurities are codeine in morphine formulations, and hydrocodone in oxycodone formulations. Impurity drugs may be detected in urine or oral fluid when low thresholds are used. When evaluating the probability that a drug is positive secondary to such incidental exposure, the impurity drug should be present at low concentrations relative to the active pharmaceutical ingredient (typically 0.5–1% or less). The opportunity for pharmaceutical impurities to cause positive test results was only recently appreciated and is a major confounding factor for test interpretation.

Unexpected negative test results can be as equally concerning as unexpected positives, as providers are tasked with determining the reason for noncompliance. Although diversion may be suspected, it is not always the reason for a negative finding; many clinical explanations exist for why a patient can test negative for prescribed drugs. A patient may have refrained from taking the drug due to concerns about side effects or potential addiction. Alternatively, if the medication is taken on a PRN basis, a patient may not have required a dose for some time prior to the test. Some patients may hoard medications for fear of running out while others may self-escalate dosing and run out early. In rare cases, patients who have undergone gastrointestinal surgery may not absorb the medication (although under these circumstances, they are also unlikely to experience analgesia). Patients with kidney failure may test negative for some drugs in blood or oral fluid if the specimen is collected following dialysis. Medications delivered via intrathecal routes may not always be detectable in urine at routine thresholds and are extremely unlikely to be detected in blood or oral fluid.

In addition to ruling out clinical factors, testing methodology should also be considered. Inclusion of the drug in question should be checked against the ordered test profile. For example, some practitioners are unaware that fentanyl is not included in testing for opiates. If the test was performed using immunoassay, cross-reactivity to the drug or its metabolite should be evaluated. Cases of patients being fired from their pain management center for negative findings for prescribed oxycodone have been reported; the providers later discovered that oxycodone did not sufficiently cross-react to the opiate test they had ordered.

Practitioners should be advised that the period of detection for each drug is a rough estimate and may be greatly impacted by medication dosing or individual differences in metabolism. Urine boasts the longest period of detection, while detection times in oral fluid and blood are relatively short. Oral fluid results may be negative for PRN drugs if these are not administered routinely; most drugs are detectable in oral fluid for a period up to 24–48 hours.

Pain management practitioners may be prone to overinterpretation of quantitative results. A common source of confusion is that urine drug concentrations do not correlate to medication dose. Consequently a provider cannot distinguish between a patient who is taking a dosage as prescribed or tripling their medication intake. Likewise, urine drug testing will not reveal if a patient is diverting some—but not all—of their prescription. Some laboratories may alert the prescriber if a measured urine drug concentration is a statistical outlier for all concentrations reported for that drug. Although these findings are not definitive indications of drug misuse, they may serve as a warning for providers to carefully assess the patient for signs of aberrancy.

Some practitioners have adopted blood testing in an effort to establish therapeutic drug monitoring. However, therapeutic ranges for opioids and benzodiazepines in blood or plasma have not been established and are not clinically meaningful given the impact of drug tolerance; likewise, pharmacokinetic changes and drug-drug interactions may affect blood concentrations, as well. Although limited information has been published on therapeutic drug monitoring for methadone (mostly for the treatment of opioid dependence), pharmacokinetic monitoring has not been proven to be effective for monitoring dosage compliance with opioids or benzodiazepines in pain management.

Laboratory Reporting and Relationship with the Practice

Studies have repeatedly demonstrated that practitioners treating patients with chronic pain have a limited understanding of drug-testing methodology or results. If used indiscriminately, drug testing may harm the doctor-patient relationship, and laboratories may spend significant resources in providing guidance in result interpretation. Toxicology reports should be streamlined and easy to read and interpret. Prescription drugs may be noted on the requisition form so that reports can indicate compliant or noncompliant

results accordingly. Laboratories are increasingly integrating reports into electronic medical record (EMR) systems used by the practice, which reduces the time spent filing documentation by clinic personnel. Additionally, laboratories that offer testing in pain management must provide available consultation with qualified experts (e.g., toxicologists with clinical experience or clinical pharmacy specialists). Requests for consultation usually occur during a patient's office visit, and responses must therefore be given in a time-sensitive manner.

For patients dismissed from clinical practice, it can be extremely difficult—if not impossible—to find another clinic to reinstate care. Drug-testing programs must be carefully designed to reduce the opportunity for error, with proper consideration given to the risk of false positives and false negatives.

Pharmacogenetic Testing

Recently, pain management practices have begun exploring options for conducting pharmacogenetic testing for their patients with the hope of individualizing drug treatment and improving outcomes. Pharmacogenetic testing has been adopted for a number of medication applications, including oncology, psychiatry, and anticoagulation, among others. Although the field of pharmacogenetic testing in pain management holds promise, it has not yet been shown to improve patient outcomes.

Genetic differences in metabolic enzymes, or pharmacogenetic polymorphisms, may exist for some enzymes involved in the metabolism of opioids and benzodiazepines. If metabolism is altered, clinical outcomes may also be affected, including increased toxicity or decreased effectiveness. Pharmacogenetic testing may be used to identify a patient's genotype for a particular enzyme and to estimate risk for drug toxicity or treatment failure. Very few drugs in pain management have been identified in product labeling as candidates for pharmacogenetic testing. The CYP2D6 enzyme is highly polymorphic; some patients lack CYP2D6 activity (poor metabolizers), have impaired metabolism (intermediate metabolizers), have normal metabolism (extensive metabolizers), or have enhanced metabolism (ultra-rapid metabolizers). Polymorphisms in CYP2D6 have been linked to variability in response to a limited number of drugs used in pain management, among them codeine and tramadol. While both hydrocodone and oxycodone are metabolized by CYP2D6, the relative contribution of their active metabolites (hydromorphone and oxymorphone, respectively) to clinical effect has not been clearly defined; to date, the CYP2D6 genotype has not been shown to directly correlate with analgesia, as studies have produced conflicting results. Methadone is metabolized by the highly polymorphic enzyme CYP2B6; however, variations in CYP2B6 are more likely to affect the relatively inactive S-enantiomer of methadone, and the CYP2B6 genotype has not been shown to influence clinical response.

In summary, knowledge of cytochrome P450 (CYP450) genotypes may not predict analgesic response for most pain medications. Further complicating this assessment is that genotypes do not always correlate to phenotypes; for example, a drug-drug interaction resulting in enzyme inhibition can turn an extensive metabolizer into a poor metabolizer. Other polymorphisms affect the pharmacodynamic response to opioids, such as the OPRM1 gene, the catechol-O-methyltransferase (COMT) enzyme, and the ATB-binding cassette B1 (ABCB1)/multiple drug resistance 1 (MDR1) gene, to name a few. Given the complexity of pain modulation and analgesic response, studies of known genotypes and their ability to predict analgesic response have yielded conflicting data.

At this time, genotypes may be regarded as risk factors but not definitive predictors of therapeutic outcomes for most opioids. Although some authors are optimistic regarding the future role of pharmacogenetic testing, it is unclear how to incorporate results into clinical practice given the conflicting evidence published to date. Currently, the only specific opioid with recommendations for pharmacogenetic testing by the National Institutes of Health's Clinical Pharmacogenetics Implementation Consortium (CPIC) guidelines is codeine, which is not commonly prescribed for chronic pain management. As a whole, the application of pharmacogenetic testing in pain management has not been demonstrated to be clinically effective.

SUGGESTED READING

1. Baselt RC. Disposition of toxic drugs and chemicals in man, 9th ed. Foster City, CA: Biomedical Publications, 2011.
2. Cone EJ, Caplan YH. Urine toxicology testing in chronic pain management. Postgrad Med 2009;121:91–102.
3. Cone EJ, Huestis MA. Interpretation of oral fluid tests for drugs of abuse. Ann N Y Acad Sci 2007;1098:51–103.
4. Gourlay DL, Heit HA, Almahrezi A. Universal precautions in pain medicine: a rational approach to the treatment of chronic pain. Pain Med 2005;6:107–12.
5. Gourlay DL, Heit HA, Caplan YH. Urine drug testing in clinical practice: the art and Science of patient care, 5th ed. Stamford, CT: PharmaGroup, 2012:1–20.
6. Heltsley R, DePriest A, Black DL, Robert T, Marshall L, Meadors VM, et al. Oral fluid drug testing of chronic pain patients. I. Positive prevalence rates of licit and illicit drugs. J Anal Toxicol 2011;35:529–40.
7. Institute of Medicine. Relieving pain in America: a blueprint for transforming prevention, care, education, and research. Washington, DC: National Academies Press, 2011.
8. Michna E, Jamison RN, Pham LD, Ross EL, Janfaza D, Nedeljkovic SS, et al. Urine toxicology screening among chronic pain patients on opioid therapy: frequency and predictability of abnormal findings. Clin J Pain 2007;23:173–9.
9. Moeller KE, Lee KC, Kissack JC. Urine drug screening: practical guide for clinicians. Mayo Clin Proc 2008;83:66–76.
10. Nafziger AN, Bertino JS. Utility and application of urine drug testing in chronic pain management with opioids. Clin J Pain 2009;25:73–9.
11. Owen GT, Burton AW, Schade CM, Passik S. Urine drug testing: current recommendations and best practices. Pain Physician 2012;15:ES119–33.
12. Peppin JF, Passik SD, Cuoto JE, Fine PG, Christo PJ, Argoff C, et al. Recommendations

for urine drug monitoring as a component of opioid therapy in the treatment of chronic pain. Pain Medicine 2012;13:886–96.

13. Reisfield GM, Goldberger BA, Bertholf RL. "False-positive" and "false-negative" test results in clinical urine drug testing. Bioanalysis 2009;1:937–52.

14. Starrels JL, Fox AD, Kunins HV, Cunningham CO. They don't know what they don't know: internal medicine residents' knowledge and confidence in urine drug test interpretation for patients with chronic pain. J Gen Intern Med 2012;27:1521–7.

CHAPTER 6

Pharmacokinetics and Pharmacodynamics

Vina Spiehler and Barry Levine

Whereas pharmacodynamics is the study of the time course of drug effects, pharmacokinetics is defined as the study of the time course of drugs in the body. Pharmacokinetic studies investigate and characterize drug bioavailability, i.e., the amount of drug absorbed relative to the amount administered, by:

- different routes of administration,
- the rates of absorption and elimination,
- the time to peak concentrations,
- the relationship between dose and blood and tissue concentrations, and
- the rates of metabolism or biotransformation and clearance.

This chapter will discuss the basic aspects of absorption, distribution, excretion, metabolism, and compartment modeling in pharmacokinetics. This discussion will be followed by demonstrations of how these principles may be applied to the practice of forensic toxicology.

ABSORPTION

Absorption is the process whereby xenobiotics enter the bloodstream. There are several mechanisms by which entry into the bloodstream can occur. The simplest mechanism is passive diffusion, the movement of a substance from an area of high concentration to an area of low concentration. Initially, at the site of absorption, there will be no xenobiotic present in the blood proximal to that site. Drug will diffuse from the site into the blood. Diffusion may also occur with the assistance of membrane proteins along a concentration gradient; this process is called facilitated diffusion.

A component common to passive and facilitated diffusion is the absence of an energy requirement. This is contrasted by active transport processes, which do require energy, act against a concentration gradient, and use carrier proteins or receptors to diffuse drug into the bloodstream. Because the concentration of these carrier proteins or receptors is finite, active transport processes can be saturable.

Drugs can enter the bloodstream through a wide variety of routes:

- *Oral.* This is one of the most common routes for drug absorption and refers to absorption through the gastrointestinal (GI) tract, i.e., the stomach and the small intestine.
- *Inhalation.* Drugs with sufficient volatility (solvents, anesthetic gases, and alkaloids with low boiling points such as nicotine) can be absorbed through the lungs.
- *Intravenous.* This is the most efficient route of administration, because the entire administered drug is placed directly into the bloodstream.
- *Intramuscular.* This is also a common route of parenteral administration of drugs, but unlike intravenous injection, it will display variable absorption.

- *Rectal.* Individuals unable to take drugs orally may be given a suppository for rectal absorption.
- *Oral mucosa.* Drugs taken by mouth that require very rapid entry into the blood may be taken sublingually. One classic example of this is the sublingual administration of nitroglycerin in patients suffering from angina pectoris.
- *Intrathecal.* Drugs requiring rapid central nervous system onset can be administered directly into the spinal fluid, thus bypassing the blood–brain barrier, a layer of cells meant to retard or prevent the entry of foreign substances into the brain.
- *Dermal.* Drugs can be absorbed through the skin. Nicotine, fentanyl, and scopolamine have been administered in this way.
- *Ocular.* Drugs used to treat eye infections or diseases may be delivered directly into the eye, usually in the form of drops.
- *Intranasal.* Cocaine has been abused by insufflation.

Unless the drug is administered intravenously, it is unlikely that all of the administered drug will be absorbed. The amount of drug absorbed relative to the amount administered, i.e., its bioavailability, can be affected by multiple factors such as the following:

- *Solubility.* In order for drugs to enter the blood, they must be in solution. For instance, a tablet, upon entry into the stomach, will disintegrate first into granules and then into particles. The rate of this disintegration will affect bioavailability. The formulation of the drug will also play a major role in the rate of this dissolution. A coated or sustained-release formulation will be absorbed more slowly than tablets or capsules. Drugs already in an aqueous medium will be more rapidly absorbed than drugs in an oily medium or in solid form. In general, salts are more water soluble than free acids or free bases.
- *Concentration.* Because absorption frequently occurs by diffusion, the greater the concentration gradient, the faster the drug absorption rate. This means that a concentrated formulation will be absorbed more rapidly than a diluted formulation.
- *Surface area.* The main function of the small intestine is the absorption of substances taken orally. The small intestine is made up of microvilli, which are designed to provide a large surface area to facilitate absorption. The stomach also has a large surface area, and some drugs are absorbed from the stomach.
- *Blood supply.* Increased blood flow can enhance absorption of a drug. Conversely, if an individual is in shock, then absorption is retarded.
- *pH.* Entry of drugs into the blood involves passage into membranes. Lipophilic drugs cross these membranes more easily than do hydrophilic drugs. Drugs that exist in an un-ionized form will be more lipophilic in the medium than drugs that exist in the ionized form. For example, suppose an acidic drug is present in the stomach, which has a pH between 1 and 3.5. This acidic drug will exist in the stomach predominantly in a nonionized (un-ionized) form; the degree to which this drug is in the nonionized form is a function of the drug's pK_a and can be calculated using the Henderson-Hasselbach equation (Fig. 1). As this acidic drug leaves the

Acid drugs:

$$pH = pK_a + \log \frac{[\text{ionized}]}{[\text{nonionized}]}$$

Basic drugs:

$$pH = pK_a + \log \frac{[\text{nonionized}]}{[\text{ionized}]}$$

Fig. 1. Henderson-Hasselbach equations for acidic and basic drugs.

stomach and enters the small intestine, the pH of the medium changes significantly. The pH of the upper portion of the small intestine, the duodenum, is 5–6 and increases to 8 at the lower part of the small intestine, the ileum. This means that as an acidic drug traverses the length of the small intestine, the amount of drug that will be in the nonionized form will decrease. The opposite reasoning can be applied if the drug is a basic drug. In the stomach, most of the drug will be ionized, thus reducing the amount absorbed. The Henderson-Hasselbach equation can also be used for basic drugs (Fig. 1). A basic drug will become increasingly nonionized as it enters the small intestine.

Because different production processes can lead to different formulations of the same active drug, the concept of bioequivalence has been developed to compare products from different manufacturers or, occasionally, lot-to-lot differences from the same manufacturer. Different formulations are said to be "biologically equivalent" if they yield similar concentrations of active drug in blood or tissues. Formulations are "therapeutically equivalent" if similar therapeutic efficacies are obtained.

DISTRIBUTION

Distribution refers to the transfer of a substance from one part of the body to another part. In pharmacokinetic terms, distribution usually refers to movement from the blood into the tissues. This movement is a function of the amount of drug presented to the tissues. Highly perfused tissues such as the heart, liver, kidney, and brain initially receive the bulk of the absorbed drug, usually within minutes. Less perfused tissues, such as muscle and fat, take longer to achieve equilibrium with the blood.

Some of the factors that affect drug absorption will also affect the distribution of drugs. The more lipid soluble the drug, the more easily the drug will move into the tissues. A sample illustration of this point would be to compare the entry into the brain of two barbiturates, thiopental and pentobarbital. The only structural difference between the two drugs is a $C=S$ for thiopental vs $C=O$ for pentobarbital on the barbiturate ring structure. This seemingly slight difference drastically changes the lipophilicity of the two drugs. Because thiopental is much more lipid soluble than pentobarbital, it distributes more rapidly into the brain than does pentobarbital. This rapid onset of action explains why thiopental is used as an anesthetic agent while pentobarbital is used as a sedative hypnotic drug.

Closely related to the lipophilicity factor is the pH effect. The Henderson-Hasselbach equation can be used to indicate the conditions under which a particular acid or basic drug will be un-ionized and to what degree. It is the un-ionized form of the drug that crosses membranes and enters tissues.

Plasma protein binding also influences the movement of drugs from blood to tissues. Albumin is the major binding protein and is present in the plasma at an approximate concentration of 40 g/L. Albumin binds preferentially to acidic drugs but may bind weakly to basic drugs. Alpha-1 acid glycoprotein is another significant plasma protein, binding preferentially to weak bases. Its plasma concentration fluctuates, but is about 0.7 g/L. In addition to these major proteins, lipoproteins and globulins are available to bind drugs. Regardless of the binding protein, the extent to which a given drug binds to a plasma protein is variable. For example, warfarin, an anticoagulant, is approximately 99% protein bound; digoxin, a cardiac glycoside used to treat congestive heart failure, is approximately 25% protein bound.

Plasma protein binding limits drug distribution in that only unbound or free drug is able to leave the blood and enter the tissues. In turn, only free drug can interact with receptors to produce pharmacologic effects. On the other hand, drug bound to protein is restricted to the blood, because the drug-protein complex is too large to leave the capillaries. Because bound drug cannot reach the tissues, it cannot produce pharmacologic actions at the intended site. Drugs that are highly protein bound will have a delayed onset of action and an extended duration of action relative to drugs that are not highly protein bound.

Potential drug interactions may occur if multiple highly bound drugs are administered simultaneously. If the protein binding of a drug is reduced, then more is in the free form and is available to enter tissues. This can lead to an unexpected increase in pharmacologic activity or toxicity.

Drugs can distribute into body fluids to varying degrees. The average 70-kg man has 42 L of total body water, divided into intracellular and extracellular fluid. Intracellular fluid makes up approximately 27 of the 42 L. The remaining 15 L exists outside the cell and consists of plasma, the fluid component of blood (3 L); interstitial fluid; cerebrospinal fluid; GI fluids; and fluids of the potential spaces.

Drugs may distribute into any or all of the total body water. This has led to the concept of apparent volume of distribution (V_d), which represents the amount of fluid in which a drug dose would appear to have been distributed if the total dose had remained in the blood.

$$V_d = \frac{D}{C} \qquad (1)$$

where D is the dose and C is the blood concentration of the drug. The volume of distribution is a function of the drug's lipophilicity, pK_a, and binding to plasma protein, tissues, etc. Drugs that are hydrophilic, such as alcohol, and that distribute mainly to body water or are strongly bound to plasma proteins such as salicylic acid or acetaminophen have a $V_d < 1$. Most psychoactive abused drugs are lipophilic, distribute into fatty tissue such as the brain, and have a $V_d > 1$. For example, the V_d of phencyclidine is 5.5–7.5 L/kg. Because V_d is a theoretical value, it is possible that the V_d is much greater than the total body water. This could suggest sequestration of a drug at a particular tissue site. For example, tricyclic antidepressants have very high apparent volumes of distribution because they are sequestered mainly in the liver.

The volume of distribution for a given drug can change as a function of the person's age, gender, disease, and body composition. The population average V_d for alcohol is 0.70 (range 0.62–0.79) for males and 0.60 (range 0.46–0.86) for females. The V_d of alcohol decreases with increasing age and is 10–15% lower in persons more than 60 years of age.

Although the brain is a highly perfused tissue, it has unique features that limit entry of xenobiotics. These serve as a protective mechanism for the brain. Endothelial cells of the brain capillary restrict aqueous bulk flow relative to endothelial cells in other tissues. There is also a layer of glial cells, which retards the diffusion of organic acids and bases in the brain.

METABOLISM

Metabolism is the process by which the structure of a xenobiotic is altered to facilitate the removal of the foreign substance from the body. These changes occur with the assistance of enzymes or biological catalysts. Enzymatic activity occurs primarily but not exclusively in the liver. Other sites of enzyme action include the kidney, lung, GI tract, and the blood. Groups of enzymes have been identified and characterized. Metabolic activity is divided into two general phases: Phase I and Phase II metabolism.

Phase I Metabolism

Phase I reactions are characterized by enzymatic transformation of functional groups (see Table 1). The most widely studied group of Phase I enzymes is the cytochrome P450 mono-oxygenases. Studies have indicated that cytochrome P450 exists in many different forms, called isozymes, which have different physical and chemical properties as well as different affinities for different drugs.

Table 1. Examples of Phase I Metabolism

Reaction	Example
N-dealkylation	Amitriptyline
O-dealkylation	Codeine
Desulfuration	Parathion
Sulfoxide formation	Cimetidine
Ester hydrolysis	Cocaine
Amide hydrolysis	Lidocaine
Deacetylation	Heroin
Aliphatic hydroxylation	Pentobarbital
Aromatic hydroxylation	Propranolol
Deamination	Chlordiazepoxide
Nitro reduction	Flunitrazepam
N-oxide formation	Atropine
Epoxide formation	Carbamazepine
Reduction	Chloral hydrate

These enzymes are embedded in the lipid bilayer of the smooth endoplasmic reticulum.

These enzymes also have a common mode of activity. The xenobiotic to be metabolized initially binds to the ferric ion component of the P450. This complex reduces the iron to the +2 valence state (ferrous ion). The reduced complex then binds molecular oxygen. As the oxygen is reduced, the xenobiotic is oxygenated. At this stage, NADPH is utilized. The final step is the release of the oxygenated product with regeneration of the enzyme. The net result of the process is the formation of water and $NADP^+$, the expenditure of NADPH and molecular oxygen, and the production of an oxidized xenobiotic.

A large number of P450 enzymes are selectively induced by drugs and environmental chemicals, including phenobarbital, antipyrine, rifampicin, polychlorinated biphenyls, polybrominated biphenyls, and aromatic hydrocarbons. Enzyme induction requires an increase in the number of enzyme-binding sites, which in turn require protein synthesis. Therefore, several weeks are required before significant enzyme induction is observed. These enzymes can also be selectively inhibited by a variety of drugs; examples of some P450 isozyme inhibitors include cimetidine, fluoxetine, diltiazem, and verapamil. Enzyme inhibition usually results from a competition for the active site between the

drug and the inhibitor. As a result, inhibition of metabolism occurs concurrently with administration of the drug and the potential inhibitor.

The significance of P450 induction and inhibition in pharmacotherapy cannot be underestimated. Many of the compounds that have been shown either to induce or to inhibit components of the P450 system are drugs routinely prescribed for a variety of medical conditions. These drugs can profoundly influence the metabolism of other therapeutically administered drugs. These drug interactions may produce an increase in metabolism of a particular drug, leading to reduced therapeutic efficacy. Conversely, a decrease in metabolism can cause an increased amount of drug in the blood and tissues, producing unexpected toxic effects.

The body contains other oxidases in addition to the P450 mono-oxygenases. Monoamine oxidase, for example, is a mitochondrial enzyme that metabolizes catecholamines and tyramine. A series of flavin-containing mono-oxygenases, which have some similarities to the P450 system, is also present in the body. These flavin-containing monooxygenases are microsomal enzymes that use NADPH and molecular oxygen to oxidize nucleophilic nitrogen, sulfur, or phosphorus atoms.

Hydrolytic enzymes are another significant group of enzymes involved in Phase I metabolism. Cholinesterase, which takes two forms in humans, is one such enzyme. Acetylcholinesterase, also known as true or red blood cell cholinesterase, is found in erythrocytes, lung, spleen, nerve endings, and the brain's gray matter. Acetylcholinesterase hydrolyzes acetylcholine and acetylbetamethylcholine. Pseudocholinesterase, produced in the liver but also located in the plasma, heart, pancreas, and the brain's white matter, lacks the substrate specificity of acetylcholinesterase. Pseudocholinesterase hydrolyzes acetylcholine, butrylcholine, and benzoylcholine. Acetylcholinesterase hydrolyzes acetylcholine in the synapse; the role of pseudocholinesterase remains unclear.

Phase I metabolism is generally viewed as a detoxification process. However, this is not necessarily the case. For example, parathion, an organophosphate pesticide, is converted to paraaxon, which is the active cholinesterase inhibitor. Moreover, some drug formulations serve as "prodrugs," compounds that become activated upon entry into the body. For instance, prazepam is a benzodiazepine prescribed as a sedative, but the sedative activity is due to its conversion to nordiazepam.

Phase II Metabolism

Phase II metabolism, or conjugation reactions, involves the derivatization of a drug or Phase I metabolite with an endogenous substance. The main purpose of these reactions is to increase the water solubility of these compounds to facilitate elimination.

The most common conjugation reaction uses uridine diphosphate-glucuronic acid and reacts with hydroxyl or amino groups to form conjugates of glucuronic acid. These reactions are catalyzed by a group of microsomal enzymes referred to as glucuronyltransferases. In general, glucuronide conjugates are inactive. One notable exception is morphine-6-glucuronide, which has a much greater analgesic potency than does morphine.

Other conjugation reactions are listed in Table 2. Drugs and metabolites may be conjugated with more than one substance. Both glucuronide and sulfate conjugates of morphine have been identified. The conjugation reaction involving acetaminophen and glutathione has been extensively studied. Acetaminophen is converted in the liver into an epoxide that is detoxified by conjugation with glutathione to form a mercaptic acid

derivative. However, if too much acetaminophen is presented to the liver, as might occur in an overdose, an insufficient amount of glutathione is available for epoxide detoxification. This reactive intermediate then binds to macromolecular components in liver tissue, ultimately leading to liver necrosis and death.

Phase II metabolism is usually but not always preceded by Phase I metabolism. The structure of the xenobiotic ultimately determines whether Phase I metabolism is needed. The benzodiazepine drug diazepam is demethylated to nordiazepam, which is then hydroxylated to oxazepam (these being the Phase 1 reactions). Oxazepam is then conjugated with glucuronic acid. Oxazepam can also be prescribed therapeutically; when taken directly, the drug is rapidly cleared by conjugation without Phase I metabolism.

First-Pass Effect

One phenomenon that may occur when drugs are administered orally is known as the first-pass effect. Enzymes in the GI tract can metabolize drugs before they enter the bloodstream. Once absorbed from the small intestine, the drug enters the portal circulation and is transported to the liver. In the liver, metabolism may occur prior to entry into the heart and the general circulation. Drugs with a significant first-pass effect may require administration by routes other than the oral route.

EXCRETION

Excretion is the final removal of xenobiotics or their byproducts from the body. Excretion can occur in a variety of ways. The most common routes are via the kidney and the liver, and these routes will be discussed in greater detail. Volatile substances can be eliminated through the lungs. Thus drivers can be tested for ethanol without the invasive procedure of blood collection. Drugs can also be eliminated into breast milk and cause a breast-fed infant to be exposed to

Table 2. Examples of Phase II Metabolism

Reaction	Example
Glucuronidation	Oxazepam
Sulfate formation	Morphine
Glutathione conjugation	Acetaminophen
Glycine conjugation	Salicylate
Acetylation	Procainamide
Methylation	Theophylline (neonates)

drugs. Foreign substances can also be excreted into sweat; the collection of sweat has begun to be employed as a means for identifying drug use. Drugs can also be cleared into sebum and semen.

Drug elimination is discussed in terms of clearance. Clearance refers to the removal of drug from plasma. It is defined as a volume cleared of a drug per unit time. Clearance does not indicate how much drug is removed, but represents the volume of plasma from which the drug is completely removed. The total body clearance is the sum of the individual organ clearances.

Hepatic Excretion

The liver weighs 1400–1700 g and is the major site of xenobiotic metabolism. The liver receives blood from two sources: the portal vein, supplying about 1100 mL/min, and the hepatic artery, which flows at about 350 mL/min. Blood from the hepatic artery supplies the liver with the nutrients and resources that it needs to perform its functions. The functional unit of the liver is the lobule, which is constructed around a central vein and empties into the hepatic vein and the vena cava. Substances cleared by the liver form the bile that is stored in the gall bladder. The bile enters the intestines, where final elimination occurs in the feces.

One factor affecting the clearance of drugs and metabolites is the blood flow to the liver. Certain physiological, pathological, and pharmacological factors influence this flow. For example, food and a reclining posture can increase hepatic flow, while exercise, an upright posture, and dehydration can reduce blood flow. Disease states such as cirrhosis, hypertension, and congestive heart failure may decrease hepatic blood flow. General anesthetics also decrease blood flow; chronic phenobarbital administration can increase blood flow.

Another factor pertaining to the clearance of drug from the liver is the ability of the liver to remove or extract the drug from the blood. Drugs may enter the liver by diffusion

or by carrier systems. Drugs cleared by the liver efficiently, such as opiates and tricyclic antidepressants, have a hepatic elimination rate not limited by processes in the liver but by the rate at which the drug in the blood gets to the liver. Conversely, elimination rates of drugs effectively removed from the blood are limited by the abilities of the liver to process the drug.

It can be difficult to assess the role of hepatic excretion. The measurement of the drug and/or metabolites in feces may indicate poor absorption rather than hepatic excretion. Moreover, drugs or their byproducts excreted into the bile enter the intestine; here they can be reabsorbed into the blood. Subsequent elimination by the kidney may occur. This is known as enterohepatic circulation and can account for an increase in the time that it takes to clear a drug from the body.

Renal Excretion

To understand how the kidney clears drugs, it is necessary to understand the kidney's basic structure. The functional unit of the kidney is the nephron, and each kidney has approximately one million of them. The nephron consists of multiple components. The glomerulus is the site where the blood entering the kidney is filtered. The kidneys are perfused by about one-fifth of the total cardiac output of about 6500 mL/min. Of this, about 130 mL of plasma is filtered each minute at the glomerulus. In fact, glomerular filtration rate (GFR), which is determined by measuring creatinine clearance, is used clinically to evaluate kidney function. Creatinine is a normal byproduct of muscle metabolism and is produced at a constant rate in an individual with a stable muscle mass. Thus an elevated serum creatinine suggests a reduced GFR and possible kidney malfunction.

Once the filtered product or ultrafiltrate is produced, it passes into the tubule component of the kidney, comprised of a proximal tubule, the loop of Henle, and the distal tubule. Changes in ultrafiltrate concentration of drugs can occur in this part of the nephron through an active secretion of drugs from the blood or a reabsorption of drugs from the ultrafiltrate into the blood. Much of the water initially filtered is reabsorbed, with the net effect being a concentration of the components in the filtrate. The remaining fluid moves into the collecting tubule, accumulates in the bladder, and is eventually excreted as urine.

The renal excretion of drugs is a function of filtration, secretion, and reabsorption. A drug will be filtered at the glomerulus if its molecular weight is less than 50,000 atomic mass units. This means that molecules such as proteins are not filtered. Therefore, any drug that is bound to plasma proteins will not be filtered. At equilibrium, a drug that is freely filtered will have the same concentration in the ultrafiltrate as appears unbound in the plasma. Drugs that are not highly protein-bound are cleared most rapidly and efficiently by filtration. The amount of free drug appearing in the ultrafiltrate is directly related to the GFR.

Highly plasma protein-bound drugs are cleared by the kidney to a greater extent by secretion, which occurs mainly in the proximal tubule. Specific carrier proteins located in the epithelium of the proximal tubule can separate bound drug from plasma proteins and carry them across the epithelium and into the tubular fluid. Secretion of drugs is an active process and requires energy.

There are separate carrier proteins for acidic and for basic drugs. These carrier proteins are saturable and subject to competition. A reduction in secretion of a particular drug can occur if another drug that is secreted with the assistance of the same carrier protein is coadministered.

Filtration and secretion increase the concentration of drugs in the tubular fluid. Reabsorption of drugs occurs mainly in the proximal and distal tubules and decreases the concentration of drug in the tubule fluid. Reabsorption may be passive or active and is affected by factors similar to those that affect the absorption of drugs into the blood, such as the drug's lipid solubility and pH characteristics. The normal pH of urine is 4.5–7.5, which is a 1000-fold range in hydrogen ion concentrations. The pK_a of weak acids is 3–7.5, while the pK_a of weak bases is 7.5–10.5. This indicates that certain drugs can have significant differences in renal clearance depending on the pH of the urine. Agents that acidify the urine, such as ammonium chloride, can lower urine pH by 2–3 units, leading to faster elimination of basic drugs. Sodium bicarbonate, which will alkalinize the urine, will lead to faster elimination of acid drugs. This phenomenon is used when treating drug intoxications.

COMPARTMENTALIZATION OF DRUGS AND ELIMINATION KINETICS

A series of mathematical models has been developed to describe the pharmacokinetics of drugs. To minimize the complexity that rapidly develops when describing these pharmacokinetics, assumptions and generalizations are required.

One assumption is the concept of body compartments. Although each tissue or tissue substructure could be viewed individually, the body is generally described as a one-compartment or a two-compartment system. The one-compartment model assumes instantaneous distribution after administration. For this model, it is also assumed that the drug distributes evenly throughout the body. The two-compartment model, rather than assuming instantaneous distribution throughout the body, assumes different distribution rates. A more rapid distribution occurs in the more highly perfused tissues and is termed the "central compartment." Distribution continues at a slower pace in less well-perfused tissues collectively termed the "peripheral compartment."

One- and two-compartment models can be demonstrated diagrammatically by plotting the natural log (ln) of plasma concentration vs time. Fig. 2 depicts a profile of an intravenously administered drug; in each case, the peak plasma concentration is reached instantaneously. In the one-compartment model, the decline in plasma concentration as a function of time proceeds in a linear

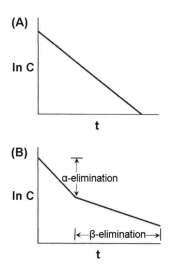

Fig. 2. Plot of natural log concentration (ln C) vs time plots for drugs with (A) one-compartment and (B) two-compartment pharmacokinetics.

fashion. In the two-compartment model, a rapid decline is initially observed. This consists of a combination of drug elimination and movement of drug into the peripheral compartment and is called the α-elimination phase. Once the distribution into the peripheral compartment has been completed, a slower decline from the plasma occurs and represents removal from the body. This is known as the β-elimination phase.

Most drugs follow first-order kinetics: a constant fraction of drug is removed from the blood per unit time. First-order elimination kinetics is defined by the following equation:

$$C = C_0 e^{-kt} \qquad (2)$$

C = concentration of drug in plasma at time, t
C_0 = the initial plasma drug concentration
k = elimination rate constant

The elimination half-life ($t_{1/2}$) is calculated using the equation

$$t_{1/2} = \frac{0.693}{k} \qquad (3)$$

By taking the natural log of both sides of Eq. 2 and rearranging, the following equation is obtained

$$\ln C = -kt + \ln C_0 \qquad (4)$$

Therefore, by plotting ln C vs t, the y-intercept is ln C_0 and the slope is –k. In first-order elimination kinetics, the blood drug concentration is decreased by one-half every half-life. By four to five half-lives, the drug is essentially removed from the blood, assuming no additional drug is absorbed.

Some drugs are eliminated by zero-order kinetics. Rather than a constant fraction of drug being removed from the blood per unit time, a constant amount of drug is cleared from the blood per unit time. For instance, ethanol will display zero-order kinetics at high blood concentrations. (This will be discussed in greater detail in Chapter 13.) The equation defining a zero-order process is as follows:

$$C = C_0 - kt \qquad (5)$$

In this scenario, a plot of C vs t yields a straight line with slope –k and intercept C_0. The elimination half-life is also dependent on the initial drug concentration:

$$t_{1/2} = \frac{(0.5)C_0}{k} \qquad (6)$$

When multiple dosing occurs, the eliminated drug is being replaced by subsequent drug administration. If the amount absorbed surpasses the amount eliminated, then a net increase in plasma drug concentration will occur until equilibrium is attained. By properly setting dosing schedules, an equilibrium will eventually be realized whereby the highest blood concentration (peak) and the lowest blood concentration (trough) each becomes the same with subsequent dosing. At this point, steady state is achieved. If the drug follows first-order kinetics and the dosing interval is the elimination half-life of the drug, steady state will be reached within four to five half-life intervals. Steady-state drug concentrations may be increased by either increasing the dose but maintaining the same dosing interval, or by increasing the frequency of the same dosing. The former method results in wider fluctuations between the maximum and minimum concentrations after each dose, while the latter method reduces the difference between the peak and trough concentrations.

APPLICATIONS TO FORENSIC TOXICOLOGY

The forensic toxicologist is asked basically four questions:

- Are drugs involved?
- How much did the subject take?
- When was it taken?
- Was it a cause of death (or, in nonfatal cases, did it affect behavior)?

The first question requires analytical toxicology, but pharmacokinetics is invoked to determine the specimen to test and the window of detection for the drug in available specimens. The second two questions on dose and time can often only be answered by pharmacokinetics. The last question on the effects of drugs and the time course of drug effects is the realm of pharmacodynamics.

Are Drugs Involved?

Analytical toxicology is the science of chemical or physical tests for drugs and poisons. The choice of test methods, target analyte(s), sensitivity, specificity, and specimen to be tested depends on knowledge of the distribution and pharmacokinetics of the drug.

For example, Fig. 3 shows the distribution of cocaine and cocaine metabolites in blood, saliva, urine, sweat, and hair. A test for cocaine metabolites in urine should target benzoylecgonine and ecgonine methyl ester. Large amounts of parent cocaine itself are not usually found in urine.

A test to determine if someone is under the influence of cocaine should be performed on blood or saliva. The test should determine the presence of active parent cocaine and the pharmacologically active metabolite cocaethylene. Testing hair for past history of exposure to cocaine requires a test procedure targeted to cocaine and lipophilic metabolites.

The specimen chosen for toxicological testing depends on the question being asked and the time course of drug or metabolites in the specimen. For example, Fig. 4 shows

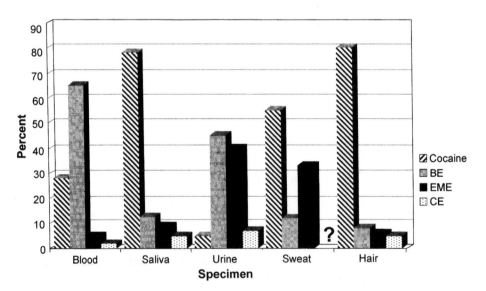

Fig. 3. Cocaine metabolic profile in blood, saliva, urine, sweat, and hair.

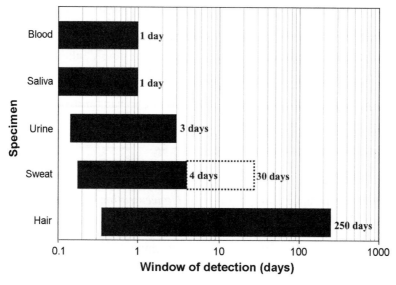

Fig. 4. Cocaine window of detection in blood, saliva, urine, sweat, and hair.

the window of detection for cocaine and metabolites in blood, saliva, urine, sweat, and hair. To find out if the person was ever exposed to cocaine, and if so, how often, the best specimens to test are bones, nails, and hair. To determine whether the person used cocaine in the past three to seven days, urine or sweat testing is indicated. To determine whether the person was under the influence of cocaine, the test must detect and quantify active drug in blood or saliva, or in brain tissue in death investigation.

How Much Drug Was Taken?

The first step to answering this question is to calculate how much drug is in the body at the time of death or at the time of obtaining the sample from a living person. Then the amount of drug eliminated from the body can be estimated. The history and observations will indicate the route of administration and give clues as to the drug's bioavailability. For example, in death investigation the autopsy record will indicate if there are tablets or capsules in the GI tract and whether the stomach is empty or contains liquids and food material. When liquid or solids are present

in the stomach lumen, it is always useful to weigh the total amount present and analyze a sample of the material for alcohol and drugs. This will aid in the estimation of total dose and may clarify route of administration and manner of death. For instance, the presence of barbiturates in the stomach and intestines might rule out later claims that a person died of homicidal injection of barbiturates. The presence of alcohol in the stomach contents at greater than 5 g/L should indicate caution in interpretation of heart blood alcohol values and the importance of obtaining and analyzing alternate specimens such as vitreous, brain, or spinal fluid for alcohol.

Abused drugs are often injected or inhaled to maximize bioavailability and avoid first-pass metabolism and inactivation by the liver. The autopsy record or the observations of a drug recognition expert will indicate presence of puncture marks and the age of the puncture wound. Drug in the nares might be observed when drugs are insufflated or snorted. Smoking cocaine often produces severe burns on lips and fingers.

The amount of drug in the body may be calculated from the person's weight in kilograms and the volume of distribution of the drug, V_d (Eq. 1).

Case History 1. Nude Female Body in River

The body of a 20- to 30-year-old woman (55 kg) was found nude, in the river, partially covered by a blanket. There were no signs of trauma and the autopsy showed that she did not drown. The lungs were congested. Toxicology findings were as follows: blood free morphine 0.45 mg/L; blood total morphine after enzyme hydrolysis 0.70 mg/L; and blood codeine 0.03 mg/L. Hair from the scalp was continuously positive along its entire length (20 cm) for morphine; 6-monoacetylmorphine (6-MAM), a metabolite of heroin, was present in her hair.

Amount
in body $= V_d \times$ weight $\times$ concentration

$V_d = 3.3 \pm 0.9$ L/kg

Amount $= 3.3$ L/kg $\times 55$ kg $\times 0.45$ mg/L

$\qquad = 81$ mg morphine

$\qquad = 103$ mg heroin

Case History 2. Asleep at the Wheel: Diazepam

A car driven by a 31-year-old white male failed to follow the road curve, crossed over the centerline, and hit a car approaching from the opposite direction, resulting in multiple fatalities. This driver was a physician known to be despondent. The driver's blood specimen obtained at the hospital 2 h after the crash contained 1.4 mg/L diazepam, 2.5 mg/L nordiazepam, and 0.04 g/dL ethanol.

Diazepam
amount in body $= 1.1 \pm 0.3$ L/kg $\times 72$ kg
$\qquad\qquad\qquad \times 1.4$ mg/L
$\qquad\qquad\quad = 110$ mg (range 96–255 mg)
Nordiazepam
in body $\qquad\quad = 79$ mg

From the amount in the body, it was concluded that the physician had injected about 10 to 11 2-mL ampoules (5 mg/mL) of diazepam and that the nordiazepam had come from multiple previous high-intravenous

doses of diazepam over previous weeks. Fifteen empty Roche Tel-E-Ject ampoules were found in the trunk of the physician's car. An open but nearly full bottle of wine was also found in the car.

The volume of distribution equation can also be solved for expected blood concentrations given a dosing history as in the following case history example.

Case History 3. Blood Alcohol Concentration from Drinking History

A 27-year-old white male, 6 feet tall and weighing 176 pounds, was observed by police officers to be driving slowly and swerving from his lane into other lanes of traffic. On approaching the driver after stopping, the officer noticed a strong odor suggestive of an alcoholic beverage. The young man had difficulty exiting his vehicle and failed the standard field sobriety tests. His breath alcohol concentration, measured at the roadside with a hand-held fuel cell device, was equivalent to 0.26 g/dL blood alcohol concentration, and his blood alcohol concentration determined on a blood specimen obtained 1.5 h after the stop was 0.25 g/dL. The young man remembered drinking five to six beers in the afternoon, ending his drinking about 4 h before the incident.

The amount of alcohol in the young man's body at the time the blood specimen was obtained can be calculated from the volume of distribution for alcohol:

Amount
in body $= V_d \times$ weight $\times$ concentration
$\qquad = 0.70$ L/kg $\times 80$ kg $\times 2.5$ g/L
$\qquad = 140$ grams [4.95 oz (w) or
$\qquad\qquad 6.19$ oz (v)] ethanol

On average, beer contains 4.5% ethanol by volume (4.8% for regular beers, 4.0% for light beers), so this is equivalent to the alcohol contained in 137.5 oz of beer or more than 10 12-oz beers. The expected blood alcohol concentration from drinking five to six beers 4 h before the incident can be calculated from the same equation rearranged for blood concentration:

$$\begin{aligned} \text{Concentration} &= \text{Dose}/V_d \times \text{weight} \\ &= 6 \times 12 \text{ oz} \times 0.045 \\ &\quad \times 0.8 / 0.70 \text{ L/kg} \times 80 \text{ kg} \\ &= 2.59 \text{ oz } (73.3 \text{ grams}) \\ &\quad \text{ethanol} / 56 \text{ L} \\ &= 0.130 \text{ g/dL} \end{aligned}$$

The highest theoretical concentration that six beers could have produced in the young man was less than that actually observed. In addition, at least 4 h had passed during which the alcohol would have been metabolized and eliminated from the body. The average rate of elimination is 0.015 g/dL/h. This would have further reduced the blood alcohol concentration:

$$\begin{aligned} \text{Concentration} &= 0.13 \text{ g/dL} \\ &\quad - (4 \text{ h} \times 0.015 \text{ g/dL/h}) \\ &= 0.07 \text{ g/dL} \end{aligned}$$

Therefore, the admitted history of drinking was not consistent with the blood alcohol concentration found, the signs and symptoms noted in the field sobriety test, or the driving behavior observed by the officers.

Cautions. Some cautions are in order regarding the application of pharmacokinetic parameters obtained in living patients or in healthy study subjects to blood specimens obtained postmortem or perimortem. In addition to interindividual variation, individual pharmacokinetics change due to disease and end-stage organ failure near the time of death. As clearance falls, half-lives will become longer and blood concentrations will increase dramatically. Drugs metabolized in the liver may accumulate in hepatic failure and drugs excreted by the kidneys will accumulate in renal failure.

Biofluids removed from the body after death may not have the same composition, hematocrit, or water content as blood and plasma from the living person. In addition, during the delay between death and the autopsy and collection of specimens, drugs can migrate from tissue reservoirs such as the liver or from the stomach or aspirated stomach contents. For example, digoxin bound to heart muscle is released into heart blood after death due to exhaustion of energy stores and beginning of tissue autolysis. For this reason, peripheral blood is generally better than heart blood for interpretation of blood concentrations. For drugs such as digoxin, the tricyclic antidepressants, and propoxyphene, which are known to increase in blood after death, it is wise to analyze an alternate specimen such as vitreous fluid, spinal fluid, brain tissue, or other organ tissues. Because of these complicating factors, it is generally unwise to predict doses from postmortem blood concentrations.

Case History 4. Digoxin

A 33-year-old white female was admitted to the hospital after taking 60 digoxin tablets. The blood concentration at admission was 45 ng/mL digoxin. Six hours later, after activated charcoal administration, digoxin concentrations were reduced to 18 ng/mL in blood sampled 1 h before death. The heart blood digoxin concentration obtained at autopsy 27 h after her death contained 36 ng/mL digoxin. In the brain, the optic chiasm contained 2.2 ng/g and the area postrema contained 1.9 ng/mL. The increase in blood digoxin after death was due to postmortem release from heart muscle into heart blood.

When Was the Drug Taken?

After a person takes a tablet or a drink, the drug is absorbed into the blood from the stomach or intestine and then distributed by the blood to the site of action. For alcohol, this absorption period is assumed complete within an hour. The rate of absorption of alcohol from an empty GI tract is said to be 0.1 g/dL/h (Fig. 5).

The bioavailability of a drug, or the percent of the drug that reaches the site of action, is the result of competing processes of

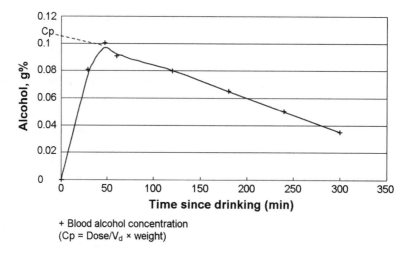

Fig. 5. Widmark curve for alcohol and alcohol pharmacokinetic (absorption, distribution, and elimination) parameters.

absorption and elimination. If a large part of the drug is metabolized in the liver or excreted in the bile, then the bioavailability of the drug when taken by mouth will be low. Cocaine is such an example. Injecting cocaine or insufflating or smoking the drug reduces the effect of hepatic first-pass metabolism.

As discussed earlier, drugs are cleared from the body by metabolism in the liver and by renal excretion. These mechanisms combine to reduce the amount of drug in the body until the drug is eliminated. The half-life ($t_{1/2}$) is defined as the time it takes for the blood concentration or the amount of drug in the body to be reduced by one-half.

Case History 5. Secobarbital

An unresponsive 34-year-old white male, 160 lb, was found and transported to the hospital where he died three days later without awakening. Serial blood samples taken at the hospital contained 47 mg/L of secobarbital at admission, 41 mg/L after 10 h, 35 mg/L after 16 h, 29 mg/L after 18 h, and 25 mg/L after 41 h. Postmortem blood contained 14.2 mg/L secobarbital. Plotting the time vs blood concentration gave a linear graph (first-order kinetics) with a slope of –0.065, or $K_1 = 0.065/2.303$ h^{-1}. This corresponds to a half-life of 40 h.

At the decedent's home, investigators found a suicide note, two different prescriptions for 30×100 mg secobarbital, and empty drug containers that had been filled at two different pharmacies the day before. A dose of 6000 mg secobarbital, if totally absorbed, would produce this blood concentration:

$$
\begin{aligned}
\text{Concentration} \\
\text{in blood} \quad &= 6000 \text{ mg} / 1.75 \text{ L/kg} \\
&\quad \times 72.7 \text{ kg} \\
&= 6000 \text{ mg} / 127.2 \text{ L} \\
&= 47.17 \text{ mg/L}
\end{aligned}
$$

This is close to the actual blood concentration found on admission. Because maximum blood concentration is reached 2–3 h after dose, it was concluded that the decedent had taken the tablets several hours before being found but not so long before that significant drug elimination had taken place.

Case History 6. Speedballing (Combined Use of Cocaine and Heroin)

A 28-year-old woman was observed driving erratically at high speed. Her car jumped the curb and came to rest against a traffic sign. She appeared agitated and shouted at witnesses, who called police. When the police arrived they found that the woman was still agitated, and then she rapidly fell asleep, with normal but fixed and nonreactive pupils (diameter 5.0 mm), a blood pressure of 140/80, and heart rate of 96, 80, and 76 beats per minute taken 15 min apart. A urine sample obtained 3 h after the incident was positive for both cocaine metabolites (benzoylecgonine) and opiate metabolites (morphine).

The half-life of cocaine is 0.8 ± 0.2 h, while the half-life of morphine from heroin is 1.9 ± 0.5 h (and morphine effects persist for 4–6 h). When cocaine and heroin are taken at the same time, the cocaine effects predominate immediately and then within about an hour the cocaine stimulant effects decrease or disappear and the narcotic effects of the morphine predominate. Urine concentrations cannot be related to dose, time of ingestion, or effect in the same manner as blood or plasma concentrations.

Parent/Metabolite Ratios

For drugs that are metabolized before elimination from the body, the ratio of parent drug to metabolite is a measure of the time elapsed since dose. The relationship between the ratio of parent to metabolite and the time since dose has been shown to be useful in forensic investigation for many therapeutic and abused drugs.

In Case History 1, the ratio of free morphine to total morphine was:

$$\text{Ratio} = 0.45 \text{ mg/L free morphine} / 0.70 \text{ mg/L total morphine}$$
$$= 64.3\%$$

The rules developed by data-mining software for interpretation of morphine-involved deaths (Fig. 6) were used to determine time and cause of death. Because the ratio of free to total morphine was >50%, this death was determined to be a rapid death occurring <3 h after dose (P = 0.85). From the presence of morphine and 6-MAM along the entire length of the deceased's hair, it was concluded that she had been a chronic user of heroin. The cause of death was morphine overdose (P = 0.75), because the blood unconjugated morphine was >0.24 mg/L, the percent of blood unconjugated morphine was >37%, and the frequency of use was chronic.

Witnesses (who were found later) admitted that the young woman had been given some high-grade heroin and then collapsed suddenly. Her body was stripped of clothes and identification and thrown into the river.

Did the Drug Account for Death or Impairment?

Many tables or compendia of therapeutic, toxic, and fatal concentrations have been published. The therapeutic doses and ranges are usually established through careful

Expert System Rules for Rapid Death	Expert System Rules for Direct Overdose
1. Percent unconjugated morphine >44%.	1. Liver morphine >0.50 to 0.75 µg/g.
2. Blood unconjugated morphine >0.09 to 0.21 µg/mL depending on other drugs present.	2. Blood unconjugated morphine >0.24 µg/mL.
3. Brain morphine >0.22 µg/mL.	3. Brain morphine >0.08 µg/mL or greater than blood unconjugated morphine.
	4. Percent blood unconjugated morphine >37%.
	5. Frequency of use: chronic.

Fig. 6. Beagle rules for morphine rapid death and direct overdose. *Source:* Spiehler VR. Computer-assisted interpretation in forensic toxicology: morphine-involved deaths. J Forensic Sci 1988;34:1104–15.

studies, but the lethal or fatal concentrations are empirical. They only record how much drug was found, not how much was required to cause death. When concentrations are gathered from published case reports, they do not represent common or expected toxic and fatal concentrations. Published papers often report the highest concentrations ever encountered or other unusual circumstances.

A second consideration in correlating a blood concentration to pharmacological effect is the time course of the drug's effect or pharmacodynamics. For drugs that display hysteresis, the effect of the drug at a given blood concentration may vary, depending on the time since dose. For instance, for alcohol, the effects at a certain blood concentration during the absorption phase are often more exciting and euphorient than at the same blood concentration during the elimination phase, when the person may feel more sedated and depressed. This is known as the Mellanby effect.

The hysteresis curve for methamphetamine is shown in Fig. 7. Shortly after dosing, the predominant effects are euphoria, relief from fatigue, nervousness, and stimulation, whereas at a later time the effects are confusion, paranoia, exhaustion, and even hypersomnolence.

The vital signs and symptoms noted during a systematic drug recognition examination are an important indicator of the pharmacologic effect of a blood concentration in a specific individual. While social and driving behavior may have many causes, observations of involuntary reflexes such as blood pressure, heart rate, temperature, pupil diameter and its accommodation to changing light levels, convergence, and nystagmus are more objective. When measured systematically and combined with psychomotor tests such as the Romberg modified attention test, the walk and turn, and one-leg stand, the resulting profiles are diagnostic of the pharmacodynamics of the drug. Conclusions as to the presence and effect of alcohol have a better than 90% predictive value. For other drugs, the predictive value range is 80–90%. The predictive value for the absence of alcohol or drugs is not as reliable (50–60%).

CONCLUSIONS

Interpretation in forensic toxicology involves three factors:

- history and observations made at the scene, at autopsy, or during the drug recognition evaluation;
- chemical tests on appropriate specimens; and
- interpretation using pharmacology, pharmacokinetics, and pharmacodynamics.

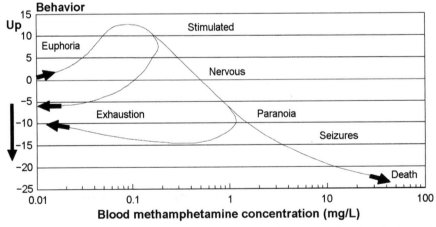

Fig. 7. Methamphetamine effect vs blood concentration over time curve showing clockwise hysteresis. *Source:* Logan B. Methamphetamine and driving impairment. J Forensic Sci 1996;41:457–64.

Pharmacokinetics and pharmacodynamics are best used to guide investigation and to test possible drug-use scenarios. Pharmacokinetic parameters derived from living subjects must be applied with caution to postmortem results. However, in death investigation, it is possible and prudent to analyze target tissues such as brain or heart or alternate specimens such as vitreous fluid or spinal fluid and to include these results in the interpretation.

SUGGESTED READING

1. Anderson WH, Prouty RW. Postmortem redistribution of drugs. In: Baselt RC, ed. Advances in analytical toxicology, vol. II. Chicago, IL: Yearbook Medical Publishers, Inc., 1989.
2. Baselt RC, ed. Disposition of toxic drugs and chemicals in man, 9th ed. Seal Beach, CA: Biomedical Publications, 2011.
3. Baselt RC, Wright JA, and Cravey RH. Therapeutic and toxic concentrations of more than 100 toxicological significant drugs in blood, plasma, or serum: a tabulation. Clin Chem 1975;21:44–62.
4. Garriott JC, ed. Garriott's medicolegal aspects of alcohol, 5th ed. Tucson, AZ: Lawyers & Judges Publishing Co., 2008.
5. Hagan RL. Basic pharmacokinetics. AACC Therapeutic Drug Monitoring and Toxicology 1996;17(9):233–46.
6. Hardman JG, Limbird LE, Molinoff PB, Ruddon RW, Gilman AG, eds. Goodman and Gilman's the pharmacological basis of therapeutics, 9th ed. New York: McGraw-Hill Co., 1996.
7. Heishman SJ, Singleton EJ, Crouch DJ. Laboratory validation study of drug evaluation and classification program: ethanol, cocaine, and marijuana. J Anal Toxicol 1996;20:468–83.
8. Logan B. Methamphetamine and driving impairment. J Forensic Sci 1996;41:457–64.
9. Pounder DJ, Yonemitsu K. Postmortem absorption of drugs and ethanol from aspirated vomitus—an experimental model. Forensic Sci Int 1991;51:189–95.
10. Spalding CT. Renal function and the elimination of drugs. AACC Therapeutic Drug Monitoring and Toxicology 1982:4(3);1–6.
11. Spiehler VR, Reed D. Brain concentrations of cocaine and benzoylecgonine in fatal cases. J Forensic Sci 1985;30:1003–11.
12. Spiehler VR, Sedgwick P, Richards RG. The use of brain digoxin concentrations to confirm blood digoxin concentrations. J Forensic Sci 1981;26(4):645–50.
13. Spiehler VR. Computer-assisted interpretation in forensic toxicology: morphine-involved deaths. J Forensic Sci 1988;34:1104–15.
14. Staub C. Hair analysis: its importance for the diagnosis of poisoning associated with opiate addiction. Forensic Sci Int 1993;63:69–75.
15. Stead AH, Moffat AC. A collection of therapeutic, toxic, and fatal blood drug concentrations in man. Human Toxicol 1983;2:437–64.
16. Tilston WJ, Stead AH. Pharmacokinetics, metabolism, and the interpretation of results. In: Moffat AC, ed. Clark's isolation and identification of drugs. London, UK: The Pharmaceutical Press, 1986:276–305.
17. Vorpal TE, Coe JI. Correlation of antemortem and postmortem digoxin levels. J Forensic Sci 1978;23:329–34.

PART II

METHODOLOGIES

CHAPTER 7

Specimen Preparation

Theodore J. Siek

Valid analytical test results depend on parameters and techniques that can be controlled by the analyst. Unless specimens are appropriately sampled and aliquoted, there is no hope for valid and reliable test results. Reasons for this will become more obvious as we discuss specimen preparation and sampling. Specimens that are homogenous at the time of sampling, such as plasma or serum, pose little difficulty other than the initial need for accurate volume or weight measurement.

Body fluids, organs, tissues, bone, hair, and other human body parts can be obtained during the autopsy or examination of a body. If properly processed in the toxicology laboratory, these specimens will yield definitive analytical data that can assist in solving a particular death case. Most often, the forensic toxicology laboratory receives whole blood, urine, and either brain or liver tissue specimens. Gastric (or stomach) content is useful in cases of suspected multiple tablet/capsule ingestion. In the more unusual cases, bile, vitreous fluid, internal tissues and organs (liver, kidney, brain, lung, and spleen), hair, nails, bone, bone marrow, skin, fat tissue, and muscle may be provided.

Fig. 1 presents an overview of the practical application of forensic toxicology. This chapter deals primarily with the sampling/aliquoting and the first step of isolating drugs, the separation from the bulk of body fluids and tissue substances.

Prior to aliquoting, a careful assessment of the task at hand must be made—for example,

how much blood, urine, tissue, or other specimen should be aliquoted for a given protocol? This depends on the testing techniques that will be employed. As a general rule, smaller sample amounts mean savings of time, materials, and solvents. Additionally, when less solvent is used, the total amount of impurities from the solvents will be reduced.

Maximizing analyte recovery is preferable to using a larger specimen amount. Therefore, when screening, take more specimen; when utilizing a specific test, take less specimen. When screening urine by a chromatographic technique such as TLC, GC, or HPLC, an aliquot of 1–10 mL is appropriate; when quantifying in blood, usually from 0.1–1 mL is sufficient.

The most direct way to obtain an aliquot of a blood specimen is to use a preselected volume by a pipetting device. Tissues are usually weighed "wet"; no effort is made to dry or remove internal blood and water from the tissue. Solid and semisolid soft tissue specimens must be homogenized with water or buffer prior to continuing with a given protocol for obtaining qualitative and quantitative information.

Other than direct sampling by pipette or by weighing, no other methods for acquiring specimen aliquots for testing purposes exist. An analytical result always contains a denominator of volume or weight to express concentration. Units used include milligram/liter (mg/L); microgram/liter (µg/L); milligram/kilogram (mg/kg); and gram/100 milliter (g/100 mL or gram%).

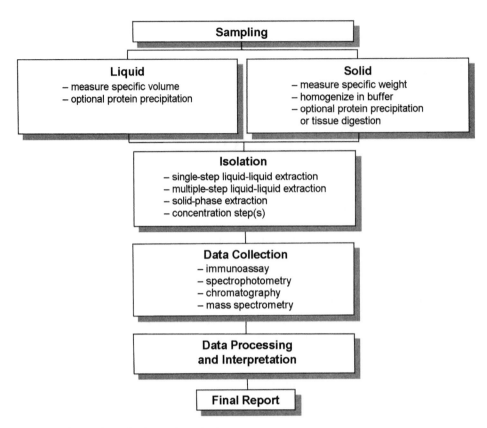

Fig. 1. Analytical overview of a forensic toxicology case.

Gas Phase Sampling for Gases and Volatile Liquids

Gases

Gases such as methane, ethane, propane, nitrous oxide, nitrogen, phosgene, and chlorine present special difficulties in preserving a given specimen prior to receipt by the toxicologist. It is imperative that specimens be frozen and secured in plastic or glass containers and held frozen until the toxicologist is ready to proceed with the analysis.

These precautions must be taken due to gas solubility—i.e., the absolute quantity (in weight, moles, volumes) in physical solution—which can be described as the volume (expressed as %) in blood or water at a given temperature and pressure. The gases named above have some solubility in blood; however, the blood will degas when its container is left open or even when its container is kept closed but standing at room temperature. Solubility is very temperature dependent, especially for inert gases such as nitrogen, hydrogen, ethane, methane, and other nonpolar organic gases. For example, the solubility of nitrous oxide (N_2O) in blood is 47/100 (47 volume %) at 37 °C and atmospheric pressure, which converts to 0.92 gram N_2O/liter blood. N_2O in blood is condensed and the concentration is more readily understood in mole/liter or gram/liter (see "Appendix 1" for how this calculation is set up). Volume percent can be converted to gram/liter by applying the ideal gas law and converting moles/liter to gram/liter.

The preparation of gas standards requires that pure gas be added to blood until saturation, that the saturation concentration be obtained from published values, and that test bloods be compared to saturation concentrations. At best, such determinations are approximate because gas solubilities in blood are temperature- and pressure-dependent, and therefore difficult to control. Gas is lost during storage and sampling.

Inert gases are usually analyzed by gas chromatography with a thermal conductivity detector or, in the case of methane, ethane, and propane, with a flame detector. Some gases are amenable to GC/MS determinations with injections of "head space," as described in the next section.

Gases such as hydrogen sulfide, hydrochloric acid, and hydrogen cyanide ionize in blood and are very water soluble. Therefore they do not behave in accordance with Henry's law. Henry's law states that the mass of a gas dissolved in a given mass of solution at constant temperature is directly proportional to the pressure the gas exerts above the solution once equilibrium is achieved.

The presence of cyanide in blood can be determined by converting ionic cyanide to hydrogen cyanide (HCN) gas by adding dilute sulfuric acid. An aliquot of blood is placed into a flat three-chamber Conway diffusion cell (middle well); reagents that react with cyanide ion are placed in the center well (two reagents plus dilute sodium hydroxide). A seal (the cover fits over the outer well) is made with the outer well, which contains dilute sulfuric acid. The cyanide in the blood is converted to hydrogen cyanide by adding 3N sulfuric acid to the blood; the HCN diffuses within 30 minutes into the reaction well (center); the outer well is also acidified, and a color reaction proportional to cyanide affords a determination.

Manipulation is the key word in dealing with gases—inert, soluble, insoluble, and reactive/ionic gas species.

Volatile Liquids

Ethanol is the most frequently analyzed substance in forensic toxicology. Ethanol, liquid at room temperature, is considered a volatile liquid, along with the other "volatiles": acetone, isopropanol, methanol, ethyl acetate, propanol, 2-butanone, and dichloromethane. Because of its adherence to

Henry's law, ethanol is readily determined as a gas by gas chromatography. The approach is generally some variation of the brief method outlined below:

1. Sample the blood or urine into a small sealable glass vial with an accurate pipette, manual or automated; 0.1–1.0 mL is typical. Vials of 5–20 mL volume are appropriate.
2. Immediately add an aqueous solution of an internal standard and cap the container. The internal standard might be 1-propanol, 2-butanone, or acetonitrile of a standard concentration. The internal standard must be separated from ethanol and other commonly occurring volatile substances.
3. Place the sealed vials into a constant temperature bath for a specified time to allow a partitioning of ethanol and the internal standard between aqueous phase and the air space above the liquid phase. The combination of heat and a salt solution in the vial (placed there prior to sampling blood) will drive ethanol and the internal standard into the gas phase or "head space" above the liquid (trapped in the sealed vial). Heating between 30 °C and 50 °C is typical in ethanol determinations.
4. Sample a measured volume of the head space in the sealed containers and place into the GC column. Exact measurement of the head space volume is not necessary because the internal standard (concentration is known) normalizes all injections.

The internal standard is added to blood, urine, and serum most often in a volume 2 to 10 times the volume of the aliquoted specimen. This is so that blood ethanol concentration can be converted to a "water" ethanol concentration, thereby avoiding calibration based on blood ethanol standards. It is more convenient to add a measured quantity of ethanol to water than to blood. The sample aliquot placed into the gas chromatography column can be an automated process; auto-samplers are available for head space gas chromatography determinations of volatile substance. Auto-samplers, when properly programmed, will provide greater precision and therefore accuracy for a given batch of specimens.

One- to four-carbon halogenated substances (chloroform, trichloroethane, dichlorethane, ethyl chloride, carbon tetrachloride, and other combinations of chlorinated and fluorinated volatiles) are liquids at room temperature, have high vapor pressures, and are sparingly water soluble. The chloro-fluoro volatile hydrocarbons substances (Chapter 28, Table 1) are used by physicians as general anesthetics. It is important to realize that when determining ethanol by gas chromatography, other volatiles may interfere if there has been exposure to volatile substances.

Protein Precipitation

The protein content of human body fluids and tissues is considerable, from about 6% by weight in plasma to greater than 50% by weight in liver and other organs. Numerous techniques have been developed to precipitate protein and remove it before extracting and concentrating drug substances.

Fig. 1 presents an outline indicating the decision process involved in bench forensic toxicology. Nonisolation and nonpurification techniques include immunoassays, test tube color tests, and some chromatography approaches in which fractionation and isolation are part of the chromatography process. Protein precipitation reagents include the following:

- *Organic solvents* (acetone, acetonitrile, methanol). One volume of blood or serum is added to two or three volumes of solvent with vortexing followed by centrifugation.
- *Zinc sulfate in methanol.* 5 g zinc sulfate are dissolved in 100 mL of water plus 43 mL methanol. It is used for precipitation at neutral pH.
- *5-Sulfosalicylic acid.* 3.2 g is added to 50 mL water plus 50 mL of methanol. It is used for serum/plasma/blood precipitations at pH 1–2.

- *Perchloric acid.* Concentrated perchloric acid (70% by weight) is diluted 10-fold with water. It is used for acidic and neutral drugs in blood or serum.
- *Trichloroacetic acid* (10–15% in water). This is one of the most frequently used protein-precipitating reagents in clinical and forensic toxicology and is strongly acidic.
- *Sodium tungstate* (10% sodium tungstate in water). This is used in conjunction with 3N sulfuric acid. Strongly acidic, it is best for recovering acidic and neutral drugs.
- *Ammonium sulfate.* The solid is added to a preheated tissue homogenate and used with dilute hydrochloric acid to complete the precipitation.

Once proteins have been precipitated, separation of aqueous and solid protein must occur by filtration or centrifugation. The purpose of protein precipitation is to obtain a cleaner preparation. Some drugs are occluded (trapped) in the precipitate, but can be at least partially recovered by washing the precipitate with hot water or hot dilute hydrochloric acid. Recovery of drugs can be monitored by the addition of an "internal standard" just prior to homogenization of the specimen. This internal standard should be chemically similar to the analytes under investigation. One way of testing recovery is to reextract the residue a second time by the identical technique and determine the ratio of the initial concentration to the second extract concentration. The formula for such a recovery study is in "Appendix 2."

Protein precipitation is appropriate in certain tests that require a nonparticle aqueous solution preparation that is to be treated with a color-producing reagent. For example, a standard and reliable test for salicylic acid (from aspirin intake) calls for treating one volume of blood or serum with 3–10 volumes of Trinder's reagent. The precipitation and color reaction occur simultaneously as the acidity causes precipitation, and salicylic acid complexing with the ferric ion in the reagent produces a visible purple color proportional to the salicylic acid concentration in the serum. Background color of serum or blood is negated by the large volume of reagent to specimen. (Other color reactions are discussed in Chapter 8.) Removal of protein makes further manipulation of the supernatant (liquid after solids filtered or centrifuged away) easier.

Those drugs readily hydrolyzed by heating under aqueous acidic or basic conditions should be either extracted without protein precipitation or extracted with a mild precipitation reagent such as zinc sulfate-methanol (see above description) without heating. Esters such as cocaine, benzocaine, meperidine, methylphenidate, and procaine need to be recovered under mild conditions. Alkaloids such as strychnine, nicotine, quinine, various opiates, and some narcotics will not be degraded by moderate heating and acid treatments to precipitate protein.

Specimen Digestion for Inorganic Determinations

Thorough analytical procedures for inorganic poisons such as arsenic, cadmium, mercury, lead, and other metal ions require that blood and tissues be "digested" so that all organic material is oxidized away (essentially burned chemically). What remains is a clean inorganic residue that can be subjected to atomic absorption spectrophotometry, atomic emission spectrophotometry, or anodic stripping voltometry. Urine and gastric contents can often be tested without digestion for some metals.

The digestion procedure involves weighing out 1 to 5 grams (usually wet weight or as received) of specimen—nails, hair, soft tissue, bone, or food and digest—and placing it in an acid-resistant fume hood with a mixture of sulfuric, nitric, and perchloric acids. The mixture is then heated to an endpoint at which sulfur trioxide (SO_3) fumes are heavily emitted. At this point various spectrophotometric techniques are applied.

Inorganic metal determination is a specialized area of forensic toxicology, and smaller laboratories are not as likely to be capable of analyzing arsenic, cadmium, and other metals. Blood lead screening programs, for example, are often carried out by state departments of health in the U.S.

Enzymatic digestion may also be used for acid-labile and strongly protein-bound drugs. One enzyme commonly used for all major drug classes is the proteolytic enzyme subtilisin Carlsberg. The procedure involves homogenizing tissue in pH 10 buffer, the pH for optimum enzyme activity. At this point, 1 mg of enzyme per gram of tissue is added to the homogenate and incubated at 55 °C for one hour. Once the incubation is completed, the pH of the homogenate can be adjusted for additional sample preparation.

Liquid-Liquid Extraction

Solvent Selection

Body fluids (blood, urine, bile) or an aqueous tissue homogenate can be extracted directly with an organic solvent to obtain organic substances. This direct method is perhaps the most frequently used in existing toxicology laboratories throughout the world. There are many reasons for this, the foremost being that blood and urine are the most frequently chosen specimens for drug substance determinations. Blood and urine, being liquids, can readily be partitioned with an organic solvent without protein precipitation after a pH adjustment of the liquid with a buffer, acid, or base. Many solvents have been employed for direct extractions, either individually or in combination. Table 1 summarizes extraction-related properties of solvents that have been used by forensic toxicologists in recent years.

Solvent polarity is one of the more important factors in choosing a solvent for extraction. Since nearly all drugs in use today have some degree of polarity, it stands to reason that petroleum ether or hexane on its own is not effective, except to recover another saturated hydrocarbon from blood. Table 1 indicates polarity in two ways: (1) the

Table 1. Key Properties of Organic Liquids Related to Their Utility as Extracting Solvents for Drug Substances

Solvent	Density (g/mL)	Boiling Point (°C)	g H$_2$O/L Saturation	Dielectric Constant	Hydrogen Bonds	
					H Donor	H Acceptor
n-Hexane	0.66	68	0.045	1.89	No	No
Toluene	0.87	111	0.46	2.38	No	No
1-Chloroform	0.89	78	0.90	7.4	No	No
Chloroform	1.49	61	1.24	4.8	Yes	No
Dichloromethane	1.34	40	11.9	9.08	No	No
Ethyl ether	0.71	35	17.0	4.33	No	Yes
Methyl t-butyl ether	0.74	55	20.3	na[a]	No	Yes
Ethyl acetate	0.90	77	29.4	6.0	No	Yes
1-Butanol	0.81	118	170	17.8	Yes	Yes
2-Propanol	0.79	82	Miscible	18.3	Yes	Yes
Acetone	0.79	56	Miscible	20.7	No	Yes
Acetonitrile	0.79	80	Miscible	37	Yes	Yes

[a]Value is not available.

solubility of water in that solvent, and (2) the dielectric constant. These two properties of solvents, as well as hydrogen bonding ability, are critical with respect to how effective a given solvent will be for a given analyte. For example, caffeine is more readily extracted by chloroform than by diethyl ether because caffeine accepts a hydrogen bond from a donor solvent (like chloroform) but has no hydrogen atoms to donate to a solvent such as diethyl ether (see Fig. 2). It is, however, logical to add an alcohol such as isopropanol, isoamyl alcohol, or butanol to hexane and achieve hydrogen bonding in all cases, since alcohols can accept and donate hydrogen atoms for hydrogen bonding with drugs. Whereas mixing solvents seems to complicate the situation, there is no denying its practicality. Hexane or heptane containing 1–5% isoamyl alcohol or isopropanol by volume effectively extracts phenothiazines from blood by direct extraction.

Adjustment of pH Prior to Extraction

Once a solvent is chosen, a buffer is usually added to convert drugs to a form that is nonionic so it will partition readily in organic solvent. Carboxylic acids (R-COOH functional groups) are fully protonated 2 pH units below their pK$_a$s (acid dissociation constants) but are ionic above their pK$_a$s. The addition of acid to blood causes some discoloring and protein precipitation. A 3N H$_3$PO$_4$ solution can lower the pH to 2 or 3 without excessive discoloration or protein precipitation. Some of the drugs containing the carboxylic acid function include salicylic acid, ibuprofen, ketoprofen, indomethacin, ampicillin, probenecid, fluoroacetic acid, citric acid, acetaminobenzoic acid, and tetrahydrocannabinol metabolites. Nitrophenols such as 2,4-dinitrophenol are as acidic as carboxylic acids, with the nitro groups making the phenol more acidic.

A second grouping of drugs by acidity includes those drugs with pK$_a$ constants above a pH of 7 or 8. Commonly occurring drugs in this group are the 1,5,5-substituted barbiturates; the 5,5-substituted barbiturates; phenytoin; acetaminophen; phenolphthalein; dicoumarol; warfarin; hydroxycoumarin; and tolbutamide.

The classification of drugs by chemical class is a convenient way to "divide and conquer" when approaching a general unknown. Drug classes are as listed below:

- strong acids (pK$_a$s from 1 to 5),
- weak acids (pK$_a$s from 5 to 9),
- neutrals (no acidic or basic functional group—extractable at all pHs),

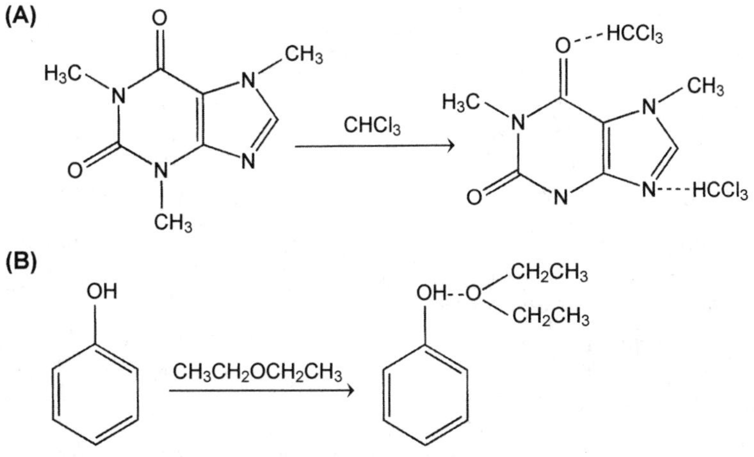

Fig. 2. Drug interaction with solvents as illustrated with (A) caffeine/chloroform and with (B) phenol/diethyl ether. Caffeine has a donor molecule.

- weak bases (neutral below pH 5 or 6),
- strong bases (un-ionized from pH 7 and greater), and
- amphoteric bases that have both amine and phenolic groups.

Fig. 3 illustrates a separation of the chemical drug groups by a sequential extraction technique. Fig. 4 lists examples of a number of these drug groups. Separations such as those shown in Fig. 3 are often applied to urine, a protein-free filtrate of liver, or to gastric contents, when a general screening for drugs is required. The aqueous fractions can be examined by ultraviolet spectrophotometry and in some instances by an immunoassay. However, chromatography techniques require a further extraction to obtain an organic concentrate or "extract" that can be chromatographed by HPLC, TLC, or GC. The several fractions shown in Fig. 3 that are in aqueous buffer are reextracted into solvent to obtain concentrated extracts that can be chromatographed. Reextractions are discussed below. The amphoteric bases and bases fractions can be readily combined for HPLC, GC, and TLC procedures. Likewise, strong and weak acids can be chromatographed together.

The key principle in adjusting pH for extraction is to create nonsalt forms of the drugs to be partitioned into the organic solvent. Amines accept protons to form hydro salt in acidic solution (for example, amphetamine hydrochloride in dilute HCL), and acidic drugs form salts in alkaline solution. The pH should be adjusted 2 pH units below the pK_a (or above in the case of amines) to produce 100% un-ionized forms. Drugs with two or more ionizable groups present some special problems. Two examples of this are morphine and benzoylecgonine (cocaine primary metabolite).

Morphine is in its "isoelectric" or least ionized form at pH 9. Morphine is not extractable above pH 10 because the phenolic group ionizes, and below pH 8, the amine accepts a proton. Benzoylecgonine is a vexing problem since it is always a salt, although between pH 7 and 8 it is primarily a "zwitter ion," an internal salt (see Fig. 4). For this reason, benzoylecgonine is only poorly recovered, even with very polar solvents, and at the isoelectric pH.

Yields of bases and acids are not improved by excessive adjustments of pH; e.g., by using 2N sodium hydroxide where 0.1N will do or using 6N sulphuric acid where 0.1N will accomplish the extraction. Norpropoxyphene (the primary metabolite of propoxyphene) rearranges rapidly in strong base, forming an amide. Bupropion decomposes in strong

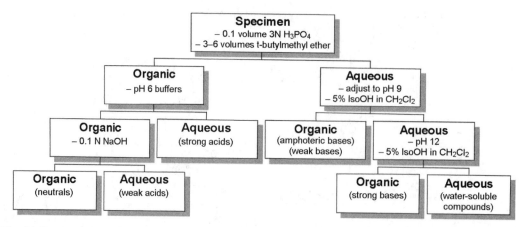

Fig. 3. Fractionation scheme for the separation of organic drug substances according to acidity/alkalinity. H_3PO_4 = phosphoric acid; IsoOH = isopropanol; NaOH = sodium hydroxide; CH_2Cl_2 = dichloromethane.

base. The use of ammonium hydroxide instead of sodium hydroxide will attenuate the pHs attained when added to blood or other body fluid. Remaining 1 to 2 pH units below or above the pK_a's is the general rule of thumb when making pH adjustments. Strong acids and alkalis will also cause emulsion problems.

A common misunderstanding is that completely neutral drugs should be extracted at pH 7. Neutral drugs extract at all pH values between 0 and 14, since the molecules are unionized at all pH points. The neutral fraction is, however, somewhat difficult to work with once isolated, since glycerides, cholesterol, and cholesterol esters are recovered with the neutral fraction from blood and tissue. The acid fraction is also contaminated with fatty acids (from glyceride hydrolysis). Removal of acids and neutrals prior to recovery of basic drugs results in a cleaner fraction. Running the chromatography of what is thought to be a "clean" extract always leaves the toxicologist asking, "What are all these peaks?" Ninety-nine percent of them are not drugs but natural pigments, food additives, dyes, phthalates, and solvent impurities.

Other Factors

Further complicating extraction is the fact that some hydrochloride salts are solvent soluble, particularly in chloroform, 1-chlorobutane, and dichloromethane. The greater the hydrocarbon content, the more readily hydrochloride salts partition into the solvent. When extracting on the acid side, use a proton-acceptor solvent such as methyl t-butyl ether, and when back-extracting from chloroform or dichloromethane, use dilute sulfuric or phosphoric acid rather than dilute hydrochloric acid, thereby creating a salt that is less soluble in organic solvent. High-molecular-weight drugs such as thioridazine and other phenothiazines form hydrochloride salts that are solvent soluble. Sulfate and phosphate salts are less soluble in organic solvents and should therefore be used in back-extractions from solvent.

There are many considerations in solvent liquid–liquid extractions, for example, cost, odor, safety, and the like. Diethyl ether, for example, has several drawbacks: an unpleasant odor that readily permeates refrigerators, high volatility and flammability, and formation of peroxides that will react with drugs. Benzene is a stated carcinogen and should be avoided. Chloroform is a suspected carcinogen, as is dichloromethane, but evidence for carcinogenicity is very weak. In the early days of urine drug testing, gallons of chloroform in large warehouses were used to extract hundreds of urine specimens for drugs of abuse. Laboratories have learned to use less solvent, but some exposure to chemists and technicians is inevitable.

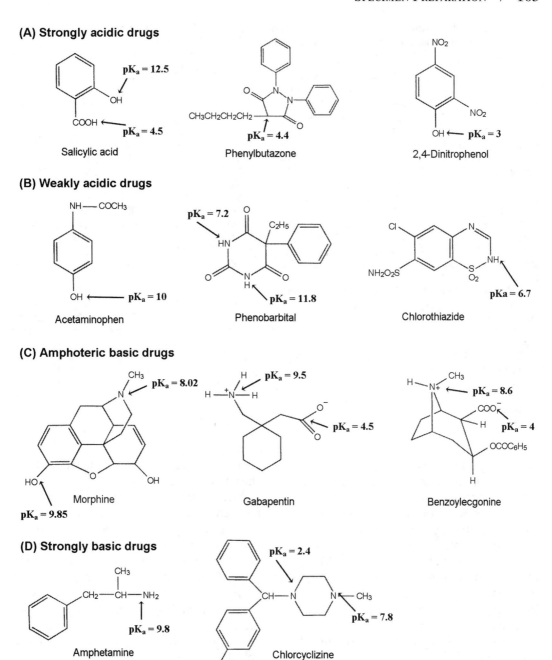

Fig. 4. Four chemical classes of drugs. The dissociation constants as pKa's are provided.

Partition constants, i.e., the distribution of drugs in organic solvent against aqueous buffer, are not specifically considered by the forensic toxicologist, mainly because toxicologists do not deal with pure systems, such as octanol–water or water–ether. However, to appreciate drug distributions between a primarily aqueous phase and the organic phase, see Table 2, which indicates recoveries of polar and nonpolar drugs using eight different solvents. Drugs with one functional group such as a tertiary amine

Table 2. Percent Recoveries of Fourteen Drugs by Extraction with Each of Eight Solvents (Extracting Solvent Partitioned Against An Equal Volume Aqueous Buffer)

Drug	Hexane	1-Chloro-butane	Dichloro-methane	Chloro-form	Isopropyl Ether	Ethyl Ether	Ethyl Acetate	1-Butanol
Chloramphenicol[a]	0	0	22	0	15	56	58	41
Hydrochlorothiazide[b]	0	4	8	0	12	30	92	84
Salicylic acid[c]	0	59	83	83	100	98	98	100
Morphine[d]	0	12	25	33	7	20	52	91
Caffeine[a]	0	10	81	90	6	9	37	54
Procainamide[e]	6	29	90	92	21	21	84	92
Pentobarbital[f]	4	66	97	96	98	95	98	99
Benzocaine[e]	29	82	100	100	88	88	94	94
Propoxyphene[e]	48	43	96	96	71	97	—	99
Imipramine[e]	35	79	88	98	84	70	99	100
Methaqualone[a]	78	90	93	93	89	91	95	97
2,5-Dimethoxy-4 methylamphetamine[e]	87	98	100	100	95	95	93	100
Cocaine[e]	89	96	95	96	94	95	99	99
Haloperidol[e]	99	99	99	100	100	100	100	100

[a]pH is 7.
[b]Extracted at pH 4; poor recoveries were obtained at all pHs, with a pH of 2–6 giving the best recoveries.
[c]pH is 1.
[d]pH is 9.
[e]pH is 11.
[f]pH is 5.

are recovered in high yield by nearly all solvents. The polar drugs such as hydrochlorothiazide, morphine, and caffeine need more polar solvents (those with higher dielectric constants). It is obvious that since caffeine can only accept a hydrogen atom (proton) for hydrogen bonding, it is better extracted by chloroform or dichloromethane plus isopropanol (hydrogen donor solvents) than by diethyl ether or ethyl acetate (hydrogen acceptor solvents). Fig. 2 illustrates how hydrogen bonding can occur with caffeine and with phenol.

Back-Extraction Techniques

The initial extraction or partitioning of blood, urine, or bile with organic solvent is the poorest yield step of the entire process. Usually, the ratio of solvent to blood should be 5:1 or even 10:1 in order to obtain good recovery (70% or greater). After the initial step, the solvent can be concentrated for chromatographic separation.

Alternatively, acids and bases may be recovered by "back-extraction" into aqueous acid or base. Here a large reduction of volume is appropriate, further concentrating and miniaturizing the procedure. One good example of this is to extract tricyclic drugs from 0.5 mL blood (pH 11–12) with 3 mL hexane-isopropanol 95/5, centrifuging and transferring the organic layer to a second tube. Next, 100 μL of a 0.1% vol/vol phosphoric acid (0.1 mL of 70% phosphoric acid to 100 mL of water) is added to the hexane-isopropanol, with vortexing. The very poor solubility of phosphate salts in hexane-isopropanol means nearly 100% recovery from organic to aqueous and achieves a concentration of 3 mL to 0.1 mL. This 0.1 mL can then be introduced directly into an appropriate HPLC column.

Getting tricyclic antidepressants from the blood to the measurement system involves a two-step extraction. For gas chromatography and thin layer chromatography, a reextraction from the aqueous mineral acid is needed (three-step extraction procedure). Needless to say, each step involves some loss of drug; the more steps, the greater the potential loss. The trade-off is purity of extract vs recovery. One-step extractions may be efficient for recovery, but are less selective since neutral substances are always present in one-step extractions. For chromatographic techniques, a three-step extraction is standard: extraction, back-extraction, re-extraction.

Solid-Phase Extraction

Because of the drawbacks and difficulties in many liquid–liquid extraction techniques, toxicologists have developed other approaches for the isolation and purification of drug-containing fractions. Solid-phase extraction (SPE) has undergone numerous changes and improvements from 1965 to present.

In-House Columns

In the 1960s and early 1970s, bench toxicologists devised their own solid-phase columns.

Toxicologists began by creating home-made columns containing sodium sulfate (to absorb water) and shredded filter paper or cotton balls (to trap the drugs of interest). These were somewhat successful, depending on the user's skill and knowledge. The procedure involved pouring the blood onto the column, then pouring a solvent through the column to recover drugs. Next, the investigator used diatomaceous earth (kieselguhr), a sedimentary rock of marine or lacustrine deposition composed primarily of silicon dioxide with 2–10% water content, in loosely packed columns.

Materials such as florisil (magnesium silicate) packed into glass pipettes or Pasteur pipettes have been employed to recover organochlorine pesticides such as lindane,

DDT, and PCBs. This technique is properly called "column chromatography" in the classical sense and involves chromatography in the purification step following an initial extraction into n-hexane. After adsorption onto florisil, nonpolar solvents such as petroleum ether or hexane are used to recover organochlorine pesticides. Lipids and proteins are highly retained by the activated florisil. Charcoal (activated carbon) columns are also used in some toxicological applications.

Commercial Preparatory (Prep) Columns

Beginning in the mid 1970s, chromatography supply companies such as Applied Science, Supelco, Alltech, Varian, and United Chemical Technologies offered manufactured columns of various phases and types, or offered purified packing materials to place into tubular glass or plastic columns. The materials included ion exchange resins, XAD resins, and finally highly purified silica gel. Silica (SiO_2) has become the mainstay of most currently used SPE columns. The raw material for the manufacture of refined silica gel is sand, obviously available in great abundance since silicon dioxide constitutes 60% (by weight) of the earth's crust. Sand is treated with sodium carbonate and water to form somewhat water-soluble H_4SiO_4. It is then treated with sulfuric acid, dried, ground, and finally sized and chemically treated to reduce "active sites," which are silol (Si-OH) groups. To make silica more useful to toxicologists and chemists, silica is sized, sorted to uniform or regular particle shapes (the more spherical the better), and then used in HPLC, TLC, and prep columns. Particle sizes of 20–40 microns are used for silica-based SPE columns.

On-Off Columns

The technology surrounding SPE silica columns involves creating short, very absorbent, fast-flow columns that (1) selectively bind drugs from an aqueous matrix; (2) allow carbohydrates, proteins, and polar lipids to pass through; and then (3) allow elution of the drugs with efficient solvents. The idea is not to chromatograph or separate drugs as in classical column chromatography or gas chromatography, but to put the drug on the column in a few minutes, remove unwanted components, and recover the drug in a few mLs of solvent, thereby highly concentrating the drugs. The appeal in solid-phase extraction is reproducibility, batch processing that is amenable to robotics, and minimizing the use of solvents. For numerous separations, this has been achieved.

Bonded Silica Sorbents

Purified silica can be reacted to form covalently chemical groups (bonded to Si or to SiOH on the silica) consisting of hydrocarbon chains (C_8, C_{18}), phenyl groups, polar groups, and anion and cation exchange sites. The bonded anion exchange sites are quaternary amines (positively charged); cation exchange sites are benzenesulfonic acid groups (pK_a approximately 0.7) that are ionic at all but very low pH values. United Chemical Technologies has developed covalent bonded SPE columns that contain hydrophobic groups and cation exchange sites (benzenesulfoic acid). With this type of "copolymeric" column, fractionation into acid plus neutrals and basic/amphoteric drugs can be achieved. Although this does not divide strong acids, weak acids, and neutrals into fractions as can be done in liquid–liquid extraction, a general unknown screen can be carried out with this column.

SPE columns can now be obtained from many scientific supply companies. Often protocols for various analytes are provided with the purchase of a bag or two of SPE columns that are shipped in the dry state and pre-packed into plastic columns that are inert to organic solvents.

The usual steps in using SPE columns are as follows:

1. Solvate or wet the column with methanol.
2. Flush the column with water to remove the methanol, then with the buffer that is used to dilute the blood specimen.
3. Pour the buffered blood onto the column.
4. Wash with water and a relatively moderate aqueous acid solution such as acetic acid or 0.1N hydrochloric acid.
5. Rinse with methanol. At this stage, basic drugs are retained, and acidic and neutral drugs are eluted.
6. Dry the columns by aspiration of air through the columns. Add a small volume of n-hexane to further dry the column bed.
7. Elute basic drugs with a weakly alkaline organic solvent mixture such as dichloromethane/isopropanol/conc. ammonia (70/20/2).

Because of the many column washings, the drying step, and the eluting solvents, this whole process may appear to be tedious. For substances that are highly partitioned from aqueous into dichloromethane (caffeine, benzodiazepines, and tricyclics), SPE uses more solvent and materials, and involves more time than a simple one-step extraction. However, for polar drugs such as benzoylecgonine that are difficult to extract directly by organic solvents, SPE is advantageous. Ceftriaxone, gabepentin, vigabatrin, and other drugs that are ionic, or internal salts from pH 1–14, defy recovery by ordinary liquid–liquid extraction. Isolation of such drugs can be achieved by an appropriate SPE technique.

As new drugs reach the public, toxicologists are constantly faced with developing analytical procedures for these new drugs. The more water soluble a drug, the more "trouble" you can expect in isolation. The key to all analytical isolation techniques is to manipulate drugs in relation to their functional groups, their hydrocarbon content, their acid/base groups, and their general water solubility.

SPE applications in forensic toxicology undoubtedly will continue to increase in versatility, size, and specificity. Some SPE columns are too resistant to flow for blood or even water-diluted blood; special columns for blood extractions are available. The columns are designed for specific determinations or specific group determinations. Procedures more in keeping with a general screening category and designed to accomplish what is outlined in Fig. 3, the liquid–liquid extraction technique, are being published. These procedures yield acids, bases, and neutrals in separate fractions.

Solid-Phase Microextraction

Solid-phase microextraction (SPME) is a newer sample technique that is being applied to alcohol and drug analysis. The main differences between SPE and SPME are the size of the sorptive surface and the phase of the extracting material. SPE requires a large sorptive surface area and extraction from liquid-phase samples; SPME uses a smaller sorptive surface area and can extract from gaseous as well as liquid samples.

SPME consists of two separate steps: (1) analyte adsorption from the matrix to a thick layer of silicone or related adsorptive material and (2) release from the adsorptive material by a gas or liquid directly into a chromatographic inlet. The extraction devices may be either a fiber with an external sorptive coating or a tube with the sorptive material inside. Some time is required for equilibrium to occur between the analyte in the specimen and the analyte in the SPME layer. Once equilibrium has occurred, the adsorbed analyte-SPME layer complex must be transferred to the chromatographic inlet. Externally coated sorbent must be physically separated from the sample. Internally coated SPME layer need not be physically separated; however, conditions must be modified to facilitate release of the analyte from the adsorbing material.

Once at the chromatographic inlet, conditions to promote desorption must be established. For externally coated fibers, insertion into a gas chromatographic inlet system as if it were a syringe will permit entry into the chromatograph. For introduction into a liquid chromatograph, there are devices that wash the SPME layer with mobile phase and pass the desorbed analyte into an injection loop. For internally coated tubes, heating is necessary prior to introduction into the gas chromatograph. For liquid chromatographic analysis, a multiple-position valve system can switch from the specimen liquid flow to the mobile phase.

Supported Liquid Extraction

A separation technique that combines elements of liquid-liquid extraction and solid phase extraction is supported liquid extraction. With this approach, the biological specimen is buffered to ensure that the analytes of interest are in the nonionized state. The buffered specimen is then applied to a column containing diatomaceous earth material. The specimen distributes throughout the porous material and is washed with a hydrophobic solvent. The high surface area of the diatomaceous earth allows greater contact with the extraction solvent, thus improving extraction efficiency. This also eliminates the formation of emulsions and precipitates that may develop when performing standard liquid-liquid extraction.

Esoteric Isolation Techniques

Some esoteric isolation techniques such as microwave extractions, soxlet extractions, countercurrent distribution, steam distillations, vacuum distillations, and Stas-Otto procedures are beyond the scope of this chapter. There is not now nor ever has there been one standard approach to isolating all potential analytes from the biological matrix. Putrefied specimens from decomposed bodies require even more innovative approaches than are discussed above.

APPENDIX 1

47 vol% = 47 mL/100 mL = 0.47 L/L.

(0.47 L/22.7 L/mol) 44 g/mol = 0.92 g N_2O/L blood.

APPENDIX 2

$\%\text{Recovery} = (1 - W_2/W_1) \times 100$ where W_1 and W_2 are weights or concentrations recovered in consecutive extractions.

SUGGESTED READING

1. Hinshaw JV. Solid phase microextraction. LC-GC North America 2003;21:1056–61.
2. Moffat AC, Osselton MD, Widdop B, ed. Clarke's analysis of drugs and poisons. London, England: Pharmaceutical Press, 2004.
3. Siek TJ. Use of organic solvents in toxicology. [Review: Winek CL, ed.] Toxicology Annual 1979;3:205–30.
4. Telepchak MJ, August TF, Cheney G. Forensic and clinical applications of solid phase extraction. Totowa, NJ: Humana Press, 2004.

CHAPTER 8

Spectrophotometry

Kenneth Cole and Barry Levine

ULTRAVIOLET-VISIBLE SPECTROPHOTOMETRY

Ultraviolet (UV)-visible spectrophotometry is one of the most useful and widely used tools available for quantitative analysis. Characteristically, this technique has broad applicability to both organic and inorganic systems, moderate to high selectivity, sensitivities that are typically in the 10^{-4} to 10^{-5} M range, reliable accuracy with typical relative uncertainties in the range of 1–3%, and convenient methods of data acquisition.

The principle of operation for UV-visible spectrophotometry is based on two phenomena: (1) substances selectively absorb or emit electromagnetic energy at different wavelengths, and (2) the energy absorption properties of a substance can be used to measure the concentration of the substance in solution. Before continuing, a review of electromagnetic radiation is in order.

Electromagnetic Radiation

Electromagnetic radiation shows both wave and particle characteristics, depending on how the radiation is observed. As a wave, electromagnetic radiation is composed of an electric field component and a magnetic field component (Fig. 1).

Electromagnetic radiation differs from other types of waves in several important respects. Familiar waves such as sound waves and water waves exist only by virtue of the media in which they exist, whereas electromagnetic waves can travel in a vacuum. Sound waves traveling through a gas consist of alternating zones of compression and rarefaction, and the molecular displacements that occur are in the direction that the waves travel. An electromagnetic wave is very different. Because it can travel through a vacuum, the medium is not essential. When such a wave comes in contact with matter, important interactions affect the wave and the material. The radiation couples with the medium, and how this occurs is best considered by referring to Fig. 1, which shows that the wave has two components: (1) an electric field and (2) a magnetic field. These components are in two planes at right angles to each other. A given point in space experiences a periodic disturbance in electric and magnetic field as the wave passes by. A charged particle, such as an electron, couples its charge with these field fluctuations and oscillates with the frequency of the wave. In other words, at the proper wavelength, an electron will interact with the electromagnetic wave and absorb energy. Conversely, an oscillating electron induces electric and magnetic fields and will also generate an electromagnetic wave or light.

Electromagnetic radiation is characterized by a wavelength (λ) and a frequency (υ). These two physical quantities are related to the velocity of light (c) by the equation $\lambda \upsilon = c$. The velocity of light is a constant in a vacuum (2.99792×10^8 m/s). Various wavelengths and the types of interactions produced in atoms and molecules are given in Table 1.

The wave model fails to account for phenomena associated with the absorption and

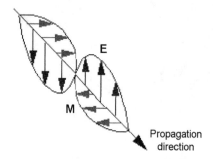

Fig. 1. Representation of electromagnetic radiation as a wave. E = electric; M = magnetic.

emission of electromagnetic energy. These processes can be better explained with a model in which electromagnetic radiation is viewed as a stream of particles or energy packets, known as photons. The energy of a photon is proportional to the frequency of the radiation. This relationship is given by the Bohr equation E = hυ = hc/λ, where E is the energy, h is Planck's constant (6.62618 × 10^{-34} Js), υ is the frequency of the radiation in hertz (Hz), c is the speed of light, and λ is the wavelength in meters. These dual views of electromagnetic radiation as waves and particles are complementary, not mutually exclusive, and this behavior has since been applied to other elementary particles such as electrons, neutrons, and protons.

The Laws of Lambert and Beer

The absorbance of light by materials was first explored by the German mathematician Johann Heinrich Lambert (1728–77).

Lambert discovered that for monochromatic radiation, absorbance was directly proportional to the path length of the incident light through the material. He formulated this discovery into Lambert's law: the proportion of radiation absorbed by a substance is independent of the intensity of the incident radiation. This means that each successive layer having a thickness of dx of a medium absorbs an equal fraction $-dI/I$ of the radiant intensity incident upon it. Mathematically this is represented as

$$-\frac{dI}{I} = bdx \qquad (1)$$

where b is a constant. Integration of this equation for a passage of light for a distance of l proceeds as follows:

$$\int \frac{dI}{I} = -b \int_0^l dx \qquad (2)$$

or

$$\ln I = -bl + g \qquad (3)$$

where g is an integration constant. Using the boundary condition that I = I_0 when l = 0 where I_0 is the intensity of radiation before passage through the medium, g can be evaluated as

$$g = \ln I_0 \qquad (4)$$

Substitution back into Eq. 3 gives

Table 1. Electromagnetic Spectrum

Type of Radiation	Frequency Range (Hz)	Wavelength Range	Type of Transition
Gamma-rays	10^{20}–10^{24}	$<10^{-12}$ m	Nuclear
X-rays	10^{17}–10^{20}	10^{-9}–10^{-12} m	Inner electron
Ultraviolet	10^{15}–10^{17}	400–1 × 10^{-9} m	Outer electron
Visible	4–7.5 × 10^{14}	750–450 × 10^{-9} m	Outer electron
Near-infrared	10^{12}–10^{14}	2.5 × 10^{-6}–750 × 10^{-9} m	Outer electron vibrations
Infrared	10^{11}–10^{12}	25–2.5 × 10^{-6} m	Molecular vibrations
Microwaves	10^{8}–10^{12}	1.0 × 10^{-3}–25 × 10^{-6} m	Molecular rotations, electron spin flips
Radiowaves	10^{0}–10^{8}	$>1 × 10^{-3}$ m	Nuclear spin flips

$$\ln I = -bl + \ln I_0 \qquad (5)$$

or

$$\ln \frac{I_0}{I} = bl \qquad (6)$$

or

$$I = I_0 e^{-bl} \qquad (7)$$

Using the more customary common logarithms, Eq. 7 is expressed as follows:

$$\log I_0/I = bl/2.303 = A \qquad (8)$$

where A is the absorbance. Absorbance has also been referred to as "extinction" or "optical density." The two terms are archaic and their use is discouraged by the International Union of Pure and Applied Chemistry (IUPAC).

Transmittance (T) is the ratio of the intensity of the transmitted radiation to the incident radiation:

$$T \equiv \frac{I}{I_0} \qquad (9)$$

Substituting transmittance into Eq. 8 gives

$$\log \frac{1}{T} = A \qquad (10)$$

The German astronomer Wilhelm Beer (1797–1850) expanded Lambert's work by studying the relationships between concentrations of a substance in solution and found that the same linear relationship existed between concentration and absorbance as Lambert had found between thickness and absorbance. For a substance in solution at concentration c, Beer's Law states that

$$\log \frac{1}{T} = A = const \times conc \qquad (11)$$

The Beer-Lambert law combines Eqs. 8 and 11 to give

$$A = \log I_0/I = \varepsilon cl \qquad (12)$$

where A is the absorbance, ε is the molar absorptivity, c is the concentration of the solution in mol/L, and l is the path length of light through the solution. The molar absorptivity constant, ε, is a proportionality constant with units of L cm^{-1} mol^{-1} and is characteristic of the substance absorbing the light and of the wavelength.

This relationship indicates that the absorbance of a solution is linearly related to the concentration of the absorbing species and that quantifications may be made by plotting concentration of a solution vs absorbance (Fig. 2).

The linearity of the Beer-Lambert law is limited by chemical and instrumental factors. Causes of nonlinearity include deviations in absorptivity coefficients at high concentrations (>0.01 M) due to electrostatic interactions between molecules in close proximity, scattering of light due to particulates in the sample, fluorescence or phosphorescence of the sample, changes in the refractive index at high analyte concentration, shifts in chemical equilibria as a function of concentration, nonmonochromatic radiation, and stray light. Deviations can be minimized by using a relatively flat part of the absorption spectrum such as the maximum of an absorption band.

Instrumentation

Instruments for measuring the absorption of UV and visible radiation are generally composed of one or more light sources,

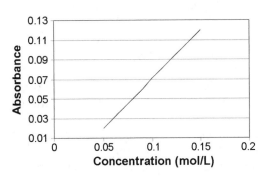

Fig. 2. Example of a Beer-Lambert law plot.

a wavelength selector, sample container, detector, signal processor, and readout devices. Some of these components are discussed below.

Sources

It is important in UV and visible spectrometry to use a continuum source whose power does not change over a considerable range of wavelengths. For the UV range of 160–375 nm, the source is usually a hydrogen or deuterium discharge lamp. These lamps use an electrical arc to produce excited molecules, which then dissociate into two atomic species plus UV photons. As such, these lamps require a regulated power supply to maintain constant intensity of light.

The tungsten filament lamp is the most common source of visible and near-infrared radiation. This lamp will produce most of its energy in the infrared region, producing usable visible light in the 350- to 2000-nm range. The lower limit of 350 nm is usually imposed by the absorption of radiation by the glass housing of the lamp. Modern instruments commonly use a tungsten/halogen lamp as the visible light source. The lifetimes of these lamps are nearly double those of tungsten lamps. Due to the high operating temperatures of tungsten/halogen lamps ($\approx$3200 °C), they are usually made of quartz. These lamps use a small amount of iodine that reacts with the gaseous tungsten that sublimes from the filament and assists in redepositing the tungsten onto the filament. These lamps are more efficient and have an output range well into the UV range.

Wavelength Selectors

Wavelength selection is accomplished with a monochromator. A modern monochromator consists of an entrance slit to provide a rectangular optical image from the source, a collimating lens or mirror to produce a parallel beam of radiation, a prism or a grating to disperse the radiation into its component wavelengths, a focusing element to reform the image of the entrance slit and to focus the light, and an exit slit that isolates the desired spectral band.

Two types of dispersing elements are found in monochromators: reflection gratings and prisms. In a prism monochromator, refraction at the two faces results in angular dispersal of the radiation. A reflection grating monochromator has a reflective surface onto which small grooves have been evenly etched. Light entering the monochromator strikes the grating at an angle and is dispersed. The grating offers advantages over a prism in that it gives linear wavelength dispersion along the focal plane of the light, whereas a prism gives greater dispersion at shorter wavelengths than at longer wavelengths.

Sample Cell

In any type of spectroscopy, the cells or cuvettes that hold the sample and solvent must be constructed of a material that is nearly transparent to the radiation in the spectral region of interest. For observing samples in the UV range (below 350 nm), a cuvette made of quartz or fused silica is desired. Both of these materials are transparent in the UV and visible range. Silicate glass and some plastics can be used in the visible range above 350 nm. The most common cell length for measuring absorbance in the UV and visible regions is 1 cm. Matched and calibrated cuvettes are available from several commercial sources. Cuvettes must be treated carefully: the use of unmatched cuvettes or the presence of fingerprints, grease, or other deposits on the walls of the cuvettes will dramatically decrease the quality of the absorbance data.

Detectors

For UV-visible spectrometry, the detector usually consists of a photon transducer. These detectors usually have an active surface capable of absorbing radiation that causes a photocurrent or enhances conductivity.

Several types of photon transducers are used in UV-visible spectrometry: photovoltaic or barrier-layer cells, phototubes, photomultiplier tubes, and silicon photodiodes. The photovoltaic cell usually consists of a copper or iron electrode that has a layer of a semiconducting material (e.g., selenium) and a layer of gold or silver on the outer surface of the semiconductor. Light striking the photovoltaic cell generates a current at the interface of the semiconductor layer and the metal. A typical cell has a maximum sensitivity around 550 nm, with the response falling to around 10% of the maximum around 350 nm and 750 nm. The photocurrent produced is directly proportional to the number of photons that strike the semiconductor surface (typically 10–100 µA). This type of detector is rugged and inexpensive and requires no external electrical source. Yet this detector also has several disadvantages. Due to the cell's low internal resistance, it is difficult to amplify its output, thus producing lower sensitivity at low levels of transmittance. In addition, the cell exhibits fatigue—its output decreases gradually during continued illumination.

The phototube is a vacuum tube that consists of a semicylindrical cathode and a wire anode. The inner surface of the cathode supports a layer of photoemissive material that ejects electrons when struck by radiation. When an electric potential is applied across the electrodes, electrons ejected from the photoemissive surface flow toward the anode, resulting in a photocurrent. The photocurrent is about one-tenth that produced by a photovoltaic cell, but because of the phototube's high electrical resistance, signal amplification is readily accomplished, accelerating the electrons that are ejected from the photoemissive surface. When an electron strikes the dynode, several electrons are ejected. This process is repeated with subsequent dynodes producing a cascade of electrons that is finally collected at the anode. It is common for a photomultiplier to generate a cascade of $>10^6$ electrons for every incident photon.

A major improvement in detector technology occurred with the photodiode array. In this detector, the photosensitive elements are small silicon photodiodes. Each diode has a dedicated capacitor and is connected to a switch register. These capacitors are charged to a specific level; when the diode is impinged by photons, the capacitors are discharged. The capacitors are then recharged at regular intervals. The amount of charge needed to recharge each capacitor is directly proportional to the light intensity.

A recent innovation in the detection system is the charge-coupled device (CCD) array. Like the diode-array detector, the CCD is capable of simultaneously measuring absorption at a range of wavelengths. CCDs are multichannel silicon array detectors in which photosensitive semiconducting silicon pixels collect incident light and transfer this charge in a stepwise process. Whereas a diode-array detector uses 512 or 1024 photosensitive diodes, a CCD uses 2048 pixels.

Instrument Configurations

Fig. 3 is a schematic of a single-beam UV-visible spectrophotometer.

Single-beam instruments vary widely in their complexity and performance characteristics. A very simple instrument may consist of a battery-powered tungsten bulb source, a set of glass filters to select wavelengths, test tubes for cuvettes, a phototube detector,

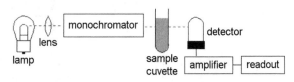

Fig. 3. Schematic of a single-beam spectrophotometer.

and microammeter for readout. A more sophisticated instrument may be a computer-controlled instrument with a range of 200–1000 nm or more. These instruments consist of interchangeable tungsten/deuterium lamp sources, high-resolution grating monochromator, rectangular silica cuvettes, a photomultiplier detector, and digitized output to permit storage and presentation in a variety of forms. Single-beam instruments have the inherent advantages of greater energy throughput, superior signal to noise ratios, and less cluttered sample compartments.

Many modern spectrophotometers are based on a double-beam design. Fig. 4 illustrates a typical double-beam instrument.

In this instrument, the beam emerging from the monochromator is split by a mirror. One beam passes through the reference solution to a detector, and the second beam simultaneously passes through the sample

of interest into a second matched detector. The two detector outputs are amplified and their ratio determined electronically and displayed by the readout device. Double-beam instruments compensate for fluctuations in output of the source and variations in source intensity and wavelength. In addition, they continuously record absorbance or transmittance spectra.

Another common type of spectrophotometer is a single-beam instrument using a diode-array detector. This type of instrument is illustrated in Fig. 5.

Radiation from the source is focused on the sample and then passes into a monochromator with a fixed grating. The dispersed radiation is then reflected onto a photodiode-array transducer, which consists of a linear array of several hundred photodiodes mounted on a silicon chip. The monochromator slit is made identical to the width of one

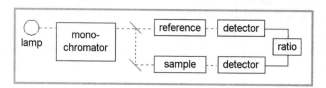

Fig. 4. Schematic of a double-beam spectrophotometer.

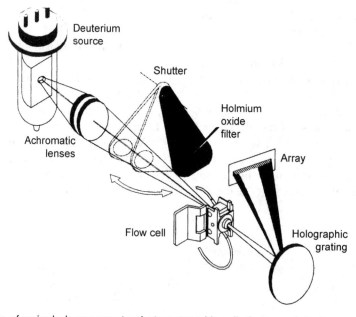

Fig. 5. Schematic of a single-beam spectrophotometer with a diode-array detector.

of the diodes. Thus the output of each diode corresponds to the radiation of a different wavelength. A spectrum is obtained by scanning these outputs sequentially. Because these electronic outputs are scanned rapidly, the data for an entire spectrum can be accumulated in <1 s. Moreover, the diode-array instrument is simple in design. It has few moving parts and needs no recalibration and minimal maintenance. A disadvantage of this instrument is its limited resolution of 1–2 nm.

Forensic Toxicology Applications

Color tests are one of the oldest forms of toxicology testing and can be viewed as assays using visible spectrophotometry. Color tests involve the reaction of a specimen, a protein-free filtrate, or an extract with a reagent or a series of reagents to produce a color or change in color. The biggest advantages to color tests are simplicity and ease of use. No sophisticated equipment is required and the time needed to train analysts is short. A negative result for a color test is helpful in ruling out a drug intoxication.

Two of the most commonly used color tests are for salicylate and acetaminophen, two over-the-counter nonnarcotic analgesics. Salicylate, the metabolite of aspirin, reacts with an acidic solution of ferric chloride to produce a purple color. This color reaction requires the presence of both the free phenolic group and the free carboxylic acid group that appears on the salicylate molecule. Therefore, aspirin itself will not produce a positive result prior to hydrolysis to salicylate. The test for acetaminophen is performed on urine or a protein-free filtrate of blood and requires heating at 100 °C after hydrochloric acid is added. A blue color after the addition of 1% o-cresol in water and ammonium hydroxide constitutes a positive test for acetaminophen. Both of these color tests have sufficient sensitivity to detect therapeutic use of the respective drugs. Although both color tests have a high degree of specificity, confirmation by an alternate analytical technique such as gas chromatography or liquid chromatography is necessary.

Other color tests may be used in the forensic toxicology laboratory. The Fujiwara test is a classic assay to identify trichlorinated compounds such as trichloroethanol. Concentrated sodium hydroxide and pyridine are added to urine or a tungstic acid precipitate of blood or tissue, and the mixture is placed in a boiling water bath for several minutes. The presence of a pink color in the pyridine layer is a positive test. It is especially critical to run a reagent blank when performing the Fujiwara test, because some of the reagents used may have contaminants that yield an apparent positive result.

Although ethchlorvynol is rarely used today as a sedative-hypnotic, a specific and sensitive color test was developed during a period of greater use. Diphenylamine is added to urine or a protein-free filtrate of blood, and concentrated sulfuric acid is gently poured down the side of the tube. A red color at the interphase represents a positive test. Some of the more esoteric color tests are listed in Table 2. (Some color tests not discussed in this chapter will be discussed at greater length in later chapters.)

Color reactions are also used to make visible thin-layer chromatographic spots. Ninhydrin is used to identify primary amines. Diphenylcarbazone and mercuric nitrate are used to identify barbiturates. Iodoplatinate reacts with nitrogenous bases to produce a purple color. Dragendorff's reagent produces orange, red-orange, or brown-orange color with nitrogenous bases. Carbamates can be detected by spraying with furfural and exposing to hydrochloric acid

Table 2. Esoteric Color Tests

Substance Identified	Color Reagent(s)
Borate	Carminic acid, sulfuric acid
Bromide	Gold chloride
Iron	2,4,6-Tripyridyltriazine, thioglycolic acid
Isoniazid	Nitroprusside, sodium hydroxide
Nitrite	Sulfanilic acid, naphthylamine
Paraquat	Dithionite

fumes. A rapid screening test for the major metabolite of marijuana uses Fast blue B.

Because many drug classes (such as barbiturates, benzodiazepines, phenothiazines, and tricyclic antidepressants) have good UV absorbance, one might expect that UV absorbance spectrophotometry would be extensively used in drug analysis. However, significant limitations restrict the use of this technique: It has low specificity, it lacks the necessary sensitivity to detect therapeutic concentrations of many drugs, and parent drugs and any active or inactive metabolites that retain the chromophore moiety will contribute to the measured UV absorbance. These limitations can be mitigated by the combination of UV spectrophotometry with a separation technique such as liquid chromatography; this can provide greater specificity and sensitivity and thus greater utility in biological specimen drug analysis.

Beside color tests, another use of spectrophotometry in forensic toxicology is in the detection systems of a number of commercially available immunoassays. Many immunoassays involve the conversion of a substrate by an enzyme into a product that causes either an increase or a decrease in absorbance at a particular wavelength. This change in absorbance can then be correlated to the amount of a drug in the specimen. For example, in EMIT®, the enzymatic activity causes the conversion of the cofactor nicotine adenine dinucleotide (NAD) to its reduced form NADH. Whereas NAD does not have any absorbance at 340 nm, NADH does; therefore, greater enzyme activity causes more production of NADH and more absorbance at 340 nm. The amount of absorbance is then used to determine the amount of drug in the specimen.

A common method in hospital laboratories for measuring serum ethanol is an enzymatic method using alcohol dehydrogenase. In this reaction, the enzyme converts the ethanol to acetaldehyde and in the process, NAD is converted to NADH. The increase in absorbance at 340 nm can then be used to determine the serum ethanol concentration.

FLUORESCENCE

Fluorescence is the emission of light from molecules that have been excited to higher energy levels after absorption of electromagnetic radiation (Fig. 6).

Because the emission of light comes from the lowest excited state of the molecule, the emitted light will likely be of a different wavelength than the light used to excite the molecule. The main advantage of fluorescence compared to absorption spectrophotometric measurements is greater sensitivity due to the very low background of fluorescence signal. A spectrophotometer used for fluorescence measurements is called a spectrofluorometer and is illustrated in Fig. 7.

Typically, the sample beam first passes through an excitation monochromator, which transmits the radiation that will excite fluorescence but excludes the wavelength that the sample will emit. Fluorescence occurs from the sample in all directions but is most conveniently observed at right angles to the excitation beam. This decreases the amount of interference that may be caused by the excitation beam and by scattered light. The emitted radiation then passes through a second monochromator and is detected. To obtain an emission spectrum on a spectrofluorometer, the excitation wavelength is held constant while scanning the emission wavelengths.

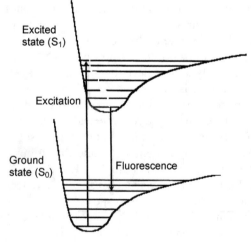

Fig. 6. Mechanism of fluorescence.

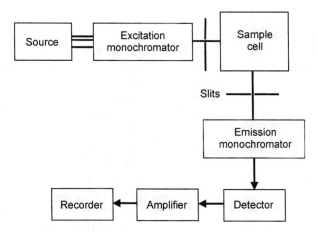

Fig. 7. Schematic of a fluorescence spectrophotometer.

When a molecule is excited by the absorption of electromagnetic radiation, there are several mechanisms by which it can relax to its original ground state. These relaxation processes may be radiative or luminescent in nature or may occur through radiationless mechanisms. Radiationless processes include vibrational relaxation and external conversion, both of which are usually brought about by collisions, internal conversion, and intersystem crossing. Luminescent methods include fluorescence or phosphorescence. Fluorescence occurs when the excited state is of the same electron spin state as the ground state. Phosphorescence occurs when the excited state is of a different electron spin state than the ground state.

The molecular structure and chemical environment will determine whether a substance will luminesce. One factor is the substance's quantum yield or quantum efficiency. This value is simply the ratio of the number of molecules that will undergo luminescence to the total number of excited molecules. For a highly fluorescent molecule, this quantum efficiency may approach unity. Nonfluorescent species have quantum efficiencies that may approach zero. Another factor is the type of transition involved. Fluorescence is found primarily with $\pi^* \to \pi$ and $\pi^* \to n$ transitions. The quantum efficiency of the $\pi^* \to \pi$ transition is ordinarily 100- to 1000-fold more efficient than the $\pi^* \to n$ transition and

therefore is more commonly associated with fluorescence.

Compounds containing aromatic functional groups with low-energy $\pi^* \to \pi$ transition levels will often provide the most useful and intense fluorescence. Aliphatic and alicyclic carbonyl compounds or highly conjugated double-bond structures may also exhibit fluorescence; however, the number of these compounds is small when compared to the number of aromatic systems that fluoresce. Most unsubstituted aromatic hydrocarbon compounds will fluoresce in solution. The quantum efficiency will typically increase as the number of rings and the amount of condensation increase, and also as the rigidity of the structure increases. Simple heterocyclic compounds like pyridine, furan, and pyrrole do not exhibit fluorescence, because these compounds have an $n \to \pi^*$ transition as a primary transition. The lower fluorescence demonstrated by these compounds is due to the likelihood that this type of transition will relax by a mechanism other than fluorescence. Quinoline, isoquinoline, and indole exhibit fluorescence, illustrating that as a heterocyclic ring is fused with a benzene ring, the likelihood of fluorescence increases.

Substitution of the benzene ring shifts the absorption and fluorescence peaks and can have a striking effect on the fluorescence behavior. For example, with halogen substitution, fluorescence decreases as the atomic number increases. Iodobenzene exhibits less fluorescence efficiency than chlorobenzene. Substitution of a carbonyl or a carboxylic acid group will usually inhibit fluorescence. This inhibition is generally attributed to the primary transition being an n→π* transition, which has a low fluorescence yield. Empirically, electron-withdrawing groups like carbonyls, nitro groups, and halogens will decrease fluorescence. Groups with valence electrons that can be donated to a ring system, such as amino, hydroxy, and ether groups, enhance fluorescence. Metal chelating agents often enhance fluorescence. This is attributed to an increase in the rigidity of the structure.

Temperature and solvent also affect fluorescence. As the temperature increases, fluorescence decreases. This is attributed to the increase in collision frequency, which allows molecules to transfer their energy by other mechanisms. Solvents such as carbon tetrabromide and compounds containing heavy atoms such as bromine or iodine decrease the fluorescence of a molecule.

The fluorescence of an aromatic compound with acidic or basic ring substituents is usually pH dependent. The ionized and nonionized forms of a compound will have a different wavelength and emission intensity. The fluorescence of different compounds as a function of pH has been used for the detection of endpoints in acid/base titrations and illustrates the importance of pH control in fluorescence measurements.

Analysis of drugs by fluorescence spectrometry has advantages and disadvantages when compared to the analysis of drugs by absorption spectrometry. One advantage of fluorescence is increased sensitivity. Fluorescence methods will have detection limits several orders of magnitude greater than detection limits of absorption methods. Another advantage is that fluorescence methods have greater specificity than absorption methods, because fewer drugs have native fluorescence. This could also be viewed as a disadvantage that limits the utility of fluorescence spectrometry. Nevertheless, the inability to distinguish between parent drug and metabolites is a limitation shared by fluorescence and absorption spectrophotometries. One example is phenothiazines. Because this class of drugs can be easily converted to fluorophores by the addition of hydrogen peroxide, it would appear that they would be good candidates for fluorescence analysis. However, phenothiazines are extensively metabolized to both active and inactive metabolites that would fluoresce. Without a technique to separate the different metabolites, it would be impossible to ascertain the amounts of active and inactive metabolites using fluorescence. As a result, the combination of liquid chromatography with a fluorescence detector provides greater utility for fluorescence in forensic toxicology.

Drugs with natural fluorescence include chloroquine, dantrolene, lysergic acid diethylamide, propranolol, and quinidine. Other drugs can be converted to derivatives that fluoresce (e.g., phenothiazines). Pancuronium can be converted into a fluorophore by reacting with Rose Bengal dye. Morphine can be converted into a fluorophore following a single-step pH 8.5 extraction, evaporation of extraction solvent, addition of sulfuric acid, pH adjustment to 9, and autoclaving.

CHAPTER 9

Chromatography

David T. Stafford

CHROMATOGRAPHIC FUNDAMENTALS

The molecular identification techniques used in forensic toxicology, the most significant being mass spectrometry (MS), require that a single molecular species be presented to the instrument at any given time. Mixed spectra are nearly uninterpretable. The most powerful separating technique available is chromatography, which has been in use since about 1900.

Definition

A nearly universal definition of chromatography is that it is a separation process based on the differential distribution of sample components between a moving and a stationary phase. This definition applies to all types of chromatography except size-exclusion chromatography, which depends on differential diffusion of sample components in closely controlled size pores of the stationary phase. There are three very important facets of this definition:

1. Chromatography is a separation process. It is not an identification technique in the sense that infrared (IR) and MS are, because it provides no molecular identification data. The fact that a component may have the same retention time as a known standard, even on several different columns, will increase the analyst's confidence that the two are the same, but identification has not been achieved.

2. The process depends on differential distribution. Distribution here refers to the relative concentrations of a component in two immiscible phases at mass transfer and temperature equilibrium as described by Nernst in 1891. If two components do not have different distribution coefficients, they cannot be separated chromatographically.

3. The process uses two immiscible phases. These may be a gas and a liquid or polymer, a gas and a solid, two liquids, or a liquid and a solid. A rather recent development uses a supercritical fluid as mobile phase.

History

Early chromatographic separations were described by a Russian botanist, Michael S. Tswett, who published some of his work involving the separation of leaf extracts using a glass tube packed with a calcium carbonate as the stationary phase and used petroleum ether as the mobile phase. The extract was placed at the head of the column, and then mobile phase was trickled through the column by gravity flow. The separation of the specimen into colored bands that could then be removed and studied gave us the term "chromatography," or color writing. This was the genesis of liquid chromatography (LC).

There was little change in the art until the mid-to late 1930s. By that time, good-quality, small-diameter silica particles were available, and a mechanism was developed to affix a thin layer of these particles to a glass plate. A sample placed near the bottom of the plate might then be separated by mobile phase rising through the stationary-phase layer by capillary action. The small particle size and concentrated specimen spot resulted in much more efficient separations than Tswett's classical column method, and because several specimens could be processed simultaneously on a single plate, analytical time decreased. Detection was frequently by ultraviolet (UV) absorption, fluorescence, or charring with sulfuric acid spray. Thus, thin-layer chromatography (TLC) was born. Izmailov and Shraiber reported separations of a number of pharmaceuticals in 1938–39.

In 1941, Martin and Synge elucidated the concept of partitioning, for which they later received the Nobel Prize. In 1951–52, Martin and James reported the development of a chromatographic process using inert gas as mobile phase, resulting in what is today called gas chromatography (GC). The first commercial gas chromatographic instrumentation was available in 1954, and the analytical capabilities were so great that there was explosive growth in analytical technique and instrumentation. In the late 1950s, an early worker in GC, M. J. E. Golay, reported dramatically improved column efficiency using narrow bore columns. This led to the development of capillary or wall-coated open tubular (WCOT)-column chromatography. The production of the first WCOT columns was difficult and expensive, and they were short lived because of their unstable performance. Not until the early 1970s, when the expiration of the patents on some of the WCOT-column technology was in sight, did better-quality columns become available. The best of these were glass columns, which were tedious to handle. In 1979, fused silica was introduced as a column material, and the inertness and handling characteristics were so superior that fused silica WCOT columns became, and are today, the most widely used GC columns.

Development of the Technology

Like GC, both classical column LC and TLC are partitioning processes. LC changed little from Tswett's time until the mid to late 1960s. At that time, dependable mobile-phase pumps and low-volume, sensitive flow-through UV detectors became available, giving rise to what was termed high-pressure LC but is today known as high-performance LC (HPLC).

The tremendous separating capability of chromatographic methods and their lack of capability to supply molecular identification data made it inevitable that attempts would be made to combine them with identification techniques such as IR and MS. Because of the relative insensitivity of IR, most of the early work concentrated on marrying GC and MS. Since this development began to be important in the late 1960s, the instrumentation developed was a combination of packed-column GC and either magnetic sector or quadrupole MS. The concurrent availability of more powerful, less expensive, and more convenient computers gave even more impetus to the development. The first GC/MS systems provided somewhat less than routine operation; however, present-day instrumentation is powerful, reliable, and, to use the current vernacular, user friendly. The GC/MS systems in analytical use are almost all WCOT-column GCs directly connected to quadrupole or ion-trap MSs.

The combination of HPLC and MS was slower to develop, primarily because HPLC instrumentation was later in development than GC, and because of the problems associated with handling the mobile phases, some of which contain salts, and of course the large volume of vapor when the liquid is vaporized. A number of innovative LC/MS interfaces are currently being marketed and successfully used.

Principles

The primary reason to subject any specimen to chromatography is to separate one or more components from the other components in order to identify (e.g., by MS), to quantify, or to do pattern recognition (e.g., accelerant analysis, which is sometimes a forensic, but not toxicologic, analysis). Fig. 1 represents a typical chromatogram of a two-component mixture, with several features

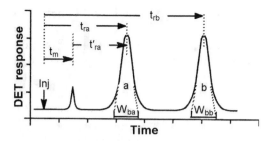

Fig. 1. Typical chromatogram.

indicated. This chromatogram is a graph of the detector response as a function of time of analysis from a GC or an HPLC determination. If the track of a TLC plate was scanned with a densitometer, a similar plot would be expected. However, the plot would be of component density as ordinate, vs distance from the origin or distance from the origin relative to the mobile-phase front, R_f, as abscissa.

The first peak after injection, with a retention time of t_m, is the time for an unretained component; it spends no time in the stationary phase. In the older GC literature, it may be referred to as t_o or the air peak. With a flame ionization detector, t_m may be determined by injecting natural gas or butane from a cigarette lighter; in HPLC, it is the negative/positive response observed as the injection solvent reaches the detector. The time from injection to a peak maximum is the retention time, t_r; t_{ra} for peak **a**, t_{rb} for peak **b**. The difference between t_r and t_m is t'_r, the adjusted retention time (e.g., t'_{ra} for peak **a**; $t'_{ra} = t_{ra} - t_m$). The average molecule of each peak spends the same amount of time, t_m, in the mobile phase; if it is in the mobile phase, it is being carried through the column with the velocity of the mobile phase. Since t_r represents the total time in the column, and t_m represents the time in the mobile phase, then t'_r represents the time spent in the stationary phase. Separation is achieved when the molecules of two components interact differently with the stationary phase, therefore spending different lengths of time in the stationary phase.

In chromatography, the distribution coefficient is designated K_d (K_{da} for analyte a) and is defined as:

$$K_{da} = \frac{\text{concentration of } a \text{ in the stationary phase}}{\text{concentration of } a \text{ in the mobile phase}} \quad (1)$$

The distribution coefficient for an analyte a is a function of temperature (T), pressure (P), stationary phase, P_s, and mobile phase, P_m:

$$K_{da} = f(T, P, P_s, P_m) \quad (2)$$

In GC, operating pressures are relatively low, with head pressures typically 25–30 psig for packed columns and 5–15 psig for WCOT columns. The nature of the inert gas, P_m, has little effect on K_d; therefore K_{da} can be considered a function of T and P_s. In HPLC, operating temperatures are frequently ambient or up to a maximum of about 60 °C. Although pressures may reach several thousand psig, K_ds between condensed phases are only slightly affected by pressure; therefore K_{da} can be considered a function of P_s and P_m. Here the nature, as well as the concentration, of P_m may have an effect. For instance, K_{da} for 30% methanol/water may be very different from K_{da} for 50% methanol/water or 30% acetonitrile/water. Although most analysts never measure K_d or have any knowledge of its numerical value, it is important to understand how it is affected, controlled, and manipulated, because it governs chromatographic performance, and most of the parameters over which the operator has control are set or changed to achieve differences in K_d between analytes.

As indicated previously, a primary purpose of chromatography is to separate, or resolve, the components of a specimen; therefore, it is convenient to have some way of describing this resolution. Chromatographically, resolution, R, between two peaks is defined as the difference in their retention times relative to average width at base, W_b. Referring to Fig. 1:

$$R = \frac{(t_{rb} - t_{ra})}{(1/2)(W_{ba} + W_{bb})}$$

$$= \frac{(t'_{rb} - t'_{ra})}{(1/2)(W_{ba} + W_{bb})} \quad (3)$$

Resolution is a dimensionless number, and as a result, all factors must be in the same units. For two Gaussian peaks of the same size, complete (baseline) resolution will be achieved at about R = 1.5. At R = 1, the two peaks will overlap by about 10%; R for the two peaks in Fig. 1 is approximately 4.

Resolution is calculated using Eq. 3 and measurements taken from the chromatogram; however, this does not address the parameters at the analyst's disposal to control or modify R. To examine these, consider the general resolution equation:

$$R = (1/4) \frac{(\alpha - 1)}{\alpha} \times \frac{(k_b)}{(k_b + 1)} \times (N^{1/2}) \quad (4)$$

$$\underbrace{\qquad}_{\text{Selectivity}} \quad \underbrace{\qquad}_{\text{Capacity}} \quad \underbrace{\qquad}_{\text{Efficiency}}$$

Eq. 4 shows that resolution is a function of the product of a selectivity (α) term, a capacity (k) term, and the square root of an efficiency term (N). These then are the factors that can be altered to control or modify R.

The capacity term does not refer to volumetric or gravimetric capacity, but rather to the capacity of the column to retard the passage of a component through the column. The capacity factor or partition ratio k (sometimes designated k′ in the older literature) is the ratio of the adjusted retention time to the time for an unretained component:

$$k = t'_{ra} / t_m = (t_{ra} - t_m) / t_m \quad (5)$$

In GC, the partition ratio is a function of temperature; in HPLC it is a function of mobile-phase concentration and composition. If the temperature of the GC oven is increased, k decreases because the K_d decreases. As temperature is increased, the analyte vapor pressure increases. Therefore, the concentration of analyte in the stationary phase decreases, the concentration in the mobile phase increases, and following Eq. 1, K_d must decrease. Every GC operator has observed this effect. At a higher temperature, an analyte will elute more quickly. Because t_r decreases and t_m remains constant, k must decrease. The retention time is manipulated by changing K_d through temperature, and

the effect is observed and can be measured as k, a dimensionless number.

The distribution coefficient and k are directly related through β, the phase ratio, a property of the column geometry:

$$\beta = \frac{\text{Column volume (or cross-sectional area)}}{\text{available to the mobile phase}}{\text{Column volume (or cross-sectional area)}}{\text{available to the stationary phase}} \quad (6)$$

β is the proportionality constant relating K_d and k:

$$K_d = \beta k \quad (7)$$

Selectivity, α, describes the relative interaction of two analytes with the stationary phase and is defined as the ratio of the two adjusted retention times:

$$\alpha = t'_{rb}/t'_{ra} \quad (8)$$

Substituting from Eq. 5 and Eq. 7 it can be shown that:

$$\alpha = k_b/k_a = K_b/K_a \quad (9)$$

In GC, temperature changes will have only a minor effect on α. The two peaks under consideration usually have very close t_rs; therefore, according to Eq. 9, their K_ds are nearly equal. A change K_a will be matched by a proportional change in K_b, and the ratio will remain constant. In order to change α, it is necessary to change stationary phase. In HPLC, α can be changed by changing stationary phase or, more conveniently, by changing mobile-phase concentration or changing the mobile-phase components. Each of these approaches manipulates the K_ds.

Column efficiency, N, in Eq. 4, relates the time an analyte remains in the column, t_r, to band broadening as described by W_b:

$$N = 16 (t_r/W_b)^2 \quad (10)$$

or using the peak width at half-peak height, $W_{1/2}$:

$$N = 5.546 (t_r/W_{1/2})^2 \quad (11)$$

Eq. 10 was derived from an analysis of the mass transfer in the chromatographic column, and Eq. 11 results from consideration of the geometry of a Gaussian peak. Column efficiency must be calculated from an *isothermal* GC or *isocratic* HPLC run. Calculation of N by either Eq. 10 or 11 yields a dimensionless number, referred to as the number of theoretical plates in the total column. This is perhaps a confusing choice of nomenclature but remember that many of the individuals who derived these relationships worked in the petroleum industry where distillation columns were used, and they frequently did have actual plates in the columns to affect vapor/liquid contact. When the efficiency of these plates was taken into consideration, the number of theoretical plates or number of vapor/liquid equilibria could be calculated. A similar concept applies to chromatography. A more convenient indicator of column efficiency, which allows efficiency between columns of different lengths to be compared, is the *height equivalent to a theoretical plate* (HETP):

$$HETP = L/N \qquad (12)$$

where L is the length of the column. HETP is conveniently expressed in millimeters, and because it has a reciprocal relation to N, the smaller the HETP, the more efficient the column. In some of the chromatographic literature, HETP is simplified to H.

Consider the general resolution equation, Eq. 4, and notice that the chromatographer has three "handles" to control R: k, α, and N. The capacity term, $k/(k + 1)$, demonstrates that it has a range of 0 to 1. A plot of $k/(k + 1)$ as ordinate and k as abscissa results in a hyperbolic curve beginning at 0 and asymptotic to 1. At $k = 2$, the capacity term contributes 67% of its maximum to R, and at $k = 10$, it is contributing about 91%. For GC, k for the first peak of interest should be ≥ 2 (≥ 1 for HPLC) and not more than about 10. In developing a method, it is desirable to have k for the first peak of interest at about 4–5. Examination of Eq. 5 reveals that k represents the ratio of the time the analyte spends in the stationary phase to that spent in the mobile phase. At very low ks,

there is too little interaction with the stationary phase; at higher ks, analytical time is being unnecessarily wasted.

Examining the selectivity term of Eq. 4 shows that for $\alpha = 1$,

$$(\alpha - 1)/\alpha = 0 \text{ and } R = 0;$$

there is no resolution. The range of $(\alpha = 1)/\alpha$ is 0 to 1, and a plot similar to that described for k results in an identically shaped curve with the difference that the ordinate is 0 at $\alpha = 1$. Selectivity describes the ratio of the times that two analytes spend in the stationary phase, and because they elute close together, their K_ds are nearly equal. Therefore, typical values of α are frequently in the range of 1.1 to 1.2. Values of α lower than this make separation difficult if not impossible, and higher values result in longer analysis time. In developing a method, if k is about 4–5 and an acceptable α is not obtained, it is time to consider a more selective GC stationary phase or change HPLC mobile-phase composition or components. This assumes that the column is reasonably efficient.

Ideally, a sample is injected into the chromatograph as a bolus. As it travels through the column, it spreads from a single plug to a peak shaped as shown in Fig. 1. The longer it remains in the column, the broader the band becomes. In 1956, van Deemter et al. described a relationship between column efficiency, diffusion, and mass transfer effects in the column. A simplified version of the van Deemter equation is given where efficiency is related to the average linear mobile-phase velocity, $\bar{\mu}$, in cm/s:

$$HETP = A + B/\bar{\mu} + C\bar{\mu} \qquad (13)$$

The terms A, B, and C represent those factors contributing most to band broadening. By minimizing each of these, it is possible to minimize band broadening and therefore increase efficiency.

The A term is related to the eddy diffusion or multipath effect. In any packed column, channels are of different lengths, and there is diffusion and mixing as the mobile phase flows around the packing particles. These factors spread the analyte band. Using uniformly sized, tightly packed particles with smaller diameter can minimize this effect. Once the column is packed, the eddy diffusion term is constant and independent of mobile-phase flow rate. Typical packing sizes are 100/120 mesh (0.125–0.15 mm diameter) for GC packings and 3–10 μm for HPLC packings.

The second term in Eq. 13 relates to the tendency of the analyte to diffuse in the mobile phase. As a component enters the mobile phase, the analyte concentration gradient drives diffusion toward areas of lower concentration. This diffusion in the mobile phase can be minimized by having a tightly packed column of closely sized particles and a higher mobile-phase flow rate. In GC, it is advantageous to use larger, heavier carrier gas molecules; the diffusion rate through nitrogen is about one-fourth of that through helium. Diffusion rates in condensed phases are minimal compared to those in gas phases, and as a result, this term can be ignored in HPLC.

The third term in the van Deemter equation addresses band broadening due to resistance to mass transfer in the stationary phase. If two analyte molecules enter the stationary phase at the same time and one spends x time before it reenters the mobile phase and the other spends $2x$ time, then the first molecule will be transported down the column some distance while the second molecule is still in the stationary phase. This spreads the analyte band. This term's effect can be minimized by using a thin, uniform film of a stationary phase with a low viscosity to promote diffusion, and by decreased mobile-phase velocity. In fact, the effect of this term will vary as the square of the film thickness.

The selection of $\bar{\mu}$ is critical. To minimize the B term, it is desirable to have a high mobile-phase flow rate; to minimize the C term, it is desirable to have a low flow rate. This problem is solved by making a van Deemter plot as shown in Fig. 2, and finding the optimum flow rate, i.e., the minimum in the curve. The optimum $\bar{\mu}$ for packed-column GC will be about 8–10 cm/s; for WCOT-

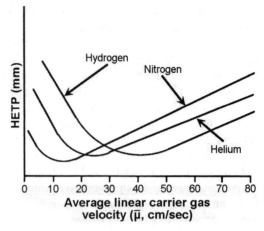

Fig. 2. WCOT-column van Deemter curves.

column GC, it will vary dramatically with carrier gas type as shown in Fig. 2. For HPLC, the optimum will be at a volumetric flow rate of about 1 mL/min, but the slope of the curve at higher rates is so low that using higher flow rates does not usually result in much loss of efficiency.

The van Deemter equation for WCOT-column GC differs from that for packed-column GC and HPLC in that there is no A term because there is only one channel. However, a $D\bar{\mu}$ term must be added to account for cross-column diffusion in the mobile phase. The effect of diffusion rates through the most commonly used carrier gases is shown in Fig. 2. For hydrogen and helium, the optima are much higher than for nitrogen, and the slopes of the curves at higher flows are lower. Nitrogen is a poor choice of carrier gas in WCOT-column GC because analysis times are much longer than with hydrogen or helium. Another factor to consider when using WCOT columns is that the analyses will almost invariably involve temperature programming, and the viscosity of gases, unlike that of liquids, increases with increased temperature. Many WCOT columns are operated at constant head pressure rather than constant flow rates. The pressure drop for flow through any channel is governed by:

$$\Delta P = (Q\mu FL)/A^2 \qquad (14)$$

where ΔP is the pressure drop across a column of length L and cross-sectional area A for a fluid of viscosity μ at a flow rate F. The proportionality constant is Q. Examination of this equation shows that if μ increases with increased temperature and ΔP is constant, then F must decrease and consequently HETP will change. The solution to this problem is to set the flow rate higher than the optimum with the oven temperature at the low point of the program. As temperature increases, the flow will decrease and HETP will decrease. If conditions are selected properly, operation will never be lower than the optimum flow rate. Referring to Fig. 2, with helium as carrier gas and a temperature program of 100–300 °C, set the flow rate at 100 °C to give a μ of about 45 cm/s. This maintains efficiency and results in faster analyses.

Characterization of Separations

The simplest, least effective mechanism to describe a separation is by the absolute retention time, t_{ra}. However, this presumes that operating conditions are exactly reproducible, which is not always the case. A second, better method is the use of relative retention time (rrt). If one or more markers, x and y, are injected with the sample, then the retention time of an analyte a can be described relative to that of the markers. For example, $rrt_x = t_{ra}/t_{rx}$; $rrt_y = t_{ra}/t_{ry}$. Relative retention times are much less subject to changes, and a library of rrt's can be very useful in making preliminary, or presumed, identifications.

In 1958 Kovats published a retention index system as part of his doctoral thesis. Beginning with the Clausius-Clapeyron equation, it is possible to derive a linear relation between log t'_r and molecular weight for a homologous series of compounds. Kovats plotted log t'_r as ordinate against carbon number, CN, multiplied by 100 as abscissa to indicate the molecular weight for a series of normal hydrocarbons chromatographed isothermally. He called 100CN the retention index (RI). RI for n-hexane is 600; RI for n-decane is 1000, etc. Having established the RI curve

for the n-hydrocarbons, it is then possible to chromatograph analyte a under the same conditions, calculate log t'_{ra}, and read its RI from the normal hydrocarbon line. Alternately, the RI can be calculated mathematically by linear interpolation between the two bracketing n-hydrocarbons. If $RI_a = 1250$, then analyte a chromatographs as if it were a normal hydrocarbon with 12.5 carbons. The Kovats RI is dependent on the analyte and the stationary phase. It is independent, over a reasonable range, of column length, stationary-phase film thickness, temperature, and mobile-phase flow rate. This means that analyte a will always have an $RI_a = 1250$ on that stationary phase and will permit the compilation of a library of RIs that can be used by any analyst in any laboratory. A similar treatment can be applied to HPLC; however, there is no widely applicable homologous series to establish the RI curve, and it is generally not used. It should be remembered that Kovats RIs result from isothermal data. In GC applications where temperature programming is used, a similar treatment can be employed, except that the retention time, t_r, is used in place of log t'_r. In this case RI_a will be a function of stationary phase, initial temperature, and temperature ramp.

Trennzahl

As indicated, column performance can be assessed or monitored using column efficiency, N. However, N must be calculated from isothermal data in order to be meaningful, and many GC separations are done under temperature program conditions. In 1961 Kaiser proposed the use of the Trennzahl or separation number (TZ) to address this issue under temperature-programmed conditions. The separation number is readily calculated from the hydrocarbon data used to establish RIs, using:

$$TZ = [(t_{rcn+1} - t_{rcn})/(W_{1/2cn+1} + W_{1/2cn})] - 1 \quad (15)$$

In Eq. 15, t_{rcn+1} and t_{rcn} represent the retention times for two adjacent normal hydrocarbons, e.g., n-C_{17} and n-C_{16}, and $W_{1/2}$ represents the corresponding peak widths at half height. For WCOT-column chromatography, TZ would be expected to be in the range 16–20. TZ represents the number of peaks, of size and shape similar to the n-hydrocarbons, that can fit evenly spaced between C_n and C_{n+1}, each with a resolution of 1.177.

By keeping a log of TZ run on a periodic basis, the column performance can be monitored with very little effort. TZ and RI data may also be used to predict whether two compounds can be separated on a particular column without ever running the compounds. If a column operated under a given set of conditions has a TZ of 19, then 19 peaks will fit between the bracketing n-hydrocarbons dividing this space into 20 equal segments. Two adjacent n-hydrocarbons have a ΔRI of 100 RI units; therefore, each of the theoretical peaks is separated by 5 RI units. If two analytes, *a* and *b*, have RIs that differ by 5 or more RI units, they can be separated with R $\geq$1.177. If the RI difference is less than 5, then they cannot be separated with this R.

PLANAR CHROMATOGRAPHY

Thin-Layer Chromatography

Tswett's classical LC was inefficient and slow, and though it was suitable for separation of milligram quantities of natural products, it was not very useful as an analytical tool. The development of the capability to produce and classify by size adsorbents such as silica and alumina in the mid-1930s quickly led to the development of TLC. Early plates were made by the laboratory and some were rather large, as much as 1 × 1 meter. Today, plates are mass produced and usually 20 × 20 cm, 10 × 20 cm, or 2.5 × 7.5 cm. Standard analytical plates have 50- to 150-µm diameter particles in layers from 150- to 500-µm thickness. High-performance (HP) TLC plates have smaller diameter particles (10–35 µm) and thinner layers (100–150 µm). Plates can be purchased with the coating divided into

channels about 1-cm wide and the length of the plate to minimize lateral diffusion. Some plates also have a preadsorbent layer, consisting of material different from the adsorbent, across one end of the plate. This allows the analyst to introduce a concentrated spot without the danger of disrupting the adsorbent layer, and helps to present a more uniform sample front to the adsorbent.

Silica is the most widely used adsorbent but others are available, including alumina and some reversed-phase materials. When calcium sulfate is used as a binding agent, plates are frequently designated by G for gypsum, e.g., Silica Gel G. Some plates also incorporate a fluorescent or other compound to aid in the visualization of spots on the developed plates. The support material for the adsorbent is frequently glass, but may be either metal or plastic.

In practice, the sample solution is spotted about 1.5–2 cm above the lower edge of the plate, either directly on the silica or near the top of the preadsorbent layer if present. Sample spots are usually delivered with a glass capillary. If samples are very dilute, then several applications may be made, with the sample solvent being allowed to dry between applications. This will result in smaller spots and less band broadening than if a larger amount of sample were applied at one time. Care must be taken not to damage the adsorbent layer if the spots are applied directly. Irregularities in the adsorbent layer can cause distorted mobile-phase flow and distorted component patterns. If channeled plates are used, then spot one sample per channel; if nonchanneled plates are used, spot samples about 1.5–2 cm apart. (One of the advantages of TLC is that several samples may be run simultaneously along with a series of standards or controls.) After spotting, the sample solvent must be allowed to vaporize. It is convenient to place a piece of tape across the top of the plate, so that the identification of the sample in that lane can be designated. The tape will not come into contact with the mobile phase.

After sample solvent has evaporated, the plate is placed in a glass developing tank containing approximately a 1-cm depth of mobile phase in the bottom. Some time is required for the atmosphere in the tank to reach equilibrium. The plate rests nearly vertically in the tank with the lower end, near where spotted, immersed in the mobile phase. The mobile phase must contact the adsorbent or preadsorbent layer uniformly without touching any spot. The tank is covered to preserve the integrity of the mobile-phase vapor/liquid atmosphere during development. It is important not to make waves. Examples of mobile phases are ethyl acetate:methanol:ammonia, 90:7:3 for acid/neutral drugs, and 85:13.5:1.5 for basic drugs separated on silica.

The mobile phase will rise up the adsorbent layer by capillary or wicking action, and each component will be distributed between the mobile and stationary phase with its K_d; those having lower K_ds migrate faster and farther from the origin than those with higher K_ds. The result is separation of the components along the mobile-phase path. When the mobile-phase front has reached about 60–80% of the plate's height, the plate is removed from the tank and the mobile-phase front is marked for reference. The plate is then allowed to dry, typically in a 50–60 °C oven for about 5 min. Developing tanks are typically glass and can hold several plates.

Visualization of the compounds separated is generally done by a combination of examination under UV radiation, fluorescence, and a series of sprays and oversprays to produce spots with colors characteristic of the drugs present. In addition to the color and sometimes the shape of the spots, each compound will have a characteristic retardation factor (R_f), which is the ratio of the distance the center of the spot travels from the origin relative to the distance the solvent front travels. Because the conditions under which TLC is done are not as precisely controlled as those of instrumental techniques, R_fs have more variability than t_rs or RIs. It is possible to scan the TLC channels with a densitometer, produce a chromatogram, measure retention times, do the calculations previously discussed, and even attempt quantitation. However, the imprecision of the data does not justify the effort and expense in most cases.

Paper Chromatography

In the early 1940s, paper began to be used as a stationary phase. Paper chromatography (PC) is similar to TLC except that the mobile-phase flow is descending rather than ascending. The samples are spotted about 10 cm from one end of the paper (usually 0.5–1 m of filter-type paper). The samples are applied more widely spaced than for TLC because more diffusion occurs. The end of the paper closest to the sample spots is placed in a glass trough and secured by a glass rod with the spots 2–3 cm over the lip of the trough and the paper hanging down. This arrangement is placed in the developing tank or box, and mobile phase is poured into the trough. As the mobile phase travels down the paper, the sample components are separated in a manner similar to TLC.

PC is seldom used in forensic toxicology and is mentioned here for completeness, but it can be useful in separating biological compounds such as proteins, amino acids, etc.

Column Efficiency

The column efficiency attainable with planar chromatography is limited to a total of about 1000 plates, using HPTLC. Eq. 4 shows that this places a severe limitation on the analytical capability, and makes it imperative that the chromatographer exercise good judgment and be innovative in the choice of mobile and stationary phases to maximize system selectivity.

Development vs Elution Chromatography

Both TLC and PC are development chromatography. After separation has been achieved, the process is stopped and the components remain in place. If documentation of the separation is required, photographs can be made to document colors and agreement with standards and controls. Because of the bulk, it is generally not feasible to save the original plates since colors tend to fade rather rapidly. Documentation in writing or on a worksheet is generally acceptable since TLC is usually a screening process and any presumed positives must be confirmed.

GC and HPLC are elution processes where each component exits from the column, is conducted through a detector, and is hardly ever trapped and saved. In fact, in many instances, it is destroyed by the detector. Paper and/or electronic documentation of the separations are readily saved for future examination and support of conclusions.

GAS CHROMATOGRAPHY

Functional Division

To get an overall view of the gas chromatographic process and to facilitate troubleshooting, it is convenient to divide the system into five functional areas: mobile-phase supply, injection, separation, detection, and data handling.

The function of the mobile-phase supply system is to provide a source of pure, clean, dry carrier gas at constant pressure or constant flow rate. The function of the injector is to take the sample from atmospheric pressure, introduce it into the instrument at system pressure, vaporize it, and conduct all or part of it onto the column with a minimum of band broadening. Separation is achieved in the GC column, which is maintained in an oven for temperature control. The detector is selected to provide a signal when each of the sample components of interest elutes from the column. Under some conditions, the signal will be proportional to the concentration or amount of component passing through the detector. The primary purpose of the data-handling operation is to provide a timed record of detector response. Depending on the degree of sophistication, it may also store and manipulate data and generate reports.

Mobile-Phase and Auxiliary Gas Selection, Supply, and Control

The selection of carrier gas is governed by several factors: type of chromatography (packed or WCOT column); detector; experience and safety; and cost. For packed-column GC with a thermal conductivity detector, the carrier gas should be helium to maximize detector response. Other packed-column separations are better done with nitrogen, because it minimizes band broadening in the column, is much less costly than helium, and does not affect detector response. For WCOT-column GC, the carrier gas should be helium or hydrogen because of the shape of the van Deemter curves (Fig. 2) and the shorter analysis times. Nitrogen should not be used because of the longer analysis times and loss of efficiency at higher flow rates and temperature-programmed conditions.

In Europe, where helium is not as available and is much more expensive than in the U.S., hydrogen is widely used as carrier gas. If hydrogen is used, an oven monitor should be used to detect any leaks. In the event of column breakage or a significant hydrogen leak, the monitor is designed to shut off hydrogen flow and, with some designs, also to discontinue electrical power to the instrument. Consideration should also be given to the experience of the operator. If the individual is relatively inexperienced with WCOT-column GC, or has demonstrated a general lack of coordination, then helium should be used. Hydrogen diffuses rapidly, and with a single GC using about 4 mL/min for septum purge and column flow and perhaps 200-mL split vent per injection, the volume of hydrogen used per day is only about 10 liters and does not represent a particular hazard under most conditions. A tank of carrier gas should last 60–90 days. Alternatively, a hydrogen generator can be used.

Carrier gas is frequently supplied in tanks holding about 225 cubic feet (6.3 m^3) at STP and a pressure of 2200–2500 psig (~150 atm). Gas is supplied to the instrument through a two-stage regulator at 30–60 psig. Further pressure and flow control are provided by the instrument's control system. Carrier gas should pass through hydrocarbon, water, and oxygen traps to remove substances that may adversely affect detector sensitivity, but primarily to prolong column life. Auxiliary gases should pass through a hydrocarbon trap, and depending on the detector type, through a water trap. If high-quality gases are purchased, traps should last for about three tanks of gas. The hydrocarbon and moisture traps can be readily regenerated in-house. Some types of oxygen traps are equipped with regeneration capability while other types must be sent back to the supplier for regeneration. There are also systems available to generate acceptable quality hydrogen, nitrogen, and air in-house. Depending on the laboratory's requirements, investing in these may be justified. The requirements for treatment to assure carrier gas quality still exist.

Traditionally, analyses were done at constant head pressure. The pressure was set to give the desired pressure, and a feedback regulator was used to keep it constant. As discussed earlier (see "Principles"), as temperature increases under temperature-programmed conditions, gas viscosity increases, and at constant pressure, flow rate will decrease. To address this problem, electronic pressure control was introduced. With this system, as the temperature and viscosity increase, the head pressure is increased in an attempt to maintain constant flow and more reproducible analytical conditions and column efficiency.

Auxiliary gases are required with most detectors; for a flame ionization detector, air at about 350–400 mL/min, hydrogen at about 30 mL/min, and perhaps makeup gas are needed. Most thermal conductivity cells require a reference gas, usually helium, the same as the carrier gas. Electron capture detectors may be operated with 5% methane in argon to help produce more capturable low-energy electrons. These gases must be clean, pure, and dry. Mass spectrometers are an exception in that they require no auxiliary gas if operated in the electron impact mode.

Makeup gas is required with some, though not all, detector designs. With 0.20–0.25 mm inner diameter (ID) WCOT columns, the carrier gas flow rate through the column will be about 1 mL/min. It can be calculated using:

$$F = [(\pi)(r^2)(L)]/t_m \qquad (16)$$

Flow, F, will be in mL/min if the column radius, r, and length, L, are in centimeters and t_m is in minutes. With such a low flow rate, any excess empty space (dead volume) will allow mixing and therefore broadening of the peaks. The effect of any dead volume in the detector can be reduced by supplying a makeup gas, frequently introduced with the hydrogen to increase total gas flow through the detector and "sweep" the component peak from the system. Nitrogen works well as a makeup gas. For packed-column instruments that have been adapted to use 0.53-mm ID fused silica or 0.75-mm ID glass columns, it frequently does not seem to make much difference whether or not makeup gas is used.

Stationary Phase

As discussed in the section "Principles," and specifically following Eq. 2, the distribution coefficient, K_{da}, for GC is nearly independent of the type of carrier gas and pressure in most GC applications. It will depend on the stationary phase and temperature. In packed-column GC, the selection of stationary phase can sometimes be difficult because of the limited number of theoretical plates available, making the stationary-phase selectivity extremely important. In WCOT-column GC, the large number of theoretical plates available somewhat reduces the dependence on selectivity (Eq. 4). One major GC supplier provides a technical bulletin addressing retention index and McReynolds constants. This publication has over 300 stationary phases listed along with their solvent compatibility, minimum and maximum recommended operating temperatures, and McReynolds constants. There is some redundancy because many trade name phases are listed; however, the point is that a large number of phases are available, and sometimes necessary, for packed-column GC. The list for the supplier's general purpose WCOT-column phases contains 15 entries. If other suppliers' comparable trade name columns were included, the list would contain about 90 entries.

The most common characteristic used in referring to stationary phases is their "polarity." It is important to define what polarity means chromatographically. A compound in which a separation of charges results in a permanent dipole, such as water, is called a polar compound. However, in addition to the strong permanent dipoles, a weaker dipole can be induced in a polarizable molecule subjected to the force field of a permanent dipole; and two polarizable molecules may interact to form even weaker mutually induced polarity. These represent respectively, dipole-dipole, dipole-apole, and apole-apole. The sum effect of these is what is referred to in chromatography as "polarity." Note that there are P_s-P_s, P_m-P_m, P_s-P_m, P_s-analyte, P_m-analyte, and analyte-analyte interactions at work and that the description of this complex situation by a single term "polarity" can be misleading.

To address this problem, W. O. McReynolds in 1970, following earlier work by L. Rohrschneider (1966, 1969), published the results of his characterization studies. As probes, he selected 10 compounds, each representative of a class of chemical compounds, e.g., alcohols, aromatics, etc. He ran these compounds isothermally at 120 °C on nearly every stationary phase available and calculated their Kovats RIs. Using squalane as the least polar stationary phase known, he tabulated McReynolds constants, the difference between the RI on a given P_s and RI on squalane, for each of the probes on each P_s. Using these data, it is possible to estimate which phase might be used to separate alcohols, separate alcohols from aromatics, and so on. They can also be used to predict elution order and compare the separation properties of stationary phases. Comparing the McReynolds constants for SE-30, OV-1, OV-101, and SP-2100 shows that these are identical as far as separating capability.

With this complex array of stationary phases available, what is the best approach to column selection? Once the separation has been defined, the fastest, easiest, and least expensive way of selecting a column is to ask someone who is doing or has done it successfully. Colleagues are a good source since they may be working in the same or a related area. The second most efficient way to approach the problem is to look in the literature. Beginning in 1969, the Institute of Petroleum in London began publishing *Gas Chromatography Abstracts*, which contained abstracts of nearly all the significant GC literature, and classified these according to a series of criteria, including compound chemical nature. In 1970, the publication was named *Gas and Liquid Chromatography Abstracts*. Today there are extensive computerized compilations of abstracts, e.g., Medline, which can readily be searched. Suppliers' catalogs and literature services are sometimes overlooked as a source. The major suppliers' catalogs contain rather extensive sections presenting chromatograms of a wide variety of separations. They also have technical bulletins and technical representatives available to discuss separation problems. These are all free except for the time invested. The least efficient approach to column selection is to go into the laboratory and experiment. This ultimately must be done in order to demonstrate that the separation can be performed on the existing system; however, good information accumulated prior to this step will shorten the time and labor involved. Automated equipment can help to reduce this phase of the effort.

Injectors

The function of the injection system is to introduce the sample, usually a measured amount, into the GC and to vaporize it immediately and completely. The most common mechanisms for measurement and injection are a syringe/septum arrangement or a direct connected loop injector, each of which may be automated.

Fig. 3 shows typical on- and off-column injectors for packed-column GC. In on-column injection, the column is positioned nearly to the septum, and the end of the column is packed with several centimeters of glass wool. Injection and vaporization occur in the glass wool packing. In off-column injection, the injector contains a liner, and injection and vaporization occur in the liner. If samples are not particularly clean or are subject to thermal degradation, e.g., injection of blood or diluted blood for alcohol analysis, then off-column injection is preferable because of relative ease of cleaning.

Fig. 4 represents a diagram of a split/splitless injector typically used in WCOT-column GC. Since WCOT columns have much less stationary phase than packed columns, they can accommodate a much smaller amount of sample. A split injector arrangement allows the chromatographer to measure an amount of sample that can be measured with reasonable accuracy, e.g., 1 μL, and have the injector conduct a portion of it, maybe 1/50th, onto the column. That part of the sample injected but not taken onto the column is vented through the split vent. In the splitless mode, the total amount of sample injected is conducted onto the column for the first 30–90 s after injection, and then any sample remaining in the injector is vented.

In the split mode, the solenoid valves (Fig. 4) are set as shown for injection. The septum purge is designed to flush out any

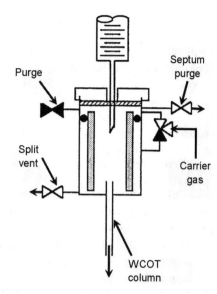

Fig. 4. Split/splitless WCOT-column injector. ⋈ = open valve; ▶◀ = closed valve.

degradation products from the septum, and remains open at a flow of 1–3 mL/min. Carrier flow is across the septum, down through the inside of the liner, and then through the column or out the split vent. Injected sample is vaporized in the liner, and then an aliquot of it is conducted onto the column, with the rest being vented out the split vent. With a standard 0.20–0.25 mm ID WCOT column, flow will be about 1 mL/min. At a split ratio of 50:1, 1/51th of the sample will go on column; 50/51ths will be vented. The column flow will be ~1 mL/min; the split flow will be

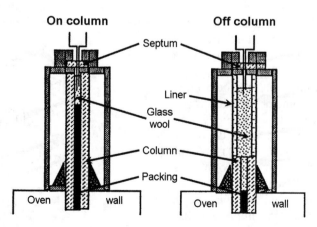

Fig. 3. Packed-column injectors: on- and off-column injection.

~50 mL/min. Since the column and split vent act as two resistances in parallel, the split vent can be closed 1–2 min after injection, and column flow will be unchanged if the column head pressure is kept constant.

The splitless mode of injection is designed to accommodate dilute samples, where it is desirable to have most of the sample injected onto the column. Referring to Fig. 4, the solenoid valves would be set as shown except that the split vent valve is closed and remains closed. The sample is injected and vaporized, and the total flow goes onto the column. After a 30–90 s delay, the purge valve (not the septum purge, which remains open) is opened, and simultaneously the carrier gas control valve is switched to cause carrier to flow around the outside of the liner to flush any remaining sample out through the purge valve. During splitless injection, the oven temperature is maintained about 20–30 °C below the boiling point of the injection solvent. This allows 85–95% of the sample injected to be focused at the head of the column. After the 30–90 s delay, as the purge and carrier gas valves are switched, the oven temperature program is initiated. The result is that the 5–15% of sample that did not get onto the column is vented so that it does not "dribble" onto the column, and the chromatography of the sample begins. Injection solvent rushes through the column, followed by the separation of the analyte components. The injection solvent must be carefully selected, and the delay time must be experimentally determined. About 1–2 min after the end of the delay time, the purge valve can be closed for the duration of the run. All of this is done at constant carrier gas pressure.

Cold on-column injection may be used in order to circumvent some of the undesirable features of split and splitless injection. In this mode of injection, the sample is deposited directly into the head of the WCOT column, which is maintained at cryogenic conditions. After deposition of the sample, the injection device (needle) is removed and the area of the column containing the sample is ballistically heated, vaporizing the sample and having it carried onto column. The advantage of cold on-column injection is that the total sample goes onto the column, there is no discrimination against higher boiling components as sometimes occurs in split injection, and there is no solvent effect to contend with as in splitless injection. The disadvantage is that it is somewhat tedious and not easily automated.

The injection of gaseous samples can be done very nicely by use of a loop injector. In this mode of injection, the sample is loaded into the fixed volume loop of the injector and then flushed onto the column by the carrier gas. The valve can be thermostated and automatically controlled. The most widely used forensic application of such an arrangement is automatic headspace analysis of alcohols and acetone in blood or urine (a schematic of a headspace injector is shown in Fig. 5). Measured amounts of specimen and internal standard are contained in a septum-sealed vial and allowed to equilibrate at an appropriate temperature, frequently about 60 °C for alcohol analyses. In the standby mode, carrier flow is as indicated, through the upper route of the tubing as well as flushing through the sample loop and out the needle. After temperature equilibration of the specimen, the vial is automatically raised, puncturing the septum and pressurizing the vial contents. When pressurization has been accomplished, the two valves in the lower leg of the tubing are switched to stop carrier flow through the loop and allow sample headspace vapors to flow to the left in the diagram, filling the sample loop and venting

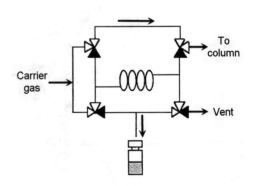

Fig. 5. Headspace injection system.

any excess. Once the loop is filled, all four valves are switched, isolating the vial and upper leg of the tubing, and closing the vent. At this point, the carrier flow is through the loop, flushing sample from the loop onto the column. Automatic headspace injectors are very reliable and demonstrate excellent analytical precision.

Detectors

In order to discuss GC detectors (there are 15 or more types in common use, and about six of these are used in forensic applications), it is necessary to define some detector characteristics: sensitivity, linear dynamic range, specificity, and sample destructiveness or nondestructiveness.

Sensitivity is the detector response to amount of analyte, the slope of the detector response vs analyte amount curve. There is some amount below which no discernible response is observed. This is frequently taken as the amount of sample that produces a response twice that of the baseline noise and is referred to as the minimum detectable quantity (MDQ) or lower limit of detection. The lower limit of detection will be lower than the lower limit of quantitation (LLQ), which is the lowest concentration that will allow acceptable quantitative results by the laboratory's criteria, e.g., a coefficient of variation of 10%.

A portion of the response vs amount or concentration curve will be linear up to some concentration; above this concentration, the increase in response will be less than that for a comparable increase in concentration within the *linear range*. This concentration, or amount, is the limit of linearity. The ratio of the limit of linearity to MDQ is referred to as the linear dynamic range. If quantitation is to be done, it should be within the linear dynamic range of the detector for best accuracy and precision. It is poor policy to do quantitation outside this range.

Specificity is the ability of the detector to selectively detect a particular type of compound. A thermal conductivity detector is nearly universal in that it will detect anything

with a thermal conductivity different from that of the carrier gas. A flame ionization detector (FID) may be thought of as a carbon counter. It will respond to most organic compounds, with varying degrees of sensitivity but will not detect many fixed gases (O_2, N_2, H_2O, CO, CO_2, NH_3, etc). An electron capture detector is rather selective in that it will detect electrophilic compounds.

Of those detectors widely in use, nearly all but the thermal conductivity detector and the infrared detector (IRD) are *sample destructive* in that the sample is burned or otherwise altered and cannot be recovered intact after passing through the detector. The most widely used detector in the early days of GC, the 1950s, was the thermal conductivity detector, initially referred to as a katharometer. In most designs, it consists of two electrically heated, high-resistance filaments, typically tungsten or tungsten/rhenium, as two legs of a Wheatstone bridge circuit. One of these is in a reference channel and sees only carrier gas; the other is in the column effluent channel and sees carrier gas plus any eluting analyte. A current of usually 100–300 amps is maintained through the filaments, which heats them, much like an incandescent light bulb filament. Heat is conducted from the filaments, most of it to the detector block, at a rate dependent on carrier gas type and flow rate. With only carrier gas flowing through both channels, the temperatures of the filaments equilibrate, the circuit is balanced, and a constant baseline can be established. Analyte molecules that elute and pass through the sample channel are much larger and less thermally conductive than the carrier gas molecules; therefore less heat is conducted away and the filament temperature rises, increasing filament electrical resistance. This causes an imbalance in the bridge circuit and a change in the output voltage, which is monitored as the detector response. Helium, being the smallest carrier gas molecule available, has the highest thermal conductivity other than hydrogen, and therefore is the carrier gas of choice to maximize sensitivity. Any analyte having a thermal conductivity different from helium will be detected, with hydrogen yielding a negative response.

The FID, introduced in the mid to late 1950s, quickly became the most widely used detector because of its sensitivity, broad applicability, and large linear dynamic range. Fig. 6 shows a schematic of the FID. A hydrogen/air flame burns at the jet tip and column effluent exits through the jet into the flame. In the environment of the flame, some of the carrier gas will be ionized, and analyte molecules that are eluted will also be ionized. A constant electrical potential of about 300 volts is maintained between the jet and the collector. The gap between them acts as a variable resistance, resistance being a function of the number of conductors, i.e., ions, in the gap. With just carrier gas exiting from the column, the current that flows in the circuit is amplified, balanced, or nulled, and monitored as baseline. As analyte molecules are ionized in the flame, the resistance decreases and more current flows; this amplified current is the detector response.

The FID is widely applicable to most volatile organic compounds. It also has a wide linear dynamic range, typically about 10^6, and MDQ in the picogram range for many compounds. The FID, like other ionization detectors, is mass flow rate dependent; that is, response is a function of mg/s passing through the detector. The thermal conductivity detector, in contrast, is concentration dependent; that is, the response is a function of mg/mL/s. Thus the ionization detectors are well matched to WCOT columns, which produce very narrow peaks with most of the mass passing through the detector in a short period of time. The thermal conductivity detector is not nearly so well suited to WCOT-column chromatography.

Another detector widely used in forensic toxicology laboratories is the nitrogen-phosphorus or thermionic detector. It is similar in design to the FID except that an alkali metal salt, typically rubidium or cesium, is positioned above the flame. The hydrogen and air flow are reduced in intensity compared to FID operation so that ionization is minimized. The hot alkali salt causes the selective ionization of compounds containing nitrogen or phosphorus. Since many drugs are nitrogen-containing compounds, they can be selectively detected with good sensitivity and minimal interference from other organic compounds that are not ionized well under the operating conditions.

The electron capture detector is constructed somewhat similar to the FID but without jet or flame. The source of ionization is a radioactive material, in almost all cases the nickel isotope weighing 63 atomic mass units (AMU). The Ni^{63} emits β particles that result in low electrical resistance, and therefore high current, in the gap between the electrodes. This "standing current" is monitored as baseline. As analyte molecules elute from the column, very little change occurs in the electrical atmosphere of the gap unless the molecules are electrophilic. If electrophilic molecules elute, they soak up or capture electrons, resulting in decreased current flow across the gap. This change is amplified and monitored as the detector output. Compounds with halogens or nitro and cyano functional groups are good candidates to be detected using the electron capture detector.

Another detector that has been developed is the atomic emission detector. This detector is capable of detecting elements contained in each component separated by the column.

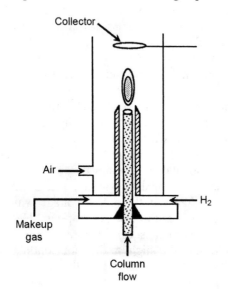

Fig. 6. Flame ionization detector.

Its use in forensic toxicology has been limited because it lacks the sensitivity of the nitrogen-phosphorus detector to compounds containing nitrogen and lacks the sensitivity of the electron capture detector to halogenated compounds.

The most widely used detector in forensic toxicology that provides structural information is the mass spectrometer. Chromatography is a powerful separating technique, but it does not identify anything. Mass spectrometry (MS) is a very powerful molecular identification technique, but it does not separate anything. By combining the two into a GC/MS system, the advantages of each are realized. By using WCOT-column GC, where the column flow rate is about 1 mL/min, the column effluent can be conducted directly into the ion source of the MS, equipped with a vacuum pump capable of handling this flow. In the ion source in electron impact (EI) ionization, analyte molecules are subjected to the force field of high-energy electrons, which imparts energy to them and raises them to an excited state. If they are sufficiently excited, they can relieve some of the excess energy by ejecting an electron and creating a "molecular ion," i.e., the intact molecule with a positive charge. If there is still excess energy in the molecule, it can fragment by selectively breaking various bonds, with the possibility of creating positive, negative, or neutral fragments. The fragmentation pattern of a particular molecular species will be reproducible under the reproducible operating conditions.

In positive-ion MS, the fragment ions are subjected to a positive electrical potential so that each of the positively charged fragments will be subjected to the same accelerating potential, imparting to them the same kinetic energy. The result is groups of singly charged ions with varying masses, therefore varying velocities. This beam of positively charged ions is focused into a mass filter where the groups of like mass:charge ratio are separated and a signal proportional to the relative number of each is monitored.

Mass spectra may be presented in several ways. One useful presentation is as a frequency diagram with the signal proportional to the number of ions in a group plotted as ordinate, and the AMU of the group plotted as abscissa. Frequently the most abundant ion in the spectrum, the "base peak," is plotted as 100, with each of the other ion abundances plotted as a percentage of it. More in-depth information about mass spectrometers, mass spectra, and GC/MS systems is presented in Chapter 11.

The IRD is being used sparsely but with increasing frequency. IR spectrometry, like MS, is valuable because it can provide identification information based on molecular structure, which the other detectors mentioned cannot. However, it is rather insensitive. With the use of an interferometer as the IR source, Fourier transform IR (FTIR) is possible, and the sensitivity is dramatically increased. In the IRD, the WCOT-column effluent is conducted through a light pipe in the path of the IR beam from the interferometer. Analyte molecules in the light pipe absorb energy from the beam. Transmitted energy is detected by an IR sensor, processed by a microprocessor, and presented as the detector output. One advantage of the IRD is that it is *sample nondestructive*; the effluent from the IRD can be presented to another detector, such as MS, to obtain additional information. Because potassium bromide is used in the optics of most IRDs, the system must be purged with dry gas. Another consideration is that in some designs, the interferometer requires the use of liquid nitrogen.

A word of caution concerning selective detectors is in order. Just because a chromatogram using a thermionic or electron capture detector shows only a few peaks, it does not mean that other compounds are not present. This same sample injected into a system using GC/MS may produce many more peaks than those seen with the selective detector.

Data Systems

Data systems used with GC systems have evolved from a simple strip chart recorder used in the 1950s to today's recorder/integrator or a much more powerful computer used as a work station. The primary purpose of a data system is to record the separation achieved, producing a chromatogram or plot of detector response as a function of retention time. A chromatogram may be all that is required, but more frequently it is desirable and necessary to do manipulations with the data: calculation of retention indices, quantitation of one or more analytes, comparison of chromatographic patterns, storage of data, control of one or more GCs, and report generation. In these cases, investment in a more versatile data system may be indicated. A review of the range of capabilities of data systems is beyond the scope of this chapter. Suffice it to say that there are data systems to suit almost every need if their cost can be justified.

Two-Dimensional Gas Chromatography

A recent development in instrumentation has allowed the use of two analytical columns of different polarities within a single gas chromatographic run. It is known as two-dimensional GC and employs a Deans switch and a cryofocusing trap. A mix of analytes is injected onto the primary column with the effluent directed to an FID. Based on the retention times of the analytes of interest, heart cuts are made, directing the effluent to a secondary column. A cryogenic focusing trap positioned at the head of the secondary column traps the analytes at the head of the secondary column. The oven temperature is then increased to move the analytes through the secondary column onto the detector. Although this system will result in longer chromatographic run times, the increased signal-to-noise ratio improves sensitivity and the removal of interfering substances improves chromatographic resolution.

HIGH-PERFORMANCE LIQUID CHROMATOGRAPHY

Applicability

To be amenable to GC separation, a material must have at least 1 torr vapor pressure at 300 °C or below, and must be stable in the vapor phase. About 18–20% of organic compounds meet these criteria. For those that do not, LC is available.

Theoretically any sample that can be dissolved can be separated by LC. Obviously, reactivity, suitable mobile and stationary phases, and detectors impose limitations; however, a much wider variety of compounds are amenable to LC than to GC separation. If a sample can reasonably be separated by GC, do it. If it cannot, consider LC.

GC is simpler, cheaper, and has much greater separating power than LC. With a WCOT-GC column, the analyst may have as many as 100,000 theoretical plates at his disposal; with HPLC he probably never has more than 15,000–20,000. This makes it difficult to separate mixtures with more than about 20 components by HPLC.

Development

As described earlier, the first publication of LC separations of any note was done by Michael S. Tswett at the turn of the century. This was classical LC in which mobile-phase flow was controlled by gravity, the columns were glass tubes packed with solid absorbent, and detection was frequently by visual observation. Separations were primarily confined to natural products. This was not high performance. In the mid-1960s, better materials for pump construction and more reliable pump designs were available, controlled porosity silica with better size classification was developed, and UV detectors with small-volume (100 μL) flow-through cells were available. Each of these contributed to a dramatic increase in interest in LC. As individuals began to build systems and test and stress their capabilities, more operable instruments with increased separation efficiency resulted, and HPLC was launched. Because of the long columns used (as much as several meters), the pump pressures required approached 10,000 psi and HPLC denoted high-pressure LC. Further developments have resulted in more reasonable operating conditions, and today we truly do have high-performance LC.

Functional Division

Division of function in HPLC is exactly as in GC: mobile-phase supply and control, injection, separation, detection, and data systems. There are, of course, differences in how these functions are achieved.

Mobile Phase and Mobile-Phase Supply

The mobile phases used in HPLC are solvents or mixtures of solvents. The terms solvent and mobile phase are frequently used interchangeably. The mobile-phase components need to be high-grade solvents of known composition; stabilizers in many solvents may cause problems. HPLC-grade solvents are available and are not inexpensive. The solvents used must be compatible with the construction materials of the system: stainless steel pump housings and tubing, sapphire pump pistons, ruby ball and ceramic check valve components, silica-based packings, and Teflon tubing and seal parts. Chlorinated solvents can corrode stainless steel under some conditions, and mobile-phase pH above about 8 can begin to dissolve the silica base of the stationary phase. Mobile phase needs to be free of any particulate matter and must be degassed. The first is usually accomplished by fitting the suction line to the pump with a metal or plastic filter with 2-μm pores. Degassing may be achieved by briefly subjecting the mobile phase to vacuum, sonication, filtering through a specially designed filter, or purging with helium (but not nitrogen).

Almost all pumps are reciprocating stainless steel pumps with a sapphire piston about 5 mm in diameter and 4 cm long. Fig. 7 shows a cross-section of a reciprocating piston pump. Pumps are fitted on both suction and discharge with single or double check valves with ceramic seats and ruby balls about 4 mm in diameter. The mobile-phase delivery rate is controlled either by limiting the length of

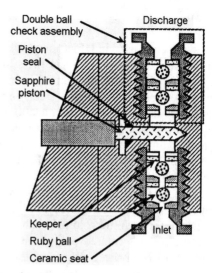

Fig. 7. HPLC reciprocating pump cross-section.

piston stroke or by having a fast, constant speed suction stroke and controlled speed delivery stroke. Operating pressures range from several hundred to several thousand psi. Because the pumps use a reciprocating action, pump delivery pressure and flow will oscillate. To minimize this, a pulse dampener is used in the delivery line. This is some sort of capacitance and will reduce, but not eliminate, pressure and flow fluctuations.

Mobile phases are usually mixtures of solvents rather than a single solvent. If a separation is done isocratically (i.e., with constant mobile-phase composition), the appropriate solvent mixture can be pumped from one reservoir with a single pump. If the composition is to be changed, a different mixture will have to be made. Some systems use several pumps, each delivering a single mobile-phase component at an appropriate rate into a mixer. This allows the composition of the mobile phase to be changed more readily. If the pump delivery rates are computer controlled, it is also possible to do gradient elution by changing the mobile-phase composition as the run progresses. Other systems use computer-controlled metering valves to meter each of 1 to 3 or 4 solvents into the suction side of a single pump. This design allows either isocratic or gradient operation.

Injectors

Most injectors used in HPLC employ a six-port loop injector somewhere in the system. Fig. 8 is a schematic of such an injector. The injector consists of a stainless steel body, a rotor, a sample loop, and six connections for tubing. In the load mode, the port from the pump communicates with the port going to the column; the port where sample is introduced communicates with the fixed volume loop and then to waste. This allows the loop to be filled at atmospheric pressure while flow is maintained through the column. In the inject mode, the rotor is rotated 60°, which allows the pump to flush the contents of the loop onto the column. These valves may be operated manually or by an actuator. Typical loop volumes are 10–20 µL. If the injector is not part of an automatic injection system, the loop is filled using a syringe. The circuit, sample injection port, loop, and waste port must be completely filled and contain no gas bubbles. If less than the full capacity of the loop is to be injected, the desired amount can be measured with the injection syringe and the remainder of the circuit filled with mobile phase. In some automatic injectors, the valve is remote and does not contact the sample. These valves are remarkably durable but must be serviced occasionally because of seal wear.

Separation

Here we look at several factors that affect separation: the column, the column packings, and gradient elution.

Columns. HPLC columns are generally constructed of 1/4″ outer diameter stainless steel tubing with IDs of 2–4.6 mm and are usually 3, 5, 10, 15, or 25 cm long. A typical HPLC column connection is shown in Fig. 9. Zero dead-volume fittings and the shortest length of 1/16″ narrow-bore interconnecting tubing practicable are used to minimize dead volume (empty space that permits mixing). Inlet and discharge end fittings are each fitted with a 2-µm porous sintered stainless steel frit to retain packing. Frequently a guard column will be placed between the injector and analytical column inlet. This is usually a 2-cm long piece of tubing packed with pellicular packing similar to the analytical column packing. The purpose is to protect the analytical column by trapping compounds that may have a very high affinity for the packing and may be detrimental to the life and performance of the column. Pellicular packing, discussed later, can be replaced fairly readily and adds minimal dead volume to the system.

Column packings. The first HPLC packings were nearly all porous silica or alumina adsorbents, irregular in shape, and with a nominal diameter of 44 µm. The size range was rather broad compared to modern packings because size classification techniques were relatively primitive. The mechanism of separation on these materials was by selective adsorption, and the intermolecular forces governing the separation could be quite strong because of the polarity of the surface hydroxyl groups (refer to discussion of polarity in GC "Stationary Phase"). When other

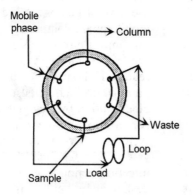
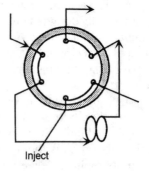

Fig. 8. Six-port loop injector.

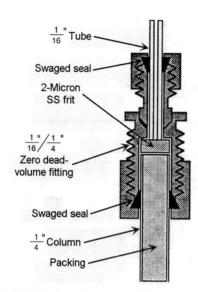

Fig. 9. HPLC column cross-section.

types of packings became available, the earlier packings were termed "normal-phase" packings. The only thing "normal" about them was that they were the first type used.

In the late 1960s, mechanisms were developed to react octadecyl-trichlorosilane, and later octadecyl,dimethyl-chlorosilane, with the hydroxyl groups of the silica surface to produce a packing that had a porous silica base with a surface covered with n-C_{18} hydrocarbon molecules, octadecylsilane (ODS). Further developments resulted in packings with various chain lengths of hydrocarbon; however, C_{18} is the most widely used. These packings are relatively nonpolar in nature and are termed "reversed-phase" packings. The mechanism of separation in reversed-phase HPLC is primarily partitioning, involving weaker intermolecular interactions than experienced in adsorption.

HPLC then is divided into two categories: normal and reversed phase. In normal phase, the stationary phase is very polar and the mobile phase has low polarity. A normal-phase mobile phase might have a base of iso-octane and then have the polarity modified with a more polar material such as chloroform. As the polarity of the mobile phase is increased, the tendency of the analyte molecules to adsorb to the silica surface is somewhat decreased. They spend less time on the stationary phase and therefore elute with shorter retention times. The more polar phase is termed a "stronger" mobile phase because it causes the analyte molecules to elute more quickly. Very polar molecules, such as organic acids, can be difficult to chromatograph by normal-phase HPLC because they are very strongly retained on the stationary phase.

In reversed-phase HPLC, the stationary phase is relatively nonpolar and the mobile phase is very polar. Typically, a reversed-phase mobile phase will have water as the base, modified with less polar materials such as methanol, acetonitrile, or tetrahydrofuran. The choice of modifier can also influence selectivity. A stronger reversed-phase mobile phase would be one that is less polar, exactly the opposite of the situation with normal-phase HPLC. Because the interactive forces in reversed phase are much weaker and an aqueous-based mobile phase can be used, it is preferable to normal phase. Reversed-phase columns equilibrate more quickly after a gradient run, they are not deactivated by water, and they are much easier to regenerate when they become "dirty."

A variety of phases is available for both normal- and reversed-phase HPLC. Careful choice of the stationary phase can provide an additional degree of selectivity. After silica, the most commonly used normal-phase packings are those containing cyano-, diol-, and amino-moieties. For reversed phase, a series of n-hydrocarbon chain lengths is available. Second to C_{18} packing in frequency of use is the C_8 packing. These are sometimes referred to as RP18 and RP8.

Packing particle diameters range from 3 to 10 μm. The smaller-diameter particles are more efficient but cannot be used in columns longer than about 5 cm; 10- to 15-cm columns use 5-μm packing; and 25-cm columns use 10-μm packing. These combinations are governed by the pressure drop through the column. Typical HPLC mobile-phase flow rates are about 1 mL/min. The slope of the van Deemter curve in the region above the optimum flow rate is very low and flat compared to that for GC. This means that once a separation has been developed, the flow rate can be increased to shorten analysis time with little loss of efficiency, assuming that the pressure drop across the column is not excessive.

In the late 1960s, pellicular (from the Greek meaning skin) packings were developed. These consist of solid-core (nonporous) glass beads covered by a thin layer of stationary phase. They are spherical and have a diameter of about 44 µm. These packings demonstrate high efficiencies, but because of the very limited amount of stationary phase, only small amounts of analyte can be separated. The low concentration of analyte in column effluent stresses the capabilities of most detectors. Columns using pellicular packing can be readily packed by the chromatographer. Analytical columns with pellicular packings are not widely used; however, they make excellent guard columns because they pack easily and contribute very little dead volume to the system.

Gradient elution. With GC, capacity and selectivity (see Eq. 4) are controlled by temperature and stationary phase, respectively. In HPLC, these are each a function of mobile-phase concentration. Additionally, selectivity is also a function of stationary phase. Since it is easier and less expensive to change mobile-phase concentration and/or components, this approach should be employed before considering a change in stationary phase. The HPLC analog to temperature programming in GC is gradient elution. In gradient elution operation, the strength of the mobile phase is increased by changing composition as the run progresses. As with temperature programming, this requires that the column be re-equilibrated at the end of the analysis. This can be done rather quickly in reversed-phase operation (~5 min) but takes much longer (perhaps 30 min) in the normal-phase mode. A drift in baseline may be observed under gradient elution operation, depending on the detector characteristics. It cannot be used with a differential refractive index detector. Gradients may be produced as indicated in the section "Mobile Phase and Mobile-Phase Supply."

HPLC Detectors

By far the most widely used detectors in HPLC are based on UV energy absorption. These are of three types: fixed wavelength; variable and, in some cases, programmable wavelength; and diode-array detectors. A schematic of a fixed-wavelength detector is shown in Fig. 10. The construction is similar to any UV spectrophotometer except that it employs a flow-through cell. Cell volumes are small, 8–18 µL, and absorption path length is usually 1 cm. In most operations, the reference cell is filled with air. The energy source is usually a 254-nm lamp with higher wavelengths available by the use of filters. In a variable-wavelength UV detector, the energy is split into various wavelengths, usually by a grating, and the desired wavelength, from about 180 to 300 nm, is focused through the sample cell. Some of these are equipped with a microprocessor that allows the wavelength to be programmed as the run progresses. A number of attempts to produce

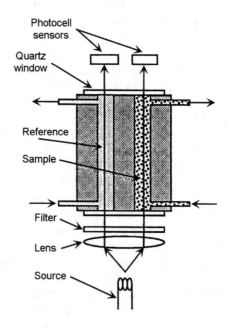

Fig. 10. HPLC fixed-wavelength detector.

scanning UV detectors have been made, but none has been very satisfactory.

The diode-array detector focuses undiffracted energy from the source through the cell and then diffracts the beam and focuses the resultant spectrum onto a series of several hundred sensors. Using this technique, a microsecond snapshot UV spectrum of the flow cell contents is obtained. A computer is necessary to capture the large amount of data produced. Once the data are obtained, they can be manipulated to compare spectra from multiple points in an eluting peak, to do library searches, and so on. The diode-array detector suffers a 3–5% loss in sensitivity compared to a fixed-wavelength detector; however, the amount of information that can be obtained is significantly greater.

UV detectors are widely used because many compounds exhibit appropriate UV absorption. Nevertheless, there are some limitations and precautions. First, the solvents used in the mobile phase must have a UV cutoff below the wavelength used for detection, or the mobile phase will not be transparent, and detectability will be low or nonexistent. Second, at the low operating wavelengths achievable with some designs (below 200–210 nm), a large number of compounds absorb, which increases potentially interfering components and decreases selectivity.

For analytes not having usable UV spectral properties, the differential refractive index detector is available. The detector compares the refractive index of the mobile phase with that of the column effluent. This detector is nearly universal in that any eluting compound that has a refractive index differing from the mobile phase will give a response. Gradient elution is not possible because the refractive index of the mobile phase entering the column will be different from that exiting the column, and baseline drift becomes significant. Since refractive indices are temperature dependent, the system must be carefully thermostated or baseline drift will not be controlled. The differential refractive index detector was originally designed for use in the polymer industry and does not find

wide use in toxicology. However, it can have some applicability for the analysis of sugars, starches, and similar compounds.

Fluorescence detectors offer a sensitive and selective analytical approach for those compounds that have natural fluorescence or that can be made to fluoresce by derivatization. They allow selection of excitation and detection wavelengths. The flow cells are generally 50–100 μL larger than those found in UV detectors. Fluorescence detectors are not widely used because of the limited number of compounds for which they are suitable.

Another detector of rather limited use in toxicological analyses is the electrochemical detector. The flow cell contains a working electrode and reference and auxiliary electrodes. The potential between the working and auxiliary electrodes is set to a value that will selectively oxidize or reduce specific compounds. The working electrode monitors electroactivity in the cell and the reference electrode provides a reproducible, stable voltage as a reference for the working electrode. For applicable compounds, this detector offers good sensitivity and selectivity.

The last detector to be considered here, and one that is increasing in use, is the mass spectrometer. The major problem with LC/MS is the large amounts of solvent that must be eliminated. An aqueous mobile-phase flow rate of 1 mL/min represents water vapor flow rates of over 1.3 L/min at ambient temperature and atmospheric pressure and over 2.4 L/min at 250 °C and atmospheric pressure. The pumping capacity of the MS system cannot begin to handle this amount of vapor.

A number of interfaces between the HPLC and the MS are currently in use. With the particle beam interface, the HPLC column effluent is mixed with helium and forced through a nozzle to form an aerosol at ambient temperature and atmospheric pressure. This aerosol is then forced through a two-stage momentum separator. Each stage consists of opposing jets and a vacuum pump. The mobile-phase molecules are lighter than the analyte molecules and are selectively pumped away. Those analyte molecules exiting the final jet are conducted into the MS ion source. This arrangement is much like the old glass jet separators formerly used in GC/MS systems, except that those used a single-stage jet. Particle beam LC/MS produces classical EI spectra with good reproducibility. The primary disadvantages of this system are that some compound volatility/stability is required and the sensitivity with water soluble analytes is not especially good.

With the thermospray interface, the HPLC column effluent is forced through a heated stainless steel capillary tube, producing a high-velocity stream of particles, droplets, and vapor. As this stream enters the hot ion source, further vaporization takes place. Ionization occurs by several mechanisms and the positive ions are repelled and focused into the mass filter. Greater pumping capacity is required, and the spectra obtained are not conventional EI spectra.

One LC/MS interface gaining widespread use in forensic toxicology is the electrospray technique. In this technique, the mobile phase is directed at high potential through a narrow metal capillary needle. As the mobile phase leaves the needle, a fine spray of charged droplets is formed. A drying gas such as nitrogen helps the solvent evaporate prior to its introduction into the mass spectrometer. The solute ions are transported into the mass spectrometer via a low-pressure transport region containing a heated capillary, a skimmer, and a series of lenses. Electrospray is a soft ionization technique, usually generating ions similar to chemical ionization.

A technique complementary to electrospray is atmospheric pressure chemical ionization. A heated nebulizer is used to form spray at atmospheric pressure. The main difference with electrospray is that chemical ionization is achieved by a corona discharge. Like electrospray, it usually produces protonated molecular ions.

See Chapter 11 for more discussion of LC/MS.

Data Systems

The same data systems available for GC can be used for HPLC.

QUANTITATION

Applicability

Analyses in forensic toxicology often require quantitation of one or more analytes in a specimen. Both GC and HPLC are well suited to quantitative analyses. With appropriate operation, analytes can be resolved so that they can be examined one at a time, and the response data are sufficiently reliable and reproducible to permit quantitation with a reasonable degree of confidence. In order to perform quantitative analyses satisfactorily and be able to support the results under rigorous examination in court, the analyst must be aware of, and adhere to, good analytical practices and understand what is being done and why. Getting a "correct" result is not enough; the analyst must understand and be able to articulate the basis for the work. Good work producing true results may be negated by cross-examination by a well-informed or well-advised attorney if the analyst cannot adequately defend his procedures. A least-squares straight line is not the slope, intercept, and correlation coefficient obtained by entering the data and stroking the correct keys on a calculator; it is the mechanism of fitting the line to the data. The analyst must have a basic understanding of such things if they are going to be used. This section will address some of these factors.

Objectives and Requirements

The goal of quantitative analysis is to determine with accuracy and precision how much of one or more analytes is present in a specimen, or the relative amounts of two or more analytes in a specimen. In order to perform quantitative analysis by GC or HPLC, several factors must be considered. First are the lower limit of quantitation (LLQ) and the linear range of the method. The analyte must be able to be detected, and quantitation must meet some acceptable criteria, e.g., controls within $\pm X\%$ of known value, a coefficient of variation of $Y\%$, etc.

In addition, the result should be within the linear range of the method and preferably bracketed by two calibrators. If a value exceeds the linear range, the specimen should be appropriately diluted and reanalyzed. It may be acceptable to report a very high value as "greater than" a certain concentration and not give a numeric result, if this is consistent with established laboratory policy. If the value is below the LLQ, it may be acceptable to report "less than" a certain concentration and not give a numeric result, again if this meets laboratory policy.

Second, resolution must be acceptable, generally 1.5 or greater, and a decision has to be made about whether to use peak area or peak height as the response from which the result is derived. For the quantitation of a small peak in the presence of a larger, closely eluting peak, it is preferable to use peak height; otherwise peak area should be used.

Third, possible sources and types of error must be considered, such as extraction efficiency, cleanliness, and reliability. Multiple analyses and an internal standard carried through the sample preparation procedure, extraction, derivatization, etc., can help to monitor these types of potential errors. The integrity of the sample should be examined. A pink, watery fluid designated as blood may, in fact, be pericardial fluid. Any apparent discrepancy should be discussed with the person who submitted the specimen, and be noted on the report.

Decisions must be made as to what standards and controls are to be run and at what frequency. Calibration methodology, single point and force through the origin, or multipoint calibration must be determined. If multipoint calibration is used, what correlation coefficient is acceptable? What is the procedure to follow if this criterion is not met? Can a single apparently aberrant value be discarded?

Calibrators are those materials used to define the calibration curve. They may be made in-house or purchased. Purity and accuracy of the accepted concentration should be demonstrated. If the calibrators are purchased, the supplier may furnish documentation

of these; however, they should be verified in the laboratory. The analyst, not the supplier, may have to testify about the validity of the results. Purity might be checked by full-scan MS, with the total ion chromatogram and spectrum meeting some acceptable criteria. Accuracy may be checked by running in parallel with a previously validated material and controls.

Controls are materials used to demonstrate the validity of the procedure and the calibration. Frequently they are purchased from a supplier who will certify their concentration. These should also be verified before using. It is not acceptable to use calibrators and controls from the same source, i.e., the same preparation or manufactured lot number. The concentrations, number, and placement of controls in the run should be established by laboratory policy. For some analyses, a single control may suffice. For others, especially where many repetitive analyses are done, such as blood alcohols, it is desirable to have controls with a series of values at the beginning, end, and spaced throughout the run.

Response Factors

Equal amounts of two different analytes will not give equal detector responses. There are two approaches to dealing with this situation. One involves response factors. The response factor for analyte a can be defined as the response (peak area or height) per unit weight of a:

$$R_{fa} = \frac{\text{Response of } a}{\text{Weight of } a \text{ Injected}} \quad (17)$$

After response factors have been determined for each analyte of interest, the amount of each can be determined from the magnitude of the detector response and Eq. 17. The concept of response factors can be of significance when dealing with a nonquantitative analysis, such as pattern recognition. For example, equal amounts of n-C_{10}, n-C_{15}, and n-C_{20} will give essentially equal responses if a FID is used. If the same mixture is subjected to MS, the areas of the total ion chromatogram will not be equal; n-C_{10} < n-C_{15} < n-C_{20}. If the MS response is not calibrated, the pattern of kerosene could be mistaken for that of diesel fuel, for example.

Calibration Curves, External and Internal Standards

It is not necessary to calculate response factors if a calibration curve is generated for each analyte. An external calibration curve is determined by injection of the same volume of each of several standards of various concentrations. The response is plotted as ordinate, and the concentration is plotted as abscissa. After the line that fits these data has been determined, the same amount of analyte solution is injected, and the concentration of the material of interest is read from the curve or calculated from the equation for the curve. The precision of analysis using external standard calibration depends on injecting the same volume of standards and sample as closely as possible. There will be some variation in amounts injected, especially if small volumes are injected with a syringe; this will affect the precision of analysis. Another consideration with the method is that there is no monitoring of sample preparation, extraction, derivatization, drying, reconstitution, etc.

An alternate to external standard calibration is the use of an internal standard. The internal standard selected should be a material that is not expected to appear in the specimen, has good stability, chromatographs satisfactorily, has a retention time reasonably close to the analyte, does not interfere with other peaks that may be present, and goes through the sample preparation process in a manner similar to the analyte. In practice, the same amount of internal standard is added to each specimen to be run. By plotting the ratio of analyte to internal standard

response of the calibrators against standard concentration, an internal standard calibration curve can be determined. This method improves analytical precision by eliminating the effect of small variations in injection volumes. Since the internal standard peak should always give nearly the same response, it also lets the chromatographer monitor method performance.

If MS is used for quantitation, a deuterated analog of the analyte can be a good choice for an internal standard. Selected ion monitoring can be used to examine the relative magnitudes of the quantitation ions and ratios of the qualifying ions of the analyte and deuterated analog. Deuterated analogs are not a good choice if MS is to be used for qualitative analysis because the presence of low concentrations of analyte is difficult to determine and the chromatographer is limited to the use of extracted ion profiles for identification rather than being able to use full-scan spectra.

There are two approaches to determining calibration curves: single- and multipoint calibration. Single-point calibration uses a single calibrator and forces a straight line through it and the origin. Some small error is automatically introduced because the origin is not the minimum detectable quantity (MDQ). This method also tends to give the false impression that the curve extends to concentrations below the LLQ.

In multipoint calibration, a series of calibrators is run, and the curve that best fits these data is determined. Using only that portion of the curve between the lowest and highest calibrators demonstrates the validity of the curve at the analyte concentration. Samples with concentrations above the highest calibrator should be diluted and rerun.

The best straight line correlating the calibration data is the least-squares line. Referring to Fig. 11, this is the line where the sum of the squares of the distances of the actual data points from the determined curve is a minimum. Another statistic of importance is the coefficient of linear correlation. The correlation coefficient indicates how well the line fits the data points, i.e., how close the data points are to the line. A value of 1.0 is a perfect fit. Generally a correlation coefficient in the range of 0.98 or better is acceptable.

In order to determine the least-squares straight line and correlation coefficient, it is necessary to examine some properties of a normal distribution (a normal distribution curve is shown in Fig. 12). Fig. 13 describes the calculation of the mean, $\bar{X}$, and standard deviation, S, of the variable X. The standard deviation, S, approximates σ of Fig. 12. These can be used to express precision; $\bar{X} \pm S$ includes about 68% of the data points; $\bar{X} \pm 2S$, 95%; and $\bar{X} \pm 3S$, 99.8%.

The calculation of covariance and the correlation coefficient, and the mechanism for obtaining the equation for the least-squares line fitting the data, are shown in Fig. 14. A set of data is given in Fig. 15 for those who want to perform the calculations; the results are given in Fig. 16.

For a set of data, (X_i, Y_i), the straight line where D ($D = \Sigma d_i^2$) is smallest, is the best straight line correlating the data; least squares line

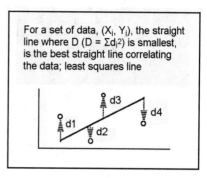

Fig.11. Definition of least-squares straight line.

To confidently and correctly use the techniques covered in this chapter, and to support them in court, the examiner must understand them sufficiently enough to be able to articulate their use and importance. The analyst must also appreciate their strengths and limitations. Chromatographic methods are powerful tools, but they cannot be used in

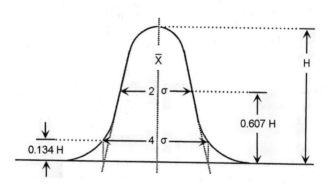

Fig. 12. Normal or Gaussian distribution. $\bar{x}$ = mean; σ = standard deviation.

For a bivariate population with paired values (X_i, Y_i) . . . . . (X_n, Y_n), e.g., (conc., pk. area):

the mean of variate X = $\frac{\Sigma X_i}{n} = \bar{X}$, and

Variance = $S^2 = \frac{\Sigma(X_i - \bar{X})^2}{(n-1)}$, where

S = Standard deviation of X

Fig. 13. Definition and calculation of mean and standard deviation.

Covariance =

$$C_{XY} = \frac{1}{(n-1)}\Sigma(X - \bar{X})(Y - \bar{Y})$$

Coefficient of linear correlation = r;

$r = (C_{XY})/(S_X S_Y)$;

for a straight line: $Y = mX + b$;

$$m = \frac{\Sigma XY - (\Sigma X)(\Sigma Y)/n}{\Sigma X^2 + (\Sigma X)^2/n} \quad b = \bar{Y} - m\bar{X}$$

Fig. 14. Calculation of least-squares lines and correlation coefficient.

For this 13-point data set, calculate $\overline{X}$, $\overline{Y}$, S_X, S_Y, r, and the least-squares straight line:					
1,	17	5,	36	9,	80
2,	21	6,	49	10,	86
3,	22	7,	56	11,	88
4,	27	8,	64	12,	92
				13,	94

Fig. 15. Practice data set.

$\overline{X}$	=	7
$\overline{Y}$	=	56.31
S_X	=	3.89
S_Y	=	29.6
r	=	0.985
Y	=	3.96 + 7.48X

Fig. 16. Results of calculations from data set (Fig. 15).

every situation. It is important to know when to use them and when not to.

SUGGESTED READING

1. Buffington R, Wilson MK. Detectors for gas chromatography. Avondale, PA: Hewlett Packard, 1987, Pub.# 5958–9433.
2. Ettre LS. Basic relationships in gas chromatography; GCD-44. Norwalk, CT: Perkin-Elmer, 1977.
3. Harris WE, Habgood HW. Programmed temperature gas chromatography. New York, NY: John Wiley, 1967.
4. Hyver KJ. High resolution gas chromatography, 3rd ed. Avondale, PA: Hewlett Packard, 1989.
5. Jennings WG. Gas chromatography with glass capillary columns. New York, NY: Academic Press, 1980.
6. Jennings WG. Comparison of fused silica and other glass columns in gas chromatography. Heidelberg, Germany: Huthig, 1981.
7. Jonsson JA. Chromatographic theory and basic principles. New York, NY: Marcel Dekker, 1987.
8. Karger BL, et al. An introduction to separation science. New York, NY: John Wiley, 1973.
9. Kirkland JJ, ed. Modern practice of liquid chromatography. New York, NY: John Wiley, 1971.
10. Klee MS. GC inlets. Avondale, PA: Hewlett Packard, 1990, Pub.# 5958-9468.
11. McNair HM, Bonelli EJ. Basic gas chromatography. Palo Alto, CA: Varian, 1968.
12. Miller JM. Separation methods in chemical analysis. New York, NY: John Wiley, 1975.
13. Ostle B. Statistics in research. Ames, IA: Iowa State Univ. Press, 1969.
14. Perry JA. Introduction to analytical gas chromatography. New York, NY: Marcel Dekker, 1981.
15. Rood D. A practical guide to the care, maintenance and troubleshooting of capillary chromatographic systems, 2nd ed. Heidelberg, Germany: Huthig, 1995.
16. Snyder LR. Principles of adsorption chromatography. New York, NY: Marcel Dekker, 1968.
17. Stafford DT. Forensic capillary gas chromatography. In: Forensic science handbook, vol. II. Safferstein R., ed. Englewood Cliffs, NJ: Prentice Hall, 1988.
18. Tebbett I, ed. Gas chromatography in forensic science. Chichester, UK: Ellis Harwood, 1992.

CHAPTER 10

Immunoassay

Michael L. Smith

Immunoassays are scientific tests that use antibodies to identify and measure amounts of a chemical substance. In forensic toxicology these assays are typically used to screen biological samples for the presence of an antigen. The original immunoassays developed in the 1950s by Rosalyn Yalow and Solomon Berson were used, conversely, to quantify human antibodies themselves in the blood of diabetics who had acquired immune responses to the bovine insulin they were taking to treat their disease. The insulin antibody concentration was determined by mixing ^{131}I-labeled insulin with the patient's blood in a test tube, separating protein-bound from unbound insulin, then measuring the gamma radiation from the labeled insulin bound to immunoglobulins. The amount of bound insulin correlated to a patient's insulin antibody concentration and this laboratory result assisted physicians in prescribing insulin dosages and determining the patient's prognosis.

Using the same theoretical basis of antibody–antigen interactions, Yalow and Berson extended this technique to measure nanogram quantities of numerous human hormones. The ability to measure submicrogram quantities of hormones revolutionized the fields of endocrinology and neuroscience. The principle they exploited was called competitive binding, and Dr. Yalow received the Nobel Prize in medicine in 1977 for developing and refining the analytical method based on this principle: radioimmunoassay (RIA).

COMPETITIVE BINDING PROCESS

The generalized competitive binding process is shown in Fig. 1.

The antigen is represented by a drug because this is the most common analyte of interest in forensic toxicology. To generate antibodies against a drug antigen, an immunogen prepared from the drug of interest is injected into an animal, and antibodies that specifically bind the drug are produced in the serum. The serum (called antiserum) collected from the animal is mixed with labeled drug and with the drug itself. Labeled and unlabeled drug compete for the antibody binding sites; at equilibrium, the concentration of drug can be determined using the law of mass action, if the equilibrium constants, concentration of labeled drug, and concentration of antibody are known. In practice, the antigen concentration is determined by comparing the amount of labeled drug bound to antibody in a sample to that of reference standards containing known concentrations of antigen. A convenient way for readers to analyze immunoassay problems in the remainder of this chapter and in the laboratory is to remember the RIA example in Fig. 2, which is a representation of a coated-tube assay in which antibodies are attached to the bottom of test tubes.

First, the same amount of radioactive ^{125}I (γ-emitter)-labeled drug is added to each of a number of assay tubes, and binds to the antibodies. Reference solutions, each containing a known concentration of drug, are

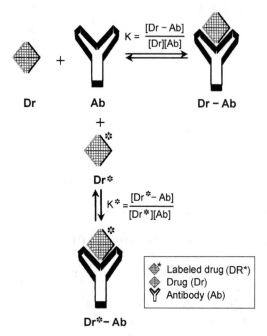

Fig. 1. Generalized competitive binding process.

then added to some of these tubes and unknown samples to the other tubes. A high concentration of drug in a reference solution or sample will displace a large amount of the labeled drug originally bound to antibodies. Samples with lower drug concentration will displace less labeled drug. The supernatant of each tube is decanted and the γ-radiation remaining in each tube (bound fraction) is measured. A calibration plot of radioactivity vs drug concentration is constructed using data from the known solutions. The concentration of drug for each unknown sample can be determined from the standard plot by correlating its radioactivity measurement on the ordinate of the standard plot with the corresponding concentration on the abscissa.

Mathematical manipulation of the data allows one to produce a linear plot (if this is desired). One common method of converting data to a linear plot is shown in Fig. 2 (see the glossary for definitions). For a qualitative

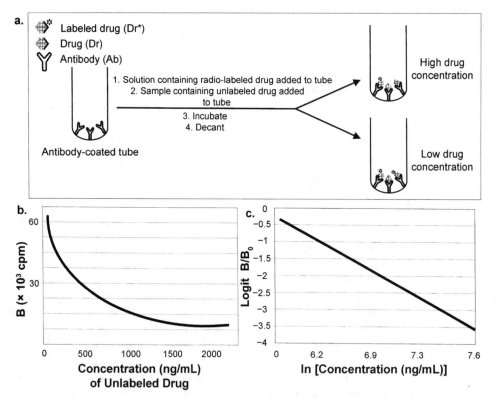

Fig. 2. Representation of a coated-tube RIA. (a) RIA procedure; (b) a plot of bound counts per minute (B) vs concentration of drug; (c) mathematical transformation of data to produce a linear plot.

screening test, standard plots are not needed. Samples with bound radioactivity equal to or less than that of a selected cutoff calibrator, i.e., equal to or higher in concentration than the cutoff calibrator, would be positive for the drug and sent for confirmation by another analytical technique.

Since the introduction of the original insulin assays, there have been many new developments in immunoassay technology. For example, assays have been developed to test for molecules smaller than peptide hormones that are of more interest to toxicologists, such as drugs, organic poisons, etc. (molecular weight [MW] of many toxicants is 100–600 daltons [Da]; MW of insulin is 6000 Da). Also, methods called homogeneous assays have been developed that do not require physical separation of bound and free antigen and can be used on large-volume automated analyzers.

The RIA described above is called a heterogeneous assay and is more labor intensive. Most of the assays used by toxicologists are commercially available in kit form, have been optimized by manufacturers, and contain simple instructions for using the kit components to screen for analytes in urine, blood, and other biological fluids. Although the kits differ in many respects, the common reagents they contain are an antiserum (antibodies), labeled drug, calibrator solutions, and control solutions. Students must understand the important scientific characteristics of these components to critically evaluate the strengths and limitations of various immunoassays.

ANTIBODIES

Production of Antibodies

Antibodies are immunoglobulins (Ig) produced by mammalian lymphocytes in response to foreign substances introduced into the body. Scientists have taken advantage of this biological phenomenon by injecting compounds of interest into hypersensitized animals and then collecting blood serum containing antibodies specific for the compound. The antiserum can be used to construct a laboratory test that identifies the compound. The serum proteins from the animal, which specifically bind the antigen, fall into at least five classes: IgG, IgM, IgA, IgE, and IgD. About 90% of Ig in the serum of hypersensitized animals are IgG, so this form will be described and is represented in Fig. 3.

IgG is a monomeric form with two light peptide chains and two heavy peptide chains connected by disulfide bonds (IgG MW = 150,000 Da). A portion of the molecule called the Fab region contains the peptide sequences that form the antigen recognition (binding) sites. Antibodies specifically bind an antigen based on the antigen's molecular composition and spatial orientation of molecules. This is an important characteristic of antibodies to remember when evaluating the specificity of immunoassays; they will exclude many substances that are dissimilar to the antigen but will also bind others that are structurally related. Binding of structurally related compounds is called cross-reactivity and is discussed under the subsection "Specificity."

Small molecules, i.e., those with molecular weights less than 2000 Da (e.g., amphetamine MW = 135 Da), are not antigenic, and scientists must "trick" an animal's immune system to produce specific antibodies. The trick is to bind the small molecule to a larger, antigenic compound before injecting it into an animal. The animal will then produce some antibodies that are specific for the small molecule. An example synthesis for preparation of such an immunogen is shown in Fig. 4. Note two important points in this figure:

1. Textbook diagrams of immunogens do not accurately represent the size difference between the small molecule, called a hapten by immunologists, and the attached protein. In this case, the MW of the methamphetamine hapten is 149 Da and the BGT protein is 150,000 Da.
2. Scientists designed the immunogen so that several bond lengths separate the hapten from the larger protein. This makes the

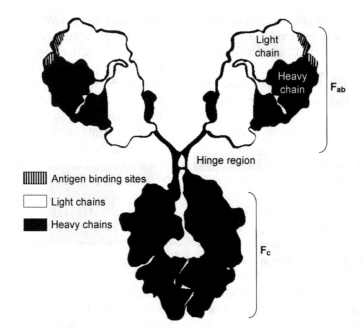

Fig. 3. Diagram of antibody (IgG) molecule. F_{ab} and F_c are names used by immunologists for regions of the molecule.

hapten more spatially unique and causes the host animal's immune system to produce a higher concentration of antibodies that specifically bind its hapten-like structure. Antiserum with high concentrations of specific antibodies is said to have a high titer. High titers are desirable and are typically described by the dilution factor needed in a standard binding assay; representative titers are 1:500 for small molecule antisera and 1:100,000 for protein antisera.

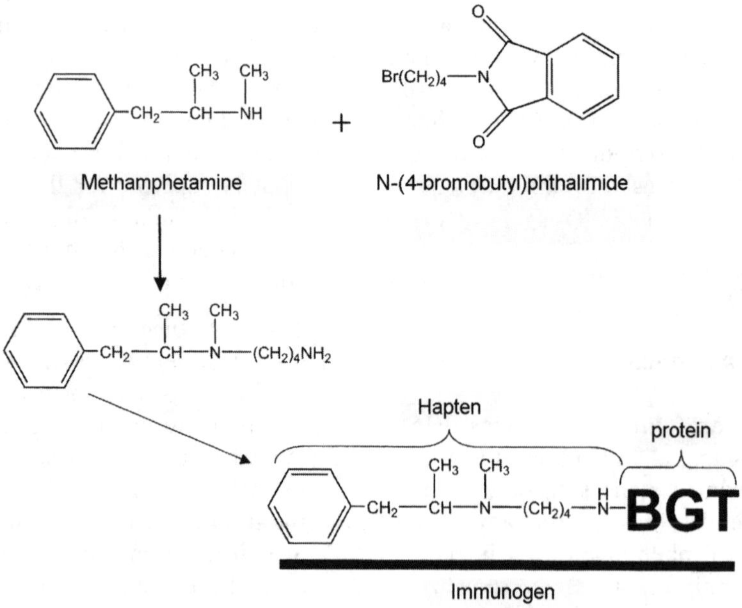

Methamphetamine

N-(4-bromobutyl)phthalimide

Hapten

protein

Immunogen

Fig. 4. Synthesis of an immunogen.

Polyclonal and Monoclonal Antiserum

Animals produce polyclonal antiserum in vivo. From the frame of reference of an analyst who uses the final product, this means that there are different types of antibodies in the antiserum, each with a different affinity for the compound of interest. These antibodies may also differ in which part of the compound they recognize. The distribution of antibodies usually differs between animals treated with the same antibody-producing regimen and within the same animal as time progresses after injection. Often a manufacturer will struggle to find an animal that produces the desired titer and specificity of antiserum only to discover with later blood drawings that these critical parameters have changed.

With the development of hybridoma technology, manufacturers began to produce monoclonal antibodies. The pictorial sum-

mary of the production of polyclonal and monoclonal antibodies is shown in Fig. 5. Production of polyclonal antiserum appears straightforward: inject an immunogen, collect blood, and then separate the serum. Variables in immune response and the time required to find the individual animal that will produce antiserum with the desired properties make this a more difficult task than it appears. The host animal, usually a rabbit, sheep, or goat (not the mouse shown in the figure), must also be large enough to allow large volumes of blood to be drawn without causing harm.

Fig. 5 also diagrams the production of monoclonal antiserum. Lymphocytes from an immunized mouse are fused to mouse myeloma cells to produce a hybridoma. The myeloma portion allows the hybridoma to propagate as long as the correct conditions are present in the culture medium. (Cancerous

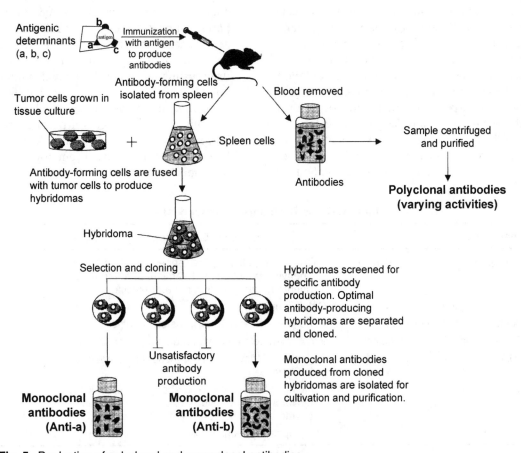

Fig. 5. Production of polyclonal and monoclonal antibodies.

cells, like the myeloma cells, are required because normal cells die after a certain number of replications.) The lymphocyte portion of the hybridoma produces antibodies. An individual hybridoma that produces the desired type of antibody is selected by cell-sorting techniques and then reproduced in culture. Each antibody in the culture medium (serum) has identical binding properties. The antiserum is very specific for the analyte and, unlike the polyclonal antiserum produced in an animal, will have the same properties as long as the selected cell line is maintained.

Specificity

Specificity is a critical characteristic of assays. It is the degree to which an assay correctly identifies only the compound of interest. (The mathematical definition may be found in the glossary.) It is often used to describe antiserum, because in immunoassays, the specific binding of the antiserum is very important, but the term specificity should more appropriately be applied to the assay using the antiserum. This is also true for the related term "cross-reactivity," which describes the degree of assay response to compounds other than the one the assay was designed to detect.

When toxicologists must identify specific toxicants in biological fluids, cross-reactivity to structurally related compounds is important, because it may lead to false-positive laboratory results if an immunoassay is not confirmed by another method. Some immunoassays and common interfering compounds reported over the years are shown in Table 1. Table 2 shows quantitative cross-reactivity figures for common interfering drugs in a representative amphetamine/methamphetamine assay.

Table 2 makes several important points:

1. First, samples containing substances with low cross-reactivity, such as *l*-ephedrine (0.55%), may appear to have a low probability of contamination in an amphetamine assay. However, one must remember that potential ephedrine concentrations in patient urine samples (10,000–200,000 ng/mL) are typically much higher than expected amphetamine concentrations (usually <5000 ng/mL). A sample containing *l*-ephedrine at the higher end of the concentration range would produce an apparent amphetamine result of 1100 ng/mL and exceed the 500-ng/mL mandated cutoff for federally regulated workplace drug-testing programs. Individuals taking ephedrine could be mistakenly identified as positive for amphetamines by this assay. For this reason, the federal program requires that immunoassay positive samples be confirmed using gas chromatography-mass spectrometry (GC/MS).

Table 1. Cross-Reactants in Immunoassays

Immunoassay	Common Cross-Reacting Substances
Amphetamine/methamphetamine	MDA, MDMA, chloroquine, ephedrine, pseudoephedrine, phenylpropanolamine, tyramine, phentermine, phenmetrazine, fenfluramine, ranitidine
Benzodiazepines	Chlorpromazine
Benzoylecgonine/(cocaine)	Ecgonine, ecgonine methyl ester, cocaine
Cannabinoids/(THC metabolites)	Ketoprofen, tolmetin, naproxen, ibuprofen, acetylsalicylic acid
LSD	Ergotamine, tricyclic antidepressants, verapamil, sertraline, fentanyl
Morphine	Codeine, dihydrocodeine, thebaine, hydrocodone, dihydromorphine, hydromorphone, oxycodone, oxymorphone, meperidine, norcodeine
PCP	TCP, diphenhydramine, dextromethorphan

Table 2. Cross-Reactivities of Common Drugs in an Amphetamine/ Methamphetamine Immunoassay

Compound	% Reactivity
d-Amphetamine	100
d-Methamphetamine	100
l-Methamphetamine	50
Phentermine	50
l-Amphetamine	16.7
l-Ephedrine	0.55
Tyramine	0.5
Phenylpropanolamine	0.3
Pseudoephedrine (100 mg/L)	0.15
Pseudoephedrine (1000 mg/L)	0.08

2. Second, there is a lower cross-reactivity for *l*-amphetamine, the stereoisomer of *d*-amphetamine, than for phentermine, the structural isomer of methamphetamine. This occurs in this assay because of the nature of the antiserum, which was produced using the immunogen in Fig. 4. The antibodies recognize the phenyl portion of methamphetamine hapten, and the phenyl portion of phentermine is more similar to *d*-methamphetamine than is the phenyl portion of the *l*-amphetamine stereoisomer. This also explains why *d*-amphetamine and *d*-methamphetamine have identical reactivities. These are theoretical concepts that are primarily the province of manufacturers who design assays, but are also important for toxicologists who need to apply them when evaluating immunoassay limitations.

3. Another characteristic of cross-reacting substances is that the response of assay antiserum to them is usually not parallel to the response to analyte as the concentration increases. Note that the cross-reactivity of pseudoephedrine in this amphetamine assay is 0.15% and 0.08% at 100 and 1000 μg/mL of pseudoephedrine, respectively. This indicates that the cross-reactivity of the assay is concentration dependent and quotations of the percent cross-reactivity for an assay should be accompanied by the concentration of the cross-reactant.

4. The last point can be made again using phentermine as an example. Its cross-reactivity is 50%. Expected urine concentrations can be as high as 5000 ng/mL. This means that most individuals taking an anorectic medication containing phentermine, e.g., Adipex or Ionamin, could produce urine that would screen positive in this assay. In workplace drug-screening laboratories, this assay would be a nemesis since many false-positive screening results would be produced and have to be confirmed as negative by more expensive techniques. These laboratories may choose to use another immunoassay with less cross-reactivity to common over-the-counter or prescribed medications such as phentermine. However, a laboratory investigating the cause of aircraft accidents, for example, may find this assay useful for detecting both amphetamines and sympathomimetic amines in the flight crew. Cross-reactivity of structurally related substances can be a boon or a bane; it is most important, in interpreting results and choosing applications, to know that it exists and how it affects immunoassay data.

SPECIFIC IMMUNOASSAY TECHNIQUES

Labeled compounds must have two important characteristics: (1) they must be immunologically similar to the compound being tested so they will successfully compete for the antibody, and (2) the labels must lend themselves to sensitive detection, free from interference by common matrices.

Labeled compounds are usually prepared by attaching a radioactive, fluorescent, enzyme or microparticle molecule to the compound of interest. The labeled molecule is added to the reaction mixture in an assay, and the assay detects the specific energy changes associated with the label when it is bound in order to measure the amount of bound labeled compound.

Many different immunoassays that test for common toxicological substances are available, and different manufacturers usually have proprietary assays available for the same target compounds. Although the antiserum and other kit components differ between competing company's assays, the primary theoretical differences are the type of labeled compound and method of detection. The most common types of assays used by toxicologists are RIA, enzyme-multiplied immunoassay technique (EMIT®; Behring Diagnostics); fluorescence polarization immunoassay (FPIA); cloned enzyme donor immunoassay (CEDIA®; Microgenics Corporation); kinetic interaction of microparticles in solution (KIMS®; Roche Diagnostic Systems); and enzyme-linked immunosorbent assay (ELISA).

Radioimmunoassay (RIA)

RIA is a heterogeneous assay, and in most current methods, ^{125}I is the label (instead of ^{131}I isotope used in the original assays) due to its longer half-life. In heterogeneous assays, it is important to completely separate bound and free labeled antigen. Supernatant (free) contamination of the precipitate (bound) will increase the bound counts per minute (cpm) and give erroneously low antigen concentration results.

Two common methods for improving separation are the double-antibody and coated-tube techniques. In the first method, an antibody (called second antibody) that binds the primary antibody is added, and the primary antibody–secondary antibody–antigen complex precipitates. (The use of two different antibodies in the same procedure makes the concept of the assay difficult to explain, but the technique works very well.) Polyethylene glycol, placed in one of the reagents, is often added to further complete the precipitation.

In the second method (see Fig. 2), primary antibody is bonded to the inside of each tube, allowing the analyst to pour off the supernatant to remove the free labeled antigen. The tube is put in a gamma counter to determine bound cpms.

Strengths

In general, these assays are very sensitive and have a large separation in assay response between drug-free and positive samples. This is because radioactivity can be measured in small amounts and is relatively free of matrix effects.

RIAs have been useful for blood and tissue analyses due to their resistance to matrix effects. For example, most other techniques cannot be applied to postmortem blood, which is commonly used for analysis after fatal accidents to determine if drivers or equipment operators were impaired by drugs or other toxicants. RIA has been successfully used to screen postmortem blood after pretreatment of the blood with acetonitrile or similar solvents to remove proteins. Untreated bile can be screened for amphetamines, barbiturates, opiates, and PCP, and treated bile for cannabinoids and benzodiazepines. The combined advantage of sensitivity and low matrix effects is also evidenced by successful assays for LSD in urine, ricin in tissue, and THC in hair. Information presented in Table 3 also shows that many adulterants added to urine samples by donors trying to avoid getting a positive drug screen do not usually produce a false-negative result. In fact, if the adulterant affects the assay, the result is often falsely positive. Other immunoassays are generally more susceptible to adulteration.

Limitations

In short,

- There are problems disposing of radioactive waste.
- Due to radioactive decay, shelf life is limited (usually ≤60 days).
- These heterogeneous assays are difficult to adapt to inexpensive automated analysis.

Many immunoassay manufacturers no longer make RIA kits for common drugs because these limitations have reduced consumer demand.

Table 3. Effects of Adulterants in Urine on Immunoassay Results

Adulterant	Immunoassay						
	Amp	Barb	Bzd	Coc	THC	Opi	PCP
NaCl	E	E	E	E	E	E	E
Base Buffer							EF
Lime-A-Way or Liquid Plumber		R		F		ER	F
Vinegar	ERK	EK	EK	EK	EFRK	ERK	EK
Bleach		C	<u>F</u>	C	EFCKR	R	K
Drano	EFCK <u>R</u>	ECK <u>R</u>	ECK	EFCK <u>R</u>	EFCK <u>R</u>	EFCK <u>R</u>	EFCK <u>RK</u>
Detergent/soap	EC <u>R</u>	EFC <u>R</u>	EC	EC <u>R</u>	EFC <u>R</u>	EC <u>R</u>	FC <u>R</u>
Visine (benzalkonium Cl)	E <u>F</u>	EK <u>F</u>	E	CE	ECK <u>R</u>	E	E
Golden Seal	C	F			EFCKR		
Urinaid (glutaraldehyde)	E <u>KR</u>	CE	E	CE <u>R</u>	EFC <u>R</u>	E <u>R</u>	CEF <u>KR</u>
Klear (KNO₂)	E <u>RK</u>	E <u>RK</u>	E <u>RK</u>	E <u>R</u>	E <u>RK</u>	E <u>RK</u>	E <u>RK</u>
DETOX					EFRK		
TEST CLEAN	EFR	EFR	EFR	EFR	EFR	EFR	EFR

E = EMIT; F = FPIA; C = CEDIA; R = RIA; K = KIMS.
Underlined abbreviations indicate a false-positive result.
Abbreviations without underlines indicate a false-negative result.
Source: Some data are from a 1998 personal communication from Sal Salamone, OraSure Technologies, Inc., Bethlehem, PA, and Yale Caplan, Baltimore, MD.

Enzyme-Multiplied Immunoassay Technique (EMIT)

EMIT assays use an enzyme-linked antigen. EMIT is a homogeneous assay, and the basic assay theory and typical standard plot are depicted in Fig. 6. The label attached to the drug in this assay is the enzyme glucose-6-phosphate dehydrogenase (G6P-DH) that oxidizes the substrate glucose-6-phosphate to gluconolactone-6-phosphate and also reduces the cofactor nicotinamide adenine dinucleotide (NAD) to NADH. Enzyme activity is determined by spectrophotometrically measuring the NADH produced, monitoring absorbance at the λ_{max} of 340 nm. The enzymatic activity of G6P-DH decreases when the attached drug is bound to antibody, so adding drug reduces the antibody available to bind to G6P-DH labeled drug and increases the rate of NADH production. The change in absorbance at 340 nm is directly related to the concentration of the drug in the biological fluid that is added.

Strengths

- Bound labeled drug can be measured without separation from free drug. These homogeneous assays are easy to automate since the reagents can be mixed, incubated, and have light measurements made in the original reaction container. Once samples are aliquoted and loaded, a typical high-volume analyzer can screen >500 samples/h, with one operator monitoring the system. Automation improves throughput, intra-assay variability, and analyst error liability.
- Shelf lives of kits are long (usually >1 year).
- Enzyme-linked assays discriminate between concentrations over a large range.
- Enzyme-related technology is well established, which improves troubleshooting and reduces costs.
- The absorbance change of the solution is measured as a function of time, i.e., as

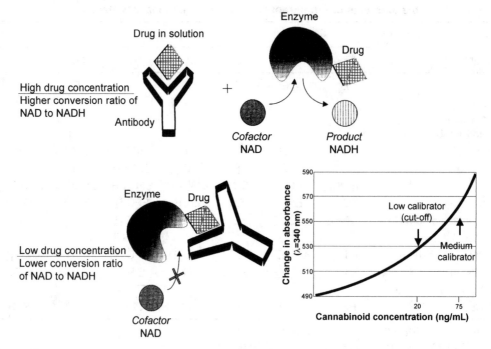

Fig. 6. Schematic of enzyme-multiplied immunoassay technique (EMIT®).

a rate measurement. Absorbances from interfering substances do not usually change with time and their contribution is minimized.
- More specialty assays, such as LSD, are available.

Limitations

- Interference results not only from compounds that cross-react with the antibody but also from substances in the matrix that interrupt the enzyme process (see Table 3).
- Urinary metabolites of tolmetin and aspirin, common analgesics, can cause false-negative assay results. Scientific studies showed that salicyluric acid, the culprit aspirin metabolite, directly interferes with measurement of the NADH product by absorbing light at $\lambda = 340$ nm. This type of interference can be detected by incorporating appropriate instrument absorbance flags in

the method parameter software. If not, they will go undetected.
- Interfering substances usually cause false-negative results (see Table 3).
- The LSD assay cited above has linear characteristics in the low pg/mL range, but has a high false-positive rate, probably due to cross-reacting substances.

Fluorescence Polarization Immunoassay (FPIA)

FPIA theory and a representative standard plot are depicted in Fig. 7. The most prevalent FPIA methods are marketed by Abbott Laboratories for operation on TDx®, ADx®, or Axysm® analyzers and use fluorescein-labeled drugs as tracers. Fluorescein can absorb light at $\lambda = 485$ nm and emit light in the range of $\lambda = 525$–550 nm. If the incoming light is polarized, emitted light will remain polarized if the fluorescein molecule is fixed in space. When the fluorescein-linked drug is bound to antibody, the fluorescein label

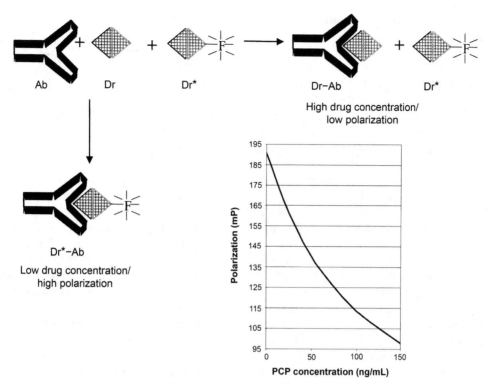

Fig. 7. Schematic of fluorescence polarization immunoassay (FPIA).

does not rotate freely and the polarized light absorbed is emitted with little loss of polarization. When the fluorescein label is free, it rotates freely in solution, and the amount of polarized light emitted is reduced. Therefore, addition of drug releases labeled drug molecules from antibody-binding sites and lowers the polarization of the light emitted. The concentration of drug in the biological fluid being measured is inversely related to the intensity of polarized light being emitted at a wavelength selected in the $\lambda = 525–550$ nm range.

Strengths

- This immunoassay is homogeneous.
- Fluorescein-labeled drug is more stable than enzyme–drug conjugates.
- Fluorescent probes provide low limits of detection. Measurement of changes in the polarization of fluorescence capitalizes on the sensitivity of fluorescence and avoids stray light interference common to measurement of direct fluorescence. Also, matrices have less effect on changes in fluorescence polarization than on changes in direct light intensity, making FPIA measurements in blood and older urine samples generally more accurate than those from an EMIT.
- Shelf lives of reagents are long (usually >1 year).

Limitations

- The assays are generally more expensive than comparable enzyme-linked assays.
- Fluorescent salts in bile occasionally give false-positive results.
- Currently, not many FPIAs are adaptable to common high-speed analyzers. Abbott methods must be performed on the company's own analyzers.

Cloned Enzyme Donor Immunoassay (CEDIA)

The theory and a standard plot for the CEDIA are depicted in Fig. 8. CEDIA is a trademark method marketed by Microgenics Corporation that uses genetically engineered fragments of *E. coli* β-galactosidase as an enzyme label. The activity of the enzyme requires assembling two fragments, termed enzyme acceptor (EA) and enzyme donor (ED) fragments. The reassociated enzyme hydrolyzes chlorophenolred-β-galactoside (CPRG) to chlorophenolred (CPR) and galactose.

CPRG does not absorb significant energy at $\lambda = 570$ nm, whereas the λ_{max} for CPR is 570 nm. Production of CPR is easily measured. A secondary wavelength (660 nm) for CPR can also be used to correct for minor changes in sample absorbance. ED is linked to the drug and will not reassociate if bound to antibody. Added drug displaces the ED-labeled drug from antibodies, reassociation occurs, and absorbance increases. The concentration of drug in biological fluid is directly proportional to the change in absorbance.

Strengths

- This immunoassay is homogeneous.
- Shelf lives of reagents are long (usually >1 year).
- Enzyme activity is almost completely stopped when antibody binding blocks reassociation of the enzyme. This phenomenon makes release of the labeled drug, subsequent enzyme reassociation, and production of colored product directly proportional to the concentration of the drug of interest, and the resulting standard plot is linear over a wide range of concentration values.
- Monitoring a second wavelength, 660 nm, provides some measure of security against interference from substances that may absorb light at the primary wavelength, 570 nm.

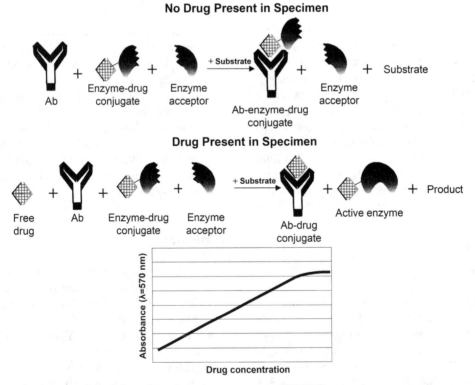

Fig. 8. Schematic of cloned enzyme donor immunoassay (CEDIA®).

- The absorbance change of the solution is measured as a function of time, i.e., as a rate measurement. Absorbances from interfering substances do not usually change with time and their contribution is minimized.
- CEDIA® has a three-component assay kit that can be used to measure LSD. The method has a large linear range and is subject to less drift than comparable immunoassays.

Limitations

Despite resistance to interference, CEDIA® methods can be affected by urine adulterants and usually yield false-negative results (see Table 3).

Kinetic Interaction of Microparticles in Solution (KIMS)

KIMS theory and a typical standard plot are shown in Fig. 9. The method was patented by Roche Diagnostic Systems and is marketed as Abuscreen Online. The labeled compound is a microparticle with several drug molecules linked to it. In the absence of the drug of interest, the conjugate of microparticle and drug molecules binds several antibody molecules and forms large aggregates that scatter transmitted light. As the aggregation reaction proceeds, the change in absorbance increases. The added drug substitutes for the conjugate attached to antibodies and prevents the formation of aggregates, which diminishes the rate of absorbance increase in proportion to the drug concentration. Plotting change in absorbance vs concentration of drug yields a negative slope. Change in transmission can also be plotted, yielding a parabolic plot with positive slopes.

Strengths

- It is an inexpensive homogeneous assay.
- Shelf lives of kits are long (usually >1 year).
- Microparticle drug conjugates are more stable than enzyme drug conjugates.

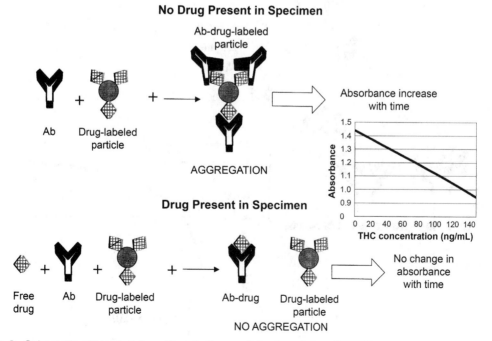

Fig. 9. Schematic of kinetic interaction of microparticles in solution (KIMS®).

- Substances that interfere with the agglutination process in KIMS usually cause false-positive results. This is an advantage because immunoassays are screening tests for identifying samples that may contain a drug. Samples containing both a drug and an interfering substance will be identified as positive by KIMS and forwarded for confirmation testing, while other techniques, such as EMIT, will produce a false-negative result and the sample will not be identified for confirmation testing. The absorbance change of the solution is measured as a function of time, i.e., as a rate measurement. Absorbances from interfering substances do not usually change with time and their contribution is minimized.

Limitations

- The microparticle solution used in KIMS assays coats the analyzer tubing and requires special system maintenance.

- The linear range for KIMS assays is generally smaller than for EMIT and CEDIA. The microparticle technology allows a steep response plot but for a narrower range than enzyme-based assays.

Enzyme-Linked Immunosorbent Assay (ELISA)

ELISA has been in use in specialty laboratories for many years, e.g., in HIV testing. Its application in drug testing is more recent; many procedures for testing oral fluid, blood, and urine have developed only within the past decade. Several companies market drug-testing methods, e.g., OraSure Technologies, Cozart Bioscience, and Immunalysis.

The theory and a representative standard plot for an OraSure method are shown in Fig. 10. When free in solution, the enzyme label (horseradish peroxidase) converts the substrate tetramethylbenzidine (TMB) to a colored product (λ_{max} = 450 nm). Enzyme

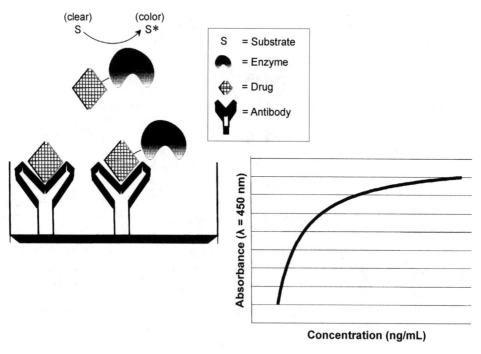

Fig. 10. Schematic of enzyme-linked immunosorbent assay (ELISA).

activity is restricted when the drug portion of the enzyme–drug complex is bound to antibodies attached to the bottom of the well in a microtiter plate. Labeled drug is released from antibody-binding sites, and enzyme activity is restored in proportion to the concentration of the drug in the sample that is added.

Strengths

- ELISA has very good sensitivity.
- Being a heterogeneous assay, it is less subject to matrix effects, especially if the double-wash technique is used. Some laboratories have investigated this technique to analyze postmortem blood samples.
- Compared to RIA, ELISA is much easier to automate. Both current and traditional methods typically used 96-well microtiter plates with automated pipetting, washing, and spectrophotometric reading.
- Because the label is an enzyme, shelf lives are longer than for RIA (usually >1 year).

Limitations

- Being a specialized heterogeneous assay, it cannot be easily adapted to common high-speed analyzers. Analyzers currently being used are specific for this technology.
- Cost per sample is generally higher than for some of the homogeneous assays, primarily because of the special analyzer needed.
- Sodium azide, a common antimicrobial agent added to preserve urine, will block the activity of horseradish peroxidase, and the method cannot be used to test these samples.

QUALITY CONTROL

In addition to antiserum and labeled antigen, most immunoassay kits contain calibrators and control solutions. A general principle of quality control is that these two solutions should be in a matrix similar to actual samples. This is very important in immunoassays because matrix effects can be significant.

In practice, limited supplies of human urine and serum force analysts to compromise. As a compromise rule, urine that is used to prepare calibrators for urine assays should not be diluted more than 50%; synthetic urine can be used with caution; controls must be in actual human urine. These are basically the guidelines used by the Food and Drug Administration to clear kits for medical testing. Very few drug-of-abuse assays are available for blood or serum that require toxicologists to compromise further when applying urine-based kits to analysis for these fluids. Calibrators from the kits may be used if quantitative values are not important. Controls must be prepared in drug-free blood or serum, respectively. More detailed discussions of quality control requirements can be found elsewhere, but a few basic principles need to be discussed here. Calibrators should be used in consonance with analytical requirements. If the immunoassay is a screening test, then a single calibrator is sufficient. For quantitative tests, multiple calibrators with concentrations that bracket those of the samples should be included in each assay. There should be sufficient control solutions, run with the samples in each assay, to demonstrate discrimination above and below the cutoff for screening tests. For quantitative tests, these controls should demonstrate good assay performance in the low- and high-concentration region of the linear range. Prior to placing an immunoassay in service, the laboratory should establish and verify a limit of detection and linear range for the method. Cross-reactivities to common interfering substances must also be verified. Performance parameters must be reverified periodically or when reagent lots change because assay response varies greatly with changes in antiserum or components that interact with it in the assay.

CUTOFFS

"Cutoff" is a term used in screening assays because these methods identify samples as either positive or negative with no quantitative results reported. A cutoff is the concentration of drug below which all specimens are considered to be negative. This can be the limit of detection of the assay or a higher concentration. For most programs using immunoassays, oversight agencies mandate administrative cutoffs well above the limit of detection of the method.

Table 4 lists the cutoffs for two workplace drug-testing programs. A cutoff above the limit of detection is usually established to ensure that most laboratories can achieve accurate results at this concentration and to meet other special program requirements. For example, the administrative immunoassay cutoff for cannabinoids was originally set at 100 ng/mL to identify active marijuana smokers but reduce the risk of identifying as positive urine samples from individuals passively exposed to marijuana smoke.

APPLICATIONS

Immunoassays have applications in postmortem investigations, workplace drug

Table 4. Immunoassay Cutoffs for Urine Drug-Testing Programs

	DoD (ng/mL)	HHS (ng/mL)
Amphetamines	500	1000
Cannabinioids	50	50
Cocaine metabolites	150	300
Designer amphetamines	500	*
Phencyclidine	25	25
Opiates (morphine/codeine)	2000	2000
Opiate (6-monoacetylmorphine)	10	*
Opiates (oxycodone/oxymorphone)	100	*

*Drug class not included in this program

testing, and human performance investigations. In a postmortem examination, the forensic pathologist collects blood, urine, tissues, and other body fluids from the victim for toxicological analyses. If there is no apparent anatomic cause of death, toxicology results are critical to the investigation. Analytically, urine is the specimen of choice for immunoassay screening because it usually has fewer interfering proteins and decomposition products, but other fluids or tissues may be the specimens of choice for interpretation. For example, some victims who die of acute heroin overdose have high concentrations of morphine in their blood but not in urine. An immunoassay screen of urine for opiates would give a negative result and the cause of death could be missed. This example supports screening blood but presents challenges for the toxicologist since blood assays have many more interfering substances. Proteins are usually precipitated before analysis using acetonitrile or a similar solvent to eliminate some of the interfering substances, and then the supernatant is pipetted for immunoassay. Historically RIA was used to screen postmortem blood. With the decreased availability of RIA methods, other techniques, primarily ELISA, are being investigated.

The following assorted facts about application of different immunoassay techniques to postmortem analysis illustrate some of the assay characteristics discussed above:

- Postmortem blood decomposes with time, producing biogenic amines. These amines often cross-react with the antibody in amphetamines immunoassays (regardless of the type) and produce false-positive results. For example, due to decomposition, tyramine and phenethylamine can accumulate in biological fluids and cross-react in the immunoassay (see monoclonal assay in Table 2).
- Salts in bile, some of which are fluorescent, can cause false-positive FPIA results.
- Some RIA and ELISA assays will give false-positive cannabinoid results in

old blood. The mechanism is not well understood.

- High concentrations of diphenhydramine cause false-positive results in some urine PCP immunoassays.
- Dihydrocodeine and codeine give false-positive results in most morphine assays.
- As mentioned, enzyme-based assays may yield false-negative results if the common preservatives NaF or NaN_3 are present in the sample.

Most urine drug-testing programs use immunoassays. The federally regulated workplace program, for example, mandates an immunoassay screen for cannabinoids, benzoylecgonine (cocaine metabolite), PCP, opiates, and amphetamines, and establishes screening cutoffs for each class of drugs. Table 4 shows cutoffs for the Department of Health and Human Services and Department of Defense programs. Samples that screen positive must be confirmed by GC/MS for both programs. Some common interfering substances in urine assays for these drugs are listed in Table 1.

Drug testing in accident, probable cause, and similar human performance investigations use immunoassays as screening tests. Immunoassay quantifications are often used in medical testing where other clinical information about the patient is available, but forensic analysis usually requires quantification and confirmation by a technique based on a different scientific principle from the immunoassay. If both blood (or serum) and urine are collected from the subject, the urine may be screened for evidence of drug use and then the blood analyzed (usually by chromatography) for evidence of the drugs found in the urine screen. It is easier to relate impaired performance to drug concentrations in blood, serum, or plasma than in urine. An elevated blood concentration of a drug also indicates more recent use of the drug, which may be important in the investigation. The relationship of blood alcohol, which is not typically measured with an immunoassay, to impairment has been investigated for many years and is well documented, but correlation of blood drug concentration to impaired performance has not been established.

SPECIAL PROBLEMS

Manufacturers of immunoassay kits are challenged by customers to produce a product that will test certain analytes in a class of drugs, but exclude others. An excellent example is the development of a method for screening the urine of employees for amphetamines. Program directors want to identify amphetamine and methamphetamine in a donor's urine with a single immunoassay and exclude other amines such as the over-the-counter cold medication pseudoephedrine. In addition, they want to identify only the d-isomers since these are the usual illicit forms of the drugs. A first approach to assay development might be to construct an immunogen with the amino function of the hapten, either amphetamine or methamphetamine, exposed. However, antibodies produced with increased specificity for d-amphetamine will have a reduced ability to detect d-methamphetamine because the amino portions of these two molecules differ. Attempts to reduce the specificity of amphetamine antiserum by hiding the amino group to achieve increased cross-reactivity to methamphetamine usually result in the capture of other unwanted amines.

One solution offered by some manufacturers is to use a mixture of two specific antibodies, one for amphetamine and one for methamphetamine. The Roche Online Amphetamines method combines antibodies and uses microparticle–amphetamine as a labeled drug. In this method, the methamphetamine antibody must have some cross-reactivity to amphetamine for the method to be effective. The TDx, EMIT, and CEDIA methods use both an amphetamine- and methamphetamine-labeled compound in the reaction mixture with the combined antibodies. The combined antibody approach increases specificity for just these two analytes, but often introduces an analytical problem. The methamphetamine antibody binds methamphetamine in a sample more strongly than the labeled amphetamine and this binding difference may increase cooperative binding. This phenomenon occurs for the Online and TDx methods. A typical cooperative binding curve is shown in Fig. 11.

These assays are good screening methods, but the characteristics of their plots complicate interpretation of assay results. For example, let us consider a urine sample from a methamphetamine user that has 500 ng/mL of methamphetamine and 500 ng/mL of its principal metabolite, amphetamine. One would expect an immunoassay with reactivity to each drug of 100% to yield a response equivalent to 1000 ng/mL of amphetamines, but might observe an assay result of 1500 ng/mL as a result of the cooperative binding phenomenon.

Another special problem of immunoassays involves cross-reactivity studies. Most manufacturers examine potential interfering substances and list these in package inserts before assays are approved for marketing. Independent research scientists expand these studies and publish a larger list of cross-reacting compounds. However, the human metabolites of these compounds are usually not readily available for study, are often elevated in urine, and can significantly influence urine immunoassay results. For example, fenfluramine, a drug once used to treat obesity, has a low cross-reactivity in studies using the TDx (FPIA) amphetamine/methamphetamine assay. Norfenfluramine, a metabolite of fenfluramine in urine, was initially unavailable and not examined in studies of cross-reactivity. Laboratories were puzzled when they observed many false-positive results from testing the urine of patients who were taking diet medications containing fenfluramine since previous studies showed little cross-reactivity to this drug. However, they later discovered that norfenfluramine with high cross-reactivity in the assay had caused the false-positive results.

The concept of administrative cutoffs for assays presents a special problem. In workplace drug-testing programs, specific cutoffs are mandated so that each person, regardless of which laboratory tests the sample, will be treated equally. That is, the cutoff must be easily achieved by most laboratories and must be the same whether the employee works in California or Maryland and regardless of the immunoassay used by the laboratory. However, as we have learned, different immunoassays have different cross-reactivities to common metabolites of the target drug. For some urine samples, one manufacturer's assay may be negative and another positive

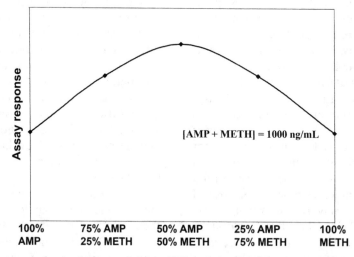

Fig. 11. Assay response for a solution containing 1000 ng/mL of total amphetamines in an amphetamine/methamphetamine immunoassay that exhibits cooperative binding.

even if both have the same cutoff for the target drug. The special problem is that the very nature of immunoassays defies the legal objectives of equal treatment. One solution is to make each immunoassay for these programs more specific for the drug of interest.

Over the years, immunoassays have in general been manufactured to be more specific to address this problem. Good examples include the immunoassays for amphetamines, benzoylecgonine, cannabinoids, morphine/codeine, and PCP that are required in the large federal workplace drug-testing program. This program emphasizes reduction of false-positive screening results and equal treatment of urine donors. To satisfy customers who are responsible for drug-testing programs, manufacturers have refined immunoassays to be more specific for the drug of interest.

One adverse result is that in other applications these assays miss more drug users. For example, original cannabinoid assays targeting the principal marijuana metabolite, 11-nor-delta-9 tetrahydrocannabinol-9-carboxylic acid glucuronide, identified more users than the current methods that use antibodies more specific for the unconjugated acid that is lower in concentration. As another example, European toxicologists in the 1990s complained that available amphetamine assays no longer detected MDMA, one of their most problematic drugs of abuse, as manufacturers made their immunoassays more specific for d-amphetamine and d-methamphetamine to satisfy the larger workplace drug-testing market in the U.S. New immunoassays that detected MDMA were not developed until use of this drug began to increase in the U.S. This problem related to specificity may be more of a lesson in marketing than science, but users must know the scientific characteristics of immunoassays to understand it.

CONCLUSIONS

Immunoassays in forensic toxicology are primarily used to screen biological samples for the presence of drugs and similar toxicants. Many commercial kit methods are available, and each kit contains an antibody reagent, labeled drug, calibrators, and controls. The assays are very sensitive, usually detecting analytes in the low ng/mL range, and many of the methods can be easily adapted to automated analyzers that test hundreds of samples per hour for several drugs. Yet cross-reactivity of structurally similar substances is a major problem with immunoassays, resulting in false-positive results. In forensic toxicology applications, immunoassay results should be confirmed by a method based on a different scientific principle. The primary theoretical difference between various immunoassays is the labeled antigen used and the method of detecting it.

GLOSSARY

Affinity (In immunology) The strength of binding between an antibody and its antigenic determinant.

Analyte A substance of interest that is being identified and measured in an assay.

Antibody A protein synthesized by animal lymphocytes in response to a foreign substance that specifically binds the foreign substance. The molecular weight of the monomeric form of an antibody is about 150,000 Da.

Antigen Any substance that stimulates an animal lymphocyte to produce an antibody that specifically binds it. Small molecules that were part of a larger immunogen when the antibodies were produced may later be referred to as antigens when they are being measured in an immunoassay, but are technically called antigenic determinants by immunologists.

Antigenic determinant The portion of an immunogenic molecule that binds to an antibody-binding site.

Avidity (In immunology) The strength of binding between antiserum, or an antibody mixture, and an antigen.

Calibrator A solution containing an analyte at a known concentration that is used to establish a measured reference concentration in an assay.

CEDIA® A type of immunoassay: cloned enzyme donor immunoassay.

Competitive binding process The process of two different substances competing for the same antibody-binding sites. In immunoassays, the competing substances are an antigen and a labeled antigen.

Cross-reactivity Qualitative definition: The degree of response in an immunoassay to a substance other than the analyte of interest.

Quantitative definition:

$$\% \text{ cross reactivity} =$$

$$\frac{\begin{array}{c}\text{concentration reading of assay}\\\text{(w/v units of assay analyte)}\end{array}}{\begin{array}{c}\text{concentration of cross-reactivity}\\\text{analyte (w/v units)}\end{array}} \times 100$$

Cutoff A concentration of an analyte established for a screening assay below which all measured values are identified as negative for the analyte.

Efficiency Qualitative definition: A characteristic of an assay that denotes the assay's ability to detect and correctly identify an analyte in samples. Also called accuracy of an assay in older literature.

Quantitative definition:

$$\text{Efficiency (\%)} =$$

$$\frac{\left[\begin{array}{c}\textit{true-positive test results}\\ + \textit{ true-negative test results}\end{array}\right]}{[\textit{all test results}]} \times 100$$

ELISA A type of immunoassay: enzyme-linked immunosorbent assay.

EMIT® A type of immunoassay: enzyme-multiplied immunoassay technique.

FPIA A type of immunoassay: fluorescence polarization immunoassay.

Hapten A small, nonimmunogenic molecule that is attached to a larger immunogenic substance, forming a new antigen that stimulates production of antibodies specific for the small molecule.

Heterogeneous immunoassay An immunoassay that requires bound and free antigen to be separated before labeled antigen is measured.

Homogeneous immunoassay An immunoassay that allows measurement of labeled antigen without separating bound and free antigen.

Immunoassay Any assay using antibodies that specifically bind an analyte to identify and measure the amount of the analyte.

Immunogen A substance injected into an animal, causing production of antibodies to the injected substance.

KIMS® A type of immunoassay: kinetic interaction of microparticles in solution.

Limit of detection (LOD) Qualitative definition: The smallest amount of analyte that can be distinguished from random assay noise.

Quantitative definition: The smallest concentration of analyte that can be distinguished from analyte-free samples in 95% of repeated measurements.

Logit B/B$_0$ A mathematical function used to linearize standard plots:

$$\ln\left[\frac{B/B_0}{1-B/B_0}\right]$$

where B = bound counts per minute (cpm) of sample, B$_0$ = bound cpm of drug free sample.

Monoclonal antiserum Antiserum containing antibodies that each have identical binding properties. This antiserum is produced in tissue culture by a set of selected lymphocytes (clones) that produce a single type of antibody.

Polyclonal antiserum Antiserum containing antibodies with a spectrum of affinities/specificities toward an antigen. Animals produce polyclonal antiserum.

Sensitivity Qualitative definition: An assay characteristic that denotes the assay's ability to detect an analyte in samples.

Quantitative definition:

Sensitivity (%) =

$$\frac{[\textit{true-positive test results}]}{[\textit{true-positive test results} + \textit{false-negative test results}]} \times 100$$

Specificity Qualitative definition: An assay characteristic that denotes the assay's ability to correctly identify an analyte in a sample.

Quantitative definition:

Specificity (%) =

$$\frac{[\textit{true-negative test results}]}{[\textit{false-positive test results} + \textit{true-negative test results}]} \times 100$$

Titer A measure of an antiserum's antibody concentration, usually expressed as the antiserum dilution that gives 50% binding of labeled antigen.

SUGGESTED READING

1. Goldberger BA, Jenkins AJ. Testing of abused drugs in urine by immunological techniques. AACC Therapeutic Drug Monitoring and Toxicology 1992;13(8):7–16.
2. Miller JJ, Valdes R. Approaches to minimizing interferences by cross-reacting molecules in immunoassays. Clin Chem 1991;37:144–53.
3. Price CP, Newman DJ, eds. Principles and practice of immunoassay. New York, NY: Stockton Press, 1991.
4. Ropero-Miller JD, Goldberger BA, eds. Handbook of workplace drug testing, 2nd ed. Washington, DC: AACC Press, 2009.
5. Stewart MJ. Immunoassays. In: Moffat AC, ed. Clarke's isolation and identification of drugs. London, UK: The Pharmaceutical Press, 1986:148–59.
6. Wild D, ed. The immunoassay handbook. New York, NY: Stockton Press, 1994.

CHAPTER 11

Mass Spectrometry

John Cody and Shawn P. Vorce

Mass spectrometry (MS) was developed about 80 years ago and has since been applied in a wide variety of scientific disciplines. The applications of MS run the gamut from the elucidation of fundamental physical and chemical properties of substances to the study of large biological molecules. The technique has come into widespread use in the last several decades, largely because of the development of small, relatively inexpensive instruments that are easy to operate. Advances in computers and sophisticated software have reduced the need for training because instruments can be controlled and data acquired with little analyst intervention. Moreover, various advances have made MS technology more usable for a wider variety of compounds in a diverse array of scientific endeavors, most recently in elucidating the nature of the genome and its encoded protein products. Although GC/MS remains the backbone of the forensic toxicology laboratory, over the past 18 years, the use of MS has begun a change toward more applications that use liquid chromatography (LC) and tandem MS (MS/MS). This trend should continue into the future.

GENERAL THEORY

Mass spectral analysis is accomplished by measuring an analyte that has been converted into an ion in the gas phase. Compared with neutral molecules, ionic species are relatively easy to manipulate because they can be affected by magnetic and electrostatic fields that allow the ions to be isolated with remarkable specificity. The fundamental physical chemistry properties of a compound's mass (m) and charge (z) make its ions unique and permit separation with resolutions of <1 Dalton (a Dalton, abbreviated Da, is equal to 1 atomic mass unit, i.e., one twelfth of the mass of a carbon atom). A molecule is introduced via one of a variety of inlet devices into an "ion source," where the molecule is ionized by one of a variety of techniques. The ions of the various molecules constituting the sample are then directed through a mass analyzer to a detector system, where a signal is generated to represent the ions that have impinged on the detector. The system requires a vacuum to allow the transfer of ions from one place to another, virtually eliminating the chance for the ions to collide with other ions or molecules. Manipulation of the electrical and magnetic fields allows the isolation of ions of a single mass-to-charge ratio (m/z). The mass resolutions available range from unit mass resolution (the ability to separate ions differing by 1 Da) to the ability to differentiate ions with the same nominal mass but different exact masses.

SCHEMATIC

Fig. 1 illustrates the basic components of the MS system. The sample enters the mass spectrometer through an inlet device. Once inside the ion source, the sample components are ionized and selectively monitored

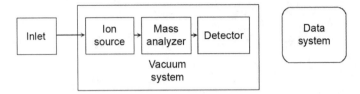

Fig. 1. Schematic representation of the basic components of a mass spectrometer.

by the mass analyzer. The ions that exit the mass analyzer enter the instrument's detector. Traditionally, these three critical components of the system were under vacuum. Recent advances that permit ionization at atmospheric pressure have led to the development of a number of ion sources that operate at atmospheric pressure. The process of ion selection and detection remains under vacuum in all systems. Data are captured by the data system (computer) and manipulated to describe the analyzed sample in a meaningful way.

SAMPLE INLET

For mass analysis, the sample must first be introduced into the mass spectrometer. Of the several different methods that have been used for this task, the most commonly used technique in forensic toxicology remains gas chromatography (GC). In recent years, however, LC and capillary electrophoresis have become more widely used. Sample introduction by direct insertion is still an option, but this method has not gained wide use, most probably because the lack of automation for the process limits its efficiency. Each method has distinct advantages and disadvantages that influence the selection of inlet type for sample analysis. Because the molecules must be in the gas phase and the mass spectrometer must be under vacuum, introducing molecules into the system poses a significant problem. Each of the sample-introduction techniques overcomes this problem differently. Likewise, each technique addresses vacuum integrity in different ways. Several of these techniques are discussed in more detail later in this chapter.

Direct-Insertion Probe

Directly inserting a sample into the mass spectrometer is the simplest form of introduction. The simplicity of this approach is its appeal, because no material is lost in the process and the amount placed into the analyzer can be easily controlled. The direct-insertion probe is also often referred to as a solids probe because it can be used to introduce solid material into the mass spectrometer. Materials that otherwise could not readily be introduced can be placed on the probe and then inserted directly into the source. Compounds that do not lend themselves to introduction through a chromatographic system can often be analyzed via direct insertion. The disadvantage of direct insertion is a lack of separation. A sample is typically placed into the probe, which is then inserted directly into the ion source through a vacuum interlock. The probe can then be heated to volatilize the compound(s) on the probe. If a mixture of compounds is on the probe, the only separation that can be effected is by heating the probe in such a manner that compounds with lower boiling points are volatilized, ionized, detected, and pumped out of the mass spectrometer before other compounds with higher boiling points are volatilized. Depending on the manufacturer, the probe may also be fitted with a cooling capability that allows for rapid temperature cycling of the probe from low to high and back to low again. This feature makes it possible to process samples in rapid succession.

A related technique uses a direct-exposure probe. Using the same principle as the direct-insertion probe, the direct-exposure probe has a small filament on which a sample is placed and then inserted into the source. A liquid sample, usually 1–2 μL, is placed directly on the wire. The solvent is evaporated, thereby depositing the residue on the wire. Solid samples can be applied directly, or they can first be dissolved in a solvent and then applied to the wire. Once inside the source, the sample wire can be heated to volatilize the sample. Both electron ionization (EI) and chemical ionization (CI) can be used to ionize samples that have been introduced by either of these probes.

Gas Chromatography

The most common method of sample introduction for MS is to pass the sample through a GC instrument. GC has been used to analyze compounds for many years, and several different detector methods besides MS have been used, with flame ionization, nitrogen–phosphorus detection, and electron capture being three of the most common.

Although each of these GC detector methods has its advantages, MS offers a significant advantage over other detectors. The ability of GC to separate compounds chromatographically is a tremendous advantage. Ideally, the GC instrument provides a pure compound to the mass spectrometer, facilitating spectral analysis. Because the mass spectrometer operates at low pressure, the amount of carrier gas introduced into the mass spectrometer must be limited so that the pumping system can keep up with the volume of incoming gas. Various types of GC interfaces can be used, depending to some extent on the pumping capacity of the system. Large-diameter packed columns have far too large a gas volume to allow all of the effluent to enter the source of most MS systems. Therefore, a number of devices have been designed to divert the bulk of the carrier gas away from the MS instrument, allowing only a small portion of the gas—along with the analyte(s)—to enter the mass spectrometer. Some large-bore capillary columns also carry too large a gas volume for some of the benchtop MS systems to handle because of their relatively low pumping capacities. For such MS systems, "macro-bore" columns require some means of separating the carrier gas from the analyte. Capillary columns that have flow rates consistent with the pumping capacity of the mass spectrometer (usually 1–2 mL/min) can be inserted directly into the source. This method, commonly called capillary direct, provides the most efficient delivery of analyte to the mass spectrometer without overwhelming the pumping system.

Liquid Chromatography

Interfacing an LC instrument with a mass spectrometer is not a new technique, but recent advances in technology have made this approach a much more common method of analysis. Many different LC procedures are available, and all allow the separation of analytes, even in very complex matrices. In many ways, LC offers advantages over GC. Typically, extraction procedures can be less extensive than for GC, derivatization is not required (thus saving time and expense), and many compounds that are not stable at high temperature fare much better with LC. The main hurdle that had been associated with coupling LC with MS was the removal of the large volumes of solvent used in LC.

Recent developments in LC interfaces have made LC a very viable technique for introducing samples for MS analysis. Several different techniques (e.g., atmospheric pressure CI [APCI], atmospheric pressure photoionization [APPI], and electrospray ionization [ESI]) are available for getting the LC effluent into the mass spectrometer. These methods, along with the ability to ionize samples at atmospheric pressure, have made LC available for use with many different analytes and with far fewer difficulties than were seen with previous methods.

IONIZATION

Several different ionization techniques are commonly used in MS. The most common techniques are EI and CI. EI produces positive ions by causing the loss of an electron, leaving a net positive charge on the molecule or its fragment. CI can lead to the production of either positive or negative ions.

These techniques are somewhat limited by the volatility of the compounds and are typically used for compounds with a mass of approximately 1000 Da or less. For larger compounds, the energy used in the process can lead to decomposition of the molecules. An approach that helps to avoid this problem with these nonvolatile compounds often involves the use of desorption-ionization techniques, including field, chemical ionization, plasma, laser, secondary-ion MS, fast atom bombardment, and laser desorption. Since this discussion is directed toward compounds of relatively small molecular weight, these desorption techniques are not discussed in detail in this chapter. Larger compounds can also be analyzed with LC/MS techniques involving multiply charged species.

Electron Ionization

EI is the most common form of ionization used in MS. This method involves a source of electrons, typically a filament, to which an electric potential is applied, causing electrons to leave the surface of the filament and move to ground. The energy potential applied to the filament is typically fixed at 70 eV. The molecules in the ion source are exposed to the beam of electrons, and the interaction between these high-energy electrons and the molecule imparts sufficient energy such that the molecule loses an electron, leaving a positively charged molecular ion (M+). Although EI is a high-energy process, the efficiency of ionization is low, with typically only one of 1000 molecules being ionized. The high energy of these electrons (70 eV) commonly destabilizes the molecule, causing rearrangement and bond breaking, ultimately resulting in fragmentation of the molecule. In some cases, virtually none of the intact molecular ion remains after exposure to this high-energy process. Some instruments allow

the user to adjust the voltage, but many, including most bench-top instruments, do not. Lowering the voltage generally leads to less ionization and less fragmentation; such information can be useful in elucidating the chemical structure of a molecule.

The ionized fragments produced by EI are characteristic of a molecule. Therefore, the ions formed and their relative proportions are reproducible, and this information can be used for qualitative identification of the compound, thus making MS a powerful analytical tool for the identification of unknown compounds. Libraries of mass spectra are commonly used in the identification of unknown compounds through comparison of spectrum of the unknown compound with spectra of known compounds. Various algorithms are used to compare ions and their relative intensities to assist in compound identification. The net result of such analyses is the identification of spectra for known compounds that are similar to the spectrum of the analyte of interest. Such comparisons are possible because the relatively high energy of the EI process produces consistent behavior by molecules exposed to the same energy. Because most instruments use the same 70-eV potential, a molecule's behavior is remarkably similar from day to day and from instrument to instrument, thus facilitating comparisons with reference spectra generated on other instruments.

Chemical Ionization

The CI process depends on electrons as the primary source of ions, but the electrons ionize a reagent gas rather than directly ionizing the analyte molecules. The reagent gas enters the ion source and is ionized by high-energy electrons. When analyte molecules are exposed to the ionized reagent gas, the analytes themselves are ionized and give rise to molecular ions. The CI source differs slightly from the EI source in that it is more "gas tight," which allows a reagent gas to be introduced into the source and to be at a sufficiently high concentration to permit reagent ion–analyte molecule reactions to occur. Due to the added reagent gas, the vacuum in the CI source is lower than typically seen in EI, thus increasing the probability that an analyte molecule will collide with a reagent gas ion. The initial ionization of the reagent gas with electrons is a high-energy process, but the ionization of analyte molecules by the reagent gas is far less energetic. Consequently, this type of ionization causes less fragmentation of the analyte molecule than EI. Ionization is most commonly due to the transfer of a proton from the ionized reagent gas to the analyte molecule.

Several different reagent gases have been used for CI (e.g., methane, ammonia, isobutane). The reaction with methane is shown below. The first reaction is the EI of the methane molecule:

$$CH_4 + e^- \rightarrow CH_4^{+\bullet} + 2e^-$$

The electrons resulting from this process are of low energy and can play a significant role in resonance electron-capture negative-ion CI, which is discussed later. The ion formed in this process may itself fragment in several ways, one of which is:

$$CH_4^{+\bullet} \rightarrow CH_3^+ + H^\bullet$$

There will also be a significant number of collisions between the ions and other neutral methane molecules, which will yield the following:

$$CH_4^{+\bullet} + CH_4 \rightarrow CH_5^+ + CH_3^\bullet$$

$$CH_3^+ + CH_4 \rightarrow C_2H_5^+ + H_2$$

When these ions interact with the analyte molecule (M), several reactions are possible. The most common reaction for most molecules, except saturated hydrocarbons, is for the molecule to acquire a proton:

$$M + CH_5^+ \rightarrow CH_4 + M+H^+$$

Ion–molecule reactions can also lead to the formation of adduct ions, such as the following:

$$M + CH_3^+ \rightarrow M+CH_3^+$$

$$M + C_2H_5+ \rightarrow M+C_2H_5^+$$

These ions ($M+H^+$, $M+CH_3^+$, $M+C_2H_5^+$) are referred to as molecular species or pseudomolecular ions. The actual molecular weight of the molecule is determined by subtracting the mass of the added proton or adduct ions, as the case may be.

Ammonia is another commonly used ionization gas that is ionized by an electron:

$$NH_3 + e^- \rightarrow NH_3^{+\bullet} + 2e^-$$

The radical ion created by this EI process reacts with another ammonia molecule in the following manner:

$$NH_3^{+\bullet} + NH_3 \rightarrow NH_4^+ + NH_2^\bullet$$

The ionization by this reagent gas depends on the kind of molecule with which it interacts. An amine-containing molecule (RNH_2) will generally undergo the following reaction:

$$NH_4^+ + RNH_2 \rightarrow RNH_3^+ + NH_3$$

Polar molecules without a strong basic group will generally form adduct ions. Importantly, molecules that do not have these characteristics are not readily ionized, thus making ammonia CI a selective ionization technique that eliminates much of the potential interference by other molecules.

The most commonly used form of CI is positive-ion CI. The reagent gas forms ions that, in turn, transfer a charge to analyte ions. This charge transfer is most commonly due to proton transfer, which yields a molecular ion with an additional proton attached, $[M + H]^+$, as described above. Commonly used reagent gases include methane, isobutane, and ammonia. Reagent gases are also sometimes combined to give a mixture that optimizes the ionization of the analyte molecules of interest. The ability of the reagent gas to transfer a proton to the molecules depends on the proton affinity of the molecules and the acidic properties of the reagent gas.

Negative-ion CI (NICI or NCI) is a valuable tool in the analysis of some analytes. The process involves the generation of negative ions by resonance electron capture, in which the analyte molecule captures a relatively low-energy electron. This process typically yields intact molecular anions that are readily detected. Because the energy is low, molecules with high electron affinity are the best candidates for this type of ionization. Almost all neutral molecules can yield positive ions, but negative-ion formation generally works with molecules containing a halogen, a nitro, an acidic, or similar electronegative group. Many biological molecules do not contain such groups and therefore do not become ionized by this method. This selectivity typically leads to a much cleaner baseline and cleaner chromatograms, which contribute to the sensitivity of this technique, often 100–1000 times as sensitive as positive-ion CI. Derivatization of molecules with highly electronegative reagents, such as trifluoroacetic, pentafluoropropionic, and heptafluorobutyryl groups, yields a derivatized molecule with a high electron affinity, thus facilitating the capture of an electron.

Atmospheric Pressure Ionization

The coupling of LC to a mass spectrometer requires the transition of analytes from a liquid medium at atmospheric pressure to the gaseous state under high vacuum in a mass spectrometer. To make this transition possible, the analytes of interest must be ionized before they enter the mass spectrometer. This process is commonly referred to as *atmospheric pressure ionization* (API). Specially designed interfaces connecting the LC instrument and the mass spectrometer are required to successfully facilitate the transition.

LC/MS interfaces have two main functions: (1) to remove and dispose of the liquid mobile phase and (2) to create and/or facilitate the transfer of ions into the mass spectrometer. Removal of the liquid mobile phase is a process called *desolvation*. Desolvation of the liquid mobile phase is accomplished with heaters, gas nebulizers, and the strategic positioning of the nebulized LC spray with respect to the capillary. Instrument manufacturers have moved away from aligning the spray directly in front of the capillary, which serves as the entrance into

the high-vacuum region. Instead, most modern interface designs are orthogonal or perpendicular to the capillary. This positioning of the spray reduces the amount of solvent and other unwanted material from entering the mass spectrometer. By allowing only ions to enter the capillary, the background signal is reduced, thereby increasing the signal-to-noise ratio and the overall sensitivity.

Ionization is the second main function of an LC/MS interface and can be accomplished in a number of ways, depending on the chemical properties of the analyte(s). Some analytes can be ionized in solution with acid/base chemistry via adjustments in the solvent pH. Two of the most common methods are ESI and thermospray (TSP). For example, alkaline drugs containing primary or secondary amines will accept a hydrogen molecule and become positively charged in acidic solutions. A second method of ionization is the transfer of a charge from a charged gas molecule to an analyte, namely APCI. A third method is APPI, which uses a UV lamp source to emit high-energy photons that can directly ionize vaporized analytes. Matrix-assisted laser desorption ionization (MALDI) is an ionization technique that uses a laser to vaporize and ionize analytes within the matrices themselves. Most MALDI applications are retained for analyses of larger macromolecules, such as proteins and polypeptides. All of these ionization techniques have been used in current LC/MS and LC-MS/MS analyses. Their applicability depends on the polarities and molecular weights of the compounds being analyzed. Fig. 2 illustrates a general guideline to the applicability of the different ionization techniques used in forensic toxicology.

Certain considerations are required when developing methods that use an API technique. Ion suppression is a major concern, and all LC/MS and LC-MS/MS ionization techniques are susceptible. Ion suppression is a matrix effect that can coincide with other factors (some of which are not really understood) to muffle the signal from the analyte. When excessive ions are present in the sample, the signal from the analyte of interest can

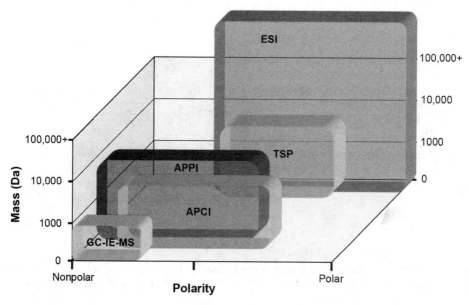

Fig. 2. The relative applications of the atmospheric pressure ionization techniques used in liquid chromatography/mass spectrometry compared with gas chromatography–electron ionization/mass spectrometry (GC-EI/MS). APCI = atmospheric pressure chemical ionization; APPI = atmospheric pressure photoionization; TSP = thermospray; ESI = electrospray ionization. *Source:* Courtesy of Agilent Technologies, Inc.

be suppressed or buried in the background noise. These effects can vary greatly between samples and between different matrices, such as blood and urine. The interferences can come from the matrices, the extraction procedure, solvents, and even the glassware or plastic tubes used in the extraction procedure. Other factors relating to the chemical properties of the analytes, such as mass, alkalinity, and concentration, can also contribute to ion suppression. The degree of suppression can negatively affect the limit of detection, the precision, and the accuracy of quantitative results. All API methods should be examined for the presence and influence of ion suppression, and appropriate steps should be taken, if needed, to minimize their effects.

Electrospray Ionization

ESI is the most commonly used API technique and is regularly used in forensic toxicology. An electrospray interface has three main components: the nebulizer, the desolvation assembly, and the mesh electrode

or repeller. Modern electrospray interfaces have pneumatically assisted nebulization, which enables larger solvent volumes and higher flow rates. Heated, highly pressurized nitrogen gas nebulizes the mobile phase as it enters the ESI interface and creates an aerosol of charged droplets. As the solvents evaporate and shrink, ions within the droplets become closer and closer to one another until the electrostatic repulsion is too great for the surface tension. At this breaking point, referred to as the Rayleigh limit, the droplet explodes into smaller droplets (Coulombic explosion). The process of desolvation (Fig. 3) continues until the solvent is evaporated and only free ions remain. Ions are drawn into the capillary via a difference in electrostatic potential between the end of the capillary and the mesh electrode. This electrode is positioned across from the capillary orifice on the opposite side of the spray. Fig. 4 is an illustration of an ESI interface.

Depending on the pK_a of the compound and the pH of the mobile phase, ions formed in solution can be either positively or negatively charged. Most modern ESI interfaces

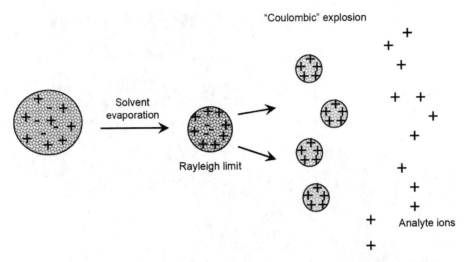

Fig. 3. The desolvation process for electrospray ionization (ESI) and thermospray (TSP) interfaces. Nebulized droplets containing ions are evaporated with heated gas (N_2) until only the free ions remain.

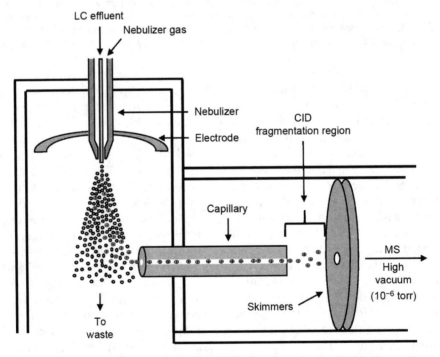

Fig. 4. Example of an electrospray ionization (ESI) interface for a liquid chromatography/mass spectrometry (LC/MS) system. CID = collision-induced dissociation.

can be programmed to analyze both positive and negative ions, either separately or simultaneously. ESI is the "softest" API technique available and often produces only the [M + 1] ion of the molecule of interest. ESI is used for very polar to slightly nonpolar compounds that can be charged in solution. For all analytes, the optimal operational parameters for fragmentation are determined by a sequential series of injections of a standard solution. This process of optimization is referred to as a flow injection analysis (FIA). During an

FIA study, such parameters as the fragmentor voltage, drying gas temperature and flow, and nebulization pressure are varied in sequential injection. Ion abundance and intensity usually determine the optimal settings.

ESI is a valuable technique in forensic toxicology because most drugs are plant alkaloids. Alkaline compounds are ideal for ESI because they can be easily charged in solution and typically have some polar properties. Typical ESI techniques are capable of analyzing a singly charged ion up to 3000 Da in size; however, analyses of large molecules such as proteins and enzymes make up the majority of ESI applications. The use of a high electrostatic potential in the ESI interface is thought to help charge the many functional groups found on large proteins and enzymes. Therefore, the use of ESI helps accomplish the goal of creating multiply charged ions. This capability greatly extends the dynamic mass range of an MS detector that differentiates molecules on the basis of the m/z ratio and enables LC-ESI/MS techniques to analyze molecules with masses greater than 100 kDa. Deconvolution software is used to decipher the cluster of peaks produced by multiple charges and to determine the molecular weight and structural identity of an analyte.

Some disadvantages are associated with ESI techniques. ESI operates most efficiently when flow rates are less than 1.0 mL/min, and loss of sensitivity occurs when this flow rate is exceeded. ESI does not work well for nonpolar analytes, thereby limiting the types of analytes that can be analyzed successfully. Additionally, the formation of such adducts as [M + Na] or [M + NH$_4$] is common with ESI and can contribute to ion-suppression effects. The formation of adducts is minimized by the use of highly pure mobile phases (HPLC grade) and low-molarity buffer solutions (<50 mmol/L).

Thermospray

TSP is an API technique very similar to ESI. Ions are created in solution with buffers that permit the analysis of polar, thermally labile, and nonvolatile analytes. The pressurized mobile phase is passed through a heated tube that vaporizes the solution. The desolvation process for the mobile phase and the subsequent production of free ions are similar to the process described for ESI. With the addition of a repeller electrode, ions are transferred into the mass spectrometer for analysis. Traditional designs for TSP differ from those for ESI only in that ESI uses a high electrostatic potential in the interface to facilitate the production and transfer of free ions. This high electrostatic potential gives ESI a significant advantage in its ability to produce multiply charged species, thus extending its mass range. Unlike ESI, for which the more efficient flow rates are <1.0 mL/min, TSP interfaces can sustain flow rates of up to 2.0 mL/min. TSP is a soft ionization technique and produces primarily pseudomolecular adduct ions, such as [M + NH$_4$]$^+$ or [M + Na]$^+$, depending on the buffer and salts used in the mobile phase. Although still used in forensic toxicology, TSP techniques have mainly been sidelined by the advances in other API techniques, such as ESI and APCI.

Atmospheric Pressure CI

An ionization method complementary to ESI is APCI. APCI is used for analyzing low- to medium-polarity molecules that are easily vaporized. Unlike ESI, for which compounds can have multiple charges, APCI usually yields a singly charged ion. Consequently, the mass range for APCI is limited by the mass spectrometer's mass range, which is typically <3000 Da.

APCI sample introduction is similar to that of ESI. An APCI interface has four basic components: the nebulizer, the vaporization tube, the corona needle, and the desolvation module. Fig. 5 illustrates an APCI interface for LC/MS system. The liquid mobile phase enters the nebulizer and flows through the needle assembly. The nebulizer blows high-pressure nitrogen (approximately 60 psi) around the needle and blasts the mobile

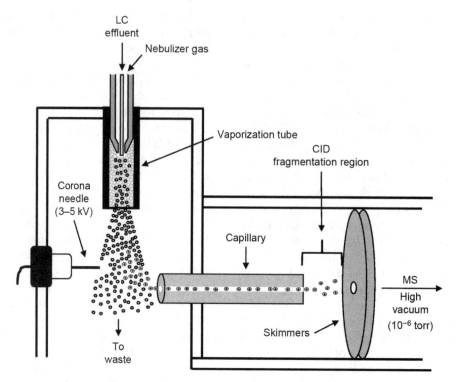

Fig. 5. Example of an atmospheric pressure chemical ionization (APCI) interface for a liquid chromatography/mass spectrometry (LC/MS) system. CID = collision-induced dissociation.

phase into a fine aerosol. The nebulizing gas then carries the aerosol containing the mobile phase and analytes through the heated (200–400 °C) vaporization tube. The temperature in this region is optimized to minimize any thermal decomposition and to maximize solvent vaporization. The vaporized mobile phase and the analytes are then ionized by a discharge from the corona needle, which is positioned at the exit of the vaporization tube. The corona needle creates a field of electrons that protonates the gas-phase solvent as it exits the tube. The charge is then transferred to the analytes in a process similar to methane positive-ion CI in GC/MS. The corona needle can produce positively or negatively charged ions, depending on the application and the analyte. The nebulizer pressure, the vaporization temperature, and the corona current are analyte dependent and are optimized with an FIA.

APCI is best used for analytes of intermediate polarity and molecular weight that do not contain acidic or basic sites. This consideration is especially true for compounds that are sensitive to acid/base solution chemistry and exhibit a poor ESI response. Samples that contain such compounds as ketones, esters, aldehydes, alcohols, and some hydrocarbons can be analyzed with APCI. APCI tolerates higher flow rates without sacrificing sensitivity and accommodates a wider range of solvents than ESI.

Applications for APCI are more limited than for ESI, and some considerations are necessary before APCI can be developed. Compounds must be moderately volatile so that they can be vaporized and ionized. A compound must have a molecular mass <3000 Da, because APCI will produce only a singly charged ion. These two limitations rule out larger, more polar molecules, such as peptides and proteins. APCI is also less effective for analyzing thermally labile analytes. The high temperature in the vaporization tube will degrade thermally sensitive molecules such as steroids. The vast majority of compounds encountered in a forensic toxicology laboratory, including most pharmaceuticals and abused drugs, can be analyzed with APCI or ESI techniques.

Atmospheric Pressure Photoionization

APPI is an interface that uses photons emitted by a light source to ionize analytes. Fig. 6 presents a schematic of an APPI interface. APPI uses a gas discharge lamp that emits UV photons at distinct energy levels that are specific to the type of gas used. Three gases frequently used in APPI are krypton (10.0 eV and 10.6 eV), argon (11.2 eV), and xenon (8.4 eV). Analytes will ionize if their ionization energies are lower than the energy emitted by the source lamp. Typically, nonpolar analytes will appear as a radical

molecular ion ($M+^{\bullet}$), and polar compounds will appear as a protonated pseudomolecular ion ($[M + 1]^+$). Depending on the composition of the mobile phase and the polarity of the analyte, the $[M+^{\bullet}]$ created can accept a hydrogen from the mobile phase (MP) to produce the $[M + 1]^+$ ion:

$$M + h\nu \rightarrow M^{+\bullet} + e^-$$
$$M^{+\bullet} + MPH \rightarrow [M + 1]^+ + MP^{\bullet}$$

APPI can operate in both positive- and negative-ion modes. In positive-ion mode, the mobile phase must contain a solvent, such as methanol, that can easily donate a hydrogen molecule. In general, one of the most popular choices for the mobile phase is a combination of acetonitrile and water. This combination is not suitable for APPI, however, because there is no hydrogen that can be freely donated. Water in its gaseous state

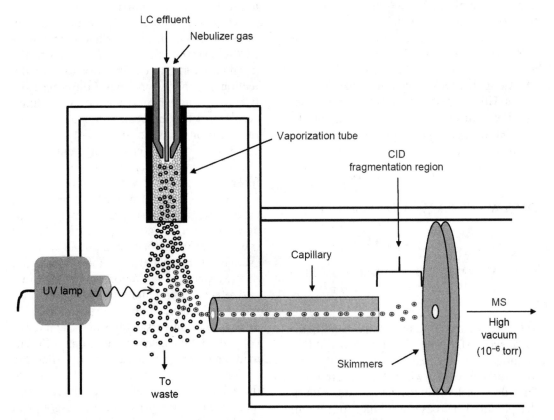

Fig. 6. Example of an atmospheric pressure photoionization (APPI) interface for a liquid chromatography/mass spectrometry (LC/MS) system. CID = collision-induced dissociation.

acts as a strong base and has a strong affinity for hydrogen. The compound must have a stronger affinity for the proton than for the solvent gas, or the ionization efficiency will be decreased severely. In negative-ion mode, the reagent gas must have a strong affinity for protons or be able to capture electrons.

APPI is not limited by acid/base chemistry or by the compound's volatility. APPI can be used to analyze nonpolar to moderately polar compounds that may not be amenable to analysis with either ESI or APCI. The energy used for ionization is relatively low but can generate doubly charged ions, thereby increasing the mass range of the mass spectrometer to slightly better than APCI but not as high as ESI.

Compounds can be ionized directly, or a dopant can be used to transfer the charge indirectly. Direct ionization occurs if the compound being analyzed has an ionization energy lower than that of the photon. Dopants are chemical additives used to increase the overall ionization efficiency of APPI for compounds that are difficult to ionize or that lose their ionization easily. Dopants (D) are added in the nebulizer to the mobile phase. Most dopants have very low ionization energies. This property makes them more easily photoionized and thereby more able to transfer their charge to the compounds of interest:

$$M + h\nu \rightarrow M^{+\bullet} + e^-$$ Direct APPI

$$D^{+\bullet} + M \rightarrow [M + H]^+ + D$$ Dopant APPI (Hydrogen addition)

$$D^{+\bullet} + M \rightarrow M^{+\bullet} + D$$ Dopant APPI (Electron transfer)

Toluene, acetone, and anisole have all been used successfully as dopants. Most APPI methods show increases in sensitivity and ionization efficiency when dopants are used. One drawback with the use of dopants is the potential increase in adduct formation, which can complicate the interpretation of mass spectra.

Collision-Induced Dissociation

Collision-induced dissociation (CID) is a fragmentation technique used in LC/MS, MS/MS, or ion-trap MS applications. CID occurs when ionized compounds accelerated in a fixed area by an electrical charge collide with neutral gas molecules (molecular nitrogen, argon, or helium) and cause fragmentation. API techniques most often produce even numbers of electron ions. CID is analyte dependent, and the degree of fragmentation is dependent on experimental parameters. In CID, fragmentation is much less energetic than with EI, and sometimes there is no fragmentation at all. Fig. 7 displays cocaine fragmentation patterns produced with three different ionization techniques. Note that the highly energetic EI technique produces greater fragmentation, whereas positive-ion CI and ESI have less energy and produce mostly the pseudomolecular ion with minimal fragmentation.

Two places where CID can occur are in the source and in the mass analyzer. For an LC/MS system, in-source *CID* refers to the fragmentation that occurs prior to mass detection. Applying a potential difference between the capillary endcap and the skimmer accelerates the molecules over a short distance, causing them to collide with the drying gas. These collisions cause fragmentation of the compounds. Increasing the potential difference (fragmentor voltage) increases the rate of collisions and produces differing degrees of fragmentation. The fragmentor voltages can be optimized to produce a desired fragmentation for each compound of interest. The distance between the endcap and the skimmer varies among manufacturers and affects the fragmentation of a particular molecule at a fixed voltage. Fragmentor voltages are not universal; the same fragmentor voltage in two instruments from different manufacturers can cause different degrees of fragmentation. In addition, the mass of the collision gas also affects the overall fragmentation. A heavy gas, such as argon, will accelerate faster and impact the molecules with more energy, causing a greater degree

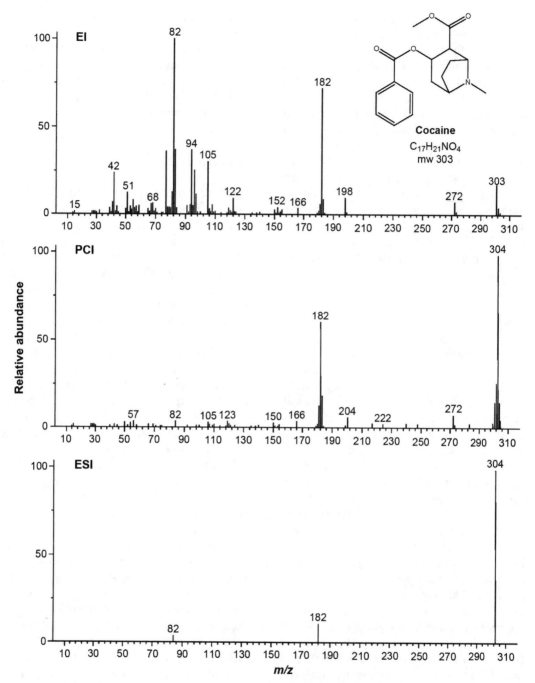

Fig. 7. Illustrated are the distinctly unique full-scan spectra of cocaine produced with three different ionization techniques: electron ionization (EI), positive-ion chemical ionization (PCI), and electrospray ionization (ESI).

of fragmentation. In-source CID can take place in the octapole region by increasing the voltage applied, thereby increasing the number of collisions.

In tandem quadrupole MS, CID occurs in the second mass analyzer (collision cell) via increasing the pressure and accelerating the ions to collide with the gas molecules.

Similarly, CID can occur inside an ion trap. Energy applied to the trap excites the ions and causes them to collide with helium gas, producing fragmentation. Helium also serves to cool and focus the ions inside the center of the trap by forming a buffer between the orbiting ions and the inside walls of the trap. Mass analyzer CID imparts greater specificity and has a higher efficiency of collision compared with in-source CID. The molecular ions are isolated prior to fragmentation, therefore eliminating the possibility of coeluting ion interferences that can occur during in-source CID. Therefore, mass analyzer CID is the preferred method for studying fragmentation patterns and identifying unknowns.

MASS ANALYZER

Magnetic Sector

Magnetic sector instruments are generally not used in the routine analytical, forensic, or clinical laboratory. They are most commonly found in the research arena. The recent requirement for high-resolution MS in sports testing may make these instruments more widely used in the future, but the discussion in this chapter is limited to a general description. Magnetic sector instruments separate ions by means of a magnetic and electrostatic analyzer. The ions are produced in a source and travel through the analyzers. Magnetic analyzers separate ions by the principle that when ions of different mass enter a magnetic field (perpendicular to the ion path), the smaller ions turn more quickly than the larger ones. Ions move through a slit that limits the mass that can exit the magnet. Sweeping the magnetic field from a high to a low field strength causes ions to pass through the slit from higher to lower mass. Electrostatic analyzers are made of two plates, each with a different charge. As ions enter the analyzer, they move along the curvature of the plates, depending on the energy of the ions. The ability to identify even very small differences in this manner allows ions of the same nominal mass to be separated. Magnetic and electrostatic analyzers can be combined in several different combinations. The most significant advantage of the sector instruments is the increased mass resolution. Resolution upwards of 100,000 Da can be achieved with these instruments.

Quadrupole

Quadrupole mass spectrometers are the most common mass analyzers in use today (Fig. 8). Classically, the quadrupole is a set of four precisely machined rods. Use of a combination of radio frequency and direct current voltages on the two sets of diagonally opposed rods allows only ions of a single m/z value to pass through the analyzer. Ions that enter the analyzer move toward the detector. All but those of the specific mass selected are deflected into the rods. The rods can be scanned, usually from lower to higher mass, allowing ions of successively higher mass to pass through the filter. In actual practice, the term quadrupole is often used to describe analyzers that have four, six, or eight rods, not just those with four.

The mass spectrum produced is referred to as a full-scan spectrum and is used when performing automated searches of mass spectral libraries. Specific masses can also be selected so that only the specified m/z values are detected. This process, commonly called selected ion monitoring (SIM), is used for qualitative and quantitative analysis of targeted analytes. Selecting a limited number of specific masses permits longer dwell times (time spent monitoring a single ion) for detecting these ions, thus increasing the sensitivity. SIM analysis provides less spectral data than a full-scan analysis but is far more sensitive. SIM analysis has better sensitivity because more time is spent monitoring fewer ions. Full-scan analysis monitors an entire range of ions over the same period of time. In SIM analysis, the loss of other m/z data is less important than determining the presence of a specific compound, often referred to as target compound analysis. With the

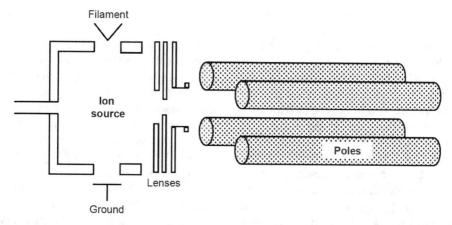

Fig. 8. Example of a quadrupole mass spectrometer. Note that various systems actually use more rods (octapole) or a single shaped device that simulates four rods (e.g., Agilent Technologies 5973 mass spectrometers). Regardless of the configuration, the basic principles are the same.

increase in sensitivity, much lower amounts of analyte can often be identified and quantified. Typically, full-scan MS methods are used for screening analysis, and SIM methods are used in quantitative analysis.

Ion Trap

The ion trap is best considered as a unique form of a quadrupole mass analyzer. Rather than being arranged parallel to each other, the four rods form a three-dimensional sphere in which ions are "trapped" (Fig. 9). The trap consists of a central ring electrode and two endcap electrodes. Applying radio-frequency voltage to these electrodes causes ions to be trapped

in the three-dimensional space of the trap. Ions are then ejected from the system by changing the applied radio frequency, which causes the trapped ions to destabilize and exit the trap. This process is often referred to as "scan out" of the trap. Ions ejected from the trap enter the detector portion of the instrument. Increasing the radio-frequency voltage destabilizes ions of increasing m/z values until all masses within the desired range are ejected. The steps in mass analysis using an ion trap can be summarized as:

1. Ion storage
2. Ion isolation
3. Collision-activated dissociation (for MS/MS)
4. Ion scan out

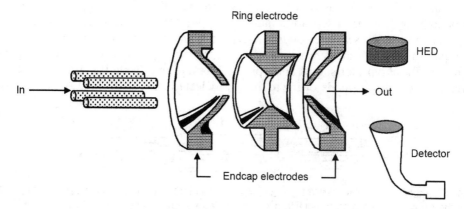

Fig. 9. Example of an ion-trap mass spectrometer. HED = high-energy dynode.

For multiple mass spectrometer (MSn) experiments, steps 2 and 3 are repeated.

The distances in the ion trap are short, which allows the use of a lower vacuum in the system. This is because the mean free path required is much shorter than in conventional quadrupole or sector instruments. Since the molecules are within a confined space, ion–molecule reactions are more likely than in a conventional quadrupole instrument. These ion–molecule reactions have the potential to generate atypical mass spectra. This potential problem can be minimized by sensing the number of ions in the trap and adjusting ionization times so that fewer molecules and ions are involved in a single scan, thus reducing the incidence of ion molecule reactions. Ion traps of older design ionized the molecules inside the trap itself. In this design, all effluent from the column entered the trap, leading to a high density of molecules and ultimately to a high probability of ion–molecule reactions. Newer designs generate the ions outside the trap and only ions enter the trap. This approach eliminates the large number of neutral molecules observed inside the trap when the ionization is accomplished within the trap.

MS/MS and MSn

In recent years, the power of MS analysis has been greatly augmented by multistage MS analysis. The method of multistage MS depends on the instrument design. MS/MS analysis can be thought of as occurring in space or in time. The process traditionally used in many instruments is based on linking several quadrupole mass analyzers together in sequence. These types of setups are typically referred to as triple quads, owing to the presence of three quadrupole analyzers in series (Fig. 10); however, today's instruments are referred to as tandem mass spectrometers because quadrupoles are not the only mass analyzers used in sequence. Typically, modern designs have a quadrupole as the first mass analyzer (Q1). The second mass analyzer region (Q2), commonly referred to as the collision cell, may contain a quadrupole, a hexapole, an octapole, or some other design. The third mass analyzer region (Q3) can contain a quadrupole or an ion trap. The instruments generate ions in the same manner as described earlier, but they usually use an ionization technique that only produces molecular ions. The most common form of MS/MS analysis that uses these instruments involves setting the Q1 region to allow only ions corresponding to the m/z of the ion of interest to pass. Once the ion has passed through the Q1 region, it enters the Q2 region where CID takes place. This is typically accomplished by putting a collision gas into this area, which generates frequent collisions between these gas molecules and the ion that has been selectively allowed to pass through Q1. The single ion passed through Q1 is referred to as the precursor ion (or, less commonly, the parent ion). The ions formed from the fragmentation of precursor ions are called product ions (or, less commonly, daughter ions). The Q3 analyzers can then be set to scan all ions produced or selectively allow only one or more of these product ions through to the detector. This method of MS/MS is referred to as MS/MS in space, whereas the other process uses time.

MS/MS in time is accomplished with ion-trap mass spectrometers. To perform MS/MS or MSn experiments in the ion trap, all ions are ejected from the trap except for the selected precursor ion. A voltage is then

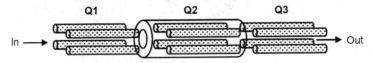

Fig. 10. Example of a tandem (MS/MS) mass spectrometer. Quadrupoles one (Q1) and three (Q3) are used in the traditional sense as mass filters. Quadrupole two (Q2) is actually a collision cell within which ions collide with collision-gas molecules, causing collisionally induced dissociation (fragmentation).

applied to the endcap electrode 180 degrees from the field generated by the radio frequency on the ring electrode. When the voltage applied to the endcap is resonant with the energy of a particular m/z value, ions with that value become destabilized and fragment. The amount of energy used can be varied to yield varying degrees of fragmentation. Following this step, the product ions are scanned out of the trap to the detector. All of these separations are accomplished within the confines of the trap; thus, it represents MS/MS in time.

The ability to trap ions can be a significant advantage in these experiments. When a single ion is trapped and then fragmented, the experiment can proceed to a third level by isolating a single product ion in the trap by scanning out all of the others and then fragmenting the remaining trapped ion. Such an analysis represents MS/MS/MS (MS^3). Theoretically, this operation can be performed repeatedly, yielding fragments that are generated as MS/MS/MS/MS (MS^4), MS/MS/MS/MS/MS (MS^5), and so on. Commercially available instruments permit MS to the 10th level; however, going beyond level three or four is unlikely—and unnecessary—in most applications.

MS/MS has tremendous advantages in the analysis of compounds. Since the first ion isolated can be the molecular ion, the likelihood of interference from other compounds that may also be in the source at the same time (i.e., chromatographically coeluting peaks) is all but eliminated. This design raises the confidence of identification and depends less on the ability of the chromatographic method to provide a single pure compound to the mass spectrometer. In addition, these methods enhance the ability to elucidate the structure of a molecule. Rather than seeing the total spectrum formed from the fragmentation of a molecule, individual ions can be isolated and their fragmentation evaluated. This ability to determine which ions come from which other fragments can be a powerful tool in the determination of chemical structure. In the case of MSn analysis, multiple levels of fragmentation can enhance the ability to elucidate chemical structure or, in the case of identification of a compound, can provide very strong analytical evidence for the presence of a compound. The elimination of other interfering ions makes the use of these techniques more sensitive and allows more rapid analysis of samples.

Other advantages of MS/MS analysis include monitoring of neutral loss for all compounds entering the mass spectrometer. This feature can be a very powerful tool in the search for metabolites of a compound or in the identification of structurally related compounds. Because this and other applications for MS/MS analysis are not commonly used in forensic toxicology, they are not discussed further.

Others

Many other mass analyzers and ionization techniques are used in the world of MS. Although not yet in wide use, one method that has potential for application in forensic toxicology is time of flight (TOF). TOF is commonly used for the analysis of large biomolecules, such as nucleic acids and proteins. As research advances to correlate genetic information and enzyme polymorphisms with their contributions to the toxicity of compounds, this analytical methodology will likely take its place in forensic toxicology. As the name implies, TOF is based on the principle that ions of different mass travel through space at different speeds when accelerated with the same energy. The time between when ions are generated and accelerated toward the detector and when they actually arrive is used to determine the mass of the ion. With one of several designs, it is possible to analyze compounds at high resolution and mass accuracy over a large mass range. TOF mass analyzers are capable of measuring a compound's mass to the fourth decimal place. This capability allows the analysis of coeluting compounds based solely on their exact elemental composition. Applications for the TOF mass analyzer in forensic toxicology have only recently been explored, but the use in the field remains limited.

APPLICATIONS

Qualitative Analysis

One of the major applications of MS is in qualitative analysis of samples to identify what compounds are present. Identification of compounds can be accomplished in several different ways, depending on the analyte. The simplest form of identification is detection of an analyte whose characteristics are well known. Identification can be as simple as monitoring several (usually three) selected ions and comparing the ratios of the detected ions with the ratios from a known reference standard, which is typically analyzed in the same analytical batch. These ions and their ratios, combined with retention-time data from a chromatographic system, are generally accepted as sufficient evidence to positively identify a compound.

Another common method of identification is comparing full-scan mass spectra with a mass spectral library. Several different search algorithms can be used to help identify compounds by comparison of the acquired spectrum with spectra in the library. For determining the presence or absence of a specific analyte, the monitoring of selected ions has several advantages; however, this method is less useful for identifying an unknown compound because the approach is based on a comparison with known characteristics, as described above. When examining a sample for what compounds might be present, the use of full-scan spectra produces more information. Coupling the spectrum with a library helps the analyst select likely candidates for the compound. Evaluation of data regarding the extraction and derivatization of the molecule can also help identify the compound. When searching for metabolites of a particular compound, the use of full-scan spectra, together with expected metabolically induced changes to the molecule (i.e., hydroxylation, demethylation), can lead to the identification of analytes of interest.

Quantitative Analysis

Another common application of MS is quantitative analysis. Quantitative applications are found across the range of available chromatographic and ionization techniques. The most common of these applications is found in GC/MS. For quantitative purposes, the internal-standard method is the most often used and is typically the most accurate of the available techniques. With the tremendous ability of the mass spectrometer to separate ions by mass, stable isotope–labeled internal standards are now in wide use for quantitative analysis. The most commonly used stable isotope is deuterium, and the incorporation of each deuterium adds one mass unit to the overall mass of the molecule or fragment observed in the mass spectrometer. A wide variety of compounds now have deuterium-labeled isotopomers available for use in quantitative analysis. Isotope-labeled compounds have some very significant advantages because the chemical and physical properties of the molecules remain almost identical to the naturally occurring compound. Therefore, the behavior of the analyte and its internal standard with respect to extraction, derivatization, and fragmentation are virtually identical. Use of stable isotope–labeled isotopomers is a special form of the internal-standard method of quantification, sometimes referred to as isotope dilution MS. When stable isotope–labeled isotopomers are not available or when the procedure is designed to analyze a large number of analytes, a number of internal standards that have chemical properties sufficiently close to those of the analytes of interest are used to yield accurate quantitative information.

Examples

There are numerous examples of analytical procedures that use MS. Analysis of amphetamines and related compounds is one interesting example. The amphetamines are abused drugs commonly found in the illicit-drug environment. Chemically, they are very simple, yet difficult to separate from many other small, naturally occurring molecules. They are easily extracted from biological fluids, but they are often coextracted with chemically related compounds. Amphetamine and methamphetamine can be separated from other compounds by means of several GC procedures. These molecules can be detected with most GC detectors, including the flame ionization detector, the nitrogen–phosphorus detector, and—when derivatized properly—an electron-capture detector. The amphetamines can also be readily derivatized, although derivatization is not required for GC analysis. If they are not derivatized, the peaks tend to tail slightly, but identification and quantification are readily accomplished. Because of the

large number of compounds often found in biological samples, the use of MS has some significant advantages for most compounds. The underivatized drugs, however, tend to yield only a single intense fragment ion at m/z 44 for amphetamine and m/z 58 for methamphetamine. Derivatization of these molecules not only improves their chromatographic behavior but also dramatically changes their mass spectra. Derivatized amphetamine and methamphetamine typically have three or more intense ions, thereby substantially increasing the confidence of identification. See Fig. 11 for an example of derivatized methamphetamine. An examination of the spectra of the derivatized compounds clearly demonstrates the advantage of using derivatization with MS. One of the significant powers of the mass spectrometer

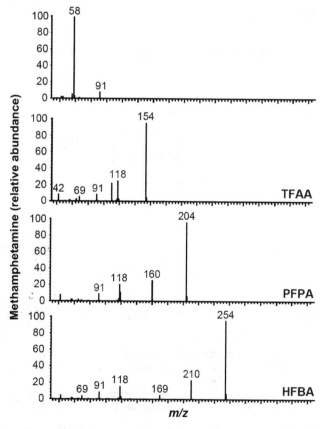

Fig. 11. Derivatized methamphetamine. This example shows mass spectra from underivatized methamphetamine and methamphetamine derivatized with trifluoroacetic anhydride (TFAA), pentafluoropropionic anhydride (PFPA), and heptafluorobutyric anhydride (HFBA). Note the increase in number and uniqueness of the ions for the derivatized compounds.

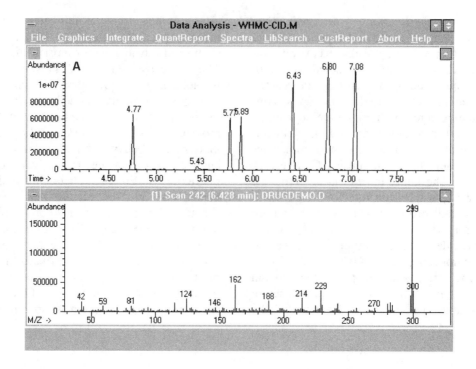

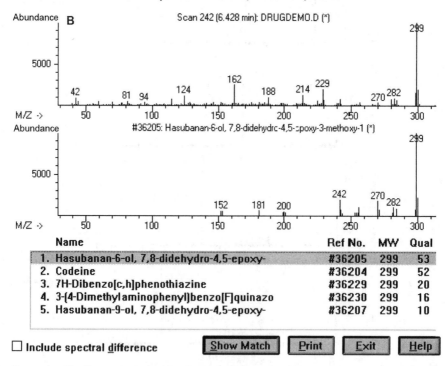

Fig. 12. Example of a library search. (A), Total-ion chromatogram and full-scan spectrum from single peak. (B), Library search results for spectrum selected at apex of chromatographic peak. (C), Library search results for spectrum selected later in chromatographic peak. First result in the list of candidate molecules is correct for C but not for B.

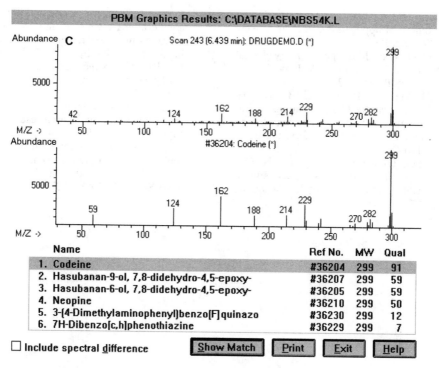

PBM Graphics Results: C:\DATABASE\NBS54K.L

Name	Ref No.	MW	Qual
1. Codeine	#36204	299	91
2. Hasubanan-9-ol, 7,8-didehydro-4,5-epoxy-	#36207	299	59
3. Hasubanan-6-ol, 7,8-didehydro-4,5-epoxy-	#36205	299	59
4. Neopine	#36210	299	50
5. 3-[4-Dimethylaminophenyl]benzo[F]quinazo	#36230	299	12
6. 7H-Dibenzo[c,h]phenothiazine	#36229	299	7

☐ Include spectral difference   [Show Match]   [Print]   [Exit]   [Help]

Fig. 12. (*Continued*)

is to determine the ions formed from the analyte of interest. Underivatized amphetamine and methamphetamine show only a single prominent ion. Although limited information, it is still more than is provided by other GC detectors, such as flame ionization. Nevertheless, it is not possible to monitor multiple ions and their relative proportions to provide a strong confirmation of the presence of the analyte. Use of the derivatized molecules permits monitoring of fragments of higher masses (generally considered more characteristic and less prone to interference) and monitoring of several ions that provide consistent ratios that can unequivocally confirm the presence of the compounds.

Full-scan analysis of a sample provides a simple demonstration of the power to identify an unknown compound. A peak is identified, and the spectrum is compared with a mass spectral library. As shown in Fig. 12, the selection of the spectrum can have a significant influence on the result of the library search. A peak with a retention time of 6.43 minutes is examined with a spectrum at 6.428

minutes (Fig. 12A), and a library search produced a result on that spectrum (Fig. 12B). A spectrum taken later in the same peak at 6.439 minutes suggests that the spectrum belongs to a different compound (Fig. 12C). The actual compound was codeine, not the first choice on the library search result for the peak's retention time. The message in this simple example is that full-scan mass spectral analysis is a tremendously powerful analytical tool, but competent professional judgment is needed in interpreting the analytical results.

SUGGESTED READING

1. Brittain R, Fiegel C. Chemical ionization and MS-MS technologies for benchtop ion trap GC-MS systems. Am Lab 1994;26:44–8.
2. Cole RB, ed. Electrospray ionization mass spectrometry fundamentals, instrumentation and applications. New York: J Wiley, 1997.
3. De Hoffman E, Charette J, Stroobant V. Mass spectrometry principles and applications. New York: J Wiley, 1996.

4. Desiderio DM, ed. Mass spectrometry clinical and biomedical applications. Volume 2. New York: Plenum, 1992.

5. Desiderio DM, ed. Mass spectrometry clinical and biomedical applications. Volume 1. New York: Plenum Press, 1992.

6. Hoja H, Marquet P, Verneuil B, Lotfi H, Penicaut B, Lachatre G. Applications of liquid chromatography-mass spectrometry in analytical toxicology: a review. J Anal Toxicol 1997;21:116–26.

7. Kitson FG, Larsen BS, McEwen CN. Gas chromatography and mass spectrometry: a practical guide. New York: Academic Press, 1996.

8. Koppel C, Tenczer J. Scope and limitations of a general unknown screening by gas chromatography-mass spectrometry in acute poisoning. J Am Soc Mass Spectrom 1995;6:995–1003.

9. Liu RH, Goldberger BA, eds. Handbook of workplace drug testing. Washington, DC: AACC Press, 1995.

10. Sparkman OD. Evaluating electron ionization mass spectral library search results. J Am Soc Mass Spectrom 1996;7:313–8.

11. Thomson BA. Atmospheric pressure ionization and liquid chromatography/mass spectrometry—together at last. J Am Soc Mass Spectrom 1998;9:187–93.

CHAPTER 12

Method Validation

Justin M. Holler and Shawn P. Vorce

Method validation in forensic toxicology is critical to ensuring quality results. The complexity of method validation in the field is certainly less stringent than in the pharmaceutical industry but no less important. With increased media attention on the forensic disciplines, government entities have identified the need for standards in forensic testing. The Scientific Working Group for Forensic Toxicology, created by the Forensic Toxicology Council, has been tasked to develop guidelines for forensic toxicology testing. Previously, the National Laboratory Certification Program in the Department of Health and Human Services had drafted requirements for forensic toxicology testing performed under its jurisdiction. In the legal arena, method validation has become important to the overall credibility of results. The questions include general scientific acceptability, method precision and accuracy, and method reliability.

The challenge for most forensic toxicology laboratories is deciding which steps are needed to validate their methods and answer these questions. This becomes more critical as new technologies and methodologies are being implemented in laboratories, including liquid chromatography-tandem mass spectrometry (LC-MS/MS) and direct injection analysis. The emergence of designer drugs also solidifies the importance of validating analytical procedures. Many of the drugs being detected and reported today have limited scientific literature associated with them; this in turn limits the peer-review process that accompanies published work.

The principle behind method validation is to demonstrate that the performance of the assay is scientifically acceptable within the parameters of its use. A method needs to work for the most pristine blood and tissue specimens, as well as clotted blood specimens or decomposed tissues; it also needs to work for urine specimens of all pH ranges. All testing aspects of the laboratory need to be validated, including initial and confirmatory testing procedures. The level of validation for initial testing procedures such as immunoassay detection is less than for confirmation procedures involving drug extraction from a matrix followed by instrument evaluation. The more complex the testing procedure, the more validation may be required to show the performance is scientifically acceptable.

Method validation responsibility is part of the quality assurance (QA)/quality control (QC) programs in forensic laboratories. The two entities of QA and QC have historically been associated together; however, most laboratories today separate them into two areas. QA is responsible for ensuring that a laboratory follows proper forensic procedures and accurately reports results. QA oversees all aspects of the laboratory, from the receipt of specimens to reporting results and litigation support. Proper method validation is essential to a QA program and is a vital part of reporting legally defensible results. Chain-of-custody documentation is often the first line of attack in litigation cases, but is often closely followed by a challenge to the documentation for proper validation of methods used to produce results.

The following information provides an overview of each validation step and explains what is involved in those processes.

TERMS AND DEFINITIONS

An **analyte** is a chemical compound that is being measured or analyzed. The analyte is extracted from a **biological matrix** that is the specimen fluid or tissue such as blood, serum, urine, or liver. To accurately quantitate the drug an **analytical reference standard** of known purity and molecular composition, often accompanied by a certificate of analysis (CoA), is required. From the analytical reference standard a concentrated solution, the **analyte standard**, is prepared. An **internal standard**, commonly a structurally related compound or deuterated analog of the analyte being measured, is also needed for accurate quantitation.

In addition to the case specimen, it is required to analyze a **blank sample**, an aliquot of the biological matrix match that contains no target analytes or internal standards. It is also necessary to analyze **positive controls** (specimen containing analyte at a known concentration used to verify calibration) and **negative controls** (specimen containing no analyte, used to verify the absence of interference with the analyte). **Interferences** are substances present in a specimen or presented during the extraction that cause chromatography or quantitation problems with the target analyte.

From the analyte standard, a series of **calibrators** are prepared. The calibrator is a solution of known concentration prepared in the biological matrix that is used to establish the relationship between what is measured, the "response," and the analyte concentration. The **calibration curve** is a plot of response vs concentration generated by the analysis of multiple calibrators. It is often desired to have a linear relationship between response and calibrator concentration. The linear range should include the concentrations expected in the different matrices. The linear relationship can be evaluated by calculating the line of regression by the method of least squares. The measure of the linear relationship between two variables is called the **correlation coefficient (r)**. The coefficient ranges between ±1, where +1 indicates a perfect positive linear relation between the two variables and -1 indicates a perfect negative linear relationship. A correlation coefficient of zero indicates that a nonlinear relationship exists. The correlation coefficient is a useful indicator of the linearity within a certain concentration range and should be above 0.985 for an analytical method. In forensic toxicology a minimally acceptable **covariance (r^2)** is required depending on the analytical technique. Typically, (r^2) must be greater than 0.980 for GC and LC/MS quantitative assays.

Specific analyte concentrations within the calibration process must be defined during the validation process. The **limit of detection (LOD)** is the smallest amount of analyte measured in relative concentration that can be detected with reasonable certainty for a given analytical procedure. The LOD must be within ±2% retention time (t_R), the ion ratios within ±20%, but the quantitative value may be outside ±20% of the target concentration. The **limit of quantitation (LOQ)** is the lowest concentration of analyte in a sample that can be measured with a defined precision and accuracy for a particular method. The LOQ must be within ±2% retention time (t_R), the ion ratios within ±20%, and the quantitative value within ±20% of the target concentration. The **upper limit of linearity (ULOL)** is the highest concentration of analyte in a sample that can be measured and identified. The ULOL must be within ±2% retention time (t_R), the ion ratios within ±20%, and the quantitative value within ±20% of the target concentration.

The **accuracy** of a method is defined as the closeness of the measured quantitative results to the actual value. **Precision** is the measurement of agreement among test results when the method is applied repeatedly to multiple samplings of a homogeneous specimen.

Repeatability is defined in two forms: intra-assay and inter-assay. **Intra-assay repeatability** is the measurement of the amount of agreement among test results when the method is applied repeatedly to multiple samplings of a homogeneous sample within the same batch. **Inter-assay repeatability** is the measurement of the amount of agreement among test results when the method is applied repeatedly to multiple samplings of a homogeneous sample between separate batches. The acceptability of these requirements is based on the **coefficient of variance (CV)**, which is defined as the measure of precision calculated by dividing the standard deviation for a series of measurements by the average measurement. The CV is also known as the percent relative standard deviation (% RSD).

Other components of the analytical process must be performed before a method is properly validated. **Selectivity** is the objective measurement of an analytical method to distinguish the analyte of interest from interfering components that may be expected in the sample matrices. These components commonly include metabolites, endogenous substances, breakdown products, and impurities. **Specificity** is the ability of the assay to identify an analyte from those compounds that are structurally related. This includes compounds in the same drug class or metabolites of the analyte of interest. The **robustness**, the ability of an assay to perform without failure over a wide range of conditions, must be evaluated to ensure consistent results are achieved. The **stability** of an analyte prior to extraction is a critical component and is defined as the measure of an analyte's ability to remain unchanged under different storage conditions including matrix temperature and time. Another important factor to analyze is **carryover**, the measure of contamination from a previous specimen analysis to the following analysis. The amount of analyte recovered through extraction and analysis compared to the amount of the analyte measured unextracted is referred to as **recovery or extraction efficiency** of the assay. In addition to recovery for LC assays, ion suppression and enhancement must be measured. **Ion suppression** is a negative signal difference between the extracted blank matrix, the mobile phase, and the unextracted standard. **Ion enhancement** is the positive signal difference between the three variables. For LC analysis a **system suitability check**, a feature used to ensure the complete testing system (LC, reagents, column, source) is operating in a sufficient manner for the intended application, is necessary.

IMMUNOASSAY METHOD VALIDATION

Most forensic toxicology laboratories include immunoassays in their testing protocol. The most common types of immunoassay technologies are enzyme-linked immunosorbent assay (ELISA), cloned enzyme donor immunoassay (CEDIA), enzyme-multiplied immunoassay technique (EMIT), fluorescence polarization immunoassay (FPIA), and kinetic interaction of microparticles in solution (KIMS). The first immunoassay technique developed, radioimmunoassay (RIA), is rarely used in forensic laboratories. The majority of the assays sold are FDA approved and manufacturers have performed multiple parts of validation. However, laboratories should perform in-house validation of these assays as well. Any deviations from the manufacturer's guidelines, such as changes in matrix to be assayed, calibrator concentration, calibrator drug, or reagent volumes, must be validated prior to placement into service. If a laboratory purchases a new immunoassay analyzer, method validation for the analyzer and all applications to be performed on it is also required. Areas that need to be validated can include: accuracy, precision, linearity, specificity, repeatability, and stability.

Accuracy and precision should be validated for all immunoassays being used in the laboratory. The most critical concentration range for immunoassays is around the cutoff, as immunoassays are often employed to distinguish between positive and negative specimens. Other critical points to analyze are 0, 25, 50, 75, 100, 125, 150, and 200% of the cutoff concentration. It is recommended to analyze a minimum of three replicates at the aforementioned concentrations over five different batches; more replicates increase statistical power. Accuracy will be measured in relation to the theoretical concentrations and precision will be a measure of coefficient of variation for both within and between runs. It is imperative that the assays are both accurate and precise. Acceptability criteria for accuracy are minimally ±20% but some laboratories will tighten the requirement to ±10%. Precision acceptability for CVs can vary widely between laboratories with a minimum requirement of ±5% up to ±20%.

Repeatability will be used to measure the effectiveness of the assay over time to ensure it produces the same results. Repeatability can be included with the precision and accuracy measurements. The assay needs to be tested both within day (intra-day) and between days (inter-day) to ensure the variability is acceptable. This may be accomplished by analyzing a minimum of three replicates per batch for a minimum of 10 batches.

Linearity is certainly less important for immunoassay testing compared to confirmation analysis. Most immunoassay techniques do not possess a large linear range; the upper limits may reach 200–400% of the cutoff concentration. Although immunoassay testing is largely qualitative, it is still important to establish the linear range. This can be accomplished by analyzing, at a minimum, three replicates at each target concentration to obtain a least squares linear regression model. Some laboratories use screening results to trigger automatic dilutions prior to extraction for confirmation. Most assays used are directly proportional for absorbance and concentration but KIMS, for example, is inversely proportional and will be evident when plotting absorbances for the linearity study. Immunoassays may also be used in a semiquantitative fashion using multiple point calibrations. Setting the calibrators to cover the linear range can allow for fairly accurate quantitations based off

immunoassay testing. This can also be used to trigger more accurate dilutions before quantitative analysis.

Most manufacturers provide specificity information in the package inserts of their assays. However, in-house validation should be completed to verify this information; in addition, other drugs of interest that may appear frequently in a lab's casework should also be included. As mentioned previously, the primary purpose of immunoassay is to serve as a qualitative screening technique. One example of this is the emergence of dimethylamylamine (DMAA), which has been detected in weight-loss supplements such as Oxy Pro-Lite®. DMAA is a simple aliphatic amine compound that cross-reacts with several amphetamine immunoassays. The military drug-testing program saw a tremendous decrease in confirmation rates for amphetamines and was unable to determine the cause until an immunoassay vendor suggested that DMAA was the problem. The military population is held to physical standards that may require the use of weight-loss supplements. DMAA caused a tremendous increase in workload until it was identified. It is very small and was never included in specificity studies for immunoassay, indicating that even existing assays may need continuous validation.

Specificity should be tested against structurally similar compounds, endogenous compounds, and common over-the-counter compounds. The increased use of monoclonal antibodies has improved the specificity of most immunoassays available. Concentrations tested for the structurally similar compounds should be pharmacologically realistic. The nonstructurally similar compounds can be analyzed at much higher concentrations to show the effectiveness of the assay. If compounds are found to cross-react, the trigger point concentration should be determined. Immunoassays for classes of drugs such as benzodiazepines use specificity to their advantage, allowing a high range of cross-reactivity with multiple benzodiazepines. It is important to verify the concentration in which an analyte of interest will trigger a positive result; just as important is verifying the concentrations that cause positives for analytes not being monitored.

Some kits allow for high sensitivity options which involve adding β-glucuronidase to a reagent to hydrolyze conjugated metabolites, thereby increasing the amount of drug capable of interacting with the antibody. The assays should be tested with and without the addition of β-glucuronidase with conjugated controls to validate the enzyme is working properly.

Stability of assays should also be measured to reflect the time planned to be used at the laboratory. Most vendors provide stability information with assays as short as one day and as long as three months. Laboratories should determine the expected time an assay will be used and verify the stability for this time period. Analysis of calibrators and controls over the period of time and comparing latter results with earlier results provides a good way to validate the stability of the assay.

The final step in the validation of an immunoassay is the analysis of real specimens. The number of specimens analyzed should minimally be 25 positive and 25 negative specimens. The immunoassay results should be compared either to a reference immunoassay method if it is replacing an existing immunoassay or to a reference confirmation method. The specificity, sensitivity, and efficiency should be calculated (see Chapter 10). The importance of sensitivity vs specificity is a function of the use of the desired assay. If specific drugs within a class are targeted, then fewer false-positive results are desired. If the immunoassay is used as part of a more comprehensive drug-testing panel, then fewer false negatives are preferred.

Another important factor in the validation process is carryover. Carryover is more a factor of instrumentation as opposed to the assay. To evaluate carryover, a specimen should be spiked at high concentrations and analyzed. Immediately following the specimen will be a blank specimen to measure the amount of carryover. The blank specimen will be compared to a true blank to see how much, if any, of the high specimen was carried over during analysis. One approach for addressing carryover has been adopted by the military drug-testing program. For many years the program implemented a second screening technique that consisted of positive screened specimens with blanks in between to verify that carryover was not the cause of the initial positive result. New immunoassay analyzers have very little carryover due to improved washing techniques of sampling and reagent needles compared to older instrumentation.

CHROMATOGRAPHIC METHOD VALDIATIONS

Confirmation methods used to quantitate results in forensic toxicology require greater method validation than immunoassay and other screening techniques. The process of developing methods will be briefly discussed in this section, as it is closely linked to validation of the final method. The results from these methods could be used in criminal or civil litigation; therefore, the generation of reliable and defensible results is imperative. Validation is necessary no matter what type of confirmation method is used. Liquid chromatography (LC) methods will require some additional validation steps compared to gas chromatography (GC); similarly, mass spectrometry (MS) requires more validation steps than other detection systems. The remainder of this section will use MS as the detector, since it requires more validation work than more general detectors.

Obviously, before a method can be validated it must first be developed. Development of methods using MS begins with analyzing full scan unextracted standards to determine which ions to monitor or by infusing standards into an MS/MS to determine transitions to be monitored as well as the collision energy and other source parameters. In most cases, extraction procedures need to be developed to allow efficient removal of the analyte or analytes from the biological matrix with minimal matrix interferences. Then separation techniques need to be established to allow detection of the drug without interference from coextracted substances. This is an extremely simplistic view of method development but all of these items are part of validating a method. The necessary validation requirements will not be met if the development of the method is inadequate.

After completing the initial steps of development, a good starting point for validation is selectivity; this allows the analyst to determine if any matrix interferences are present. Obviously more matrix sources increase the confidence that the method is free from interference. Minimally, six different matrices should be used for this experiment. They should be analyzed with and without the internal standard to be used. The analysis of the matrix without internal standard will determine if there is interference from the matrix. Analysis with the internal standard will allow the analyst to determine if the internal standard is free from structural interferences. When using a deuterated analog as an internal standard, it is important to note that many of these analogs are contaminated to some extent with the nondeuterated compound. If an endogenous interference is detected, it must be resolved by either modification to the extraction procedure or through the separation technique. Some guidelines for postmortem laboratories suggest that each different source of blood be validated. The practicality of this for most postmortem laboratories is unrealistic. However, if possible, laboratories should make an attempt to at least analyze as many different sources as they can.

The specificity of a method may be the most important factor to be assessed during validation. As stated earlier, specificity is the ability to identify an analyte from those compounds that are structurally similar, either a drug metabolite, another member of the drug class, or other structural analogs. To assess specificity, the matrix should be analyzed with and without the drug in the presence of interfering compounds. Ideally the drug should be spiked at the limit of quantitation of the assay since this is the minimal concentration for accurate quantitation. The

tough question is determining which compounds to use for the interference studies. Every method should be analyzed using common over-the-counter drugs and common drugs of abuse with their metabolites. Additionally, structurally similar compounds for the drug of interest should be analyzed. If a laboratory is located in a region where use of a certain drug or drug class is prevalent, this also should be analyzed for potential interference. The concentrations of the potentially interfering compounds to be evaluated vary. Some recommend 5 mg/L across the board regardless of therapeutic concentrations. Each laboratory should assess the concentration based on historical information of concentrations seen at their facilities.

The linearity of the assay is also a critical part of validation, as it establishes the range in which accurate quantitation can be achieved. Prepare a calibration curve and then spike a minimum of three concentrations below the lowest level of the curve and analyze in duplicate. The lowest concentration at which the established ion ratios are acceptable but quantitation is outside 20% is the limit of detection (LOD). The lowest concentration at which both the ion ratios and the quantitation are acceptable is the limit of quantitation (LOQ) of the assay. Repeat this procedure for the upper end of the calibration curve to determine the upper limit of linearity. The highest concentration in which both the ion ratios and the quantitation is within 20% of the target is the upper limit of linearity (ULOL). Several factors can be changed to adjust if the desired quantitation range is not achieved. The sample volume can be adjusted, reconstitution volume can be changed, and injection volume and split ratios can also be changed to achieve the desired linearity range. These changes come with a give-and-take caveat, as sensitivity on the lower end could be lost to gain a higher upper limit of linearity. The laboratory must decide the critical points the linear range should cover. A laboratory could also administratively assign the LOD/LOQ/ULOL of an assay if they have concentrations that meet acceptability requirements and do not want to attempt to extend the range. If they are assigned administratively, they must also meet all acceptability requirements for chromatography as if they were established experimentally.

The accuracy and precision of the method are necessary factors included in validation. The assay needs to be validated for both within-day and between-day acceptability. Accuracy and precision can be analyzed concurrently during validation. Minimally, the laboratory should prepare three controls in the desired matrix that cover the concentration range of the assay. These controls will then be analyzed over a number of batches to determine the accuracy and precision of the method. Each laboratory will need to determine the minimum number of batches they deem acceptable; ideally it would be at least five batches. The results of the three controls prepared will be used to determine the accuracy and precision of the method. Acceptability criteria should minimally be a CV less than 20% for precision. Accuracy should at least be within 20% of the expected result. In addition to this interassay statistical determination, the laboratory should also determine intra-assay variation. The three controls minimally should be analyzed five times within the batch and have less than 20% variation. The accuracy and precision studies will allow a laboratory to show the method's ability to reproduce results, critical in forensic toxicology.

Carryover needs to be assessed for confirmation methods, as is done with immunoassays. Some laboratories analyze a solvent in between case specimens to address carryover but determining an experimental level can prove beneficial. Analysis of a high concentrated control followed by an extracted blank will determine the observed concentration carryover. The analyst can adjust instrument factors to address carryover by adding more needle washes to the method or changing the wash solvent for LC analysis.

Ion suppression is a major concern for all LC/MS and LC-MS/MS ionization techniques and must be assessed during method validation. Ion suppression is a matrix effect

that can coincide with other factors to muffle the signal of the analyte. When excessive ions are present in the sample, the signal from the analyte of interest can be suppressed or buried in the background noise. The signal in some instances can also be enhanced. These effects can vary greatly between samples and between different matrices such as blood and urine. The interferences can come from the sample matrices, the extraction procedure, solvents, mobile phase, and, even, the glassware or plastic tubes used in the extraction procedure. Other factors relating to the chemical properties of the analytes, such as mass, alkalinity, and concentration, can also contribute to ion suppression. The degree of suppression or enhancement can negatively affect LOD and the precision and accuracy of quantitative results.

Ion suppression and extraction efficiency studies are performed by comparing the unextracted standards to extracted samples with the compounds added post- and pre-extraction. These experiments are usually performed at three different concentrations throughout the linear range of the assay; minimally, two concentrations should be used. The ion suppression is determined to be the signal loss between the unextracted standards and samples where the standards were added postextraction. Extraction efficiency is also calculated from the difference between the samples where the standards were added postextraction (the ion suppressed signal) vs preextraction. If the instrument has an infusion pump, the ion suppression of the mobile phase can be measured directly. By infusing the compound of interest into the MS, monitoring the ion response, and then simultaneously infusing the mobile phase, the ion suppression effects from the mobile phase can be calculated. Ion suppression effects can be minimized and/or accounted for by doing sample preparation, using deuterated internal standards, and minimizing the salt content in the mobile phase (using formic acid, not ammonium formate).

Ion suppression experiments only measure the effects of negative matrices used in that particular laboratory. Real specimens are always different and true matrix effects and variations associated with real specimens can never be measured in practical applications, only minimized through thorough method validation. This is an important fact to consider if direct injection or dilute and shoot methods are to be used.

Another factor in validation of LC methods is developing a system suitability check. A system suitability test is an analysis designed to ensure that the complete analytical testing system (i.e., LC, reagents, columns, software, source, and the mass spectrometer) is operating adequately for the intended application. Regardless of whether a LC-MS/MS instrument has an automated autotune or checktune feature, a system suitability test should be performed on a daily basis. Many manufacturers do not have a built-in autotune feature that many in forensic toxicology are accustomed to with GC/MS analysis. Therefore, there is no record of instrument performance if a system suitability test is not used.

Typically, a system suitability test is analyzed before a batch is started. However, to ensure the system is operating correctly throughout the entire batch, system suitability tests can be analyzed throughout the analysis. System suitability samples should consist of compounds that are the same, structurally similar, or in the same class as the compounds being analyzed in the assay. The compounds should cover the entire retention time and mass range of the analytes of interest. Parameters that can be monitored include: MRM transitions, retention time, peak area counts, peak widths at half height, and chromatography parameters such as peak resolution and capacity factor. Historical values should be established, recorded, and monitored over time to determine if any system degradation has occurred. For instance, a shift in retention times can indicate the incorrect or contaminated mobile phase. It could also be an indication of column degradation. A dramatic decrease in the area counts can indicate a dirty source and missing peaks could indicate the instrument needs a mass calibration. Experiments during method development are used to define

system suitability acceptance limits and guidance should be provided when those limits are exceeded.

One decision left to the discretion of the laboratory is when and to what extent a method validation is required. At a minimum, a full validation is required when a new method is put online. If a change is made to instrumentation, such as a new model GC/MS, a minivalidation should be completed. This should include side-by-side comparison of at least three batches of real specimens as well as reestablishing the linearity of the method. If the method changes from GC to LC, then a more in-depth validation should be accomplished. This should include side-by-side comparison of real specimen batches, linearity, matrix effects, specificity, and ion suppression. The necessity of the expanded validation due to instrument change is because of the impact LC can have on an analyte. The ionization technique used is very different from GC, which requires the matrix effects, specificity, and ion suppression to be validated. The separation technique can lead to drugs that did not interfere by GC to be problematic with LC.

Changes made to the extraction will also require some revalidation of a confirmation method. For example, if a laboratory chooses to switch from a liquid/liquid extraction to a solid-phase extraction it will need to analyze side-by-side batches, matrix effects, specificity, linearity, ion suppression (if LC), and recovery. If the method change is washing a column with a different buffer to enhance the clean-up process, it may require only specificity and recovery to be validated.

Another questionable area of method validation requirement is for infrequently analyzed drugs. Many postmortem laboratories are expected to be able to analyze for any drug and it is not feasible to perform the above steps for each drug. A laboratory needs to determine the frequency of testing in which it decides what is infrequently tested. The lab should attempt to analyze infrequent drugs in the same fashion from analysis to analysis and keep a record of what was done.

MASS SPETROMETRY SCREENING METHOD VALIDATION

Mass spectrometry screening methods are becoming more popular as advancement in the technology of multiple quadrupole systems allows their applications to be more efficient, specific, sensitive, and practical. They are emerging as a viable replacement for immunoassays that cannot adapt fast enough to the ever-changing world of designer drugs. MS screening methods can utilize a variety of techniques for analysis such as MRM transition screen with or without LC separation and high-resolution time of flight (TOF) MS, capable of identifying a compound using exact mass calculations. Regardless of the technique, method validation is required to ensure the method will be reliable and accurate for the intended application. For screening procedures the validation emphasis should be on the detection of the compounds of interests. There should be extensive specificity and selectivity experiments to ensure no compounds could interfere with the assay. Numerous negative controls for each of the matrices used in the assay should be investigated for possible interference and matrix effects. Recovery experiments should be performed if the method involves LC introduction or separation and the ion suppression effect also needs to be measured. Cutoffs can be established administratively or experimentally and thus the limit of detection (LOD) must be determined and criteria for positive identification established. If a semi-quantitative method is being developed, then intraday and interday precision studies need to be performed. These experiments should cover at least three separate concentrations over the proposed linear range. Upper limits of detection can also be determined if necessary for the specific application. Carryover also needs to be evaluated to determine if and when washes are needed in a batch.

SUMMARY

Method validation is a necessity in forensic toxicology laboratories. Governing bodies are providing guidelines for requirements of method validations but they can vary greatly. Each laboratory is responsible for determining what is required for their validation based on their certifications, casework, workload, and budget. This chapter should provide laboratories with a template of what is needed based on the analysis being performed.

SUGGESTED READING

1. Clinical and Laboratory Standards Institute. Gas chromatography/mass spectrometry confirmation of drugs; approved guidelines—2nd ed. Document C43-A2. Wayne, PA: CLSI, 2010.
2. National Laboratory Certification Program. Manual for urine laboratories. Research Triangle Park, NC: RTI International Center for Forensic Sciences, 2010.
3. Scientific Working Group for Forensic Toxicology. SWGTOX Doc 003: Standard practices for method validation in forensic toxicology. Draft version. SWGTOX, 2012.
4. Society of Forensic Toxicologists and American Academy of Forensic Sciences. Forensic toxicology laboratory guidelines. Mesa, AZ: SOFT/AAFS, 2006.
5. Swartz M, Krull I. Validation of bioanalytical methods—highlights of FDA's guidance. LCGC N Amer 2003;21:136–42.
6. U.S. Department of Health and Human Services, Food and Drug Administration, Center for Drug Evaluation and Research. Guidance for industry: bioanalytical methods validation. Rockville, MD: FDA, 2001.

PART III

ANALYTES

CHAPTER 13

Alcohol

Barry Levine, Yale H. Caplan, and Alan Wayne Jones

Alcohol, better known to chemists and toxicologists as ethanol (CH_3CH_2OH), is the psychoactive substance most commonly encountered in forensic toxicology casework when blood or other body fluids from living and deceased persons are analyzed. Ethanol tops the list of drugs identified in medical examiner or coroner cases, impaired drivers (traffic cases), sexual assault and date rape victims, as well as workplace accident investigations. Between 20–50% of all drivers killed in road-traffic crashes, according to various epidemiological surveys, had been drinking alcohol before the crash and their blood alcohol concentration (BAC) at autopsy exceeded the statutory limit for driving.

Ethanol is probably man's oldest psychoactive drug and is produced in nature by microbial fermentation of sugars contained in fruits, honey, or other vegetable matter. Alcohol is a legal drug and is available for purchase by adults almost without restriction. Moderate drinking, such as 10–20 g ethanol daily (one to two drinks), has no detrimental effects on a person's health or wellbeing, and there is growing evidence that this amount, especially in the form of red wine, has a protective effect against cardiovascular diseases such as stroke. Unfortunately, for about 10% of the population, especially among men, initial moderate drinking escalates into overconsumption and abuse, with serious consequences for the individual, family, and society as a whole.

Efforts to prevent alcohol-related problems have a long history, and one example is the enactment of prohibition during the first decades of the twentieth century in the U.S. Examples of medical complications caused by excessive drinking are disease of the liver (hepatitis, cirrhosis), acute and chronic pancreatitis, gout, various cancers, and cardiomyopathy. The prevalence and deaths from these medical conditions is highly correlated with total alcohol consumption in society.

CLASSIFICATION OF ALCOHOLS

Textbooks devoted to organic chemistry classify alcohols according to their chemical structure, such as carbon chain length, the degree of branching, or the number of hydroxyl groups (-OH) contained in each molecule. Alcohols with one hydroxyl group are referred to as mono-hydroxy (e.g., ethanol and methanol), two hydroxyl groups are di-hydroxy (e.g., ethylene glycol), whereas glycerol is a tri-hydroxy alcohol and mannitol and sorbitol are poly-hydroxy alcohols. The various aliphatic alcohols are also denoted as primary (ethanol), secondary (*iso*-propanol), or tertiary (*t*-butanol), depending on whether one, two, or three alkyl groups are bonded to the saturated carbon atom containing the hydroxyl (-OH) radical.

Table 1 shows examples of the alcohols commonly encountered in clinical and forensic toxicology, along with their main physicochemical properties and toxic metabolites formed in the body during metabolism in the liver.

Table 1. Physicochemical Properties of Various Alcohols Often Encountered in Clinical and Forensic Toxicology

Property	Methanol	Ethanol	n-Propanol	Isopropanol	Ethylene Glycol
CAS-number[a]	65–46–1	64–17–5	71–23–8	67–63–0	107–21–1
Molecular weight	32.04	46.07	60.09	60.09	62.07
Chemical formulae	CH_3OH	CH_3CH_2OH	$CH_3CH_2CH_2OH$	$(CH_3)_2CHOH$	$(COOH)_2$
Structure	Primary aliphatic alcohol	Primary aliphatic alcohol	Primary aliphatic alcohol	Secondary aliphatic alcohol	Dihydroxy aliphatic alcohol (diol)
Common name	Wood alcohol	Beverage or grain alcohol	Propyl alcohol	Rubbing alcohol	Antifreeze
Boiling point	64.7 °C	78.5 °C	82.6 °C	82.5 °C	197 °C
Melting point	–95.8 °C	–114.1 °C	–126.5 °C	–88.5 °C	–13 °C
Density (20 °C)	0.791	0.789	0.805	0.785	1.11
Solubility in water	Mixes completely	Mixes completely	Mixes completely	Mixes completely	Mixes completely
Toxic metabolites	Formaldehyde and formic acid	Acetaldehyde and acetic acid	Propionaldehyde and propionic acid	Acetone	Glycolic, glyoxylic, and oxalic acid

[a] Chemical abstract service number.

206

In general, the narcotic effects of aliphatic alcohols on cell membranes increase with the number of carbon atoms in the molecule with the notable exception of methanol (CH_3OH). Methanol is commonly referred to as wood alcohol because it was originally made from the distillation of wood under vacuum. Although methanol is comparable with ethanol in terms of its acute intoxicating effects, wood alcohol is much more dangerous owing to toxicity of its metabolites, namely formaldehyde and formic acid (Table 1). Another common alcohol is isopropanol, or rubbing alcohol, which is widely used in clinics as an antiseptic to clean the skin before taking blood samples. The additional carbon atom in isopropanol makes it more lipid soluble and easier to penetrate cell membranes, giving a greater depression of the central nervous system. Occasionally, chronic alcoholics resort to drinking industrial alcohol products that contain more toxic alcohols, such as methanol or isopropanol, in addition to varying amounts of ethanol.

Another toxic alcohol encountered in clinical and forensic toxicology is the sweet-tasting solvent ethylene glycol, a major component of antifreeze. The two hydroxyl groups in ethylene glycol are oxidized successively by hepatic enzymes, first to aldehydes (-CHO) and then to carboxylic acids (-COOH), and the end product of metabolism is oxalic acid (Table 1). Oxalic acid can react with intracellular calcium ions to produce insoluble calcium oxalate crystals, which get trapped in the kidney tubuli, eventually causing renal failure and death. In a poisoned patient, the analysis of ethylene glycol and/or its metabolites in body fluids and the extent of metabolic acidosis furnish proof of toxic alcohol ingestion. In medical examiner cases, ethylene glycol fatalities are often recognized from the presence of calcium oxalate crystals in sections of the kidney or from the presence of these crystals in the urine when examined under polarized light.

Because the boiling point of ethylene glycol (197 °C) is much higher than that of ethanol (78 °C), methanol (65 °C), and isopropanol (82 °C), this aliphatic diol is not identified in biological specimens during routine gas chromatography (GC) analysis of volatiles. Ethylene glycol is usually determined by an enzymatic method (e.g., with glycerol dehydrogenase) or after protein precipitation and direct injection into a GC instrument fitted with a flame ionization detector (FID) or by GC-FID after making a suitable chemical derivative, such as the phenyl bornate ester.

On entering the blood stream, primary alcohols are oxidized in the liver to aldehydes whereas secondary alcohols, such as isopropanol, are converted into ketones such as acetone. Tertiary alcohols are resistant to oxidation and usually undergo phase II conjugation reactions to form glucuronides, which are excreted in the urine. The method used to determine ethanol in blood and other body fluids must be able to distinguish acetone, isopropanol, and methanol, which are commonly encountered together with ethanol in forensic casework.

PRODUCTION OF ALCOHOLIC BEVERAGES

The initial step in the production of alcoholic beverages is fermentation, one of the oldest known organic reactions dating back approximately 3,000 years. Fermentation requires adding yeast to an aqueous solution of some carbohydrate substrate, and one molecule of a six-carbon sugar, such as glucose, is converted into two molecules of ethanol and two molecules of carbon dioxide:

$$C_6H_{12}O_6 \rightarrow 2CH_3CH_2OH + 2CO_2$$

Any natural product with sufficient amounts of starch or sugar can undergo fermentation by the enzymes contained in yeast or by other microorganism depending on appropriate conditions of temperature and time. Brewer's yeast (*Saccharomycas cerevisae*), a type of fungus, has been around for a long time. During the fermentation process, ethanol concentrations up to 12–14 vol% are produced whereas on reaching higher concentrations the yeast is inactivated and fermentation stops. Beverages with higher concentrations of ethanol are produced by distillation or by spiking fermented drinks with extra ethanol.

In addition to ethanol and water, alcoholic beverages contain small amounts of other substances broadly classified as congeners, which, according to the *Oxford English Dictionary*, means "one of the same kind, allied in nature or origin." Accordingly, congeners are other types of alcohols (e.g., methyl, pentyl, or amyl), aldehydes, and ketones, as well as other low molecular weight substances that might be produced during the fermentation process depending on source and type of raw materials used. Other congeners are imparted when fermented or distilled beverages are stored in oak casks during the aging process prior to bottling.

The congeners contribute to the smell and taste and give color to certain types of alcoholic beverages such as whiskey or cognac. The "cleanest" alcoholic drink in terms of low congener content is vodka, which after distillation is filtered through activated charcoal to remove any trace impurities. Distilled alcoholic beverages usually contain 40–60 vol% ethanol (80–120 proof), and in some nations this alcohol content is regulated by statute. Beers might contain from 4–12 vol% alcohol depending on the manufacturing process, whereas table wines are 8–14 vol% and fortified wines 14–24 vol% ethanol. The so-called alcohol-free beers, which are widely available, are usually about 1 vol% or less, which makes them safe to consume by drivers and others engaged in safety-sensitive work.

FATE OF ALCOHOL IN THE BODY

Absorption

Absorption describes the process by which a drug or poison (e.g., alcohol) passes from outside the body into the bloodstream. The oral route of administration (by mouth or drinking) is how drinks are consumed in real-life situations. However, in emergency medicine, sterile solutions of ethanol in saline (8–10 vol%) might be administered intravenously to treat patients admitted to hospital poisoned from drinking methanol or ethylene glycol. High blood alcohol concentrations can also be reached after rectal administration.

The absorption of alcohol into the portal venous blood starts in the stomach but the rate of uptake is much faster when the stomach contents empty into the duodenum and jejunum, owing to the much larger surface area provided by the villi and microvilli that project from the surface of the mucosa of the small intestines. Accordingly, factors that affect gastric emptying have a major influence on the rate of absorption of ethanol into the bloodstream. A more rapid rate of absorption is associated with a higher and earlier occurring peak blood ethanol concentration (C_{max}) and thus a greater impairment of the central nervous system.

Small amounts of ethanol may be absorbed into the blood via the dermal route (intact skin) or by inhalation through the lungs, although these methods are ineffective in elevating the BAC above 0.01 g/100 mL. The slow absorption through the skin is balanced by simultaneous metabolism in the liver at a rate of 7–8 g/hour. If the skin is damaged with cuts or abrasions and there are open blood vessels, this might enhance uptake but is still not an effective way to increase the BAC. The absorption of ethanol into the bloodstream by inhalation via the lungs depends on the concentration in the ambient air breathed and the degree of lung ventilation. However, even under extreme conditions, when concentrations in the inhaled air are high this is not a practical way to increase a person's BAC owing to simultaneous metabolism of any absorbed ethanol.

Because absorption is a passive diffusion process one can expect that ethanol contained in distilled liquors (40 vol%) is absorbed faster than ethanol in wine (10 vol%) or beer (5 vol%), as predicted by Fick's principle. However, this simple rule is offset by the fact that beers and wines, as well as fruit brandies, contain sugars and other constituents that delay gastric emptying. The type of mixer used with spirit drinks also impacts speed of absorption by delaying gastric emptying. The ethanol in carbonated (CO_2) beverages such as champagne seems to be absorbed faster than decarbonated drinks with the same alcohol content, such as white wine. When neat spirits are consumed on an empty stomach, this often irritates the gastric mucosa and results in a pyloric spasm, which leads to a delayed gastric emptying and a slower rate of absorption of ethanol into the blood.

The results from hundreds of controlled drinking studies show that peak BAC occurs at between 10–120 min after the end of drinking and on average after about 60 min. However, in social drinking situations, when multiple drinks are consumed over longer time periods, the absorption takes place progressively as more and more alcohol is consumed and the peak concentration in blood is reached earlier, usually within 30 min after cessation of drinking. Fig. 1 gives examples of blood alcohol curves obtained from experiments with N = 16 healthy men after they drank a standard dose of alcohol (0.85 g/kg) as neat whiskey on an empty stomach in 25 min. These BAC curves show the magnitude of intersubject variation, which is greatest during the absorption phase as reflected in variations in C_{max} and t_{max} before the postabsorptive phase starts at about 60–90 min postdrinking.

Some absorption of alcohol occurs through the mucous surfaces of the stomach, but the bulk of the dose administered is absorbed via the upper part of the small intestine. Estimates of the relative amounts of ethanol absorbed from the stomach (20%) and intestines (89%) are only approximate because much depends on stomach emptying, including the presence of food in the stomach before drinking, the type of beverage consumed, and use of certain prescription drugs. Absorption of ethanol from different parts of the gastrointestinal (GI) tract depends on the concentration present in the individual structures, blood flow (vascularity), and the absorption surface area.

Factors that increase GI motility will increase the rate of ethanol absorption into the blood and a delayed gastric emptying (gastroparesis) decreases the absorption of ethanol. Inflammation of the GI tract, for example, increases blood flow to that region, resulting in a more rapid absorption of alcohol. Prokinetic drugs increase gastric motility (e.g., cisapride or metaclopramide) and lead to a faster rate of absorption of ethanol into the portal blood. Heavy cigarette smoking delays gastric emptying and slows rate of ethanol absorption. However, the single most important factor delaying the absorption of ethanol is the presence of food in the stomach, such as when alcohol is consumed immediately after eating a large meal. The

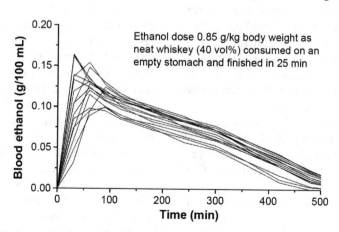

Fig. 1. Interindividual variations in concentration-time profiles of ethanol in 16 healthy men after they consumed the same dose of ethanol (0.85 g/kg body weight) as neat whiskey (40 vol%) on an empty stomach (overnight fast) in a drinking time of 25 min.

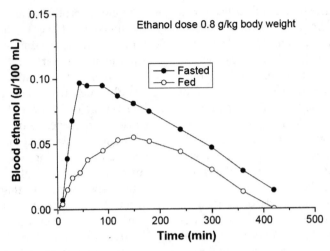

Fig. 2. Blood alcohol curves in a male subject after drinking the same dose of ethanol (0.8 g/kg) either on an empty stomach (overnight fast) or after eating a standardized breakfast.

amount of food eaten seems more important than its composition in terms of protein, fat, or carbohydrate content. Fig. 2 shows blood alcohol curves obtained when the same dose of ethanol (0.8 g/kg) was consumed on an empty stomach (overnight fast) or immediately after eating a standardized breakfast.

The peak concentration of ethanol in blood was higher and occurred earlier when ethanol was consumed on an empty stomach compared with the same dose after eating a meal. Food mixes with and dilutes the concentration of ethanol in the stomach so that it remains unabsorbed for a much longer time. The BAC curve obtained in the fed state gives the impression that a smaller dose of ethanol had been administered, but this was not the case (Fig 2). It seems that food not only lowers the bioavailability of ethanol but also increases the rate of metabolism as reflected in a smaller area under the curve and a shorter time to reach zero BAC. For the most part, the rate of ethanol metabolism is independent of the concentration in blood provided the oxidative enzymes are saturated with substrate (BAC > 0.02–0.03 g/100 mL).

Eating a meal increases hepatic blood flow and consequently there is a more effective clearance of ethanol, which is one mechanism that helps to explain the food effect. This was demonstrated when subjects ate a meal when the alcohol was given by intravenous infusion, thus sidestepping any influence of gastric emptying. Some investigators suggested that when alcohol is retained in the stomach for longer, such as when drinking and eating occurs, a larger amount undergoes presystemic metabolism owing to alcohol dehydrogenase located in the gastric mucosa.

Distribution

After absorption into the portal venous blood, ethanol is transported first to the liver and then to the right side of the heart and to the lungs before oxygenated blood returns to the left side of the heart and is transported throughout the whole body. When blood enters the pulmonary circulation, some of the ethanol in solution diffuses across the alveolar-capillary membrane and is exhaled in the breath. This forms the basis of the widely used breath-alcohol test, which will be covered in more detail later in this chapter. During the absorption phase, the concentration of ethanol in alveolar air and hence in the expired air runs closer to the arterial blood concentration rather than the venous blood concentration. Tissues that are initially free of alcohol extract alcohol from the arterial blood so that the venous blood returning to the heart with deoxygenated blood has a lower concentration of alcohol.

The magnitude of the arterial-venous (A–V) difference in alcohol content is greatest when a bolus dose is consumed on an empty stomach. After the end of drinking, the magnitude of the A–V difference progressively decreases and eventually becomes zero (A = V), which marks the point when ethanol is fully absorbed and distributed in all body fluids and tissues. Studies have shown that venous blood contains a slightly higher concentration of ethanol than arterial blood during the postabsorptive elimination phase of the BAC curve.

The speed of equilibration of ethanol between blood and other body fluids and tissues depends on the ratio of blood flow to tissue mass, which means that organs with a rich blood supply, such as the brain and kidneys, rapidly equilibrate with the concentration of ethanol in arterial blood, whereas bulky skeletal muscles, with their lower ratio of blood flow to tissue mass, require a longer time to equilibrate. Body fluids containing more water than blood (e.g., saliva, vitreous humor, and urine) will also have higher concentrations of ethanol when equilibration is reached.

An important concept in pharmacokinetics is how a drug distributes between the blood or plasma and the other tissues of the body. Known as volume of distribution (V_d), this important pharmacokinetic parameter relates the concentration of a drug in the blood or plasma to the total amount of the drug in the body. A drug's V_d depends on lipid solubility and the degree of binding to plasma proteins. From a knowledge of V_d it is easy to calculate the amount of drug absorbed and distributed in all body fluids and tissues from the concentration determined in a sample of blood. The V_d for a water-soluble drug like ethanol depends on the person's age and gender and the proportion of fat to lean tissue in the body.

Total body water (TBW) comprises about 60% of body weight in men and 50% in women as determined by isotope dilution experiments. The V_d for ethanol varies twofold between individuals from a low of 0.4–0.5 L/kg in obese females to a high of 0.7–0.8 L/kg in lean male subjects. Results from alcohol drinking experiments gave average values of V_d of 0.7 L/kg in healthy adult men and 0.6 L/kg in healthy adult women. The water content of blood is easy to determine by desiccation or freeze drying and is ~80% w/w with a small but statistically significant gender difference, owing to lower hematocrit (less red cells and more plasma) in female blood.

Because ethanol distributes into the water fraction of all body fluids, the distribution ratio of ethanol between the blood and the body as a whole should be similar to the distribution of water, namely 60/80 or 0.75 for men and 50/80 or 0.62 for women. In practice, much depends on body composition, especially the amount of adipose tissue in relation to fat-free mass. A clinical measure of obesity is given by body mass index (BMI), calculated as the ratio of body weight in kg to height in meters squared (kg/m^2). A person with BMI 30 kg/m^2 can be expected to have a lower ethanol V_d than a person with normal BMI of 20–25 kg/m^2.

Blood consists of the straw-colored plasma (92 % w/w water) and red cells (erythrocytes), which are 68% w/w water. This suggests a plasma/blood distribution ratio of ethanol of 1.15:1 (92/80 = 1.15) and a red-cell/blood ratio of 0.85 (68/80 = 0.85) depending in part on hematocrit and lipid content of the blood specimen. Most people can be expected to have a plasma/blood distribution ratio of ethanol ranging from 1.1:1 to 1.2:1 depending on their state of health. In people suffering from anemia (low hematocrit), with more plasma (and water) per unit volume of blood, the plasma/blood distribution of ethanol should be closer to 1.10:1 or lower. Plasma and serum contain the same amount of water and therefore the amount of ethanol and ethanol distribution ratios are the same.

If a clinical laboratory reports a serum ethanol concentration of 0.1 g%, then for forensic purposes the expected concentration in whole blood is 0.087 g/100 mL

(0.1/1.15 = 0.086), but might range from 0.083 g/100 mL (0.1/1.2) to 0.091 g/100 mL (0.1/1.1). The results from analysis of ethanol in plasma and serum done at hospital clinical chemistry laboratories should not be used for legal purposes without making this conversion to the expected concentration in whole blood.

The distribution of ethanol between blood and other biological fluids and tissues has been extensively studied and the values depend on water content of specimens and the time after drinking when samples are taken. Results from many such studies are summarized (Table 2) if samples are taken after absorption and distribution is complete. The concentrations in vitreous humor, saliva, spinal fluid, and urine are 15–20% higher than in an equal volume of blood, as expected from differences in water content. However, in practice the distribution ratios of ethanol between CSF and blood and urine and blood are higher (1.3:1) because of a lag time in the formation of these alternative body fluids. Concentrations of ethanol in the liver, kidneys, and brain are less than in blood in part due to lower water content in these tissues and the fact that some are metabolically active after death, which leads to a decrease in the concentrations of ethanol.

Table 2. Average Distribution Ratios of Ethanol Between Blood and Other Biological Specimens at Equilibrium

Specimen Analyzed	Specimen/Blood Concentration Ratio[a]
Mixed saliva (oral fluid)	1.12
Vitreous humor	1.20
Bile	1.0
Cerebrospinal fluid	1.3
Liver tissue	0.6
Kidney tissue	0.7
Brain tissue	0.8
Urine	1.3

[a] The concentration ratios show wide variation depending on, among other things, time after drinking when samples are taken and equilibration of ethanol in all body fluids and tissues.

Metabolism

More than 90% of the dose of ethanol consumed undergoes oxidative metabolism in the liver by various enzymatic reactions, as shown in Fig. 3. The first step involves oxidation of ethanol to acetaldehyde and this reaction is catalyzed by a cytosolic enzyme alcohol dehydrogenase (ADH). ADH is polymorphic and various isozymes exist with slightly different amino acid sequences and kinetic properties (V_{max} and k_m), which might account for individual differences in rates of ethanol metabolism. Zinc is a necessary element for enzyme activity of alcohol dehydrogenase. During oxidative metabolism of ethanol, the cofactor nicotinamide adenine dinucleotide (NAD^+) is simultaneously reduced to NADH and the reoxidation of NADH to NAD^+ is the rate-limiting step in the overall redox reaction.

Acetaldehyde is a toxic and highly reactive substance but luckily the primary metabolite of ethanol is rapidly oxidized to acetic acid by the action of low k_m aldehyde dehydrogenase (ALDH) located in the mitochondria. The acetate becomes transported with blood away from the liver and enters the aerobic respiration process (citric acid cycle), eventually breaking down into the end products of carbon dioxide and water. The oxidative metabolism of ethanol via the ADH and ALDH pathway is the primary route of alcohol elimination from the body. However, in the early 1960s it was discovered that the smooth endoplasmic recticulm of liver cells contained an enzyme that oxidized ethanol denoted microsomal ethanol oxidizing system (MEOS). MEOS formed part of the cytochrome P450 family of enzymes and CYP2E1 was the variant mainly responsible for oxidation of ethanol. The same P450 enzyme is responsible for metabolism of certain drugs such as acetaminophen and chlorinated and aromatic hydrocarbons. The P450 system is inducible after chronic exposure to substrate, which accounts for the finding that some alcoholics during detoxification have higher rates of metabolism of ethanol compared with occasional drinkers.

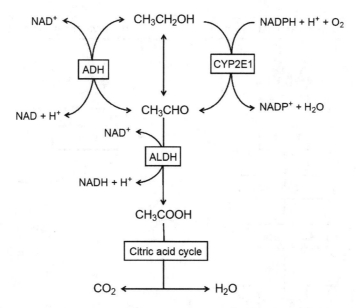

Fig. 3. Scheme showing the main pathway for oxidative metabolism of ethanol, where ADH is alcohol dehydrogenase, ALDH is aldehyde dehydrogenase, NAD$^+$ and NADH are oxidized and reduced forms of coenzyme nicotinamide adenine dinucleotide, and CYP2E1 is a microsomal enzyme.

Nonoxidative Metabolism

Since the previous edition of this textbook, considerable research has focused on the nonoxidative metabolites of ethanol (Fig. 4). A small fraction of the dose of ethanol ingested (0.1–0.2%) undergoes Phase II conjugation reactions to give ethyl glucuronide (EtG) and ethyl sulfate (EtS) as metabolites via glucuronosyltransferase and sulfotransferase enzymes, respectively. EtG and EtS are detectable in blood and urine for considerably longer than ethanol itself and can serve as biomarkers to disclose recent drinking after ethanol has been eliminated from the body. However, care is needed when results of EtG are interpreted because ethanol is a constituent of many household products, including mouthwash, cosmetics, cough medication, and hand sanitizers. This requires use of conservative and reasonable cutoff concentrations when urinary EtG is analyzed and reported, such as 100–500 ng/mL (0.1–0.5 mg/L). Lower cutoffs are acceptable for EtS, such as 25–100 ng/mL (0.025–0.1 mg/L), before a person is accused of drinking alcoholic beverages.

Analysis of EtG and EtS find applications in postmortem toxicology to distinguish ethanol produced during decomposition from antemortem ingestion of alcoholic beverages. If EtG and/or EtS conjugates are verified present in postmortem blood or urine, this speaks for consumption of alcoholic beverages during life. Ethanol must undergo metabolism to produce these conjugates and must therefore have passed through the liver as opposed to being produced after death by action of bacteria or yeasts.

Another nonoxidative metabolite of ethanol is phosphatidylethanol (PEth), which is formed in a reaction between ethanol and phosphatidylcholine and the enzyme phospholipase D. Peth also remains elevated after ethanol has been cleared from the bloodstream. However, a heavier drinking period is needed to produce elevated levels of PEth compared with EtG and EtS.

Ethanol undergoes an enzymatic reaction with both saturated and unsaturated fatty acids (e.g., palmitic, linoleic, stearic, etc.) to give fatty acid ethyl esters (FAEE). The incorporation of FAEE into various body organs (heart, brain, and pancreas) has been suggested as a possible mechanism for

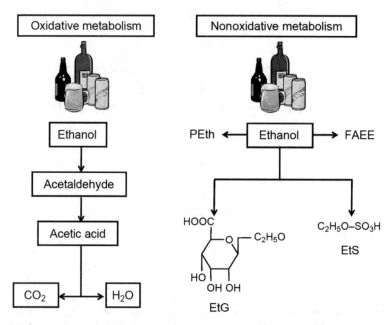

Fig. 4. Pathways of oxidative metabolism of ethanol via acetaldehyde, acetate, and end products carbon dioxide and water (left part) and nonoxidative metabolism to ethyl glucuoride (EtG) and ethyl sulfate (EtS) conjugates, phosphatidylethanol (PEth), and fatty acid ethyl esters (FAEE).

alcohol-related tissue damage, which is often seen in chronic alcoholics. FAEE can also be determined in hair strands and used to monitor abstinence in people required to refrain from drinking for various reasons.

Excretion

Excretion refers to the removal of ethanol from the body in an unchanged form, and this occurs via the lungs (in breath), the kidneys (in urine), and through the skin (in sweat). However, all three routes of excretion combined account for at most 5–10% of the dose of ethanol administered. Ethanol can also be detected in the saliva, which, however, is usually swallowed and reabsorbed into the blood.

Urine has a long history as a biological specimen for forensic analysis of alcohol because large volumes are available. In the past, the UAC was used to estimate the BAC but this conversion is not advisable owing to large variations in the UAC/BAC ratio depending on sampling time after end of drinking. Concentration-time pro-

files of ethanol in blood and bladder urine are shown in Fig. 5 when 0.85 g ethanol/kg body weight was consumed as neat whiskey on an empty stomach. Note that after a bolus dose the concentration in urine is less than in blood during the absorption phase and higher than in blood after about 100 min and remains higher for the duration of the postabsorptive period. The insert graph shows the ethanol-induced dieresis, which is greatest (6 mL per min) during the absorption phase of the blood alcohol curve returning to normal (~1 mL per min) during the postabsorptive period.

The physiological principles of ethanol excretion in urine are well-known, and as renal artery blood enters the kidney, about 20% is filtered at the glomerulus. Most of this filtrate is reabsorbed, with <1% of the filtrate being excreted as urine in the bladder. Analysis of near simultaneous samples of blood and bladder urine show that UAC/BAC concentration ratios range from 1.2–1.3 after absorption of alcohol is complete. However, individual ratios vary widely depending on status of absorptive and the time of storage of urine in the bladder before voiding. Blood ethanol decrease by

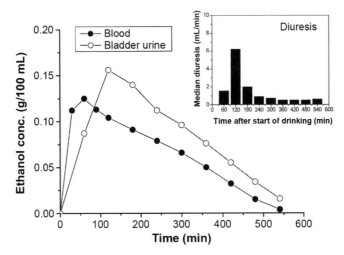

Fig. 5. Concentration-time curves of ethanol in blood and bladder urine in one subject who drank ethanol (0.85 g/kg) as neat whiskey on an empty stomach. Note that the bladder was emptied before drinking started and the insert graph shows ethanol-induced dieresis at different times after end of drinking.

metabolism as urine is produced whereas there is no metabolism of ethanol in urine after it collects in the bladder. During the absorptive phase of the BAC curve, the UAC/BAC ratio is <1.0, and during the postabsorptive phase, the concentration in urine is 25–30% higher than in blood. The variations in urine-to-blood concentration ratios for an individual in the postabsorptive phase can be so large that it is generally considered unacceptable to estimate a blood ethanol concentration from the ethanol concentration of a randomly collected urine specimen. Better correlations are obtained for ethanol in urine and blood when two consecutive urine specimens are collected. The second voided specimen, collected 30–60 min after the first, shows a closer correlation with BAC and the average UAC/BAC is about 1.3:1.

Pharmacokinetics

Pharmacokinetics is concerned with absorption, distribution, metabolism, and excretion (ADME) of drugs and how these processes can be described in quantitative terms. The Swedish scientist Erik MP Widmark (1889–1945) made extensive studies of ADME of ethanol in the 1930s when he plotted BAC time profiles and used these to derive a set of alcohol parameters under well-controlled drinking conditions. A Widmark-type BAC curve is shown in Fig. 6, along with the pharmacokinetic parameters of ethanol C_0, C_{max}, t_{max}, β, min_0, and rho.

A male subject drank a moderate dose of ethanol (0.8 g/kg) on an empty stomach in 30 min. The peak concentration in blood (C_{max}) and time of reaching the peak (t_{max}) are read directly from the graph. At about 80 min postdosing after C_{max} is reached, the BAC decreased at a constant rate per unit time in accordance with zero-order saturation kinetics. The slope of this rectilinear elimination part of the BAC profile is determined from the dashed diagonal line in Fig. 6, denoted β-slope with y-intercept C_0 (g/100 mL) and x-intercept min_0 (min or h), where $C_0/min_0 = \beta$ (g/100 mL per h). In the example shown, the rate of ethanol elimination from blood (β-slope) was 0.014 g/100 mL per h. The other important pharmacokinetic parameter is the distribution volume of ethanol derived from the ratio of alcohol in the entire body (g/kg) to concentration in the blood at time zero given by C_0 (g/L). This latter parameter is the concentration of ethanol in blood that would be obtained if the entire dose was absorbed and distributed in the body before any metabolism occurred. In Fig. 6, the volume of distribution (V_d) was calculated to be

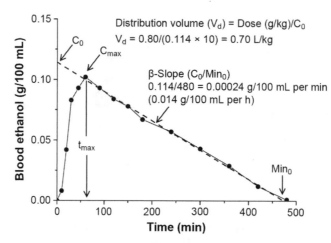

Fig. 6. Blood alcohol curve resulting from drinking a dose of ethanol (0.8 g/kg) on an empty stomach in 30 min. Shown on the graph is calculation of pharmacokinetic parameters including zero-order elimination rate constant (β-slope) and volume of distribution (V_d).

0.70 L/kg and represents a good average for male subjects.

On reaching low concentrations of ethanol in blood (<0.01–0.02 g/100 mL), the ADH metabolizing enzyme is no longer saturated with substrate and zero-order kinetics change to first-order kinetics. The entire postabsorptive elimination phase from high to low concentrations is best described by saturation kinetics described mathematically by the Michaelis-Menten equation. Table 3 compares the properties of zero-order, first-order, and Michaelis-Menten kinetics when applied to BAC profiles.

The Michaelis constant (k_m) for human Class I ADH is about 0.005–0.01 g/100 mL. Table 3 shows that if the Michaelis constant is much greater than the substrate concentration

(BAC), the equation collapses into first-order kinetics. In contrast, if the substrate concentration (BAC) is much greater than the Michaelis constant (e.g., >0.02 g/100 mL), then the elimination kinetics of ethanol are adequately described by zero-order kinetics.

The results from many alcohol dosing studies show that the average elimination rate of ethanol from blood is 0.015 g/100 mL per hour for men and 0.018 g/100 mL per hour for women. Several factors can affect this elimination rate. Enhanced rates of ethanol elimination from blood are likely in alcoholics during detoxification owing to a process of enzyme induction involving CYP2E1. Genetic factors may also be involved in controlling rates of metabolism, as seen in some ethnic groups such as Asians with slightly faster

Table 3. Examples of Various Pharmacokinetic Models Used to Describe Blood Alcohol Concentration-Time Profiles in Blood or Plasma

Pharmacokinetic Model	Rate Equations Describing the Process	Important Kinetic Parameters
Zero-order	$-dC/dt = kC^0$ Integration gives a linear equation $C_t = C_0 - k_0 t$	C_0 = y-intercept Zero-order rate constant (k_0)
First-order	$-dC/dt = kC^1$ Integration gives $C_t = C_0 e^{-kt}$ Log transformation gives $Ln\ C_t = Ln\ C_0 - k_1 t$	$Ln\ C_0$ = y-intercept First-order rate constant (k_1) Elimination half-life ($t_{1/2}$) = 0.693/k_1
Michaelis-Menten (saturation kinetics)	$-dC/dt = (V_{max} \times C)/(k_m + C)$ When $C >>> k_m$ then $-dC/dt = V_{max}$ (zero order) When $C <<< k_m$ then $-dC/dt = kC$ (first order) Note that $k = V_{max}/k_m$	Maximum reaction velocity (V_{max}) Michaelis constant (k_m)

elimination rates of ethanol from blood compared with Caucasians. Because most of the ethanol consumed is eliminated in the liver, any disease state in that tissue can potentially impair the clearance of ethanol. Administration of fructose, glycine, or alanine may enhance ethanol elimination. Recent work has suggested that food, as well as affecting the absorption of ethanol, might slightly enhance the elimination of ethanol.

There is some evidence that metabolism of ethanol occurs in the gastric mucosa before the blood reaches the liver, which would contribute to the observed first-pass metabolism (FPM) of ethanol when drinking occurs after a meal. The relative importance of FPM and whether this occurs in liver or stomach or both organs is still an open question, although most investigators seem to consider the liver as more important because of the greater amount of oxidative enzyme present. The area under the BAC curve is smaller when the same dose is administered orally compared with intravenously, which indicates a lower systemic availability. Gastric ADH would facilitate metabolism of some of the ethanol the longer it remains unabsorbed in the stomach. This implies that any drug that affects the activity of gastric ADH impacts on the FPM of ethanol. Drugs such as cimetidine and ranitidine, which inhibit the activity of gastric ADH, are therefore expected to allow more of the dose of ethanol to become absorbed into the blood and thus increase the bioavailability. Activity of gastric ADH also varies as a function of age and gender and between different racial groups. With all these factors to consider it is not surprising that the absorption phase of the BAC curve shows large intersubject variations and speaks against making predictions of the BAC expected after drinking a given dose.

The Widmark Equation

Blood alcohol curves are characterized by a rising phase mainly reflecting the absorption process, which initially occurs faster than elimination through metabolism and excretion. As time passes and the amount of alcohol still unabsorbed decreases, the BAC eventually reaches a peak or maximum concentration, usually at 30–90 min postdrinking. At this time the rates of absorption and metabolism are now about equal. During the postabsorptive declining portion of the BAC curve, absorption has already ended and elimination is the dominant process.

The relationship between a person's blood alcohol concentration and the amount of alcohol in the body has been thoroughly investigated and is expressed by the well-known Widmark equation:

$$A \text{ (g)} = BAC \text{ (g/L)} \times \text{body weight (kg)} \times V_d \text{ or rho (L/kg)}$$

In the above equation, A is the amount of alcohol (g) absorbed and distributed in all body fluids and tissues at the time of sampling blood, BAC is the blood alcohol concentration in g/L (g/100 mL × 10), and V_d is the apparent volume of distribution (rho factor = L/kg), which expresses the ratio of ethanol concentration in the whole body (g/kg) to that in the blood (g/L).

Blood alcohol calculations are commonly requested when alcohol-related crimes are investigated, such as driving under the influence of alcohol. For example, if a male person (V_d = 0.7 L/kg) with a body weight of 80 kg has a BAC of 0.1 g/100 mL then 56 g ethanol are absorbed and distributed in all body fluids and tissues. If drinking began 6 h before the blood was taken, the total amount of ethanol consumed is easy to calculate by adding on the amount lost through metabolism. Ethanol is eliminated from the whole body in moderate drinkers at a rate of 0.1 g/kg per h, so over 6 h a person has disposed of 48 g ethanol (0.1 × 80 × 6). The total amount consumed is easy to calculate from the equation below and this comes to 104 g (56 + 48 = 104), which if necessary can be converted to the number of standard drinks consumed.

$$A \text{ (g)} = [BAC \text{ (g/L)} \times \text{body weight (kg)} \times V_d \text{ or rho (L/kg)}] + [0.1 \times \text{kg} \times \text{h}]$$

The main sources of variation are uncertainty in the distribution factor V_d or rho and the elimination rate of alcohol from the body (g/kg/h). The results from many controlled drinking studies show that average V_d for ethanol is 0.70 for men and 0.60 for women and with an interindividual variation of about ± 20%. The lower average V_d of ethanol in females leads to a higher BAC for a given dose of ethanol ingested and this gender difference needs to be considered when blood alcohol calculations are made. The ± 20% variability in V_d stems from differences in body composition, especially the proportion of fat to lean tissue. There is scant evidence that the menstrual cycle and female sex hormones impact on the disposition and fate of ethanol in the body.

Other Alcohols

Forensic toxicologists are often required to analyze and interpret the concentrations of other aliphatic alcohols in blood samples, such as methanol (wood alcohol), isopropanol (rubbing alcohol), and ethylene glycol (antifreeze). These alcohols are widely available in household and commercial products and are sometimes consumed as ethanol substitutes for intoxication purposes by problem drinkers and alcoholics. The acute intoxication effects of ethanol are similar to these more toxic alcohols, which means that people are initially unaware they are in danger of poisoning and therefore don't seek emergency hospital treatment.

The metabolism of methanol is blocked as long as blood ethanol concentration exceeds 0.02 g/100 mL. Below this concentration methanol is converted in the liver first to formaldehyde and then formic acid and the elimination half-life is about 2–4 h. Formic acid is a strong organic acid (pKa = 3.77), which causes a disordered acid-base balance and a dangerous state of metabolic acidosis. Patients complain of nausea and they may vomit and suffer from abdominal pains after drinking methanol. A well-recognized clinical observation in methanol poisoning is blurred vision and blindness, owing to the interaction of formaldehyde with the retina or the eye. Methanol poisoning is associated with high mortality because people seek emergency treatment too late when life-threatening acidosis has already developed. Clinical diagnosis of methanol poisoning might include measuring osmolal gap and anion gap metabolic acidosis, although specificity is improved if blood methanol and/or serum formate are also determined. When methanol poisoning deaths are investigated, fatalities often depend on whether this alcohol was consumed alone or mixed with ethanol. The presence of ethanol prevents conversion into toxic metabolites and during this time methanol is eliminated in urine and breath.

Ethylene glycol is metabolized in the liver by the same enzymes involved in the metabolism of ethanol and methanol and the elimination half-life of the diol is 2.5–3.5 h in the absence of antidote treatment. The first product of metabolism is glycoaldehyde, which is further oxidized to glycolic acid. Oxidation of the second hydroxyl group produces glyoxylic acid and finally oxalic acid. Glycolic, glyoxylic, and oxalic acids contribute to the metabolic acidosis seen in patients poisoned with ethylene glycol. The clinical presentation of glycol toxicity is usually considered in three stages depending on time elapsed after ingestion. The first stage occurs after 0.5–2 h, when concentrations of the diol in blood are fairly high, leading to acute intoxication and depression of the central nervous system and also a raised osmolal gap. The second stage is seen after 12–24 h, when anion gap metabolic acidosis increases and osmolal gap decreases. Patients might experience difficulties breathing, with hyperventilation and hypoxia. The third stage is after 24–72 h, when concentration of the diol in blood is low or zero but there is a high anion gap and patients complain of pain in the lower back. Many cannot urinate (oliguria) and victims eventually die from renal failure and metabolic acidosis.

The traditional first-aid treatment for patients poisoned with methanol or ethylene glycol was to administer ethanol (8–10 % v/v) to reach and maintain a BAC of 0.1–0.15 g% for several hours. The higher affinity of liver ADH for ethanol meant that methanol and ethylene glycol were not converted into toxic metabolites. The unchanged alcohols as well as any metabolites formed could be removed from the blood by hemodialysis. Because dialysis also removes ethanol from the bloodstream, the infusion must be continued even during treatment.

A more modern alternative to ethanol as antidote for methanol and ethylene glycol poisoning is the drug fomepizole (Antizol®), which chemically is 4-methyl pyrazole. This heterocyclic molecule is a potent competitive inhibitor of liver ADH and like ethanol blocks conversion of the toxic alcohols into their more dangerous metabolites. Fomepizole also undergoes metabolism and needs to be administered as a series of IV injections to be an effective treatment for the poisoned patient. Unlike ethanol, fomepizole does not depress the central nervous system and is the preferred antidote for treatment of children or skid-row alcoholics, who might suffer from hepatic dysfunction (cirrhosis or other liver diseases). The disadvantage of fomepizole is the high cost of the medication compared with ethanol.

Treatment of patients poisoned with isopropanol is less complicated and requires only a general supervision to ensure they don't vomit and thus keep the airways clear and wait for the alcohol to become metabolized. The secondary alcohol is converted in the liver into acetone as the principal metabolite so patients have a sweetish smell of this ketone on the breath. The elimination half-life of isopropanol (3–5 h) is much shorter than that of acetone (15–20 h), which means acetone can be measured in blood and breath for a lot longer than isopropanol.

EFFECTS OF ETHANOL

Ethanol exerts a wide spectrum of biochemical and physiological effects on the body depending on the amounts consumed on each occasion (the dose) as well as duration (years) of exposure to the drug. The acute intoxicating effect of ethanol depends on the dose, the speed of drinking, and gastric emptying.

Metabolic Effects

A variety of metabolic disturbances occur during hepatic oxidation of ethanol as a direct result of an altered redox state of the liver, which is shifted to a more reduced potential. Acetaldehyde, the first product of oxidation, is a highly reactive chemical species that binds to proteins and other endogenous molecules, and toxicity of acetaldehyde has been incriminated in alcohol-related diseases, including the development of various cancers. When ethanol is oxidized to acetaldehyde, one atom of hydrogen is transferred to the cofactor nicotinamide adenine dinucleotide (NAD), which is converted to its reduced form (NADH). Further reduction of NAD to NADH occurs when acetaldehyde is oxidized to acetate in the second stage of ethanol biotransformation. The acetate generated from ethanol metabolism is transported with the blood away from the liver and is oxidized in the citric acid cycle into end products carbon dioxide and water (Fig. 3). When people were given ethanol labeled with ^{14}C, this radioactive tracer was immediately afterwards detected in the expired air as $^{14}CO_2$, verifying a rapid oxidative metabolism.

The markedly raised NADH/NAD$^+$ ratio and excess of reducing equivalents associated with the hepatic metabolism of ethanol have important consequences for other NAD-dependent biochemical reactions in the liver. The lactate/pyruvate ratio increases, which leads to hyperlactatemia and a metabolic acidosis; this diminishes the capacity of the kidneys to excrete uric acid and eventually leads to hyperuricemia and attacks of gout. Furthermore, an elevated NADH/NAD ratio favors triglyceride accumulation and also promotes fatty acid synthesis and lipogenesis, hence the clinical syndrome of fatty liver. Another metabolic consequence of elevated NADH/ NAD is inhibition of hepatic gluconeogenesis, which explains why heavy drinkers and alcohols often suffer from hypoglycemia. This condition is worsened by an inadequate diet in alcoholics, who obtain most of their calories from the combustion of ethanol (7.1 kcal per gram). However, these are referred to as "empty calories" because the body cannot store alcohol for later use and alcoholic drinks lack essential proteins, vitamins, and minerals contained in normal foods so many alcoholics are also malnourished.

Cardiovascular System

Moderate ethanol consumption has no significant effect on blood pressure, cardiac output, and cardiac contractile force. Moderate doses increase high-density lipoprotein, which has been associated with reduced cardiovascular disease. Ethanol does cause vasodilatation of the cutaneous vessels, which creates the feeling of warmth often associated with the consumption of alcoholic beverages. This vasodilatation does not occur uniformly over the vasculature. In fact, moderate doses of ethanol can cause vasoconstriction in the heart and brain.

Central Nervous System

Ethanol easily crosses the blood-brain barrier to interact with nerve cell membranes and receptor proteins, with the overall effect of depressing the central nervous system. At fairly low BAC (0.03–0.05 g/100 mL) people feel less inhibited; they become more talkative and social, which is often incorrectly conceived as stimulation. After higher doses and increasing BAC, depression of simpler and more basic functions occurs. At very high blood ethanol concentration (>0.4 g/100 mL) the respiratory center in the brain is depressed and coma and death ensue. Scientific studies performed over many years have established general relationships between BAC and effects on the brain as reflected in clinical signs and symptoms of drunkenness, and one widely cited and recently updated compilation is shown in Table 4.

Table 4 shows a broad overlap in the signs and symptoms of alcohol influence for different ranges of BAC. The mild euphoria at low BAC (<0.05 g/100 mL) is actually caused by disinhibition. As the blood ethanol concentration increases (0.03–0.12 g/100 mL), judgment and decision-making abilities are influenced, and perception and reaction to events are impaired. This impairment develops prior to the onset of more overt symptoms of ethanol intoxication such as difficulties in walking, speaking, and maintaining balance (0.09–0.25 g/100 mL). The signs and symptoms described in Table 4 are what might be expected for an adult person with moderate drinking habits. Habituation to alcohol alters the relationship and some people are able to function at high BAC, especially when relatively simple tasks are performed. The pattern of drinking is also important in relation to ethanol-induced impairment, which is more pronounced after rapid drinking and when the BAC is in the rising phase. When the BAC curve enters the postabsorptive phase, several hours postdosing, one observes a marked recovery in the intoxication/impairment effects of alcohol, which does not necessarily mean that a person is a safe driver, owing to anxiety and fatigue.

Gastrointestinal Tract

Consumption of ethanol preceding or in combination with meals stimulates the production of gastric juices rich in acid and poor in pepsin. Concentrated ethanol (e.g., at concentrations above 40%) can irritate mucosal membranes, which may lead to hyperemia or gastritis. Many chronic alcoholics have chronic GI problems due to the irritating effects of ethanol on the stomach. In general, gastric motility is not directly affected by ethanol.

Table 4. Stages of Acute Alcoholic Influence or Intoxication in Relation to Blood-Alcohol Concentration (BAC)

Blood Alcohol Conc. g/100 mL (g%)	Stage of Alcohol Influence	Clinical Signs or Symptoms
0.01–0.05	Subclinical	Behavior nearly normal by ordinary observation Influence/effects usually not apparent or obvious Impairment detectable by special tests
0.03–0.12	Euphoria	Mild euphoria, sociability, talkativeness Increased self-confidence; decreased inhibitions Diminished attention, judgment, and control Some sensory-motor impairment Slowed information processing Loss of efficiency in critical performance tests
0.09–0.25	Excitement	Emotional instability; loss of critical judgment Impairment of perception, memory, and comprehension Decreased sensatory response; increased reaction time Reduced visual acuity and peripheral vision and slow glare recovery Sensory-motor in-coordination; impaired balance; slurred speech Vomiting; drowsiness
0.18–0.30	Confusion	Disorientation, mental confusion; vertigo; dysphoria Exaggerated emotional states (fear, rage, grief, etc.) Disturbances of vision (diplopia, etc.) and of perception of color, form, motion, dimensions Increased pain threshold Increased muscular in-coordination; staggering gait; ataxia Memory loss Apathy with progressive lethargy
0.25–0.40	Stupor	General inertia; approaching loss of motor functions Markedly decreased response to stimuli Marked muscular in-coordination; inability to stand or walk Vomiting; incontinence of urine and feces Impaired consciousness; sleep or stupor; deep snoring
0.35–0.50	Coma	Complete unconsciousness; coma; anesthesia Depressed or abolished reflexes Subnormal temperature Impairment/irregularities of circulation and respiration Possible death
Mean, Median = 0.36 90% = 0.21–0.50	Death	Death from respiratory or cardiac arrest

Source: Copyright© 2012 by Kurt M. Dubowski, Ph.D., Oklahoma City, Oklahoma, USA.

Kidneys

The ingestion of ethanol produces a diuretic effect in part because of an increase in volume of liquid consumed, especially in beer drinkers who frequently need to urinate. However, the main diuretic action of ethanol is by inhibition of the secretion of antidiuretic hormone (vasopressin). Antidiuretic hormone is produced by the pituitary gland and is responsible for the renal tubular reabsorption of water. In general, about 99% of the water filtered by the kidneys is reabsorbed, with the remaining water (1%) entering the bladder as urine. The increased production of urine after drinking ethanol is only evident during the absorption part of the BAC curve as shown in Fig. 5. In the postabsorptive elimination phase of the BAC curve, the production of urine returns to normal at about 1 mL per minute.

Liver

The acute ingestion of ethanol has little effect on hepatic function. Damage to the liver will develop as a result of long-term, regular consumption of ethanol. Injury first occurs from the accumulation of fat in the liver. The amount of ethanol presented to the liver after drinking is large in comparison to the concentration of other substances. For the liver to process the ethanol, it reduces the activity of other biochemical processes. One of the processes reduced is the oxidation of fat, causing excess fat to remain in the liver. Furthermore, ethanol ingestion leads to increased acetaldehyde formation, which can also have a toxic effect on the liver by increasing lipid peroxidation. Initially, these fatty changes are reversible; however, over time continued heavy drinking requires repair of liver damage through the deposition of collagen. This leads to fibrotic changes in the liver that eventually become irreversible, developing into liver cirrhosis, liver failure, and death.

Miscellaneous Effects

Ethanol may cause either an increase or a decrease in a variety of secretions. For example, ethanol increases the production of hydrocortisone but decreases plasma testosterone concentrations. Plasma catecholamines also increase following the consumption of ethanol.

Ethanol is also associated with teratogenic effects. These effects have been defined collectively as the "fetal alcohol syndrome" and are described by lower intelligence, slower growth, and facial abnormalities. As a result, drinking alcoholic beverages during pregnancy is not recommended.

While the vasodilatation of ethanol gives the feeling of warmth, it in fact causes increased sweating, which leads to heat loss. Therefore, ethanol may cause a slight lowering of body temperature.

Tolerance

It is common knowledge that people differ in their response to the same dose of a drug and the legal drug ethanol is no exception. Ethanol's effects are biphasic, with stimulation being more pronounced during the rising part of the BAC curve and sedation and depression on the declining part of the BAC curve.

Tolerance is defined as a decrease in response to a given dose of a drug after repeated intake, and in pharmacology this is reflected in a shift in the dose-response curve to the right. Two main types of tolerance are recognized for ethanol: dispositional and cellular tolerance. Dispositional tolerance has to do with altered absorption, distribution, or elimination after repeated exposure to the drug, whereas cellular tolerance is reflected in an altered pharmacological response. Another name for dispositional tolerance is metabolic tolerance, reflected in an increased rate of metabolism owing to induction of the microsomal CYP2E1 enzyme after a period of chronic heavy drinking. The slope of the postabsorptive elimination phase in alcoholics might range from 0.02–0.035 g/100 mL per hour compared with 0.01–0.02 g/100 mL per hour in moderate drinkers. The dose of alcohol and frequency of drinking necessary to cause an induction of the microsomal enzyme has not been established in humans.

Acute tolerance refers to diminished effects of the drug on performance and behavior during a single exposure. Acute tolerance is sometimes referred to as the Mellanby effect, named after the British pharmacologist who first observed the phenomenon in dogs receiving alcohol by stomach tube. Acute tolerance is a robust finding and has been confirmed by many investigators using various behavioral measures of alcohol influence. Impairment is more pronounced on the ascending limb of the blood alcohol curve compared with the descending phase. A steeper slope on the ascending limb of the BAC curve produces a greater degree of intoxication and can be reinforcing for some drinkers but aversive for others, causing nausea and vomiting especially in novice drinkers. Gulping drinks and drinking on an empty stomach is associated with a steeper rise in BAC and a greater effect on the brain. The mechanism behind the development of acute tolerance is, however, not completely understood.

The other aspect of tolerance is chronic or functional tolerance, reflected in diminished effects of alcohol after the same dose or the need to drink greater amounts (higher dose) to achieve the same effects before development of tolerance. Many people are capable of functioning despite an elevated BAC as exemplified by drunk drivers, many of whom when examined by physicians were judged not under the influence of alcohol despite a high BAC. Apart from the smell of alcohol on the breath, when people arrested for public intoxication were admitted to emergency hospital departments for treatment they were coherent and could be interviewed despite some having a BAC of 0.3 g/100 mL or more. Whether caused by learning or previous experience, these individuals were able to compensate for the behavioral impairment effects of ethanol and in this way conceal the more overt symptoms of intoxication.

Also of interest is cross-tolerance between ethanol and other classes of drugs, such as barbiturates and benzodiazepines, which act as agonists at the $GABA_A$ receptor complex. Larger doses of these drugs might be necessary to achieve a desired effect in individuals who are tolerant to alcohol. This calls for caution when drugs such as benzodiazepines are prescribed to alcoholics and other people susceptible to abuse and dependence.

BLOOD ALCOHOL ANALYSIS

Sampling

The proper sampling of blood for determination of ethanol and other drugs requires assistance from a registered nurse,

physician, or phlebotomist legally entitled to draw blood. In some jurisdictions medical laboratory technicians might also be trained and permitted to take blood samples for forensic analysis. Obviously, when ethanol is the substance analyzed in blood, an alcohol swab should not be used to disinfect the skin at the site of the needle puncture. This would raise suspicion that the blood might have been contaminated with alcohol from the swab even though the risk of this happening is minimal when blood is drawn by venipuncture. To avoid unnecessary discussion and debate in legal cases, a nonalcohol skin disinfectant should be used such as providone-iodine or chlorhexidine. Simply washing the skin with soap and water would suffice because the needle used to penetrate the skin is sterile. Many alcohol-type antiseptics contain isopropanol and not ethanol; these alcohols are easily separated when using gas chromatography for analysis. Evacuated tubes used for sampling blood intended for ethanol analysis should contain an anticoagulant (potassium oxalate or heparin) as well as sodium fluoride (1% w/v) as an enzyme inhibitor. The latter is necessary to quash any notion that ethanol was produced by the action of yeasts or bacteria on blood glucose, which is not very likely anyway because the tubes and needle are sterile.

Three principal methods are available for analysis of ethanol in biological specimens: (1) chemical oxidation and titrimetric or photometric analysis; (2) enzymatic oxidation and measuring reduced coenzyme NADH by UV absorption at 340 nm; and (3) gas chromatography either by liquid injection or headspace analysis after equilibration of blood at a fixed temperature.

Chemical Oxidation

Methods of alcohol analysis based on chemical oxidation have been used for more than 100 years, and the most common oxidizing agent is a mixture of potassium dichromate and sulfuric acid. Before starting the chemical reaction it was necessary to remove ethanol from the sample by distillation, aeration, diffusion, or protein precipitation. The aqueous solution of ethanol produced was then reacted with the dichromate-acid mixture and the end point determined by titrimetric analysis or photometric analysis.

Wet-chemical oxidation methods of analysis were not specific for ethanol, and other volatiles such as acetone, methanol, or ether, if also present in blood, were oxidized, leading to false high concentrations of ethanol. This was a particular problem in postmortem toxicology when alcohol poisonings were investigated and the deceased had consumed denatured industrial alcohol. Special preliminary tests were necessary to identify the presence of these interfering substances.

One of the most successful wet-chemical oxidation methods was described by Widmark in 1922 and was used in several countries for legal purposes. This microdiffusion method required only 80–100 mg of capillary blood for each analysis. Widmark flasks resemble the Conway diffusion cells (a dish containing two concentric wells). The blood or other biological specimen (~100 mg) enters the outer well and an excess of the dichromate oxidizing agent is added to the inner well. The flask was sealed and allowed to stand at room temperature or heated until the reaction was completed. Ethanol and any other volatile substances in the blood diffuse into the center well where the chemical reaction occurs. The amount of oxidizing agent that remained after the reaction was over was determined by iodometric titration. Crystals of potassium iodide were added to react with dichromate and liberate iodine, which was determined by volumetric analysis using standard sodium thiosulfate and starch indicator to detect the endpoint.

The dichromate ion (Cr^{+6}) is converted to the chromic ion (Cr^{+3}), which causes a change in color from yellow to green, which was observed visually providing a simple screening test for alcohol. Semiquantitative results were possible by making a series of ethanol standards and allowing them to react with dichromate in exactly the same way as case specimens. However, methods based on chemical oxidation are labor intensive and nonspecific, making them more or less obsolete in modern clinical and forensic laboratories.

Enzymatic Oxidation

Enzymatic methods were first applied to blood alcohol analysis in the 1950s and coincided with the isolation of the liver enzyme alcohol dehydrogenase (ADH) in a pure crystalline form. The enzymes contained in yeast were found to be more selective for oxidation of ethanol than mammalian ADH, which was an important consideration for specificity of the method. Because the ADH-NAD^+ oxidative is reversible, the acetaldehyde formed must be trapped so that the reaction is driven to completion. The buffer solution of coenzyme NAD^+ also had semicarbizide present, which reacted with acetaldehyde to produce a stable semicarbazone. The NADH produced from NAD^+ is measured spectrophotometrically at 340 nm and used for quantitative analysis. Although this assay was designed for serum, it works equally well with urine and also whole blood after precipitation of proteins with perchloric acid.

Enzymatic methods had the advantage in that they were easier to automate and several procedures became available including use of a Technicon AutoAnalyzer or an Abbott X series analyzers. In the latter method NADH produced by the ADH-catalyzed reaction of ethanol reacts with a thiazoyl blue dye, forming a chromagen. This technique is called radiative energy attenuation (REA) and is based on the principle that the measured fluorescence intensity of a solution containing a fluorophore and a chromagen is related to the absorbance of the solution. In this assay, fluoroscein is the fluorophore and has been used successfully to measure ethanol in serum and urine, as well as in blood from living and deceased persons.

Gas-Liquid Chromatography

The "gold standard" method for qualitative and quantitative determination of ethanol in biological specimens in both clinical and forensic laboratories is gas-liquid chromatography (GLC) equipped with a flame ionization detector (FID). GLC is highly sensitivity and specific and provides accurate and precise results in a minimum of time. Moreover, other volatiles that might be present in blood together with ethanol, such as other alcohols, aldehydes, and ketones, can be determined simultaneously and can be distinguished by their retention times, that is, the time after injection until the appearance of the apex of the peak on the gas chromatogram. Quantitative analysis by FID gives a linear response over a wide range of ethanol concentrations in blood from 0.01–0.5 g/100 mL and the limit of quantitation in routine case work is usually 0.01 g/100 mL. The FID detector has the advantage in that it is insensitive to water vapor but sensitive to substances containing carbon, hydrogen, and oxygen atoms. The analytical sensitivity can be increased by saturating the blood sample with an inorganic salt, such as sodium chloride or potassium carbonate, which might be necessary if endogenous concentrations of ethanol are of interest.

The two most widely used GLC methods are direct injection of a liquid sample (1–2 μL) or analysis of the headspace vapor in equilibrium with the blood sample in a closed glass vial. The biological specimen should first be diluted (1:10) with an aqueous solution of internal standard (I.S.), such as n-propanol or t-butanol, before GLC analysis. Diluting with an internal standard reduces the amount of biological substance that enters the GC instrument, which prolongs the life of the analytical column, and measuring peak area ratios helps to compensate for any variations in operating conditions. A calibration plot is constructed by plotting peak area ratio (ethanol:I.S.) for known strength aqueous standards and using this to deduce the ethanol concentration in blood samples.

The problem posed by making repeated injections of the biological matrix into the GC instrument is avoided when headspace GC analysis is done. The diluted blood sample is transferred to a glass vial, which is then fitted with a rubber septum and a crimped-on aluminum cap. The vial is allowed to equilibrate at 50 or 60 °C and then headspace vapor samples are removed with a gas-tight syringe and injected into the GC instrument for analysis. At a fixed temperature, the amount of any volatile in the air space is proportional to the concentration of the volatile substance in the solution. Therefore, sampling the headspace of heated specimens and similarly treated ethanol calibrators allows calculation of the ethanol concentration in the specimen. Furthermore, aqueous calibrators can be used if the specimen is diluted 10 times, which eliminates matrix effects.

The traditional gas chromatographs used packed columns measuring about 2-m long and 3-mm inside diameter and containing polar stationary phases such as polyethylene glycol (Carbowax) or porous polymer materials (Porapak), which separated the volatile substances. Today, capillary columns are the norm for GLC analysis of ethanol and other substances, and specialist columns are available for blood alcohol and related volatiles. These substances are separated according to the size of the molecules and their volatility. A thermal conductivity detector can be used but is not advisable because of the large response to water vapor in the sample. The flame ionization detector is the most appropriate for carbon-hydrogen molecules and has high sensitivity and good linearity. The effluent from the GC column could also be analyzed by mass spectrometry and the electron impact spectrum contains mass fragments at m/z 31 (base peak), m/z 45, and m/z 46 (molecular ion), which are characteristic of ethanol and "fingerprint" the molecule. The theory behind each of these detectors is explained in Chapter 9. An example of a gas chromatogram from a calibrator containing multiple volatiles is shown in Fig. 7.

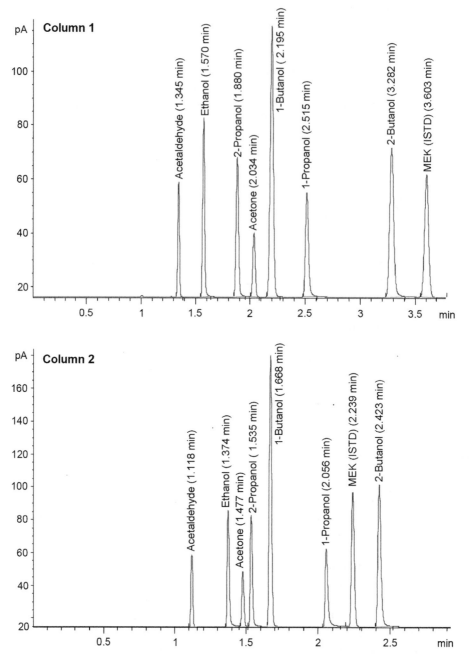

Fig. 7. Typical gas chromatogram obtained from analysis of a mixture of volatiles containing acetaldehyde, ethanol, acetone, isopropanol, 1-propanol, 1-butanol, and 2-butanol using 2-butanone (MEK) as the internal standard on two different columns (Restek Rtx®-BAC1 and -BAC2).

Analysis of Alcohol in Breath

A maximum of 10% of the total amount of alcohol consumed leaves the body unchanged by excretion via the lungs (exhaled air), the kidney (urine), and the skin (sweat). The small amount eliminated via the lungs forms the basis of the use of breath analyzers in traffic law enforcement as evidence of driving under the influence of alcohol. Roadside breath alcohol tests are routinely done by police authorities worldwide to test people suspected of driving under the influence of alcohol. There are several advantages of breath alcohol analysis over sampling blood for laboratory analysis, including noninvasive sampling and obtaining results immediately afterward so that decisions can be made to arrest the driver or repeat the test.

Three special characteristics of ethanol facilitate use of breath analysis: (1) ethanol is volatile; (2) the concentrations in blood and breath are highly correlated; and (3) after drinking alcohol the concentration of ethanol exhaled in breath far exceeds that of other endogenous volatile substances. However, acetone is a potential interfering substance and high concentrations are exhaled in breath in poorly treated diabetics or after a prolonged fast or eating low-carbohydrate diets.

Two types of breath alcohol analyzer are currently available: hand-held electronic devices mainly intended for screening purposes and highly sophisticated stationary units used at police stations for evidential purposes. The hand-held units are denoted PBTs (preliminary breath testers) and they capture a sample of breath as the suspect exhales through a disposable plastic mouthpiece. Ethanol content in the breath is determined by electrochemical oxidation (fuel cell). Breath alcohol analyzers intended for evidential purposes determine ethanol content of breath by infrared spectrometry and by measuring the stretching frequency of C-H bonds (3.5 μm) or the C-O bond (9.5 μm) in ethanol molecules. Some modern breath alcohol analyzers incorporate both infrared and electrochemical methods of analysis, which is highly desirable in forensic toxicology because this furnishes two independent methods of analysis. Test subjects are required to make a prolonged end exhalation into the instrument for at least 6 s and the concentration profile of exhaled ethanol is monitored as a function of time.

The physiological principles of breath alcohol testing are well founded scientifically. The distribution of ethanol between blood and alveolar air obeys Henry's law, which states that at a given temperature, a direct relationship exists between the amount of a volatile substance (ethanol) dissolved in a liquid (blood) and the amount of the substance in the vapor (alveolar air) above the solution. Commercially available evidential breath-testing devices are based on the relationship that the amount of ethanol in 2100 mL of breath equals the amount of ethanol in 1 mL of blood at 34 °C, the temperature of expired air. This 2100:1 ratio was based on early scientific studies; more recent work indicates that 2300:1 is a better representation of the actual breath-to-blood ratio. This means that breath-testing devices based on a 2100:1 ratio will underestimate the actual blood ethanol concentration for the overwhelming majority of individuals.

Several scientific safeguards are necessary when breath alcohol analyzers are used for legal purposes; the most important of which is to observe the subject for at least 15–20 min prior to taking a sample and to ensure that nothing enters the mouth. Belching or vomiting could return ethanol from the stomach, possibly leading to an erroneous result. Evidentiary breath tests are confirmation tests that require a deprivation period of 15 min and are preceded by a blank reading from analysis of room air. At least two breath samples should be collected and analyzed, with the replicate analyses agreeing within 0.02 g/210L for approval. Breath ethanol results should be reported in terms of a mass of ethanol per volume of breath, which avoids any assumptions about a particular blood:breath ratio. Instrument performance should be validated with the testing of each subject using either a wet bath simulator or a calibrated dry gas standard as an ethanol control sample.

Many analytical methods have been developed for forensic breath alcohol analysis, including the classic Breathalyzer® instrument developed by Robert F Borkenstein in the 1950s. The sampling of breath was done in a stainless steel cylinder and piston device with a vent that allowed discarding of the initial top-lung exhaled breath. The last part of the exhalation that was considered to reflect alveolar air was trapped and saved for analysis. The sample chamber was heated to 50 °C to prevent condensation of water vapor and ethanol in the breath sample. The breath sample was analyzed by oxidation with a mixture of potassium dichromate and sulfuric acid and a small amount of silver nitrate catalyst, which was contained in a glass ampoule. The oxidation reaction was allowed to proceed for 90 s, the optimal time to prevent interference from any acetone that might be present in the breath sample. The actual photometric measurement of ethanol was done at an absorbance of 440 nm.

Infrared (IR) Spectrophotometry

The absorption of infrared (IR) radiation is a characteristic property of a molecule depending on its structure and the types of chemical bonding. Absorption of IR light at certain wavelengths is characteristic of certain bonds, such as C-H, O-H, or C-O. Molecules can undergo stretching and bending vibrations when exposed to IR radiation and the usual range of wavelengths span from 2.5 to 25 μm corresponding to wave numbers 4000–400 cm^{-1}.

The use of IR technology for the analysis of ethanol in breath has become a mainstay in evidential breath-testing devices. Ethanol has several types of bonds: C-H, C-C, C-O, and O-H. Selecting a wavelength where these bonds specifically absorb IR energy allows partial identification and quantification of ethanol in breath. Because many other compounds have the same chemical bonding and absorb IR energy at the same wavelength, there is a risk for interference with analysis of ethanol in breath. This potential interference problem is mitigated by the fact that an interfering substance must be volatile enough to appear in significant concentration in human expired air. Specificity can be enhanced by using multiple wavelengths achieved with a series of filters between 3.3–3.5 μm.

IR breath analyzers differ in certain respects, such as volume of breath sampled, wavelength monitored, number of wavelengths used, and manner in which the exhalation is controlled for time and pressure characteristics. However, the basic principle is the same and an end-expired sample of breath enters a heated chamber or cell where it is irradiated with IR energy. If ethanol is present in the sample, it will absorb some of the IR energy in proportion to the amount of ethanol in the sample. Absorption of IR energy by ethanol means that less energy reaches the detector in comparison to an air sample not containing ethanol. By calibrating the instrument using known strength air-ethanol vapor mixtures, the ethanol concentration in the subject's breath can be determined.

Electrochemical Oxidation

Electrochemical detectors oxidize ethanol in the vapor phase to acetaldehyde and further to acetic acid, and such detectors have been incorporated into a range of instruments intended for forensic breath alcohol analysis. This detector is constructed as a fuel cell, which consists of two platinum-coated conduction electrodes separated by an ion-conducting electrolyte layer, such as phosphoric acid. The conversion of ethanol present in breath to acetic acid produces a current. The flow generated is directly proportional to the amount of ethanol present in the sample. The fuel cell may react minimally with other alcohols like methanol and isopropanol but does not respond to any great extent to acetone.

Fuel cell technology has been used since the 1970s in hand-held instruments for breath alcohol analysis. These devices are intended as roadside screening tests to furnish police officers with probable cause to arrest a driver for further testing. Fuel cells might also be used in evidential breath analyzers, especially in combination with an IR detector. Because the IR detector is nondestructive of ethanol, a fuel cell can be placed in series after an IR detector. The fuel cell does not oxidize acetone, which is the major endogenous volatile in the breath under some circumstances. However, acetaldehyde is oxidized but the concentrations in breath, even after drinking alcoholic beverages, are so low that this ethanol metabolite is not a serious problem as an interfering substance.

Gas chromatography has also been adapted for breath alcohol analysis, because ethanol is already in the gaseous state when exhaled in the breath. Small and compact GC instruments incorporated a pressurized cylinder containing a mixture of hydrogen and nitrogen as combustible gas for the flame detector and a sampling loop to capture a portion of the exhaled air. One such instrument was the GC Intoximeter (FID detector) and another the AlcoAnalyzer (thermal conductivity detector). However, the complexity of GC analysis, the need for more intensive training of operators, and the need for more frequent recalibrations meant that GC methods, although more specific, were abandoned in favor of infrared breath alcohol analyzers.

Examples of hand-held PBT instruments include Alcolmeter, Alcotest, Lifeloc, and AlcoSensor, all of which incorporate fuel cell sensors for determination of ethanol. Electrochemistry is not completely specific for ethanol because methanol and other alcohols (but not acetone) are oxidized at different reaction rates. The instruments used for evidential breath alcohol testing are mostly based on multiple wavelength infrared (IR) detectors at 3.4 μm and/or 9.5 μm ranges (e.g., Intoxilyzer, DataMaster, and Evidenzer). One evidential breath analyzer (Intoximeter EC/IR) uses electrochemical oxidation as the primary means of detection, whereas others use a combination of IR and electrochemistry (Alcotest).

STABILITY OF ETHANOL IN BLOOD AND URINE

Compared with many other drugs and intoxicants encountered in forensic toxicology, the concentrations of ethanol in blood are remarkably stable during short- and long-term storage of specimens. A small decrease in concentration of ethanol in blood of about 0.003 g/100 mL per month occurs

when specimens are stored refrigerated (4 °C) in evacuated tubes until analyzed. The loss of ethanol is higher if the tubes are opened periodically to remove aliquots for analysis. Besides a diffusion of ethanol from the liquid into the air space, exposure to room air replenishes the oxygen content in the air space above the blood, and one mechanism suggested to account for this loss of ethanol is nonenzymatic oxidation via oxyhemoglobin. Hence, ethanol concentrations might be more stable in blood samples from smokers with higher concentrations of carboxyhemoglobin compared with nonsmokers. Stability is improved if specimens are stored frozen.

The evacuated tubes used to collect blood samples for ethanol analysis should contain chemical preservatives in powder form. Use of potassium oxalate, EDTA, or heparin is suitable as an anticoagulant, and sodium fluoride (~1% w/v) is included as an enzyme inhibitor. A widely used 10 mL grey-stopper evacuated tube used for collecting blood samples for ethanol analysis has potassium oxalate (25 mg) as an anticoagulant and sodium fluoride (100 mg) as an enzyme inhibitor.

Ethanol concentrations in blood from living persons are rarely found to increase during long-term storage. But the situation is different in autopsy work because the specimens might already be contaminated with bacteria when the autopsy was performed. Ethanol can be produced by fermentation of substrates such as glucose and various fatty acids or amino acids in the presence of bacteria or yeasts. It is always a challenge in postmortem toxicology to establish whether a measured BAC resulted from antemortem ingestion or postmortem synthesis (neoformation). This can be investigated in a number of ways, although knowledge of the circumstances surrounding the death, especially witness statements and police reports about possible drinking by the deceased, is important information.

In postmortem toxicology, the concentrations of ethanol in different biological specimens should be compared and contrasted because this furnishes useful information to rule out postmortem synthesis having occurred. Finding acceptable agreement in results based on known water content of the materials analyzed speaks toward antemortem ingestion of ethanol and not postmortem synthesis. If the body emits a bad smell at autopsy this is a strong indication that decomposition has already commenced and care is needed when toxicological results are interpreted. Finding an elevated concentration of ethanol in blood but negligible concentrations in vitreous humor or urine, which are both resistant to the putrefaction process, speaks toward postmortem production of ethanol.

Low concentrations of ethanol in blood, such as 0.01 g/100 mL, are easily produced after death even when there are no obvious signs of decomposition or putrefaction. This suggests that in postmortem toxicology a blood ethanol cutoff concentration of 0.02 g/100 mL would be more appropriate when positive results are reported. Low BACs of 0.01–0.03 g/100 mL need to be verified by analysis of ethanol in alternative specimens, such as vitreous humor (VH) or urine. Occasionally, blood ethanol concentrations exceeding 0.10 g/100 mL are seen with zero concentrations in alternative specimens, especially in highly traumatic deaths. On the other hand, a measurable concentration found in vitreous humor or urine specimens speaks toward antemortem ingestion of alcohol, especially if the concentrations ratios VH:blood or urine:blood are in the expected range of 1.2–1.3 based on relative water content of the specimens analyzed.

Other evidence that ethanol was produced in the body after death comes from finding other volatile substances besides ethanol (e.g., acetaldehyde, acetone, n-propanol, or n-butanol). Although ethanol is the main product of bacterial activity, it is not the exclusive product. However, because acetaldehyde is a normal metabolic product of ethanol metabolism and acetone might be elevated in blood of diabetics or malnourished individuals, the presence of these substances can occur by mechanisms other than fermentation.

Recent research demonstrates the possibility to determine nonoxidative metabolites of ethanol in body fluids as evidence that ethanol has undergone metabolism in the body during life. Methods involving GC/MS or LC/MS with deuterium-labeled internal standards are widely used to determine ethyl glucuronide or ethyl sulfate in postmortem specimens, including hair strands. The analysis of EtG and EtS verifies that ethanol has undergone a phase II conjugation reaction, which points toward antemortem consumption rather than postmortem synthesis. Use of realistic cutoff concentrations for positive EtG and EtS are necessary to avoid extraneous sources of ethanol in foodstuffs, medication, and various household products.

Numerous studies show a good stability of ethanol in antemortem blood specimens when they are properly stored in evacuated tubes and contain a chemical preservative. Potassium oxalate is commonly used as an anticoagulant to prevent clotting and is used in conjunction with sodium fluoride as an enzyme inhibitor. Under these conditions, in properly sealed tubes, the blood ethanol concentration will remain stable for at least a month, even if kept at room temperature.

As alluded to earlier, ethanol is rarely produced after voiding if the urine specimens are obtained from healthy subjects. The situation is different in diabetics, who might secrete glucose in the urine and who may also suffer from a urinary tract or *Candida* infection. Under these circumstances, after 24–48 h storage at room temperature high urinary concentrations of ethanol are produced. However, all three components (sugar, microorganism, or yeast) and time are necessary for the in vitro production of ethanol after sampling. Storage of samples in the cold at +4 °C or better still frozen (–20 °C) prevents microbial synthesis of ethanol even when there is no NaF in the tubes. However, because urinary tract infections or candidiasis are common in diabetics, the inclusion of a fluoride preservative should be mandatory if ethanol is the substance to be analyzed.

LEGAL AND REGULATORY ASPECTS

Driving under the Influence

Epidemiological surveys verify that overconsumption of alcohol and drunkenness play a major role in many types of accidents in the home, at work, and on the roads. Therefore, the analysis of alcohol in blood and other body fluids forms a critical component in any criminal or civil investigation of alcohol-related accidents. To address this problem, state legislatures have set limits on the concentration of ethanol permitted in blood or breath when an individual operates a motor vehicle.

Most countries have enacted blood alcohol limits ranging from 0.02–0.08 g/100 mL depending on activity, such as driving on the highway or engaging in safety-sensitive work (Table 5). The blood alcohol concentrations are expressed in different concentration units, such as mg/100 mL (UK and Canada), g/L (France and Spain), and g/kg (Nordic countries and Germany). SI concentration units (mmol/L) are also given for comparison because these units are increasingly used in hospital clinical chemistry laboratories when alcohol is analyzed and reported.

As early as 1971, the U.S. National Safety Council Committee on Alcohol and Other Drugs stated that any driver with a blood alcohol concentration of 0.08 g/100 mL or more was impaired in terms of driving performance.

Subsequent statements by the committee have emphasized that driving impairment occurs at lower concentrations in some individuals. Almost all states have moved away from "presumption" statutes where the issue of an individual's intoxication is rebuttable by other evidence, regardless of the ethanol concentration. Instead, "per se" laws have been adopted that make it a violation of the law to have above a fixed ethanol concentration in blood or breath at time of driving.

The National Committee on Uniform Traffic Laws and Ordinances (NCUTLO) developed the Uniform Vehicle Code to be adopted by the various states and the District of Columbia. The document consists of two parts: (1) the Uniform Vehicle Code, a set of motor vehicle laws designed and advanced as a comprehensive guide or standard for the state motor vehicle traffic laws; and (2) the Model Traffic Ordinance. Within the Uniform Vehicle Code several recommendations are important to alcohol testing:

- Revocation of license for refusal to submit to a chemical test or having a BAC of 0.08 g/100 mL or g/210 L or more, generally referred to as the "implied consent law." Any person who drives a motor vehicle on public highways shall be deemed to have given his consent to have a chemical test of breath, blood, or urine to determine the alcohol concentration or the presence of other drugs.

Table 5. Threshold Blood Alcohol Concentration (BAC) Limits Expressed in Different Units and Used for Regulatory and Legal Purposes

g/100 mL (g%)	mg/100 mL (mg%)	g/L (mg/mL)	mmol/L[a]	g/kg (mg/g)[b]	Threshold or Legal Standard
0.08	80	0.80	18.2	0.76	Federal blood alcohol limit for driving in all 50 U.S. states.
0.05	50	0.50	11.3	0.47	Medical standard for alcohol influence and the statutory limit for driving in most EU countries.
0.04	40	0.40	9.1	0.38	Federal highway safety standard for commercial vehicle drivers and also workplace violations.
0.02	20	0.20	4.5	0.19	Blood alcohol limit for novice drivers in U.S. states and also some EU nations.

[a] Molecular weight of ethanol = 46 (0.1 g/100 mL = 21.7 mmol/L)
[b] Density of blood = 1.055 g/mL

- Revocation of license for refusal to submit to a chemical test or having a BAC of any measurable and detectable amount (0.02 g/100 mL or g/210 L or more) for persons under 21 years of age.
- The administration of a preliminary breath test when a law enforcement officer has probable cause to believe the person may be impaired by alcohol.
- A driver may be compelled to submit to a chemical test if involved in a serious personal injury or fatal crash.
- The State Department of Health is authorized to approve techniques or methods for the analysis of alcohol in blood, breath, and urine and to promulgate guidelines to determine competence of individuals to conduct such analysis.
- The sample for analysis of blood may only be drawn by a physician, registered nurse, or other person qualified to withdraw blood acting at the direction of a police officer.
- The defendant may have an additional test administered in addition to the test administered at the direction of the officer.
- Alcohol concentration shall mean either grams of alcohol per 100 mL of blood or grams of alcohol per 210 L of breath.

- If alcohol concentration is measured at 0.08 g/100 mL or g/210 L or more, it shall be presumed that the person was under the influence of alcohol.

The Uniform Vehicle Code serves as a basis for standardizing laws and practices among the states.

Fig. 8 shows relative frequency distributions of blood alcohol concentrations in men and women apprehended in Sweden (statutory BAC limit 0.02 g/100 mL) for drunken driving. Mean blood alcohol concentrations, regardless of gender, were 0.16–0.17 g/100 mL, which signifies a period of heavy drinking and suggests that many drunk drivers are problem drinkers or alcoholics. Males dominated over females among traffic delinquents by 88% to 12%, although BAC did not seem to vary much in relation to the person's age.

Alcohol in the Workplace

Some workplace activities obviously entail greater hazards than others, including significant risks to the worker, the workplace, and other individuals. In particular, the transportation workplace in all modalities presents a variety of basic safety hazards, which are increased by the effects of alcohol use by workers performing various safety-sensitive

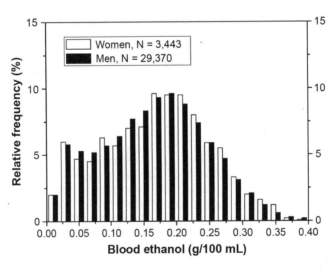

Fig. 8. Relative frequency distributions of blood alcohol concentration in men and women apprehended for drunken driving in Sweden where the statutory limit is 0.02 g/100 mL.

functions. Many nontransportation industries and workplaces also involve transport of persons, goods, and materials. In others, activities and operations occur that are inherently hazardous or associated with potential risks. The risk of error or adverse events is increased when tasks are performed by alcohol-impaired workers. Fundamentally, workers should be free of alcoholic influence at all times while at work. It is, therefore, recommended that:

- Employees abstain from alcohol intake for 12–24 h prior to undertaking critical and safety-sensitive tasks.
- An appropriate program of on-site and off-site alcohol testing be implemented.
- Breath alcohol concentrations <0.01 g/210 L, and blood and saliva alcohol concentrations <0.01 g/100 mL, should be deemed alcohol-free.

The universe of alcohol testing in the workplace is readily divided into governmentally regulated and nonregulated testing (testing for alcohol that is not required by law). In addition to testing performed under federal mandates, increasing numbers of states have enacted laws that control testing for alcohol and other drugs in workers. Further, such groups as the National Football League and the National Basketball Association require testing for alcohol and other abused drugs in professional athletes.

There are several important differences between alcohol and other abused drugs. Principally, alcohol is a licit drug and consumption of alcoholic beverages by adults is lawful, with limited exceptions, such as while driving motor vehicles. The mere presence of alcohol in the body and in body fluids (breath or saliva) does not imply a violation of law. Alcohol in the body has a short half-life, meaning that its elimination from the body is significantly faster than that of other commonly abused drugs (hours rather than days or weeks). Thus the timing of specimen collection for alcohol testing is more critical and demanding.

The National Safety Council's Committee on Alcohol and Other Drugs in 1995 developed "A Model Program for the Control of Alcohol in the Workplace." The program was designed primarily to assist employers and others required to establish testing programs in response to the Omnibus Transportation Employee Testing Act of 1991. It suggests that the purpose of alcohol-testing programs is to help prevent accidents and injuries resulting from the misuse of alcohol by employees who perform safety-sensitive functions.

Workplace alcohol testing regulated by the U.S. Department of Transportation (DOT) is mandated by the Omnibus Transportation Employee Testing Act of 1991 (Public Law 102–143, 1991) for certain transportation modalities. Performance of safety-sensitive functions by a covered employee in a DOT-regulated entity is prohibited:

1. When such a person has an alcohol concentration of 0.04 g/210 L or greater, as indicated by a breath alcohol test, or temporarily when such person has an alcohol concentration of 0.02 g/210 L or greater but less than 0.04 g/210 L.
2. While such person is using alcohol.
3. Within 4–8 h after using alcohol.

In addition, an employee involved in an accident may not refuse alcohol testing or consume alcoholic beverages until tested or until 8 h after an accident.

The categories for alcohol testing in the workplace are largely self-explanatory and include:

- Applicant testing.
- Reasonable suspicion and reasonable cause testing.
- Fitness-for-duty testing.
- Postaccident testing.
- Return-to-duty and follow-up testing.
- Random testing.

Testing for alcohol under the DOT regulations has the following features:

- Alcohol is defined as "the intoxicating agent in beverage alcohol, ethyl alcohol, or other low molecular weight alcohols including methyl or isopropyl alcohol."

- Alcohol concentration is defined as "the alcohol in a volume of breath expressed in terms of grams of alcohol per 210 liters of breath as indicated by a breath test."
- All alcohol testing is to be carried out on-site at the workplace, except in some postaccident situations.
- Breath and saliva are the only acceptable specimens for initial "screening" tests.
- "Screening" and "confirmation" tests are required in specific situations. Breath is the only acceptable specimen for "confirmation" tests, with some exceptions for postaccident testing.

Testing is categorized into two varieties:

- Initial tests, sometimes referred to as screening or preliminary tests, are intended to establish whether the tested person is alcohol-free or not. Alcohol-free individuals do not require any further testing. To be most practical, screening tests must be simple and rapidly performed with minimal training.
- Confirmatory tests are performed with evidential-grade testing devices after an initial test has indicated the presence of alcohol in the tested person. The results of the confirmatory test are relied upon for personnel actions such as removal from current safety-sensitive duties.

All testing for alcohol in breath or saliva must be carried out with testing and associated devices appearing on NHTSA Conforming Products Lists. Screening tests on breath or saliva must use approved breath or saliva alcohol screening test devices or be performed on breath with approved evidential breath testers (EBTs). Confirmation tests must be carried out on breath and must use EBTs that are:

1. Capable of providing a printed result in triplicate.
2. Capable of assigning a unique and sequential number to each completed test and displaying the same before test.
3. Capable of printing on each copy of the result the manufacture's name for the device, the device serial number, the time of the test, the test number, and the test result.
4. Able to distinguish alcohol from acetone at an alcohol concentration of 0.02 g/210 L.
5. Capable of testing an air blank prior to each collection of breath, and of performing an "external calibration check."

Confirmation tests must be carried out within 30 min of the completion of a screening test that reports an alcohol concentration of 0.02 g/210 L or greater. A deprivation period of not less than 15 min and an air blank yielding a 0.00 g/210 L result must precede the breath collection for a confirmation test. (Air blanks are not required before or after a breath-screening test.) Testing must be performed by a breath alcohol technician (BAT) who has successfully completed a course of instruction equivalent to the DOT model course and who has "demonstrated competence in the operation of the specific EBT(s)" that the BAT will use. Law enforcement officers who have been certified by state or local governments to conduct breath alcohol testing with the EBT concerned are deemed by DOT to be qualified as BATs.

The following documents define the criteria for evaluation and provide notice of acceptable products that meet the established criteria:

1. Model Specifications for Evidential Breath-Testing Devices (58 FR 48705–10, September 17, 1993).
2. Conforming Products List of Evidential Breath Alcohol Measurement Devices (77 FR 35747–35751, June 14, 2012).
3. Model Specifications for Screening Devices to Measure Alcohol in Bodily Fluids (73 FR 16956–16960, March 31, 2008).
4. Conforming Products List of Screening Devices to Measure Alcohol in Bodily Fluids (74 FR 66398–66400, December 15, 2009).
5. Model Specifications for Calibrating Unit for Breath Alcohol Testers; Conforming Products List of Calibrating Unit for Breath Testers (72 FR 34742–34748, June 25, 2007)

Updated notices of conforming products appear periodically in the Federal Register.

SUGGESTED READING

1. Caplan YH, Zettl JR. The determination of alcohol in blood and breath. In: Saferstein R, ed. Forensic science handbook, 2nd ed. Englewood Cliffs, NJ: Prentice-Hall, Inc., 2002:635–95.

2. Dubowski KM. Absorption, distribution, and elimination of alcohol: highway safety aspects. J Stud Alc 1985;Suppl 10:98–108.

3. Dubowski KM. The technology of breath-alcohol analysis. DHHS publication (ADM) 92–1728, Rockville, MD: National Institute on Alcohol and Alcoholism, 1992.

4. Garriott JC, ed., Garriott's medicolegal aspects of alcohol, 5th ed., Tucson, AZ: Lawyers and Judges Publishing, Inc., 2008.

5. Jones AW. Physiological aspects of breath-alcohol measurement. Alc, Drugs, and Driving 1990;6:1–25.

6. Jones AW. Measuring alcohol in blood and breath for forensic purposes—a historical review. Forensic Sci Rev 1996;8:14–43.

7. Jones AW. Urine as a biological specimen for forensic alcohol analysis and variability in the urine-to-blood relationship. Toxicol Rev 2006;25:15–35.

8. Jones AW. Biochemical and physiological research on the disposition and fate of ethanol in the body. In: Garriott JC, ed. Medical-legal aspects of alcohol, 5th ed. Tucson, AZ: Lawyers & Judges Publishing Co., Inc., 2008.

9. Jones AW. Evidence based survey of the elimination rates of ethanol from blood with applications in forensic casework. Forensic Sci Int 2010;200:1–20.

10. Jones AW. Pharmacokinetics of ethanol—issues of forensic importance. Forensic Sci Rev 2011;23:91–136.

11. Kugelberg FC, Jones AW. Interpreting results of ethanol analysis in postmortem specimens: a review of the literature. Forensic Sci Int 2007;165:10–29.

12. O'Neal CL, Poklis A. Postmortem production of ethanol and factors that influence interpretation: a critical review. Am J Forensic Med Path 1996;17:8–20.

13. Porter WH. Ethylene glycol poisoning. Quintessential clinical toxicology, analytical conundrum. Clin Chim Acta 2012;413:365–77.

14. Walsham NE, Sherwood RA. Ethyl glucuronide. Ann Clin Biochem 2012;49:110–7.

CHAPTER 14

Benzodiazepines

Rebecca A. Jufer-Phipps and Barry Levine

As a class, benzodiazepines are one of the most widely prescribed drugs in the world and have largely replaced barbiturates as the major class of CNS-depressant drugs. Data from 2004 indicated that five benzodiazepines rank among the top 200 drugs in the U.S., as determined by the number of prescriptions dispensed. These top-ranking benzodiazepines were alprazolam (#11), lorazepam (#33), clonazepam (#43), diazepam (#64), and temazepam (#111). Currently, approximately 20 benzodiazepines are approved for use in the U.S. and are prescribed as anxiolytics, muscle relaxants, anesthetic adjuncts, anticonvulsants, and treatment for obsessive-compulsive disorders. The properties of selected benzodiazepines are summarized in Table 1.

Dr. Leo Sternbach of Hoffmann-La Roche is credited with the discovery of benzodiazepines. During an assistantship in Poland in the 1930s, Dr. Sternbach studied a class of compounds called heptoxdiazines. His interest in these compounds resurfaced in the mid-1950s when he began to evaluate heptoxdiazines as potential tranquilizers. During his investigation, he discovered that these compounds were not heptoxdiazines as previously thought, but they were quinazoline 3-oxides. After several years of synthesizing numerous quinazoline 3-oxide compounds with disappointing pharmacological test results, Dr. Sternbach initiated a "clean up" of the laboratory and expected to complete this work with at least some publishable material. During the clean up, a coworker drew his attention to a compound that formed when quinazoline N-oxide was treated with methylamine. This compound was subsequently submitted for animal pharmacological testing, which yielded promising results. Further testing indicated that this compound was the product of an unusual ring enlargement, which had created a benzodiazepine derivative (Fig. 1). Clinical trials with this benzodiazepine compound were initiated in 1958, leading to its approval by the FDA in February 1960. One month later it was marketed as Librium (chlordiazepoxide), the first benzodiazepine approved for therapeutic use.

CHEMISTRY AND USE

The general benzodiazepine structure is shown in Fig. 2. The name of the class is derived from the combination of a benzene ring (A) with a seven-member diazepine ring (B). Included in the structure is a phenyl ring (C) attached to the 5-position of the diazepine ring. This phenyl group (C) appears to be a requirement for benzodiazepine activity. Moreover, the benzene component of the benzodiazepine structure needs an electron-withdrawing group present at R_7 to have enhanced activity; a chlorine atom and a nitro group are the most common entities attached. Potency can be improved by adding an electron-withdrawing group in the ortho position ($R_{2'}$) on the phenyl ring attached to the benzodiazepine nucleus (i.e., lorazepam, clonazepam, flunitrazepam). An electron-withdrawing group at this position also produces a greater amnesic effect.

Table 1. Selected Properties of Benzodiazepines

Benzodiazepine	Trade Name(s)	Uses	Primary Metabolite(s)	Half-Life	V_d	Dose	Therapeutic Concentrations
Alprazolam	Xanax	Antidepressant Anxiolytic	α-Hydroxyalprazolam	11–15 h	0.7–1.3 L/kg	General anxiety: 0.75–4 mg/day Panic disorder: up to 10 mg/day	5–50 ng/mL
Bromazepam	Lectopam Lexotan	Anxiolytic Muscle relaxant	3-Hydroxybromazpam glucuronide 2-Amino-5-bromo-3-hydroxy-benzoylpyridine glucuronide	8–19 h	0.9 L/kg	3–18 mg daily (max 60 mg daily)	0.08–0.15 mg/L
Chlordiazepoxide	Librium	Anxiolytic Alcohol withdrawal	Norchlordiazepoxide Demoxepam Nordiazepam Oxazepam	5–30 h (CDP) 30–100 h (Nordiazepam)	0.3–0.6 L/kg	Anxiety: 30–100 mg daily Alcohol withdrawal: up to 300 mg daily	0.4–4 mg/L
Clobazam	Frisium Urbanyl	Anticonvulsant Anxiolytic Panic disorder Sedative	Desmethylclobazam	10–30 h (Clobazam) 2–3 d (Des-methylclobazam)	0.9–1.8 L/kg	20–60 mg daily	0.1–0.4 mg/L
Clonazepam	Clonopin Klonopin	Anticonvulsant Panic disorder	7-Aminoclonazepam	19–60 h	2–4 L/kg	1.5–20 mg daily	0.005–0.07 mg/L
Clorazepate	Tranxene	Anticonvulsant Anxiolytic Alcohol withdrawal	Nordiazepam Oxazepam	2 h (Clorazepate) 30–100 h (Nordiazepam)	0.5–2.5 L/kg	Up to 60 mg daily	0.02–0.8 mg/L Nordiazepam

Generic	Trade name	Clinical use	Metabolite	Half-life	Volume of distribution	Dose	Concentration
Diazepam	Valium	Anticonvulsant, Anxiolytic, Muscle relaxant	Nordiazepam	20–50 h (Diazepam) 30–100 h (Nordiazepam)	0.5–2.5 L/kg	2–40 mg daily	0.1–1.5 mg/L
Flunitrazepam	Rohypnol	Anesthetic induction agent, Hypnotic	7-Aminoflunitrazepam	9–25 h	3.5–5.5 L/kg	0.5–2 mg	0.005–0.015 mg/L
Flurazepam	Dalmane	Hypnotic	N-1-Desalkylflurazepam, N-1-Hydroxyethyl-Flurazepam	1–3 h (Flurazepam) 80 h (N-1-desalkylflura-zepam)	3.4–5.5 L/kg	15–30 mg daily	0.0005–0.03 mg/L
Halazepam	Paxipam	Anxiolytic	Nordiazepam	14–16 h	1.0 L/kg	20–40 mg, 3–4 × daily	0.037–0.125 mg/L
Lorazepam	Ativan	Anxiolytic, Preoperative	Lorazepam glucuronide	9–24 h	1–2 L/kg	1–10 mg daily	0.05–0.24 mg/L
Midazolam	Versed	Anesthetic induction agent, Preoperative, Sedative	α-Hydroxymidazolam	1.5–2.5 h	1.0–2.5 L/kg	0.05–0.5 mg/kg	0.08–0.25 mg/L
Nitrazepam	Mogadon	Hypnotic	7-Aminonitrazepam	16–48 h	2–5 L/kg	5–10 mg daily	0.03–0.12 mg/L
Oxazepam	Serax	Anxiolytic	Oxazepam glucuronide	4–15 h	0.5–2.0 L/kg	15–60 mg daily	0.5–2.0 mg/L
Prazepam	Centrax, Vertran	Anxiolytic	Nordiazepam	1.3 h (Prazepam) 30–100 h (Nordiazepam)	12–14 L/kg	20–60 mg daily	0.02–0.8 mg/L Nordiazepam
Temazepam	Normison, Restoril	Hypnotic, Preoperative	Oxazepam	5–15 h	0.8–1.4 L/kg	15–60 mg daily	0.3–0.9 mg/L
Triazolam	Halcion	Hypnotic	α-Hydroxytriazolam	1.5–5.5 h	1.1–2.7 L/kg	0.125–0.25 mg daily	0.002–0.02 mg/L

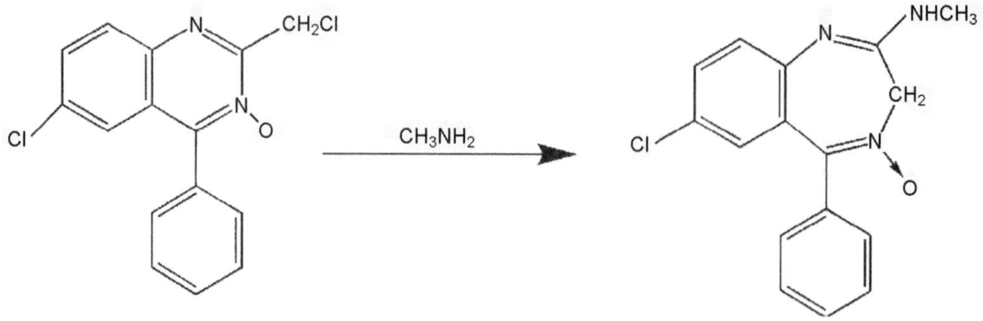

Fig. 1. The first benzodiazepine was synthesized by the reaction of a quinazoline N-oxide with methylamine.

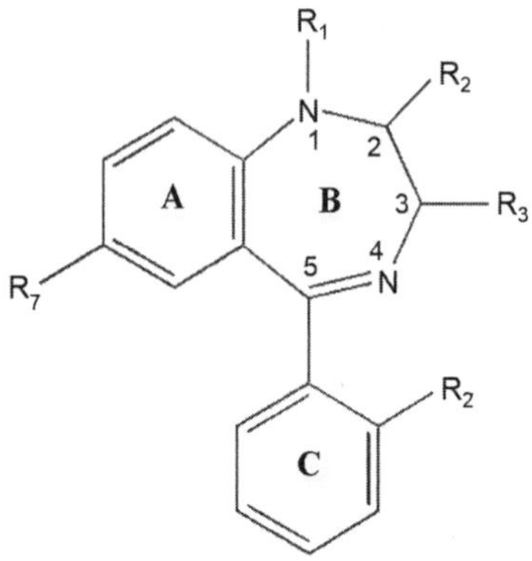

Fig. 2. The benzodiazepine structure.

Other structural modifications are possible and can affect both potency and duration of action. Groups commonly bonded to the N_1 position include hydrogen, a substituted alkyl group, or a fused triazolo ring. Benzodiazepines with smaller substituents on position N_1 tend to have higher intrinsic activity; however, some drugs with larger N-1 substituents are effective (e.g., flurazepam), largely due to metabolic dealkylation to an active metabolite. Most benzodiazepines have a double-bonded oxygen attached to C_2 (the exceptions are chlordiazepoxide, which has a methylamino group, and quazepam, which has a double-bonded sulfur). Replacing a hydrogen with a hydroxyl group on C_3 reduces the drug's duration of action. The addition of the hydroxyl group allows direct conjugation of the parent drug to an inactive glucuronide conjugate. An additional ring can be added to positions 1 and 2 of the diazepine ring, resulting in the highly potent imidazo- and triazolo-benzodiazepines. Selected benzodiazepine structures are illustrated in Figs. 3 and 4.

As therapeutic agents, benzodiazepines have many advantages over barbiturates; namely, they have fewer side effects and are much safer in overdose. Benzodiazepines display selective rather than generalized central nervous system depressant actions. This gives them a uniquely wide margin of safety. There is less liver enzyme induction with benzodiazepines, which presents fewer complications when multiple drugs are coadministered. While withdrawal effects after discontinuing benzodiazepine use do occur, the symptoms are milder than those observed with barbiturates.

Benzodiazepines have been approved for treating many illnesses. One of the most common therapeutic uses of benzodiazepines is to treat anxiety. Diazepam gained widespread use in the 1970s as an anxiolytic drug. Alprazolam was introduced in the U.S. pharmaceutical market in the 1980s and has largely replaced diazepam for this use. The anxiolytic effects of benzodiazepines are likely related to their ability to produce inhibitory effects in areas of the brain that are associated with anxiogenesis. Additionally, it has been reported that benzodiazepines act to suppress noradrenergic and/or serotonergic pathways in some areas of the brain, which appears to play a role in their anxiolytic effects. The major advantages of benzodiazepines as anxiolytics include their

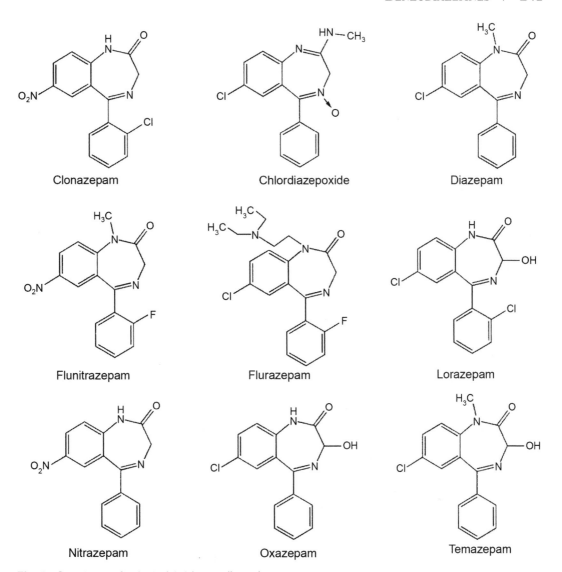

Clonazepam

Chlordiazepoxide

Diazepam

Flunitrazepam

Flurazepam

Lorazepam

Nitrazepam

Oxazepam

Temazepam

Fig. 3. Structures of selected 1,4-benzodiazepines.

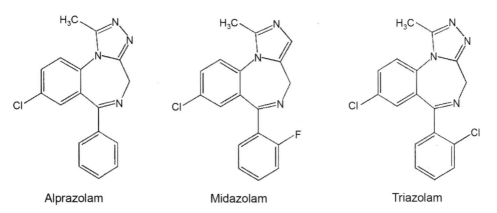

Alprazolam

Midazolam

Triazolam

Fig. 4. Structures of selected imidazo- and triazolo-benzodiazepines.

rapid onset of action and their safety. The major disadvantages of benzodiazepines as anxiolytics include the development of tolerance and/or dependence with long-term use, and their potential negative effects on psychomotor performance.

Another use of benzodiazepines is as hypnotic agents for treating insomnia. Insomnia is a fairly common condition, affecting 30–40% of the U.S. adult population within a given year. Insomnia is more common in women, and its prevalence increases with age. To be an effective hypnotic, a drug should have a rapid onset of action, assuming that it is taken at bedtime. Ideally, the duration of action should be long enough to allow a complete night's sleep but not so long that the drowsiness persists into the following day (the hangover effect). Benzodiazepines effectively treat insomnia; their use often results in a more rapid sleep onset, decreased night-time awakenings, and an increased total sleeping time. However, benzodiazepine-induced sleep differs from natural sleep, resulting in prolonged periods of light sleep and decreased duration of REM and slow wave sleep. The major disadvantages associated with benzodiazepine hypnotics include the development of tolerance and dependence, rebound insomnia with discontinuation of use, hangover effects, and respiratory depression that can aggravate some respiratory conditions.

The benzodiazepines are also used in the treatment of seizures. For example, diazepam has long been the drug of choice in the treatment of status epilepticus. Clonazepam can be used to treat a variety of seizures (with the exception of generalized tonic-clonic seizures). The major disadvantages of benzodiazepines as antiepileptics are the development of tolerance in many patients and potential sedation and psychomotor impairment.

In addition to their use as therapeutic agents, benzodiazepines produce sedative and amnesic effects for brief medical procedures and are used to premedicate patients. An intravenous dose of a short-acting benzodiazepine, midazolam, assists in the induction of surgical anesthesia. Diazepam and lorazepam are also administered as preanesthetic medications. Diazepam is an effective muscle relaxant. It has been used in this capacity to treat various motion disorders. Chlordiazepoxide and diazepam have been used to treat alcohol dependence. They are administered during alcohol detoxification to prevent withdrawal seizures.

Benzodiazepines are often used in combination with illicit drugs. The combination of benzodiazepines with opiates has been reported to produce an enhanced high. Benzodiazepines in combination with cocaine decrease seizure threshold and ease users down from a binge. Benzodiazepine use may also reduce the withdrawal symptoms that drug abusers experience. The most commonly encountered benzodiazepines among illicit drug abusers are diazepam and alprazolam.

When benzodiazepines are prescribed as therapeutic agents, they are recommended for short-term (four weeks or less) or intermittent use in most cases, since tolerance and dependence can occur with extended use. Tolerance to the sedative effects of benzodiazepines develops rapidly, usually within a week of the initiation of benzodiazepine therapy. However, tolerance to the anxiolytic effects appears to develop more slowly and to a lesser degree. Long-term benzodiazepine use has been associated with dependence. It has been reported that approximately 35% of patients taking benzodiazepines for more than four weeks—regardless of whether the dosage is therapeutic or excessive—develop dependence, as evidenced by the appearance of withdrawal symptoms following dosage decrease or termination. In addition, patients who are on benzodiazepines for extended periods (without dose escalation) may exhibit withdrawal symptoms such as anxiety, agitation, irritability, increased sensitivity to light and sound, muscle cramps, myoclonic jerks, insomnia, fatigue, headache, dizziness, concentration difficulties, paresthesias, nausea, seizures, loss of appetite, weight loss, and depression. Benzodiazepines with higher potency and shorter elimination half-lives appear to be associated with an increased risk of dependence.

Although benzodiazepines are considered relatively safe drugs, overdose can produce life-threatening effects. Data from the 2004 Annual Report of the American Association of Poison Control Centers Toxic Exposure Surveillance System indicated 65,998 benzodiazepine exposures, of which 2954 (4.4%) resulted in major toxicity and 202 (0.3%) resulted in death. When benzodiazepine intoxication occurs, it can be treated with a variety of measures, including generalized supportive care, monitoring of vital signs, maintenance of adequate airway, and administration of vasopressors to treat hypotension. Activated charcoal administration is most beneficial within 2 to 4 h of ingestion and when risk of aspiration is minimal. Flumazenil, a GABA antagonist, may be administered if appropriate. However, flumazenil must be used with caution because it reduces seizure threshold and may actually precipitate seizure activity in a patient who has co-ingested a substance that induces seizures (e.g., tricyclic antidepressants), or in a patient with an underlying seizure disorder. When a patient presents with suspected benzodiazepine intoxication, it is important to identify any cointoxicants, as they may alter the recommended course of treatment.

PHARMACOLOGY

Mechanism of Action

Benzodiazepines mediate their CNS-depressant activity through the neurotransmitter gamma-amino butyric acid (GABA). GABA is the major inhibitory neurotransmitter in the brain and consists of two subtypes: (1) $GABA_A$ and (2) $GABA_B$.

$GABA_A$ receptors are a set of ligand-gated ion channels that convey GABA's effect on fast synaptic transmission. Benzodiazepines bind to $GABA_A$ receptors and potentiate the inhibitory action of GABA. Activating the $GABA_A$ receptor opens an ion channel and allows chloride ions to enter the cell. As a result, neuronal activity slows down because of hyperpolarization of the cell membrane potential. Specifically, the binding of the drug increases the amount of chloride current generated by the $GABA_A$-receptor complex, increasing inhibitory effect. Benzodiazepine binding to the $GABA_A$ receptor does not open the chloride ion channel directly, but increases the effectiveness of GABA by decreasing the concentration of GABA required to open the channel. There are also multiple subtypes of $GABA_A$ receptors, and benzodiazepines appear to interact with many of these subtypes. This accounts for the varied pharmacologic uses of the drugs.

Pharmacokinetics

Benzodiazepines may be administered orally, intravenously, or intramuscularly. When taken orally, they are completely absorbed—their high lipid solubility aids absorption. However, the rate of absorption depends on the benzodiazepine. For example, diazepam reaches peak blood concentrations within an hour after ingestion. Other benzodiazepines require several hours to reach their peak. Several benzodiazepines, such as clorazepate and prazepam, serve as prodrugs, being rapidly broken down to nordiazepam, which is the active drug.

Generally, benzodiazepines display a significant first-pass effect prior to general distribution. Their volume of distribution is around 2 L/kg, and they are highly protein bound. Typically, the fraction-bound portion is >80%. The major binding protein for benzodiazepines is albumin; however, it appears that triazolobenzodiazepines bind to all acid glycoprotein. Like barbiturates, benzodiazepines are classified according to their elimination half-lives. Midazolam and triazolam are considered short acting because their elimination half-lives are only several hours. Many (such as alprazolam, lorazepam, oxazepam, and temazepam) have elimination half-lives of 6–24 h and are classified as intermediate acting. Long-acting benzodiazepines, such as diazepam and quazepam, have elimination half-lives >24 h.

One difficulty in the establishment of this classification is the presence of active metabolites that may have substantially different half-lives than the parent drug. For example, flurazepam has an elimination half-life of several hours, but an active metabolite has an elimination half-life of several days.

Benzodiazepines are extensively metabolized in the liver. Microsomal enzymes play a prominent role in this metabolism. Phase I metabolic routes include hydroxylation, dealkylation, deamination, and reduction. Substituents are usually removed from the B-ring, with larger or further removed alkyl substituents often removed more rapidly than smaller ones. Hydroxylation, a slow process that can take about 100 h, usually occurs at position R_3 of the B-ring. Structural modifications, such as the presence of a pyridyl ring (e.g., bromazepam) can greatly enhance the rate of hydroxylation. The cytochrome P450 3A3 and 3A4 enzyme subtypes mediate many hydroxylation and dealkylation reactions.

Table 2 gives specific examples of each type of metabolic pathway. As previously stated, many of these metabolites have CNS-depressant activity that affects potency and duration of action. Once hydroxyl products are formed, phase II metabolism or conjugation with glucuronic acid then occurs. These conjugated metabolites are the major urinary products of benzodiazepines.

Performance Effects of Benzodiazepines

As central nervous system depressants, benzodiazepines can have significant effects on psychomotor function, even in recommended doses. Such effects include prolonged reaction times; impaired judgment; impaired coordination, alertness, and concentration; and impaired short-term memory. Clinical studies have demonstrated that typical doses of diazepam, nitrazepam, flunitrazepam, flurazepam, lorazepam, and triazolam can impair some skills necessary for driving. Concomitant use of ethanol and benzodiazepines will increase impairment. Tolerance to some of these effects can develop with prolonged use. However, considering the scale on which benzodiazepines are prescribed, their effects on driving skills and potential contribution to traffic and other accidents are a major concern.

Interactions

When administered alone, benzodiazepines are relatively safe drugs. There are few reports of fatal overdoses due solely to benzodiazepine toxicity. However, benzodiazepine use in combination with other CNS depressants can increase toxicity: recent Drug Abuse Warning Network data indicated that 78% of benzodiazepine-related emergency department visits involved two or more drugs. The drugs most often combined with benzodiazepines were alcohol, illicit drugs, and opiates.

Since the cytochrome P450 3A enzyme family is involved in the metabolism of many benzodiazepines, it is important to consider the potential effects of drugs that induce or inhibit this enzyme system. Some of the more commonly encountered drugs

Table 2. Examples of Benzodiazepine Phase I Metabolism

Reaction	Precursor	Product
Dealkylation	Diazepam	Nordiazepam
	Temazepam	Oxazepam
	Flurazepam	N-1-desalkylflurazepam
Deamination	Chlordiazepoxide	Demoxepam
Hydroxylation	Alprazolam	α-Hydroxyalprazolam
	Diazepam	Temazepam
	Nordiazepam	Oxazepam
Reduction	Clonazepam	7-Aminoclonazepam
	Demoxepam	Nordiazepam

that inhibit the CYP3A enzymes include cimetidine, diltiazem, fluoxetine, fluvoxamine, paroxetine, verapamil, antifungals, and protease inhibitors. Coadministration of some of these inhibitors and benzodiazepines has been reported to produce clinically significant effects, including increased blood benzodiazepine concentrations and increased benzodiazepine elimination half-life. Drugs that induce the CYP3A enzyme family include barbiturates, phenytoin, carbamazepine, and rifampicin. Drugs that alter glucuronyl transferase activity may also affect the metabolism of 3-hydroxy benzodiazepines.

Special Considerations

There is limited data on the effects of benzodiazepines on the fetus and nursing infants. The available data suggest that benzodiazepine administration during pregnancy does not increase the risk of congenital malformations. However, the data are insufficient to definitively state that there is no risk of injury to the fetus with benzodiazepine exposure. Withdrawal can occur in infants of mothers receiving chronic benzodiazepine therapy, especially if benzodiazepines are administered near term or during delivery. Although benzodiazepines are not contraindicated in lactating mothers, there is evidence that some benzodiazepines are excreted into breast milk, at concentrations about 10–20% of plasma concentrations. If benzodiazepines are administered to mothers who breast feed, their infants should be closely watched for lethargy, sedation, and weight loss.

Benzodiazepines are widely administered to the elderly. It has been estimated that elderly patients receive 50% of all benzodiazepine prescriptions, although they account for less than 13% of the population. Studies have indicated that the elderly show increased sensitivity to the effects of some benzodiazepines. This is partially due to the decrease in the rate at which the elderly oxidize some benzodiazepines. The decreased rate of metabolism is a result of the decreased CYP3A4 activity that occurs

with age. The pharmacokinetic profiles of benzodiazepines that are metabolized primarily by conjugation, including temazepam and oxazepam, are not significantly altered in the elderly. These benzodiazepines may be more suitable choices for benzodiazepine therapy in elderly patients.

Renal disease can significantly affect benzodiazepine elimination. Because most parent benzodiazepines are highly protein bound, glomerular filtration is low and their metabolism is less affected by renal disease. However, metabolites such as glucuronide conjugates can accumulate because the kidney's ability to excrete these substances is compromised. Another consequence of renal disease is decreased plasma protein binding of benzodiazepines, which increases the concentrations of circulating free drug.

Conditions that cause hypoalbuminemia can increase the concentrations of free active drug. Hypoalbuminemia can occur as a result of liver disease (decreased synthesis of albumin), renal disease (extravascular protein loss), ascites and congestive heart failure (hemodilution), and severe burns (direct loss of albumin from the skin, a major site for albumin storage).

INDIVIDUAL BENZODIAZEPINES

Alprazolam

Alprazolam is an intermediate-acting triazolobenzodiazepine that is primarily used to treat anxiety and depression. Its potency is about 20 times that of diazepam. A white powder with a pK_a of 2.4, alprazolam is soluble in methanol and ethanol and insoluble in water. Following oral administration, alprazolam is well absorbed, with a bioavailability of approximately 90%. Alprazolam is metabolized to α-hydroxyalprazolam and 4-hydroxyalprazolam by cytochrome P450 3A4. Both metabolites are less active than alprazolam and are typically detected in plasma at concentrations <10% of alprazolam concentrations. Almost all of a single dose of alprazolam is excreted within 72 h, with 80% excreted in urine and 7% in feces; 20% is excreted as unchanged alprazolam.

Clonazepam

Clonazepam is a long-acting benzodiazepine indicated for the treatment of seizure disorders and panic disorder. Clonazepam is a white to light yellow crystalline powder that is soluble in acetone, chloroform, and methanol. Following oral administration, clonazepam is well absorbed, with a bioavailability close to 100%. Clonazepam is primarily metabolized by reduction of the nitro group to form 7-aminoclonazepam, which is detected in plasma at concentrations similar to clonazepam. Cytochrome P450 3A4 mediates the formation of 7-aminoclonazepam. Up to 70% of a dose is eliminated in the urine over seven days, mainly as 7-aminoclonazepam and 7-acetamidoclonazepam. Clonazepam is relatively unstable in postmortem specimens due to bacterial and thermal degradation.

Diazepam

Diazepam is a long-acting 1,4-benzodiazepine that is commonly prescribed for the management of anxiety, as an adjunct for the treatment of skeletal muscle spasm and status epilepticus, and as a minor tranquilizer or sedative. It is also used to reduce the effects of alcohol withdrawal. Diazepam is a white or yellow crystalline powder with a pK_a of 3.3 that is soluble in ethanol and chloroform and slightly soluble in water. Its oral bioavailability is about 100%. Following administration, diazepam is demethylated to form its primary active metabolite, nordiazepam, which accumulates in plasma with repeated administration. The CYP2C19 and CYP3A4 enzymes mediate the demethylation of diazepam; the CYP3A4 enzyme is involved in the formation of 3-hydroxy metabolites of diazepam, oxazepam, and temazepam. Following oral administration, much of a diazepam dose is eliminated in the urine as oxazepam glucuronide and conjugates of nordiazepam and temazepam.

Flumazenil

Flumazenil is an imidazo-benzodiazepine derivative that acts as a competitive GABA antagonist in humans. The structure of flumazenil is illustrated in Fig. 5. Flumazenil does not antagonize the action of drugs binding to the GABA receptor at sites other than the benzodiazepine binding site (i.e., barbiturates, ethanol, and general anesthetics). Flumazenil can be used to reverse benzodiazepine effects such as sedation, respiratory depression, memory impairment, and psychomotor impairment. The duration and degree of antagonism are related to the dose administered and to the concentrations of flumazenil in plasma. Flumazenil is administered intravenously and its actions are usually observed within minutes of administration. The complications associated with flumazenil administration are related to the reversal of benzodiazepine effects: flumazenil has been reported to precipitate withdrawal in patients who have been on benzodiazepine therapy long enough to develop tolerance and/or dependence. In addition, seizure activity can occur with flumazenil administration, especially if the patient has coingested a substance that causes seizure activity.

Flumazenil is not as highly protein bound as most benzodiazepines, with only about 50% of the drug protein bound. Following intravenous administration, flumazenil is rapidly distributed and eliminated; its half-life is 40 to 80 min. When flumazenil is administered as an antidote for

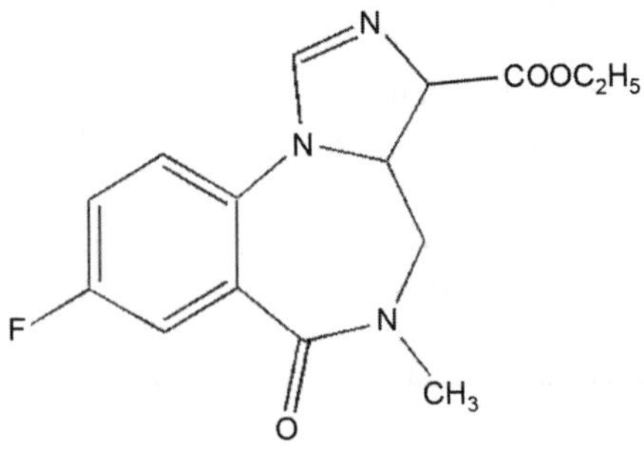

Fig. 5. Structure of flumazenil, a benzodiazepine antagonist.

benzodiazepine intoxication the patient must still be monitored for signs of benzodiazepine intoxication because the flumazenil may be eliminated earlier than the ingested benzodiazepine. Up to 95% of a dose of flumazenil is eliminated in the urine in three days, and about 5–10% is eliminated in the feces. Flumazenil is excreted mainly as a des-ethyl carboxylic acid derivative and its glucuronide conjugate; less than 1% of unchanged drug is excreted in the urine.

Flurazepam

Flurazepam is a white crystalline hypnotic agent, soluble in chloroform, that is used to treat insomnia. Following oral administration, flurazepam is rapidly metabolized to N-1-desalkylflurazepam and N-1-hydroxyethylflurazepam, which may be responsible for much of flurazepam's observed effects. N-1-desalkylflurazepam accumulates in blood with repeated administration, achieving steady-state concentrations after 7–10 days of dosing. Steady-state N-1-desalkylflurazepam plasma concentrations are generally five to six times the concentrations observed following a single dose. Up to 60% of a flurazepam dose is eliminated in the urine within 48 h and about 9% of a dose is eliminated in the feces. The primary urinary metabolite of flurazepam is conjugated N-1-hydroxyethylflurazepam.

Lorazepam

Lorazepam is an intermediate-acting benzodiazepine that is indicated for the treatment of anxiety. It is also used as a preanesthetic to alleviate anxiety, produce sedation, and decrease the ability to recall events related to a procedure. Following oral administration, lorazepam is well absorbed, with a bioavailability of 95% and a primary metabolic pathway of inactive glucuronide conjugate formation. Lorazepam glucuronide accumulates in plasma and attains concentrations greater than lorazepam.

Approximately 75% of a lorazepam dose is eliminated over five days as lorazepam glucuronide in the urine; only a very small amount of lorazepam is eliminated as unchanged drug. Lorazepam can be difficult to detect, as most commercially available immunoassay screening tests do not have high cross-reactivity to this benzodiazepine.

Phenazepam

Phenazepam is a benzodiazepine that was developed in the former Soviet Union in the 1970s and has been used in Russia to treat insomnia, anxiety, alcohol withdrawal, and seizures. It is not approved for use in the U.S. It is a relatively potent benzodiazepine, and doses of 0.5 to 1.0 mg can produce significant central nervous system depression. After oral ingestion, the peak plasma concentration occurs at 4 h. It has a longer half-life than most benzodiazepines, approximately 60 h. Because of its availability over the internet and a lack of control of its use by the Drug Enforcement Agency, it has become an abused benzodiazepine in certain parts of the U.S. One report of phenazepam use in eight drugged driving cases found an average blood concentration of 0.22 mg/L with a range 0.10 to 0.52 mg/L.

Temazepam

Temazepam is a hypnotic agent indicated for the short-term treatment of insomnia. It is a white crystalline powder that is slightly soluble in water and freely soluble in methylene chloride. Temazepam is well absorbed following oral administration, with a bioavailability close to 100%. The major metabolic pathway for temazepam is glucuronidation; smaller amounts of oxazepam and oxazepam glucuronide are formed. Approximately 80% of a dose is eliminated in the urine, and 12% in the feces. Because the primary metabolic route is conjugation, temazepam pharmacokinetics are not significantly altered by changes in CYP3A4 activity.

ANALYSIS

Many difficulties are associated with the attempt to take a comprehensive approach to benzodiazepine analysis. A large number of benzodiazepines with different functional groups exist on the benzodiazepine nucleus. Many metabolites of benzodiazepines are pharmacologically active and should be quantified to assess the overall effects of benzodiazepines in a particular case. Benzodiazepine potencies may vary by several orders of magnitude, so analytical methodologies need different detection limits to identify therapeutic use. With many benzodiazepines, establishing a simultaneous method for blood and urine specimen analysis is difficult because the target compound is often different. Moreover, urinary benzodiazepine products are conjugated, and a hydrolysis step is required to improve detectability.

There are many commercially available screening tests for benzodiazepines. Some are designed to test urine, while others test a wide range of matrices, making them applicable to postmortem toxicology. Often the target analyte is oxazepam or nordiazepam, and good cross-reactivity to a number of benzodiazepines can be achieved. More recently, specific assays for flunitrazepam have been developed. Typically, no specimen pretreatment is necessary; however, sensitivity of these assays may be enhanced by an enzymatic hydrolysis step because the predominant urinary products are conjugated species. One limitation to the use of immunoassays is that certain benzodiazepines, such as lorazepam, do not have sufficient cross-reactivity with the assay antibody to identify that benzodiazepine's therapeutic use.

Benzodiazepines can be separated from biological specimens by liquid–liquid extraction or by solid-phase extraction. When analyzing urine specimens, hydrolysis is necessary to cleave the glucuronide conjugate. Enzymatic hydrolysis is preferred over acid hydrolysis; some benzodiazepines are unstable in acid and rearrange to form benzophenones. Adjusting the pH to 9–10 allows extraction of benzodiazepines into an immiscible organic solvent. Solid-phase extraction procedures also rely on pH adjustment, with the final pH dependent on the type of solid phase being used. After application of the pH-adjusted specimen to the column, buffers and solvents are used to wash the column of endogenous substances or other drugs. This is followed by solvent elution of the benzodiazepines from the column.

Another general screening method for benzodiazepines involves their conversion to benzophenones. Hydrochloric acid and heat will cleave the benzodiazepine ring to form a benzophenone. Many common benzodiazepines can be converted in this manner to a small number of benzophenones. Hydrolyzing diazepam and temazepam forms N-methyl-2-amino-5-chlorobenzophenone (MACB); hydrolyzing nordiazepam, chlordiazepoxide, and oxazepam produces 2-amino-5-chlorobenzophenone (ACB); lorazepam hydrolysis generates 2-amino-5,2'-dichlorobenzophenone. Triazolobenzodiazepines like alprazolam and triazolam do not form benzophenones, however, and this constitutes a major disadvantage in using this screening method to identify benzodiazepine use because alprazolam is widely used. (There is one additional disadvantage to using this screening method: it does not identify the specific benzodiazepine used.)

The benzophenones produced can be identified by using one of several methods. After hydrolysis, the hydrolysate is alkalinized and extracted. The extract can be spotted on a silica gel thin-layer chromatographic plate and developed in a solvent of toluene:acetic acid (97:3). This is useful for the analysis of bile and urine specimens. The benzophenones are visualized as diazotized derivatives after spraying with nitrous acid, ammonium sulfamate, and N-(1-naphthyl)ethylenediamine (this is known as the Bratton-Marshall reagent). A red-blue spot is positive for a benzophenone. Alternatively, the extract can be injected into a gas chromatograph or gas chromatograph–mass spectrometer.

Gas chromatography (GC) can analyze many benzodiazepines without derivatization, among them chlordiazepoxide, diazepam, nordiazepam, flurazepam, and alprazolam. The benzodiazepine structure contains certain atoms that facilitate analysis using specialized gas chromatographic detectors that provide enhanced detection limits. An electron capture detector affords excellent sensitivity due to the presence of a halogen in all benzodiazepines. Benzodiazepines also contain several nitrogen atoms that enable detection with a nitrogen-phosphorus detector. Disadvantages to using GC analysis of benzodiazepines include the thermal instability of chlordiazepoxide, which poses a problem with the high temperature needed to get the drug through the column. The biggest drawback to using GC is that some of the more polar drugs within the class do not elute well from common gas chromatographic columns. Some of the diazolobenzodiazepines and triazolobenzodiazepines require high temperatures for elution from a GC column; these compounds are also very sensitive to chromatographic conditions, and less than optimal results may be obtained if regular instrument maintenance is not performed. Drugs with a hydroxyl group (such as oxazepam, temazepam, and lorazepam) or a nitro group (such as clonazepam and nitrazepam) would display poor chromatographic characteristics. Derivatization by gas chromatography is often necessary for the analysis of these compounds. A specialized GC column that facilitates the analysis of underivatized benzodiazepines, including lorazepam, temazepam, and clonazepam, is available. This column contains a trifluoropropyl stationary phase that is thermally stable at temperatures up to 360°C. Fig. 6 displays an example chromatogram from a benzodiazepine analysis by gas chromatography.

Liquid chromatography (LC) can also be used to detect individual benzodiazepines and their metabolites without derivatization. A reverse-phase C_8 or C_{18} column is commonly used to provide analytical separation. Isocratic mobile phases can provide adequate separation for most applications. Benzodiazepines have good UV absorbance at around 240 nm, and this can be used for detection. If a photodiode-array detector is used, then a UV spectrum of the benzodiazepine can be collected in real time to enhance specificity. The liquid chromatographic method also alleviates the problem with thermally labile benzodiazepines. Since a number of forensic laboratories have acquired the capability to perform liquid chromatography/mass spectrometry (LC/MS), this technique has become more widely applied to benzodiazepine analysis. It is a technique of high sensitivity and high specificity that is well suited to more polar or thermally labile benzodiazepines.

Gas chromatography/mass spectrometry (GC/MS) remains the most common methodology for identifying and measuring specific benzodiazepines in biological specimens. The limitations of GC would also apply to GC/MS because the gas chromatograph remains the route of introducing the sample into the mass spectrometer. Nevertheless, GC/MS also has some advantages. The electron impact mass spectrum of benzodiazepines produces multiple abundant ions with high mass-to-charge ratios, which aid in the qualitative identification of the drug or metabolite. Selected ion monitoring can improve sensitivity to benzodiazepines present in low concentrations. A variety of derivatives can be made to improve the chromatographic characteristics of the more polar benzodiazepines and metabolites. The more common derivatives are silyl, acyl, or alkyl derivatives; various derivatizing reagents are available. Silylation is typically performed by heating the final extract with BSTFA (N,O-bis[Trimethylsilyl] trifluoroacetamide) or MTBSTFA (N-methyl-N-[tert-butyldimethylsilyl] trifluoroacetamide), which form trimethylsilyl and tert-butyldimethylsilyl derivatives, respectively. Benzodiazepine silyl derivatives prepared with MTBSTFA are generally more stable and produce larger mass peaks when analyzed by GC/MS. Chemical ionization is also useful for benzodiazepine analysis. The presence of halogen permits negative chemical ionization, which affords the greatest sensitivity for

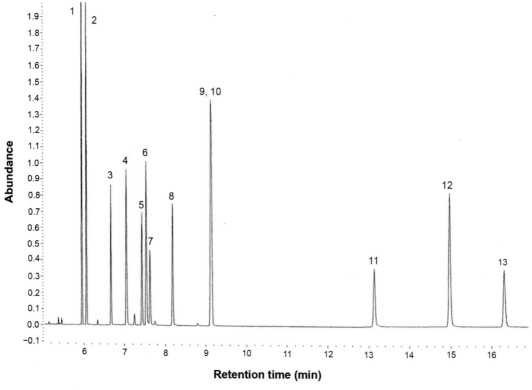

Fig. 6. Chromatogram of MTBSTFA-derivatized benzodiazepines on an RTX-200 capillary column. Benzodiazepines elute as follows: nordiazepam (1); desalkylflurazepam (2); oxazepam (3); diazepam (4); lorazepam (5); midazolam (6); 7-aminoclonazepam (7); temazepam (8); clonazepam (9); 1-hydroxymidazolam (10); alprazolam (11); 1-hydroxyalprazolam (12); and 1-hydroxytriazolam (13).

benzodiazepine analysis by GC/MS. Fig. 7 illustrates the electron impact and chemical ionization mass spectra for diazepam.

INTERPRETATION

Therapeutic ranges for benzodiazepines reflect their differences in potency. Many drugs, like diazepam and chlordiazepoxide, have therapeutic concentrations around 2 mg/L. Others, like alprazolam and lorazepam, have therapeutic concentrations in the 0.05- to 0.1-mg/L range. Active metabolites are also a factor to be considered when evaluating the amount of active benzodiazepine in the blood.

Although the presence of benzodiazepines is a relatively common finding in postmortem cases, few intoxication cases due exclusively to benzodiazepines have been reported due to their high therapeutic indices. However, there have been some studies that suggest alprazolam is relatively more toxic in overdose situations than other benzodiazepines. Generally, benzodiazepines are involved in drug deaths as a result of being combined with alcohol or other drugs, with the cause of death attributable to alcohol and drug or multiple drug intoxication.

One complication in the interpretation of postmortem benzodiazepine concentrations is that some display in vitro instability. For instance, chlordiazepoxide is broken down in the blood to demoxepam and nordiazepam. Drugs with a nitro group, such as clonazepam and nitrazepam, can be reduced in vitro to their respective amino products. Chlordiazepoxide standards are unstable in water or methanol and should

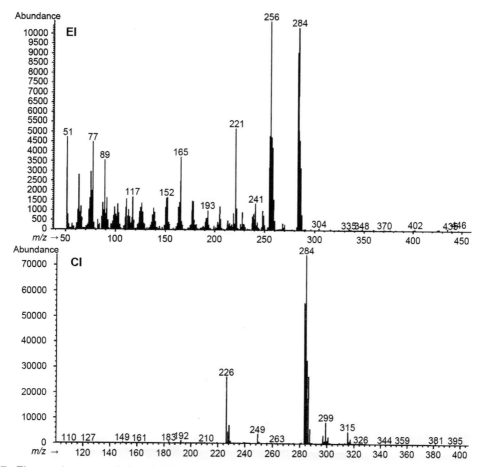

Fig. 7. Electron impact and chemical ionization mass spectra of diazepam.

be prepared fresh or in aprotic solvents such as acetonitrile.

A negative result of a benzodiazepine screen must be interpreted in the context of the methodology used. The discussion of benzodiazepine analysis in the previous section clearly indicated that different methodologies have different abilities to identify certain benzodiazepines. If the case history indicates the presence or involvement of a particular benzodiazepine, then a method must be selected that would identify the drug or metabolite of interest.

SUGGESTED READING

1. Baselt RC, ed. Analytical procedures for therapeutic drug monitoring and emergency toxicology, 2nd ed. Littleton, MA: PSG Publishing Co., 1987.

2. Baselt RC, ed. Disposition of toxic drugs and chemicals in man, 6th ed. Foster City, CA: Biomedical Publications, 2002.

3. Fitzgerald R. Analytical toxicology of the benzodiazepines. AACC Therapeutic Drug Monitoring and Toxicology 1995;16(7): 169–79.

4. Hardman JG, Limbird LE, Molinoff PB, Ruddon RW, Gilman AG, eds. Goodman and Gilman's the pharmacological basis of therapeutics, 9th ed. New York: McGraw-Hill Co., 1996.

5. Wians FH. Benzodiazepine update. AACC Therapeutic Drug Monitoring and Toxicology 1989;11(4): 7–20.

6. Zherdev VP, Caccia S, Garattini S, Ekonomov AL. Species differences in phenazepam kinetics and metabolism. Euro J Drug Metab Pharm 1982;7:191–6.

CHAPTER 15

Gamma-Hydroxybutyric Acid (GHB)*

Marc LeBeau

GHB is a simple hydroxylated, short-chain fatty acid composed of four carbon, eight hydrogen, and three oxygen atoms (Fig. 1). It has a molecular weight of 104.1 amu and is usually supplied as the sodium salt with a molecular weight of 126.1 amu. The salt is typically a white or off-white powder that is readily soluble in water.

When in solution, GHB coexists in a state of equilibrium with its lactone, gammabutyrolactone (GBL). The conversion of GHB to GBL is dependent upon the matrix it is in, as well as the pH and temperature of the matrix. Because GHB has a pK_a of 4.72, it will predominate when the pH of the matrix is greater than 4.72; GBL will predominate if the pH is below 4.72. Additionally, the presence of the enzyme lactonase in plasma will also affect the equilibrium because it converts GBL to GHB.

GHB has a history of clinical and recreational abuse and has been utilized in drug-facilitated crimes.

USE AND ABUSE OF GHB

GHB was first introduced in Europe in the 1960s as an intravenous general anesthetic agent that lacked analgesic properties. A short time later this use diminished due to reported side effects of grand mal seizures and coma. GHB has also been studied for its ability to suppress the symptoms of alcohol dependence and opiate-withdrawal syndrome and for the management of narcoleptic patients. In 2002, the U.S. Food and Drug Administration (FDA) approved GHB for clinical use in patients suffering from cataplexy. In its prescription form, GHB is a Schedule III substance; however, street formulations of GHB and illegal trafficking of the prescription formulation carry Schedule I penalties.

Historically, GHB abuse has been widespread across a variety of populations. One group includes bodybuilders, who believe it to be a steroid alternative for building muscle mass based on reports indicating that GHB increases the release of human growth hormone. Other GHB abusers include those who use it for the strong central nervous system (CNS) depressant effect that leads to euphoria, reduced inhibitions, and sedation. As with other CNS depressants, the effects largely depend upon the amount consumed and the individual's tolerance to the drug. Thus an individual consuming GHB may experience a range of effects, from wakefulness and euphoria to deep sleep or coma.

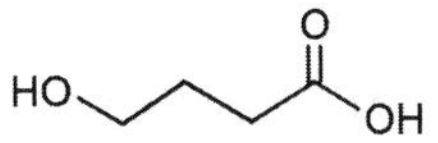

Fig. 1. Structure of gamma-hydroxybutyrate (GHB).

*This is publication 13-05 of the Federal Bureau of Investigation (FBI). Names of commercial manufacturers are provided for identification purposes only, and inclusion does not imply endorsement by the FBI. The views expressed are those of the author and do not necessarily reflect the official policy of the FBI or the U.S. government.

In 1993, actor River Phoenix collapsed and died of a drug overdose at a Los Angeles nightclub. Although never confirmed, rumors linked his death to GHB. Phoenix's death seemed to popularize the recreational use of GHB.

GHB is nearly always abused orally, most often diluted in an aqueous matrix where it can be disguised as bottled water, a sport drink, or juice. As law enforcement agencies have recognized these attempts to conceal GHB, sellers and abusers have disguised it in other containers such as those for hairspray, eye drops, and mouthwash. Usually consumed by the capful or by the teaspoon, a dose of GHB is usually 0.5 to 3 grams. As with all recreational drugs, GHB has a number of street names (Table 1). It should also be noted that there are metabolic precursors of GHB (e.g., gamma-butyrolactone [GBL] and 1,4-butanediol [1,4-BD]) that, once ingested, exhibit the same pharmacological effect as GHB. Table 1 also lists common street names for these analogs.

DRUG-FACILITATED SEXUAL ASSAULT

As a result of its strong sedative and amnesiac effects, GHB has been implicated in a number of drug-facilitated sexual assault (DFSA) cases. These assaults occur after a victim is rendered unconscious or otherwise incapable of consenting to a sexual act following the voluntary or involuntary use of drugs. Of all the drugs used to commit this crime, GHB and its analogs are probably among the most favored by rapists, although statistically it is very difficult to prove; GHB is naturally present in the body, so evaluating its role in cases of suspected DFSA can be complicated. Further, its rapid elimination after ingestion leaves only low concentrations of GHB in the body, concentrations that often cannot be readily differentiated from what is considered endogenous.

While the time will vary based on dose and interindividual differences, in general it may not be possible to differentiate between exogenous and endogenous concentrations of GHB if a blood or urine sample is collected later than 2 h or 6 h, respectively, after ingestion. As is often the case in DFSA, victims may not report the crime or provide evidentiary samples until this time period has elapsed, thus preventing detection of the drug if it were actually used. Another factor that makes GHB, GBL, and 1,4-BD attractive to rapists is that the drugs are readily available. It is simple to make GHB in an ordinary kitchen, and these drugs remain relatively easy to buy online, on the street, in numerous fitness facilities, and in dance clubs.

GHB and its related products have characteristics unlike many other drugs used to commit DFSA. In particular, GHB, GBL, and 1,4-BD can cause the victim to pass from a completely alert state to deep unconsciousness within 10 to 15 min after ingestion. Additionally, GHB demonstrates an amnesiac effect upon the individual under its influence. It has been reported that a GHB-assisted sleep lasts only 1.5–5 h, after which the user awakes feeling unusually refreshed. This latter effect is likely due to GHB's rapid clearance from the body.

A bystander who sees an individual under the influence of GHB is likely to assume the individual has consumed too much alcohol. To a rapist, this is another attractive characteristic of these drugs, as witnesses may claim the victim was intoxicated, a factor that many juries weigh when deliberating a DFSA case. Rapists may also be aware that many forensic and clinical laboratories do not include this drug among those commonly screened for in blood or urine specimens. Unless the investigator has the foresight to specifically request that a specimen be tested for GHB, the laboratory may not perform the test, and the drug may go undetected no matter how quickly the specimen is collected.

Finally, because GHB, GBL, and 1,4-BD have become such popular recreational drugs, the rapist may not need to slip the drug into the victim's drink in order to incapacitate her. Many victims voluntarily

Table 1. Chemical Synonyms and Street Names for GHB, GBL, and 1,4-BD

Compound	Chemical Synonyms	Street Names and Trade Names
γ-Hydroxybutyrate (GHB)	γ-Hydroxybutyric acid 4-Hydroxybutyrate Sodium 4-hydroxybutyrate Sodium oxybate Sodium oxybutyrate	Cherry Menth Easy Lay Energy Drink Everclear Fantasy G G Juice GBH G-Riffick Gamma 10 Gamma Hydrate Gamma OH Georgia Home Boy Gook Great Hormones at Bedtime Grievous Bodily Harm Liquid Ecstasy Liquid E Liquid G Liquid X Nature's Quaalude Organic Quaalude Salty Water Scoop Soap Somsanit Somatomac Somatomax PM Vita G Water Xyrem Zonked
γ-Butyrolactone (GBL)	Dihydro-2(3H)-furanone Butyrolactone 1,2-Butanolide 1,4-Butanolide γ-Hydroxybutyric acid lactone 3-Hydoxybutyric acid lactone 4-Hydroxybutanoic acid lactone	BLO Blow Blue Moon Blue Nitro Firewater G3 Gamma G G.H. Revitalizer Insom-X Invigorate Longevity N-force Pure Raine Regenerize Remedy GH Remforce

continued

Table 1. Chemical Synonyms and Street Names for GHB, GBL, and 1,4-BD (*continued*)

Compound	Chemical Synonyms	Street Names and Trade Names
γ-Butyrolactone (GBL) (*continued*)		Renewtrient Revivarant Thunda Verve X-12
1,4-Butanediol (1,4-BD)	Butanediol Butane-1,4-diol Butylene glycol 1,4-Butylene glycol 1,4-Dihydroxybutane 1,4-Tetramethylene glycol Tetramethylene 1,4-diol	Enliven Diol 14B Dormir FX GHRE Inner G NRG3 One Comma Four One Four B One Four B-D-O Revitalize Plus Serenity Soma SomatoPro Sucol B Thunder II Thunder Nectar Weight Belt Cleaner White Magic

consume these products for the euphoric effect they provide at low doses.

EFFECTS

Although GHB affects nearly every organ system, its primary effect is as a CNS depressant from perturbations of several neurotransmitter systems. Within the CNS, GHB mediates sleep cycles, temperature regulation, cerebral glucose metabolism and blood flow, memory, and emotional control. After typical doses, GHB levels in the CNS increase 100- to 500-fold.

The neurodepressant effect of GHB may be mediated by its affinity for two receptor sites in the CNS: a GHB-specific receptor and the $GABA_b$ receptor. The GHB receptors appear to be localized to neuronal cells and, more specifically, to the synaptosomal membrane. Following exogenous adminis-

tration of GHB, these GHB receptors are saturated. In the human brain, the pons and hippocampus exhibit the highest density of GHB receptors, followed by the cerebral cortex and caudate. GHB binds to the $GABA_b$ receptor at a much lower affinity than to the GHB receptor. Physiological levels of GHB would not bind to this receptor sufficiently to cause a pharmacological effect. However, supraphysiological levels that are achieved following exogenous administration could cause significant binding of the $GABA_b$ receptor, leading to membrane hyperpolarization and CNS depression.

Experimental findings indicate that some dopaminergic activity is mediated by the GHB receptor following GHB administration. GHB administration increases dopamine concentrations in the striatum and cortex in a dose-dependent fashion. The increase occurs due to stimulation of tyrosine hydroxylase, the enzyme necessary for dopamine synthesis, and is not related to a decrease in the catabolism of dopamine. A dose-dependent effect of GHB has been reported in which lower doses inhibit and higher doses stimulate the release of dopamine. Further, GHB inhibits dopamine release in awake animals, while it stimulates dopamine release in anesthetized animals.

The cholinergic and serotonergic systems also seem to be affected by GHB. Some studies suggest that GHB interacts with CNS opioids, as well.

Both behavioral and neurological effects are observed in subjects who have ingested GHB. Low doses of GHB (approximately 0.5–1.5 g) induce a state of relaxation and tranquility, placidity, sensuality, mild euphoria, a tendency to verbalize, emotional warmth, and drowsiness. Higher doses, such as those probably involved in drug-facilitated crimes (1.5 grams or more), can induce more obvious clinical manifestations and adverse effects including confusion, dizziness and drowsiness, nausea and vomiting, agitation, nystagmus, loss of peripheral vision, hallucinations, short-term amnesia, somnolence, uncontrollable shaking or seizures, combativeness, bradycardia, respiratory depression, apnea, and coma. One study found that blood concentrations exceeding 260 mg/L were associated with deep sleep; levels of 156–260 mg/L with moderate sleep; 52–156 mg/L with light sleep; and < 52 mg/L with wakefulness. In animal experiments, the median lethal dose is 5 to 15 times the coma-inducing dose.

There have been reported cases of physical dependence on GHB, with symptoms attributed to GHB withdrawal that include hallucinations, tremors, tachycardia, hypertension, sweating, anxiety, agitation, paranoia, insomnia, confusion, and aggression. Additionally, there have been numerous fatalities resulting from GHB overdose, sometimes in combination with other drugs.

Since GBL and 1,4-BD are rapidly metabolized to GHB after oral ingestion, the pharmacological effects of these drugs are analogous to the effects observed when GHB is ingested.

PHARMACOKINETICS

Due to its highly hydroscopic nature, GHB is usually administered as an oral solution and is rapidly absorbed, with plasma concentrations peaking within about 30 min and urinary concentrations peaking at about 1 h. Research suggests that GHB absorption is capacity limited and may be enhanced when the drug is consumed on an empty stomach. Oral bioavailability of GHB in rats is 59–65%. Initial clinical effects occur 15–20 min after oral administration, with peak effects occurring 30–60 min after ingestion. Extensive first-pass metabolism of GHB occurs following oral administration.

The lipid-soluble nature of GHB allows it to readily cross the blood-brain barrier where it exerts its primary effect. No appreciable plasma protein binding occurs with GHB. Distribution to target tissues occurs rapidly and follows a two-compartment model with an apparent volume of distribution (V_d) of 0.4 L/kg and 0.6 L/kg.

The primary pathway for GHB metabolism involves conversion to succinic semialdehyde before it is converted to succinic acid (Fig. 2). After succinic acid enters the Krebs cycle, it is ultimately expired as carbon dioxide. A small amount of GHB may be metabolized to succinic acid via a beta-oxidation pathway in the liver before entering the Krebs cycle. Due to the extensive biotransformation of GHB, less than 5% of an oral dose is excreted unchanged in the urine.

Pharmacokinetic studies demonstrate capacity-limited, nonlinear, and dose-dependent elimination of GHB with a half-life of 20–53 min in healthy human subjects. As mentioned previously, GBL and 1,4-BD are both metabolized to GHB following their ingestion (Fig. 3). The conversion to GHB is rapid and can be complete within 10 min of ingestion. Once this has occurred, GBL and 1,4-BD mimic the pharmacokinetics and pharmacodynamics of GHB.

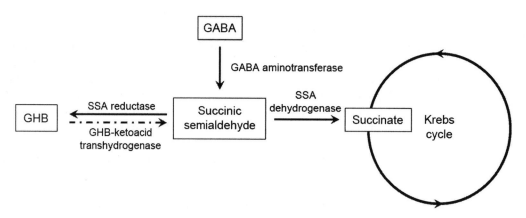

Fig. 2. GHB synthesis and metabolism.

ANALYTICAL METHODS

The analytical method used to measure GHB can have a significant effect on the obtained results. Because of the in vitro conversion between GHB and GBL, it may be important to ensure that the method employed measures the "total" of these two compounds. This conversion is unpredictable due to its dependence on pH, temperature, and time; therefore, the most conclusive analysis incorporates the "total" GHB into the measurement. Methods that do not take into account the presence of GBL may have significantly lower measurements of GHB, and care must be used when comparing data obtained from different analytical methods.

Numerous approaches exist for analyzing GHB's presence in biological specimens. One approach uses a concentrated dehydrating acid, such as sulfuric acid, to force the conversion of GHB to GBL followed by extraction into an organic solvent and direct injection into a gas chromatograph (GC) or gas chromatograph/mass spectrometer (GC/MS). This approach increases column and injection port maintenance because the extraction procedure does not include a back-extraction step. The conversion of GHB into GBL is important, as this allows one to account for both the GHB and GBL within the sample. Another approach involves copolymeric solid-phase extraction coupled with a solvent cleanup. Some authors have analyzed the extract by liquid chromatography–tandem mass spectrometry techniques. Others have utilized trimethylsilyl (TMS) derivatization of GHB in the extract and analyzed by GC or GC/MS. Yet other methods have involved headspace or solid-phase microextraction (SPME). One such method incorporates the use of methane chemical ionization GC/MS for the identification of the lactonized GHB.

INTERPRETATION

The endogenous nature of GHB in the body results, in part, from the normal metabolism of GABA in the CNS (Fig. 2) and from its production outside the CNS. In the CNS, GABA is converted into succinic semi-

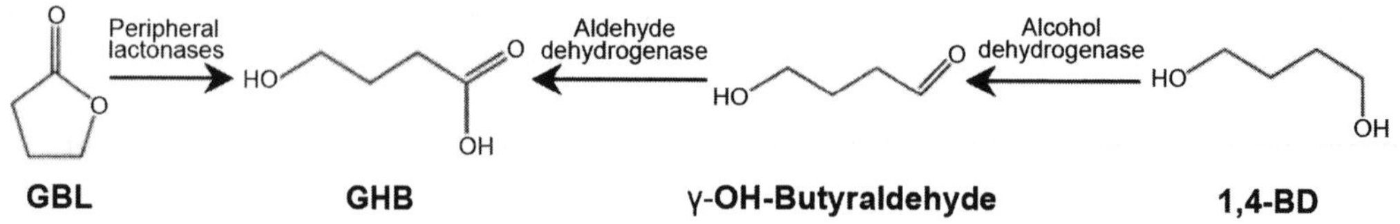

Fig. 3. Metabolism of 1,4-BD and GBL.

GBL   GHB   γ-OH-Butyraldehyde   1,4-BD

aldehyde (SSA) via GABA aminotransferase. Most of the formed SSA is oxidized to succinic acid (SA) via SSA dehydrogenase, where it enters the Krebs cycle and is converted to water and carbon dioxide. However, a small amount of the SSA is reduced to GHB via SSA reductase. GHB is typically oxidized back to SSA via GHB ketoacid transhydrogenase, where it, too, is converted to SA before entering the Krebs cycle, but a small amount of GHB may instead undergo oxidation to 3,4-dihydroxybutyric acid and 3-keto-4-hydroxybutyric acid. Research has suggested that these metabolites of oxidized GHB may only occur at measurable levels when the ketoacid transhydrogenase pathway is blocked.

There is evidence that there are sources of endogenous GHB in the body other than GABA. For example, GHB is present in extraneural sites (i.e., heart, lung, liver, skeletal muscle, kidney, and hair) that have either no or very little amounts of GABA present. Research has also shown that 1,4-BD is an endogenous product from fatty acids and may be a source of GHB in peripheral tissues.

A number of published cases reported urinary GHB concentrations following ingestion of the chemical. In one study, a driver found asleep in his car and unable to stand unassisted had a urinary GHB concentration of 1975 mg/L approximately 2 h postingestion. Another study found GHB in the urine of two impaired drivers at concentrations of 1086 and 1041 mg/L, respectively. A third case reported a comatose emergency room patient with a urine GHB concentration of 141,000 mg/L 1 h after ingestion of ethanol and GHB. It should be emphasized that the subjects were still under the influence of the drug when the urine specimens were collected in all three reports. This is not likely to be the situation when dealing with instances of DFSA. In one such case, a 27-year-old female was invited to a male friend's home for dinner and to watch a movie. After dinner, she agreed to have a cocktail but did not remember any of the events that followed. She awoke a couple of hours later, confused and completely nude in the man's bed. She

left his house and got immediate medical attention. Approximately 4 h after consuming the cocktail, she provided blood and urine specimens for testing. The results identified GHB in both the blood and urine specimens at concentrations of 47 and 308 mg/L, respectively.

The endogenous nature of GHB makes interpreting results in clinical and forensic specimens difficult at times. Most investigators agree that GHB concentrations exceeding 10 mg/L in urine samples are evidence of exogenous GHB exposure. However, potential in vitro formation of GHB may complicate interpretation if analysis of the urine sample is delayed more than a few months. Findings in blood specimens from living patients can also be complicated because it has been reported that the use of citrate-buffered specimen collection tubes may cause a falsely elevated amount of GHB in these tubes. Generally, GHB concentrations that exceed 2 mg/L in a blood sample stored in a noncitrate buffered tube provide additional evidence of exogenous GHB exposure. Whenever interpreting GHB findings in clinical specimens, it should be remembered that in most cases the maximum detection time of GHB after ingestion is 2 h in blood and 6 h in urine. Further, it is entirely possible that blood and urine concentrations of GHB will drop to endogenous concentrations in much less time than this.

Postmortem samples provide an additional challenge to the interpretation of GHB results. It is now well documented that GHB concentrations will artificially increase in postmortem blood specimens within a very short period of time. To minimize this increase, postmortem blood specimens should be preserved with sodium fluoride and stored at temperatures <5 °C. One study found that GHB concentrations in blood samples remained stable for several years if preserved with sodium fluoride and stored at -20 °C. Generally, in vitro increases in GHB concentrations have not been observed in postmortem vitreous humor specimens. A good rule of thumb for interpreting GHB findings in postmortem blood is that a GHB concentration >50 mg/L suggests the ingestion of GHB. However, as with all death investigations, the blood findings should be complemented by findings in other specimens and must be consistent with the case history.

SUGGESTED READING

1. Borgen LA, Okerholm RA, Lai A, Scharf MB. The pharmacokinetics of sodium oxybate oral solution following acute and chronic administration to narcoleptic patients. J Clin Pharmacol 2004;44:253–7.
2. Borgen LA, Okerholm R, Morrison D, Lai A. The influence of gender and food on the pharmacokinetics of sodium oxybate oral solution in healthy subjects. J Clin Pharmacol 2003;43:59–65.
3. Brailsford, AD, Cowan, DA, Kicman, AT. Pharmacokinetic properties of gamma-hydroxybutyrate (GHB) in whole blood, serum, and urine. J Anal Toxicol 2012;36:88–95.
4. Brenneisen R, Elsohly MA, Murphy TP, Passarelli J, Russmann S, Salamone SJ, et al. Pharmacokinetics and excretion of gamma-hydroxybutyrate (GHB) in healthy subjects. J Anal Toxicol 2004;28:625–30.
5. Craig K, Gomez HF, McManus JL, Bania TC. Severe gamma-hydroxybutyrate withdrawal: a case report and literature review. J Emerg Med 2000;18:65–70.
6. Doherty JD, Hattox SE, Snead OC, Roth RH. Identification of endogenous gamma-hydroxybutyrate in human and bovine brain and its regional distribution in human, guinea pig, and rhesus monkey brain. J Pharmacol Exp Ther 1978;207:130–9.
7. Elian AA. Determination of endogenous gammahydroxybutyric acid (GHB) levels in antemortem urine and blood. Forensic Sci Int 2002;128:120–2.
8. Elliott SP. Further evidence for the presence of GHB in postmortem biological fluid: implications for the interpretation of findings. J Anal Toxicol 2004;28:20–6.
9. Ferrara SD, Zotti S, Tedeschi L, Frison G, Castagna F, Gallimberti L, et al. Pharmacokinetics of gamma-hydroxybutyric acid in alcohol-dependent patients after single and repeated oral doses. Br J Clin Pharmacol 1992;34:231–5.
10. Fieler EL, Coleman DE, Baselt RC. Gammahydroxybutyrate concentrations in pre- and postmortem blood and urine. Clin Chem 1998;44:692.
11. Frison G, Tedeschi L, Maietti S, Ferrara SD. Determination of gamma-hydroxybutyric acid (GHB) in plasma and urine by headspace solid-phase microextraction and gas chromatography/positive ion chemical ionization mass spectrometry. Rapid Commun Mass Spectrom 2000;14:2401–7.
12. Galloway GP, Frederick SL, Staggers F Jr. Physical dependence on sodium oxybate. Lancet 1994;343:57.
13. Jakobs C, Bojasch M, Monch E, Rating D, Siemes H, Hanefeld F. Urinary excretion of gammahydroxybutyric acid in a patient with neurological abnormalities. The probability of a new inborn error of metabolism. Clin Chim Acta 1981;111:169–78.
14. Kavanagh PV, Kenny P, Feely J. The urinary excretion of gamma-hydroxybutyric acid in man. J Pharm Pharmacol 2001;53:399–402.
15. Kerrigan S. In vitro production of gammahydroxybutyrate in antemortem urine samples. J Anal Toxicol 2002;26:571–4.
16. LeBeau MA, Christenson RH, Levine B, Darwin WD, Huestis MA. Intra- and interindividual variations in urinary concentrations of endogenous gamma-hydroxybutyrate. J Anal Toxicol 2002;26:340–6.
17. LeBeau MA, Miller ML, Levine B. Effect of storage temperature on endogenous GHB levels in urine. Forensic Sci Int 2001;119:161–7.
18. LeBeau MA, Montgomery MA, Jufer RA, Miller ML. Elevated GHB in citrate-buffered blood. J Anal Toxicol 2000;24:383.
19. LeBeau MA, Montgomery MA, Miller ML, Burmeister SG. Analysis of biofluids for gammahydroxybutyrate (GHB) and gamma-butyrolactone (GBL) by headspace GC-FID and GC/MS. J Anal Toxicol 2000;24:421–8.
20. McCusker RR, Paget-Wilkes H, Chronister CW, Goldberger BA. Analysis of gamma-hydroxybutyrate (GHB) in urine by gas chromatography/mass spectrometry. J Anal Toxicol 1999;23:301–5.
21. Palatini P, Tedeschi L, Frison G, Padrini R, Zordan R, Orlando R, et al. Dose-dependent absorption and elimination of gamma-hydroxybutyric acid in healthy volunteers. Eur J Clin Pharmacol 1993;45:353–6.
22. Snead OC III, Liu CC. Gamma-hydroxybutyric acid binding sites in rat and human brain synaptosomal membranes. Biochem Pharmacol 1984;33:2587–90.
23. Wood M, Laloup M, Samyn N, Morris MR, de Bruijn EA, Maes RA, et al. Simultaneous analysis of gamma-hydroxybutyric acid and its precursors in urine using liquid chromatography/tandem mass spectrometry. J Chromatogr A 2004;1056:83–90.
24. Zachmann M, Tocci P, Nyhan WL. The occurrence of gamma-aminobutyric acid in human tissues other than brain. J Biol Chem 1996;241:1355–8.

CHAPTER 16

Miscellaneous Central Nervous System Depressants

Barry Levine

BARBITURATES

Chemistry, Classification, and Use

Barbiturates are one of the oldest classes of general CNS depressants. A wide variety of barbiturates is available today; they are primarily indicated for use as sedative-hypnotics, as anticonvulsants, in migraine therapy, and for reduction of cerebral edema secondary to head injury. The first barbiturate to be used therapeutically dates back to the early 1900s when diethylbarbituric acid (or barbital) was introduced. Shortly thereafter, phenobarbital was approved for use as a hypnotic agent. Barbituric acid results from the reaction of urea and malonic acid, with the resulting loss of water. The general formula of barbiturates (as well as the structural components of commonly used barbiturates) is shown in Fig. 1.

Modification of the general barbiturate structure to produce the various therapeutic barbiturate analogs can occur at multiple sites. For example, most barbiturates have a double-bonded oxygen attached to C_2, but some have a double-bonded sulfur at that position. Hydrogen is usually bonded to the N_3 position, but some barbiturate analogs substitute a methyl group at that position. However, the major structural modifications for barbiturates occur at the C_5 position, where two groups can be changed. One group, the C_{5a} position, may have an ethyl group or an allyl group. The other position, C_{5b}, may have a variety of aliphatic or aromatic side chains.

Since barbiturates have been around for approximately 100 years, numerous structural modifications have been attempted. The result is a great deal of information regarding the structure–activity relationships of barbiturates. For instance, increasing barbiturates' lipid solubility increases the potency but decreases the drugs' duration of activity. Lipid solubility can be increased by increasing the length of the aliphatic chain at the C_{5a} or C_{5b} position. Lipid solubility also is increased by substituting sulfur for oxygen at the C_2 position. However, once the carbon chain length on the C_{5b} position reaches or exceeds seven, CNS stimulation and not CNS depression results. Adding polar groups on the alkyl side chains, such as a hydroxyl group, removes hypnotic activity. Moreover, alkylating the N_3 position with a methyl group increases potency and decreases duration of activity. These methylated barbiturates are rapidly demethylated in vivo, resulting in active desmethyl metabolites.

A classification system for barbiturates based on their duration of action has been developed. The ultrashort-acting barbiturates act with great potency for a short period of time. Thiopental, thiamylal, and methohexital fall within this classification. The short-acting barbiturates include pentobarbital and secobarbital. The intermediate-acting

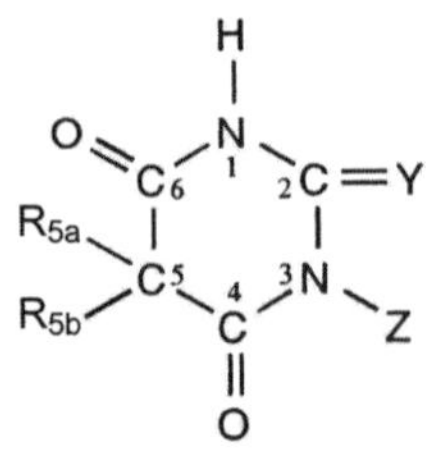

Fig. 1. The general barbiturate structure and structures of common barbiturates.

Drug	R_{5a}	R_{5b}	Y	Z
Amobarbital	ethyl	isopentyl	O	H
Butabarbital	ethyl	sec-butyl	O	H
Butalbital	allyl	isobutyl	O	H
Methohexital	allyl	1-methyl-2-pentynyl	O	CH₃
Pentobarbital	ethyl	1-methylbutyl	O	H
Phenobarbital	ethyl	phenyl	O	H
Secobarbital	allyl	1-methylbutyl	O	H
Thiamylal	allyl	1-methylbutyl	S	H
Thiopental	ethyl	1-methylbutyl	S	H

barbiturates, as the name implies, act for a longer period of time than the previously grouped drugs; amobarbital, butalbital, and butabarbital are classified as such. Phenobarbital is the most commonly prescribed drug in the long-acting barbiturate group.

The therapeutic uses of barbiturates are developed from this classification system. The ultrashort-acting barbiturates are used to induce surgical anesthesia. The short- and intermediate-acting barbiturates have been prescribed as sedative-hypnotic agents. Pentobarbital has also been used to relieve intracranial pressure in head trauma cases. Butalbital has been prescribed to treat migraine headaches. Phenobarbital is used to control seizures.

The use of barbiturates as sedative-hypnotic agents has declined over time. Because barbiturates have general CNS-depressant activity, they have significant impairing effects. Moreover, tolerance occurs to a greater extent with barbiturates than with other CNS-depressant drugs. Barbiturates have largely been replaced as sedative-hypnotic agents by other drugs, mainly benzodiazepines, which have a shorter duration of action and a higher therapeutic index, thus providing a greater margin of safety when administered.

Pharmacokinetics

Barbiturates may be administered either orally or parenterally. The oral route is preferred when the drug is prescribed as a sedative-hypnotic or as an anticonvulsant drug. Barbiturates as sodium salts are well absorbed orally. Despite the pH characteristics of the drugs (weak acids with pK$_a$s ranging from 7 to 8), the small intestine is the major site for oral absorption. The intravenous route is used to administer ultrashort-acting barbiturates during the induction of anesthesia. Seizure emergencies may also be handled through the intravenous administration of phenobarbital. Sodium salts of barbiturates are not usually administered intramuscularly because of alkalinity, which results in poor absorption of the drugs from muscle depots.

Barbiturates distribute throughout the major tissues of the body. Binding to plasma proteins is variable, depending on the drug. Ultrashort-acting thiobarbiturates show a biphasic distribution within the brain. A rapid initial distribution of the drug into the gray matter occurs within seconds of intravenous administration; this is the reason for their utility as anesthetic agents. Subsequently, the drug redistributes into other components of the brain.

Elimination half-lives vary with the particular barbiturate and form the basis for the classification system. The short-acting barbiturates have a half-life of about 1 day, while the intermediate-acting barbiturates have a half-life of about 2 days. The elimination half-life of long-acting barbiturates is 2–5 days.

Barbiturates are extensively metabolized in the liver. Except for phenobarbital, less than 10% of a dose appears in the urine as unchanged drug. Hydroxylation at the C_{5b} constituent is a common metabolic route. Oxidation of the end carbon of the C_{5b} constituent to a carboxylic acid can also occur in barbiturates with an aliphatic structure at that position. In addition, a ring nitrogen can form a glucoside metabolite by reacting with glucose.

One of the most important characteristics of barbiturates is their ability to induce microsomal enzymes in the liver. This can significantly influence the therapeutic action of drugs that are metabolized via this mechanism when they are coadministered with barbiturates. Doses of these drugs may need adjustments to correct for this increased metabolism.

Analysis

Barbiturates can be easily separated from biological specimens. Adjustment of the pH to approximately 5–7 and extraction with an immiscible organic solvent will cause the barbiturates to enter the organic layer. Alternatively, solid-phase extraction can be performed. Once separation has taken place, various identification techniques are available.

A color reaction using mercuric nitrate and diphenylcarbazone can be performed on the evaporated extract. An orange-blue color will be produced if a barbiturate is present. The color varies with the barbiturate structure. To qualitatively identify the barbiturate present, this color reaction can be used after application of the extract to a silica gel thin-layer chromatographic plate and development using the Davidow system

(ethyl acetate:methanol:ammonium hydroxide, 85:10:5). A purple spot will be produced if a barbiturate is present.

A classical ultraviolet (UV) spectrophotometric method was developed to identify barbiturates. The solvent extract is back extracted into a dilute base such as sodium hydroxide. At this point, the dilute base is divided into two aliquots. One portion is adjusted to pH 10 with ammonium chloride, and the other is adjusted to pH 13 with sodium hydroxide. The pH 10 portion is placed in the reference compartment of the spectrophotometer and the pH 13 portion is placed in the sample compartment. An absorption spectrum between 220 and 280 nm is obtained, with the absorption difference between 240 and 260 nm being proportional to the amount of barbiturate present.

Gas chromatography (GC) is a common method for separating and analyzing different barbiturates. The common drugs can be separated on a dimethyl or phenylmethyl silicone analytical column using temperature programming. Although sufficient resolution and acceptable chromatographic characteristics are obtained without derivatization, chromatography is improved by derivatization of the barbiturates with a methylating agent. In one common technique, "flash methylation," an extract is reconstituted with a methylating agent such as trimethylphenylammonium hydroxide. Injection into the hot injection port of the gas chromatograph permits the derivatization to occur. An example of a chromatogram containing five commonly detected barbiturates and an internal standard (cyclopal) is illustrated in Fig. 2.

High-performance liquid chromatography (HPLC) is an acceptable technique for separating and quantifying individual barbiturates. A C_8 or C_{18} reverse-phase analytical column can provide separation using a variety of mobile phases. One disadvantage to liquid chromatography (LC) is the low wavelength of detection when using an ultraviolet (UV) detector. A wavelength of approximately 200 nm is required to obtain acceptable detection limits. However, significant interferences from endogenous

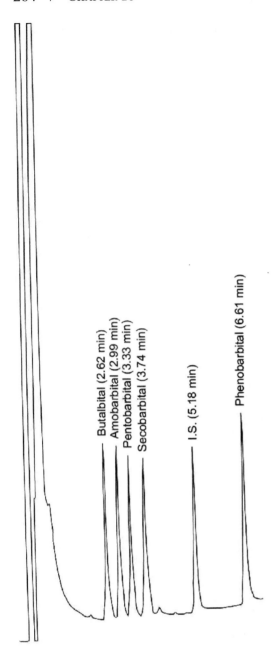

Fig. 2. Gas chromatogram of methyl derivatives of common barbiturates.

components at this wavelength can occur, especially when analyzing postmortem blood or tissue specimens.

Barbiturates can be rapidly screened in urine specimens using commercially available immunoassays. Most of these immunoassays are targeted to detect secobarbital but have sufficient cross-reactivity to other bar-

biturates to identify therapeutic use. Immunoassays have also been designed to screen serum for barbiturates in emergency toxicology. Therapeutic drug monitoring immunoassays are also available for phenobarbital.

Common oxybarbiturates have mass spectral similarities based on their constituents at the C_5 position. For example, butabarbital, amobarbital, and pentobarbital each have an ethyl group at the C_{5a} position but different aliphatic groups at the C_{5b} position. The mass spectrum of each compound has major ions at 141 and 156 amu, with smaller ions at 183 and 197 amu (Fig. 3). Therefore, relying exclusively on a mass spectrum to identify these compounds could potentially lead to a misidentification. Fortunately, these compounds can be easily separated chromatographically; therefore, the combination of chromatographic retention time and mass spectrum can provide conclusive identification of the barbiturate present. Similarly, drugs with an allyl group at the C_{5a} position, such as butalbital and secobarbital, have mass spectra with many common ions.

Interpretation

The therapeutic ranges of barbiturates in blood have been well established. The short-acting barbiturates have a therapeutic range of 0.5–2 mg/L. The intermediate-acting barbiturates have an expected range of 1–5 mg/L. When phenobarbital is used as a sedative-hypnotic, targeted blood concentrations are 5–15 mg/L. To treat seizures, a phenobarbital concentration of 15–40 mg/L is considered therapeutic. These ranges can be subject to exceptions. Occasionally with epileptics, higher phenobarbital concentrations are necessary to control seizures. When an apparently elevated phenobarbital concentration is measured, a review of the history is in order before deciding that a drug intoxication has occurred. Patients being treated with pentobarbital to relieve intracranial pressure may reach blood concentrations of an order of magnitude above the generally reported therapeutic range. Hospital record analysis

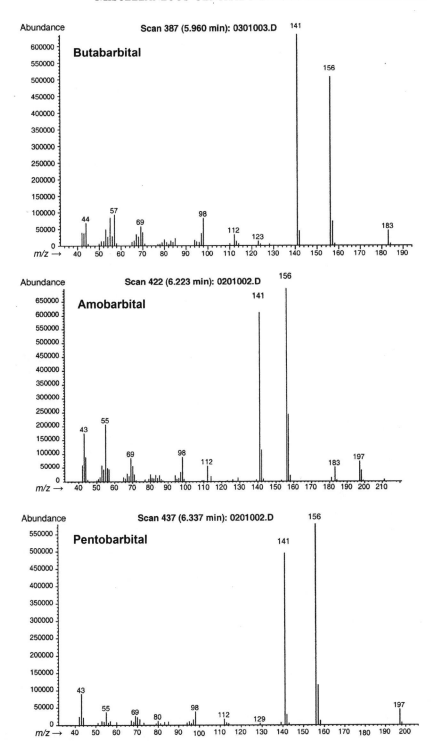

Fig. 3. Full-scan electron impact mass spectra of several common barbiturates.

should clarify this and thus prevent an erroneous interpretation of the analytical results.

OTHER CNS DEPRESSANTS

Barbiturates and benzodiazepines (Chapter 14) represent the major classes of drugs when CNS depression is desired. However, over the years, other CNS-depressant drugs have been developed that reportedly have certain advantages over these drug classes. Some of these alleged benefits were a higher therapeutic index and the lack of abuse potential. However, once these drugs gained widespread use, many of these benefits failed to materialize. Fig. 4 gives the chemical structures of the drugs that are discussed here.

Buspirone

Buspirone is an azapirone drug approved for use in the U.S. in 1986. Unlike benzodiazepines and zolpidem, the drug does not mediate its CNS-depressant activity through GABA. Instead, buspirone acts as a partial agonist at the $5HT_{1A}$ receptor site. Buspirone does not have any anticonvulsant or muscle relaxant activity.

One advantage to using buspirone to treat anxiety is its relatively short half-life, <6 h. It is metabolized to 5-hydroxybuspirone and to 1-(2-pyrimidinyl) piperazine (1-PP). This latter metabolite appears in higher concentrations in the blood than does the parent drug, and it is pharmacologically active. Blood buspirone concentrations <0.01 mg/L result from therapeutic administration.

Due to the low drug concentrations that appear in the blood, the analysis in biological specimens may be difficult. Buspirone can be separated from blood, urine, or tissue specimens by liquid–liquid extraction at alkaline pH or by solid-phase extraction. GC/MS with selected ion monitoring can measure buspirone and 1-PP. Buspirone does not require derivatization, but 1-PP, a secondary amine, requires derivatization for adequate detection limits. LC of parent and metabolite, using UV detection, electrochemical detection, or mass spectrometry, has also been reported.

Carisoprodol/Meprobamate

Carisoprodol, N-isopropyl meprobamate, is a carbamate derivative used as a muscle relaxant. It is metabolized by dealkylation to meprobamate. Meprobamate is also an older CNS depressant originally marketed as an alternative to barbiturates without the risk of abuse or overdosage. The safety that was advertised failed to develop, because meprobamate produced toxic effects similar to other sedative-hypnotic drugs. Meprobamate is further metabolized by hydroxylation to an inactive metabolite and is excreted as a glucuronide conjugate. The average elimination half-life is about 12 h.

Carisoprodol and meprobamate, both neutral drugs, are easily separated from the biological matrix by extraction with an immiscible organic solvent. A color test designed to detect carbamates can also be used to identify both drugs; acid furfural is the color reagent. This color reaction can also be applied to a thin-layer plate after the application of an extract to a thin-layer plate and development in chloroform:methanol (9:1). Carisoprodol and meprobamate can also be detected by GC with flame ionization or nitrogen-phosphorus detection. After therapeutic use of carisoprodol, serum concentrations of both parent drug and meprobamate are in the range of 2–5 mg/L. When meprobamate was used as a sedative/hypnotic, concentrations of 5–25 mg/L range were observed.

Chloral hydrate

Chloral hydrate is the oldest sedative-hypnotic still in use today. Although not widely prescribed for adults, it is used to reduce agitation in neonates and infants requiring mechanical ventilation. Spontaneous extubation in chronically ventilated infants occurs less often when they are treated with chloral hydrate. One advantage over other CNS-depressant drugs in these patients is that there appears to be no depression in respiratory drive. Chloral hydrate serves as a prodrug, as it rapidly loses water to form trichloroethanol. Trichloroethanol is the active metabolite of chloral hydrate. Trichloroethanol may be excreted as a glucuronide conjugate or be oxidized to trichloroacetic acid, conjugated, and cleared.

Trichloroethanol can be analyzed rapidly using the Fujiwara test for chlorinated hydrocarbons. Urine or a protein-free filtrate of blood can be alkalinized with strong base and heated after the addition of pyridine. The presence of trichloroethanol is indicated by a yellow color in the pyridine layer. Trichloroethanol can also be analyzed by GC.

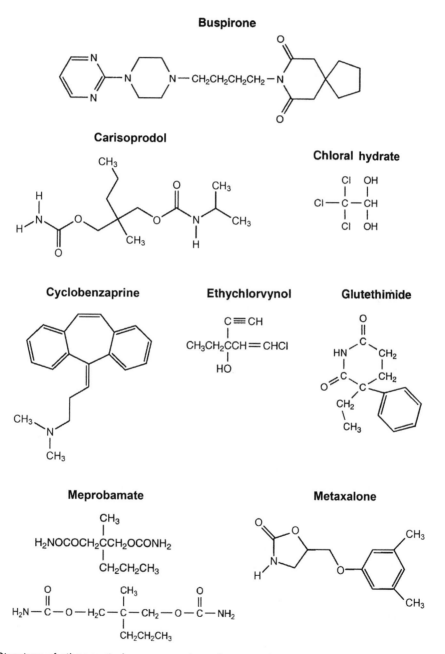

Fig. 4. Structure of other central nervous system–depressants.

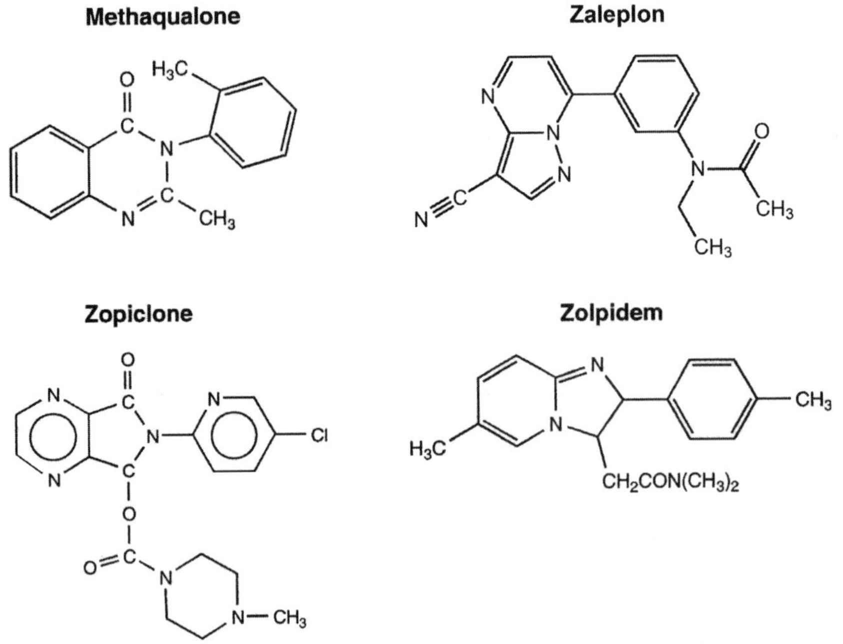

Methaqualone

Zaleplon

Zopiclone

Zolpidem

Fig. 4. (*Continued*)

A flame ionization detector has adequate sensitivity to permit detection of therapeutic chloral hydrate use. Use of an electron capture detector can greatly enhance sensitivity because there are three halogens in this compound. A general therapeutic range for trichloroethanol is 2–12 mg/L.

Cyclobenzaprine

Cyclobenzaprine is structurally similar to amitriptyline, with a double bond in the cycloheptane ring as opposed to a single bond with amitriptyline. Despite the structural similarities, it lacks the antidepressant properties possessed by amitriptyline and is used therapeutically as a muscle relaxant. Like amitriptyline, it is metabolized by demethylation, hydroxylation, and N-oxide formation; unlike amitriptyline, hydroxylation occurs on the phenyl ring. A diol on the cycloheptane ring has also been identified as a metabolite. Cyclobenzaprine extracts under alkaline conditions and chromatographs similar to the tricyclic antidepressants. Therapeutic concentrations are in the range of 0.01–0.03 mg/L.

Ethchlorvynol

Ethchlorvynol was approved for use in the 1950s as a sedative-hypnotic drug with a shorter duration and more rapid onset of action than barbiturates. Its rapid onset of action is related to its high lipophilicity. In fact, it is one drug that has significant distribution into fat. As such, ethchlorvynol shows biphasic elimination from the blood. There is a rapid α-elimination half-life of several hours, which represents rapid distribution. This is followed by a β-elimination half-life of approximately 1 day. Ethchlorvynol is metabolized to hydroxyethchlorvynol, which is the major urinary metabolite.

As with trichloroethanol, a color reaction is available for the analysis of ethchlorvynol. Urine or protein-free filtrate of blood can be reacted with concentrated sulfuric acid and diphenylamine. A pink color constitutes a positive test. Ethchlorvynol can also be measured by GC with a flame ionization detector. The drug has one chlorine atom, thus permitting detection using an electron capture detector. Because the drug does not have a nitrogen atom, a nitrogen-phosphorus detector would be of little use for the analysis of ethchlorvynol. A blood concentration of 2–8 mg/L is expected after therapeutic use.

Glutethimide

Glutethimide is structurally similar to phenobarbital; one of the nitrogen atoms is replaced with a carbon atom. Although it shares phenobarbital's CNS-depressing properties, the change in this one atom eliminates anticonvulsant properties. Glutethimide has also been abused, especially in combination with opiate drugs. Its half-life is approximately 12–24 h. Glutethimide is metabolized to hydroxyglutethimide, which has greater CNS-depressant activity than the parent drug and can be a source of significant toxicity.

Glutethimide can be separated from biological specimens by liquid–liquid extraction at weak acid or neutral pH. Identification can be achieved by thin-layer chromatography following visualization with diphenylcarbazone and mercuric nitrate. As with phenobarbital, both GC and LC can also be used to identify and quantify glutethimide. Immunoassays designed to detect barbiturate use cannot be used to identify glutethimide use. Glutethimide concentrations <5 mg/L would be expected in blood following therapeutic use. Excessive CNS depression is often seen at concentrations >10 mg/L. These expected effects would vary according to the concentration of the hydroxyglutethimide in the blood.

Metaxalone

Metaxalone is an oxazolidine derivative that acts centrally as a skeletal muscle relaxant. It is marketed either as a single product or as a component of combination products. At lower doses, it depresses polysynaptic reflexes as measured by the loss of the righting reflex. At high doses, it produces depression of monosynaptic reflexes. Metaxalone does not directly relax "tense" skeletal muscle because it has no direct effect on the contractile mechanism of striated muscle, the motor endplate, or the nerve fiber. The onset of action is 1 h with a duration of action of 4–6 h and a half-life of 2–3 h. Plasma concentrations following a single 400–800 mg dose were in the range of 1–4 mg/L. Metaxalone is extensively metabolized to at least 3 metabolites primarily excreted in the urine. One metabolite is formed by the oxidation of one of the methyl groups to the carboxy analog and appears in the urine as the glucuronide conjugate. Drowsiness is the most frequently reported adverse effect of this drug.

Methaqualone

Methaqualone (Quaalude) was another sedative-hypnotic drug developed in the 1950s. During the 1960s and 1970s, it became a popular drug of abuse. Allegedly, a feeling of euphoria was achieved without the drowsiness caused by barbiturates. By 1984, it had been removed from the market in the U.S. Methaqualone has an elimination half-life of approximately 2 days. Methaqualone is extensively metabolized, with numerous positions on the ring structures capable of being hydroxylated.

Methaqualone has different analytical characteristics than the older nonbarbiturate CNS-depressant drugs. Because of the abuse potential, commercially available immunoassays were developed specifically to detect methaqualone use. In addition, methaqualone has significant UV absorbance at 230–235 nm. Methaqualone can be extracted under weak alkaline, neutral, or weak acid conditions, and can be identified or quantified by GC without derivatization.

Zaleplon

Zaleplon is a pyrazolpyrimidine derivative that has been used to treat insomnia since 1999. Like the structurally similar zolpidem, zaleplon is a selective agonist at the benzodiazepine type I receptor subtype on the GABAA receptor complex in the brain. The recommended dose is 5–20 mg per night. Neither tolerance nor withdrawal effects have been reported. Although administered orally, zaleplon undergoes significant first-pass metabolism, leading to a bioavailability of approximately 30%. It is extensively metabolized to inactive metabolites, including N-desethylzaleplon and 5-oxozaleplon. Peak plasma concentrations following a 20 mg dose are in the range of 0.05 mg/L.

Zopiclone

Zopiclone has a cyclopyrrolone structure and is structurally unrelated to barbiturates, benzodiazepines, or other previously marketed CNS-depressant drugs. It is a short-acting CNS depressant used to treat insomnia and anxiety, but also has muscle relaxant and anticonvulsant activities. Zopiclone is metabolized by decarboxylation, oxidation, and demethylation. The N-oxide metabolite has CNS-depressant activity.

The analysis of zopiclone in biological specimens is complicated by several factors. It is unstable in methanol, forming a methoxy adduct. To make calibrators for analysis, the stock standard solution should be prepared in acetonitrile. It is also unstable in acidic or basic media and must be extracted at neutral pH. Zopiclone and its metabolites can be measured by LC with either UV or fluorescence detection. Analyzing the drug by GC can result in thermal degradation depending on the operating conditions. Either a nitrogen-phosphorus or electron capture detector can be used. Blood concentrations of about 0.1 mg/L are seen following therapeutic use.

Zolpidem

Zolpidem is the prototype of a class of sedative-hypnotic drugs that are derivatives of imidazopyridine. Although not considered a benzodiazepine, zolpidem does possess some structural similarities to this class of drugs. Whereas benzodiazepines bind nonspecifically to many $GABA_A$ receptor subtypes, zolpidem binds specifically to the $GABA_A$ receptor responsible for sedative activity. Thus, zolpidem is used for the short-term management of insomnia. It has an elimination half-life of several hours.

Zolpidem is separated from biological specimens after adjusting the pH to alkaline conditions. The drug can easily be identified by GC on a dimethyl or phenylmethyl silicone column without derivatization. Nitrogen-phosphorus detection provides adequate sensitivity. LC with either UV or fluorescence detection can also be used. Following therapeutic use, blood zolpidem concentrations are in the 0.1–0.2 mg/L range.

SUGGESTED READING

1. Baselt RC, ed. Analytical procedures for therapeutic drug monitoring and emergency toxicology, 2nd ed. Littleton, MA: PSG Publishing Co., 1987.
2. Baselt RC, ed. Disposition of toxic drugs and chemicals in man, 9th ed. Seal Beach, CA: Biomedical Publications, 2011.
3. Brunton LL, Lazo JS, Parker KL, Gilman AG, eds. Goodman and Gilman's the pharmacological basis of therapeutics, 11th ed. New York: McGraw-Hill Co., 2006.
4. Cannon DJ. Glutethimide. AACC Therapeutic Drug Monitoring and Toxicology 1992;13(10): 3–4.
5. Gupta RN. Review: drug level monitoring: sedative hypnotics. J Chromatogr 1985;340:139–72.
6. Ionescu-Pioggia M, Bird M, Orzack MH, Benes F, Beake B, Cole JO. Methaqualone. Int Clin Psychopharmacol 1988;3:97–109.
7. Langtry HD, Benfield P. Zolpidem: a review of its pharmacodynamic and pharmacokinetic properties and therapeutic potential. Drugs 1990;40:291–313.
8. Zebelman AM. Ethchlorvynol. AACC Therapeutic Drug Monitoring and Toxicology 1992;13(15):3–4.
9. Zebelman AM. Meprobamate. AACC Therapeutic Drug Monitoring and Toxicology 1993;14(12):303–4.

CHAPTER 17

Opioids

Sarah Kerrigan and Bruce A. Goldberger

Used for more than 2000 years, opiates are naturally occurring alkaloid analgesics obtained from the opium poppy, *Papaver somniferum*. The milky exudate obtained upon incision of the unripe seed contains several pharmacologically active compounds, including morphine and codeine. Morphine, the principal alkaloid of opium, is named after Morpheus, the god of dreams.

First isolated in 1806, morphine was the primary building block in the subsequent development of many semisynthetic opioid analgesics. The term *opioid* is used to describe natural and semisynthetic alkaloids prepared from opium, as well as synthetic surrogates whose pharmacologic effects, rather than their structures, mimic those of morphine. This term also includes the natural or endogenous neuropeptides (opiopeptins), such as enkephalins, endorphins, and dynorphins, which are not within the scope of this discussion.

The semisynthetic derivative heroin was first synthesized from morphine in 1874 and was made available as a pharmaceutical preparation in 1898. Heroin is unavailable in the U.S. for therapeutic use, but widespread abuse of the drug has persisted since the 1970s. The first fully synthetic opioid without a morphine-like structure was meperidine (prepared serendipitously in 1939). Another fully synthetic opioid, methadone, was synthesized shortly thereafter, in 1946.

Nalorphine, the original opioid antagonist, was first synthesized in 1942. A significant pharmacotherapeutic advance, nalorphine is able to reverse the respiratory depression produced by morphine and facilitate abstinence in drug-dependent individuals. This capability, in combination with its analgesic properties, is due to its mixed agonist–antagonist effect. Further discoveries led to the development of other drugs, such as naloxone, that possess an almost exclusive antagonistic binding behavior. The design of new synthetic opioids is concomitant with investigations into interactions with opioid receptors, in the hope that current understanding in this area will further the discovery of potent analgesics with fewer side effects.

CHEMISTRY AND MECHANISM OF ACTION

The characteristic pharmacologic effects of opioids are due to the somewhat selective binding to receptors at several sites in the central nervous system (CNS). Structural modification of the polycyclic framework of morphine can considerably alter the pharmacology of the drug and its potency as an analgesic. The limbic system, which is rich in opioid-binding sites, is primarily involved in the arousal of emotion in humans. Opioids produce an analgesic effect by blocking the transmission of painful stimuli. The interaction between the opioid and specific receptors at terminal nerve endings impedes the release of neurotransmitter, thus interrupting the pain. This interaction prevents the recognition of painful sensations, inhibits the negative emotional component of pain, and can produce euphoria in some instances.

Opioid Receptors

The pharmacologic profile of different opioids is characterized by their interaction with certain receptors (Table 1), of which there are at least three major types: μ (mu), κ (kappa), and δ (delta).

- μ receptor interactions produce central depression, which is clinically manifested as supraspinal ($μ_1$) and spinal ($μ_2$) analgesia, respiratory depression, miosis, euphoria, reduced gastrointestinal motility, hypothermia, bradycardia, and physical tolerance and dependence.
- κ receptor interactions produce spinal analgesia, sedation, miosis, diuresis, mild respiratory depression, and low addiction liability.
- δ receptors are the binding sites for most endogenous peptides. Interactions at these sites mediate spinal analgesia, dysphoria, delusions, hallucinations, and respiratory and vasomotor stimulation.

The analgesic effect of morphine and several of its congeners is mediated through the μ opioid receptor. κ receptor interactions can also produce analgesia, but this effect is sometimes accompanied by psychomimetic effects that may limit their clinical utility. Opioids may also bind to σ (sigma) receptors to produce central excitation, causing tachycardia, hypertension, tachypnea, mydriasis, and hallucinations.

Agonist and Antagonist Behavior

Opioids are broadly classified into three groups, depending on their mode of action. The term *full agonist* refers to compounds that have an affinity for opioid receptors of a certain type. Drugs with an agonistic effect at one class of receptor and an antagonistic effect at another are called *mixed agonist–antagonists*. *Full antagonists*, which inhibit agonist binding, tend to have reduced analgesic effects and are primarily indicated for the treatment of opioid intoxication.

An antagonist can preferentially displace an opioid from a receptor's binding site because of an increased affinity or competitive potency. For example, substitution of the N-methyl group in morphine with an allyl moiety tends to produce antagonistic binding behavior. Naloxone, which is an extremely potent antagonist, has no analgesic effect when administered alone. Consequently, the antagonistic properties of these drugs have been exploited clinically for the treatment of intoxication, including the rapid reversal of opioid-induced respiratory depression. After morphine intoxication, the antagonistic effect of naloxone can dramatically reverse the opioid effect within a few minutes and effectively normalize respiration.

The pharmacologic profile of an agonist–antagonist analgesic is generally consistent with the type of opioid receptor involved. Pentazocine interacts preferentially with κ receptors, which advantageously mediate analgesia with limited respiratory depression, whereas its interactions with σ receptors may produce behavioral and dysphoric side effects. In some instances, multiple modes of action are responsible for an array of pharmacologic responses. For example, the analgesic effect of tramadol is due to μ agonism and a nonopioid pathway involving inhibition of noradrenaline and serotonin uptake. A current understanding of the different classes of receptors and their pharmacologic characteristics facilitates the design of potent narcotic analgesics with reduced side effects and reduced addiction liability.

Structure–Activity Relationships

Major qualitative and quantitative changes in pharmacologic response are brought about by variations in conformation, rigidity, and the nature of the moieties substituted into the ring system of morphine. The degree of complement, or goodness of fit, between the receptor binding site and the drug determines the extent of analgesia and the duration of effects. Consequently, drugs within this class exhibit a wide range of potencies relative to morphine (Table 1).

The pharmacodynamics of a particular opioid are largely predetermined by the steric

Table 1. Mode of Action and Analgesic Potency of Opioids

Drug	Mode of Action	Analgesic Potency (Morphine = 1)
Buprenorphine	Partial μ agonist, κ antagonist	25–50
Butorphanol	Strong κ agonist, μ antagonist	4–8
Codeine	Weak μ agonist, weak δ agonist	0.1
Dihydrocodeine	μ agonist	0.3
Fentanyl	Strong μ agonist	100–200
Heroin	Strong μ agonist	1–5
Hydrocodone	μ agonist	1–2
Hydromorphone	Strong μ agonist	7–10
Levorphanol	Strong μ and κ agonist	4–5
Meperidine	Strong μ agonist	0.1
Methadone	Strong μ agonist	1
Morphine	Strong μ agonist, weak κ and δ agonist	1
Nalbuphine	Strong κ agonist, σ agonist, μ antagonist	0.5–1.0
Oxycodone	μ agonist	1–2
Oxymorphone	Strong μ agonist	8–15
Pentazocine	Mixed κ, μ, and σ agonist	0.2
Propoxyphene	μ agonist	<0.1
Tapentadol	μ agonist, norepinephrine reuptake inhibition	0.05
Tramadol	μ agonist, norepinephrine, serotonin reuptake inhibition	0.1–0.2

and electronic characteristics of the drug. An opioid's binding interactions with the receptor, which are responsible for the pharmacologic effect, are determined not only by the molecular structure of the drug but also by its stereospecificity. For example, only the levorotatory isomer of morphine, which occurs in nature, is a potent analgesic. Within the drug molecule, one region is responsible for the goodness of fit, and another region facilitates the conformational changes that are necessary for receptor binding to occur. These factors ultimately determine whether the drug behaves as an agonist or an antagonist. Opioids exert their pharmacologic effects by mimicking the activities of enkephalins and endorphins, which are the body's own analgesic resource.

Despite the wide variation in size and functionality, the opioids are characterized by their aromatic core and basic nature (Fig. 1). Typical pK_a values (approximately 7.6–8.9) ensure some degree of protonation at physiological pH, which is believed to facilitate the binding interaction with the receptor. Various conformations and molecular structures facilitate the initial pharmacophoric interaction between the drug and the opioid receptor, and aspects of secondary structure may enhance or impede their association.

Relatively minor changes in molecular structure can profoundly affect the pharmacologic properties of a drug. For example, replacement of the C3 hydroxyl (phenolic) group of morphine can substantially reduce the affinity for μ opioid receptors, as is the case for both heroin and codeine. Substitution of the N-methyl substituent in morphine with a larger group can result in binding activity with antagonistic receptor, as in nalbuphine. The pharmacokinetics are affected by the replacement of the C3 and C6 hydroxyl (aliphatic) groups of morphine. Methylation of these groups (e.g., codeine, oxycodone) decreases the susceptibility to first-pass metabolism and significantly increases the potency of orally administered drugs. Similarly, acetylation of morphine to produce diamorphine (heroin) facilitates penetration of the blood–brain barrier.

The evolution of drug design to optimize therapeutic analgesic effects has led to the production of a number of useful natural,

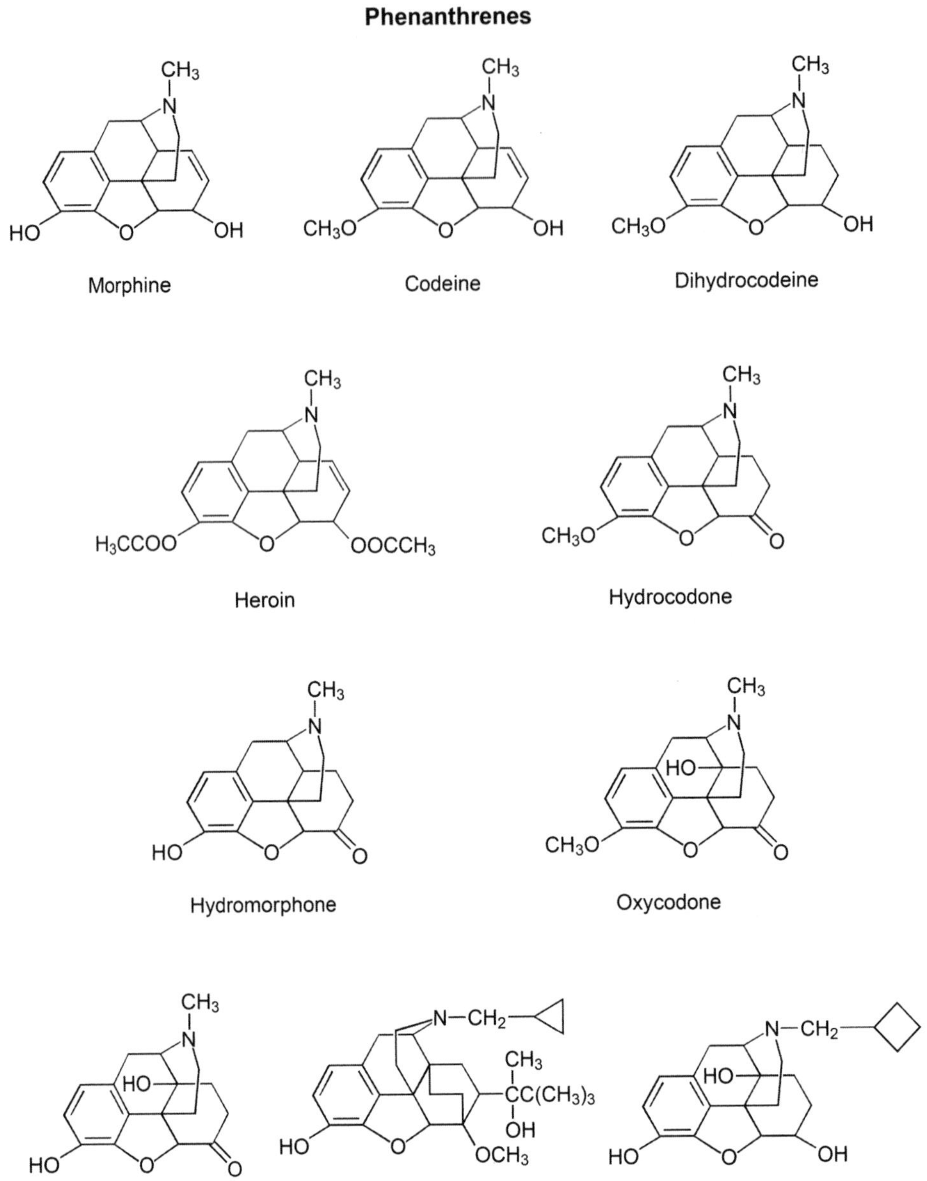

Phenanthrenes

Morphine

Codeine

Dihydrocodeine

Heroin

Hydrocodone

Hydromorphone

Oxycodone

Oxymorphone

Buprenorphine

Nalbuphine

Fig. 1. Chemical structures of opioid analgesics.

semisynthetic, and synthetic opioids, which are broadly classified as:

- Phenanthrenes: morphine, codeine, dihydrocodeine, heroin, hydrocodone, hydromorphone, oxycodone, oxymorphone, buprenorphine, nalbuphine
- Morphinans: butorphanol, levorphanol
- Phenylheptylamines: methadone, propoxyphene

- Phenylpiperidines: meperidine, fentanyl
- Benzomorphans: pentazocine
- Cyclohexanols, Phenols: tramadol, tapentadol

The phenanthrenes, also called 4,5-epoxymorphinans, include the major opiate alkaloids obtained from the opium poppy. Derivatization of these natural alkaloids has expanded this class, which is now the largest

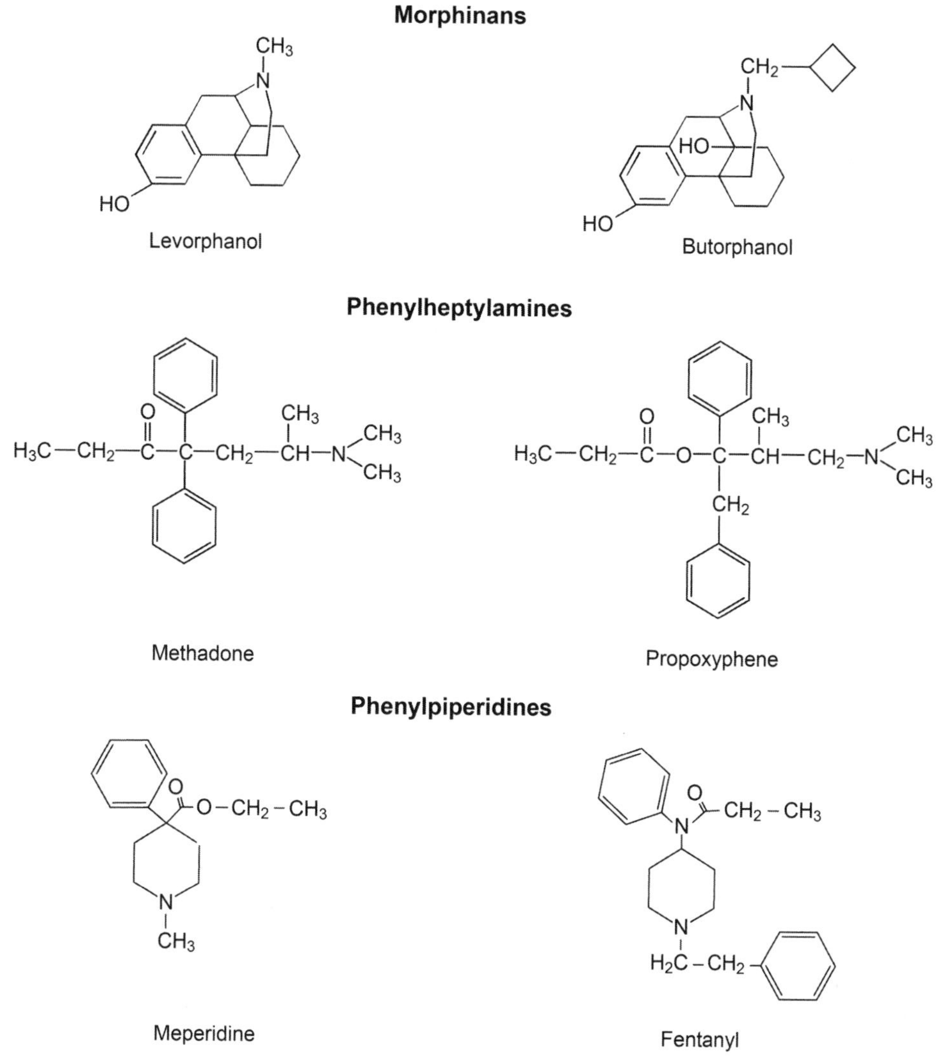

Morphinans

Levorphanol

Butorphanol

Phenylheptylamines

Methadone

Propoxyphene

Phenylpiperidines

Meperidine

Fentanyl

Fig. 1. *(Continued)*

and best characterized group of opioids. Structural alterations of the basic morphine framework include the methylation or acetylation of the C3 and C6 hydroxyl groups, saturation of the C7=C8 double bond (dihydro derivatives), oxidation to a ketone at position 6 (hydro derivatives), and subsequent hydroxylation of the C14 atom (oxy derivatives). Simplification of the morphine structure by removing the furan bridge (in morphinans) or by ring exclusion to yield a bridged naphthalene (in benzomorphans) can produce congeners that retain analgesic activity. In addition to these semisynthetic analogs, relatively simple synthetic opioids, such as the piperidines, may have analgesic properties that in some cases exceed the effectiveness of the principal alkaloid, morphine.

USE AND EFFECTS

The therapeutic uses of opioids include postoperative analgesia and indications in surgical and medical emergencies, including myocardial infarction, trauma, burns, and orthopedic pain. Other major indications include the management of chronic pain associated with cancer and terminal illness and

Benzomorphan

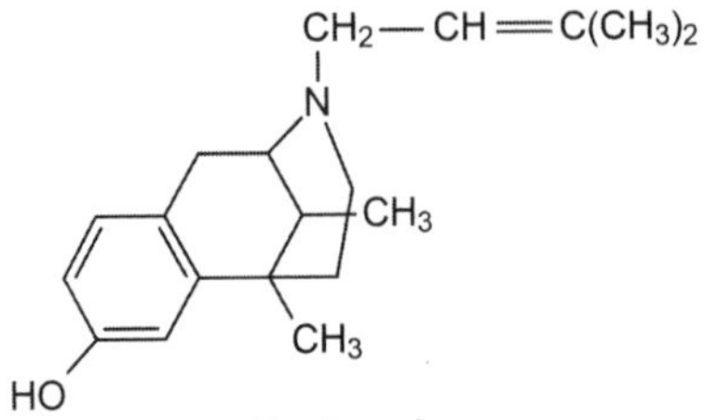

Cyclohexanol

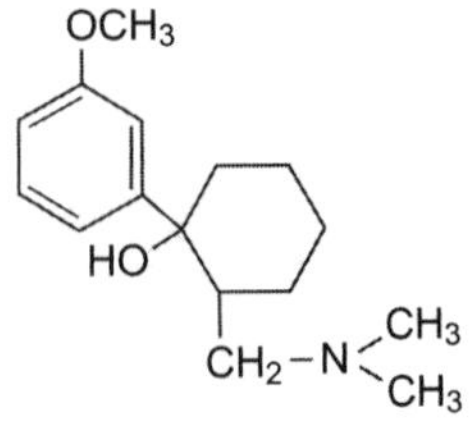

$CH_2—CH=C(CH_3)_2$

OCH_3

CH_3

HO

CH_3

HO

$CH_2-N\begin{smallmatrix}CH_3\\CH_3\end{smallmatrix}$

Pentazocine

Tramadol

Phenol

$H_2C\begin{smallmatrix}CH_3\end{smallmatrix}$

HO

$CH-CH$

$CH_2-N\begin{smallmatrix}CH_3\\CH_3\end{smallmatrix}$

CH_3

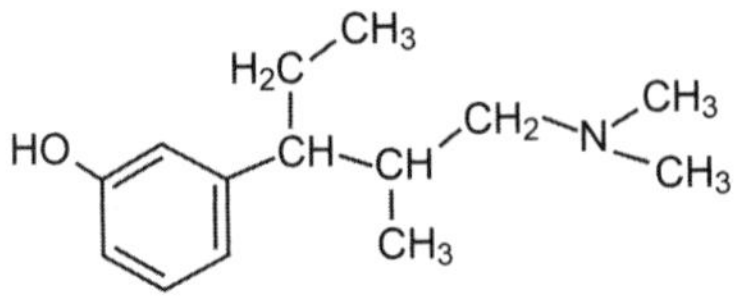

Tapentadol

Fig. 1. *(Continued)*

use as anesthetic and sedative supplements. Opioids are also used clinically for their antitussive and antidiarrheal properties and for detoxification of patients after opioid intoxication. Table 2 summarizes specific uses of individual opioids.

Opioids exert their major pharmacologic effect on the CNS. Their clinical importance lies in their ability to provide analgesia without the loss of consciousness. Analgesia is often accompanied by euphoria, sedation, and mental clouding. In addition, opioids may produce pulmonary and gastrointestinal effects, including respiratory depression, nausea, vomiting, and constipation. Other risks associated with opioid toxicity are coma, hypothermia, seizure, and hypotension. Table 3 provides a more thorough description of the therapeutic and adverse effects of opioids, which act both centrally and peripherally.

The major disadvantages associated with the use of opioid analgesics include the risk of respiratory failure, which is the major cause of death in intoxication cases, and addiction liability, which can cause physical dependence. Associated with these disadvantages is the increasing tolerance of the drug with sustained use, which necessitates the administration of a higher dose to produce an equivalent therapeutic effect.

Opioid tolerance is initiated after the first dose but is not usually clinically significant until the second or third week of chronic use. Depending on the drug, the degree of tolerance may necessitate a 35-fold increase for an equipotent analgesic dose. Cross-tolerance also exists between opioids that have the same mode of action, e.g., μ receptor agonists such as morphine, methadone, and meperidine. Habituation and drug dependence is related to the analgesic potency of the drug. Repeated administration of opioid analgesics that act as μ receptor agonists invariably leads to drug dependence. Mixed agonist–antagonists, such as buprenorphine, pentazocine, or nalbuphine, have the lowest potential for addiction and subsequent misuse (Table 2).

Discontinuation of opioid use or administration of an opioid antagonist following overdose can produce characteristic withdrawal symptoms (also known as abstinence syndrome), the features and chronology of which are described in Table 4. Typical effects include increased heart rate, irritability, profuse sweating, and piloerection, as well as uncontrollable muscle spasm and pain. Physiological withdrawal manifests itself clinically 6–8 h after the last dose and becomes heightened at 36–72 h. The severity of symptoms varies, depending on the frequency and

Table 2. Therapeutic Uses, Effectiveness, and Abuse Potential of Opioids

Drug	Uses	Pain Relief	Abuse Potential
Buprenorphine	Myocardial infarction, anesthetic supplement, orthopedics, obstetrics	Moderate to severe	Low
Butorphanol	Migraine, obstetric, musculoskeletal, postoperative, and cancer pain	Moderate to severe	Low
Codeine	Injuries, musculoskeletal, neuralgia	Mild to moderate	Moderate
Dihydrocodeine	Injuries, musculoskeletal, neuralgia	Mild to moderate	Moderate
Fentanyl	Pre-/postoperative medication, anesthetic supplement	Moderate to severe	High
Hydrocodone	Postoperative, pulmonary disease	Moderate to severe	Moderate
Hydromorphone	Cancer, surgery, trauma, biliary and renal colic, MI, burns	Moderate to severe	High
Levorphanol	Cancer, biliary and renal colic, MI, anesthetic supplement	Moderate to severe	High
Meperidine	Postoperative pain, anesthesia, obstetrics	Moderate to severe	High
Methadone	Detoxification, maintenance	Severe	High
Morphine	Cancer, preoperative sedation, anesthetic supplement, obstetrics	Moderate to severe	High
Nalbuphine	Pre-/postoperative anesthesia, childbirth	Moderate to severe	Low
Oxycodone	Bursitis, injuries, neuralgia, postoperative, obstetrics	Moderate to severe	Moderate
Oxymorphone	Preoperative, obstetric analgesia, anxiety, dyspnea	Moderate to severe	High
Pentazocine	Pre-/postoperative analgesia, surgical anesthesia	Moderate to severe	Low
Propoxyphene	Detoxification	Mild to moderate	Low
Tapentadol	Postoperative, dental	Moderate to severe	Low
Tramadol	Postoperative, gynecologic, obstetric, cancer	Moderate to severe	Low

duration of drug use. Physiological effects generally subside within 7–10 days, whereas psychological dependence may last for prolonged periods. Intense drug craving, which may prove unbearable, is a common cause of recidivism among recovering individuals. Withdrawal is not life threatening.

Opiate intoxication is treated with a variety of antidotal and supportive measures that generally include ventilation and cardiovascular, cardiac, and respiratory monitoring; oxygen and anticonvulsants to combat seizures; intravenous fluids and vasopressors to normalize blood pressure; and naloxone to reverse CNS and respiratory depression (Table 5).

Reversal of opioid intoxication with naloxone is carried out at the risk of precipitating severe acute-withdrawal symptoms. Additional care is necessary for the reversal of effects caused by opioids with long half-lives. Careful monitoring and treatment over several days may be necessary for the complete reversal of effects.

Methadone is frequently used for detoxification and maintenance of opioid-dependent persons; the withdrawal effect of methadone is milder but longer lasting than that of morphine. Tolerance and physical dependence to methadone develop more slowly than with morphine. During maintenance therapy, daily oral methadone doses of 80–120 mg substantially reduce the severity of withdrawal symptoms, thus minimizing the likelihood of drug craving and

Table 3. Therapeutic and Adverse Effects of Opioids

Central Nervous System Effects	
Nervous	Euphoria
	Analgesia
	Sedation
	Mental clouding and mood swings
Pulmonary	Respiratory depression
	Decreased responsiveness
Gastrointestinal	Nausea
	Vomiting
Other	Cough suppression
	Miosis
	Truncal rigidity
	Flushing and warming of the skin
	Sweating and itching
	Vertigo
Peripheral Effects	
Cardiac	Bradycardia
	Orthostatic hypotension when system is stressed
	Stroke
Gastrointestinal	Constipation
	Decreased motility
	Increased tone
	Decreased gastric secretions
	Biliary tract constriction of smooth muscle
Genitourinary	Decreased renal plasma flow
	Increased urethral and bladder tone
	Prolongation of labor
	Menstrual abnormalities
	Sexual dysfunction
Neuroendocrine	Increased release of antidiuretic hormone

resumption of compulsive use. This response is due to the cross-tolerance that exists between methadone and heroin, which allows the addiction-reinforcing effect of heroin to be blocked. While the individual is receiving methadone treatment, self-administered heroin fails to produce the desired euphoric effect. Buprenorphine is a detoxification alternative to methadone.

Other treatments that can alleviate symptoms include increased electrolyte and fluid intake, antispasmodics (propantheline), sedative-hypnotics (phenobarbital), anti-adrenergics (clonidine), and nitrous oxide. The effectiveness of maintenance therapy in drug detoxification is highly dependent on the individual. For the recovering addict, abstinence may be due to morphine-like analgesia following regular dosing, abatement of withdrawal symptoms, or the blocking effect against self-administered drugs.

Opioids have the potential to impair human performance because of their depressant effects on the CNS. The indications of impairment are mixed and frequently complicated by tolerance (in chronic use) and concurrent use of other drugs (polypharmacy). Opioids have an additive effect with respect to other CNS-depressant drugs and may greatly increase the deleterious effects of alcohol on driving competence. Most prescription opioids are accompanied by a warning from the manufacturer that the drug may impair the mental and/or physical

Table 4. Chronology of Opioid Abstinence Syndrome in Humans

8–12 h	Lacrimation
	Yawning
	Rhinorrhea
	Perspiration
12–14 h	Irritability
	Piloerection ("goose flesh")
	Restless sleep
	Weakness
	Mydriasis
	Tremor
	Anorexia
	Muscle twitching
48–72 h (peak of syndrome)	Increased irritability
	Increased heart rate
	Insomnia
	Hypertension
	Marked anorexia
	Hot and cold flashes
	Sneezing
	Alternating sweating/flushing
	Nausea and vomiting
	Piloerection
	Hyperthermia
	Hyperpnea
	Abdominal cramps
	Aching muscles
Syndrome duration	7–10 days

Table 5. Clinical Treatment for Symptoms of Opioid Overdose

1. Monitoring of cardiovascular and respiratory status
2. Ventilation for reestablishment of respiratory exchange
3. Oxygen for seizure
4. Antidotal naloxone to counteract CNS[a] and respiratory effects
5. Intravenous fluids for hypotension
6. Therapeutic intervention
   a. Doxapram as a respiratory stimulant
   b. Vasopressors for hypotension
   c. Anticonvulsants for seizure treatment
7. Other supportive measures
   a. Rewarming (<90 °F) for hypothermia
   b. Mechanical ventilation

[a]CNS, central nervous system.

abilities required for the performance of potentially hazardous tasks. Table 6 summarizes common psychological and physiological effects that may be important in impaired-driving cases. Although significant psychomotor impairment may not be evident in tolerant individuals, opioids have the potential to increase subjective feelings of sedation, to decrease consciousness, and to impair reaction time, visual acuity, and information processing in a dose-dependent fashion. More-pronounced effects are expected in naive drug users. Observations of drivers apprehended for driving under the influence

Table 6. Opioids and Human Performance

Psychological effects	Drowsiness, sedation, lethargy, dizziness, mental clouding, mood swings (euphoria/dysphoria), depressed reflexes, altered sensory perception, stupor, coma
Physiological effects	Analgesia, headache, dry mouth, facial flushing, nausea, constipation, respiratory depression, muscle flaccidity, pupil constriction (nonreactive to light stimulus), low blood pressure, low pulse, droopy eyelids, low body temperature
Driving effects	Slow driving, weaving, poor vehicle control, poor coordination, slow response to stimuli, delayed reactions, difficulty following instructions, falling asleep at the wheel

have included slow driving, weaving, poor vehicle control, poor coordination, slow response to stimuli, delayed reactions, difficulty in following instructions, and falling asleep at the wheel.

GENERAL PHARMACOKINETICS

Absorption and Distribution

Most opioids are absorbed readily after subcutaneous or intramuscular injection. Gastrointestinal absorption is generally good, although the bioavailability and pharmacologic effects of opioids vary considerably, depending on the extent of first-pass metabolism. Lipid-soluble opioids are effectively absorbed via the nasal or buccal mucosa besides via the usual routes. Highly lipid-soluble drugs can be absorbed transdermally and act quickly after subcutaneous administration because of their accelerated absorption and entry into the CNS.

Intravenous administration is common in opioids consumed for illicit purposes because of its rapid effect; however, because of the increasing purity of street drugs and a greater concern about the spread of human immunodeficiency virus, smoking, nasal insufflation (snorting), and inhalation of vapors ("chasing the dragon") have become popular for some abused drugs, such as heroin. These routes of administration may not provide the user with the same euphoric "rush" that is typical after intravenous injection, however.

Opioids are bound to plasma proteins in the blood to varying degrees (Table 7).

Subsequent localization in highly perfused organs such as the lungs, liver, brain, kidneys, and spleen may also occur. Accumulation in fatty tissues becomes important for highly lipophilic opioids, which can also accumulate in skeletal muscle reservoirs and cross the placental barrier to varying degrees. Transfer across the blood–brain barrier is impeded for highly amphoteric opioids such as morphine but is somewhat easier for less polar congeners, such as codeine and diamorphine.

Metabolism and Excretion

Some opioids undergo significant first-pass metabolism, which decreases the efficacy of the orally administered drug. Metabolism takes place primarily in the liver to form mostly polar metabolites, which are eliminated via enterohepatic or renal recirculation. Metabolites are excreted primarily in the urine, with relatively small amounts of the glucuronidated drug eliminated in the feces.

Table 8 lists metabolites for individual opioids that, despite variation in the molecular structure from the parent drug, share a number of common biotransformations, including oxidation, hydroxylation, O-demethylation, and N-demethylation. The N-demethylation pathway yields a nor-derivative, which frequently undergoes conjugation before elimination. Glucuronidation is the major metabolic route for opioids that contain available hydroxyl groups, such as morphine and levorphanol. After conjugation, these products undergo principally biliary and urinary excretion.

Table 7. Pharmacokinetic Parameters of Opioids

Drug	Half-life (h)	Volume of Distribution (L/kg)	Duration of Analgesia (h)	Protein Binding (%)	Common Routes of Administration
Buprenorphine	2–4[a] 18–49[b]	1.4–6.2	4–8	96	PO, IM, IV, SL, E, T
Butorphanol	2.9–8.4	5–10	3–4	83	IM, IV, SC, N
Codeine	1.2–3.9	2.5–3.5	3–4	7–25	PO, SC
Dihydrocodeine	3.4–4.5	1.0–1.3	3–4[c] 12[d]	20	PO
Fentanyl	3–12	3–8	1–1.5[c] >12[e]	79	IM, IV, N, SL, T
Heroin	0.03–0.10	25	3–5	<5	PO, IM, IV, SC, N
Hydrocodone	3.4–8.8	3.3–4.7	3–5[c] 12[d]	25	PO
Hydromorphone	3–9[c] 10–22[d]	2–4	4–5[c] 12–24[d]	19	PO, IM, IV, SC, PR
Levorphanol	11–16	10–13	4–5	40	SC, PO
Meperidine	2–5	3.7–4.2	2–4	45–64	PO, IM, IV, SC
Methadone	15–55	4–7	4–6	87	PO, IM, IV, SC
Morphine	1.3–6.7	2–5	4–5[c] 8–24[d]	35	PO, IM, IV, SC, E
Nalbuphine	1.9–7.7	2.4–7.3	3–6	25–40	IM, IV, SC
Opium	2–4	3–4	4–5	35	PO, PR, N
Oxycodone	3–6	1.8–3.7	4–6[c] 12[d]	45	PO, IM, IV, SC, PR
Oxymorphone	4–12	2–4	4–6[c] 12[d]	10–12	PO, IM, IV, SC
Pentazocine	2.1–3.5	4.4–7.8	3–4	61	PO, IM, IV, SC
Propoxyphene	8–24	12–26	4–5	78	PO
Tapentadol	3–5	6–9	4–6	20	PO
Tramadol	4.3–6.7	2.6–2.9	4–6[c] 12–24[d]	15–20	PO, IM, IV, SC PO, IM, IV, SC

[a] Parenteral.
[b] Sublingual.
[c] IV and immediate release.
[d] Extended release.
[e] Transdermal.
PO = oral; PR = rectal; IV = intravenous; IM = intramuscular; SC = subcutaneous;
SL = sublingual or transmucosal; T = transdermal; E = epidural or intrathecal; N = smoking or intranasal.
Source: Adapted from *1, 5, 6, 8*. Reprinted with permission from Ropero-Miller JD, Goldberger BA, Reisfield GM. Opioids. In: Kwong TC, Magnani B, Rosano TG, Shaw LM, eds. The clinical toxicology laboratory: contemporary practice of poisoning evaluation, 2nd ed. Washington, DC: AACC Press, 2013.

Drug Interactions

Opioids should be administered with caution to patients who have reduced metabolic capability or certain medical conditions, particularly pulmonary or hepatic disease. Caution in the administration of opioids is also advised because a number of centrally acting drugs can initiate adverse reactions or additive effects when coadministered with opioids. Such drugs include CNS depressants, alcohol, general anesthetics, tranquilizers,

Table 8. Metabolism of Opioids

Drug	Major Metabolites
Buprenorphine	Norbuprenorphine[a], buprenorphine[a]
Butorphanol	3-Hydroxybutorphanol, norbutorphanol[a]
Codeine	Codeine[a], morphine[a], norcodeine[a]
Dihydrocodeine	Dihydromorphine[a], nordihydrocodeine[a], dihydrocodeine[a]
Fentanyl	Despropionylfentanyl, norfentanyl, hydroxyfentanyl, hydroxynorfentanyl
Heroin	6-Acetylmorphine[a], morphine[a], normorphine
Hydrocodone	Hydromorphone[a], norhydrocodone, hydrocodol, hydromorphol[a]
Hydromorphone	Hydromorphol[a], hydromorphone[a]
Levorphanol	Norlevorphanol[a], levorphanol[a]
Meperidine	Normeperidine, meperidinic acid[a], normeperidinic acid[a]
Methadone	EDDP[a], EDMP[a], methadone[a], methadol, normethadol
Morphine	Morphine[a], normorphine[a]
Nalbuphine	Nornalbuphine[a], nalbuphine[a]
Oxycodone	Noroxycodone, oxymorphone[a], oxycodone[a]
Oxymorphone	6-Oxymorphol[a], oxymorphone[a]
Pentazocine	Pentazocine[a], cis- and trans-hydroxypentazocine[a], trans-carboxypentazocine[a]
Propoxyphene	Norpropoxyphene[a], dinorpropoxyphene[a], cyclic dinorpropoxyphene
Tapentadol	Tapentadol[a], N-desmethyltapentadol
Tramadol	O-monodesmethyltramadol[a], N,O-didesmethyltramadol[a], N-desmethyltramadol

[a]Conjugation occurs prior to elimination.
EDDP = 2-ethylidene-1,5-dimethyl-3,3-diphenylpyrrolidine; EMDP = 2-ethyl-5-methyl-3, 3-diphenylpyrroline.

sedative-hypnotics, tricyclic antidepressants, dextroamphetamine, and monoamine oxidase inhibitors (the monoamine oxidase inhibitors are a contraindication because of the increased risk of seizures, hyperpyrexic coma, and hypertension). Because of the dual mode of action of tramadol, patients receiving selective serotonin reuptake inhibitors or other antidepressants may experience serotonin toxicity after use of this drug. Other dangers arise from the coadministration of opioids with drugs such as carbamazepine, phenobarbital, tricyclic antidepressants, and warfarin because of a significantly reduced capability to metabolize these drugs.

SPECIFIC OPIOIDS

Buprenorphine

Buprenorphine is a derivative of thebaine that has mixed agonist–antagonist properties. Its high affinity for binding to receptors produces longer-lasting morphine-like analgesia and has potential for use in detoxification and maintenance in cases of heroin dependence. Its long duration of action is due to its slow dissociation from μ receptors. Therefore, reversal of respiratory depression with naloxone is not an effective measure. Biotransformation occurs via N-dealkylation to form the pharmacologically active metabolite norbuprenorphine, which is subsequently glucuronidated. The drug is eliminated primarily in the feces with only a small amount excreted in the urine and usually is detectable only within 1–3 days of use.

Butorphanol

Butorphanol is a synthetic benzomorphan agonist–antagonist that has been used since 1978 to treat pain. A widely used analgesic, butorphanol is absorbed rapidly and effectively via the transnasal route with a bioavailability of 60–70%, which is several times greater than that of oral administration. Extensive first-pass metabolism occurs primarily by hydroxylation of the cyclobutyl ring and by N-demethylation with subsequent conjugation. Approximately 70% of the drug is excreted in the urine within 5 days, 5–10% of which is excreted within 24 h as the unchanged drug. Butorphanol should not be used in opioid-dependent patients who are incompletely detoxified because it can initiate withdrawal-like symptoms.

Codeine

A semisynthetic agonist obtained by the methylation of morphine, codeine is a moderately low-potency analgesic that is incorporated into a number of proprietary formulations, including some over-the-counter remedies. It is often used in combination with nonopioid analgesics, such as acetaminophen or aspirin. Illicit synthesis of morphine and heroin from commercially available codeine products has been reported.

Following a typical dose, approximately 10–20% of the drug is excreted in the urine within 24 h as unchanged codeine. N- and O-demethylation followed by glucuronidation and sulfation are the primary metabolic routes. Approximately 10% of the administered dose is metabolized to morphine, accounting for most of the analgesic effect. Further metabolism can produce the active metabolite morphine-6-glucuronide (M6G),

which is more potent than morphine itself. During the early phase of excretion, codeine conjugates predominate, but morphine conjugates become the major products over a period of 20–40 h. Approximately 3 days after codeine use, the composition of the metabolites in the urine is similar to that following morphine or heroin use; however, the presence of norcodeine in the urine, which is not a metabolite of either morphine or heroin, is indicative of codeine use.

Dihydrocodeine

Hydrogenation of codeine in the C7–C8 position yields a semisynthetic agonist that has increased potency relative to the parent compound. The drug is frequently combined with either aspirin or acetaminophen in pain-relief formulations. The metabolic fate of dihydrocodeine is analogous to codeine, with N- and O-demethylation followed by conjugation being the most likely route. Approximately 20–60% of the drug is excreted in the urine within 24 h, depending on urinary pH and route of administration and is principally (30–45%) excreted in the conjugated form.

Fentanyl

Fentanyl is an extremely fast-acting, potent synthetic agonist that was originally introduced in 1963 as an anesthetic supplement. Despite an increased analgesic potency relative to morphine, it has comparable tolerance and physical-dependence liability. Because of its lipophilicity, fentanyl and its derivatives quickly cross the blood–brain barrier to the brain, where they have a pronounced effect on the CNS, including severe respiratory depression and heightened euphoria.

Transdermal fentanyl is used for managing chronic pain, although therapeutic concentrations may not be reached for 12–24 h. Abuse of this drug has become popular among healthcare workers because of the drug's euphoric effects and its availability.

Rapid metabolism to inactive metabolites takes place in the liver. N-demethylation accounts for 26–55% of the total dose, with less than 6% eliminated in the urine as the unchanged drug over 3–4 days.

Sufentanil, a derivative of fentanyl that is used as an analgesic/anesthetic in cardiac surgery, is five to seven times more potent than the parent drug. Alfentanil, which is less potent than fentanyl, has a very short duration of action and is reserved for minor surgeries. Additional derivatives include lofentanil (6000 times more potent than morphine), which is used in trauma patients, and carfentanil (3200 times more potent than morphine), which is used in veterinary medicine as an immobilizing agent for wild animals.

Fentanyl derivatives, such as p-fluorofentanyl and 3-methylfentanyl, have also been found as street drugs.

Heroin

Heroin, which is obtained synthetically via the acetylation of morphine, has an analgesic potency one to five times that of the parent drug and has better penetration across the blood–brain barrier because of the two acetyl groups. Heroin itself is rarely present in body fluids in detectable quantities. With a half-life of only a few minutes, the drug undergoes rapid deacetylation to 6-acetylmorphine (6-AM), which is about four times as potent as morphine. Heroin is different from most other opioids in that it has little or no affinity for opioid receptors in the brain. Therefore, the analgesic effects of the drug are attributed to the combined effect of 6-AM, which has a half-life of 0.6 h, and its subsequent biotransformation to morphine.

The presence of 6-AM is conclusive evidence of heroin use, because 6-AM is not a product of either morphine or codeine metabolism; however, it is detectable in urine only up to about 8 h after administration. Approximately 80% of the drug is eliminated in the urine within 24 h, mostly as morphine-3-glucuronide; only about 0.1% is eliminated as the free drug.

The clinical use of diamorphine in the U.S. is prohibited, although it is used in Canada and the U.K. for the management of chronic pain in terminal illness.

Heroin is one of the most widely abused opioids. Peak plasma concentrations are achieved within a few minutes of drug administration, and the prolonged duration of its effects is due to its active metabolites. Illicit heroin may contain several related opium alkaloids and synthetic artifacts, including acetylmorphine, acetylcodeine, codeine, papaverine, and morphine, among others. Subsequent adulteration at the street level uses various common diluents, such as sugars, talc, baking soda, flour, or other drugs. The average purity of illicit heroin in the U.S. depends on the geographic location and can range from <10% to >80%. Death following administration of heroin is typically due to profound respiratory depression, which can be rapidly reversed by naloxone administration.

Hydrocodone

Hydrocodone is a semisynthetic analgesic agonist derived from codeine. Despite its increased toxicity and addiction liability, it is widely used in cough syrup. Approximately 26% of the drug is excreted in the urine within 72 h, 12% as the unchanged drug. Principally metabolized by demethylation (to hydromorphone) and reduction of the 6-keto group, the unconjugated metabolites are believed to be pharmacologically active and therefore thought to contribute to the analgesic effect of the drug. Hydromorphol and hydrocodol may be present as stereoisomers of the drug.

Hydromorphone

Hydromorphone, a metabolite of hydrocodone, is a hydrogenated ketone derivative of morphine, and it exhibits an increased potency relative to morphine. This semisynthetic agonist undergoes rapid first-pass metabolism following oral administration, with only about 6% of the unmetabolized drug being excreted in the urine after 24 h. The primary metabolic route is believed to produce active metabolites via reduction of the 6-keto group and formation of 6α- and 6β-hydroxy derivatives.

Levorphanol

A synthetic analgesic agonist with properties similar to morphine, levorphanol provides an increased potency and longer-lasting effects. Data on humans is lacking, but animal studies indicate that levorphanol is metabolized primarily by 3-glucuronidation. Approximately 7% of the drug is eliminated unchanged in the urine of rats.

Meperidine

Meperidine is a synthetic narcotic agonist and is commonly abused by healthcare professionals. Less potent than morphine, it has shorter duration of action and is slightly faster acting. Following oral administration, meperidine is readily absorbed and extensively distributed in the tissues. Only about 7% of the total drug is excreted in the urine unchanged, although this percentage increases with decreasing urinary pH and in women taking oral contraceptives. In addition to the usual N-demethylation and conjugation, deesterification occurs to produce acidic metabolites. Normeperidine, which has a potency about half that of the parent drug, is several times more toxic than meperidine itself and has a longer half-life.

Clandestine production of the meperidine derivative MPPP (1-methyl-4-phenyl-4-propionoxypiperidine) may produce the highly neurotoxic by-product MPTP (1-methyl-4-phenyl-1,2,5,6-tetrahydropyridine), which poses a significant hazard to the drug user.

Methadone

Methadone is a synthetic analgesic agonist that, because of its oral effec-tiveness and moderately long-lasting effect, is largely used for detoxification and maintenance of individuals with narcotic addiction. Methadone is also used in pain-management programs to treat moderate to severe pain. Only the levorotatory isomer is pharmacologically active in small doses. When administered acutely, the duration of analgesia is 3–6 h; however, long-term use can extend the pharmacokinetic and pharmacodynamic profile of methadone to alleviate drug craving over a 24-h dosing interval. It can be administered orally for relief of opiate-withdrawal symptoms during detoxification/induction. After initial stabilization, the full treatment dose for maintaining opiate-dependent patients is typically 80–120 mg/day. Despite the acute toxicity of methadone, doses of 200 mg/day may be tolerated after prolonged administration (>21 days).

Methadone is rapidly absorbed after oral administration and is widely distributed in the tissues, particularly the liver, lungs, and kidney. Following mono- and di-N-demethylation, cyclization of the unstable intermediates produces the inactive metabolites 2-ethylidene-1,5-dimethyl-3,3-diphenylpyrrolidine (EDDP) and 2-ethyl-5-methyl-3,3-diphenylpyrroline (EMDP). Hydroxylation and glucuronidation occur, but approximately 75% of the drug remains unconjugated. As much as 33% of the drug may be excreted unchanged within 24 h in the urine of a patient receiving methadone maintenance treatment.

Morphine

The principal alkaloid of opium, morphine is rapidly absorbed after parenteral administration. Considerable first-pass metabolism following oral administration significantly reduces the effectiveness of the drug, which becomes widely distributed, mainly in the kidneys, liver, lungs, and spleen. Major metabolic routes are 3- and 6-glucuronidation and sulfation, N- and O-demethylation, and

N-oxide formation. Both morphine-3-gluc-uronide and normorphine are pharmaco-logically inactive metabolites. The analgesic potency of M6G is approximately twice that of morphine. In addition, an equianal-gesic dose of M6G instead of morphine has decreased potential for respiratory depres-sion and therefore can be effective in its own right as an analgesic for the manage-ment of chronic pain.

Surprisingly, the glucuronidated drug has been shown to cross the blood–brain bar-rier despite the increased polarity of this metabolite. A theoretical explanation for the unexpectedly high lipophilicity of gluc-uronidated morphine is that intramolecular folding takes place to minimize the surface area of the polar moieties. Another issue is whether the major metabolite morphine-3-glucuronide, which has a very low affin-ity for opioid receptors, can antagonize the analgesic effect of morphine and therefore have a mechanistic role in the development of tolerance. Following parenteral adminis-tration, up to 90% of the drug is excreted in the urine, and 10% is eliminated in the bile. About 10% is excreted as free morphine, but this fraction increases with decreasing urinary pH. The presence of free or con-jugated morphine may also be indicative of either codeine or heroin use because it is the principal active metabolite of both these drugs.

Nalbuphine

A synthetic opioid of the phenanthrene type, nalbuphine has agonistic and antagonis-tic properties. As an antagonist, nalbuphine has one quarter the potency of nalorphine and 10 times that of pentazocine. It has been successfully used for the treatment of respi-ratory depression after postsurgical opioid administration. Approximately equivalent to morphine in analgesic potency, nalbuphine acts within 2–15 min of injection, and its ef-fects last 3–6 h. Following N-demethylation and conjugation, approximately 71% of the administered dose is excreted in the urine,

with the remainder eliminated in the feces via biliary excretion.

Opium

Opium is a complex mixture of more than 20 alkaloids obtained from the dried exu-date of *P. somniferum*. The composition of opium varies from one geographic region to another, but the major constituents are mor-phine (10%), noscapine (6%), papaverine (1%), codeine (0.5%), and thebaine (0.2%). Having been replaced by synthetic opioids such as fentanyl and meperidine, opium it-self is no longer used medically as an analge-sic, but it is used as the starting material for the extraction and purification of other alka-loids. Morphine and codeine are the major active constituents of opium. The remaining components do not produce morphine-like euphoria. Noscapine (narcotine) and pa-paverine have antitussive and vasodilator properties, respectively, and thebaine is an important reactive starting material for the synthesis of other drugs.

Oxycodone

Frequently used in combination with nonopioid analgesics such as acetaminophen or aspirin, oxycodone is a semisynthetic opioid agonist derived from thebaine. It is as potent as morphine when administered par-enterally but has a higher oral-to-parenteral efficacy ratio. N- and O-demethylation occur, and the latter produces the active metabo-lite oxymorphone, which contributes to the analgesic potency of the drug. Metabolites undergo glucuronidation before elimina-tion, with 13–19% typically excreted as the unchanged drug within 24 h of an oral dose.

Oxymorphone

Oxymorphone is a semisynthetic opi-ate agonist derived from thebaine. It has an increased analgesic potency relative to morphine and is itself a metabolite of oxycodone. It is extensively metabolized by conjugation and reduction of the keto group, and only about 2% of the unchanged drug is excreted in the urine after 5 days. It is used therapeutically in a sustained-release form; because of the increased amount of drug in this formulation, it is prone to abuse by administration in forms other than the oral route.

Pentazocine

A synthetic benzomorphan derivative with agonist and antagonist activity, pentazocine is used in combination with acetaminophen or aspirin to increase the analgesic effect. Having only about 2% of the potency of nalorphine, pentazocine only weakly antagonizes morphine.

Metabolism of pentazocine principally involves the oxidation of the dimethylallyl group to produce *cis*- and *trans*-hydroxypentazocine; the latter is carboxylated to form *trans*-carboxypentazocine. After an oral dose, up to 13% of the drug may be excreted unchanged in the urine within 24 h; however, the rate of metabolism is variable and may be significantly increased (up to 40%) in smokers. Administration of pentazocine in combination with tripelennamine produces heroin-like effects that increase the risk of death. Pentazocine can also initiate withdrawal-like symptoms in opioid-dependent patients.

Propoxyphene

A mild analgesic structurally and pharmacologically similar to methadone, propoxyphene has been used clinically since 1957 and is often formulated with acetaminophen. The dextrorotatory and levorotatory isomeric forms of the drug have different uses—the former as an analgesic, the latter as an antitussive. Propoxyphene napsylate (800–1400 mg/day) has been used successfully for the treatment of opiate withdrawal or maintenance. Following N-demethylation, the active metabolite norpropoxyphene can become harmful, owing to its longer half-life. The drug is rapidly distributed and accumulates in the brain, lungs, liver, and kidneys. Further demethylation and dehydration of dinorpropoxyphene results in cyclization. Deesterification, hydroxylation, and conjugation also occur. Approximately 35% of the total drug is excreted in the urine within 24 h, 5% as the unchanged drug. Cardiotoxicity of the parent drug and its metabolites is a drawback, however, and there have been a number of fatalities. As a result, it has been removed from the market in a number of countries.

Tapentadol

Tapentadol is the most recent synthetic opioid to become available; it was approved for use in the U.S. in 2008. It undergoes Phase I metabolism by N-demethylation and alkyl hydroxylation; none of the metabolites have analgesic activity. The primary urinary metabolite is tapentadol O-glucuronide.

Tramadol

Tramadol has an analgesic potency similar to that of codeine but with reduced respiratory effects. It is extensively metabolized and is excreted primarily through the kidneys. About 90% of an oral dose is excreted in the urine after 3 days, 30% as the unchanged drug. N- and O-demethylation of the drug is followed by conjugation with glucuronic acid and sulfate. O-Monodesmethyltramadol is an active metabolite with twice the potency of the parent drug and a longer half-life; it is believed to contribute to the toxicity of the drug.

ANALYSIS

Sample Preparation

Polar opioids and their metabolites tend to undergo conjugation before elimination, so sample pretreatment is often necessary to measure the total amount of drug in a sample. Acid or enzyme hydrolysis with hydrochloric acid, β-glucuronidase, or sulfatase can be used to cleave off the conjugated group at elevated temperatures. Acidic hydrolysis, which is generally faster, should be used with caution, however, because 6-AM may be degraded in the process.

Opioids may be extracted from the biological matrix by either liquid–liquid extraction or solid-phase extraction. Organic solvents, such as chloroform modified with 2-propanol, n-butanol, or isoamyl alcohol, are commonly used to extract opioids from aqueous mixtures in the pH range of 8–10. Increasing the sample pH reduces the tendency of the unconjugated drug to ionize, because the pK_a value of the basic nitrogen is about 8. Solid-phase extraction, which uses a copolymeric bonded phase, can be used to adsorb drug via a combination of hydrophobic and cation-exchange mechanisms. A drug can usually be isolated after column-conditioning and sample-washing steps with mixtures of basic solvents, such as methylene chloride/2-propanol/ammonium hydroxide (volume ratio, 78:20:2). As a general rule, this method produces cleaner extracts with fewer coextractive interferences than liquid–liquid extraction, but it is more expensive.

Screening Techniques

Immunoassays are the most frequently used screening technique because of their high sample throughput, ease of automation, and lack of sample preparation. These immunoassays generally allow a drug to be detected in the urine up to about 3 days after exposure. A variety of immunochemical tests are available, such as the enzyme-multiplied immunoassay technique (EMIT®) and cloned enzyme donor immunoassay (CEDIA®). A variety of manufacturers produce numerous class- and analyte-specific enzyme-linked immunosorbent assays for phenanthrene-type drugs (opiates), buprenorphine, fentanyl, methadone, meperidine, oxycodone, oxymorphone, propoxyphene, and tramadol.

In general, most opiate immunoassays are not specific. Cross-reactivity toward structurally related morphine-like compounds, such as various metabolites, is common. The overall specificity of the assay is dependent on the characteristics of the antibody reagent and the assay methodology. Heterogeneous immunoassay formats may provide fewer nonspecific interferences than their homogeneous counterparts, but the former may take longer to perform. Typically, morphine or morphine-3-glucuronide is used as the target molecule, but cross-reactions between the antibody and dihydrocodeine, hydrocodone, and hydromorphone commonly occur. Immunoassays for the synthetic opioids tend to be more specific and undergo fewer cross-reactions; however, immunoassays for methadone may cross-react with l-α-acetylmethadol (LAAM), which is a long-acting methadone analog.

Thin-layer chromatography can detect most opioids in urine down to concentrations of 500–1000 ng/mL for a 10-mL sample. The advantages of this technique are its relative speed, simplicity, and low cost. Specific thin-layer chromatography systems are commercially available, including the Toxi-Lab LTD™ system, which detects codeine, dihydrocodeine, hydrocodone, hydromorphone, morphine, and 6-AM down to 200 ng/mL.

Gas chromatography (GC) coupled with nitrogen–phosphorus or mass spectrometry (MS) detection is often used by emergency and postmortem toxicology laboratories as a component of a comprehensive drug screen. Many of the opioids and their metabolites chromatograph well without derivatization. In addition, blood and urine concentrations are often sufficiently high for detection to be easily achieved. Drugs commonly detected via these methods include codeine, hydrocodone, meperidine, methadone, oxycodone, oxymorphone, propoxyphene, and tramadol.

Confirmatory Procedures

The initial screening technique may yield a number of presumptive positive samples that must then be retested with a more rigorous technique. The most frequently used confirmation methods include GC, GC/MS, and liquid chromatography/mass spectrometry (LC/MS). The drawback is that these methods are more labor intensive and require pretreatment and extraction of the drug from the biological matrix before analysis.

LC methods may be advantageous because of their ability to separate both the free drug and the conjugated drug simultaneously. GC methods typically necessitate derivatization before separation in order to increase the volatility of the drug and improve the chromatographic resolution. Polar groups on the drug may be derivatized with trimethylsilyl, perfluoroester, heptafluorobutyryl, or trifluoroacetyl groups, among others. Detection can be achieved by electron capture, nitrogen–phosphorus, or flame-ionization methods. MS, which offers improved specificity in identification, is the method of choice for opiate detection in many drug-testing facilities. Detection limits with MS are typically 1–50 ng/mL. The structural similarities of many of the opioids, particularly the metabolites of morphine and codeine, may produce interferences; however, derivatizing and optimizing the separation conditions can usually eliminate the potential interferences.

Recently, opioids have been analyzed by HPLC/MS or HPLC-tandem MS. These methods can simultaneously measure parent drugs and metabolites, free and conjugated, with minimum specimen preparation.

INTERPRETATION

Blood

Individuals suspected of drug impairment or overdose are frequently investigated for the presence of opioids and their metabolites. The results of drug and drug metabolite measurements are essential for developing diagnoses in such cases. In addition, depending on the drug detected, many laboratories will measure the free and total drug concentrations. The free and total drug measurements are particularly useful after morphine overdose to determine the mode of death. For example, rapid deaths are often characterized by a higher ratio of the concentrations of free morphine to total morphine.

The interpretation of opioid-related deaths is often complicated by other findings. Such findings can include the individual's prior exposure to opioids and potential pharmacologic tolerance, and the presence of other centrally acting drugs, including ethanol. For example, the drug concentrations found in opioid-related deaths often overlap with those found in deaths not related to drugs. These factors also complicate the interpretation of drug concentrations in the blood in cases of impaired driving. Drug concentrations must be interpreted within the context of the case: driving performance, observed effects, and the measure of impairment.

Urine

The detection time for morphine or codeine is usually 48 h, but this time varies according to individual differences in metabolism, excretion, route of administration, and frequency of drug use. Illicit drug use must be distinguished from inadvertent exposure to opioids through ingestion of certain foodstuffs or over-the-counter and prescription medications. A number of opioids, such as codeine, hydromorphone, hydrocodone, and oxycodone, are contained in widely available analgesic and cough expectorant formulations. These and other factors may produce results that are difficult to interpret. In some instances, it may not be possible to distinguish between heroin, morphine, and codeine use, particularly if illicit heroin preparations are contaminated with acetylcodeine, which is subsequently metabolized to codeine. The presence of morphine alone in the urine indicates exposure to heroin, morphine, or poppy seeds, whereas detection of codeine with low concentrations of morphine is consistent with codeine use. Unequivocal identification of heroin use is indicated by the presence of 6-AM; however, the short urinary half-life of the metabolite limits the detection time to 2–8 h after exposure.

Poppy seeds may contain morphine and codeine at concentrations of up to 300 µg/g and 5 µg/g, respectively. Therefore, ingestion of poppy seeds as food may expose the unwitting individual to a significant quantity of opiate. Urinary concentrations of morphine and codeine peak within 2–4 h of ingestion of such food. Such opiates may remain detectable for up to 72 h, posing a particular problem for employment or rehabilitation drug-testing programs. Thebaine, which is also present in poppy seeds, has been used as a marker for poppy seed ingestion. After the consumption of certain foods, thebaine was present in the urine at concentrations of 2–81 ng/mL. Because of its short half-life, however, thebaine may be difficult to detect more than 12 h after ingestion.

Other Matrices

Although blood (serum or plasma) and urine are generally the preferred specimens, opioids can be detected in a variety of other matrices. The concentration of opiate in sweat typically accounts for about 1–2% of the total dose administered. Sweat contains mostly the parent opioid and lipophilic metabolites, e.g., heroin and 6-AM following heroin use. Such findings are in contrast to the metabolic profile of heroin in other matrices, which contain predominantly free (saliva) or conjugated (blood and urine) morphine.

Despite minimal sample preparation, saliva typically contains low concentrations of drug, and the concentrations decline rapidly. Saliva measurements may be used to estimate the amount of circulating drug, but its quantitative significance has not yet been established. In cerebrospinal fluid, the concentrations of morphine and M6G have been shown to correlate with those found in blood. Morphine and its conjugates can also be detected in vitreous humor, typically at concentrations lower than those found in either blood or cerebrospinal fluid.

The detection of opioids in hair may provide useful information regarding the pattern of drug use over a period of months to years. This fact has been applied in employment drug testing, investigation of drug overdose, and prenatal exposure. Widespread use of the technique has been hampered by sample-preparation requirements and the difficulty in interpreting the quantitative significance of results.

Hair tends to accumulate higher concentrations of the parent (lipophilic) drug rather than metabolites. Consequently, hair may be particularly useful for the detection of drugs that are rapidly excreted, such as heroin. After heroin use, hair may contain heroin, morphine, and 6-AM. The last of these, the presence of which is considered conclusive evidence of heroin use, has successfully been detected in hair of heroin users at typically greater concentrations than for morphine.

Opioids and other drugs are incorporated into the hair internally via the blood that circulates at the root or externally via contamination, passive deposition, or perspiration. Hair samples, ideally taken from the posterior vertex, should be thoroughly decontaminated, and the washing solutions should be analyzed. After digestion or extraction, opioids are assayed in the usual way, typically by immunoassay and GC/MS or LC-MS/MS. Sample-preparation methods that involve strong acid or alkali may be unsuitable for the detection of hydrolyzable opioids such as 6-AM, which may require methanolic or enzymatic extraction.

There is some controversy as to whether the analysis of hair is substantive in its own right or whether it should be viewed in a supportive context only. There are still no established cutoff values for drugs detected in hair; however, according to the distribution of quantitative findings in the literature, a 6-AM cutoff value of 0.5 ng/mg has been suggested as an indicator of heroin use.

SUGGESTED READING

1. Baselt RC, ed. Disposition of toxic drugs and chemicals in man, 9th ed. Foster City, CA: Biomedical Publications, 2011.

2. Brunton LL, Chabner B, Knollman B, eds. Goodman & Gilman's the pharmacological basis of therapeutics, 12th ed. New York: McGraw-Hill, 2010.

3. Couper FJ, Logan BK. Drugs and human performance fact sheets. Washington, DC: National Highway Traffic Safety Administration, U.S. Department of Transportation, 2004. DOT HS 809 725.

4. Katzung BG, Masters S, Trevor A, eds. Basic and clinical pharmacology, 12th ed. New York: McGraw-Hill, 2011.

5 Leiken JB, Paloucek FP, eds. Poisoning and toxicology compendium. Cleveland, OH: Lexi-Comp, 1998.

6. Moffat AC, Osselton MD, Widdop B, Watts J, eds. Clarke's analysis of drugs and poisons, 4th ed. London: Pharmaceutical Press, 2011.

7. Nelson LS, Lewin NA, Howland MA, Hoffman RS, Goldfrank LR, Flomenbaum NE, eds. Goldfrank's toxicologic emergencies, 9th ed. New York: McGraw-Hill, 2010.

8. Physicians' desk reference, 67th ed. Montvale, NJ: PDR Network, 2013.

9. Stout PR, Farrell LJ. Opioids—Effects on human performance and behavior. Forensic Sci Rev 2002;15:29–59.

10. Wu A, ed. Tietz clinical guide to laboratory tests, 4th ed. Philadelphia: WB Saunders, 2006.

CHAPTER 18

Cocaine

Daniel S. Isenschmid

INTRODUCTION

History

Cocaine is an alkaloid found in *Erythroxylon coca*, which grows principally in the northern South American Andes and, to a lesser extent, in India, Africa, and Indonesia. Cultivation of the plant, which may reach 9 feet in height, is favored at higher elevations (up to 6000 feet) because at lower elevations (below 1500 feet), the alkaloid content is significantly diminished because of more rapid growth. Coca leaves may first be harvested about two years after planting. Then, the leaves may be harvested up to three times a year, depending on the altitude. The leaves are dried and converted into a coca paste, which eventually is used to produce cocaine hydrochloride. The yield from 100 kg of coca leaves is about 1 kg of coca paste or 800 g of cocaine hydrochloride.

Cocaine is a psychotropic drug that has been used for 2000 years. The Incas of Peru chewed the leaves of the coca plant in their religious ceremonies. Later, during the Spanish conquest, the Spaniards found that the Peruvian Indians could not perform their heavy labor in the mines when deprived of the plant.

In the mid-19th century, Carl Wöhler, the chemist who synthesized urea, had coca leaves imported to Germany and presented them to his graduate student, Albert Niemann, to analyze. Niemann was the first to successfully isolate cocaine from the coca plant. From the 1860s through the turn of the century, cocaine appeared in various elixirs and tonics purported to have "magic" properties. Some of the more famous preparations included Vin Mariani, a mixture of wine and cocaine, and the original Coca-Cola® recipe developed by John Pemberton.

The Italian physician Paolo Mantegazza was the first to spark interest in the medicinal uses of cocaine. Several papers had been written in the 1870s about cocaine's potential use for treating morphine addiction, but not until Sigmund Freud popularized the drug in his famous 1884 treatise "Über Coca" did it become well known in the scientific community. In 1884, Carl Koller became the first physician to use cocaine as a topical anesthetic in ophthalmologic surgery. It was popularly reported to be a wonder drug that would satiate the hungry, give strength to the fatigued, and cause people to forget their misfortune. Freud, a proponent of cocaine use, gave the drug to his fiancée and many of his patients and friends. After the death of a friend who had been given the drug to treat morphine dependence, Freud finally admitted cocaine's hazards.

Despite numerous early reports of cocaine toxicity, including cardiac arrhythmias and fatalities, cocaine-containing products became ever more popular. In 1914, as cocaine abuse began to be viewed as a problem, the drug was labeled a narcotic (albeit incorrectly) under the Harrison Narcotic Act, and over-the-counter sales were discontinued. In 1970, under the Controlled Substances Act, cocaine was scheduled as a drug with some medicinal value but with a high potential for abuse (Schedule II). It continues to have some medical use, which is almost exclusively limited to topical administration as a local anesthetic in ear, nose, and throat surgery (as the hydrochloride salt in 10–20% solutions) and in ophthalmologic procedures (as a 1–4% solution).

Today cocaine is one of the most common illicit drugs of abuse. It has acquired numerous street names, including blow, coke, crack, dust, flake, gold dust, happy dust, lady, nose, nose candy, rock, snow, speedball (when mixed with heroin and injected), stardust, tick (when smoked with phencyclidine), toot, and white. It was originally reputed to be a "drug for the rich," but lower prices and less expensive (per purchase) forms of the drug, such as crack, have resulted in widespread cocaine use in all populations. A 2004 National Survey on Drug Use and Health reported that 34.14 million Americans (14.7% of the total U.S. population older than 12 years) have used cocaine in their lifetimes, and 2 million are current users.

Cocaine is sold on the street in two forms: the hydrochloride salt and crack. The salt form varies considerably in purity but, according to statistics compiled by the U.S. Drug Enforcement Administration, is generally greater than 50% by the time it reaches the purchaser of gram-sized packets. The salt form is typically diluted ("cut") with agents such as mannitol, lactose, and sucrose to add bulk. In addition, readily available central nervous system stimulants (caffeine, phenylpropanolamine, ephedrine) and other local anesthetics (lidocaine, procaine, benzocaine) are sometimes used as diluents to simulate the actual drug. Other drugs, such as levamisole and diltiazem, are also frequently detected in cocaine samples. Levamisole, in particular, has received a lot of attention due to its association with agranulocytosis. Levamisole is further metabolized to aminorex, which is also potentially toxic.

The cocaine powder supplied by dealers is often clumpy and first needs to be chopped. This is usually done with a mirror and a razor blade. The cocaine is then arranged into thin lines about 30–60 mm long and 2 mm wide (for an average dose of 25 mg) and then snorted through a straw or "tooter." Alternatively, cocaine may be snorted from a "coke spoon" or a "bullet" (a vial containing cocaine is inverted over a closed chamber and the chamber is rotated for convenient snorting). A single long fingernail may serve as a natural coke spoon.

Crack is a freebase form of cocaine that produces a characteristic crackling sound when smoked. It should not be confused with "freebasing," which is no longer commonly practiced. Freebasing was a process in which the user purified regular cocaine hydrochloride by mixing an aqueous solution of cocaine with baking soda or ammonia and adding ether, thereby extracting the free form of the drug into the organic solvent, which was then evaporated to dryness. The drug could then be smoked in a pipe (with the risk of igniting any remaining ether). Crack, on the other hand, is sold in the freebase form before sale. It is prepared by adding baking soda to aqueous cocaine hydrochloride and heating it to remove the water. After heating, the mixture is cooled and filtered; the freebase cocaine then precipitates into small pellets or "rocks." These rocks can then be smoked in a crack pipe. Crack pipes range from elaborate glass pipes to a soda can with a hole. A typical rock weighs about 20 mg and costs US$10–20, much less expensive per unit than the salt form, which is typically sold at up to US$150/g.

Chemistry

Cocaine (methylbenzoylecgonine), an ester of benzoic acid and the amino alcohol methylecgonine, which contains a tropine moiety, is chemically but not pharmacologically related to atropine. The ecgonine portion of the molecule has four chiral carbon atoms and can exist as four racemates (eight optically active isomers). Cocaine is commercially synthesized from (−)-ecgonine in the presence of methanol and benzoic acid after hydrolysis of the ester alkaloids extracted from the plant material. In (−)-cocaine, the benzoyl and methyl ester are located cis to the nitrogen bridge. (+)-Pseudococaine, with the methyl ester located trans to the nitrogen bridge, is also active.

Cocaine is structurally different from other local anesthetics by virtue of its tropine moiety; however, cocaine, like other local anesthetics, consists of a hydrophobic region and a hydrophilic region. The hydrophobic region contains a benzene ring, whereas the hydrophilic region consists of a secondary or tertiary amine. Cocaine is also similar to other local anesthetics owing to its ester linkages, which allow the body to hydrolyze and deactivate the drug. The ester group is also susceptible to in vitro hydrolysis.

PHARMACOLOGY

Effects

Cocaine is used medicinally as a topical local anesthetic. Clinically, its most important mechanism of action lies in its ability to block sodium channel conductance and to thereby increase the threshold required to generate an action potential. Cocaine has additional actions, however, that make it unique among local anesthetics, including its ability to block reuptake of the neurotransmitters norepinephrine, dopamine (DA), and serotonin (5-HT). Norepinephrine is responsible for the classic adrenergic effects seen with cocaine use, including mydriasis, vasoconstriction, hypertension, tachycardia, and tachypnea. Although these effects may be the most important toxicologically, the behavioral effects of cocaine are due to its dopaminergic actions. The desirable effects of cocaine, which are mediated by DA, include intense euphoria, psychic energy, heightened sexual excitement, and self-confidence (elevation of mood). Potential undesirable effects include paranoia, hallucinations, and dysphoria.

After an acute dose of cocaine, brain concentrations of DA increase briefly and then decrease markedly to below normal concentrations, corresponding to the central stimulatory effects ("rush") and depression ("crash") that the cocaine user experiences. Cocaine prevents the reuptake of DA into the presynaptic dopaminergic neuron by binding to receptors on the DA transporter located on the dopaminergic nerve terminal. This DA reuptake, which is mediated by sodium, chloride, and energy-dependent active transport, is inhibited when cocaine binds to the sodium-binding site on the transporter and alters the chloride-binding site, thus preventing the binding of both ions. Because translocation of DA across the membrane of the presynaptic neuron is inhibited, increased extracellular DA concentrations chronically stimulate the DA receptor in the postsynaptic neuron.

Positive emission tomography studies have demonstrated that 47% of DA transporters are occupied by cocaine before its effects become recognized, with 60–77% of sites occupied after doses consistent with cocaine abuse. The time course for the high in humans parallels that of the cocaine concentration in the striatum, a region in the brain implicated in the control of motivation and reward. For equivalent plasma cocaine concentrations and DA transporter blockade, smoked cocaine induces significantly greater self-reports of "high" than intranasal (IN) cocaine and shows a trend for a greater effect than intravenous (IV) cocaine. Such reports and the fact that the time to reach peak subjective effects is significantly faster for smoked cocaine (1.4 min) than for IV cocaine (3.1 min) and IN cocaine (14.6 min) demonstrate the importance of speed of cocaine delivery into the brain for its reinforcing effects.

Chronic cocaine administration alters the DA transporter in the mesolimbic regions of the brain. Increased densities in the DA transporter have been observed postmortem in the brains of cocaine abusers and in vivo in acutely abstinent cocaine users. Up-regulation of cocaine-binding sites in the brain produces a need for additional cocaine to continue experiencing its rewarding effects. Chronic cocaine users repeatedly administer cocaine, increasing the synaptic levels of DA. This process becomes cyclical and demonstrates how a cocaine binge or "run" is followed by a crash and why the temptation to self-medicate is so strong.

Cocaine-excited delirium, which is associated with hyperthermia, delirium, agitation, cardiorespiratory arrest, and sudden death, may be due to an inability of the DA transporter to up-regulate as it does in most chronic cocaine users. In these individuals, increased densities of DA receptors are not observed, and the lack of increased receptor sites has been postulated to produce insufficient DA reuptake, leading to excessive DA concentrations in the synapse. The extreme hyperthermia in these individuals may be related to the observed down-regulation in DA-2 receptors in the hypothalamus, which are responsible for decreasing body temperature. DA-1 receptors, which are responsible for increasing the body temperature, are not affected. Individuals with a high body mass index (body weight in kilograms divided by the square of the height in meters) appear to be at highest risk because they generate the most heat through skeletal muscle activity. This finding may also explain why the majority of excited-delirium cases occur during the summer and in young black males. An up-regulation of κ_2 opiate receptors has been observed in the amygdala after death due to excited delirium. These receptors are a subtype of the receptors that have been reported to produce psychosis in phencyclidine intoxication.

Cocaine also binds to the 5-HT transporter and inhibits 5-HT reuptake. Acutely, 5-HT would be expected to partially antagonize the stimulatory effects of cocaine in the naive user (this expectation was the basis for investigating the use of 5-HT reuptake inhibitors for the treatment of cocaine dependence). Withdrawal from cocaine after chronic use produces a decrease in synaptic 5-HT concentrations by altering the function of the presynaptic 5-HT receptor that controls the amount of 5-HT available for release. Alterations in the sensitivity of postsynaptic receptors to 5-HT also occur. These alterations have been implicated in the depression and craving seen after cocaine withdrawal.

These effects are more than just psychological. They are negatively reinforcing, making it very difficult for an individual to discontinue cocaine use. Some investigators therefore believe that cocaine can produce physical as well as psychological dependence;

however, because cocaine lacks the classic narcotic-type withdrawal symptoms, some medical scientists do not concede that cocaine is physically addicting. The withdrawal effects diminish gradually over 1–3 weeks.

Repeated doses of cocaine have been shown to produce both diminished effects (tolerance) and increased effects (sensitization). Acute tolerance to cocaine typically occurs during a binge in which the users dose themselves repeatedly, leading to an acute depletion of DA and a diminished response. Sensitization tolerance, or reverse tolerance, typically occurs with chronic cocaine use and longer dosing intervals and does not appear to be related to brain catecholamine concentrations. Such observations support early theories that sensitization to cocaine may occur via changes to receptors that make them more sensitive to cocaine or its action at other receptors. The excitatory glutamate receptor (the N-methyl-D-aspartate receptor) has recently been linked to cocaine sensitization. Other agents with pharmacologic actions similar to cocaine, such as methylphenidate and amphetamines, have shown considerable cross-sensitization and cross-tolerance to cocaine.

The most common clinical manifestations following acute cocaine intoxication include profound central nervous system stimulation, with psychosis and repeated grand mal convulsions, ventricular arrhythmias, respiratory dysfunction with Cheyne–Stokes breathing, and, ultimately, respiratory paralysis. Other symptoms include mydriasis, hypertension leading to hypotension, and small-muscle twitching. The ability of cocaine to cause increased muscular activity and vasoconstriction may produce extreme hyperthermia. The patient may also lapse into a coma. Acute myocardial infarctions have occurred after even therapeutic doses of cocaine.

Symptoms of chronic cocaine use, other than psychiatric disturbances, include rhinitis (with possible nasal septum perforation), shortness of breath, cold sweats, tremors, violent protective behavior, distorted perception, tachycardia, tachypnea, dyspnea, and hyperkinetic behavior. The drug can injure cerebral arteries, and an acute hypertensive episode following a single dose in a chronic user can cause cerebral vessels to rupture. Cocaine may induce epilepsy and angina and worsen preexisting coronary heart disease to the point of a heart attack. Tolerance to the cardiovascular effects of cocaine does not occur, and during a cocaine binge the chronic cocaine user may self-administer more cocaine than the cardiovascular system can tolerate. Poor personal grooming and malnutrition, which can lower immune defenses and precipitate other diseases, may also be observed after chronic cocaine use.

The chronic cocaine user may become quite self-confident and egocentric. Psychological dependence becomes dominant by virtue of the drug's unusually high rewarding effects. The phrase "coked out" has been used to describe the psychological changes in chronic users. Such individuals have difficulty concentrating and remembering; they may grow short-tempered and suspicious and may undergo a schizophrenic psychosis similar to that seen with amphetamine abuse. They may also become aggressive and experience attacks of paranoia, panic, or auditory, visual, and tactile hallucinations. Symptoms may be severe enough to require hospitalization and antipsychotic pharmacotherapy.

Treatment of symptoms is critical, although death may occur so suddenly that treatment cannot be instituted. In addition to respiratory and cardiovascular support, hyperthermia should be treated with external cooling. Diazepam may be useful for controlling seizures and helping to sedate the patient, and chlorpromazine may be useful by virtue of its antidopaminergic, antiadrenergic, antihyperthermic, and sedative effects. Arrhythmias may be controlled with beta-blockers such as propranolol and the ultrashort-acting esmolol.

PHARMACOKINETICS

Absorption

Cocaine may be administered via IN, IV, oral (PO), or smoking (SM) routes. Cocaine is usually not administered PO because first-pass effects produce low bioavailability (about 20%) and reduced euphoric effects due to inefficient delivery to the brain. The IV route of administration, sometimes called "mainlining," is the only route that consistently produces 100% drug bioavailability. The bioavailability of cocaine by IN or SM administration is quite variable; however, the convenience of these two routes of administration and the latter's rapid, intense onset of effects make them the most commonly used.

IN bioavailability has been suggested to possibly be dose dependent, with increased bioavailability at higher doses being a function of the amount of drug available for absorption. Bioavailability estimates range from 25% to as high as 94%. The IN route delivers cocaine to the brain more efficiently than the PO route, but this route delays absorption because of the vasoconstrictive action of the drug and its propensity for being swallowed in various amounts during insufflation.

Smoked cocaine produces a rapid and intense high similar to that of the IV route, reflecting its efficiency in delivering the dose to the brain. Despite this similarity in effects, studies have indicated that the average bioavailability by the SM route is only 57–70%, with considerable variation within studies. Interindividual variation in smoking technique, the temperature and nature of the smoked cocaine, and the construction of the pipe may all play a role in the erratic absorption of cocaine by the SM route. It has been postulated that cocaine may undergo pyrolysis in the pipe and that the first few "hits" provide greater bioavailability than later ones. The recoveries of residual cocaine obtained from pipes after smoking studies demonstrate that approximately 25% of the original cocaine dose remains in the pipe.

Metabolism

Cocaine is metabolized primarily to benzoylecgonine and ecgonine methyl ester via different mechanisms (Fig. 1). The mechanisms of cocaine metabolism are not

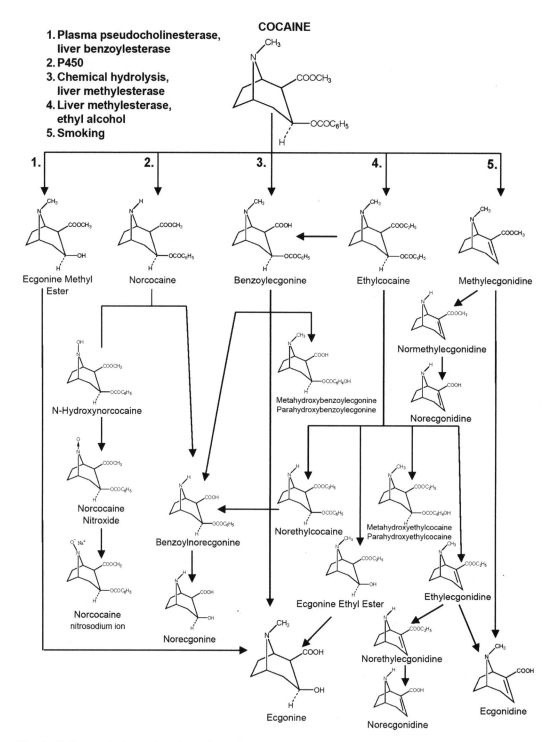

Fig. 1. Pathways in the metabolism of cocaine.

straightforward, however, and the interpretation of cocaine and metabolite concentrations in blood and other samples is complicated by complex metabolic reactions in vitro and in vivo.

The results of stability studies support the long-held belief that cocaine is metabolized to ecgonine methyl ester via enzymatic hydrolysis by pseudocholinesterase and to benzoylecgonine via spontaneous hydrolysis at physiological and alkaline pH (see "Interpretation of Results"). Cocaine can also be hydrolyzed to benzoylecgonine and ecgonine methyl ester by liver carboxylesterases. Two types of esterases have been isolated and purified from nonspecific carboxylesterases in the human liver. Liver methylesterase catalyzes the conversion of cocaine to benzoylecgonine and the transesterification of cocaine to ethylcocaine. In the absence of ethyl alcohol, this enzyme hydrolyzes cocaine exclusively to benzoylecgonine. A separate and distinct human liver esterase, benzoylesterase, catalyzes the conversion of cocaine to ecgonine methyl ester.

Norcocaine, an N-demethyl metabolite of cocaine produced by liver cytochrome P450, has received considerable study because of its conversion into a hepatotoxic metabolite. Norcocaine is metabolized to N-hydroxynorcocaine and then to norcocaine nitroxide. The nitroxide was thought to be a free radical that produced hepatotoxicity, but a further oxidative product, norcocaine nitrosodium ion, has since been demonstrated to be responsible. In humans, norcocaine is a minor metabolite, and reports of hepatotoxicity attributed to cocaine use are rare.

Appreciable amounts of norcocaine have been quantified in the plasma of individuals receiving chronic PO cocaine, however. Peak norcocaine concentrations in these individuals averaged about 10% of peak cocaine concentrations. In addition, peak concentrations of benzoylnorecgonine, a metabolite of norcocaine, have been detected at concentrations two to three times those of norcocaine. Two additional metabolites, p-hydroxycocaine and p-hydroxybenzoylecgonine, were also measured in the plasma of individuals

receiving chronic PO cocaine. Both m- and p-substituted forms of hydroxylated and hydroxymethoxylated cocaine have been identified in urine samples from cocaine users. Some of these metabolites have also been identified as their methyl de-esterified analogs. One of these metabolites, m-hydroxybenzoylecgonine, has been shown to be an important metabolite in the meconium of cocaine-exposed babies.

Both benzoylecgonine and ecgonine methyl ester are metabolized to ecgonine. Although the pathways have not been fully studied, enzymatic hydrolysis of the benzoyl ester and chemical hydrolysis of the methyl ester would be expected to varying degrees. Ecgonine is difficult to extract from an aqueous matrix; hence, analysis of ecgonine has been limited. When it has been analyzed, however, ecgonine has been found in significant quantities in urine and blood. As one of the end products of cocaine metabolism, it is particularly useful for documenting exposure to cocaine from urine samples when concentrations of other metabolites may be below reportable thresholds.

Anhydroecgonine methyl ester (methylecgonidine) has been identified as a unique cocaine metabolite in postmortem blood and urine after SM cocaine administration. Although it has been reported to be produced in the injection port of a gas chromatograph, <1% of the cocaine is converted to anhydroecgonine methyl ester if the injection port of the gas chromatograph is maintained at 250 °C. The related metabolites ecgonidine and norecgonidine methyl ester have been identified in urine samples.

The coadministration of cocaine and ethanol produces ethylcocaine (cocaethylene) through the transesterification of cocaine with ethanol. In addition to being formed by liver methyl esterase in simultaneous cocaine and ethanol users it can also be formed by fatty acid ethyl synthase. Because it is structurally similar to cocaine, it is not surprising that this metabolite has similar physicochemical properties to cocaine and has been found to enhance the euphoria associated with concurrent cocaine and alcohol use in animals. In vitro studies suggest that ethylcocaine may also be cardiotoxic. The appearance of ethylcocaine in the blood after simultaneous cocaine and ethanol use is delayed by 10–30 min. The average half-life of ethylcocaine based on various reports is about 120 min, slightly longer than average reports for cocaine.

Ethylcocaine is a pharmacologically important metabolite of cocaine, when it is present. The self-reported "high" after administration of pure ethylcocaine was lower than for an equivalent amount of cocaine administered to the same individuals; however, in studies in which cocaine-dependent individuals were administered cocaine (1 mg/kg IN every 30 min for 2 h) while they maintained a blood ethyl alcohol concentration of 100 mg/dL, the cocaine–ethanol combination produced a greater euphoria and perception of well-being than cocaine alone. In vitro studies suggest that ethylcocaine may also be cardiotoxic.

Metabolites of ethylcocaine include ecgonine ethyl ester, norethylcocaine, ethylecgonidine, and hydroxylated ethylcocaine. Many of these compounds have been identified in postmortem blood and urine samples. Anhydroecgonine ethyl ester has been identified in cocaine smokers also using ethyl alcohol. Ethylcocaine is also expected to be metabolized to benzoylecgonine via the same processes that convert cocaine to benzoylecgonine. Because liver methylesterase catalyzes the transesterification of cocaine to ethylcocaine 3.5 times faster than it hydrolyzes cocaine to benzoylecgonine, enzymatic conversion of ethylcocaine to benzoylecgonine would not be expected until the cocaine or ethyl alcohol has been consumed. This fact may explain in part the longer half-life of ethylcocaine compared with cocaine, which may contribute to the former's increased toxicity.

Plasma Concentrations

Many pharmacokinetic studies of cocaine have been performed. Although there is considerable interindividual variation, several observations can be made. When bioequivalent doses of cocaine are administered by the IV and SM routes, similar absorption and elimination curves for cocaine are obtained. Administration of two different cocaine doses by the same route (IV, SM, or PO) to the same individuals produced mean peak plasma cocaine concentrations that were related to the dose. When cocaine was administered IN, the dose and the mean peak plasma concentration showed a poor correlation because of dose-dependent differences in bioavailability. Peak plasma concentrations occurred almost immediately after IV and SM administration but were delayed 30–60 min and a mean of 60 min after the last cocaine dose administered IN and PO, respectively.

Peak plasma cocaine concentrations in most single-dose pharmacokinetic studies by the SM route (up to 100 mg), the IV route (up to 64 mg), and the IN route (up to 100 mg) averaged between 200 ng/mL and 400 ng/mL. Chronic multiple-dosing studies measured up to 1000–2000 ng/mL cocaine administered by the SM, IV, or PO routes without adverse effects (it is important to note, however, that these concentrations overlap with those associated with cocaine toxicity, a finding that will be discussed later).

Studies with both one- and two-compartment models indicate that cocaine follows first-order elimination after IV and SM administration. For both routes, the mean half-life of cocaine is about 60 min, according to the literature. The similar elimination rates obtained for the IV and SM routes are consistent with the similar effects seen via the IV or SM route of administration. Generally, the half-life of cocaine does not appear to be dose dependent, although dose-dependent kinetics have been reported after very high plasma cocaine concentrations were achieved via IV cocaine administration.

IN cocaine pharmacokinetics have generally been described with one- or two-compartment models with first-order input. One study found evidence for dose-dependent elimination. Published data indicate that the mean absorption half-life for cocaine after

IN administration is 12 min and that the mean elimination half-life is 84 min. Studies that used extended sampling times and more sensitive analytical measurements have shown that the terminal half-life of cocaine, especially administered via the SM and IN routes, may be much longer than had originally been reported—a mean of 4 to 5 h. Such results suggest that small amounts of cocaine may be stored in lipid-soluble tissue, similarly to marijuana.

Few pharmacokinetic studies have measured concentrations of cocaine metabolites in addition to cocaine or compared different routes of administration within the same individuals. In a study of 10 individuals who received IV or SM cocaine, the mean peak plasma cocaine concentrations approximated those of benzoylecgonine, with only trace amounts of ecgonine methyl ester. This result suggests that cocaine is metabolized primarily to benzoylecgonine in the blood and that ecgonine methyl ester may not be a major metabolite in the blood of healthy individuals. Although the time course in this study was too short to sufficiently evaluate the pharmacokinetics of the metabolites, another study that used a more extended collection period also failed to demonstrate appreciable quantities of ecgonine methyl ester in plasma after cocaine administration via the IV, SM, or IN route. This study showed that peak plasma benzoylecgonine concentrations usually occurred within 90 min after SM and IV administration and were about half the peak cocaine concentration. After IN administration, peak benzoylecgonine concentrations were not reached until 3 h; they were about twice those of cocaine and remained elevated for the next 5 h. The higher metabolite concentrations observed after IN administration is not surprising, because absorption is delayed after IN administration and significant metabolism of cocaine may occur during the absorption process. The rate of benzoylecgonine elimination was reported to be slow compared with its rate of formation, accounting for its accumulation in plasma while cocaine concentrations were decreasing. The elimination half-lives for benzoylecgonine were 347, 324, and 213 min after administration by the IV, SM, and IN routes, respectively.

Some studies have detected ecgonine methyl ester in the plasma after cocaine administration, however. A possible explanation for this disparity is that at the plasma cocaine concentrations reached, the preservative (sodium fluoride) did not adequately inhibit plasma pseudocholinesterase from the time of sample collection until analysis (see "Interpretation of Results"). The action of sodium fluoride as an inhibitor of plasma pseudocholinesterase has been shown to be reversible, especially at the low concentrations in standard gray Vacutainer® tubes.

A study that used PO cocaine administration suggests another explanation. Significant concentrations of ecgonine methyl ester and benzoylecgonine were detected in cocaine-abusing volunteers given 500–2000 mg PO cocaine daily in five equal hourly doses for up to 16 sessions. This study was unique in that PO cocaine was administered in a chronic rather than a single-dosing study and the investigators quantified the metabolites in properly preserved plasma samples following extended collection periods. Peak ecgonine methyl ester and benzoylecgonine concentrations were detected in the plasma of these individuals close to the time of peak cocaine concentrations. Peak benzoylecgonine concentrations were up to 10 times higher than peak cocaine concentrations. Peak ecgonine methyl ester concentrations were consistently lower than the peak benzoylecgonine concentrations but varied considerably. Studies of single PO doses by the same investigators also showed appreciable amounts of ecgonine methyl ester. Thus, it appears that the route of administration plays a greater role than the dosing regimen in determining whether ecgonine methyl ester is found in blood. Conversion of cocaine to ecgonine methyl ester via the PO route of administration is probably facilitated by first-pass effects of liver benzoylesterase. This hypothesis is supported by the absence of ecgonine methyl ester in plasma samples collected during different chronic-dosing studies that used the IV, SM, and combined IV and SM routes of administration in a regimen of seven doses over 90 min daily for up to nine sessions.

Outside of controlled laboratory studies, it does appear that some ecgonine methyl ester can be detected after SM and IN cocaine administration. This is probably due to some minor gastrointestinal absorption of the drug. Further research is still needed to determine the relationship between frequency of use, chronicity of use, route of administration, and the role that recently identified enzymes play in cocaine metabolism. In addition, enzymatic reactions not yet identified may play a role in cocaine metabolism.

Excretion

Cocaine and its metabolites are excreted into the urine almost exclusively by simple filtration. Thus, the urinary excretion rates and plasma concentrations of cocaine and benzoylecgonine parallel one another, indicating that the elimination rate of the drug is proportional to the plasma concentration. After a single cocaine dose, 64–69% is recovered in the urine within three days, regardless of the route of administration, and 86% of this amount is recovered within the first day. Some reports have indicated that up to 90% of a dose may be recovered in a 24-h urine sample. A review of published data has indicated that 1–9% of the drug is excreted unchanged (depending on the pH), 26–54% is excreted as benzoylecgonine, 18–41% is excreted as ecgonine methyl ester, and 2–3% is excreted as ecgonine. Anhydroecgonine methyl ester and various demethylated and hydroxylated metabolites appear to be minor metabolites in urine. After continuous prolonged IV cocaine infusions, the mean urinary half-lives for cocaine, benzoylecgonine, and ecgonine methyl ester were 0.8 h, 4.5 h, and 3.1 h, respectively, compared with 2.9 h, 4.8 h, and 4.9 h, respectively, after a single smoked dose of cocaine. Unfortunately, many controlled excretion studies have been limited to low doses of cocaine for short durations. Postmortem data suggest that with chronic use, cocaine concentrations in the urine are much higher than would be expected on the basis of pharmacokinetic data.

Urine concentrations of ecgonine, initially thought to be a minor urinary metabolite, have been shown to significantly exceed those of benzoylecgonine in certain situations. In 104 of 139 urine samples in which ecgonine was present at ≥50 ng/mL, the mean ecgonine concentration was approximately five times the comparable benzoylecgonine concentration. On the basis of the benzoylecgonine concentrations, this scenario appears to be most likely during the late stages of urinary excretion of a cocaine dose. In vitro hydrolysis of benzoylecgonine and ecgonine methyl ester in urine may also contribute to ecgonine concentrations detected to a minor degree.

DIRECT METHODS OF ANALYSIS

Immunoassay

Immunoassays are commonly used for screening purposes because they are readily amenable to large-batch analysis, are relatively sensitive, and require little or no sample preparation. Under current U.S. federal rules for workplace drug testing, immunoassay is the required initial testing technique for the detection of cocaine and its metabolites in urine. Because immunoassays are targeted to detect benzoylecgonine, they are particularly well suited for screening urine samples. Several types of immunoassays are on the market; depending on the product selected, immunoassays use the principle of enzyme immunoassay (EIA), microparticle immunoassay (KIMS), cloned enzyme donor immunoassay (CEDIA), or enzyme-linked immunosorbent assay (ELISA). Although all immunoassay techniques are targeted to benzoylecgonine, cross-reactivities to cocaine and other metabolites vary considerably by manufacturer and analytical principle. Immunoassays that possess substantial cross-reactivity to cocaine and ethylcocaine are particularly useful for screening oral fluid, hair, and postmortem blood, where significant concentrations of the parent drug might be found. Depending on the immunoassay selected, analysis of postmortem blood and tissue homogenates may be performed directly or after protein precipitation and/or solvent extraction. ELISA is especially well suited to postmortem analyses of whole blood because these assays generally do not require any sample preparation other than dilution. These assays can also be used successfully with tissue homogenates. Although the cutoff concentration for benzoylecgonine in U.S. federal workplace drug testing is 150 ng/mL, most immunoassays can reliably detect far lower concentrations.

INDIRECT METHODS OF ANALYSIS

Sample Preparation

Before cocaine and its metabolites can be analyzed with chromatographic techniques, the drugs must be separated from the biological matrix. This may be accomplished by liquid–liquid extraction, solid-phase extraction (SPE), or solid-phase microextraction procedures. SPE and solid-phase microextraction can be readily adapted to laboratory-automation devices. Several important issues must be considered before choosing an extraction procedure, however. Cocaine and many of its metabolites are esters that are susceptible to hydrolysis under alkaline conditions and at high temperatures. In addition, plasma and liver esterases contribute to their hydrolysis. During sample preparation, the amount of time the biological sample remains in conditions unfavorable for cocaine stability must be minimized; otherwise, esters may hydrolyze in vitro and complicate the interpretation of the analytical results (see "Interpretation of Results"). Consideration must also be given to the targeted analytes, because the polarities of cocaine and its metabolites vary considerably.

Other than stability concerns, the extraction of cocaine and ethylcocaine is straightforward. These compounds are readily extracted into n-butyl chloride at pH 8–9. A chloroform–2-propanol mixture (9:1) is also commonly used. These conditions will also extract benzoylecgonine and ecgonine methyl ester, although not with optimal recoveries. SPE procedures, also used for these analytes, commonly use a protein-precipitation step before applying the buffered supernatant to the extraction column. Elution is typically accomplished with a mixture of methylene chloride, 2-propanol, and ammonium hydroxide (78:20:2), although other elution solvents have been used as well, depending on the analytes targeted and the column used.

The extraction of the most polar analyte, ecgonine, presents a unique challenge. Because it is both a carboxylic acid and an alcohol, it cannot be extracted with common liquid–liquid procedures. Liquid–liquid procedures that use ion-exchange extraction have been attempted, but recoveries have been low. SPE procedures with anion-exchange cartridges have been described for urine but not for postmortem blood and tissue samples. The most promising method to date for such samples uses a protein-precipitation step with acetonitrile. After centrifugation, the upper layer is decanted, evaporated, and derivatized via a two-step conversion to p-nitro-n-propylcocaine, after which the product can be extracted with conventional liquid–liquid procedures.

Thin-Layer Chromatography

Thin-layer chromatography (TLC) is a simple technique that can be used to analyze for both cocaine and benzoylecgonine, but its lack of sensitivity generally limits it to the analysis of urine or bile samples, if it is used at all. After extracting 5 mL of urine for basic drugs and spotting the concentrated extract on a silica TLC plate, one can expect a sensitivity of about 1000–2000 ng/mL for benzoylecgonine with the standard Davidow solvent and visualization with Dragendorff's reagent or iodoplatinate. The sensitivity for benzoylecgonine may be increased up to 10-fold by an initial spraying with Dragendorff's reagent followed by an overspray with 20% sulfuric acid and exposure to iodine vapors. Sensitivity for cocaine by TLC is generally better than for benzoylecgonine with most schemes for extracting basic drugs. High-performance TLC has considerably improved detection limits. As a qualitative tool, TLC may be used to confirm immunoassay results when positive forensic identification is not required. TLC is particularly useful for benzoylecgonine, because it does not migrate up the plate very far, thus allowing it to be readily distinguished from many other basic drugs. TLC procedures for ecgonine methyl ester with similar sensitivities have also been described. Ecgonine methyl ester can be extracted from urine with a chloroform–2-propanol mixture (9:1). After solvent evaporation and reconstitution with methylene chloride and methanol (1:1), separation is achieved on a standard silica plate with the Davidow procedure. Ninhydrin and iodoplatinate are used for visualization of ecgonine methyl ester, which appears as a deep blue spot with a retardation factor (R_f) of 0.74.

Gas Chromatography

Gas chromatography (GC) is the separation technique most frequently used for the analysis of cocaine and its metabolites. Cocaine, ethylcocaine, and their N-desmethyl metabolites can be readily assayed without derivatization by means of nitrogen–phosphorus detection and by mass spectrometry (MS) detection in both the electron ionization and positive chemical ionization modes. Detection by flame ionization may also be used but is not nearly as sensitive. Ecgonine methyl ester and related compounds can be detected without derivatization but tend to tail on most analytical columns because of free hydroxyl moieties. Benzoylecgonine and related compounds must be derivatized prior to analysis. Various derivatization procedures have been used. Acylation procedures (e.g., pentafluoro) and silylation (e.g.,

trimethylsilyl) derivatize both benzoylecgonine and ecgonine methyl ester. Alkylation procedures (e.g., n-propyl) will derivatize N-desmethyl metabolites in addition to benzoylecgonine. Sequential derivatization allows the simultaneous detection of multiple analytes. For example, ecgonine, ecgonine methyl ester, benzoylecgonine, and norcocaine can be derivatized with 1-propyliodide followed by p-nitrobenzoylchloride to yield p-nitro-n-propylcocaine, p-nitrococaine, n-propylcocaine, and N-propylcocaine, respectively. Electron-capture detectors are very sensitive and have been used to analyze benzoylecgonine after acylation. The major disadvantage of this detector is that cocaine must be reduced prior to acylation.

Detection by MS provides the highest degree of specificity of all GC detectors and is virtually a requirement for forensic confirmation of cocaine and its metabolites today. The high sensitivity required for the detection of cocaine and metabolites in alternative matrices (sweat, oral fluid, hair) may require tandem MS (MS/MS) although two-dimensional GC/MS (operated with a Dean switch) appears to be a suitable, less costly option. A particular advantage with MS detection is that deuterated analogs of cocaine and its major metabolites are available and, by virtue of their chemical characteristics being nearly identical with their nondeuterated analogs, permit excellent reproducibility and accurate analysis. If other detectors are used, the selection of internal standards should be carefully considered so that they undergo the same chemistry as the analyte.

Liquid Chromatography

Liquid chromatography (LC) is very useful because cocaine, ethylcocaine, and benzoylecgonine can be analyzed simultaneously without derivatization when using ultraviolet (UV) detection. Although UV detection has a sensitivity of at least 0.05 mg/L for cocaine and benzoylecgonine, detection of other metabolites requires MS detection. In addition, UV detection is not as selective as other detection methods and does not allow the use of deuterium-labeled internal standards. The lack of selectivity can be a particular problem when trying to select an appropriate internal standard. For example, lidocaine may interfere with cocaine and meperidine may interfere with tetracaine, a commonly used internal standard. A further disadvantage of UV detection is that ecgonine methyl ester and related compounds as well as ecgonine do not possess a UV chromophore and would need derivatization for detection.

On the other hand, LC coupled with MS may be the ideal separation and detection techniques for cocaine and its metabolites without the need for derivatization. Although LC/MS and LC tandem mass spectrometry (LC/MS/MS) instruments are still quite expensive, their appearance in clinical laboratories has increased over the past several years. The biggest advantage to LC/MS/MS is its ability to analyze both parent drug and virtually all metabolites within a single chromatographic run without derivatization and with minimal specimen preparation. Both atmospheric pressure chemical ionization and electrospray ionization prior to MS/MS analysis have been used to measure cocaine and multiple metabolites in urine specimens.

INTERPRETATION OF RESULTS

Pathology

Many pathologic conditions may predispose an individual to cocaine toxicity that may cause death at cocaine concentrations lower than expected. The diagnosis of such conditions will ultimately affect the toxicologic interpretation. Chronic cocaine use may also contribute to the development of pathologic conditions that may cause sudden death. Excellent texts on the pathology of drug abuse are available, so only the most important conditions will be considered here.

A significant number of deaths have been associated with a cocaine-induced psychosis now commonly known as cocaine-induced excited or agitated delirium. This syndrome is characterized by severe hyperthermia (104–108 °F), extreme agitation and delirium, respiratory arrest, and sudden death. These individuals exhibit bizarre and violent behavior and extreme strength, and they frequently can be seen running around—often naked—shouting, fighting, breaking things, and causing injury to themselves and others. Death may occur from these injuries, but death more frequently occurs suddenly after agitation has ceased. Unfortunately, the police have usually intervened by this time, and the restrained individual then dies in police custody. At autopsy, minor injuries, especially head injuries that may occur during attempts to restrain an individual, may lead to overinterpretation and litigation. Other autopsy findings are relatively nonspecific, but cardiomegaly is a consistent finding. In these cases, the stress from restraint may produce catecholamine surges on an already sensitized myocardium, producing a terminal arrhythmia. The use of Tasers to try to subdue these individuals further complicates interpretation. In a multiyear review of 75 Taser-related deaths, cardiovascular disease was found in 54.1% of the cases with available autopsy reports. Illegal substances were found in 78.4% of the cases, of which 86.2% involved stimulant drugs and 75.7% had a diagnosis of excited delirium. In 27% of the cases, the use of a Taser was considered a potential or contributory cause of death. This topic remains very controversial, however.

In noncustody excited-delirium cases, decedents are frequently found in places where they may have attempted to cool themselves, such as the bathroom. Other evidence of attempts at cooling (e.g., wet towels and ice cube trays) may also be present at the scene. Toxicology results in excited-delirium cases have demonstrated cocaine-to-benzoylecgonine ratios similar to those found for other accidental deaths due to cocaine toxicity. A large percentage of excited-delirium victims die after they have survived 1–12 h. When the survival time is <6 h, cases featuring high cocaine concentrations also tend to have high benzoylecgonine concentrations, and cases with low cocaine concentrations tend to have low benzoylecgonine concentrations. Because the half-life of benzoylecgonine exceeds that of cocaine, these findings suggest that the development of excited delirium is associated with binge cocaine use.

Although chronic cocaine use may produce toxicity in a variety of organ systems, cardiovascular diseases are most commonly associated with sudden death due to cocaine. Coronary artery disease with or without myocardial infarction, myocardial diseases including myocarditis, hypertrophy, dilated cardiomyopathy, and contraction band necrosis due to catecholamine toxicity, valvular heart disease, and aortic dissection have all been attributed to complications of cocaine abuse. Unfortunately, few features distinguish cocaine-induced disease from naturally occurring pathology. Neurologic disorders have frequently been associated with chronic cocaine use and may be related to sensitization. Subarachnoid and intracerebral hemorrhages, berry aneurysms, cerebral infarction, and cocaine-induced seizures have all been reported in addition to cocaine-induced excited delirium. At autopsy, chronic cocaine users have a statistically significant decrease in body mass index compared with nonusers, an observation consistent with cocaine's anorectic properties. Interestingly, cocaine users who die after cocaine-induced excited delirium tend to have a high body mass index. Physical signs of cocaine or drug use are also important (e.g., puncture wounds, needle tracks, a perforated nasal septum, evidence of seizures such as lip bites, and drug paraphernalia at the scene or with the individual).

Occasionally, it may be possible to attribute cocaine toxicity or death to "body packing." Body packers may try transporting cocaine by swallowing a cocaine-filled condom (or other container) or concealing it rectally or vaginally. These containers have occasionally ruptured, releasing a large dose of the drug. Blood cocaine concentrations in postmortem cases are usually huge, sometimes >100,000 ng/mL, making interpretation straightforward.

Blood

Many factors must be considered when interpreting cocaine and metabolite concentrations in the blood. As previously discussed, plasma cocaine concentrations in single-dose pharmacokinetic studies generally average 200–400 ng/mL. Plasma concentrations >1000 ng/mL have been reported without adverse effects in some studies after chronic oral dosing and after repeated doses of smoked cocaine. In one instance, a plasma concentration of 3870 ng/mL was documented after IV cocaine administration without symptoms of toxicity. A search of the literature suggests that cocaine concentrations of <300 ng/mL are generally considered clinically therapeutic; however, clinical and postmortem studies have clearly shown that therapeutic, toxic, and lethal cocaine concentrations overlap. Tolerance and sensitization may play a significant role in the poor correlation observed. In a study of 130 patients who presented to an emergency room with acute cocaine toxicity, the mean plasma cocaine concentration was 340 ng/mL (range, 0.00–3920 ng/mL). The median cocaine concentration in these patients was only 70 ng/mL; however, the mean and median benzoylecgonine concentrations in these patients were 1570 ng/mL and 1060 ng/mL, respectively. There was no correlation of the cocaine and metabolite concentrations in these patients with their clinical state or outcome, but the degree of symptoms of toxicity—most notably hyperthermia, heart rate, and psychosis—was a better predictor of patient outcome.

Studies that evaluated the relationship between blood cocaine concentrations and their effects have demonstrated a good correlation between peak plasma cocaine concentrations and peak pharmacologic and behavioral effects. Because the high associated with cocaine use is related to the plasma concentration, not to the dose, it is easy to understand how self-administration of toxic amounts of cocaine can occur during rapidly repeated cocaine administration (binging). The time to peak plasma concentration and maximal effect depends on the route of administration. After bioequivalent IV and SM administrations of cocaine, systolic and diastolic blood pressures, heart rate, and pupil diameter increase almost immediately. Both routes of administration produce an equally rapid onset of behavioral effects (self-reported high, liking, euphoria, and dysphoria); however, the intensity and duration of pleasurable effects after SM administration was markedly higher than after IV administration. One possible explanation for this observation is that after injection into the antecubital vein, the bolus of cocaine in the blood becomes substantially diluted by the time it reaches the heart and aorta, where a portion of the bolus is shunted into the carotid artery. In contrast, when cocaine is smoked, the majority of the dose is deposited in the lung where the arterial bloodstream may deliver a more concentrated bolus dose to the cocaine receptors in the brain, producing greater effects. This explanation accounts for why studies have found that smoked cocaine is more desirable and potentially more addictive than other routes of administration. After IN administration, the physiological effects are delayed, and their intensities are diminished. Behavioral effects peak later (about 20 min) and remain elevated longer than after SM and IV administration.

Peak cocaine concentrations occur rapidly after IV and SM routes of administration; consequently, cocaine toxicity or death may be delayed until after considerable amounts of the cocaine dose have been metabolized, producing the lower-than-expected plasma concentrations. If toxicity is delayed long enough, high concentrations of cocaine metabolites may be found in the absence of the parent drug. Conversely, toxicity or death may occur close to the time of peak cocaine concentration after IN and PO administration because of the delayed peak in cocaine concentration. Disease may also play a role in the analytes that are measured. In postmortem cases with chronic renal failure, very high blood benzoylecgonine concentrations (>10,000 ng/mL) have been observed in the absence of any cocaine, suggesting a difficulty in eliminating this polar metabolite. These findings may also be consistent with delayed toxicity due to cocaine. The route of administration may also play a significant role in the amounts of metabolites that are measured. Higher concentrations of ecgonine methyl ester have been observed after PO cocaine administration and in individuals who have swallowed their cocaine contraband.

Given that cocaine is typically used in a binge of multiple doses over the course of many hours, blood concentrations of cocaine and its metabolites are usually not useful for estimating the dose or time of administration. Because the half-life of benzoylecgonine is considerably longer than that of cocaine, one would expect benzoylecgonine concentrations to increase out of proportion to the cocaine concentration during a cocaine binge. High blood benzoylecgonine concentrations with significant cocaine concentrations (>100 ng/mL) may indicate binge cocaine use, whereas similar cocaine and benzoylecgonine concentrations are more typical of a recent single dose or multiple doses within a very short period of time. Hydrolysis of the collected sample, however, may create analytical artifacts that may alter interpretation of the results.

Cocaine contains two ester moieties that render it susceptible to hydrolysis in vitro and in vivo (see "Metabolism"). In unpreserved blood, in vitro stability studies have shown that cocaine is hydrolyzed almost exclusively at the phenyl ester by plasma pseudocholinesterase to yield ecgonine methyl ester. The rates of hydrolysis of both esters have been shown to be temperature and pH dependent, with higher temperatures and pH increasing the rate of hydrolysis. The loss of cocaine in unpreserved blood can be dramatic. Benzoylecgonine is considerably more stable than ecgonine methyl ester in unpreserved blood (pH 7.4) at room temperature. A 50% loss of ecgonine methyl ester occurred over a 35-day period, compared with a 25% loss for benzoylecgonine. Little loss of either compound was observed when the blood sample was refrigerated for the same period of time. Cocaine and metabolite stability will be discussed in greater detail in the chapter on drug stability. The conditions to which samples are exposed during analysis are another factor affecting the stability of cocaine and the interpretation of cocaine and metabolite measurements. Primary samples and aliquots should not be allowed to remain at room temperature for extended periods during the analytical process. Because cocaine is a basic drug, many procedures use basic conditions (pH 8–11) to extract it from the biological matrix into organic solvents. This process may be repeated during a back extraction. The duration of exposure to these alkaline conditions, especially at room temperature, is critical and may contribute to artifactual hydrolysis of cocaine and its metabolites.

The appropriate blood samples must be collected, properly identified as to origin, and preserved and frozen as quickly as possible. In postmortem cases, heart blood should be collected only during the autopsy to ensure that the hypodermic syringe is aspirating blood directly from the heart. If no autopsy is performed, only peripheral blood should be collected, because samples collected by "blind stick" are prone to contamination. In addition, trauma may yield contaminated blood samples. Ideally, both peripheral blood and heart blood should be collected. The occurrence of higher cocaine concentrations in the arteries than in the veins shortly after SM or IV administration suggest that cocaine distribution is not immediately uniform. These factors may affect blood concentrations found in acute cocaine-intoxication cases. Other specimens, such as vitreous humor, may be useful in trauma cases, but cocaine concentrations have been shown to change after death in this specimen as well.

In conclusion, the evidence in the literature suggests that cocaine concentrations of 0.0–3800 ng/mL in the blood are associated with therapeutic, toxic, and lethal events. In simultaneous ethyl alcohol and cocaine users, ethylcocaine concentrations should also be considered when interpreting results. Cocaine concentrations >5000 ng/mL have generally been observed only in fatalities, although cocaine may not have always been the direct cause of death. These findings strongly suggest that toxicologic findings must be placed in the contexts of a good medical/legal investigation and comprehensive pathology studies for their proper interpretation. Many pathologic conditions consistent with natural disease may be determined to be cocaine related if positive toxicology results for cocaine or its metabolites, even at low concentrations, are provided. On the other hand, a gunshot wound through the brain stem rules out even large cocaine concentrations as an immediate cause of death. Investigation may also play a key role. A documentable history of cocaine-induced excited delirium, even in the absence of significant cocaine concentrations or other pathology, may provide the needed evidence to determine a cause of death. If a decedent was initially treated at a hospital, considerable survival time may have passed, and a postmortem blood analysis may yield negative results. Even if hospital samples are available, they are usually unpreserved, unrefrigerated serum samples and may be of little use by the time they are analyzed. Investigations, laboratory findings, and clinical presentation or autopsy results must be considered together, because any factor taken out of context may produce an incorrect interpretation.

Urine

Urine is currently the required specimen in U.S. federal workplace drug-testing programs. Under the federal program, a government-certified laboratory assays a urine sample for benzoylecgonine by an immunoassay that uses a 150-ng/mL cutoff concentration. Confirmation is performed by GC/MS analysis with a 100-ng/mL cutoff concentration. Only benzoylecgonine may be assayed in workplace urine drug-testing programs.

Urine is suitable only for determining an exposure to cocaine. Quantitative measurements of benzoylecgonine concentration (especially if corrected for creatinine) in serial urine samples may be useful in substance-abuse treatment programs to detect a relapse during a period of abstinence, but single samples collected in a forensic setting cannot be similarly interpreted, because only a randomly collected urine sample is typically analyzed.

In general, cocaine and metabolite concentrations measured in urine cannot be correlated with the time of drug use or the degree of impairment. Once alternative medical explanations are ruled out, positive benzoylecgonine results in a workplace drug test have few interpretative concerns. Typically, urinary benzoylecgonine concentrations may be detectable from 2 to 4 days after cocaine use, depending on the dose, frequency of use, urinary pH, and clearance.

The urinary-elimination half-lives for cocaine and its metabolites have been determined through the consolidation of several published studies. These data indicate half-lives of 1.5 h for cocaine, 7.5 h for benzoylecgonine, and 3.6 h for ecgonine methyl ester, although there is considerable interindividual variation. In a study that simulated chronic cocaine use with PO dosing, longer terminal excretion curves were observed. The mean initial elimination rates were 4.1 h for cocaine, 7.2 h for benzoylecgonine, and 5.6 h for ecgonine methyl ester. The mean terminal half-lives were 22.8 h for benzoylecgonine (range, 15.0–34.5 h) and 32.8 h (range, 22.3–52.4 h) for ecgonine methyl ester. A terminal excretion curve for cocaine was observed in only 3 of the individuals, with a mean half-life of 19.0 h (range, 13.5–27.4 h). Prolonged positive immunoassay results for 5 to 10 days have been reported after compulsive cocaine use, with continuous positive results for up to 16 days with a longer terminal half-life after chronic, heavy cocaine use. The increased binding of benzoylecgonine to plasma proteins compared with the negligible binding of cocaine may also explain the extended detection times seen in urine samples from chronic high-dose cocaine users.

Issues concerning the stability of benzoylecgonine have been raised, particularly with regard to retesting a sample previously reported as positive. Benzoylecgonine, although relatively stable in urine at freezing temperatures, is susceptible to hydrolysis in alkaline conditions and at higher temperatures. (See the chapter on drug stability.)

One defense to the identification of benzoylecgonine in regulated testing is that exogenous cocaine was added to the urine specimen after collection and was subsequently hydrolyzed to benzoylecgonine. When cocaine (1000 ng/mL) was added to buffers at different pHs (5, 7.4, and 10) and stored at 4 °C and 25 °C, the rate of cocaine hydrolysis to benzoylecgonine increased with temperature and pH. Ecgonine methyl ester was tested for but not detected as a hydrolysis product of cocaine in buffers, suggesting its presence could be indicative of endogenous cocaine use. Another study, however, showed that when high cocaine concentrations (155,000 ng/mL) are fortified into a negatively testing urine sample adjusted to alkaline pH, significant hydrolysis to both benzoylecgonine and ecgonine methyl ester occurs, even though the esterases that hydrolyze cocaine are not present in urine. As a percentage of the initial amount of cocaine added, the detected amounts of benzoylecgonine and ecgonine methyl ester were 34% and 36%, respectively, in urine adjusted to pH 8.0 and stored at room temperature (25 °C) for three days. The comparable data for urine samples adjusted to pH 9.0 were 43% for both benzoylecgonine and ecgonine methyl ester. No appreciable cocaine loss was observed at pH 5.0 or pH 7.0. For this reason, some investigators have suggested the measurement of the hydroxybenzoylecgonines when benzoylecgonine and ecgonine methyl ester are alleged to be present because of in vitro adulteration. The measurement of ecgonine has also been suggested.

Issues are frequently raised regarding unknowing exposure or ingestion of cocaine. In a study in which six individuals were exposed to up to 200 mg cocaine freebase (200 °C) for 1 h in a room of $2.1 \times 2.5 \times 2.4$ m, urine samples collected periodically up to 34.7 h after exposure contained maximal benzoylecgonine concentrations (range, 22–123 ng/mL). The individuals, however, never tested positive for benzoylecgonine above the 300-ng/mL cutoff with the EMIT assay. The amount of cocaine the individuals inhaled according to the room air measurements was 0.25 mg. For comparison, the same individuals were also given a 1-mg IV injection of cocaine hydrochloride. Four of the six individuals tested positive (>300 ng/mL) after the injection (indicating that the minimum amount of cocaine in these individuals necessary to produce a positive result was approximately 1 mg). It was concluded that passive exposure conditions that would lead to absorption of ≥1 mg cocaine could produce positively testing samples at a cutoff of 300 ng/mL benzoylecgonine. Such conditions are not likely, however.

Another issue often raised is that cocaine ingestion was unknowing because the cocaine had been added to a beverage. Most studies of cocaine ingestion in a beverage have not involved fortified beverages but rather beverages that naturally contained cocaine. Specifically, in the 1980s, Health Inca Tea, which was sold in health food stores in the U.S., was found to contain trace amounts of cocaine. The U.S. Food and Drug Administration has since banned the importation of any tea containing residual cocaine, yet several studies of Health Inca Tea and other teas imported from South American countries have clearly shown that even very low amounts of cocaine in a beverage can produce a positive result in a urine drug test. For example, after brewing tea that contained 1.87 mg cocaine in a cup, the peak urinary benzoylecgonine concentrations in four individuals ranged from 1400–2800 ng/mL at 4–11 h after ingestion. Positive immunoassay results (>300 ng/mL) determined by FPIA were obtained for 21–26 h after ingestion. Benzoylecgonine concentrations measured by GC/MS exceeded the 300-ng/mL cutoff for 17.5 h after ingestion and exceeded 150 ng/mL for 22 h after ingestion. No pharmacologic effects were reported in any of the studies in which coca teas were ingested.

In a study in which 6 ounces of cola fortified with 25 mg cocaine hydrochloride was consumed by a 165-lb male, peak urinary concentrations of cocaine (269 ng/mL) and benzoylecgonine (7940 ng/mL) were obtained at 1 h and 12 h respectively. Urine benzoylecgonine concentrations remained at >300 ng/mL for 48 h. The individual reported a very slight local-anesthetic effect on the lips and tongue when consuming the beverage but noted no unusual taste. About 1 h after ingestion, the individual noted some dryness of the mouth, lightheadedness, and a slight headache that lasted about 1.5 h; however, the physiological effects described should be considered in the context of a study of a single individual without placebo.

These studies demonstrate that very small amounts of cocaine (<5.0 mg or about one fifth of a typical IN dose or line) added to or contained in a beverage are sufficient to produce a positive result in a drug test for cocaine metabolites in urine in an unsuspecting individual. In such cases, the detection of unique cocaine metabolites, such as methylecgonidine or ecgonidine, which are produced after smoking crack cocaine, may prove to be useful for refuting alleged oral ingestion of cocaine after a positive drug-test result for benzoylecgonine.

Concern has also been raised regarding passive exposure to cocaine in personnel who come in frequent contact with the drug. The issue of dermal exposure to cocaine has been investigated in several studies, all of which demonstrated that with appropriate personal protective equipment, casual exposure to cocaine is not likely to produce a benzoylecgonine concentration greater than the 150 ng/mL U.S. federal workplace drug-testing cutoff concentration. If testing occurs at lower cutoff concentrations, studies suggest that the data need to be evaluated carefully.

Tissues

Brain may be a useful specimen for the measurement of cocaine and its metabolites, because cocaine is relatively stable in the brain and is not subject to postmortem redistribution. Because cocaine rapidly crosses the blood–brain barrier, brain cocaine concentrations in cases of acute cocaine intoxication have been shown to be much higher than concentrations in the blood. In addition, because benzoylecgonine probably does not cross the blood–brain barrier, the presence of this metabolite in the brain has been attributed to cocaine that entered the brain. Thus, the brain may be particularly helpful in estimating the pattern of cocaine use before death. In a study of 34 acute cocaine deaths, the mean brain-to-blood ratio of cocaine concentration was 9.6 (median ratio, 3.8), compared with a mean ratio of 2.5 in 14 incidental cases in which both analytes could be detected. Cocaine was also detected in the brain in 11 incidental cases in which only benzoylecgonine was detected in the blood. The mean cocaine-to-benzoylecgonine ratio was also higher in the brain than in the blood, both in acute cases (14.7 vs 0.64) and in incidental cases (0.87 vs 0.27). These observations have been replicated in other studies. The main disadvantage of the brain is the difficulty of working with fatty homogenates, although SPE technology has simplified sample handling to some degree. Properly stored and preserved cerebrospinal fluid may simplify sample collection and preparation issues while retaining the potential advantage of brain tissue analysis. Because the pH of cerebrospinal fluid increases during storage, samples should be preserved with sodium fluoride and acidified with sodium citrate or acetic acid and frozen as soon as possible.

Other tissues may be useful when biological fluids are not available, but they do not provide additional interpretive information. In the few cases studied, kidney and spleen have been found to have the highest cocaine concentrations.

Hair

Cocaine and metabolites may be detectable in hair for longer periods of time than urine. For this reason, analysis of hair may be useful in determining a past history of cocaine use. It takes 4 to 5 days for ingested cocaine to begin to appear in the hair. The ability to detect cocaine in hair is based more on the concentration than on a pharmacologic "time window," because as long as the hair is not cut, the incorporated drug will remain in it. However, the utility of hair is limited to obtaining historical information about drug use and is not useful for determining an acute use, such as in postaccident testing. As such, hair testing may be extremely useful in postmortem cases in which no other specimen is available. Hair has even been used to identify cocaine in ancient Peruvian mummies.

Although appropriate forensic methodologies exist for the analysis of cocaine and metabolites in hair, their use for employment-related drug testing is controversial because of a lack of the data required for accurately interpreting the results. Still under study are many important issues related to hair testing, including environmental contamination, washing techniques, racial bias in hair due to the concentration of certain types of melanin, sex bias, sample adulteration, quality-control procedures, proficiency testing, and the establishment of cutoff concentrations.

The primary analyte detected in hair after cocaine use is the parent cocaine, but to minimize environmental-contamination issues and to demonstrate cocaine ingestion, the proposed guidelines for hair testing in federal workplace drug-testing programs require a benzoylecgonine/cocaine ratio of 0.1 in the confirmatory testing process in order to report a positive result. Still, some studies suggest that benzoylecgonine arises primarily from hydrolysis of cocaine in hair, not from biological incorporation. Other possible target analytes in hair for demonstrating in vivo cocaine use include norcocaine and ethylcocaine.

Oral Fluid

Oral fluid may be a useful specimen for detecting recent cocaine use in clinical studies and workplace testing. There is generally a good correlation between saliva and plasma cocaine concentrations. Saliva cocaine concentrations have also been correlated to behavioral effects. In addition, saliva may be collected by direct observation without any invasive procedure.

Appropriate sample-collection procedures are critical for minimizing contamination from the oral cavity, especially after SM and IN administration. The use of benzoylecgonine as a target analyte in workplace testing should help minimize this issue. Despite cocaine being the predominant analyte in saliva after acute cocaine use, benzoylecgonine is detected more frequently and at higher concentrations than cocaine after cessation of chronic cocaine use. Detection times for benzoylecgonine after chronic PO cocaine administration were comparable for saliva and plasma (45 h vs 47 h, respectively; cutoff, 10 ng/mL) but were far less than for urine, which had an mean *minimum* detection time of 165 h for the same low cutoff concentration. On the other hand, cocaine could be detected for nearly twice as long in saliva than in plasma (15 hs vs 9 h; cutoff, 10 ng/mL). The saliva/plasma cocaine ratio can also be affected by saliva pH and saliva flow rate after stimulation. For this reason, it is important to develop standardized collection protocols.

Sweat

Sweat may be a useful, noninvasive specimen for monitoring drug use. Sweat may be collected by means of a collection patch placed on the skin for a predetermined period. This collection procedure allows a continuous period of monitoring or accumulation of any excreted drug. In sweat, cocaine is excreted primarily as the parent drug, offering the added advantage of simple GC analysis. Depending on the device used to collect sweat, any attempt at tampering with the collection device would be evident. Although wearing a sweat patch for monitoring cocaine use may provide a wider detection window than for urine, any correlation between the accumulated sweat cocaine concentration with the degree of impairment or time of use is not likely. Because trace amounts of cocaine can be detected in sweat after IV administration of as little as 1 mg cocaine, some concerns regarding passive exposure have been raised.

Meconium

Meconium is the first stool excreted by the neonate. Because meconium accumulates throughout gestation, it is a useful specimen with which to monitor fetal drug exposure due to maternal drug use. Neonates appear to metabolize cocaine differently than adults. In meconium, *m*-hydroxybenzoylecgonine is the metabolite most frequently present. Fortunately, this metabolite cross-reacts with many of the available immunoassays; however, it is important to include this analyte in confirmation procedures, because GC/MS confirms up to 25% fewer cases when only testing for benzoylecgonine is carried out. In addition to the parent cocaine, most of the cocaine metabolites that have been reported in urine have also been reported in meconium, including anhydroecgonine methyl ester, which is suggestive of maternal crack use. Meconium analysis for the measurement of cocaine in stillborn babies has also been shown to be useful. Cocaine has been identified in meconium from a 17-week-old fetus, suggesting that fetal drug exposure can be determined early in gestation. Because meconium forms layers in the intestine as it is being deposited, it is not homogeneous. As with other heterogeneous specimens, such as gastric contents, it is important that the entire sample be collected and thoroughly mixed before sampling. Caution should be taken when interpreting cocaine and metabolite ratios if the meconium sample has been collected from a diaper because it may have been contaminated with urine.

EFFECT OF COCAINE ON DRIVING

Apart from the effects of cocaine, driving performance entails many factors that may affect driving, including coordination skills, reaction time, risk taking, emotional state (e.g., anger, fear, stress, hostility), personality style (relaxed, tense, aggressive), fatigue, physical and mental health, and distractions (radio, cell phone, smoking, thoughts, conversation, children). Whether an accident could have been prevented in the absence of a drug(s) given the inherent driving performance variables is difficult to determine.

Relatively few scientific studies have evaluated the effects of cocaine on driving performance. The euphoric effects of cocaine during acute intoxication may give a driver the feeling of increased mental and physical abilities, and this optimism has been suggested to prompt increased risk-taking behavior and perhaps increase the probability of accidents, particularly in conjunction with ethyl alcohol use. In one study, 62% of cocaine smokers reported symptoms of suspiciousness, distrust, and paranoia. These effects have led to high-speed chases with police. It is not surprising that the use of stimulants has also been associated with road rage.

These findings appear consistent with an examination of 253 motor vehicle fatalities that occurred in metropolitan Detroit (Wayne County, Michigan) over a three-year period. Cocaine and/or its metabolites were detected in the blood of 25 (10%) of these cases. An analysis of the histories confirmed that aggressive driving (as determined by high speed and loss of control) was the most common finding in all of the accidents and occurred in all but three cases. Ethyl alcohol was detected in 14 of the 25 cases, 10 of which were also positive for parent cocaine and/or ethylcocaine in the blood, confirming the high incidence of acute combined cocaine and ethanol use. However, although high-risk driving appeared to be associated with cocaine use (with or without ethyl alcohol), fault is more likely to occur when ethyl alcohol is present, indicating that alcohol may play a larger role in accident occurrence than cocaine. This fact is consistent with other studies that compared crash responsibility with drug and alcohol use and may be related to the combined effects of a stimulant drug with a drug that depressed inhibitions.

There was no evidence to suggest that the concentration of cocaine and its metabolites was related to accident occurrence.

In a study of more than 25,000 drivers in Sweden arrested for driving under the influence of drugs, 795 were positive for cocaine and/or benzoylecgonine in the blood (in the absence of alcohol). In the 20 cases with the highest cocaine concentrations in the blood, drivers were observed to be driving dangerously, including weaving, speeding, and ignoring red lights. Typical findings reported by police officers included increased pupil diameters, bloodshot eyes, agitation, difficulty standing or sitting, incoherent speech, and increased pulse rate. However, a review of 44 reports by drug-recognition experts in cocaine-related driving-under-the-influence cases in Washington state showed that although increased pupil diameter (especially in a dark room) and pulse rate were frequently observed, the magnitude of these changes did not appear to be related to cocaine concentration.

The ability of cocaine to produce mydriasis appears to have significant effects in self-reported observations. After IN cocaine use, 43% of individuals reported increased sensitivity to light, halos around bright objects, and difficulty focusing. More than 34% of cocaine smokers reported blurred vision, often accompanied by glare-recovery problems. Hallucinations were reported by 50% of cocaine smokers and 18% of IN users. "Snow lights," flashes or movements of light in the peripheral field of vision, were the most commonly reported hallucination. Reaction to snow lights included moving in their direction or trying to avoid or evade them.

When self-reported driving behaviors were compared for individuals in treatment for cocaine or cannabis abuse, individuals reported reckless driving 29.7% of the time when driving under the influence of cocaine, compared with only 2.4% of the time when driving under the influence of cannabis. Conversely, individuals driving under the influence of cannabis reported that they were more likely to attempt to drive carefully or cautiously (27.9%) than when driving under the influence of cocaine (11.8%).

Because the effects of cocaine are brief, the crash that follows cocaine use may be a particularly dangerous time for driving; however, samples collected from individuals in such a state may be positive only for cocaine metabolites, making assessment difficult. The presence of cocaine metabolites suggests past use and cannot be used to determine impairment or withdrawal without additional information, such as witnessed driving and/or observations by a trained drug-recognition expert. This is particularly the case when only a urine sample is available. Of 150 individuals arrested for reckless driving and who tested negative for alcohol, 13% tested positive for cocaine metabolites, 33% were positive for cannabinoids, and 12% were positive for cannabinoids and cocaine metabolites in the urine. Nearly half of the drivers testing positive for prior cocaine use performed normally on field-sobriety tests, including two individuals who were stopped for driving directly into oncoming traffic. Of those testing positive for cocaine, 21% were sleepy or slow, 39% were happy, carefree, and talkative, and 39% were combative, argumentative, and paranoid.

Double-blind laboratory studies have demonstrated that low doses of cocaine may actually improve driving performance and counteract some of the performance decrements of ethyl alcohol and other depressant drugs. In a study of more than 4000 individuals, an increased risk of injury was associated with the use of psychoactive substances, but the risk was lower when cocaine was used with other depressant drugs. Although stimulants (amphetamines or cocaine) may acutely enhance performance of simple tasks, this enhancement may disappear as the complexity of the task increases. For example, cocaine-induced hyperexcitability has led to rapid steering or braking reactions in response to sudden sounds, such as horns or sirens.

The current data suggest that it is very difficult to predict driving impairment on the basis of the presence of cocaine and or its metabolites in biological samples alone. Witnessed driving behavior and examination by a drug-recognition examiner, coupled with laboratory studies, is the triad that appears most appropriate for determining driving impairment.

SUGGESTED READING

1. Ambre J. The urinary excretion of cocaine and metabolites in humans: a kinetic analysis of published data. J Anal Toxicol 1985;9:241–5.
2. Ambre J, Ruo T, Nelson J, Belknap B. Urinary excretion of cocaine, benzoylecgonine, and ecgonine methyl ester in humans. J Anal Toxicol 1988;12:301–6.
3. Barnett G, Hawks R, Resnick R. Cocaine pharmacokinetics in humans. J Ethnopharmacol 1981;3:353–66.
4. Baselt RC, Chang R. Urinary excretion of cocaine and benzoylecgonine following oral ingestion in a single subject. J Anal Toxicol 1987;11:81–2.
5. Bertol E, Trigano C, Di Milia MG, Di Padua M, Mari F. Cocaine-related deaths: an enigma still under investigation. Forensic Sci Int 2008;176:121–3.
6. Brogan WC, Lange RA, Glamann DB, Hillis RD. Recurrent coronary vasoconstriction caused by intranasal cocaine: possible role for metabolites. Ann Int Med 1992;116:557–61.
7. Brookoff D, Cook CS, Williams C, Mann CS. Testing reckless drivers for cocaine and marijuana. N Engl J Med 1994;331:518–22.
8. Byck R. The effects of cocaine on complex performance in humans. Alcohol Drugs Driving 1987;3:9–12.
9. Clouet D, Asghar K, Brown R, eds. Mechanisms of cocaine abuse and toxicity. Rockville, MD: Department of Health and Human Services, 1988. National Institute on Drug Abuse research monograph nr 88.
10. Cone EJ. Pharmacokinetics and pharmacodynamics of cocaine. J Anal Toxicol 1995;19:459–78.
11. Cone EJ, Yousefnejad D, Hillsgrove MJ, Holicky B, Darwin WD. Passive inhalation of cocaine. J Anal Toxicol 1995;19:399–411.
12. Dean RA, Christian CD, Sample RHB, Bosron WF. Human liver cocaine esterases: ethanol-mediated formation of ethylcocaine. FASEB J 1991;5:2735–9.
13. Ellenhorn M, Barceloux D, eds. Medical toxicology. New York: Elsevier, 1988.
14. Grabowki J, ed. Cocaine: pharmacology, effects and treatment of abuse. Rockville, MD: Department of Health and Human Services, 1984. National Institute on Drug Abuse research monograph nr 50.

15. Hornbeck CL, Barton KM, Czarny RJ. Urine concentrations of ecgonine from specimens with low benzoylecgonine levels using a new ecgonine assay. J Anal Toxicol 1995;19:133–8.

16. Isenschmid DS. Cocaine: effects on human performance and behavior. Forensic Sci Rev 2002;14:61–100.

17. Isenschmid DS, Fischman MW, Foltin RW, Caplan YH. Concentration of cocaine and metabolites in plasma of humans following intravenous administration and smoking of cocaine. J Anal Toxicol 1992;16:311–4.

18. Isenschmid DS, Levine BS, Caplan YH. A comprehensive study of the stability of cocaine and its metabolites. J Anal Toxicol 1989;13:250–6.

19. Jackson GF, Saady JJ, Poklis A. Urinary excretion of benzoylecgonine following ingestion of Health Inca Tea. Forensic Sci Int 1991;49:57–64.

20. Jatlow PI, Barash PG, Van Dyke C, Radding J, Byck R. Cocaine and succinylcholine: a new caution. Anesth Analg 1979;58:235–8.

21. Jones AW, Holmgren A, Kugelberg FC. Concentrations of cocaine and its major metabolite benzoylecgonine in blood samples from apprehended drivers in Sweden. Forensic Sci Int 2008;177:133–9.

22. Jufer RA, Walsh SL, Cone EJ. Cocaine and metabolite concentrations in plasma during repeated oral administration: development of a human laboratory model of chronic cocaine use. J Anal Toxicol 1998;22:435–44.

23. Jufer RA, Wstadik A, Walsh SL, Levine BS, Cone EJ. Elimination of cocaine and metabolites in plasma, saliva, and urine following repeated oral administration to human volunteers. J Anal Toxicol 2000;24:467–77.

24. Karch S. A brief history of cocaine. Boca Raton, FL: CRC Press, 1997.

25. Karch S, ed. Drug abuse handbook, 2nd ed. Boca Raton, FL: CRC Press, 2007.

26. Karch S, ed. The pathology of drug abuse, 3rd ed. Boca Raton, FL: CRC Press, 2002.

27. Klette KL, Poch GK, Czarny R, Lau CO. Simultaneous GC/MS analysis of meta- and para-hydroxybenzoylecgonine and norbenzoylecgonine: a secondary method to corroborate cocaine ingestion using nonhydrolytic metabolites. J Anal Toxicol 2000;24:482–8.

28. Kump D, Matulka R, Edinboro L, Poklis A, Holsapple M. Disposition of cocaine and norcocaine in blood and tissues of B6C3F1 mice. J Anal Toxicol 1994;18:342–5.

29. Logan BK. CNS stimulants. Is the driver impaired by drugs? Can blood drug concentrations and DRE evaluation answer this question? Workshop nr 27. American Academy of Forensic Sciences Annual Meeting, 2002; Atlanta, GA.

30. Logan BK, Blaho K, Mandrell T, Berryman HE, Goff ME, Goldberger BA, et al. Effects of death and decomposition on concentrations of cocaine and metabolites in juvenile swine [abstract]. Abstract nr K54. American Academy of Forensic Sciences Annual Meeting, 1998; San Francisco, CA.

31. Logan BK, Peterson KL. The origin and significance of ecgonine methyl ester in blood samples. J Anal Toxicol 1994;18:124–5.

32. Logan BK, Smirnow D, Gullberg RG. Lack of predictable site-dependent differences and time-dependent changes in postmortem concentrations of cocaine, benzoylecgonine, and cocaethylene in humans. J Anal Toxicol 1997;20:23–31.

33. MacDonald S, Mann R, Chipman M, Pakula B, Erickson P, Hathaway A, MacIntyre P. Driving behavior under the influence of cannabis or cocaine. Traffic Inj Prev 2008;9:190–4.

34. Majewska M, ed. Neurotoxicity and neuropathology associated with cocaine abuse. Rockville, MD: Department of Health and Human Services, 1996. National Institute on Drug Abuse research monograph nr 163.

35. Rapaka R, Chiang N, Martin B, eds. Pharmacokinetics, metabolism, and pharmaceutics of drugs of abuse. Rockville, MD: Department of Health and Human Services, 1997. National Institute on Drug Abuse research monograph nr 173.

36. Regidor E, Barrio G, de la Fuente L, Rodriguez C. Non-fatal injuries and the use of psychoactive drugs among young adults in Spain. Drug Alcohol Depend 1996;40:249–59.

37. Romberg RW, Past MR. Reanalysis of forensic urine specimens containing benzoylecgonine and THC-COOH. J Forensic Sci 1994;39:479–85.

38. Saady JJ, Bowman ER, Aceto MD. Cocaine, ecgonine methyl ester, and benzoylecgonine plasma profiles in rhesus monkeys. J Anal Toxicol 1995;19:571–5.

39. Siegel RK. Cocaine hallucinations. Am J Psychiatry 1978;135:309–14.

40. Siegel RK. Cocaine smoking. J Psychoactive Drugs 1982;14:271–359.

41. Siegel RK. Cocaine use and driving behavior. Alcohol Drugs Driving 1987;3:1–8.

42. Smirnow D, Logan BK. Analysis of ecgonine and other cocaine biotransformation products in postmortem whole blood by protein precipitation-extractive alkylation and GC-MS. J Anal Toxicol 1996;20:463–7.

43. Spiehler VR, Reed D. Brain concentrations of cocaine and benzoylecgonine in fatal cases. J Forensic Sci 1985;30:1003–11.

44. Strote J, Range Hutson H. Taser use in restraint-related deaths. Prehosp Emerg Care 2006;10:447–50.

CHAPTER 19

Cannabis

Marilyn A. Huestis

INTRODUCTION

Marijuana (cannabis), hashish, and sinsemilla are psychoactive products of the *Cannabis sativa* plant complex and have been used for its euphoric effects for over 4000 years. Cannabis is self-administered for its mood-altering properties; it is a dependence-producing drug characterized by reversible psychological impairment, by the development of tolerance after frequent cannabis use throughout the day for an extended period, and by an abstinence syndrome after cessation of chronic drug use. A mixture of depressant and stimulant effects is noted at low doses; cannabis acts as a central nervous system (CNS) depressant at high doses. Cannabinoids share effects with other psychoactive drugs yet have a distinct pattern of effects that distinguishes this unique pharmacologic drug class.

The Assyrians incorporated cannabis into their religious rites and as medicine for neurologic and psychiatric diseases. Medicinal properties of the plant were recognized in China 2700 years ago for the relief of pain, muscle spasms, convulsions, epilepsy, asthma, and rheumatism. As with other herbal preparations, however, the unreliability of its potency contributed to the decline in its therapeutic use. Currently, there is growing interest in the biology, chemistry, pharmacology, and toxicology of cannabinoids and in the development of potential cannabinoid medications. It is clear that the endogenous cannabinoid system, which consists of cannabinoid neurotransmitters, receptors, metabolic enzymes and transporters, plays a critical role in physiological and behavioral processes and that cannabis ingestion disrupts normal biological functions.

Cannabis is also the most commonly abused drug in the world, the drug with the highest prevalence in cases involving driving under the influence of drugs, and the source of more positive results in workplace drug tests than any other drug of abuse. For these reasons, it is essential that toxicologists understand cannabis' cognitive, physiological, biochemical, and behavioral effects, as well as the disposition of the drug and its metabolites in biological fluids and tissues.

CHEMISTRY

Cannabis preparations include loose cannabis, kilobricks (the classic Mexican-produced material), buds, sinsemilla, Thai sticks, hashish (cannabis resin), and hash oil. The various parts of the plant differ in their chemical composition. Sinsemilla, a seedless and more potent form of cannabis produced from the unfertilized flowering tops of female cannabis plants, first appeared in 1977 and is usually produced in the U.S.

Δ^9-Tetrahydrocannabinol (THC), the primary psychoactive analyte, is found in the plant's flowering or fruity tops, leaves, and resin. Fig. 1 shows the structure of THC. About 95% of the THC in cannabis is a mixture of monocarboxylic acids that readily decarboxylate upon heating. It was originally believed that a person who orally ingested cannabis without heating would absorb little THC but that if one heated the cannabis prior to ingestion, e.g., baked in marijuana brownies, significant quantities of THC would become available. Later research demonstrated that an individual also can absorb THC from cannabis that has been dried in the sun because decarboxylation releases variable amounts of THC.

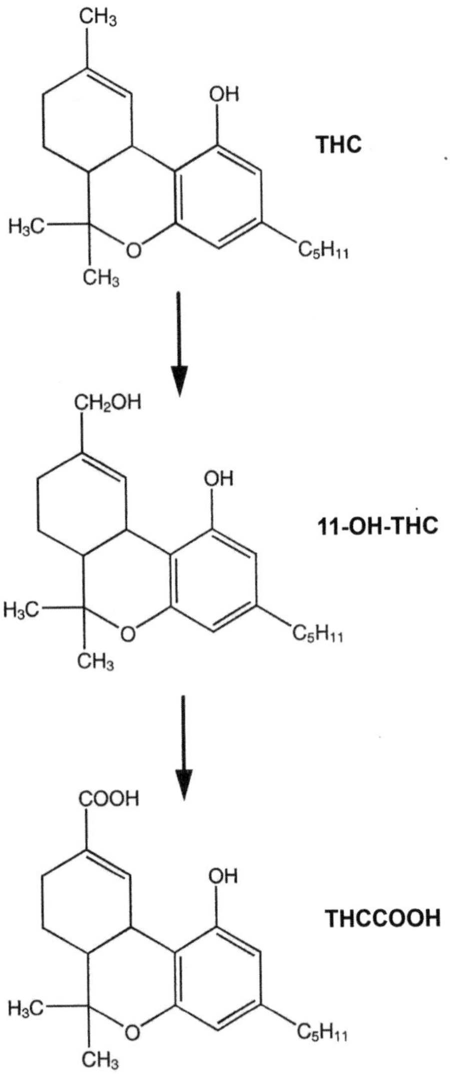

Fig. 1. Major metabolic route for Δ^9-tetrahydrocannabinol (THC), the primary psychoactive component of cannabis, to its equipotent metabolite 11-hydroxy-THC (11-OH-THC) and its primary inactive metabolite, 11-nor-9-carboxy-THC (THCCOOH). THC, 11-OH-THC, and THCCOOH also undergo phase II metabolism with glucuronic acid and sulfates.

Cannabis contains >421 different chemicals, including >60 cannabinoids, nitrogenous compounds, amino acids, hydrocarbons, sugars, terpenes, and simple and fatty acids. Pyrolysis of the drug during smoking yields >2000 compounds, including those that contribute to cannabis' known pharmacologic and toxicologic properties. Other cannabinoids include cannabinol, which is approximately 10% as psychoactive as THC, and cannabidiol, which is not a mood-altering agent but is the subject of extensive research into its therapeutic properties. THC decomposes when exposed to air, heat, or light; exposure to acid can oxidize the compound to cannabinol. Cannabinol is essentially a chemical-degradation product, and its relative abundance increases as samples age. The ratios of these unique cannabinoids depend on the age of the sample, its geographic origin, and the plant strain. The potency of a preparation is described by its THC concentration, usually as the percentage of THC per dry weight of material. Selective cultivation over the years has steadily increased its potency, and there are hydroponic farms capable of growing cannabis with a THC content as high as 40%. A cane-like variety that is devoid of psychoactive effects provides an important source of hemp fiber.

Nomenclature

The structure of THC was elucidated in 1964. Consisting of a tricyclic 21-carbon structure, THC is a volatile, viscous oil that is insoluble in water but highly soluble in lipids. THC contains no nitrogen and has two chiral centers in trans configurations. The pK_a of THC is 10.6. Two different numbering systems, the dibenzopyran (Δ^9) and monoterpene (Δ^1) nomenclatures, are commonly used to describe THC; the dibenzopyran system is used throughout this chapter.

Mechanisms of THC Action

Early research with racemic THC suggested that its mechanisms of actions were nonspecific, perhaps due to disruption of protein structures contained within lipids of cellular and organelle membranes, similar to the effects of anesthetics. It is now clear, however, that the effects of cannabinoids are highly stereospecific. Another hypothesis suggested that THC and the endogenous cannabinoids interacted with specific cannabinoid receptors. Cannabinoids are natural (–) enantiomers with (3R,4R) stereochemistry. Structure–activity investigations have demonstrated that the tricyclic structure, the aromatic ring, and the phenolic group are required for THC's central activity. In addition, animal studies have shown that a C5 hydroxyl group confers potent peripheral activity. Delineating mechanisms of action has been difficult because of THC's demonstrated activity at many sites, including the opioid and benzodiazepine receptors, and its noted effects on prostaglandin synthesis, DNA, RNA, and protein metabolism. Cannabinoids inhibit macromolecular metabolism in a dose-related manner and have a wide range of effects on enzyme systems, hormone secretion, and neurotransmitters. These numerous and diffuse effects have lent support to the nonspecific-interaction hypothesis.

In the last 20 years, our knowledge of cannabinoid pharmacology has increased tremendously. The discoveries have included the identification of central (CB1) and primarily peripheral (CB2) cannabinoid receptors, multiple endogenous ligands termed *eicosanoids* (anandamide, arachidonyl ethanolamine, and others), enzymes for inactivating anandamide (fatty acid amide hydrolase, or FAAH) and arachidonyl ethanolamine (monoacylglycerol lipase), and transporters of endocannabinoids across cell membranes. Many of these findings were made possible by the development of specific cannabinoid receptor antagonists, pharmacologic tools for investigating the endogenous cannabinoid system. Mapping of CB1 receptors in the brain indicated that the distribution of the high-affinity, stereoselective, and pharmacologically distinct brain receptors were anatomically selective. Dense binding was documented in the cerebral cortex, hippocampus, amygdala, striatum, and cerebellum, which are functional areas associated with the most prominent behavioral effects of cannabinoids. CB1 receptors, which are expressed predominantly at nerve terminals, mediate neurotransmitter release. Cannabinoid receptors, which belong to the G protein class of receptors, are present in high amounts and are desensitized and internalized during chronic exposure. The distinct CB2 cannabinoid receptor is involved in immunomodulation.

The endogenous cannabinoid system is involved in the control of locomotion, emotional behavior, cognitive function, cardiovascular responses, pain, feeding behavior, and addiction. THC acts on dopaminergic projections in the brain in a fashion similar to that of noncannabinoid drugs of abuse. THC is thought to stimulate reward circuits in the brain and to act as a direct or indirect dopamine agonist in the projections of the medial forebrain bundle. Stimulation of the brain's reward circuits is an essential characteristic of drugs of abuse. Cannabis produces substantial changes in human behavior that are linked to physiological and biochemical changes. Subjective responses and performance effects are interrelated with other bodily functions, behavior being the highest level of human response. It is the integration of all of cannabis' pharmacologic effects that modifies behavior.

EFFECTS

Cannabis' behavioral effects include feelings of euphoria and relaxation, altered time perception, lack of concentration, impaired learning and memory, and mood changes such as panic reactions and paranoia. This spectrum of behavioral effects is unique and prevents the drug's classification as a stimulant, sedative, tranquilizer, or hallucinogen. Subjective effects of cannabis, such as drug "liking" and "feeling drug effects," may appear after the first puff of a cigarette. Cannabis smoking produces rapid changes in physiological effects, including heart rate, conjunctival suffusion, dry mouth and throat, and increased appetite. Although tachycardia is an expected cannabis effect, less well known is the pronounced hypotension and dizziness that we have observed in our controlled THC research in approximately 25% of participants approximately 10 min after the end of smoking. Individuals who experienced symptomatic hypotension had peak plasma THC concentrations that were about two-thirds higher than those who did not. Also underappreciated is the substantial paranoia that many cannabis smokers experience. Most behavioral and physiological effects of THC return to baseline levels within 3–8 h after exposure, although some investigators have demonstrated residual effects in specific behaviors up to 24 h after drug intake.

By showing that rimonabant, a specific CB1 cannabinoid receptor antagonist, could significantly reduce tachycardia and the subjective effects of smoked THC, we documented for the first time in humans that the cardiovascular and behavioral effects of cannabis were mediated through CB1 cannabinoid receptors.

The most common neurocognitive deficit observed during acute intoxication is impairment of short-term memory. Individuals who are acutely intoxicated during memory encoding demonstrate deficits in spontaneous recall; however, information processed prior to intoxication is unaffected. Memory impairment corresponds well with the distribution of CB1 receptors in brain regions associated with memory, such as the hippocampus and the anterior cingulate. Research studies have indicated that cannabis may decrease accuracy in cognitive and psychomotor tests, impair time estimation, and reduce learning and memory functions. Deficits in motor inhibition, decision making, and inhibitory control were documented for up to 6 h after smoking a high dose (13%) of THC. Less consistent results have been obtained with respect to risk taking after cannabis use.

The acute toxic effects of cannabis include behavioral effects (e.g., panic attacks and psychosis), increased heart rates, and CNS depression. The Drug Abuse Warning Network of the National Institute on Drug Abuse reported 290,563 cannabis-related visits to hospital emergency rooms in 2006, 9.1% of the total number of drug-related visits. The increase in potency of cannabis in the U.S. over the last two decades has led to an increased demand for cannabis treatment. Serious CNS depression may be observed in children after they inadvertently ingest cannabis; however, with supportive care such cases resolve successfully with few residual effects. Although cannabis does not cause death directly, owing to its few effects on respiratory function, the drug is a major contributing factor to motor-vehicle and other accidents.

Simultaneous collection of pharmacodynamic and pharmacokinetic data during controlled cannabis administration has provided insight into the relationship of the drug-induced effects to the concentrations of THC and its metabolites in the blood. THC is rapidly absorbed and distributed to tissues; the initial changes in blood concentration are out of phase (hysteresis) with the physiological and behavioral changes. The counterclockwise hysteresis displayed in plots of effect vs time for heart rate and subjective assessments of the "high" indicates a delay between the effects and plasma THC concentrations (Fig. 2). A counterclockwise hysteresis is generally indicative of a prominent distribution phase, i.e., distribution of drug from the vascular compartment to the drug's site of action, the brain. The subjective "high" effect was found to be directly proportional to the mean plasma THC concentration from approximately 1–4 h after cannabis smoking. This hysteresis makes it difficult to interpret cannabinoid concentrations. For example, the effects observed at the same plasma concentration (e.g., 100 µg/L) can be different, depending on whether the sample was collected during the absorption phase, when effects and concentrations are rapidly increasing, or during the distribution phase after the end of smoking, when concentrations are dropping rapidly (Fig. 2).

Effects remain stable at high concentrations, however. To demonstrate the hysteresis concentration–effect relationship, we continuously collected samples from the start of smoking until approximately 20 min after the end of smoking and collected samples frequently thereafter. These data were the first to demonstrate that peak THC effects occur before the end of smoking, suggesting that individuals titrate their smoked dose to their own comfort level of physiological and behavioral effects. Fortunately, most collections of cannabinoid samples in forensic investigations occur after the end of smoking, and in many cases, after the initial distribution phase is completed, approximately 45–60 min after the start of smoking.

Additional research is needed to define the onset, magnitude, and duration of cannabis' behavioral effects and to characterize the development of tolerance after long-term, frequent exposure. Controversy exists as to whether long-term exposure produces irreversible changes in brain function. Short-term (24-h) neurocognitive impairment of verbal memory, language function, and processing speed compared with controls has been reported, and impairment of memory, executive function, inhibitory control, and psychomotor speed has been documented in frequent cannabis users after 28 days of abstinence. Seven light users [mean (±SD), 10.5 ± 4 joints/week for 3.4 ± 1.6 years], eight moderate users (42 ± 18.2 joints/week for 5.4 ± 4.2 years), and seven heavy users (93.9 ± 15.4 joints/week for 5.3 ± 2.4 years) were tested for multiple neurocognitive measures. All measures were significantly affected by cannabis (P <0.05). Impairment according to the Symbol-Digit Paired Associate Learning, Stroop, reaction-time, and Grooved Pegboard measures were dose dependent (i.e., joints/week) with R^2 values >0.44. Nearly all participants reported smoking cannabis at least daily, often several times per day or several cigarettes per session.

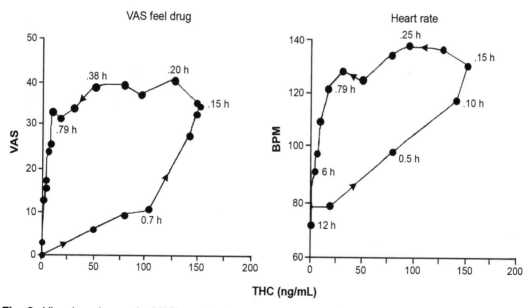

Fig. 2. Visual analog scale (VAS) results for a question ("How strongly do you feel the drug now?") and heart rate in beats per minute (BPM) for a study participant after the smoking of a 3.55% Δ⁹-tetrahydrocannabinol (THC) cigarette. The results (time in hours) illustrate a counterclockwise hysteresis for the concentration–effect curves. *Source:* Modified with kind permission of Springer Science+Business Media. Huestis MA, Smith ML. Human cannabinoid pharmacokinetics and the interpretation of cannabinoid concentrations. In: ElSohly MA, ed. Marijuana and the cannabinoids. Totawa, NJ: Humana Press, 2007:215 (Fig 6).

In our investigation of cognitive function in frequent cannabis users, we compared 45 former heavy users (>5000 occasions in lifetime, <12 occasions in the preceding 90 days), 63 current heavy users (>5000 occasions in lifetime), and 72 nonusers (<50 occasions in lifetime) on tests of neurocognitive ability. The battery of tests assessed executive function, abstract reasoning, sustained attention, verbal fluency, and learning and recall. Assessments occurred on days 0, 1, 7, and 28 after last reported use. Current heavy users performed more poorly than controls on verbal memory tests at baseline and for 7 days of abstinence. Furthermore, the observed impairment in performance was correlated with the concentrations of the inactive THC metabolite 11-nor-9-carboxy-THC (THC-COOH) in urine on admission. By day 28 of abstinence, there were no longer any differences in neurocognitive performance.

Inconsistency in results between studies may be due to differences in the study individuals, methodologies, concurrent use of other illicit drugs, and the abstinence period. We hypothesize that cannabinoids are removed from the brain with sustained cannabis abstinence, eventually normalizing performance. We recently reported residual THC in the whole blood, plasma, and urine of long-term daily cannabis smokers, suggesting that residual THC in the brain could be a mechanism for sustained impairment. Abstinence might permit elimination of cannabinoids from the brain and a return to normal performance.

There are conflicting reports in the literature on cannabis' chronic toxic effects. Such discrepancies may be due in part to differences in experimental protocols, types and potencies of the cannabis materials, schedules and lengths of exposure, characteristics of study participants, and defined end points of effect. Impaired health consequences, including lung damage, behavioral changes, and reproductive, cardiovascular, and immunologic effects, are associated with cannabis use. The condensate yield of cannabis smoke, including potential mutagens, was >50% higher than that of cigarette tobacco smoke, although usually fewer cannabis cigarettes are smoked daily. Cannabinoids readily cross placental membranes and expose the developing fetus. Cannabinoids may affect embryo implantation and sterility, affect child development, and increase vulnerability to substance-abuse problems later in life. Endogenous cannabinoids modulate immune functions via cannabinoid receptors. Cannabinoids alter immune function and decrease host resistance to microbial infections in experimental animal models and in vitro. Given this important immunomodulatory role, cannabinoids may be therapeutic for conditions involving pathologic immune responses.

DRIVING IMPAIRMENT

Driving under the influence of drugs is a serious and preventable problem worldwide. It would be helpful if drug concentrations in biological samples could be linked to performance impairment, as is the case with ethanol; however, the interpretation of data for drugged driving is complicated by such factors as the lack of a linear concentration–effect relationship (hysteresis), drug tolerance, the age and health of the driver, driving experience, drug interactions, road and weather conditions, and, of course, intra- and interindividual differences. The specific effects of cannabis on driving include decreased car-handling performance, increased reaction times, impaired time and distance estimation, inability to maintain headway, lateral travel, subjective sleepiness, lack of motor coordination, and impaired ability to sustain vigilance. These operational effects are consistent with the described behavioral effects. Evaluations of cannabis's effects on driving have taken three approaches: epidemiologic studies of cannabis use and rates of accidents or fatalities, laboratory studies of cognitive or psychomotor impairment, and driving/flying simulator or closed- or open-course driving tests. Each of these approaches offers a valuable and unique perspective on cannabis's effects on driving performance.

Epidemiologic Studies

The advantages of epidemiologic studies are that they examine the effects of drugs on driving skills under authentic conditions. In case-study analyses (e.g., the Grand Rapids study of the effects of alcohol on driving), large numbers of drivers are stopped, performance is evaluated, and biological samples are collected. These types of data provide definitive information about impaired driving performance but are expensive and difficult to conduct, especially if a more invasive collection of samples is required. An important advantage of studying alcohol's effects on driving is that breath concentrations of alcohol, which are less invasive to ascertain than venipuncture, are suitable for estimating blood concentrations; such sampling is not possible for any other drug class. Unfortunately, many of the studies that have examined the frequency of accidents or fatalities among individuals who consume drugs have lacked proper control groups. The value of these studies in predicting possible impairment and linking drug use to increased rates of accidents or fatalities is weakened because the incidence rates of cannabis use in control populations are frequently unknown. An exciting new opportunity available to the field of traffic safety is the advent of sensitive and noninvasive monitoring of oral fluids for drugs. The introduction of on-site oral-fluid tests provides the opportunity for roadside testing and large case–control studies for drugs of abuse. Despite the limitations of earlier work, a number of conclusions can be drawn from them. Cannabis is almost always the most common illicit drug noted in epidemiologic driving studies, and THC concentrations are generally low, <5 µg/L. Such low values are due to the rapid decline in THC concentration after smoking and to the time required to obtain blood samples from drugged drivers. In a high percentage of cases, THC is found in combination with ethanol or other drugs. Driving impairment is frequently evident in THC-positive cases, as witnessed by failures in roadside sobriety checks and by police stops for erratic driving.

Other approaches include responsibility analyses that statistically prove that drivers under the influence of a drug have a higher odds ratio for having an accident than drivers who are on the same road at the same time and who are not under the influence of a drug. Investigators blind to the drug status of each party assign responsibility for the accident under the conditions present at the time of the accident. If a statistically greater number of drivers with cannabis-positive samples are judged responsible for the accident than drivers without cannabis, cannabis is considered to significantly increase the odds for an accident. Many attempts have been made to prove that cannabis increases the odds ratio for driving accidents; however, none of these studies were successful until Drummer et al. (2004) demonstrated that individuals with measurable THC in the blood were significantly more likely to die in a car crash than those without THC in the blood. Moreover, the odds ratio increased to 6.6 if the THC concentration was >5 µg/L. There were many reasons why this proof of cannabis-caused driving impairment was difficult to achieve. First, analysis of cannabinoids is challenging, and a low limit of quantification (LOQ) is difficult to obtain for blood. Second, early investigations did not differentiate between THC and THCCOOH and thus included measurement of the inactive THCCOOH metabolite as an indicator of impairment. Finally, THC concentrations frequently fell below the LOQ before sample collection, which was often more than 4 h after the accident.

Performance Studies

A review of the literature requires careful evaluation of the study design, including appropriate placebo controls, double-blind dose presentation, dosage and route of drug administration, inclusion of more than one dose to demonstrate a dose–response effect, performance task difficulty, and individuals' experience with the task. Generally, the more complex the task, the more sensitive the task is to cannabis impairment. In addition, tasks that are well practiced, such as driving, tend to be more resistant to drug effects. Therefore, laboratory tests that require a divided attention and response to stressful, demanding situations are more likely to demonstrate performance impairment. Another key factor in evaluating reported effects is the availability of simultaneously collected blood samples for measuring THC concentrations. Few performance studies have included measurement of drug concentrations in the blood. Measurements of drug concentration are important because of the difficulty in delivering a specified THC dose via the smoking route. Clinical studies that have included strict controls on smoking dynamics (e.g., number of puffs, time between puffs, hold time, and inhalation time) have reported wide intra- and interindividual variation in blood THC concentrations because of an individual's ability to titrate drug dose.

In general, studies of laboratory performance have demonstrated that sensory functions are not highly impaired but that perceptual functions are significantly affected. Perceptual errors are the most frequently cited errors leading to driving accidents involving ethanol, and such errors could be significant factors in cannabis impairment. The user's ability to concentrate and maintain attention may be decreased during cannabis intoxication. Perceptual motor skills, decision making, and car-handling skills also may be reduced. Impairment of hand–eye coordination is dose related over a wide range of cannabis dosages, and the impairment effects of cannabis and ethanol exposures are additive. Coordination and body-sway decrements have been documented. Stability of stance and deficits in information processing decrease in a dose-related manner after cannabis use. Impairment in immediate and delayed free recall has been observed, but not in recognition memory. The most consistently reported cognitive effect following cannabis use is a disruption of short-term memory.

In 2006, Ramaekers et al. defined performance impairment as a function of THC concentration in serum and oral fluid in or-

der to provide a scientific framework for the development of limits per se for driving under the influence of cannabis. Twenty adults who smoked high-potency THC (up to 500 µg THC/kg) demonstrated impaired executive function in the Tower of London problem-solving task, impaired motor control in the critical-tracking task, increased stop-reaction time in the stop-signal task, and increased commission and omission errors in a choice reaction-time task. THC-induced impairments were still present in the last test period 6 h after smoking. A strong and linear correlation between the THC concentrations in serum and oral fluid was shown, but there was no linear relationship between the magnitude of performance impairment and THC concentrations in oral fluid and serum. The proportion of observations showing impairment or no impairment was evaluated at different THC concentrations to define threshold levels of impairment. Impairment increased progressively in all tasks as a function of the serum THC concentration. The critical-tracking task indicated impairment at serum THC concentrations of 2–5 µg/L, and all tasks were affected at 5–10 µg/L. These investigators suggested that serum THC concentrations between 2 µg/L and 5 µg/L establish the lower interval of THC impairment. The impairment of executive function is consistent with the general observation that the greater the multitasking and reasoning demands placed on a driver, the greater the cannabis-induced impairment. Furthermore, Grotenhermen et al. (2007) concluded from a metaanalysis of existing performance studies that a limit on serum THC concentrations of 7–10 µg/L was appropriate.

Jones et al. (2008) reported blood THC concentrations for individuals who had driven under the influence of cannabis in Sweden over the previous 10 years. Eighteen percent and 30% of individuals suspected of driving under the influence of drugs had THC concentrations ≥0.3 µg/L alone or with other drugs, respectively. The median THC concentration for 8794 cases was 1.0 µg/L. Even when THC was the only identified drug, the individuals in 41% of the cases had

THC concentrations <2.0 µg/L. The authors stated that even if a 2.0-µg/L limit were enacted, the rapid decrease in THC concentrations would allow many individuals to evade prosecution for impaired driving. They suggested that zero-tolerance or LOQ laws are a more pragmatic approach to enforcing legislation for driving under the influence of drugs.

Driving- and Flying-Simulator Studies and Closed-/Open-Course Driving Studies

In general, cannabis use impairs performance in driving-simulator tasks and on open and closed driving courses. Cannabis decreases car-handling performance, increases reaction times, impairs time and distance estimation in a dose-related manner, and affects decision making that relies on these skills; however, improvement in driving performance has been observed in some participants in low-dose cannabis studies. Cannabis use reduced the number of attempts at passing cars or other risky behavior, in contrast to ethanol use, which increased risk taking. As previously mentioned, the more difficult the task, the more apparent is the impairment in performance.

Impairment for up to 24 h was reported in flying-simulator studies following cannabis smoking. Short-term memory, attention, and concentration were affected. Impairment was also related to the difficulty of the task and the age of the pilot. One of the most important aspects of the studies was the lack of pilot awareness of decreased performance or impairment.

In 1998, Robbe conducted a series of driving-simulator and on-the-road driving tests of individuals after they had smoked cannabis. The task most consistently altered was the standard deviation of lateral position, or weaving. The impairment at the highest study dose, 300 µg/kg (approximately 21 mg THC), was equivalent to that of a blood alcohol concentration of ≥0.05 g ethanol/100 mL of blood. In less experienced cannabis users, 100–200 µg/kg (about 7–14 mg THC)

impaired fundamental road tracking in a dose-related manner and reduced the individual's ability to maintain a constant headway with the preceding vehicle for 2.5 h. Combining cannabis with alcohol had an additive effect on impairment of headway maintenance and reaction time.

DEVELOPMENT OF TOLERANCE

Hunt and Jones evaluated the development of tolerance to THC's effects by following the effects of oral 30-mg THC administrations every 4 h for 10–12 days. Subjective ratings of intoxication after 9 days on the maximum daily dose were significantly lower than ratings on the first day of dosing. The heart rate increase produced by smoking a cannabis cigarette also was reduced significantly. Significant loss of tolerance occurred within 24 h, and full recovery to predrug tolerance levels still had not occurred by 12 days after the last oral THC dose. Few pharmacokinetic changes were noted during chronic administration, although the mean total metabolic clearance and the mean initial apparent volume of distribution increased from 605 to 977 mL/min and from 2.6 to 6.4 L/kg, respectively. The finding that the pharmacokinetic changes observed after chronic oral THC administration could not account for the observed behavioral and physiological tolerance suggested that tolerance was due to pharmacodynamic adaptation.

In general, multiple THC exposures throughout the day are needed to develop tolerance to the behavioral and physiological effects of cannabis. Smoking a single cigarette of 1% or 2% THC each day for 28 days did not produce tolerance to cannabis-induced tachycardia. Another study found a possible "reversal" of tolerance in 16 participants who smoked 2–6 cannabis cigarettes per day ad libitum (125–190 mg THC/day) over 3 days. In 1977, Nowlan and Cohen induced tolerance to subjective "high" ratings and heart rate changes in 30 moderate and heavy users who were exposed to 33.7–198.7 mg THC/day for 64 days. Participants smoked 1.7 to 10 cigarettes/day, but only between 4:00 PM and midnight and with 9–12 h of abstinence between days. Subjective "high" ratings and mean heart rates after smoking during the first week were significantly greater than during weeks 5 and 9. After 1 week of abstinence, tolerance recovered only partially to these measures.

In another study in 1976, Jones et al. established substantial cannabinoid dependence and tolerance in participants via administration of 30 mg THC every 4 h (total daily dose, 210 mg) for up to 21 days. The heart rate increase produced by smoking a cannabis cigarette was reduced by >50%. The intensity of subjective effects diminished by 60–80% after 10 days of consuming 10 or 30 mg THC every 3–4 h. Tolerance developed to many other physiological effects, such as on heart rate, orthostatic hypotension, skin and body temperature, salivary flow, intraocular pressure, electroencephalograms, sleep duration and quality, eye tracking, and psychomotor performance. Increasing the single THC dose by 30–50% usually produced a prompt and temporary return of the drug's subjective effects. In addition, tolerance developed more rapidly with a dosing schedule of 20 mg THC every 3 h than with 30 mg every 4 h.

Mild tolerance to the effects of oral THC has been achieved over shorter periods. In 1999, Haney et al. administered 20 or 30 mg THC four times a day for 4 days and monitored the development of tolerance with visual-analog scales. Three of 50 items on the visual-analog scale ("good drug effect," "high," and "stimulated") showed a statistically significant change (50% decrease) from the first to the fourth day of dosing.

THERAPEUTIC USES

There has long been hope that cannabinoids might provide novel approaches to treating human diseases and disorders. The therapeutic usefulness of oral cannabinoids is being investigated for medicinal applications, including analgesia, treatment of acquired immunodeficiency syndrome (AIDS) wasting disease, counteracting spasticity of motor diseases, antiemetic agents following chemotherapy, and antispasmodics in multiple sclerosis. Despite active research into the therapeutic uses of cannabis, behavioral effects have not yet been successfully separated from therapeutic effects. Synthetic analogs and cannabis itself have been used. Dronabinol (Marinol®; Solvay Pharmaceuticals), a synthetic THC, has been available in the U.S. since 1986. Dronabinol is licensed for the treatment of nausea and vomiting associated with cancer chemotherapy. Some oncologists have indicated that smoked cannabis is more effective than the synthetic oral medication because of dronabinol's low and less reliable bioavailability, some patients' inability to tolerate the oral medication, and the absence of other active compounds found in cannabis plant material.

More recently, research has focused on the other cannabinoids present in cannabis, specifically cannabidiol. Cannabidiol does not produce THC's well-known behavioral effects, and evidence exists for its efficacy as an analgesic, anti-inflammatory, antitumor, and antiepileptic medication. In 1999, the National Institutes of Health Institute of Medicine acknowledged the therapeutic potential of cannabinoids and encouraged that well-designed clinical trials be conducted to document efficacy. The dangers and health risks associated with cannabis smoking were deemed inappropriate for pharmacotherapies; however, the development of less toxic forms of delivery was requested. The Volcano Vaporizer delivers THC and other cannabinoids from cannabis plant material without requiring the high pyrolytic temperatures obtained during cannabis smoking. The THC concentrations and pharmacodynamic effects are similar to those obtained after cannabis smoking. Potential therapeutic applications and the passage of medicinal-cannabis laws in multiple states will complicate the interpretation of cannabis test results and drugged-driving laws.

PHARMACOKINETICS

Absorption

Smoked Administration

The smoking route, the principal means of cannabis administration, provides a rapid and highly efficient method of drug delivery, although oral use is not uncommon. Smoked drugs are highly abused in part because of the efficiency and speed of drug delivery from the lungs to the brain. Intense pleasurable and strongly reinforcing effects may be produced, owing to the almost immediate exposure of the CNS to the drug. Prior to harvesting, cannabis plant material contains little active THC. When smoked, the THC carboxylic acids spontaneously decarboxylate to produce THC, with nearly complete conversion upon heating. Pyrolysis during smoking destroys approximately 30% of the THC. Drug availability is further reduced via loss of the drug in the sidestream smoke and that remaining in the unsmoked cigarette butt. The number, duration, and spacing of puffs, the hold time, and the inhalation volume greatly influence the degree of drug exposure. These factors contribute to the high variability (18–50%) in drug delivery by the smoked route; the actual dose is much lower than the amount of THC and THC precursor present in the cigarette. THC can be measured in the plasma within seconds of inhalation of the first puff of cannabis smoke (Fig. 3). Mean (± SD) THC concentrations of 7.0 ± 8.1 µg/L and 18.1 ± 12.0 µg/L were observed after the first inhalation of a low-dose (1.75% THC) and high-dose (3.55% THC) cigarette, respectively. Concentrations continued to increase rapidly, reaching mean peaks of 84.3 µg/L (range, 50–129 µg/L) and 162.2 µg/L (range, 76–267 µg/L) for the low-dose and high-dose cigarette, respectively. Peak concentrations occurred at 9.0 min, prior to initiation of the last puff sequence at 9.8 min. Intra- and interindividual variation in smoking dynamics or topography contributes to the uncertainty in dose delivery and to the actual peak THC concentration achieved, even when the drug is administered under controlled conditions (Fig. 4).

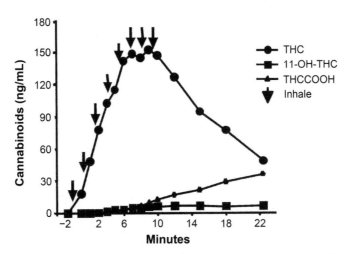

Fig. 3. Mean plasma concentrations (n = 6) of D^9-tetrahydrocannabinol (THC, ●), 11-hydroxy-THC (11-OH-THC, ■), and 11-nor-9-carboxy-THC (THCCOOH, ▲) by gas chromatography–mass spectrometry during smoking of a single 3.55% THC cigarette. Each arrow represents one inhalation or puff on the cannabis cigarette. *Source:* Reprinted with kind permission of Springer Science+Business Media. Huestis MA, Smith ML. Human cannabinoid pharmacokinetics and the interpretation of cannabinoid concentrations. In: ElSohly MA, ed. Marijuana and the cannabinoids. Totawa, NJ: Humana Press, 2007:209 (Fig 1).

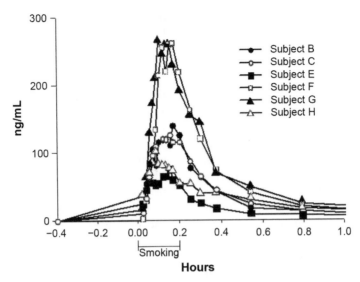

Fig. 4. Individual plasma Δ⁹-tetrahydrocannabinol (THC) time course by gas chromatography–mass spectrometry for six individuals after controlled administration by smoking of a single 3.55% THC cigarette. *Source:* Reprinted from (32) by permission of Preston Publications, A Division of Preston Industries, Inc.

Mean peak plasma concentrations of 11-hydroxy-THC (11-OH-THC) were 6.7 µg/L and 7.5 µg/L for the low and high doses, respectively. THCCOOH concentrations gradually increased and peaked between 0.54 h and 4 h (mean, 1.9 h) at mean concentrations of 24.5 µg/L (range, 15–54 µg/L) and 54.0 µg/L (range, 22–101 µg/L), respectively.

Oral Administration

After oral and sublingual administration of THC, THC-containing food products, or cannabis-based extracts, THC and 11-OH-THC concentrations are much lower than after smoked administration. Bioavailability is reduced to 6–18% after oral use, partly because of degradation of the drug in the stomach and significant first-pass metabolism in the liver to active and inactive metabolites. Two THC peaks are frequently observed because of the enterohepatic circulation. Peak plasma concentrations of THC and THC-COOH after daily oral doses of 10–15 mg Marinol were 2.1–16.9 µg/L within 1–8 h and 74.5–244 µg/L within 2–8 h, respectively.

We recently studied the oral administration of THC-containing hemp oils (in liquid and capsules) and dronabinol (synthetic THC). Six volunteers ingested liquid hemp oil (0.39 and 14.8 mg THC/day), hemp oil in capsules (0.47 mg THC/day), dronabinol capsules (7.5 mg THC/day), and placebo for five consecutive days. THC and 11-OH-THC concentrations were low and never exceeded 6.1 µg/L. Analytes were detectable 1.5 h after initiating dosing with the regimen of 7.5 mg THC/day and 4.5 h after starting the sessions of 14.8 mg THC/day. Tests results for plasma THC and 11-OH-THC were negative for all participants and all doses by 16 h after the last THC dose. THCCOOH was generally detected 1.5 h after the first dose. Plasma THCCOOH concentrations peaked at 3.1 µg/L during dosing with the low-dose hemp oils, whereas the much higher concentrations (up to 43.0 µg/L) found after the higher doses persisted for at least 39.5 h after the end of dosing. These data demonstrate that individuals who use hemp oil with a high THC content (347 µg/g) as a dietary supplement have THC and metabolite concentrations in the plasma comparable to those of patients who use dronabinol for appetite stimulation. Body mass index, maximal drug concentration, and the number of samples positive for THC and 11-OH-THC showed significant correlations.

Compared with THC administered by the smoking route, the onset, magnitude, and duration of pharmacodynamic effects generally occur later with the oral route, and the effects are lower in magnitude and have a delayed return to baseline. The pharmacodynamic effects of cannabis taken orally are due to both THC and its equipotent metabolite, 11-OH-THC.

Oromucosal Administration

Because of the chemical complexity of cannabis plant material compared with synthetic THC, cannabis extracts are being explored as therapeutic medications. Reproducible extracts of *C. sativa* plants containing high percentages of THC and cannabidiol are combined in different ratios to target specific diseases or illnesses. The efficacies of these extracts are being evaluated in clinical trials for analgesia, migraine, and treatment of spasticity and related complications in affected patients. THC–cannabidiol extracts are administered sublingually to avoid first-pass metabolism by the liver. Sativex® (GW Pharmaceuticals), a new cannabis-based medicinal extract, contains equivalent amounts of cannabidiol and THC and has been approved in Canada to treat neuropathic pain and spasticity associated with multiple sclerosis and in three European countries to treat related syndromes. THC and 11-OH-THC concentrations peak at about 120 and 160 min, respectively, after a 20-mg dose and are low, approximately 3–7 µg/L and 6–8 µg/L.

Distribution

THC has a large volume of distribution (initially reported as 10 L/kg but recently estimated to be approximately 4 L/kg), and 97–99% of the drug is bound to proteins in the plasma, primarily albumin and lipoproteins.

Highly perfused organs, including the lung, heart, brain, and liver, are rapidly exposed to the drug. Tissues that are less highly perfused accumulate the drug more slowly as the THC redistributes from vascular into peripheral compartments. The high solubility of THC in lipids promotes the concentration and prolonged retention of the drug in fat. Detectable concentrations of THC have been found in fat biopsies obtained >4 weeks after smoking. The formation of fatty acid conjugates of THC and 11-OH-THC has been suggested, and such conjugates may increase the stability of the compounds in fat. Slow release of the drug from fat and significant enterohepatic recirculation contribute to THC's long drug half-life in plasma, reported to be >4.1 days when isotopically labeled THC and sensitive analytical procedures have been used. Less sensitive methods and shorter monitoring periods yield much lower estimates of the terminal half-life.

In 2005, Mura et al. reported THC concentrations in paired samples of postmortem blood and brain. THC concentrations in brain exceeded those in blood in all 12 cases, but the two matrices showed no significant correlation. THC was still detectable in the brain when it was no longer measurable in blood. 11-OH-THC, the equipotent metabolite, was found in the brain at similar but lower concentrations, and concentrations of THCCOOH, the inactive metabolite, were equivalent to or slightly higher than those for THC. We recently documented measurable THC in whole blood and plasma for at least 7 days, and for as long as 24 days in the urine of the heaviest cannabis users during 24 h of monitored abstinence in our research unit. Yet to be determined is whether chronic daily cannabis users also demonstrate cognitive impairment at times when residual THC is still measurable, albeit at low concentrations, in the blood and brain.

Metabolism

Fig. 1 summarizes the primary metabolic route and metabolites of THC. Hydroxylation of THC at C9 by the hepatic cytochrome

P450 enzyme system yields the equipotent metabolite, 11-OH-THC, which early investigators believed to be the true psychoactive analyte. Cytochrome P450s 2C9, 2C19, and 3A4 are involved in the oxidation of THC. More than 100 THC metabolites, including di- and trihydroxy compounds, ketones, aldehydes, and carboxylic acids, have been identified. Although 11-OH-THC predominates as the first oxidation product, significant amounts of 8β-OH-THC and lower amounts of 8α-OH-THC are formed. Much lower plasma 11-OH-THC concentrations (approximately 10% of the THC concentration) are found after cannabis smoking than after oral administration (50–100% lower). Mean peak 11-OH-THC concentrations occur approximately 13 min after the start of smoking. Other tissues, including lung, may contribute to the metabolism of THC, although alternative hydroxylation pathways may be more prominent. Cytochrome P450 2C9 is believed to be primarily responsible for the formation of 11-OH-THC, whereas P450 3A catalyzes the formation of 8β-OH-THC, epoxy-hexahydrocannabinol, and other minor metabolites. Excretion of 8β,11-dihydroxy-THC in urine has been proposed as a good biomarker of recent cannabis use, although other investigators have not validated the use of this compound. To our knowledge, it has not been used in forensic or clinical investigations.

Oxidation of active 11-OH-THC produces the inactive metabolite, THCCOOH. THCCOOH and its glucuronide conjugate are the major end products of biotransformation in most species, including humans. Phase II metabolism of THCCOOH involves addition of glucuronic acid and, less commonly, other moieties (such as sulfate, glutathione, amino acids, and fatty acids) via the C11 carboxyl group. The phenolic hydroxyl group may also be a target. It is also possible to have two glucuronic acid moieties attached to THCCOOH, although steric hindrance at the phenolic hydroxyl group may be a limiting factor. To date, the degree of cannabinoid glucuronidation in the plasma remains unclear. It appears that THC glucuronidation is low after both oral and smoked administration; less is known about the percentages of free and total 11-OH-THC and THCCOOH in plasma. In general, conjugate concentrations are believed to be lower in the plasma after intravenous or smoking administration of cannabis, but they may be much greater after oral drug administration. There is no indication that the glucuronide conjugates are active, although data to support this supposition are lacking. Further complicating the issue is the lack of knowledge of the stability of cannabinoid glucuronides in authentic samples of plasma and whole blood stored under different conditions. Additional research to define these important pharmacokinetic parameters is necessary to improve the interpretation of cannabinoid tests and to determine these compounds' influence, if any, on models estimating the time of last cannabis use.

Addition of the glucuronide group improves water solubility, thereby facilitating excretion, but renal clearance of these polar metabolites is low because of their extensive binding to proteins. No significant differences between males and females have been reported with respect to metabolism of these compounds. Owing to the rapid decrease in THC concentrations, THCCOOH concentrations gradually increase and surpass concurrent THC concentrations shortly after the completion of smoking. The time course of the detection of THCCOOH in plasma is much longer than for either of the active analytes.

Elimination

Mean THCCOOH amounts of 93.9 ± 24.5 µg and 197.4 ± 33.6 µg were measured in urine over a 7-day period following the smoking of 1.75% and 3.55% THC cigarettes containing approximately 18 and 34 mg THC, respectively. These amounts represented a mean of only 0.54% ± 0.14% and 0.53% ± 0.09% of the original amount of THC in the low-dose and high-dose cigarettes, respectively. The small percentage of the total dose that was found in urine as THCCOOH is not surprising, considering the many factors that influence THCCOOH excretion after smoking. Most of the THC dose is excreted in the feces (30–65%) rather than in urine (20%). Another factor affecting the low amount of recovered dose is the measurement of a single metabolite, THCCOOH, in urine. Humans produce numerous cannabinoid metabolites, most of which are not measured or included in the calculation of percent dose excreted.

Eighty percent to 90% of the urinary elimination of a single THC dose occurs within 5 days, and the excreted products are primarily hydroxylated and carboxylated metabolites. Approximately 20% of acidic urinary metabolites are conjugated and unconjugated THCCOOH. The acid-linked THCCOOH glucuronide conjugate has an excretion half-life of 3–4 days. Urinary THCCOOH concentrations generally decrease rapidly until a concentration of 20–50 µg/L is reached, even in the most frequent cannabis smokers. At this point, the concentration decreases at a much slower rate. The subsequent slow release of the THC stored in the tissues extends the window of drug detection.

Interestingly, in almost all cases after smoked or oral THC administration and near the end of the drug's elimination in the urine, negatively and positively testing samples become interspersed. This phenomenon appears to be due to several factors, including variable release of THC from the tissues and inconsistent dilution in the urine. The presence of a positive result in a urine test after one or more negative test results may be misinterpreted as new cannabis use. Creatinine normalization of urinary cannabinoid concentrations is a method for dealing with this phenomenon (see below). No significant pharmacokinetic differences between chronic and occasional cannabis users have been substantiated.

Terminal Elimination Half-Lives of THCCOOH

The elimination of THC and THCCOOH is described with models of two or more compartments. Initially THC and THCCOOH are eliminated rapidly, followed by much longer terminal elimination half-lives. Accurately determining terminal half-lives requires sensitive procedures for quantifying low cannabinoid concentrations and a monitoring period of 4–5 half-lives. Many investigations have used short sampling intervals of 8–72 h, which underestimate terminal half-lives. Slow release of THC from lipid storage compartments and significant enterohepatic circulation contribute to THC's long terminal half-life in the plasma, which has been reported as >4.1 days in chronic cannabis users. A plasma elimination half-life of up to 12.6 days was observed in a chronic cannabis user when THCCOOH concentrations were monitored for 4 weeks. Elimination half-lives for plasma THCCOOH were measured with isotopically labeled THC and sensitive analytical procedures, yielding mean values of 5.2 ± 0.8 days and 6.2 ± 6.7 days for frequent and infrequent cannabis users, respectively. Similarly, the terminal urinary-excretion half-life of THCCOOH was estimated as 3–4 days.

Most data for the plasma THC concentration have been collected following acute exposure; less is known of plasma THC concentrations in frequent users. Mean plasma concentrations of THC, 11-OH-THC, and THCCOOH in frequent cannabis users of 0.86 ± 0.22 µg/L, 0.46 ± 0.17 µg/L, and 45.8 ± 13.1 µg/L, respectively, were noted a minimum of 12 h after the last smoked dose. Recent research on the heaviest cannabis users participating in our studies over the last 15 years showed quantifiable THC in the blood and plasma for >7 days during sustained cannabis abstinence. Of 28 daily cannabis users residing on a closed research unit with no access to the drug, 15 tested positive for >24 h for whole-blood THC concentrations greater than the method LOQ of 0.25 µg/L. The whole-blood samples of six participants had THC concentrations that were still greater than this limit after 7 days of monitored abstinence, with three of the six participants having THC concentrations >1 µg/L. We stress that these concentrations were found only in individuals who were long-term daily cannabis smokers; individuals who smoked less frequently than daily produced negative results in tests of whole blood within 8 h of cannabis use. In addition, the 0.25-µg/L LOQ that was achieved via two-dimensional gas chromatography–mass spectrometry (2D-GC/MS) with cryofocusing is much lower than the limit of most analytical procedures and lower than the cannabinoid-reporting threshold of most laboratories.

Plasma Cannabinoid Concentrations

THC can be detected in the plasma immediately after the first cannabis puff. Concentrations continue to increase rapidly. After the smoking of one cannabis cigarette of 1.75% or 3.55% THC, peak concentrations were 50–129 µg/L (mean, 84.3 µg/L) and 76–267 µg/L (mean, 162.2 µg/L), respectively. Mean THC concentrations 15 and 30 min after smoking were approximately 60% and 20% of peak concentrations, respectively. Within 2 h, THC concentrations were ≤5 µg/L. The time of detection of THC (GC/MS LOQ, 0.5 µg/L) was 3–12 h after the low-THC dose (1.75%) and 6–27 h after the high-dose cigarette (3.55% THC).

Plasma concentrations of 11-OH-THC were approximately 6–10% of concurrent THC concentrations for up to 45 min after the start of smoking. Peak 11-OH-THC concentrations were noted at a mean of 13.5 min (range, 9.0–22.8 min) after the start of smoking. 11-OH-THC concentrations decreased gradually, with mean detection times of 4.5 h and 11.2 h after the two doses. THCCOOH concentrations in the plasma increased slowly and plateaued for up to 4 h. This inactive metabolite was detected in the plasma of all participants by 8 min after the start of cannabis smoking. Peak concentrations were consistently lower than peak THC concentrations but were higher than peak 11-OH-THC concentrations. Mean peak THCCOOH concentrations were 24.5 µg/L (range, 15–54 µg/L) and 54.0 µg/L (range, 22–101 µg/L) after the low- and high-dose cannabis cigarettes, respectively. Following the smoking of a 1.75% THC cigarette, THCCOOH was detected from 48 to 168 h (mean, 84 h). Detection times ranged from 72 to 168 h (mean, 152 h) after the smoking of a 3.55% THC cigarette.

Peak plasma concentrations after oral administration occur after approximately 2–3 h and reach concentrations of 4.4–11 µg/L after a 20-µg dose. THC concentrations decline to <10 µg/L by 4–6 h after ingestion. Peak effects were noted to occur 2.5–3.5 h after the ingestion of cannabis-laced brownies.

Interpretation of Plasma Cannabinoid Concentrations

Scientific advances have improved our ability to identify and quantify cannabinoids in body fluids; however, the interpretation of results remains a difficult task. Forensic scientists receive frequent requests to interpret the significance of cannabinoid concentrations in blood samples from individuals involved in accidents, criminal investigations, and traffic violations. Relevant facts, such as the amount of drug used, the route of administration, and history of use, are generally unknown. Unlike the situation with blood ethanol concentrations, practical presumptive concentrations of blood THC are more difficult to relate to measurable impairment. Because of the chemical and pharmacokinetic differences between cannabis and ethanol, we cannot use ethanol as a model for relating drug concentrations to effects. Consequently, the patterns of distribution to and elimination from active sites are quite different for these two molecules. Pharmacokinetic and pharmacodynamic models that account for the dispositional differences of THC may be more successful in defining blood concentrations that can be associated with the psychoactive effects of THC.

THC and THCCOOH are found predominantly in the plasma fraction of blood, where 95% to 99% of these cannabinoids are bound to albumin and lipoproteins. Cannabinoid concentrations in whole blood are approximately one-half the concentrations in plasma, due to the low partition coefficient of drug into erythrocytes.

Although the interpretation of blood cannabinoid results continues to be controversial, some general concepts have wide support. A dose–response relationship has been demonstrated for smoked THC and the THC concentration in plasma. It is well established that plasma THC concentrations begin to decline before the occurrence of peak effects, although THC effects appear rapidly after the initiation of smoking. We found peak cannabis effects at the time of equivalent THC and THCCOOH concentrations, within 30–45 min after initiation of smoking. Individual drug concentrations and ratios of the cannabinoid metabolite concentration to the parent drug concentration have been suggested as potentially useful indicators of recent drug use. Measurement of 8β,11-dihydroxy-THC, a cannabinoid biomarker with a short time course of detection, has not found widespread use as a biomarker of recent use. Accurate prediction of the time of cannabis exposure would be helpful in establishing the role of cannabis as a contributing factor to accidents.

Mathematical Models for Predicting Elapsed Time Since Last Cannabis Use

We have presented two mathematical models for predicting the elapsed time after smoking from cannabinoid measurements of single plasma samples from individuals who smoke cannabis less frequently than daily. The models were derived from cannabinoid data obtained from a controlled clinical study of acute smoking and were validated with cannabinoid data from the literature. Model I is based on the plasma THC concentration, and model II is based on the ratio of the concentrations of plasma THCCOOH to plasma THC (Fig. 5). The models were applied to all published studies at the time that included plasma concentrations; both models correctly predicted times of cannabis exposure within 95% confidence intervals (CIs) for >90% of the samples evaluated. Initially, plasma THC concentrations <2.0 μg/L were excluded for two reasons: the possibility of residual THC concentrations in frequent smokers and concerns at the time about accuracy of quantification at low concentrations. In the following formulas, T represents the elapsed time in hours between the beginning of cannabis smoking and blood collection, and CI represents the 95% CI for the estimate of T. Subscripts 1 and 2 refer to models I and II, respectively, and brackets denote the concentrations of THC or THCCOOH in micrograms per liter.

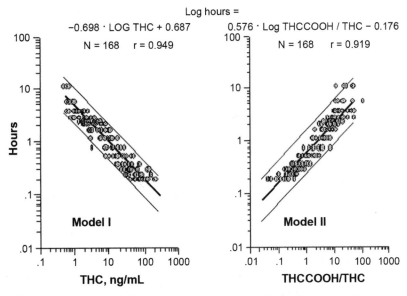

Log hours =

−0.698 · LOG THC + 0.687   0.576 · Log THCCOOH / THC − 0.176

N = 168   r = 0.949   N = 168   r = 0.919

Model I

THC, ng/mL

Model II

THCCOOH/THC

Fig. 5. Predictive mathematical models for estimating the elapsed time in hours of last cannabis use from plasma Δ⁹–tetrahydrocannabinol (THC) and 11-nor-9-carboxy-THC (THCCOOH) concentrations measured by GC/MS. *Source:* Reprinted from (33) by permission of Preston Publications, A Division of Preston Industries, Inc.

Model I: $\quad \log T = -0.698 \cdot \log[\text{THC}] + 0.687$

$$\log \text{CI}_1 = \log T \pm 1.975 \sqrt{0.030 \left\{ 1.006 + \frac{(\log[\text{THC}] - 0.996)^2}{89.937} \right\}}$$

Model II: $\quad \log T = (0.576 \cdot \log[\text{THCCOOH}]/[\text{THC}]) - 0.176$

$$\log \text{CI}_2 = \log T \pm 1.975 \sqrt{0.045 \left\{ 1.006 + \frac{(\log[\text{THCCOOH}]/[\text{THC}] - 0.283)^2}{123.420} \right\}}$$

The models predict last cannabis use within a specified interval of time. The magnitude of the interval is smaller when the elapsed time between cannabis use and blood collection is shorter.

More recently, the validation of these predictive models was extended to include the estimation of the time of use after multiple THC doses and at low THC concentrations (0.5–2 µg/L), situations that were not included in the development of the original models. Model I was less accurate with primarily overestimates that benefit the accused. After single doses, model II had primarily underestimates that are less favorable in forensic testing because they tend to predict earlier cannabis use that could be misinterpreted as a period of impaired performance. Model II was more accurate and had no underestimates for multiple doses. The most accurate approach applied a combination of models I and II by predicting a single time interval defined by the lowest and highest 95% confidence limits of the two models. For all 717 plasma samples, 99% of the predicted times of last use were within this combination interval, 0.9% were overestimated, and none were underestimated. For 289 plasma samples collected after multiple doses, 97% were correct with no underestimates. All time estimates were correct for 77 plasma samples with THC concentrations between 0.5 µg/L and 2 µg/L, a low concentration interval not previously examined.

These models also appeared to be valuable when they were applied to the small amount of data from published studies of oral ingestion that was available at the time the models were developed. Additional studies were performed to determine if the predictive models could estimate last use after multiple oral doses, a route of administration more popular with the advent of cannabis therapies. Eighteen study participants received oral THC as Marinol or as hemp oil containing THC. The actual times between THC ingestion and blood collection spanned 0.5 to 16 h. Use of the combined CI yielded correct predicted times 96.7% of the time, with one overestimate (0.65 h) and two underestimates (0.13 h, 0.57 h).

When used in combination, the models correctly predict the time of cannabis use within a 95% CI for more than 95% of cases involving a single smoked cannabis cigarette, two smoked cannabis cigarettes, or multiple oral doses of THC-containing preparations in individuals who use cannabis less than daily. Most controlled studies of cannabis administration have indicated impairment of tasks related to normal driving functions for up to 6–8 h after use. A small number of studies have extended this time interval to 24 h for complex, multitasking operations. The predictive models provide an objective means of estimating recent cannabis use within the 95% CI. Such estimation can be combined with evidence derived from the known pharmacodynamic effects of cannabis to develop a case of impairment. It is important to remember that the models are not designed to predict time of last use in daily cannabis users, who may have significant residual THC concentrations. To date, no controlled studies have applied the models to daily cannabis users. In addition, because of the limited distribution of THC and THCCOOH into red blood cells, it is important to remember that when comparing whole-blood and plasma concentrations of THC and/or THCCOOH, it is necessary to double the whole-blood concentrations before applying the models.

In 1996, Daldrup developed a model for predicting cannabis impairment that calculates a cannabis influence factor (CIF) from plasma THC, 11-OH-THC, and THCCOOH concentrations expressed in micrograms per liter. Cannabinoid concentrations and CIFs were compared with driving errors and impairment in >100 cases of drivers stopped by the roadside in Germany. A CIF ≥10 indicated impairment of driving ability.

Urine Cannabinoid Concentrations

The interpretation of positive results in urine tests requires an understanding of the excretion pattern of cannabinoid metabolites in humans; however, there are limited urinary-excretion data available from controlled clinical studies to aid in such interpretation. Substantial interindividual and interdose variation exists in the patterns of THCCOOH excretion. The THCCOOH concentration in the first sample collected after smoking is indicative of how rapidly the metabolite appears in urine. Mean THC concentrations in the first urine sample were 47 ± 22.3 μg/L and 75.3 ± 48.9 μg/L after smoking one 1.75% THC cigarette and one 3.55% THC cigarette, respectively. Approximately 50% of the study participants' first urine samples after the low dose and 83% of the first urine samples after the high dose were positive by GC/MS analysis (THCCOOH cutoff concentration, 15 μg/L). THCCOOH concentrations in the first urine sample are dependent on the relative potency of the cigarette, the elapsed time following drug administration, smoking efficiency, and individual differences in drug metabolism and excretion. Mean peak urine THC-COOH concentrations were 89.8 ± 31.9 μg/L (range, 20.6–234.2 μg/L) and 153.4 ± 49.2 μg/L (range, 29.9–355.2 μg/L) following the smoking of approximately 15.8 mg and 33.8 mg THC, respectively. Mean times of peak urine concentration were 7.7 ± 0.8 h after the 1.75% THC dose and 13.9 ± 3.5 h after the 3.55% THC dose. Although peak concentrations appeared to be dose related, individual values varied by as much as 12-fold.

The drug-detection time, i.e., the time after drug administration that an individual tests positive, is an important factor in the interpretation of urine drug results. Detection time is dependent on pharmacologic factors (e.g., drug dose, route of administration, rates of metabolism and excretion) and analytical factors (e.g., assay sensitivity, specificity, accuracy). Mean detection times in urine following smoking vary considerably among individuals, even in controlled smoking studies in which cannabis dosing is standardized and smoking is paced by computer. During the terminal elimination phase, consecutive urine samples may fluctuate between testing positive and testing negative as the THC-COOH concentrations approach the cutoff concentration. After smoking a 1.75% THC cigarette, three of six study participants had additional positive urine samples interspersed among negatively testing samples. This intermittent pattern had the effect of producing much longer detection times for the last positive sample. When the 15-μg/L cutoff for THCCOOH currently required by the Department of Health and Human Services (DHHS), the Department of Transportation, and the Department of Defense for regulated urine drug testing in the U.S. is applied, mean GC/MS THCCOOH-detection times for the last positive urine sample following the smoking of a single 1.75% or 3.55% THC cigarette were 33.7 ± 9.2 h (range, 8–68.5 h) and 88.6 ± 23.2 h (range, 57–122.3 h), respectively. GC/MS detection times were shorter than those obtained with less specific immunoassays.

Significant differences exist between the available immunoassay products, and these differences affect the efficiency of detection of cannabinoid use. Therefore, knowledge of the sensitivity and specificity of an immunoassay is essential for its proper use. Reports of prolonged drug excretion are the basis for the common assumption that cannabinoid metabolites can be detected in the urine for a week or more. The accuracy, sensitivity, and specificity for detecting cannabinoids and their metabolites are unique to a particular immunoassay and may change over time. It is important that individuals who select assays and those who interpret the test results be aware of the qualitative and quantitative changes that can and do occur. In general, the detection times of cannabinoid metabolites in urine have decreased as the specificities of the various immunoassays have increased. This decrease has improved not only the correlations between immunoassays but also the correlations between immunoassays and confirmation procedures; however, the increase in specificity also has contributed to the noted decrease in the time course of detection of acute cannabis use.

Detection times for urinary cannabinoids vary substantially across assays, individuals, doses, and cutoff concentrations. Monitoring acute use by a cannabinoid immunoassay with a 50-µg/L cutoff concentration provides only a narrow window of detection (1–2 days) after one 1.75% or 3.55% THC cigarette. GC/MS detection times with the federally mandated 15-µg/L cutoff were approximately twice as long as mean detection times with a 50-µg/L immunoassay cutoff. Immunoassay thresholds are higher than GC/MS thresholds because multiple cannabinoids cross-react in the immunoassay and only THCCOOH (after basic or enzymatic hydrolysis) is quantified in the confirmation assay. Mean detection times were longer (1–6 days after smoking) with an immunoassay with a 20-µg/L cutoff. Consecutive urine voids may produce positive or negative results as drug concentrations approach the cutoff concentration. Quantitative results that are not adjusted for creatinine concentration reflect the typical variation in cannabinoid excretion values caused by differences in the water content of urine samples. Cannabinoid concentration or dilution in urine has an important effect on detection times for the last positive urine sample and in interpreting results of urine tests.

Interpretation of Urine Cannabinoid Concentrations

The detection of cannabinoids in the urine is indicative of prior cannabis exposure, but the long excretion half-life of THC in the body, especially in chronic cannabis users, makes it difficult to predict the timing of past drug use. In a single extreme case, the individual's urine was positive by immunoassay at a concentration of >20 µg/L for up to 67 days after the last drug exposure. This individual had used cannabis heavily for >10 years. Urine samples from a naive user, however, may test negative by immunoassay only a few hours after smoking of a single cannabis cigarette. Nevertheless, a positive result in a urine test for cannabinoids indicates only that drug exposure has occurred. The result provides no information on the route of administration, the amount of drug exposure, when drug exposure occurred, or the degree of impairment.

Normalization of Urine Cannabinoid Concentrations to the Urine Creatinine Concentration

Normalization of the cannabinoid drug concentration to the urine creatinine concentration aids in distinguishing new cannabis use from prior cannabis use and reduces the variation in drug measurements due to variable dilution of the urine. Given the long half-life of drug in the body, especially in chronic cannabis users, toxicologists are frequently asked to determine whether a positive result in a urine test represents a new episode of drug use or continuing excretion of residual drug. The amount of creatinine in random urine samples varies, depending on the degree of urine concentration. In 1983, Hawks first suggested creatinine normalization for urine test results to account for variation in the urine volume in the bladder. Whereas urine volume is highly variable because of changes in liquid, salt, and protein intake, exercise, and age, creatinine excretion is much more stable. In 1984, Manno et al. recommended that an increase of 150% in the creatinine-normalized cannabinoid concentration above that of the previous sample be considered indicative of a new episode of drug exposure. If the increase is greater than or equal to the selected threshold, then new use is predicted. This approach had received wide attention for potential use in treatment and employee-assistance programs, but there was limited evaluation of the usefulness of this ratio under controlled-dosing conditions.

We conducted a controlled clinical study of the excretion profile of creatinine and cannabinoid metabolites in cannabis smokers. Fig. 6 shows that normalization of the urinary THCCOOH concentration to the urinary creatinine concentration produces a smoother excretion pattern and facilitates interpretation of consecutive results of urine drug tests. A receiver operating characteristic (ROC) curve was constructed from sensitivity and specificity data for 26 different cutoffs that ranged from increases of 10% to increases of 200% in the ratios of two creatinine-normalized urine cannabinoid concentrations. The most accurate (85.4%) ratio was 50% in cannabis users who smoked less than daily (sensitivity, 80.1%; specificity, 90.2%; false-positive prediction, 5.6%; false-negative prediction, 7.4%). When the previously recommended increase of 150% was applied as the threshold for new use, the sensitivity of detecting new use was only 33.4%, the specificity was high at 99.8%, and the overall accuracy of prediction was 74.2%. To further substantiate the validity of the derived ROC

curve, we evaluated urine cannabinoid metabolite and creatinine data from another controlled clinical trial that specifically addressed water dilution as a means of sample adulteration. Values for sensitivity, specificity, accuracy, percent false positives, and percent false negatives were 71.9%, 91.6%, 83.9%, 5.4%, and 10.7%, respectively, when the 50% criterion was applied. These data indicate that selecting a threshold to evaluate sequential creatinine-normalized drug concentrations in urine can improve the ability for distinguishing residual excretion from new drug use.

An increase of >50% in the creatinine-normalized cannabinoid concentration above that of the previous sample is considered indicative of a new episode of drug exposure in individuals who are less-than-daily users. In long-term daily cannabis users, THCCOOH concentrations initially drop off rapidly, with the 50% criterion proving accurate for predicting new cannabis use, according to cannabis treatment providers; however, heavy chronic users have smaller decreases in urinary cannabinoid excretion later in the elimination time course. Increases of >150% in creatinine-corrected concentrations for urine samples collected from chronic users have been suggested as an indicator of new cannabis use.

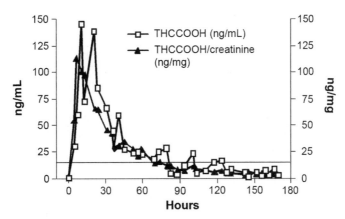

Fig. 6. Urinary excretion profile of 11-nor-9-carboxy-Δ^9-tetrahydrocannabinol (THCCOOH, □) as measured by GC/MS in one study participant following the smoking of a single 3.55% THC cigarette. The horizontal line at 15 ng/mL represents the current GC/MS cutoff used in most testing programs. The urinary THCCOOH concentrations (nanograms per milliliter) normalized to urine creatinine concentrations (milligrams per milliliter) are illustrated (▲). *Source:* Reprinted from (26) by permission of Preston Publications, A Division of Preston Industries, Inc.

We recently reported the time course of THCCOOH elimination in the urine for 60 cannabis users during 24-h monitored abstinence on a closed research unit for up to 30 days. We screened 6158 urine samples by immunoassay. Samples with values ≥50 µg/L were classified as positive, and results were confirmed by GC/MS for measurements ≥15 µg/L. The maximum creatinine-normalized THCCOOH concentration occurred in the first urine sample in 60% of the individuals; in 40%, peaks occurred as long as 2.9 days after admission. The creatinine-corrected initial THCCOOH concentrations were divided into three groups (0–50 µg/g, 51–150 µg/g, and >150 µg/g). There were statistically significant correlations between groups and the number of days until the first negatively and the last positively testing urine samples (mean number of days were 0.6 and 4.3 days, 3.2 and 9.7 days, and 4.7 and 15.4 days for the three groups, respectively). These data provide guidelines for interpreting the results of urine tests for cannabinoids and suggest appropriate detection windows for differentiating new cannabis use from residual drug excretion.

Measurement of THC and 11-OH-THC in Urine as Indicators of Recent Cannabis Use

For many years, THC and 11-OH-THC were believed to be absent in urine samples after cannabis administration. Kemp et al. discovered that THC and 11-OH-THC could be detected if urine was hydrolyzed with β-glucuronidase from *Escherichia coli* rather than from *Helix pomatia* (a snail) prior to GC/MS analysis. The authors proposed that the presence of THC and 11-OH-THC in the urine indicated recent cannabis use; however, urine samples were collected for only 8 h after controlled THC administration. Recently, we monitored urinary cannabinoid excretion in 33 chronic cannabis smokers, who all resided on our secure research unit under 24-h continuous medical surveillance. All urine samples were collected individually ad libitum for up to 30 days, hydrolyzed

with a tandem *E. coli* β-glucuronidase/base procedure, and analyzed for THC, 11-OH-THC, and THCCOOH with an LOQ of 2.5 µg/L. Although many of the chronic cannabis users had no detectable THC in their urine, extended THC excretion of greater than 72 h was observed in 7 individuals during monitored abstinence. THC was detected in urine for up to 24 days after cessation of cannabis use. 11-OH-THC and THCCOOH were detectable in samples from these individuals for up to 30 days. This study was the first time that extended urinary excretion of THC and 11-OH-THC had been documented. These results negated their effectiveness as biomarkers of recent cannabis exposure and substantiated the long terminal elimination times for urinary cannabinoids following chronic cannabis smoking.

Cannabinoids in Oral Fluid

Oral fluid also is a suitable sample for monitoring cannabinoid exposure and is being evaluated for driving under the influence of drugs, drug treatment, workplace drug testing, and clinical trials. Oral fluid offers advantages, including ease and noninvasiveness of collection, possible use as an indicator of recent cannabis smoking (depending on the cutoff used), a closer relationship to blood concentrations than urine, and reduced potential for sample adulteration because of observed collection procedures. Proponents of this matrix for roadside drug testing in Europe initially advanced the development of oral-fluid technologies. The Roadsite Testing Assessment studies (ROSITA and ROSITA II) evaluated the best biological matrices (urine, oral fluid, or sweat) for monitoring drugged driving. Although police, toxicologists, and policy personnel selected oral fluid as the most promising matrix, the available oral fluid–collection devices and assays did not perform with acceptable sensitivity, specificity, and reliability. One of the major problems of measuring cannabinoids in oral fluid is the low recovery from the collection device. Investigators have reported that THC recoveries from many of these collection devices are <50%. Most screening methods are adapted from urine testing and target THCCOOH with cutoffs that are too high and detection rates that are too low. These technical problems are being addressed, and testing procedures for oral fluid are improving at a rapid pace. Many drug-testing programs are converting from urine monitoring to monitoring of this new alternative matrix.

THC, rather than 11-OH-THC or THC-COOH, is the primary cannabinoid analyte in oral fluid after cannabis use. The oral mucosa is exposed to high concentrations of THC during smoking and is the major source of THC found in oral fluid. After intravenous administration of radiolabeled THC, no radioactivity could be demonstrated in oral fluid at a LOQ of 0.5 µg/L. Despite these reports, we found that THC concentrations in oral fluid correlated well with plasma concentrations after the initial contamination of oral fluid by smoking was cleared (Fig. 7). After smoking a 3.55% THC cigarette, one individual had a THC concentration of 5800 µg/L in the first oral fluid sample collected at 0.2 h and a concentration of 81 µg/L in the sample collected at 0.33 h. Initially, THC concentrations in oral fluid were up to 20-fold higher than the concentrations in simultaneously collected plasma samples. From 0.4 to 4.0 h, the mean (± SD) ratio of the THC concentration in oral fluid to that in plasma was 1.18 ± 0.62. In addition, we found no measurable 11-OH-THC or THCCOOH in oral-fluid samples collected immediately and up to 7 days after cannabis smoking at a GC/MS LOQ of 0.5 µg/L. Similarly, we detected no 11-OH-THC and THCCOOH in oral-fluid samples from 22 documented cannabis users. Oral fluid collected with the Salivette collection device (Sarstedt) was positive for THC in 14 of these 22 participants. Although no 11-OH-THC or THCCOOH was identified, cannabinol and cannabidiol were found besides THC. THC concentrations in oral fluid correlate temporally with plasma cannabinoid concentrations and behavioral and physiological effects, but wide intra- and interindividual variation precludes the use of oral-fluid concentrations as indicators of drug impairment.

In a study reported in 2007, Kauert et al. collected serum samples from 10 individuals who smoked cannabis containing 18 mg and 36.5 mg THC. The mean concentrations at the end of smoking (47.8 ± 35.0 µg/L and 79.1 ± 42.5 µg/L, respectively) decreased to <1 µg/L at 6 h. The highest THC concentrations in oral fluid occurred in the first collection at 0.25 h (900 ± 589 µg/L and 1041 ± 652 µg/L for the low and high doses, respectively).

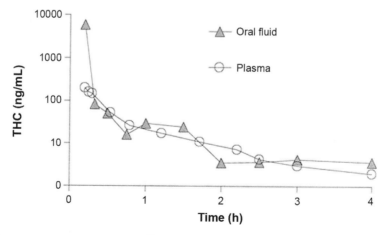

Fig. 7. Simultaneous measurement of Δ^9-tetrahydrocannabinol (THC) in oral fluid and plasma by GC/MS (cutoff concentration, 0.5 mg/mL) in a human study participant over 4 h after the smoking of a single cannabis cigarette (3.55%). *Source:* Reprinted from (27) by permission of Preston Publications, A Division of Preston Industries, Inc.

THC concentrations decreased in oral fluid to 18 µg/L over 6 h. The interpretation of cannabinoid results for oral fluid depends on the assay LOQ, the cannabinoid analyte of interest, and cutoff concentrations.

GC-MS/MS and 2D-GC/MS procedures with LOQs of 10 ng/L have been developed for THC and its metabolites. These low detection limits have permitted investigators to quantify cannabinoids in oral fluid for longer periods after smoking and to measure the THCCOOH present in oral fluid at concentrations of picograms per milliliter. With these methods, THC can be detected for 24 h, and THCCOOH can be detected for 48 h. One report identified THCCOOH glucuronide in oral fluid and noted that THCCOOH glucuronide constituted 64.5% of the total THCCOOH concentration 48 h after smoking. Identifying THCCOOH glucuronide in oral fluid might have the advantages of longer detection windows and an absence of passive contamination by cannabis smoke.

Current practice is to measure THC in oral fluid, but sidestream cannabis smoke has been shown to contaminate oral fluid with THC. The peak THC concentration reported for oral-fluid samples collected from passively exposed individuals was 7.5 µg/L. Studies of passive cannabis exposure appear to indicate that positive THC results in tests of oral fluid can occur shortly after cannabis smoke exposure, but results become negative within an hour. Consequently, when very recent passive exposure to cannabis smoke can be ruled out, one can conclude that a positive result in an oral-fluid test provides credible evidence of active cannabis use.

Cannabinoids in Sweat

Sweat testing is a noninvasive technique for monitoring drug exposure over a 7-day period and is useful in treatment, criminal justice, and employment settings. The advantages of sweat testing include noninvasive collection, reduced potential for adulteration, and continuous monitoring during the sweat-patch wear period. Disadvantages

include the availability of only a single commercially available sweat-collection device (the PharmChek™ patch from PharmChem), minor allergic reactions to the patch, variable sweat production within and between individuals, and the paucity of data for interpreting test results. Typically, the patch is worn for 7 days and exchanged for a new patch once each week during visits to the treatment clinic or parole officer. Theoretically, this approach permits constant monitoring of drug use throughout the week, thereby extending the window of drug detection and improving test sensitivity. As with oral-fluid testing, however, the development of this analytical technique is ongoing, and much has yet to be learned about the pharmacokinetics of cannabinoid excretion in sweat, the potential for THC reabsorption by the skin, possible degradation of THC on the patch, and the adsorption of THC onto the patch itself. The collection device does not accurately measure the volume of sweat collected; therefore, the amount of drug collected per patch is reported, rather than the concentration of the drug in sweat. Furthermore, the amount of sweat excreted and collected varies, depending on the amount of exercise and the ambient temperature.

Cannabinoids were first detected by radioimmunoassay in apocrine sweat in 1989. THC is the primary analyte detected in sweat, with little 11-OH-THC and THCCOOH. THC concentrations ranged from 4–38 ng/patch in 20 heroin abusers who wore the PharmChek patch for 5 days during detoxification. Sweat was extracted with methanol and analyzed by GC/MS.

The Substance Abuse and Mental Health Services Administration (SAMHSA) guidelines proposed for testing of cannabinoids in sweat with the PharmChek patch are a screening cutoff of 4 ng THC/patch and a confirmation cutoff of 1 ng THC/patch. To date, only one study on the excretion of cannabinoids in sweat following controlled THC administration has been published. We tested daily and weekly sweat patches from seven individuals who were administered oral doses of up to 14.8 mg THC/day for five consecutive days. In this study of oral THC administration, no daily or weekly patches had THC concentrations above the LOQ; concurrent plasma THC concentrations were all <6.1 µg/L. Oral ingestion of up to 14.8 mg THC daily does not produce a THC-positive sweat patch. No similar studies that followed the controlled smoking of cannabis have been reported.

We had the opportunity to monitor THC excretion from previously self-administered cannabis in 11 daily smokers after initiation of abstinence. Participants resided on our secure research unit under continuous medical monitoring. PharmChek sweat patches worn for 7 days were analyzed for THC by GC/MS. The LOQ for the method was 0.4 ng THC/patch. Sweat patches worn the first week of abstinence had THC amounts greater than the SAMHSA-proposed 1 ng-THC/patch cutoff concentration for federal workplace testing. The mean (± SE) amount of THC detected was 3.85 ± 0.86 ng THC/patch. Eight of 11 individuals had negatively testing patches by the second week, and one study participant produced THC-positive patches for 4 weeks of monitored abstinence (Fig. 8). With the proposed federal cutoff concentrations, most daily cannabis users will have a positively testing sweat patch in the first week after ceasing drug use and a negative patch in subsequent weeks, although patches may remain positive for 4 weeks or more.

Cannabinoids in Hair

Tests of drugs in hair are frequently used in forensic investigations, drug-treatment research, and drug testing in nonfederal workplaces. There are multiple mechanisms for the incorporation of cannabinoids in hair. THC and its metabolites may diffuse from the blood into the hair bulb from the surrounding capillaries, from sebum secreted onto the hair shaft, and/or from sweat excreted onto the skin surface. Drug may also be incorporated into hair from the environment. That cannabis is primarily smoked provides an opportunity for contamination of hair by THC in the air. Controlled experiments have shown that drugs in solution applied to hair strands can be incorporated. Environmental contamination of hair remains a controversial subject, with most investigators having demonstrated drug incorporation despite extensive washing procedures. Others contend that the use of a combination of polar and nonpolar washing solvents and comparisons of drug concentrations in wash solutions and hair extracts reveal external contamination. A concern for reducing the possibility of external contamination has motivated SAMHSA to propose guidelines for screening cutoffs for cannabinoids in hair at 1 pg/mg for cannabinoids and 0.05 pg/mg for THC-COOH for confirmation testing.

Monitoring drug use with hair testing has distinct advantages, including a wide window of drug detection, a less invasive procedure for sample collection, and the ability to collect a similar sample at a later time; however, one of the weakest aspects of testing for cannabinoids in hair is the low sensitivity of drug detection in this alternative matrix. Basic drugs such as cocaine and methamphetamine concentrate in hair because of ionic bonding to melanin, the pigment in hair that determines hair color. The more neutral and lipophilic THC is not highly bound to melanin, thus producing much lower THC concentrations in hair compared with other drugs of abuse. Usually, THC is present in hair at a higher concentration than its THCCOOH metabolite (usually in low concentrations in the range of picograms per milligram). The advantage of measuring THCCOOH is its absence in cannabis smoke; the issue of passive THC exposure from the environment can thus be avoided.

The analysis of cannabinoids in hair is challenging because of the high analytical sensitivity that is required. Tandem GC/MS and 2D-GC/MS are the most common analytical techniques. A novel approach to screening hair samples for cannabinoids uses a rapid, simple GC/MS screening method for THC, cannabinol, and cannabidiol without derivatization. The method is a sensitive screen for cannabis detection, with GC/MS

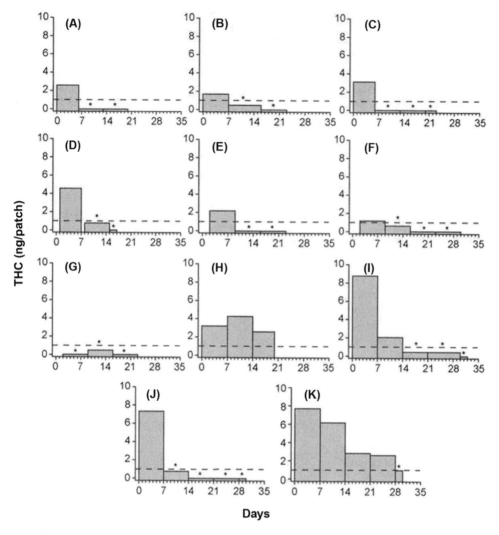

Fig. 8. Δ⁹-Tetrahydrocannabinol (THC) excreted in the sweat of 11 tested individuals. Dashed line indicates the cutoff concentration of 1.0 ng/patch proposed by the Substance Abuse and Mental Health Services Administration. Asterisk indicates a THC amount less than the assay's limit of quantification (0.4 ng/patch). *Source:* Reprinted from (*37*) with permission from Elsevier.

identification of THC recommended as a confirmatory procedure.

It is difficult to conduct controlled cannabinoid-administration studies on the disposition of cannabinoids in hair because of the inability to differentiate administered drug from previously self-administered cannabis and the low rates of incorporation of cannabinoids into hair. We studied THC and THCCOOH in 53 hair samples from 38 documented cannabis users: 18 daily users and 20 who smoked cannabis 1–5 days/week.

History of cannabis use was documented by questionnaire, urinalysis, and controlled, double-blind administration of smoked or oral THC. All participants had tested positive for urine cannabinoids at the time of hair collection. Additional hair samples were collected after the participants had smoked two 2.7% THC cigarettes or taken multiple oral THC doses. Cannabinoid concentrations in hair were measured by ELISA and GC-MS/MS. Positive ELISA screening results (5 pg cannabinoids/mg hair) occurred in only 65% of daily smokers and 35% of nondaily smokers. Detection rates before and after the smoked or oral doses were not significantly different. Thirty-six percent of the participants had no detectable THC or THCCOOH at the LOQs of 1.0 pg/mg and 0.1 pg/mg of hair, respectively. THC only, THCCOOH only, and both cannabinoids were detected in 3.8%, 26%, and 34% of the study participants, respectively. GC-MS/MS detection rates for daily cannabis users and nondaily users were significantly different (85% and 52%, respectively). Detection rates in hair samples from African Americans (n = 40) and Caucasians (n= 13) were not significantly different. For samples with detectable cannabinoids, the concentration ranges were 3.4–>100 pg THC/mg and 0.10–7.3 pg THCCOOH/mg of hair. THC and THCCOOH concentrations were positively correlated. Eighty-three percent of the samples that screened positive were confirmed by GC-MS/MS at a cutoff concentration of 0.1 pg THCCOOH/mg of hair.

Hair grows at a rate of about 1 cm/month, providing an opportunity to segment hair to determine periods of drug use over time. Studies that have tried to relate time of drug use with its presence in specific hair segments have had inconsistent results. Kintz et al. used segmental hair analysis to indicate the time of drug exposure in drug-facilitated sexual assault, and others have measured antibiotics in hair to monitor hair growth and to tie the presence of drugs to known times of drug administration. Other investigators have administered deuterated cocaine and shown that the drug can be found throughout the hair shaft. These data are consistent with the theory that drugs in sweat may bathe the hair shaft and deposit drug along the length of the hair follicle. Despite these issues, it does appear that higher and more frequent drug use is usually reflected in higher hair concentrations. Most of our knowledge of drug concentrations in hair is derived from basic drugs such as cocaine, amphetamines, and opiates. There are almost no data from research with controlled cannabinoid administration to help interpret the results of cannabinoid hair tests. The lack of findings can be attributed to the fact that THC is neutral and not bound to hair via ionic mechanisms that are important to the incorporation of basic drugs.

Passive Inhalation

Environmental exposure to cannabis smoke can occur through passive inhalation of sidestream and exhaled smoke. Several research studies have indicated that it is possible to produce detectable concentrations of cannabis metabolites in the urine and plasma after passive inhalation of cannabis smoke, although the conditions required to produce such positive results were unrealistic and extreme. It is generally agreed that passive exposure is not a valid explanation for a positive result in a urine test, although this conclusion remains commonly used in workplace and forensic settings.

ANALYSIS

THC binds readily to glass and plastic. This fact must be taken into consideration throughout all analyses, including preparation and storage of cannabinoid calibrators and quality-control materials. THC adsorption from solutions can be minimized with storage in amber silylated glassware at a basic pH or in an organic solvent.

Screening

The objective of the initial screening test is to identify true positive samples with a minimum number of unconfirmed positive results. To accomplish this goal, high immunoassay sensitivity must be balanced with high specificity to reduce the number of samples that require expensive and time-consuming GC/MS confirmation. Selecting an appropriate testing methodology requires knowledge of the type of available sample, the analyte's metabolic profile, and the assay's characteristics. The nature and abundance of specific metabolites in different biological matrices must be known. Initial testing or screening methodologies for cannabinoids in body fluids include immunoassays and thin-layer chromatography (TLC). A wide variety of immunoassays are available, including enzyme immunoassays, fluorescence polarization immunoassays, radioimmunoassays, cloned enzyme donor immunoassays, kinetic interaction of microparticles in solution, and recently introduced biochip assays (Randox) that screen for multiple drug classes simultaneously in a single sample.

Urine is usually tested without sample preparation because of the high concentrations of drug and/or metabolites and the low concentrations of other interfering components, such as proteins and lipids. The cross-reactivity of the immunoassay's antibodies to drug metabolites, including glucuronides, is important in method selection. Most immunoassays contain antibodies directed against THCCOOH, the primary urinary metabolite, although cross-reactivities vary considerably for THC, 11-OH-THC, cannabidiol, cannabinol, and the glucuronides. This specificity toward THCCOOH makes these assays appropriate for urinalysis because little free THC or 11-OH-THC is present in urine; however, a much greater percentage of the cannabinoids in oral fluid, sweat, and hair is parent THC. Glucuronide metabolites constitute a high percentage of the cannabinoid metabolites excreted in urine, but the combined cross-reactivity of glucuronide metabolites and the abundance of free carboxy metabolites provide adequate sensitivity to obviate hydrolysis of urine before screening. Cutoff values for initial screening tests of urine include 20 µg/L, 50 µg/L, and 100 µg/L. In April 1988, DHHS guidelines for testing urine for the federal sector established the initial test (screen) cutoff for cannabinoids at 100 µg/L but subsequently lowered the cutoff to 50 µg/L. We conducted a controlled study of cannabis administration via smoking and collected individual urine samples for evaluating multiple immunoassays at three cutoff concentrations and

for GC/MS confirmation. The advantages of the use of authentic samples instead of fortified samples supplemented to contain only the target analyte include the presence of a variety of conjugated and nonconjugated human cannabinoid metabolites. A further advantage is the information gained from urine samples collected over an extended period after smoking. The nature and relative concentrations of cannabinoid metabolites change over time, and a controlled clinical study provides the opportunity to evaluate urine samples with distinct metabolic patterns. Lowering the cutoff concentration to 50 µg/L increased sensitivity in all immunoassays (sensitivity range, 57.0–79.5%) with minimal loss in specificity. Specificity, or the true-negative rate, decreased slightly when the cutoff concentration was lowered to 50 µg/L. Unconfirmed positive screening results (false-positive tests) increased from 1.0% to 2.6%. The correlation between screening and confirmation also is important, considering the high labor and instrumentation costs of the confirmation assay. Thus, we demonstrated that lowering the cutoff to 50 µg/L greatly increased the identification of true-positive samples with little increase in false-positive screening results.

Additional challenges have arisen in immunoassay tests for cannabinoids in urine. The introduction of nonsteroidal anti-inflammatory drugs initially increased the number of nonconfirmed positive results in immunoassays, but manufacturers rapidly changed antibodies to eliminate the source of cross-reactivity. Another challenge arose with the widespread popularity of THC-containing foodstuffs. Hemp oil, a health food product prepared by crushing hemp seeds, was found to contain up to 300 µg/g THC in some U.S. products and up to 1500 µg/g in Swiss hemp oil. THC content is dependent on the effectiveness of cannabis seed cleaning and oil-filtration processes. Ingestion of these materials could produce positive results in immunoassay and confirmatory cannabinoid tests. Government pressure to eliminate the illicit THC in these products was successful in reducing the probability of a positive result in a urine test from this source. New challenges will continue to occur. Currently, the therapeutic usefulness of oral cannabinoids is being investigated for various medicinal applications, as mentioned above. Use of these products could produce positive results in urine drug tests, depending on the potency, route of administration, and magnitude and chronicity of use. We demonstrated with a controlled oral-administration protocol that low-concentration hemp oils (total daily dose, 0.39–0.47 µg/day) taken in accordance with the manufacturer's recommendations produced few positive results in cannabinoid immunoassay screens, whereas high-concentration hemp oils (total daily dose, 14.8 µg/day) and synthetic THC in the form of Marinol (7.5 µg/day) produced frequent and long-lasting positive results in urine tests.

TLC may also be a sensitive screening method for cannabinoids in urine. Early studies of THC metabolism used classic TLC methods. Commercial applications of these systems are available for the identification of THCCOOH in urine, and although both the times required for testing and technologist times may be greater than with immunoassays, a number of samples may be tested simultaneously and at a reduced cost in some instances. TLC methods are specific for the THCCOOH metabolite and include alkaline hydrolysis, extraction, concentration, separation, and visualization steps. Fast Blue BB is the staining reagent of choice for visualization; sensitivity limits of 5–10 µg/L THCCOOH have been achieved.

Oral fluid also is a suitable specimen for screening for the presence of cannabinoids. SAMHSA proposed a screening cutoff for oral fluid of 4 µg/L for cannabinoids and a confirmation cutoff of 2 µg/L for THC. Oral fluid contains much higher concentrations of parent THC than THCCOOH, which is present in the range of picograms per milliliter. Oral fluid–screening kits generally have adapted urine assays to function for oral fluid, in some cases limiting assay sensitivity. Another common difficulty encountered in oral-fluid testing is the adsorption of can-nabinoids to the oral fluid–collection device. Different manufacturers have resolved this problem by developing buffers that free cannabinoids from the device; however, these buffers dilute the cannabinoid concentrations in oral fluid and frequently interfere with liquid chromatography–MS (LC-MS) analysis because of the salts and proteins in the buffer. With a cannabinoid screening cutoff for oral fluid of 3 µg/L and a confirmation THC cutoff of 1.5 µg/L, 3.22% of 77 218 oral fluid samples sent to a large drug-testing laboratory were positive. This result is similar to the urine cannabinoid–positive rate for laboratories of 3.17% with federally mandated cutoff concentrations. Unfortunately, the data available from well-controlled clinical studies to aid in our interpretation are limited.

Whole blood, plasma, and tissues also are screened for the presence of cannabinoids, generally in postmortem and human-performance laboratories (for drugged driving). Cannabinoid concentrations in whole blood are approximately one-half the concentrations in plasma samples, because of the low partition coefficient of the drug into erythrocytes. Simple preparation steps, such as dilution, protein precipitation, or single-step solvent extraction, may be required with some methodologies; more-extensive extraction and concentration schemes may be required for other immunoassays. It is essential that calibrator and quality-control samples be prepared in the same matrix as the samples to be tested in order to account for matrix effects. The cutoff concentration of the immunoassay also may require adjustment for adequate screening of cannabinoid concentrations in different matrices. Method validation is essential for each matrix to instill confidence in the accuracy of the screening process. THC cross-reacts poorly with the antibodies found in most of the commercially available reagents, and a small number of cases featuring high THC concentrations and low THCCOOH concentrations (e.g., samples collected immediately after smoking) may produce negative results when assayed with THCCOOH-specific reagents.

However, THCCOOH concentrations begin to rise during smoking, increase over time, and have a much longer time course of detection than the parent compound.

Drugs that have been eluted from sweat patches may also be screened with appropriate immunoassay reagents. The cutoff concentrations for THC, the primary analyte in sweat, are much lower than for cannabinoids in urine screening. It is essential that immunoassays be validated for the sweat matrix. Sweat contains many additional compounds, including various oils that may interfere with some immunoassays. Only a single commercial laboratory offers sweat collection and testing; sweat testing in research settings generally involves analyzing sweat directly via confirmation procedures, bypassing the screening step.

Drug testing of hair is increasing in workplace drug testing and in forensic investigations. The screening assay is highly important because of the high cost of confirmatory testing with this matrix. Sample-preparation steps are necessary, including carefully washing the hair to reduce external contamination and to remove natural oils and hair-care products. Extraction of drugs from the hair sample is necessary before screening, and a wide variety of methods has been applied, from simple organic extractions to full dissolution of the hair matrix with enzyme mixtures or strong base. Many times, a hair sample is cut into small segments before or after hair washing or reduced to a powder by grinding in a ball mill after hair washing to improve homogenization of the sample and analyte-extraction efficiency. The extract may require neutralization of the pH and buffering before the immunoassay or radioimmunoassay. One of the most difficult aspects of hair testing is verifying that the extraction of the drugs from the complex matrix is complete. Fortification of hair segments or samples of powdered hair does not ensure that the analytes have been incorporated into the hair in the same manner as after drug consumption in vivo. Thus, quality-control and proficiency tests frequently include hair samples from authenticated drug users to compare performance within and between laboratories. Sensitive immunoassays that are capable of measuring the low nanogram-per-milligram concentrations of cannabinoids in hair and that have good cross-reactivity to THC are preferred for hair testing. Method validation and preparation of calibrators in the hair matrix are critical for adequate performance.

Confirmation

Confirmation of cannabinoid results requires a chemical technique based on a scientific principle that is different from that of the initial test (e.g., immunoassay for screening and chromatography for confirmation). Confirmation methodologies include TLC, GC, high-performance liquid chromatography, and GC/MS. Ideally, the sensitivity of the confirmation assay should be equal to or greater than the sensitivity of the initial test method. Selected ion monitoring, full-scan ion monitoring, chemical-ionization methods, and direct probe insertion GC/MS are used for cannabinoid confirmation. Sample preparation for cannabinoid testing frequently includes a hydrolysis step to free cannabinoids from their glucuronide conjugates. Most GC/MS confirmation procedures for urine measure total THCCOOH after either enzymatic hydrolysis with β-glucuronidase or, more commonly, alkaline hydrolysis with sodium hydroxide. Alkaline hydrolysis appears to efficiently hydrolyze the THC-COOH–glucuronide ester linkage.

GC/MS confirmation of THC, 11-OH-THC, and THCCOOH provides adequate sensitivity and specificity for a wide variety of biological tissues. Several deuterated THCCOOH materials are available as internal standards and are recommended to obtain results of the highest accuracy. Also available are compounds with multiple deuterium ions, which provide adequate resolution of deuterated ions from native ions for use in full-scan ion-monitoring techniques. Carboxyl and hydroxyl groups on the THC, 11-OH-THC, and THCCOOH molecules require derivatization to increase their volatility and improve chromatographic performance. Trimethylsilyl and methyl derivatizing reagents are frequently used to achieve acceptable chromatography and sensitivity. Electron-ionization MS of cannabinoids after alkaline hydrolysis and derivatization with one of a wide variety of derivatization reagents was made achievable for most forensic toxicology laboratories by the availability of low-cost, bench-top GC/MS instruments. The increased selectivity of chemical-ionization techniques has also become readily available with the release of several new bench-top instruments. One of the most sensitive methods for THCCOOH detection uses negative-ion chemical-ionization MS of the methyl ester trifluoroacetate derivative. Sensitivity limits of 10 ng/L THC-COOH in blood, plasma, or urine matrices can be achieved because of the high ionization efficiency and selectivity. Metastable ion–detection techniques are also available for applications that require highly sensitive methods, e.g., pharmacokinetic studies. GC/MS confirmation is still superior to LC-MS/MS applications for cannabinoids, although LC-MS/MS has the advantage of permitting direct analysis of metabolites that are more polar and their glucuronides without hydrolysis and derivatization.

Compared with other drugs of abuse, the analysis of cannabinoids presents difficult challenges. THC and 11-OH-THC are highly lipophilic and are present in low concentrations in body fluids and tissues. Complex sample matrices, i.e., blood, sweat, and hair, require multistep extractions to separate cannabinoids from endogenous lipids and proteins. Care must be taken to avoid low cannabinoid recoveries caused by their high affinities to glass and plastic containers and to collection devices for alternative matrices. Cannabinoid-extraction techniques include liquid–liquid extractions and solid-phase extraction with multiple single- and mixed-mode polymeric and ion-exchange columns. Sample preparation for urine cannabinoid testing may include enzymatic hydrolysis with β-glucuronidase or, more commonly, alkaline hydrolysis to free THC-COOH from the glucuronide conjugate. Most GC/MS procedures used for confirmation of urine results use a 15-µg/L cutoff and are specific for THCCOOH. Assays may include a hydrolysis step before the analysis of cannabinoids in blood or plasma, but this step is rarely used. The importance of glucuronide derivatives of cannabinoids in blood and plasma remains a contested issue. The efficiency of glucuronide hydrolysis in cannabinoid-extraction methods should be routinely evaluated by inclusion of a THC-COOH glucuronide quality-control sample. This sample can be prepared from a pool of cannabinoid-positive samples or from samples spiked with THCCOOH glucuronide.

2D-GC/MS with cryofocusing is superior to one-dimensional systems in the separation of analytes from interfering substances, as in the detection of drugs in complex matrices. The technology frequently yields improved sensitivity and reduces labor and time-intensive extraction procedures. Enhanced resolution is achieved by means of a pneumatically controlled switch (Deans switch) and cryofocusing with the cryotrap. The Deans switch diverts column flow from a primary (1°) column to a secondary (2°) column of different stationary phase. A short section (<1 m) of capillary column (restrictor) connects the 1° column to the primary detector. The choice of primary detector is selected according to the analytes of interest. Restrictor dimensions vary depending on the dimensions of the 1° and 2° columns, column pressures, and flow rates. Sections (heart cuts) of the chromatogram containing analytes from the 1° column are rerouted to the 2° column for further chromatographic separation and final detection by mass analysis. Cryofocusing sharpens the chromatographic signal by decreasing the signal band width of the target analytes. Compounds eluting off the 1° column are trapped in a 10-cm region at the head of the 2° column, which is maintained at low temperature. Analytes are released for further chromatographic separation on the 2° column by rapidly increasing the cryotrap temperature.

In many procedures, sensitivity is the limiting factor in cannabinoid analysis. The measurement of THCCOOH in oral fluid and hair represents two of our most challenging confirmation assays. THC is present in oral fluid and hair in higher concentrations but also can be deposited via passive exposure of oral fluid to THC in environmental smoke and external contamination of hair from environmental sources of THC. The advantage of measuring THCCOOH in oral fluid and hair is that it is a biomarker of in vivo ingestion of cannabis and eliminates the concern of passive exposure and environmental contamination. GC-MS/MS has been required in most cases to accurately quantify low THC-COOH concentrations in these matrices, but 2D-GC/MS now offers a lower-cost alternative, and with equipment currently available in most toxicology laboratories.

CONCLUSIONS

Cannabinoids are one of the most important classes of illicit drugs for the toxicologist. Understanding its pharmacodynamic effects and pharmacokinetics in a wide variety of matrices is critical for the analysis and interpretation of cannabinoid concentrations in biological fluids and tissues.

SUGGESTED READING

1. Agurell S, Halldin M, Lindgren JE, Ohlsson A, Widman M, Gillespie H, Hollister L. Pharmacokinetics and metabolism of delta 1-tetrahydrocannabinol and other cannabinoids with emphasis on man. Pharmacol Rev 1986;38:21–42.
2. Ameri A. The effects of cannabinoids on the brain. Prog Neurobiol 1999;58:315–48.
3. Azorlosa JL, Heishman SJ, Stitzer ML, Mahaffey JM. Marijuana smoking: effect of varying delta 9-tetrahydrocannabinol content and number of puffs. J Pharmacol Exp Ther 1992;261:114–22.
4. Barnett G, Licko V, Thompson T. Behavioral pharmacokinetics of marijuana. Psychopharmacology (Berl) 1985;85:51–6.
5. Blows S, Ivers RQ, Connor J, Ameratunga S, Woodward M, Norton R. Marijuana use and car crash injury. Addiction 2005;100:605–11.
6. Cone EJ, Huestis MA. Relating blood concentrations of tetrahydrocannabinol and metabolites to pharmacologic effects and time of marijuana usage. Ther Drug Monit 1993;15:527–32.
7. Cone EJ, Johnson RE. Contact highs and urinary cannabinoid excretion after passive exposure to marijuana smoke. Clin Pharmacol Ther 1986;40:247–56.
8. Cone EJ, Johnson RE, Paul BD, Mell LD, Mitchell J. Marijuana-laced brownies: behavioral effects, physiologic effects, and urinalysis in humans following ingestion. J Anal Toxicol 1988;12:169–75.
9. Daldrup T. Cannabis im Straßenverkehr. Abschlußbericht des im Auftragdes Ministeriums für Wirtschaft und Mittelstand, Technologie under Verkehr des Landes Nordrhein-Westfalen durchgeführten Untersuchungsvorhabens. Düsseldorf: 1996.
10. Devane WA, Dysarz FA 3rd, Johnson MR, Melvin LS, Howlett AC. Determination and characterization of a cannabinoid receptor in rat brain. Mol Pharmacol 1988;34:605–13.
11. Devane WA, Hanus L, Breuer A, Pertwee RG, Stevenson LA, Griffin G, et al. Isolation and structure of a brain constituent that binds to the cannabinoid receptor. Science 1992;258:1946–9.
12. Drummer OH, Gerostamoulos J, Batziris H, Chu M, Caplehorn J, Robertson MD, Swann P. The involvement of drugs in drivers of motor vehicles killed in Australian road traffic crashes. Accid Anal Prev 2004;36:239–48.
13. Giroud C, Ménétrey A, Augsburger M, Buclin T, Sanchez-Mazas P, Mangin P. Δ^9-THC, 11-OH-Δ^9-THC and Δ^9-THCCOOH plasma or serum to whole blood concentrations distribution ratios in blood samples taken from living and dead people. Forensic Sci Int 2001;123:159–64.
14. Goodwin RS, Darwin WD, Chiang CN, Shih M, Li SH, Huestis MA. Urinary elimination of 11-nor-9-carboxy-Δ^9-tetrahydrocannabinol in cannabis users during continuously monitored abstinence. J Anal Toxicol 2008;32:562–9.
15. Goodwin RS, Gustafson RA, Barnes A, Nebro W, Moolchan ET, Huestis MA. Δ^9-tetrahydrocannabinol, 11-hydroxy-Δ^9-tetrahydrocannabinol and 11-nor-9-carboxy-Δ^9-tetrahydrocannabinol in human plasma following controlled oral administration of cannabinoids. Ther Drug Monit 2006;28:545–51.
16. Grotenhermen F, Leson G, Berghaus G, Drummer OH, Krüger HP, Longo M, et al. Developing limits for driving under cannabis. Addiction 2007;102:1910–7.

17. Gustafson RA, Kim I, Stout PR, Klette KL, George MP, Moolchan ET, et al. Urinary pharmacokinetics of 11-nor-9-carboxy-Δ^9-tetrahydrocannabinol after controlled oral Δ^9-tetrahydrocannabinol administration. J Anal Toxicol 2004;28:160–7.

18. Gustafson RA, Levine B, Stout PR, Klette KL, George MP, Moolchan ET, Huestis MA. Urinary cannabinoid detection times following controlled oral administration of Δ^9-tetrahydrocannabinol to humans. Clin Chem 2003;49:1114–24.

19. Hall W, Solowij N. Adverse effects of cannabis. Lancet 1998;352:1611–6.

20. Haney M, Ward AS, Comer SD, Foltin RW, Fischman MW. Abstinence symptoms following oral THC administration to humans. Psychopharmacology (Berl) 1999;141:385–94.

21. Haney M, Ward AS, Comer SD, Foltin RW, Fischman MW. Abstinence symptoms following smoked marijuana in humans. Psychopharmacology (Berl) 1999;141:395–404.

22. Hawks RL. Developments in cannabinoid analyses of body fluids: implications for forensic applications. In: Agurell S, Dewey W, Willette R, eds. The cannabinoids: chemical, pharmacologic, and therapeutic aspects. Rockville, MD: Academic Press, 1983:1–12.

23. Heishman SJ, Arasteh K, Stitzer ML. Comparative effects of alcohol and marijuana on mood, memory, and performance. Pharmacol Biochem Behav 1997;58:93–101.

24. Hollister LE. Health aspects of cannabis: revisited. Int J Neuropsychopharmcol 1998;1:71–80.

25. Huestis MA. Pharmacokinetics and metabolism of the plant cannabinoids. Handb Exp Pharmacol 2005;(168):657–90.

26. Huestis MA, Barnes A, Smith ML. Estimating the time of last cannabis use from plasma Δ^9-tetrahydrocannabinol and 11-nor-9-carboxy-Δ^9-tetrahydrocannabinol concentrations. Clin Chem 2005;51:2289–95.

27. Huestis MA, Cone EJ. Differentiating new marijuana use from residual drug excretion in occasional marijuana users. J Anal Toxicol 1998;22:445–54.

28. Huestis MA, Cone EJ. Relationship of Δ^9-tetrahydrocannabinol in oral fluid to plasma after controlled administration of smoked cannabis. J Anal Toxicol 2004;28:394–9.

29. Huestis MA, Cone EJ, Mitchell J. Detection times of marijuana metabolites in urine by immunoassay and GC-MS. J Anal Toxicol 1995;19:443–9.

30. Huestis MA, Elsohly M, Nebro W, Gustafson RA, Smith ML. Estimating time of last oral ingestion of cannabis from plasma THC and THCCOOH concentrations. Ther Drug Monit 2006;28:540–4.

31. Huestis MA, Gorelick DA, Heishman SJ, Preston KL, Nelson RA, Moolchan ET, Frank RA. Blockade of smoked marijuana effects in humans by the oral CB1-selective cannabinoid receptor antagonist SR141716. Arch Gen Psychiatry 2001;58:322–8.

32. Huestis MA, Gustafson RA, Moolchan ET, Barnes A, Bourland JA, Sweeney SA, et al. Cannabinoid concentrations in hair from documented cannabis users. Forensic Sci Int 2007;169:129–36.

33. Huestis MA, Henningfield JE, Cone EJ. Blood cannabinoids. I. Absorption of THC and formation of 11-OH-THC and THC-COOH during and after smoking marijuana. J Anal Toxicol 1992;16:276–82.

34. Huestis MA, Henningfield JE, Cone EJ. Blood cannabinoids. II. Models for the prediction of marijuana exposure from plasma concentrations of Δ^9-tetrahydrocannabinol (THC) and 11-nor-9-carboxy-Δ^9-tetrahydrocannabinol (THCCOOH). J Anal Toxicol 1992;16:283–90.

35. Huestis MA, Mitchell J, Cone EJ. Lowering the federally mandated cannabinoid immunoassay cutoff increases true-positive results. Clin Chem 1994;40:729–33.

36. Huestis MA, Mitchell JM, Cone EJ. Urinary excretion profiles of 11-nor-9-carboxy-Δ^9-tetrahydrocannabinol in humans after single smoked doses of marijuana. J Anal Toxicol 1996;20:441–52.

37. Huestis MA, Sampson AH, Holicky BJ, Henningfield JE, Cone EJ. Characterization of the absorption phase of marijuana smoke. Clin Pharmacol Ther 1992;52:31–41.

38. Huestis MA, Scheidweiler KB, Saito T, Fortner N, Abraham T, Gustafson RA, Smith ML. Excretion of Δ^9-tetrahydrocannabinol in sweat. Forensic Sci Int 2008;174:173–7.

39. Hunt CA, Jones RT. Tolerance and disposition of tetrahydrocannabinol in man. J Pharmacol Exp Ther 1980;215:35–44.

40. Johansson E, Agurell S, Hollister L, Halldin M. Prolonged apparent half-life of Δ^1-tetrahydrocannabinol in plasma of chronic marijuana users. J Pharm Pharmacol 1988;40:374–5.

41. Jones AW, Holmgren A, Kugelberg FC. Driving under the influence of cannabis: a 10-year study of age and gender differences in the concentrations of tetrahydrocannabinol in blood. Addiction 2008;103:452–61.

42. Jones RT, Benowitz N, Bachman J. Clinical studies of cannabis tolerance and dependence. Ann NY Acad Sci 1976;282:221–39.

43. Kalant H. Adverse effects of cannabis on health: an update of the literature since 1996. Prog Neuropsychopharmacol Biol Psychiatry 2004;28:849–63.

44. Kauert GF, Ramaekers JG, Schneider E, Moeller MR, Toennes SW. Pharmacokinetic

properties of Δ^9-tetrahydrocannabinol in serum and oral fluid. J Anal Toxicol 2007;31:288–93.

45. Kemp PM, Abukhalaf IK, Manno JE, Alford DD, McWilliams ME, Nixon FE, et al. Cannabinoids in humans. II. The influence of three methods of hydrolysis on the concentration of THC and two metabolites in urine. J Anal Toxicol 1995;19:292–8.

46. Kintz P, Villain M, Ludes B. Testing for the undetectable in drug-facilitated sexual assault using hair analyzed by tandem mass spectrometry as evidence. Ther Drug Monit 2004;26:211–4.

47. Kirk JM, de Wit H. Responses to oral Δ^9-tetrahydrocannabinol in frequent and infrequent marijuana users. Pharmacol Biochem Behav 1999;63:137–42.

48. Laumon B, Gadegbeku B, Martin JL, Biecheler MB, and the SAM Group. Cannabis intoxication and fatal road crashes in France: population based case-control study. BMJ 2005;331:1371.

49. Law B, Mason PA, Moffat AC, Gleadle RI, King LJ. Forensic aspects of the metabolism and excretion of cannabinoids following oral ingestion of cannabis resin. J Pharm Pharmacol 1984;36:289–94.

50. Leirer VO, Yesavage JA, Morrow DG. Marijuana carry over effects on aircraft pilot performance. Aviat Space Environ Med 1991;62:221–7.

51. Liguori A, Gatto CP, Jarrett DB. Separate and combined effects of marijuana and alcohol on mood, equilibrium and simulated driving. Psychopharmacology (Berl) 2002;163:399–405.

52. Liguori A, Gatto CP, Robinson JH. Effects of marijuana on equilibrium, psychomotor performance, and simulated driving. Behav Pharmacol 1998;9:599–609.

53. Lowe RH, Karschner EL, Schwilke EW, Barnes AJ, Huestis MA. Simultaneous quantification of Δ^9-tetrahydrocannabinol (THC), 11-hydroxy-Δ^9-tetrahydrocannabinol(11-OH-THC), and 11-nor-Δ^9-tetrahydrocannabinol-9 carboxylic acid (THCCOOH) in human plasma using two-dimensional gas chromatography, cryofocusing, and electron impact-mass spectrometry. J Chromatogr A 2007;1163:318–27.

54. Lundqvist T. Cognitive consequences of cannabis use: comparison with abuse of stimulants and heroin with regard to attention, memory and executive functions. Pharmacol Biochem Behav 2005;81:319–30.

55. Macavoy MG, Marks DF. Divided attention performance of cannabis users and non-users following cannabis and alcohol. Psychopharmacologia 1975;44:147–52.

56. Manno JE, Ferslew KE, Manno BR. Urine excretion patterns of cannabinoids and the clinical application of the EMIT-d.a.u. cannabinoid urine assay for substance abuse treatment. In: Agurell S, Dewey WL, Willette RE, eds. The cannabinoids: chemical, pharmacologic, and therapeutic aspects. Orlando, FL: Harcourt Brace Jonanovich, 1984:281–90.

57. Ménétrey A, Augsburger M, Favrat B, Pin MA, Rothuizen LE, Appenzeller M, et al. Assessment of driving capability through the use of clinical and psychomotor tests in relation to blood cannabinoids levels following oral administration of 20 mg dronabinol or of a cannabis decoction made with 20 or 60 mg Δ^9-THC. J Anal Toxicol 2005;29:327–38.

58. Moskowitz H. Marihuana and driving. Accid Anal Prev 1985;17:323–45.

59. Mura P, Kintz P, Dumestre V, Raul S, Hauet T. THC can be detected in brain while absent in blood. J Anal Toxicol 2005;29:842–3.

60. Mura P, Kintz P, Ludes B, Gaulier JM, Marquet P, Martin-Dupont S, et al. Comparison of the prevalence of alcohol, cannabis and other drugs between 900 injured drivers and 900 control subjects: results of a French collaborative study. Forensic Sci Int 2003;133:79–85.

61. Nowlan R, Cohen S. Tolerance to marijuana: heart rate and subjective "high." Clin Pharmacol Ther 1977;22(Pt 1):550–6.

62. Peat MA. Distribution of Δ^9-tetrahydrocannabinol and its metabolites. In: Baselt RC, ed. Advances in analytical toxicology, vol. II. Chicago: Yearbook Medical Publishers, 1989:186.

63. Perez-Reyes M, Di Guiseppi S, Davis KH, Schindler VH, Cook CE. Comparison of effects of marihuana cigarettes to three different potencies. Clin Pharmacol Ther 1982;31:617–24.

64. Perez-Reyes M, Owens SM, Di Guiseppi S. The clinical pharmacology and dynamics of marihuana cigarette smoking. J Clin Pharmacol 1981;21(Suppl):201S–7S.

65. Pope HG Jr, Gruber AJ, Hudson JI, Cohane G, Huestis MA, Yurgelun-Todd D. Early-onset cannabis use and cognitive deficits: what is the nature of the association? Drug Alcohol Depend 2003;69:303–10.

66. Pope HG Jr, Gruber AJ, Hudson JI, Huestis MA, Yurgelun-Todd D. Neuropsychological performance in long-term cannabis users. Arch Gen Psychiatry 2001;58:909–15.

67. Ramaekers JG, Berghaus G, van Laar M, Drummer OH. Dose related risk of motor vehicle crashes after cannabis use. Drug Alcohol Depend 2004;73:109–19.

68. Ramaekers JG, Moeller MR, van Ruitenbeek P, Theunissen EL, Schneider E, Kauert G. Cognition and motor control as a function of Δ^9-THC concentration in serum and oral fluid: limits of impairment. Drug Alcohol Depend 2006;85:114–22.

69. Ramaekers JG, Robbe HW, O'Hanlon JF. Marijuana, alcohol and actual driving performance. Hum Psychopharmacol 2000;15:551–8.

70. Reeve VC, Grant JD, Robertson W, Gillespie HK, Hollister LE. Plasma concentrations of Δ^9-tetrahydrocannabinol and impaired motor function. Drug Alcohol Depend 1983;11:167–75.

71. Robbe H. Marijuana's impairing effects on driving are moderate when taken alone but severe when combined with alcohol. Hum Psychopharmacol 1998;13:S70–8.

72. Schwilke EW, Karschner EL, Lowe RH, Gordon AM, Cadet JL, Herning RI, Huestis MA. Intra- and inter-subject whole blood/plasma cannabinoid ratios determined by 2-dimensional, electron impact-gas chromatography mass spectrometry with cryofocusing. Clin Chem 2009;55:1188–95.

73. Walsh JM, Verstraete A, Huestis MA, Mørland J. Guidelines for research on drugged driving. Addiction 2008;103:1258–68.

CHAPTER 20

Amphetamines/Sympathomimetic Amines

Michele L. Merves and Karla A. Moore

INTRODUCTION

The compound "amphetamine" has come to represent a class of phenethylamine compounds that have varying degrees of sympathomimetic activity. Sympathomimetic drugs mimic the actions of the endogenous neurotransmitters that stimulate the sympathetic nervous system. This growing class of structurally related compounds may also stimulate the sympathetic nervous system through many other mechanisms of action, such as by affecting the release of endogenous neurotransmitters or inhibiting their reuptake.

Amphetamine was synthesized in 1877. During the 1930s, amphetamines were first used clinically as a central nervous system (CNS) stimulant for the treatment of narcolepsy and depression, where its abuse potential first became evident. Since that time, the ability of amphetamines to alleviate fatigue, improve performance of simple mental and physical tasks, elevate mood, increase confidence, and produce euphoria has led to their misuse and abuse.

Amphetamine use, including amphetamine, methamphetamine, phenmetrazine, methylphenidate, diethylpropion, and propylhexedrine, reached epidemic proportions during World War II, notably by soldiers, factory workers, and prisoners of war in Japan. After World War II, a surplus on the Japanese market permitted sales without a prescription, with peak use occurring about 1954. In the 1960s, methamphetamine abuse became a social problem in the U.S. By 1970, 50% of legally manufactured amphetamine and related compounds were being sold on the black market.

Increasing abuse of these drugs eventually led to their classification as a Schedule II controlled substance under the Controlled Substances Act (Public Law 91-513) of 1970. Schedule II substances have a high abuse potential with severe psychic or physical dependence liability. This classification limited the acquisition of these compounds through legitimate channels and stringently regulated their production, forcing manufacturers to decrease sales to retail pharmacies. Because methamphetamine is easily synthesized even in crude laboratories, it quickly became the "stimulant of choice." Illicit production and use of methamphetamine hydrochloride remains a significant drug abuse problem. Endemic areas for this increase include the Pacific Coast states, Hawaii, and other Pacific Rim countries such as Japan and Korea.

Methamphetamine is one of the most frequently encountered clandestinely produced controlled substances in the U.S. Unlike *d*-amphetamine, *d*-methamphetamine is easy to synthesize. Laboratories producing methamphetamine accounted for more than 50% of all lab seizures by the Drug Enforcement Administration (DEA) during a 45-month period ending in September 1981. In 2006, a National Association of Counties survey identified methamphetamine as the top drug problem.

In the 1970s, the most popular method of synthesis was reductive amination using phenyl-2-propanone (P2P), methylamine, aluminum foil, mercuric chloride (catalyst), and alcohol. In a second popular method, the product of an acetaldehyde/methylamine reaction was refluxed with benzylmagnesium chloride. A third method used the Leukart reaction, refluxing P2P with either methylamine and formic acid or N-methylformamide with hydrochloric acid. An important precursor in these syntheses was P2P, which, until 1981, was available commercially. Because of its importance in illicit synthetic methods, it is now a Schedule II controlled substance. As a result of its control, some clandestine laboratories now synthesize only P2P.

During the late 1970s and early 1980s, the conversion of ephedrine to methamphetamine by reductive cleavage of the hydroxyl group using either thionyl chloride or hydroiodic acid (HI) and red phosphorus was relatively uncommon; only 10 of the laboratories seized used this synthetic method. In fact, through the late 1980s, the DEA reported that significantly more laboratories were synthesizing methamphetamine using one of the reductive amination methods or synthesizing P2P. However, with the growing difficulty in obtaining precursors for the reductive amination routes and with the increasing availability of (-)-ephedrine and (+)-pseudoephedrine, methamphetamine synthesized from ephedrine flooded the market in both the U.S. and the Far East. From 1991 through 1993, the DEA seized more than 500 illicit methamphetamine laboratories, mostly on the West Coast and in Houston, Texas. The ephedrine (EPH) reduction method was used in 81% of these laboratories, whereas the P2P method was used in only 16%. This represented a direct reversal of trends noted in the 1980s. Forensic laboratories in New Mexico also reported that in the first six months of 1994, there was a decided increase in the number of methamphetamine seizures, all using the EPH process. Additionally, the California Bureau of Narcotic Enforcement reported

that the use of the precursor chemical EPH in California had rapidly increased with the availability of the chemical from Mexico. The value of ephedrine as a precursor in methamphetamine manufacture spread quickly in the Mexican drug community, causing it to become a significant smuggling commodity and resulting in a significant price drop in the U.S. market.

In March 1994, the *Federal Register* documented a DEA proposal to make all regulated transactions of EPH, regardless of size, subject to the reporting and record-keeping requirements of the Chemical Diversion and Trafficking Act of 1988 (CDTA). This proposal was intended to subject all transactions involving bulk EPH and single-entity EPH drug products to the applicable provisions of the CDTA. In 2006, the U.S. passed into law the Combat Methamphetamine Epidemic Act of 2005. This law attempted to limit the availability of pseudoephedrine (PE) and phenylpropanolamine (PPA), as well as EPH. All purchases of products containing these drugs were to be recorded and the records kept for two years. In addition, proof of identity was required prior to purchase. Solid dosage forms containing these drugs were to be sold only in unit dose packaging, and these products were to be stored in locked cabinets behind retail counters. There were also limits in daily and monthly purchases of these drugs.

Almost since the inception of the pharmaceutical industry, slight changes in the molecular structure of various classes of compounds have been used to circumvent patent restrictions and allow drug manufacturers to gain a share of the lucrative drug market. This concept has not been lost on the chemists who provide materials for the illicit drug market. Their primary impetus, however, in molecular redesign and modification is finding ways to circumvent scheduling restrictions. This has been particularly true of the "designer" group of compounds in the amphetamine/methamphetamine class, especially 3,4-methylenedioxymethamphetamine (MDMA; "Ecstasy"; "Adam";

"XTC") and its N-demethyl metabolite, 3,4-methylenedioxyamphetamine (MDA). MDMA and MDA are two of the oldest so-called "designer drugs." MDMA is a derivative of methamphetamine whereas MDA is a derivative of amphetamine.

Newer designer drugs with stimulant, entactogenic, and hallucinogenic properties continue to emerge in today's culture, either from recent synthesis or reintroduction of drugs discovered almost a century ago. In general, minor changes to the chemical structures of phenethylamines, piperazines, piperidines, and tryptamines provide similar effects on the central nervous system as their more traditional counterparts, although their potency may be altered. Furthermore, some of these derivatives are biotransformed into other pharmacologically active substances. With such a large, complex, and ever-changing assortment of compounds, it is often difficult for lawmakers to control manufacturing, distributing, selling, and use of these compounds designed as "legal highs." With global access through the Internet, many new compounds can become available as older ones become controlled. With this in mind, it can be challenging for researchers to elucidate the pharmacological and toxicological properties of these newer drugs within the current cultural context. The complexity of this research increases especially with the concept of drug-drug interactions. Many of these designer drugs may be ingested in combination with other drugs with the intent to enhance euphoric effects; however, these interactions may also increase the risk of toxicity.

As part of the movement to keep designer drugs legal, many are marketed as "not for human consumption." Alternatively, they are sold in products labeled as bath salts, plant foods, stain removers, and insect repellants. Although several derivatives exist, methylone, mephedrone, and 3,4-methylenedioxypyrovalerone (MDPV) are three common ones that have gained media attention in recent years.

Some naturally occurring alkaloids can also be targets for recreational use. A common example is the ephedrine found in the *Ephedra* plant. *Ephedra* also contains norpseudoephedrine but in lesser quantities. Interestingly, norpseudoephedrine is an alkaloid found in larger quantities within the *Catha edulis* plant (i.e., khat) and, therefore, it is commonly referred to as cathine. Although cathine is present in large quantities within the plant, the stimulatory effects from khat are believed to be primarily from a structurally similar alkaloid, cathinone. Many synthetic analogues marketed as "designer drugs" are derived from cathinone. Fig. 1 displays the drugs that will be discussed in this chapter.

EFFECTS

Methamphetamine stimulates the CNS by displacing dopamine from nerve terminal storage vesicles. This release causes the hyperstimulation of dopaminergic receptor neurons in the synaptic cleft. Amphetamine and methamphetamine are substrates for serotonin (5-HT), norepinephrine (NE), and dopamine (DA) transporters and lead to transmitter release by a process of transport-mediated exchange. Upon entry to the cytoplasm, the amphetamines further reduce accumulation of NE/DA in the synaptic vesicles. Catecholaminergic vesicles use an interior-acidic proton gradient for transmitter uptake. These drugs compete for protons with neurotransmitter already present in the granules. The resulting uncharged neurotransmitter then diffuses out of the granules down its concentration gradient. This mechanism causes a continuous release of neurotransmitter at low doses of stimulant, accounting for the locomotor stimulant and reinforcing effects of these compounds. Direct peripheral and organ stimulation at the various α- and β-adrenergic receptors also occurs, resulting in elevation of systolic and diastolic blood pressures and weak bronchodilator and respiratory stimulant action. At therapeutic doses, the heart rate may be slowed; large doses may produce cardiac arrhythmias.

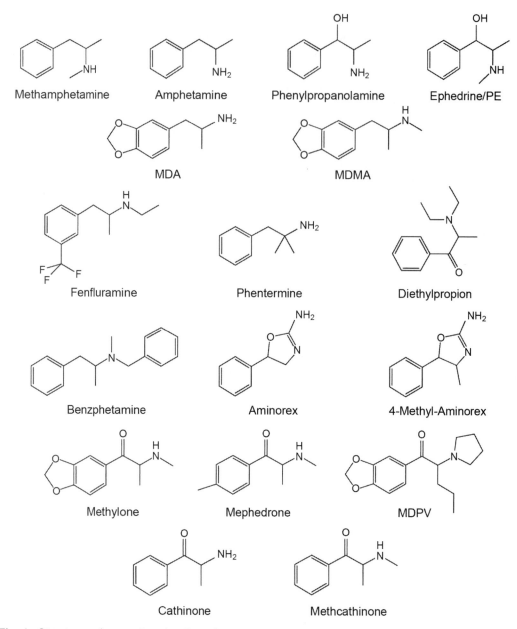

Fig. 1. Structures of sympathomimetic amines.

D-methamphetamine has greater CNS efficacy than d-amphetamine, most likely because of its greater ability to penetrate the CNS. The euphoric effects produced by methamphetamine, cocaine, and designer sympathomimetic amines are difficult to distinguish clinically. The only notable exception is the difference in half-life; for example, methamphetamine has a significantly longer half-life than cocaine, sometimes as much as 10 times longer.

PPA, EPH, and PE are members of the class of sympathomimetic amines with primarily peripheral effects. These compounds stimulate α-adrenergic receptors of vascular smooth muscle, producing vasoconstriction, changes in blood pressure, and nasal decongestion. Although EPH and PE retain some β-adrenergic properties (this effect of EPH leads to its occasional use in cardiac resuscitation procedures), a large part of the peripheral action of PPA is due to NE release stimulated through β-adrenergic receptors. This β-agonist effect of PPA can produce elevated blood pressure due to vasoconstriction and cardiac stimulation. Systemically, the products have muted α-effects, allowing decongestion without drastic changes in blood pressure, vascular redistribution, or cardiac stimulation. Constriction of the vessels in the mucous membranes results in their shrinkage, thus promoting drainage and improving ventilation. Other minor α-effects include contraction of gastrointestinal (GI) and urinary sphincters, mydriasis, and decreased pancreatic beta-cell secretion. EPH is a potent stimulator of the CNS, but less so than amphetamine. PPA has the weakest CNS effects of this class of drugs. This is probably due to its decreased lipid solubility because of the lack of an alkyl group on the nitrogen.

Phentermine has a spectrum of pharmacological effects similar to that of the amphetamines with weaker CNS stimulation. This drug increases the concentrations of NE and DA in the brain but with less potency than amphetamines. It has no effect on 5-HT.

MDMA and MDA display marked sympathomimetic activity similar to amphetamine as demonstrated by peripheral vasoconstriction, tachycardia, pupillary dilatation, and effects on other smooth muscles. CNS stimulatory effects also mimic those of amphetamine and, in cases of overdose, convulsions, hyperthermia, and behavioral changes may occur. Other severe complications, such as rhabdomyolysis, intravascular coagulation, acute renal failure, and hepatonecrosis, have been reported with MDMA overdose. Both MDMA and MDA produce perceptual distortions and pronounced subjective effects including intensification of feelings, an apparent facilitation of self-insight, an overwhelming desire to communicate, profound empathy, and euphoria.

Following doses of 150–225 mg in conjunction with psychotherapy sessions, MDMA users reported experiencing positive mood changes, improvements in attitude, beliefs, relationships, occupation, and spiritual-physical condition, and a transient decrease in substance abuse. However, MDMA ingestion has also been reported to cause tachycardia, an occasional "wired" feeling, jaw clenching, nystagmus, a nervous desire to be in motion, transient anorexia, panic attacks, nausea and vomiting, ataxia, urinary urgency, diplopia, insomnia, and, rarely, transient hallucinations.

Newer designer drugs with similar chemical structures to amphetamine, methamphetamine, and MDMA seem to exhibit similar effects. Although the mechanisms of action for this growing class of drugs have not been fully elucidated, research suggests they may have similar sites of action but affect them to different degrees when compared to their more traditional counterparts. Drugs such as cathinone, methcathinone, MDPV, mephedrone, and methylone seem to have mechanisms of action that inhibit the reuptake of norepinephrine, dopamine, and/or serotonin in varying proportions and/or increase the release of one or more of these neurotransmitters. Adverse effects for these types of drugs include some of the classic signs and symptoms such as tachycardia, hypertension, insomnia, hyperthermia, nausea, vomiting, and anxiety. Reports even suggest that paranoia and hallucinations can occur.

THERAPEUTIC USES

Pharmaceutical dosage forms for amphetamine and methamphetamine include 5-, 10-, and 15-mg tablets or sustained-release capsules. Amphetamine is also available as a 5-mg/mL elixir. Clinical indications for amphetamine and methamphetamine include narcolepsy, attention deficit disorder, and appetite suppression in the treatment of exogenous obesity, where they function as a short-term adjunct to a regimen of weight reduction based on caloric restriction. In the Department of Defense (DoD), stimulants, particularly amphetamines, were once used in "go/no go" packs as countermeasures to fatigue induced by circadian desynchronosis (disruption of the natural day/night circadian rhythms) and extended flight operations. However, because of the tight DEA control of these substances and the advent of newer drugs with fewer side effects and less abuse potential, these compounds are currently rarely prescribed. The DoD has also discontinued use of these substances in "go/ no go" packs. However, studies are still being conducted to make recommendations concerning the use of dextroamphetamine for some operational tasks and flying requirements.

PE is primarily used as a decongestant, administered directly to swollen membranes (e.g., via sprays and drops) or systemically via the oral route. It is commonly found in over-the-counter cold and allergy medications in combination with antihistamines and analgesics. Until November 2000, PPA was also used as a decongestant and as an anorexiant in many over-the-counter diet aids. On November 3, 2000, the FDA announced a decision to initiate rule making to classify PPA as not generally safe and effective because of an association between PPA and hemorrhagic stroke. At the urging of the FDA, drug companies voluntarily ceased marketing over-the-counter products containing this compound. In 2005, the FDA removed PPA from over-the counter products.

Appetite suppression is a common use of drugs in this class. At one time, fenfluramine was used as an anorexiant, but it was voluntarily removed from the U.S. market in 1997 by the manufacturer due to concerns of cardiac toxicity. Phentermine and diethylpropion are two amphetamine analogs still commonly prescribed for this purpose. In addition, there are nonamphetamine anorexiants that are indirect-acting sympathomimetic amines; they include mazindol, phenmetrazine, and phendimetrazine.

Unlike other types of designer drugs, MDMA and MDA were legally synthesized in the early decades of the twentieth century and have experienced a brief history of legitimate, therapeutic use. MDMA was first synthesized by Merck in 1914 as an appetite suppressant but never marketed as such. In the 1970s and 1980s, MDMA gained brief popularity as an adjunct to psychotherapy, but was never officially approved for that use. MDA, the drug originally known as "Ecstasy," chemically resembles mescaline and is related to saffrole, a psychoactive agent in mace and nutmeg. It was first synthesized in 1910 and had been used variously as an antitussive, an ataractic, and as an anorexiant.

ABUSE

Because of its ease of manufacture and ready availability, methamphetamine has become the sympathomimetic amine of choice among stimulant abusers. Illicit methamphetamine is available as a water-soluble white crystalline powder (methamphetamine hydrochloride) known as "speed," "crank," "go," "crystal," or, simply, "meth." This compound is adulterated with a variety of substances such as dimethylsulfone, sugars (usually added to give more volume to the final product), or cheaper stimulants (e.g., caffeine, PPA, or EPH/PE). Methamphetamine in this form can be used for intravenous injection, oral consumption, smoking, or (rarely) insufflation. Moreover, a form of methamphetamine hydrochloride called "ice" can be smoked. The term "ice" originated in the Far East and refers to the large crystals of methamphetamine hydrochloride produced through the ephedrine-reduction method. The popularity of ice is due to the immediate clinical effects of euphoria resulting from the drug's rapid absorption from the lungs.

Both MDMA and MDA have been gaining in popularity as drugs of abuse. While both isomers of MDMA are mild hallucinogens, the S(+)-isomer of MDA is thought to be more amphetamine-like, whereas R(-)-MDA is hallucinogenic. While never legally available in the U.S., MDA became widely abused in the 1960s and 1970s because of its reported hallucinogenic and psychoactive properties. From 1978 through 1981, 16 clandestine MDA laboratories were seized. More than 65% of these labs used the reaction of isosafrole with hydrogen peroxide and formic acid followed by formamide/ammonium formate and hydrochloric acid. The synthetic methods used for amphetamine analogs have been extensively reviewed by legitimate researchers. Some methods, including very sophisticated processes, have also been described in many "underground" publications. Regardless of the source, all of the methods result in the synthesis of racemic mixtures. While these syntheses can be modified to allow for the resolution of racemates, such modifications are rarely used in the illicit labs due to the unavailability of optically pure precursors or lack of sophistication/interest on the part of the "garage" chemist.

On July 1, 1985, the DEA placed MDMA in Schedule I on an emergency basis. Because of its structural similarity to MDA, which by that time had been shown to selectively damage 5-HT nerve terminals in the rat, dangerous side effects to MDMA's abuse were considered likely. They cited that its widespread use was proof of its abuse. Despite this scheduling, the recreational use and abuse of MDMA increased significantly in the 1990s, especially on college campuses. Partly as a result of this resurgence in popularity, numerous studies have been initiated to explore the drug's neurochemical effects. These studies indicate that MDMA is a selective 5-HT neurotoxin, causing retrograde destruction of 5-HT neurons following large doses. The S(+)-isomer of MDMA has been reported to be a more potent neurotoxin than the R(-)-isomer. Additionally, the S(+)-isomer of MDMA is preferentially metabolized, resulting in the stereoselective formation of the S(+)-isomer of MDA. Unlike MDMA, however, both isomers of MDA cause long-term 5-HT neurotoxicity. In fact, much of the neurotoxicity originally attributed to MDMA may actually be a result of its more potent neurotoxic metabolite, MDA.

It has been demonstrated that both enantiomers of MDMA cause an acute depletion of cortical 5-HT, but only S(+)-MDMA results in significant depletions of 5-HT and 5-HT uptake sites. It was later reported that the S(+) isomers of both MDA and MDMA

were more potent at depleting 5-HT and in depressing tryptophan hydroxylase (TPH), the rate-limiting enzyme in 5-HT synthesis. It has since been shown that while S(+)-MDMA is more potent than R(-)-MDMA in eliciting some stereotyped behaviors, S(+)-MDA is more potent than both of its parent enantiomers in eliciting these behaviors and produces "wet-dog shake" behavior, as well. This may indicate that S(+)-MDA has additional harmful effects on other CNS systems in addition to the serotonergic system.

S(+)-MDA stereoselectively accumulates in the blood of animals following a racemic dose of MDMA. This is due to the stereoselective metabolism of S(+)-MDMA to S(+)-MDA, resulting in peak plasma concentrations approximately three times that of R(-)-MDA and almost twice as much S(+)-MDA being excreted in the urine as compared to R(-)-MDA.

Occasional reports of abuse have surfaced about another member of this class of drugs, 4-methylaminorex (4-MAX; "u4euh"). 4-MAX was described in 1963 as an indirect-acting sympathomimetic drug with anorectic properties. 4-MAX is similar in structure to pemoline (a Schedule IV CNS stimulant) and aminorex, an anorectic marketed in Europe in 1965 but withdrawn in 1968. Recently, 4-MAX has come to the forefront as a new stimulant of abuse. Users have described the effects of 4-MAX to be like those of amphetamine and cocaine.

In addition, naturally occurring alkaloids such as cathinone have abuse potential due to their amphetamine-like effects. Cathinone is present in *Catha edulis*, a plant that grows primarily in regions of East Africa and the Arab Peninsula. A common name for this plant is khat, which often refers to the leaves. Leaves can be brewed as a type of tea or chewed to obtain stimulatory effects. More sophisticated techniques can extract cathinone from the plant in order to prepare other herbal preparations.

More recently, synthetic cathinone derivatives have been recognized for their abuse potential due to their stimulatory, entactogenic, and/or hallucinogenic effects. Many of them seem to have similar mechanisms of action to amphetamine and, often, MDMA, which may be explained by the similarity in their chemical structures. Methcathinone is one of the earliest derivatives of cathinone. It was originally synthesized in the late 1920s, although it wasn't recognized by recreational drug users until the early 1990s. It is also known by other chemical names such as ephedrone, N-methylcathinone, and monomethylpropion and the recreational names Cat and Jeff. Mephedrone (4-methylmethcathinone or 4-methylephedrone) is a synthetic derivative of methcathinone and, therefore, cathinone. It has primarily entactogenic properties. Mephedrone may be marketed under such names as MCAT and "meow." Methylone (chemical names 2-methyl-amino-1-[3,4-methylenedioxyphenyl]propan-1-one and 3,4-methylenedioxy-N-methylcathinone) is an additional cathinone and methcathinone derivative with entactogenic effects like MDMA. Another drug becoming widely abused is MDPV (3,4-methylenedioxypyrovalerone). As a derivative of cathinone and pyrovalerone, MDPV has stimulatory effects and is one of the more recent synthetic amphetamines to be scheduled. These aforementioned synthetic derivatives are only a few of the many analogues that have been synthesized as designer drugs. Collectively, many of these compounds have been marketed as bath salts, stain removers, plant foods, or insect repellants. Although they are marketed as "not for human consumption," the goal of recreational users seems to be to create "legal" highs. As more information becomes available about the dangers of these synthetic derivatives, a movement to ban them has been ongoing over the past few decades.

PHARMACOKINETICS

Amphetamine and methamphetamine display essentially the same pharmacokinetic profile. Methamphetamine is highly lipid soluble and well absorbed orally, with a bioavailability of approximately 67% and a volume of distribution of 3–7 L/kg. A single oral methamphetamine dose of 0.125 mg/kg given to human male volunteers produced a peak plasma concentration of 0.020 mg/L at 3.6 h with an average elimination half-life of approximately 10 h. In another study that evaluated the effect of d-methamphetamine on circadian rhythms, 10 male volunteers were given 0.43 mg/kg d-methamphetamine during two test sessions, one week apart. Peak serum concentrations ranged from 0.06–0.3 mg/L at 3.6 h after administration during the day session and 0.03–0.08 mg/L at 4.8 h during the night session. After oral administration of 30 mg amphetamine base to 8 adults, an average peak plasma level of 0.11 mg/L was observed at 2.5 h, decreasing to 0.08 mg/L by 4.5 h.

In one study, the bioavailability of an average inhaled dose of 21.8 mg was approximately 90%. The mean half-life was 11.1 h, compared to 12.2 h for an intravenous injection of 15.5 mg. The volume of distribution was 3.24 L/kg for the smoked dose and 3.73 L/kg for the intravenous dose. Because of the more rapid and intense drug effect, patients describe a "high" distinct from that produced by snorting or ingesting the drug.

Methamphetamine is excreted in the urine largely as unchanged parent drug; under normal conditions, up to 45% of a dose in a 24-h period. Approximately 7% of an administered dose undergoes N-demethylation to amphetamine (Fig. 2). Amphetamines are also metabolized in the liver via aromatic hydroxylation. Accumulated hydroxylated metabolites have been implicated in the development of amphetamine psychosis. Elimination of the sympathomimetic amines is highly dependent on urinary pH. Urinary acidification to a pH <5.6 decreases the plasma half-life from 11–12 h to 7–8 h. Alkalization increases the half-life to 18–34 h. For every 1-unit increase in urinary pH, there is an average 7-h increase in plasma half-life. In acidic urine, up to 76% of a dose can be found as unchanged drug, whereas in alkaline urine <2% of a given dose will be detected as unchanged drug and <0.1% as

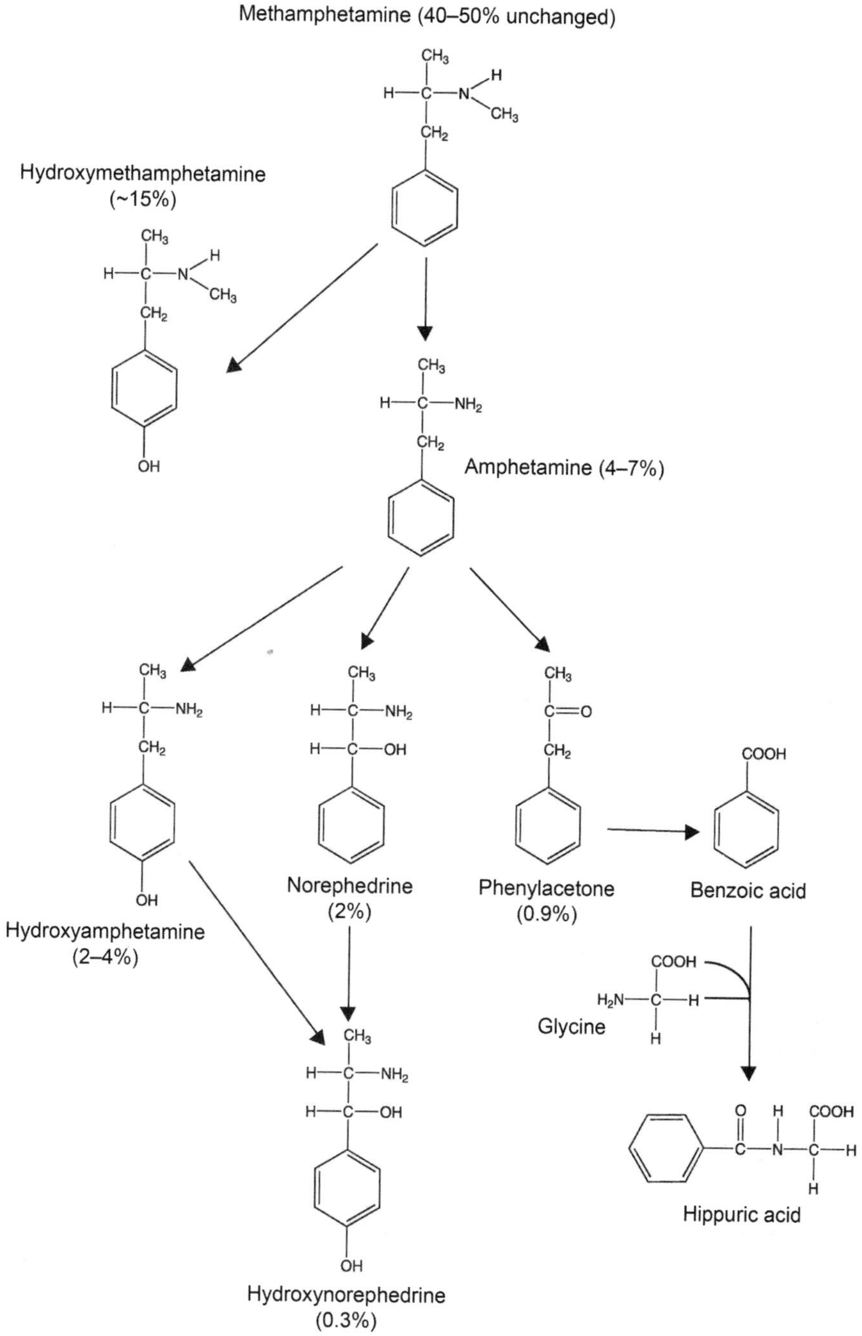

Fig. 2. Metabolism of methamphetamine.

amphetamine. Approximately 15% of a dose is excreted as p-hydroxymethamphetamine. After ingestion of 10 mg of methamphetamine, urine concentrations of methamphetamine can range from 0.5–4.0 mg/L during the first 24 h. Long-time abusers, who may be using 5000–15,000 mg per day, can have urinary methamphetamine concentrations >20 mg/L and amphetamine concentrations >10 mg/L.

EPH, PE, and PPA are all well absorbed orally. EPH, when used as a vasopressor in resuscitation, is administered parenterally—intravenous, subcutaneous, or intramuscular—where it is completely and rapidly absorbed. Onset of action by the intramuscular route is more rapid than by the subcutaneous route. Pressor and cardiac responses to EPH last about 60 min. EPH and PE are not stored to any significant extent in the body, both having a volume of distribution of 3–4 L/kg. Readily absorbed from the GI tract, PPA reaches peak plasma concentrations in 1–2 h with a plasma half-life of 3–4 h. Its volume of distribution is approximately 4 L/kg. All of these compounds are excreted primarily unchanged in the urine. EPH and PE are metabolized to a small extent (<10% of a given dose) in the liver by N-demethylation to PPA. Small amounts of PPA are metabolized in the liver to active hydroxylated metabolites with 80–90% excreted unchanged. Much like amphetamine and methamphetamine, the excretion of these compounds is highly urine pH-dependent, resulting in increased elimination with acidification of the urine. Elimination half-life can be increased from 3 h to 6 h with a pH change of 5 to 6.

Phentermine is well absorbed from the small intestine. Peak plasma concentrations occur within 8 h following oral administration, with therapeutic concentrations lasting for approximately 20 h ($t_{1/2}$ = 20–24 h). In one study of 21 individuals, once-daily dosing for 14 days with 30 mg extended-release phentermine produced mean plasma concentrations of 0.08–0.142 mg/L.

Diethylpropion is well absorbed from the GI tract, with peak plasma concentrations occurring approximately 2 h after administration. It is metabolized in the liver to numerous active metabolites that have an elimination $t_{1/2}$ of 8 h. It is likely that these metabolites contribute significantly to the efficacy of this compound. Both diethylpropion and its active metabolites readily cross the blood–brain barrier and the placenta. One of the minor metabolites of diethylpropion that is pharmacologically active is cathinone. As mentioned previously, cathinone is key constituent of khat.

Like many other drugs, the metabolism of MDMA is complex and involves multiple enzymatic pathways. Research suggests the half-life of MDMA is 5–9 h. MDMA has the potential to exhibit nonlinear pharmacokinetics as well as inhibit its own metabolism at various concentrations. MDMA metabolizes to 3,4-dihydroxymethamphetamine (HHMA) primarily through CYP 450 2D6, and HHMA is then metabolized to 4-hydroxy-3-methoxymethamphetamine (HMMA) using the catecholamine-O-methyltransferase pathway. Less than 5% of MDMA is metabolized to MDA, an N-demethylation of MDMA via the cytochrome P450 pathway. Further demethylation occurs to form 3,4-dihydroxyamphetamine (HHA) and then O-methylation to form 4-hydroxy-3-methoxyamphetamine (HMA). These multiple pathways also result in many sulfate and glucuronide conjugates.

Cathinone and its derivatives have β-keto functional groups that decrease their lipophilicity. Therefore, they are generally less potent than their amphetamine counterparts. With this in mind, larger doses of these drugs may be required to achieve similar euphoric effects. Research indicates cathinone has a half-life of 2.7–6 h and is primarily biotransformed to norephedrine with one of its minor metabolites as norpseudoephedrine. Similarly, methcathinone metabolizes to ephedrine and then to norephedrine. Analogous to other drugs, cathinone and its derivatives extensively metabolize through various Phase I and Phase II pathways via demethylation, hydroxylation, oxidation, reduction, O-methylation, glucuronidation, and sulfation. Excretion of these drugs and their metabolites are dependent on urine pH.

ANALYSIS

Immunoassay

Since the introduction of the Syva Co. enzyme-multiplied immunoassay technique drug abuse (EMIT-dau®) assays in the mid-1970s, immunoassays based on the competitive binding of labeled drugs and specimen drugs for specific drug antibody binding sites have proved successful for rapid screening for amphetamines and other drugs of abuse. This is particularly useful for screening purposes in many types of forensic toxicology laboratories, including but not limited to postmortem, human performance, and urine drug-testing labs. With this in mind, many types of immunoassay products are available to meet the needs of a diverse industry. Some products provide minimal cross-reactivity to target specific drugs monitored by the federal government in urine drug-testing laboratories. Other products offer a wide range of cross-reactivity in diverse biological matrices to aid postmortem and human performance investigations. There are even products designed to give instant results, which may prove helpful in clinical or roadside settings that require immediate action.

The historical basis of the EMIT-dau® technique was the detection of a change in ultraviolet (UV) absorbance (340 nm) as the coenzyme NAD is reduced to NADH. The EMIT-dau® amphetamine class assay (EC) contained polyclonal antibodies and had a cutoff calibrator of 300 ng/mL d-amphetamine. The assay readily cross-reacted with ephedrine, pseudoephedrine, phentermine, and other phenylisopropylamines. The EC was indicated when low detection limits for amphetamines or high cross-reactivity to other structurally related stimulants was desired. Thus, EC was used in athletic drug testing and in screening patients in substance abuse rehabilitation programs. In an effort to further confront the issue of cross-reactivity of these assays with EPH, PE, and PPA, Syva Co. also supplied an optional amphetamine confirmation kit. The kit contained sodium hydroxide and sodium periodate, which were added to the specimen before testing. These reagents eliminated cross-reacting compounds with a hydroxyl group in the α-position, such as PPA and PE/EPH through oxidative cleavage of the α– and β–carbon bonds.

Due in part to workplace testing requirements and needs, the EMIT-dau® monoclonal amphetamine/methamphetamine assay (EM) was developed with a cutoff calibrator of 1000 ng/mL d-methamphetamine. The assay displayed much less cross-reactivity with phenylisopropylamine derivatives than the EC. However, the assay readily detected low concentrations of MDA and MDMA. This was subsequently upgraded to the EMIT-II amphetamine/methamphetamine assay (EII). EII contained monoclonal antibodies with a cutoff calibrator of 1000 ng/mL d-methamphetamine. Unlike the EM assay, EII required 1000 ng/mL d-amphetamine to produce a positive response. The EII assay had low cross-reactivity to phenylisopropylamine derivatives and was configured for high volume, high-speed analyzers, and high selectivity for amphetamine, methamphetamine, MDMA, and MDA.

In addition to EMIT products now supplied by Siemens Healthcare Diagnostics, Inc., a number of other immunoassay technologies are available for the rapid detection of sympathomimetic amines in blood, urine, and/or alternative biological specimens. This variety of products has been designed to meet the needs of many forensic applications. One challenging aspect of product design for postmortem toxicology is the cross-reactivity of decomposition amines such as phenethylamine and tyramine. Many companies are designing products to cost-effectively improve efficiency and selectivity for the broad spectrum of chemical structures that compose the amphetamine class of drugs. Among the immunoassay technologies are KIMS, CEDIA®, and ELISA, which provide a diverse range of cross-reactivity.

Kinetic interaction of microparticles in a solution (KIMS) is a homogenous assay used in many immunoassay products designed by the Roche Diagnostics Corporation. Its technology has been used to create products with different target analytes. For example, Roche Diagnostics has created at least three different assays with amphetamine, methamphetamine, and MDMA as the primary target analytes. However, there is a range of cross-reactivity to related structures such as MDA, MDEA, and N-methyl-1-(3,4-methylenedioxyphenyl)-2-butanamine (MBDB).

CEDIA®, a homogenous assay manufactured by Thermo Fisher Scientific, can be an alternative tool for screening purposes. Currently there are two CEDIA® products designed to detect amphetamines. The target analyte for one of the products is *d*-amphetamine, but there is significant cross-reactivity to structures such as *d*-methamphetamine and MDMA. The second product has cross-reactivity with several compounds such as *d*-amphetamine, *d*-methamphetamine, MDA, MDEA, MDMA, p-methoxymethamphetamine (PMMA), and N-methyl-1-(3,4-methylene-dioxyphenyl)-2-butanamine (MBDB).

ELISA, a heterogenous assay, is used by multiple manufacturers. Immunalysis Corporation has developed an ELISA kit with *d*-amphetamine as the target analyte. It can also detect MDA and phentermine, but has minimal cross-reactivity with *l*-amphetamine, methamphetamine, ephedrine, pseudoephedrine, and MDMA. Due to the limited cross-reactivity, Immunalysis offers a second ELISA kit designed to detect methamphetamine and MDMA. Randox Laboratories Limited also uses ELISA technology to target amphetamine-related compounds including, but not limited to, amphetamine, methamphetamine, MDMA, pseudoephedrine, mephedrone, methcathinone, and MDPV.

An alternative immunoassay technique supplied by Randox is the Biochip Array system. It uses a drug labeled horseradish peroxidase and a chemiluminescent detection system that offers detection of amphetamine and related compounds, including synthetic amphetamines. Several products target amphetamine, methamphetamine, MDMA, MDPV, methcathinone, and/or mephedrone. Each of these products has different target analytes with a range of selectivity for similar chemical structures.

Thin-Layer Chromatography

Thin-layer chromatography (TLC) is an older chromatographic system that has been used in systematic toxicological analysis for more than 50 years. It uses a mobile phase and stationary phase to separate the components of a mixture. The mobile phase is typically a solvent system with opposite polarity of the stationary phase, which is bound to the TLC plate. Typically, the TLC plate contains a silica-based stationary phase. The difference in polarity between the mobile and stationary phases aids in the separation of the components.

When separating drugs from a biological matrix, additional sample preparation is needed to concentrate the drugs in an appropriate solvent. Following a solvent extraction of the biological specimen, some of the solvent may be evaporated. This step concentrates the sample, and the remaining sample is applied to the bottom of a thin-layer plate coated with a silica stationary phase. After the plate is spotted with case extracts and standards, it is placed in a development tank saturated with various solvents. After development, the plate is removed from the tank and allowed to dry. Drug separation occurs as different drugs migrate to differing heights on the plate. An important term used in TLC is R_f. The R_f value for each compound is determined by dividing the distance the drug migrated by the distance of the solvent front. After removal from the developing tank and drying, a variety of coloring reagents can be applied to the plate so that drug movement can be visualized. A number of color reagents will permit visualization of amphetamines and sympathomimetic amines. For example, Dragendorff's reagent and iodoplatinate reagents produce a color change with all nitrogenous bases, while others, such as ninhydrin, produce a color change more specific to primary or secondary amines.

Some companies have combined the plates, solvents, and reagents into a single commercially available product line. The most common commercially available TLC system is Toxi-Lab® (Agilent Technologies). First steps include extraction, concentration onto a silica gel disk, placement onto a larger silica gel plate, and then development. Next the plate is removed, warmed to remove any solvent, and placed in a tank of formaldehyde vapors. Visualization is a multistep process that allows for the elucidation of hundreds of drugs of toxicological significance, including many of the amphetamines and sympathomemetic amines. In Stage 1, the plate is dipped in concentrated sulfuric acid. Many of the amphetamine and sympathomimetic amines have a yellow to yellowish-brown color at this stage, with the notable exception of MDMA, which appears blue. At Stage 2, the plate is dipped in water, where many analytes fade, but amphetamine, methamphetamine, MDA, and MDMA remain visible. In the next stage, the chromatogram is viewed with 366 nm transmitted UV light. Amines will appear blue upon exposure to UV light. In the final stage, the plate is dipped into a modified Dragendorff's reagent. At this stage, the amines are orange-brown in color. R_f values, often compared to standards run at the same time, are important in the identification of these drugs and their metabolites.

Gas Chromatography/Mass Spectrometry

Gas chromatography (GC) is a useful tool in the analysis of amphetamine and other structurally related amines. Various detectors such as nitrogen-phosphorus or mass spectrometry are coupled to GC. It is a separation technique that uses a gaseous mobile phase to carry the sample through the GC column. This GC column is coated with a stationary phase with particular physicochemical properties. Samples are typically introduced as a liquid, but are quickly volatilized by the high temperature of the injection port. Depending on the polarity of the stationary phase, amphetamine and other sympathomimetic amines will elute at various times. The time it takes to elute from the column is known as the retention time. Amphetamines and other structurally related compounds can be separated using dimethyl silicone and phenylmethyl silicone analytical columns without derivatization. They elute very early, prior to other drugs

such as narcotic analgesics, antidepressants, benzodiazepines, and antihistamines. Using nonpolar or slightly polar columns, the elution order of some of the more common ones are as follows: amphetamine, phentermine, methamphetamine, PPA, ephedrine, PE, MDA MDMA, MDEA, mephedrone, methylone, and MDPV.

Although not required, derivatization offers a number of advantages for qualitative and quantitative analysis of stimulant amines. One advantage is that peak tailing is reduced by forming a derivative. Reducing peak tailing improves peak shape, which allows for better peak integration and, consequently, more accurate quantitations. Derivatization also reduces the volatility of these compounds, increasing their retention time and enhancing their separation from potentially interfering endogenous compounds. While many derivatives are available for GC/MS use, those most commonly used with primary and secondary amines include heptafluorobutyric anhydride (HFBA), pentafluoropropionic anhydride (PFPA), trifluoroacetic anhydride (TFAA), and 4-carbethoxyhexfluorobutyryl chloride (4-CB). As an example, Table 1 provides GC/MS ion characteristics for HFBA derivatives of amphetamine, methamphetamine, and other amines.

A variety of detection systems are compatible with GC, but mass spectrometry is the most common for the detection of amphetamine and other sympathomimetic amines. Caution should always be taken when interpreting the mass spectral data because many of the compounds are very similar in size and structure, resulting in similar mass spectra. Retention time is helpful in the identification process. Furthermore, amphetamine and many other structurally similar compounds are volatile and precautions may need to be taken to increase recovery of these compounds in the sample preparation steps. For example, an acidic methanolic solution may be added to extracts prior to evaporating away the excess solvent in preparation of GC and GC/MS analysis.

Table 1. GC/MS Ion Characteristics for HFBA Derivatives of Sympathomimetic Amines

Compound	Retention Time (Min)[a]	Ions Monitored	Comments
β-Phenethylamine	4.6	104, 118, 99, 149/150	
d,l-Amphetamine	4.7	240, 118, 91	
Phentermine	4.8	254, 91	No 210 ion
Phenylpropanolamine	5.4	240, 160, 330, 275	
d,l-Methamphetamine	5.5	254, 118, 210	
Ephedrine	5.7	254, 210, 344	No 118 or 91 ions
Pseudephedrine	6.0	254, 210, 344	No 118 or 91 ions
Phenylephrine	6.5	240, 169	No 91 ion
MDA	7.1	135, 162, 240, 169	No 91 ion
MDMA	7.7	162, 254, 210, 162	No 118 or 91 ions
Benzphetamine	7.9	148, 91, 65, 149	Not derivatized

[a]HP-1 capillary column [12 m × 0.2 mm(id) × 0.33 μm] initial oven temperature = 100 °C; injection port = 250 °C; ramped from an initial temperature of 100 °C (held for 2 min) to 280 °C at 20 °C/min.

Liquid Chromatography

Like GC, liquid chromatography (LC) is a useful tool to separate constituents of a mixture. However, it requires a liquid mobile phase instead of a gaseous one to move a sample through the LC column. The LC column contains a stationary phase with particular physicochemical properties and, depending on the polarity of the stationary phase compared to the mobile phase, amphetamine and other sympathomimetic amines will elute at various times. LC can be coupled with a variety of detection systems. However, LC with detection systems other than mass spectrometry (MS) or tandem mass spectrometry (MS/MS) in the analysis of amphetamines and other amines have limited utility. For example, LC systems commonly use UV energy absorption technology in their detectors, but these amines do not have strong UV absorbance. Therefore, very low wavelengths would be necessary if UV absorbance or photodiode array detection were desired. Unfortunately, this increases the potential for endogenous substance interference. Improved detection limits could potentially be obtained with alternative detection systems such as fluorescence detection, but these drugs do not have native fluorescence. Furthermore, amphetamine and similar chemical structures do not lend themselves to electrochemical detection.

Derivatization of the stimulant amines can be performed for LC analysis. Unlike GC, where the primary reason for derivatization is improved chromatographic characteristics, the main advantage for derivatization in LC is improved detectability. Derivatizing reagents that have been used include 9-fluorenylmethylchloroformate and phenylisothiocyanate for UV detection and dansyl chloride and naphthaquinone-4-sulphonate for fluorescence detection.

The detector of choice is the mass spectrometer. LC/MS technology evolved with the development of atmospheric pressure ionization sources (API) for MS. API sources facilitate the ionization and transfer of analytes from a liquid medium (mobile phase) into the high-pressure region of the MS. Two main types of API sources are used for LC/MS and LC-MS/MS analysis of CNS stimulants: electrospray ionization (ESI) and atmospheric pressure chemical ionization (APCI). There are several advantages to using LC/MS vs GC/MS in the analysis of amines, including minimal sample extraction/preparation and greater specificity in the resultant MS data. A protein precipitation with methanol or acetonitrile may be all of the specimen preparation required for LC/MS analysis, as opposed to liquid-liquid extraction or solid-phase extraction for GC/MS. Furthermore, the more gentle ionization of ESI or APCI typically allows for the identification of the parent ion, which is useful with structurally similar compounds such as the amphetamines and sympathomimetic amines.

Chiral Separations

Many of the drugs in this class of compounds contain a chiral carbon and therefore exist as enantiomers. In many cases, pharmaceutical companies in the development of drugs have exploited the presence of the chiral carbon and its ability to bind with chiral receptors. Examples include methamphetamine, amphetamine, EPH/PE, and fenfluramine/dexfenfluramine. *D*-methamphetamine and *d*-amphetamine are used therapeutically for narcolepsy, attention deficit disorder, and weight loss. *L*-methamphetamine has one-tenth the CNS stimulation effect of the *d*-isomer but has greater peripheral vasoconstrictive properties and thus has been used in over-the-counter nasal inhalers. As a result, the *d*-form of amphetamine and methamphetamine are the primary abused drugs and often the target analytes for forensic and urine drug-testing laboratories. Since standard GC/MS procedures are unable to distinguish between enantiomers, special testing may be necessary.

Chromatographic identification of *d*- and *l*-isomers depends on the enantiomers reacting with optically active substrates to form diastereomers. This can be accomplished in one of two ways: (1) a chiral, optically active stationary phase can be used to form transient diastereomers with the optically active drug causing different partition coefficients, or (2) a chiral derivatizing reagent may be used to achieve separation on an achiral stationary phase.

Chiral stationary phases are available for both GC and LC systems. However, chiral derivatizing reagents have gained popularity since they allow chiral analysis on the same instrument used for other routine analyses.

The main disadvantage of using a chiral derivatizing reagent is the difficulty in ensuring the optical purity of the derivatizing reagent; four possible isomers can result from the reaction of an asymmetric sample with an asymmetric reagent rather than the two desired. The four derivative isomers consist of two diastereomeric pairs of chromatographically unresolvable enantiomers. Experiments must also be done to demonstrate both that racemization is not occurring during the derivatizing process and that stereoselective formation of one pair of diastereomers is not occurring.

Amines have been converted to diastereomeric amides with several chiral acid chloride reagents for GC analysis, such as *O*-methylmandelyl chloride, α-phenylbutyryl chloride or anhydride, and *N*-trifluoroacetyl-L-prolyl chloride (L-TPC). L-TPC is the most popular of this type of reagent. First used as a chiral derivatizing reagent for the separation of amino acids, it has since become popular for both the on-column and preinjection derivatization of amphetamine and methamphetamine. There have been some reports of racemization with the use of L-TPC. Amide derivatives can also be prepared with acyclimidazole reagents and with chiral acids in the presence of *N,N'*-carbonyldiimidazole. Diastereomeric sulfonamide derivatives have been created using (+)-camphor-10-sulfonyl chloride and menthyl carbamates, such as menthyl chlorformate. These reagents have been used for sympathomimetic amines and amino acid analysis.

INTERPRETATION

Impairment

At low doses, methamphetamine-induced CNS stimulation manifests clinically as euphoria, increased alertness, intensified emotions, increased feeling of self-esteem and well-being, sensations of extreme physical and mental power, and allegedly increased sexuality. Most abusers begin by taking amphetamines orally, usually 150–250 mg/day. Doses in this range generally produce plasma concentrations of 0.1–0.2 mg/L. Progression to intravenous use is usually a result of the desire to intensify the euphoric feelings that often accompany use of these drugs.

Intravenous use of amphetamines begins with 20- to 40-mg doses, three to four times a day. As tolerance develops, the dose and frequency of injection increase considerably and sleep cycles may be affected. For example, if the drug is injected every 2–3 h around the clock, the user never sleeps. A wide range of injection patterns exists, but there is potential for some drug abusers to inject repeatedly over several days, possibly up to 10–12 days. Following a run, users "fall out," i.e., become so exhausted, disorganized, tense, or paranoid that they cease using the drug and go to sleep. This sleep could last 12–18 h following a 3–4 day run. Upon awakening, the paranoid state is diminished, but lethargy may persist. At this point, a new run terminates the lethargy. When use becomes well established, individual injections range from 100 to 300 mg. Long-time abusers may use as much as 5000–15,000 mg/day.

Smoked doses of approximately 20 mg methamphetamine hydrochloride produce peak plasma concentrations of 0.04 mg/L in less than 1 h. Although methamphetamine levels peak rapidly after smoking, they remain high for a considerable time, declining with a half-life of 11–12 h. This long plateau effect and much longer half-life of smoked methamphetamine (vs oral or intravenous use) suggests significant danger in repeated smoking of methamphetamine, because if the dose is repeated, even at fairly long intervals, markedly higher plasma concentrations would be expected.

In toxic doses, amphetamine and drugs with similar structures begin to produce unpleasant CNS symptoms such as anxiety, agitation, hallucinations, delirium, seizures, and death. Long-term, high-dose use of stimulants can induce an acute psychotic state in previously healthy individuals or precipitate a psychotic episode in those with psychiatric illness. Hyperthermia may result from CNS-induced abnormalities, seizures, or muscular hyperactivity. Secondary rhabdomyolysis may also be seen.

Cardiovascular manifestations of amphetamine use include hypertension, tachycardia, atrial and ventricular arrhythmias, and myocardial ischemia. Cerebrovascular accidents may also be seen, precipitated by elevated blood pressures or drug-induced vasospasms.

Evidence suggests that the neurochemical basis underlying the behavioral effects and increased motor activity associated with sympathomimetic amines involves dopaminergic systems. By enhancement of neurotransmitter release/blockade of reuptake, stimulants facilitate catecholaminergic neurotransmission. One of the defining characteristics of psychomotor stimulants (methamphetamine, amphetamine, cocaine, etc.) is their ability to elicit increases in spontaneous motor activity. At low doses, these drugs produce an alerting response characterized by increases in exploration and locomotion. As the dose increases, locomotor activity decreases and the behavioral patterns become more stereotyped (i.e., a continuous repetition of one or several types of behavior). The "rewarding effects" (those responsible for psychomotor stimulant abuse) are also thought to result from enhanced DA release in the limbic regions such as the nucleus accumbens.

This mechanism causes a continuous release of neurotransmitter at low doses of stimulant, accounting for the locomotor stimulant and reinforcing effects of these compounds. As the dose increases, the cytoplasmic concentrations of neurotransmitter continue to increase and the phenomenon of intracellular oxidative stress becomes prominent. Ultimately, this results in neurotoxicity and selective degeneration of DA neuron terminals. When the monoamine neurotransmitters are redistributed from the reducing environment of the synaptic vesicle to extravesicular oxidizing environments, generation of oxygen radicals and reactive metabolites by monoamine oxidase within the neuron may trigger selective terminal loss. Similar effects are believed to occur with other weakly basic drugs (including fenfluramine, MDMA, and phencyclidine) that are toxic to monoamine systems. Chronic cocaine abusers also have been shown to have decreased neurofilament proteins in midbrain DA regions, suggesting that cocaine may also selectively damage neuronal processes.

Clinically, damage to or complete loss of these neurons would present as Parkinson's-like symptoms, choreoathetoid disorders (irregular, writhing/spasmodic, involuntary movements of the limbs or facial muscles, especially the fingers and hands), memory loss, irregular moods, anxiety, aggression, and changes in sleep patterns.

Impairment caused by designer amphetamines seems to manifest in similar ways to their more traditional counterparts. However, potency may be affected because of the minor modifications in the chemical structures that alter their physicochemical properties. In other words, the dose required to achieve the desired euphoric effect may be vastly different from one compound to the next. With this in mind, some of the packaging may have dosing listed in creative ways, especially if the product states that it is not for human consumption. Purity of the products may also be of concern, since many of these compounds are not manufactured and distributed in a regulated manner.

Postmortem

As is true with most abused drugs, tolerance makes it very difficult to use blood and tissue concentrations as predictors of cause or contribution to death. Steady-state amphetamine blood concentrations of 2–3 mg/L have been seen in tolerant addicts, while methamphetamine/amphetamine concentrations in fatal cases have ranged from <1 mg/L to >14 mg/L. Since the degree of tolerance for any drug is impossible to determine at autopsy, attributing significance to isolated postmortem concentrations or attempting to back-calculate to a dose is unwise. Furthermore, the redistribution of drugs within various postmortem tissues may also affect interpretation.

Fatalities have been reported after ingestion as low as 1.5 mg/kg. Low blood concentrations, thought to be incidental findings, are hard to interpret. Very low concentrations (<0.5 mg/L) have been observed in patients dying of what is now described as "classic stimulant toxicity" with agitation, hypertension, tachycardia, and hyperthermia. It is safe to say that, in the absence of any other pathological or anatomical causes of death, the detection of any amount of methamphetamine or amphetamine in the blood is significant and may have contributed to the cause of death. Recently, there has been an increase in reports of fatalities due to synthetic amphetamines and other designer drugs with similar structures.

Seizures, while also often associated with stimulant abuse, tend to occur only at very high doses. Convulsions are a common sequel to long-term, high-dose use of stimulants such as cocaine, the amphetamines, amphetamine analogs (MDMA, MDA, etc.), pemoline, aminorex, and 4-MAX. The mechanisms of seizure induction appear to be as varied as the drugs themselves; however, 5-HT depletion has been implicated in several models of convulsions, neurotoxicity, and clinical syndromes such as depression, multiple sclerosis, schizophrenia, and "stimulant psychosis." Depletion of the amine in the brain increases susceptibility to seizures, whereas agents that increase 5-HT concentration decrease susceptibility.

Stimulants achieve this final common pathway to seizurgenesis/5-HT reduction through a variety of mechanisms, including decreased synthesis, decreased release, increased metabolism, or death of serotonergic neurons. Chronic or subacute administration of amphetamine or methamphetamine produces prolonged decreases in regional tryptophan hydroxylase activity and concentrations of 5-HT.

4-MAX also has potent convulsant actions; it produces a substantial reduction in neostriatal TPH activity. Dramatic decreases in TPH activity have also been noted in other brain regions (hippocampus and frontal cortex) following 4-MAX administration.

Therapeutic Drugs Converted to Amphetamine/Methamphetamine

A number of drugs are metabolized to amphetamine and methamphetamine. This group includes benzphetamine, clobenzorex, deprenyl, famprofazone, fenethylline, and fenproporex. There are several ways to document the use of these drugs as an explanation for a positive urinalysis result. Examination of medical history is a straightforward approach. Alternatively, it may be possible to identify the parent drug in the urine specimens. Unfortunately, this is not always possible given the short half-lives of many of these drugs. Instead, the identification of a metabolite unique to these drugs may provide analytical verification that these drugs were ingested.

Enantiomer analysis can be used to document selegiline use. Prescription selegiline is the *l*-enantiomer; it is converted in the body exclusively to *l*-methamphetamine and *l*-amphetamine. Therefore, any findings of the *d*-isomers of these compounds would be inconsistent with selegiline use. Conversely, fenethylline is a racemic for the amphetamine portion of the molecule, which would most likely cause the detection of equal amounts of the *d* and *l* isomers in urine.

SUMMARY

Amphetamine and compounds with similar chemical structures represent a key class of drugs that stimulate the sympathetic nervous system. In various forms, a selective few of these drugs have become important therapeutic agents while many are targeted by recreational users. Extensive research has been conducted to better understand the pharmacokinetic and pharmacodynamic properties of these drugs. Laboratories have invested significant resources to optimize methods for detecting such compounds in various biological matrices.

SUGGESTED READING

1. Baselt RC. Disposition of toxic drugs and chemicals in man, 9th ed. Seal Beach, CA: Biomedical Publications, 2011.
2. Caldwell J. The metabolism of amphetamines in mammals. Drug Metab Rev 1976;5:219–80.
3. Cook CE, Jeffcoat AR, Hill JM, Pugh DE, Patetta PK, Sadler BM, et al. Pharmacokinetics of methamphetamine self-administered to human subjects by smoking *S*-(+)-methamphetamine hydrochloride. Drug Metab Disposition 1993;21:717–23.
4. Cook CE, Jeffcoat AR, Sadler BM, Hill JM, et al. Pharmacokinetics of oral methamphetamine and effects of repeated daily dosing in humans. Drug Metab Disposition 1993;20:856–62.
5. Cook CE. Pyrolytic characteristics, pharmacokinetics, and bioavailability of smoked heroin, cocaine, phencyclidine, and methamphetamine. NIDA Research Monograph 1991;115:6–23.
6. Drug Facts and Comparisons. St. Louis, MO: Wolters Kluwer Health, 2008.
7. Hoffman BB, Lefkowitz RJ. Catecholamines and sympathomimetic drugs. In: Gilman AG, Goodman LS, Rall TW, Murad F, eds. Goodman and Gilman's the pharmacological basis of therapeutics, 8th ed. New York, NY: Pergammon Press, 1990:187–220.
8. Jickells S, Negrusz A, eds. Clarke's analytical forensic toxicology. London UK: Pharmaceutical Press, 2008.
9. Kalix P. The pharmacology of psychoactive alkaloids from ephedra and catha. J Ethnopharmacol 1991;32:201–8.
10. Kelly JP. Cathinone derivatives: a review of their chemistry, pharmacology, and toxicology. Drug Test Anal 2011;3:439–53.
11. Kolbrich EA, Goodwin RS, Gorelick DA, Hayes RJ, Stein EA, Huestis MA. Plasma pharmacokinetics of 3,4-methylenedioxymethamphetamine after controlled oral administration to young adults. Ther Drug Monit 2008;30:320–32.
12. Moffat AC, Osselton MD, Widdop B, Watts J, eds. Clarke's analysis of drugs and poisons, 4th ed. London UK: Pharmaceutical Press, 2011.
13. Samanin R, Garattini S. Neurochemical mechanism of action of anorectic drugs. Pharmacol Toxicol 1993;73:63–8.
14. Silverstone T. Appetite suppressants: a review. Drugs 1992;43:820–36.

CHAPTER 21

Hallucinogens

Amanda J. Jenkins

Hallucinogen is a term commonly applied to a group of drugs that are capable of altering perception of reality. These are also known as psychedelic, psychotomimetic, or psychotogen drugs.

Under certain conditions, or at toxic doses, several classes of drugs can induce illusions, hallucinations, or delusions. These include anticholinergics, bromides, antimalarials, opioid antagonists, cocaine, corticosteroids, and certain volatile solvents. There is no distinct line dividing psychedelic compounds from other centrally acting drugs. However, one feature that distinguishes the psychedelic agent is the capacity to reliably induce states of altered perception, thought, and feeling that are not experienced otherwise except in dreams or at times of religious exaltation. Historically, there have been several attempts to define the term "hallucinogenic." Hollister defined hallucinogens by the following criteria:

1. Changes in thought, perception, and mood should dominate among the effects of the drug.
2. Memory or intellectual impairment should be minimal.
3. Stupor or excessive stimulation should not be a major effect.
4. Autonomic nervous system adverse effects should be minimal.
5. Addictive craving should be absent.

Most descriptions of the hallucinogenic state include several major effects, including a heightened awareness of sensory input and diminished control over what is experienced.

There may be a feeling that the self is divided in two, with one part a passive observer while the other part participates in the sensory experience. Frequently the attention of the individual is turned inward, with mild sensations having deep meaning. The user may experience a diminished capacity to differentiate the boundaries of one object from another and also of the user from the environment.

Most hallucinogens are New World alkaloids of plant origin. Although only 60 of the hundreds of thousands of plant species in existence have been used as hallucinogens, approximately 20 are considered clinically important. Hallucinogens have been classified generally into nitrogen-containing and non-nitrogen-containing compounds. Marijuana is an example of the latter and is discussed in Chapter 19. An alternate classification system also divides hallucinogens into two categories: the indolylalkylamines and the phenylalkylamines. The indolylalkylamines are subdivided as follows:

1. β-Carbolines, e.g., harmala alkaloids
2. Ergolines, e.g., lysergic acid diethylamide
3. α-Methyltryptamines, e.g., 5-methoxy α-methyltryptamine
4. Tryptamines, e.g., N,N-dimethyltryptamine, psilocin

Phenylalkylamines may be subdivided as follows:

1. Phenylalkylamines, e.g., mescaline
2. Phenylisopropylamines, e.g., 1-(2,5-dimethoxy-4X-phenyl-)-2-aminopropane

This chapter will discuss several examples of hallucinogens and also phencyclidine, which, although classified as a dissociative anesthetic, is primarily abused for its hallucinogenic properties. In addition, ketamine, another anesthetic agent, may now be added to the list of abused substances.

PHENCYCLIDINE

Phencyclidine (PCP, 1-[1-phenylcyclohexyl] piperidine) is an arylcyclohexylamine with a chemical formula of $C_{17}H_{25}N$ and a molecular weight of 243.4. It is structurally similar to ketamine (Fig. 1). PCP was first synthesized in 1926 but its utility as an anesthetic was not discovered until 1956, when Victor Maddox of the Product Development Department of Parke-Davis and Co. in Detroit, Michigan, investigated chemical reactions to Grignard reagents with nitriles. Maddox submitted several compounds to a pharmacologist at Parke-Davis, Graham Chen, for pharmacological testing. Experiments with laboratory animals (cats) led Chen to categorize this new compound as a "cataleptoid anesthetic." Further experiments with rhesus monkeys demonstrated its ability to produce serenity, tranquility, and peace.

Clinical trials in 1957 demonstrated phencyclidine's usefulness as an anesthetic in individuals with compromised cardiac function. In 1960 and 1963, the U.K. and U.S. governments, respectively, permitted use of PCP (under the trade name Sernyl™) as a short-acting analgesic or general anesthetic in humans. Shortly thereafter, adverse psychological reactions were observed in humans after surgery. These included delusions, delirium, hallucinations, muscle rigidity, and seizures. In 1963, Parke-Davis and Co.

discontinued marketing PCP for human use. PCP continued to be used, however, as a large-animal veterinary tranquilizer under the trade name Sernylan™. The legal manufacture of PCP continued until 1979.

PCP first appeared illicitly in 1967, when it was sold in the Haight-Ashbury district of San Francisco. At that time it was known as the "peace pill" and was self-administered orally. The adverse psychological effects of PCP resulted in a brief decrease in use in the late 1960s. Because illicit synthesis is relatively easy and inexpensive, abuse became widespread in the 1970s and early 1980s. Today, use of PCP tends to be highly regionalized in the U.S., apparent particularly in Los Angeles, New York, and the Baltimore–Washington, D.C., corridor. According to the National Survey Results on Drug Use from the Monitoring of the Future Study, 1975–1994, PCP use among high school seniors fell sharply between 1979 and 1982, from an annual prevalence of 7.0% to 2.2%. It reached a low in 1988 of 1.2%, rising slightly thereafter to 1.6% in 1994. In the same study, the prevalence rate was reported as 0.3% for young adults (19–32 years of age). More recent data suggest a continued decline in PCP use, with past year initial use declining from 123,000 in 2002 to 45,000 in 2010. However, these figures do not reflect the use of marijuana cigarettes laced with PCP. According to the Highlights of the 2010 Drug Abuse Warning Network (DAWN) of the U.S. Department of Health and Human Services, of the 4.9 million drug-related emergency department visits, approximately 1.1 million involved illicit drugs. PCP was involved in 21.1 ED visits/100,000 population of persons 21 or older, compared with 210.7 visits/100,000 for cocaine.

Drug-Abuse Patterns

PCP has many street names, including angel dust, killer weed, crystal, PeaCe Pill, hog, horse tracks, embalming fluid, and busy bee (Table 1). It may be sold as flakes or "angel dust" of high (80%) purity or in a

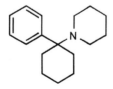

Fig. 1. Structure of phencyclidine.

Table 1. Phencyclidine Street Names

Angel dust	Lovely
Busy bee	Mist
Cadillac	Monkey tranquilizer
CJ	Peace
Crystal	Peace pill
Crystal joints	Peace weed
Elephant tranquilizer	Sheets
Embalming fluid	Sherman
Gorilla biscuits	Snorts
Hog	Super kool
Horse tracks	T
Jet fuel	Tick
Killer weed	White powder

less pure form (10–30%), resulting from soaking a tobacco or marijuana cigarette in liquid PCP or mixing with vegetable matter such as mint or parsley leaves. A single dose is approximately 5 mg, with a range of 1–10 mg.

Experimental and chronic-abuse patterns have been described. First-time users are introduced to PCP by friends; these friends may misrepresent the drug as a more desirable hallucinogen such as lysergic acid diethylamide (LSD). Many first-time users do not continue experimentation with PCP, disliking the sensory isolation PCP produces. Those who continue to use PCP are most likely polydrug abusers, already experienced with ethanol, marijuana, and sedatives. To these individuals, the disassociation and perceptual distortions that occur with PCP use are welcomed. PCP use may also result in feelings of power and strength, which users find attractive. Chronic use increases the likelihood of undesirable and unpredictable side effects.

Synthesis

PCP is controlled under Federal Schedule II of the Controlled Substances Act of 1970. Its salts, isomers, and salts of isomers are also controlled. Two of the precursors are also controlled: 1-phenylcyclohexylamine (PCH) and 1-piperidinocyclohexanecarbonitrile (PCC) (Fig. 2).

Fig. 2. Structure of phencyclidine precursors: 1-phenylcyclohexylamine (PCH) and 1-piperidinocyclohexanecarbonitrile (PCC).

To synthesize PCP, PCC is prepared by adding potassium cyanide and sodium bisulfite to piperidine and cyclohexanone. A Grignard reaction between phenylmagnesium bromide and PCC gives PCP as the product, with a yield of approximately 65% if care is exercised to remove water during synthesis. Several analogs of PCP have been clandestinely manufactured, including a thiophene analog, an n-ethyl analog, and a pyrolidine analog, all controlled under Schedule I (Fig. 3). 1-(1-Thiophenecyclohexyl)piperidine (TCP) is prepared as above, except that

Fig. 3. Structure of phencyclidine analogs: 1-(1-thiophenecyclohexyl) piperidine (TCP); 1-(1-phenylcyclohexyl) pyrrolidine (PHP); and 1-(1-phenylcyclohexyl) ethylamine (PCE) or cyclohexamine.

bromothiophene is used in the Grignard reagent. In the synthesis of 1-(1-phenylcyclo-hexyl)ethylamine (PCE) or cyclohexamine, ethylamine replaces piperidine. For the pyrolidine analog PHP or 1-(1-phenylcyclo-hexyl)pyrolidine, pyrolidine is used in place of piperidine.

Organic solvents, such as diethyl ether, are used during this procedure for extraction purposes. PCP may be converted to the hydrochloride salt by the addition of concentrated hydrochloric acid followed by air evaporation or by passing anhydrous hydrochloric acid into an ether solution of the base. Typically, the salt is sold on the street, but the base is also available. Unreacted PCC is not completely removed during this procedure and therefore will appear in the final product unless further cleanup is conducted. The colorless crystalline base has a melting point of 46 °C and a boiling point of 135–137 °C. Ultraviolet (UV) maxima in 0.1N hydrochloric acid occur at 252, 257.5, 262, and 268.5 nm. The octanol/water partition coefficient is 6600 at 25 °C. The hydrochloride salt of PCP has a molecular weight of 279.9 amu and is a stable white crystalline powder with a melting point of 233–235 °C. UV maxima in ethanol occur at 254, 258, 262.5, and 269 nm.

Mechanism of Action

PCP is classified pharmacologically as a dissociative anesthetic, but it exhibits stimulant, depressant, hallucinogenic, and analgesic properties. These effects appear to depend upon the dose, the route of drug administration, the personality of the individual, and also, possibly, genetic predisposition.

PCP interacts with many neurotransmitter systems, including the cholinergic, adrenergic, and dopaminergic systems. The relationship between specific receptor binding and the signs and symptoms observed in PCP users is unclear. PCP interacts with the N-methyl-D-aspartate (NMDA) receptor in the brain cortex, hippocampus, basal ganglia, and limbic system. Binding of excitatory amino acids such as glutamate and aspartate to the NMDA receptor permits cations to move across cell membranes. PCP binds to the glutamate receptor, blocking the channel, thus preventing the flux of cations such as calcium.

The actions of PCP on the dopaminergic system are thought to account for the principal effects on behavior (via the meso-limbic pathway) and on motor control (via the nigrostriatal pathway). PCP is thought to inhibit dopamine (DA) presynaptic uptake, promote the spontaneous release of DA, and stimulate the enzymes adenylate cyclase and tyrosine hydroxylase. PCP also increases glucose metabolism in those areas of the brain responsible for regulating or controlling emotional behavior, namely the frontal cortex, the hippocampus, and the caudoputamen.

PCP receptors have been described in the rat brain. Specific [3H]PCP binding was highest in the hippocampus, and binding in the cervical spinal cord was approximately one-third that of the hippocampus. Intermediate binding was observed in the hypothalamus, caudate nucleus, frontal cortex, and cerebellum, followed by the medulla/pons and amygdala. [3H]PCP binding was also found in hepatic and renal homogenates. This binding did not correlate with binding in the central nervous system or with behavioral tests. Therefore, specific binding sites may exist in the human brain and also to a lesser extent in other organs such as the liver and kidney. PCP may interact with non-cAMP-mediated DA_2 dopamine receptors rather than DA_1 receptors. In addition, PCP interacts with central sigma opiate receptors and affects endorphin-mediated behavior in laboratory animals. Sigma receptors are found in the central nervous system and also in endocrine, immune, and peripheral tissues. Stimulation of sigma receptors is thought to be responsible for several adverse effects of opiate use. Interaction with sigma receptors may explain similarities in the behavioral effects of different drugs that bind to them.

PCP may also bind to cholinergic receptors and potentially interact with cholinesterase enzymes. Mild anticholinergic effects are observed. For example, in the periphery, the antimuscarinic effects of PCP are several orders of magnitude less than atropine, resulting from action upon the ion channel of the motor endplate. PCP blocks nicotinic receptors.

PCP is an adrenergic agonist, elevating blood pressure and causing a pressor response at low doses. At high doses, PCP is a direct myocardial depressant. PCP reduces norepinephrine concentrations in the brain by causing the release of stored catecholamines. It also blocks certain sensory inputs, such as pain. PCP interferes with the sensory association pathways, thereby diminishing the user's ability to integrate sensory input into meaningful behavior.

Pharmacokinetics

The most common form of PCP encountered is the water-soluble hydrochloride salt. The base form is insoluble in water. PCP is a lipophilic weak base with a pK_a of 8.5. When produced for use as an anesthetic, PCP was administered intravenously. Illicit use as a "peace pill" was by oral ingestion. More recently, PCP has been self-administered by smoking. Flakes of crystalline PCP may be sprinkled on marijuana ("lovely"). Conversely, marijuana cigarettes or regular tobacco cigarettes may be "dunked" in liquid PCP ("Sherman") and then smoked. Alternatively, vegetable matter, such as parsley flakes, may be mixed with liquid PCP and then rolled into cigarettes. Powdered PCP may also be mixed with cocaine ("tick"). Smoking as a route of drug administration has the advantage of allowing the smoker to control the dose by varying the frequency and depth of puffs. The pharmacokinetic characteristics of absorption vary depending upon route of administration. Several pharmacokinetic parameters of PCP are listed in Table 2.

PCP is typically self-administered by the oral, intravenous, or smoked routes. After oral administration to healthy human volunteers, the bioavailability was found to vary

Table 2. Pharmacokinetic Parameters of Phencyclidine

Weak base	
Lipophilic	
pK_a	8.5
V_d	5.3–7.5 L/kg
Fb	0.65
Blood/plasma ratio	1
$T_{1/2}$	7–46 h
Clearance	0.14–0.77 L/min

V_d = volume of distribution; Fb = fraction plasma protein bound; $T_{1/2}$ = elimination half-life.

between 50% and 90%. In this study, peak plasma concentrations were achieved after 1.5 h and appeared to correlate with the time to reach maximum pharmacological effects. However, because there have been no comprehensive clinical controlled studies of phencyclidine, correlation between PCP blood concentrations and pharmacological effects has not been definitively documented. Maximum serum PCP concentrations ranged between 2.7 and 2.9 ng/mL after 1 mg PCP administered orally.

PCP is commonly self-administered by the smoked route. Upon smoking, PCP is partially volatilized to 1-phenylcyclohexene (PC). One study found that 69 ± 5% of the PCP available in the cigarette was inhaled, 39% as PCP and 30% as PC. Losses of drug also occurred in main and sidestream smoke. The pharmacological and toxicological properties of PC have not been established. Peak plasma concentrations of PCP were reached within 5–20 min. In 80% of the subjects, a second peak was observed in plasma PCP concentrations, occurring 1–3 h after the end of smoking. This may have been due to trapping of PCP in the mouth, where it could be released and absorbed by the gastrointestinal tract, or alternatively, it could be due to absorption by the lung and bronchial tissue with slower release into the systemic circulation. Long-term users of PCP report feeling the effects of the drug within 2–5 min of smoking, with a peak effect after 15–30 min and residual effects for 4–6 h.

Plasma protein binding of PCP in healthy individuals remains relatively constant between 60% and 70% over the concentration range of 7–5000 ng/mL. PCP binding to serum albumin accounts for only 24% of the binding; this suggests that binding to another protein may occur to a significant extent. When studied in vitro, α1-acid glycoprotein was also found to bind PCP. The volume of distribution has been shown to be large (5.3–7.5 L/kg), providing evidence of extensive distribution to extravascular tissues.

The pharmacokinetics of PCP have been described by a two-compartment model with a plasma half-life for PCP of 7–16 h, or a more complex three-compartment pharmacokinetic model with reported half-lives for each compartment of 5.5 min, 4.6 h, and 22 h. The specific tissues and organs represented by the multicompartment model were not identified. Half-lives >3 days have been reported in cases of PCP overdose.

PCP is metabolized by the liver through oxidative hydroxylation. Unchanged PCP and one dihydroxylated and two monohydroxylated metabolites have been identified in urine after oral and intravenous administration. The monohydroxylated metabolites have been identified as 4-phenyl-4-(1-piperidinyl)-cyclohexanol (PPC) and 1-(1-phenylcyclohexyl)-4-hydroxypiperidine (PCHP). These metabolites are pharmacologically inactive in humans, and PPC is present in both cis- and transisomeric forms. The cis/trans ratio was found to be 1:1.4 in human urine. The dihydroxylated metabolite was identified as 4-(4-hydroxypiperidino)-4-phenylcyclohexanol (HPPC). These metabolites are present in urine as glucuronide conjugates, as well as in their unconjugated forms.

Approximately 30–50% of a labeled intravenous dose was excreted over a 72-h period in urine as unchanged drug (19.4%) and 80.6% as polar metabolites, PPC. Only 2% of a dose is excreted in feces. After 10 days, an average of 77% of an intravenous dose is found in the feces and urine. Urine PCP concentrations of 40–3400 ng/mL have been reported in ambulatory users.

Urine pH is an important determinant of renal elimination of PCP. In a study in which urine pH was uncontrolled (6.0–7.5), the average total clearance of PCP was 22.8 ± 4.8 L/h after intravenous administration. In the same study, renal clearance was 1.98 ± 0.48 L/h. When the urine was made alkaline, the renal clearance of PCP was found to decrease to 0.3 ± 0.18 L/h. If the urine was acidified (pH 6.1) in the same subjects, renal clearance increased to 2.4 ± 0.78 L/h. There is disagreement about the utility of urine acidification in the treatment of PCP overdose, even though excretion may be increased by as much as 100-fold. It should be noted that acidification may increase the risk of metabolic complications.

Effects

Pollack noted that PCP intoxication is "a clinical condition that is defined by clinical signs and symptoms, ranging from mild, moderate, to severe, with coma and eventual death." Intoxication is influenced by several variables mentioned previously, such as preparation, route of administration, dose, age, personality, and medical, drug, and behavioral history. These factors result in variable responses to given doses and poor correlation between blood concentrations and behavior. However, generalized statements can be made.

The effects of PCP administration are observed within a few minutes after smoking or intravenous administration and within 1 h after oral ingestion. The typical high from PCP lasts 4–6 h, with a "come down" period of 6–24 h. A dose of 1–5 mg generally produces feelings of euphoria and numbness. At this stage an observer may liken the effect to alcohol intoxication. Disinhibition and emotional liability may also be observed in the user. A dose of 5–10 mg will likely produce an excited but confused individual who may exhibit repetitive motor movements, fever, diaphoresis, myoclonus, vomiting, decreased peripheral sensations, and horizontal and vertical nystagmus. At these doses, catatonia and paranoid schizophrenia may occur. Coma and death from respiratory depression caused by seizure activity may occur at doses ≥20 mg. Table 3 lists the pharmacological effects of PCP according to approximate dose. Generally, impaired thought or psychotic reactions are more likely to occur with phencyclidine use than with LSD or mescaline. In one study, despite adverse effects 72% of individuals continued to use PCP due to its powerful psychological effects, availability, and relatively low cost.

A PCP-abuse syndrome has been described. It is distinguished by four behavioral phases, namely: acute toxicity, toxic psychosis, PCP-precipitated psychotic episodes, and PCP-induced depression. Acute PCP toxicity is characterized by the four *c*'s: combativeness and catatonia at low doses and convulsions and coma at higher doses. Toxic psychosis includes impaired judgment, paranoid delusions, visual and auditory hallucinations, and agitations. This may occur

Table 3. Pharmacological Effects of Phencyclidine

Physiological	Psychological
Low Dose (<5 mg)	
Increased blood pressure	Agitative behavior
	Euphoria
Increased deep tendon reflexes	Disorganization of thought
Perspiration	Body image changes
Facial grimacing	Apprehension/anxiety
Tremors	Dissociation
Incoordination	
Moderate Dose (5–10 mg)	
Spontaneous nystagmus	Feelings of inebriation
	Insomnia
Hypersalivation	Loss of appetite
Nausea and vomiting	Rage
Repetitive motor movements	Amnesia
	Hypnotic state
Muscle rigidity	Fever
High Dose (>10 mg)	
Hypertension	Catatonia
Arrhythmias	Eyes open or closed
Tonic-clonic seizures	Cerebral bleeding
Absent peripheral sensations	Coma
	Death

from 24 h to 7 days. The PCP toxic psychosis is typically observed in chronic users. Toxic psychosis may be followed by the psychotic episode, which may last 7–30 days. PCP-induced depression may occur after any of the preceding three stages and may last from one day to several months. During this time, the individual is at high risk of suicide.

Additional medical complications of PCP intoxication include generalized tonic-clonic seizures, elevation of systolic and diastolic blood pressure, hyperthermia, and rhabdomyolysis with or without renal failure due to myoglobinuria. There is no antidote for PCP overdose. Seizures and respiratory depression are more frequently observed in children. Treatment of the PCP-intoxicated individual involves stabilization, such as maintaining airway and ventilatory adequacy. This is followed with supportive care to correct medical complications only and not to restrain individuals unnecessarily. Therefore, if body temperature is elevated above 105 °F, the individual is rapidly cooled. Hypertension is observed in approximately 50% of PCP intoxications. Complications are unusual even with systolic pressures of 250 mm Hg. Once agitated or violent behavior is controlled, blood pressure typically drops. However, if the diastolic blood pressure remains above 140 mm Hg or symptoms related to hypertension occur, treatment with sublingual nifedipine or intravenous nitroprusside should be administered. The agitated state or any violent behavior may be treated with 5–10 mg (in adults) of diazepam, administered intravenously. Psychoses may be treated with haloperidol or chlorpromazine. Response appears to be better with haloperidol, a specific DA_2 receptor antagonist, than with chlorpromazine, a mixed DA_1 and DA_2 antagonist. Airway hyperactivity may be treated with aminophylline while dystonic reactions respond to diphenhydramine. Rhabdomyolysis is the main complication of PCP intoxication; it is thought to result from the use of restraints in agitated people. Therefore, it is recommended that restraints not be used but that the individual be placed in a quiet room with minimal stimuli.

Rhabdomyolysis is treated with fluid replacement and monitoring of urinary output. Retention of the urine may require catheterization. Generally, elimination enhancement procedures are not recommended treatment for the PCP-intoxicated patient.

Analysis

PCP has been measured in drug seizures using the techniques of colorimetry, UV spectrophotometry, thin-layer chromatography (TLC), gas chromatography (GC), and gas chromatography/mass spectrometry (GC/MS). PCP has also been detected on U.S. paper currency in microgram quantities using GC/MS technology. Similarly, PCP, its analogs, and metabolites have been determined in biological specimens using the techniques of immunoassay, TLC, GC, and GC/MS. UV-SPEC, although routinely used to detect and quantify PCP in solid dose samples, is not sufficiently sensitive for detecting PCP in biological specimens.

A presumptive color test has been described for PCP in urine using tetrabromophenolphthalein ethyl ester reagent after buffering the sample to pH 6–7. The limit of detection is 1000 ng/mL. TLC was the first analytical technique used for detecting PCP in urine. Indeed, today the commercial paper chromatography system, Toxi-Lab® system A, is routinely used for measuring PCP in urine. It is detected as a brown spot at Stage IV with an R_f of 0.85 and a detection limit of 500 ng/mL. Other TLC systems and visualization reagents have been described. Urine specimens are routinely screened for PCP by immunoassay. This technique was first developed in the 1970s, and today immunoassays that target PCP are available utilizing EMIT®, CEDIA®, RIA, FPIA, ELISA, and KIMS® technologies. Vendors generally provide reagents using the federally mandated cutoff for workplace drug testing of 25 ng/mL. On-site drug testing or point-of-care testing devices are also typically based on competitive binding immunoassay technology. Commercial immunoassays

for PCP cross-react to a varying degree with several analogs such as TCP. In addition, false-positive results have been reported for venlafaxine and metabolite, tramadol and metabolite, dextromethorphan, ibuprofen, 3,4-methylenedioxypyrovalerone (MDPV), and methoxetamine.

PCP may be extracted from biological specimens by traditional liquid–liquid extraction procedures or by solid-phase extraction. Solid-phase extraction techniques typically exhibit recoveries >85%. Many of these assays, especially those analyzed by GC/MS, use a deuterated internal standard (d_5-PCP). Classic liquid–liquid extraction procedures alkalinize the biological matrix, add an organic solvent such as n-butyl chloride, and back extract by adding acid followed by another base and then an organic solvent such as methylene chloride. This solvent is evaporated to dryness and the extract reconstituted with isopropanol or an alternate organic solvent. Solid-phase extraction procedures typically buffer the matrix to pH 4–6, precondition the column, and elute the analyte with a basic organic solvent such as 2% ammonium hydroxide in ethyl acetate or methanol. PCP may be analyzed qualitatively and quantitatively by GC with capillary columns. Flame ionization detection has been used with limits of detection of 50 ng/mL. Several procedures have been described using nitrogen phosphorus detection with limits of quantification around 10 ng/mL. PCP exhibits good chromatographic characteristics without the need for derivatization. However, methods described in the literature include derivatization with heptafluorobutyric anhydride.

High-performance liquid chromatographic procedures for the analysis of PCP in biological specimens have been described. One procedure used a C_{18} reversed-phase column, a buffered mobile phase containing 65% methanol and 1% triethylamine, and UV detection at 254 nm.

Several GC/MS procedures have been described to measure PCP and its hydroxylated metabolites in biological matrices using electron impact ionization. Full-scan and selected ion monitoring (SIM) modes have been used. When performing SIM analysis, m/z 200, 242, and 243 ions are commonly monitored. Reported limits of detection for these assays are 1–5 ng/mL. Chemical ionization GC/MS has also been used to quantify PCP and its metabolites. In one report, ions selected for monitoring were m/z 159 and 243 for PCP and m/z 164 and 248 for the pentadeuterated PCP internal standard. LC/MS/MS procedures have been developed for the measurement of PCP using deuterated internal standards. These methods typically involve little sample preparation while achieving lower limits of quantitation close to 5 ng/mL. More novel techniques using microfluidic chip based nano liquid chromatography-tandem mass spectrometry and capillary zone electrophoresis with ultraviolet detection have also been described.

Interpretation of PCP Concentrations

As previously discussed, no controlled pharmacokinetic studies have been performed in humans using psychoactive doses. In 26 individuals arrested for driving under the influence of drugs or exhibiting disorderly behavior in public, blood phencyclidine concentrations were 7–240 ng/mL, with an average of 75 ng/mL. In a study reporting PCP blood concentrations in Drug Recognition Expert (DRE) cases, blood concentrations were measured in 259 people over a two-year period. The mean PCP concentration for those cases in which only PCP was identified by both the DRE and toxicology was 51 ng/mL, with a range of 12–118 ng/mL. No correlation was found in this study between PCP concentration and behavior.

Another study described the incidental intoxication of a 62-year-old woman who lived above a clandestine PCP laboratory and visited a hospital emergency room complaining of odors in her bathroom that made her dizzy. A serum PCP concentration of 8 ng/mL was determined by GC with nitrogen phosphorous detection (NPD) and later confirmed by GC/MS. On admission, the woman appeared fully oriented, alert, and cooperative but depressed. GC-NPD was also used to measure phencyclidine in blood and urine specimens obtained from two law enforcement personnel who handled confiscated PCP preparations. One individual had a blood PCP concentration of 28 ng/mL that declined to 4 ng/mL after two weeks, during which time he continued to handle PCP cases. The second individual had a blood PCP concentration of 70 ng/mL, declining to <1 ng/mL after two weeks. PCP was detected in the urine of the first individual but not the second.

PCP has been measured in saliva obtained from 100 emergency room patients. Paired serum and saliva samples were measured. Seventy-four of the 100 saliva samples and 75 of the paired serum samples were positive for PCP. PCP protein binding in saliva is approximately 7%. Saliva concentrations usually exceed plasma concentrations with a saliva:plasma concentration ratio of 2:4. PCP has also been detected in cerebrospinal fluid, usually exceeding serum concentrations. PCP has been identified in human hair at 0.1–23 ng/mg of hair. This drug has also been measured in sweat. In one study, radiolabeled PCP was detected in axilla perspiration for 54 h following intravenous administration. The appearance of PCP has been studied in cord blood, amniotic fluid, and breast milk. PCP was detected in 12% of cord blood samples in a large urban teaching hospital with concentrations of 0.1–5.8 ng/mL. In the same study, PCP was identified in amniotic fluid on the 36th day of pregnancy in one individual. The PCP concentration in the maternal blood was 0.77 ng/mL with a concentration of 3.42 ng/mL reported in the amniotic fluid. In the same case, PCP was identified in the breast milk five days later at a concentration of 3.9 ng/mL.

The majority of PCP-related deaths occur due to the behavioral toxicity of the drug. This includes jumping from high buildings and drowning. In a Los Angeles County study in 1983 of 104 PCP-related fatalities, only 15 deaths were determined to be due to PCP overdose. The deaths were usually accidental or homicidal. Individuals who commit suicide while under the influence of PCP typically choose very violent methods, such as leaping from a building or a freeway overpass or plunging a large knife into the chest or running into a wall. Death by direct PCP toxicity is usually due to respiratory arrest, hyperpyrexia with cardiovascular collapse, status epilepticus, or coma with multiple organ failure. Death has been reported after the ingestion of 120 mg of PCP.

In a study in Maryland, PCP was detected in 37 cases in a medical examiner population over a two-year period in the mid-1970s. However, in only two cases was death a result of acute PCP toxicity. Blood PCP concentrations in these cases were 1500 and 25,000 ng/mL. In the other 35 cases, blood concentrations ranged from 20–700 ng/mL with a median concentration of 100 ng/mL. Individuals were typically white males age 16–42 (mean age, 21). Causes of death in these cases included gunshot wounds, asphyxia, stab wounds, smoke and soot inhalation, drowning, multiple injuries, and intravenous narcotism. The manner of death in 38% of the PCP-positive cases in this study was suicide. In another study in California, nine fatal cases attributed to PCP overdose had blood PCP concentrations of 300–12,000 ng/mL and liver concentrations of 999–80,000 ng/g. Two of the cases were determined to be suicides. These investigators compared blood and tissue concentrations in deaths due to PCP toxicity vs deaths due to other causes. They determined that the two groups could not be separated based upon PCP concentrations.

In a five-year retrospective study (2003–2007) conducted by the New York City Office of the Chief Medical Examiner, PCP was identified in postmortem blood (in 95% of cases the heart was the site of collection) in 138 cases. The concentration of PCP in blood in mixed-drug intoxications [N=52, 38%] ranged from <1–598 ng/mL. Of the 80 violent deaths, concentrations ranged from <1–581 ng/mL. Similar to the Maryland study 30 years earlier, these deaths included sharp-force injuries, firearms injuries, smoke inhalation, drownings, falls from a height, and asphyxia. Blood PCP concentrations in five nonviolent deaths ranged from 53–361 ng/mL. It was concluded that underlying medical conditions could have contributed to the death of these individuals.

In cases of PCP intoxication, there are no specific pathologic findings. At autopsy, pulmonary congestion is often found in probable acute PCP intoxication. In addition, acute posterior lobar pneumonia, or bronchopneumonia, or numerous alveolar macrophages have been reported in several cases. No neuropathologic changes have been documented from autopsy studies of PCP intoxications.

Precursors and Analogs

Contamination of street samples of PCP with the precursor PCC is not uncommon. During synthesis, incomplete reaction with the Grignard reagent results in the presence of PCC in the finished product. PCC is present in approximately 20% of street samples and is approximately equipotent to PCP in producing lethality in mice. Its toxicity is reported to be three times greater than PCP, with a lethal synergism between PCC and PCP. The mechanism of toxicity appears to be different with the labile cyano group resulting in the in vivo release of hydrogen cyanide. Toxic symptoms include vomiting, abdominal pain, and diarrhea. Upon degradation, PCC produces piperidine that has a fish-like smell.

The analog cyclohexamine (PCE) has similar pharmacological properties as PCP, with a potency in rats six times greater than PCP. It is usually available as a powder or tablet in a range of colors from off-white to pink to brown. It may be self-administered by routes similar to those for PCP. Two fatalities resulting from PCE use have been documented in the literature. The first, a 24-year-old male, had a blood PCE concentration of 3100 ng/mL. The cause of death was determined to be drug overdose. The second individual, also a young male in his 20s, had a blood PCE concentration of 1000 ng/mL and a liver concentration of 1900 ng/g. In the latter case, the cause of death was determined to be drowning. In both cases, no other drugs, including ethanol, were detected.

The physiological properties of the analog TCP appear to be similar to PCP in humans. In rats, TCP may be slightly more active. Approximately 9% of PCP seizures also contain TCP. The analog PHP produces similar pharmacological effects as PCP. The presence of PHP was reported in specimens obtained from the autopsy of an individual shot while acting in a bizarre manner and resisting police arrest.

Other PCP analogs have been reported: TCM or 1-[1-(2-thienyl)cyclohexyl] morpholine; PCM or 1-(1-phenylcyclohexyl) morpholine; and PCDEA or N,N-diethyl-1-phenyl-cyclohexylamine.

LYSERGIC ACID DIETHYLAMIDE

D-lysergic acid diethylamide (LSD; 9, 10-didehydro-N,N-diethyl-6-methylergoline-8β-carboxamide) is an indolealkylamine (Fig. 4) discovered by Albert Hoffman of Sandoz Laboratories in 1943 after he inadvertently ingested the compound. It may be synthesized from lysergic acid and diethylamine. Lysergic acid, a naturally occurring ergot alkaloid, is present in grain parasitized by the fungus *Claviceps purpurea,* which may grow on certain rye plants. A closely related alkaloid, lysergic acid amide, is present in morning glory seeds and the Hawaiian baby wood rose.

LSD is a colorless, odorless, tasteless liquid that is very potent. As a result, it is almost always diluted and self-administered in low doses. It is available illicitly as a powder,

tablet, gelatin capsule, or impregnated in sugar cubes, gelatin squares, blotter paper, or postage stamps. Impregnation is achieved by pouring an aqueous solution of LSD evenly over the absorbent. Blotter paper is typically perforated into squares that are often imprinted with figures, logos, and other designs. Clandestine laboratories may manufacture tablets that are usually small and colored. They are often referred to by their color, such as orange sunshine, purple haze, and yellow microdots. One tablet typically contains 0.05–0.1 mg LSD. Another form of LSD known as windowpanes was popular in the 1970s and consisted of small (1 × 2 mm) gelatin rectangles.

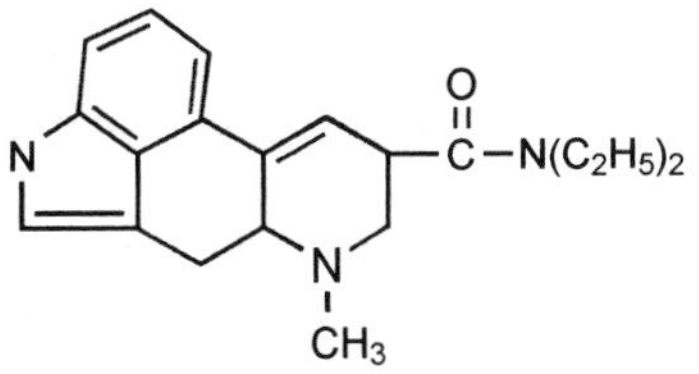

Synthesis

LSD may be synthesized by adding cold trifluoroacetic anhydride in acetonitrile to a cold solution of lysergic acid. After standing for a few hours, a solution of diethylamine in acetonitrile is added, the mixture is allowed to stand for 2 h, and then the acetonitrile is removed by vacuum. The crude LSD should be dissolved in chloroform and washed with water. Purification may be achieved by evaporating the chloroform and then pouring on an alumina column with a 3:1 benzene:chloroform solution. The resulting mixture contains d-LSD and d-iso-LSD that may be separated using a carbonate column.

Drug-Abuse Patterns

In the 1950s, LSD was used in medicine as an aid in the treatment of alcoholism, opioid addiction, psychoneurosis, and sexual disorders. Currently it is classified under Schedule I of the Federal Controlled Substances Act of 1970, with no accepted medical use in the U.S. Its precursor, lysergic acid, is controlled under Schedule III, which restricts distribution. According to the National Institute on Drug Abuse's Monitoring the Future Study, LSD lifetime use increased 1% among 8th graders (from 2.7% to 3.7%) from 1991 to 1994;

Fig. 4. Structure of LSD.

1.7% among 12th graders (from 8.8% to 10.5%); and remained stable among young adults (at approximately 13%) throughout the same period. According to recent DAWN data, LSD-related emergency room episodes have remained relatively stable since 1988, at 3300–3900 annually. More recently among youths ages 12–17 the number of lifetime users of LSD has remained fairly stable since 2004, with a prevalence estimate in 2010 of 0.9%. During the same period the estimate decreased from 12.1 to 6.4% among young adults ages 18–25. Current trends suggest that more than 300,000 individuals aged 12 or older will initiate LSD use within a given year.

Of all illicit drugs, LSD is probably the least adulterated. More than 90% of alleged LSD street samples are genuine with diethylamine present as a contaminant. The typical street dose is 50–300 µg (average, 100 µg) with a minimum effective dose of about 25 µg. The optimal psychedelic dose is considered 100–1000 µg. LSD is approximately 3000 times more potent on a per weight basis than mescaline. It is typically self-administered orally, with intermittent use (a "binge") more common than intense and sustained use. LSD users are typically polydrug users, experimenting with ethanol, marijuana, and amphetamines. Concurrent sedative-hypnotic and opiate use is uncommon in this group of drug users. Tolerance to the effects of LSD does occur but physical withdrawal symptoms upon discontinuation do not occur although a user may be psychologically dependent. Development of tolerance depends upon the dose and frequency but typically develops after 3–4 daily doses. Tolerance disappears 4–5 days after drug withdrawal. Cross-tolerance develops between LSD, psilocybin, and mescaline but not d-amphetamine.

Mechanism of Action

LSD is a potent centrally acting drug. The d-isomer is pharmacologically active while the l-isomer is apparently inactive. Neuropharmacological studies have shown that LSD exerts a selective inhibitory effect on the brain's raphe system by causing cessation of the spontaneous firing of serotonin-containing neurons of the dorsal and median raphe nuclei. In this way, LSD acts as an indirect serotonin antagonist. However, inhibition of raphe firing is not sufficient to explain the psychotomimetic effects of LSD, because the compound lisuride is a more potent inhibitor of the raphe system yet does not demonstrate hallucinogenic potential in humans. Therefore, other postsynaptic mechanisms such as action on glutamate or serotonin receptors may be involved. In addition, there is evidence that LSD indirectly exerts effects on the cytoskeleton by reducing the amount of serotonin released by the raphe system.

Effects

The effects of LSD may be divided into physiological, psychotomimetic, and psychiatric. Physiological effects are primarily sympathomimetic, parasympathomimetic, and neuromuscular, such as mydriasis, lacrimation, tachycardia, piloerection, hyperglycemia, and elevated body temperature. Pupil dilation of 3–5 mm is the most frequent and consistent sign of LSD use. After large doses, salivation, tremor, nausea, vomiting, hyperactivity, and hyperreflexia may occur. Rhabdomyolysis has been reported after LSD ingestion.

Psychological experiences include perceptual alterations such as visual illusions and alterations in sound or in intensity of colors. Misrepresentation of sensory cues is the most notable and consistent alteration. Fixed objects undulate and flat surfaces assume depth. Amplification of background noise may occur with an overflow of sensory input such that colors are heard and music is palpable. Thought processes are affected to the degree that body image changes with depersonalization. Typically, orientation is preserved but judgment may be poor due to paranoia or ideas of persecution. Behavioral patterns after LSD use are difficult to predict because they depend upon the setting, expectations, the individual's underlying personality, and emotional stress in addition to the dose. Individuals tend to be quiet, passive, self-centered, and withdrawn. However, the mood may be labile.

No single factor guarantees a pleasurable LSD experience. An acute panic attack is the most common side effect of LSD use and frequently accompanies accidental consumption. Other psychiatric effects include flashbacks (the recurrence of drug effect without drug use), acute psychotic reactions, and behavior-induced trauma. Flashback experiences include visual alterations, time distortions, and body image changes after a period of abstinence. Flashbacks may be precipitated by physiological and emotional stress and occur in approximately 15% of users for several years following ingestion. The etiology of flashbacks is unknown. Acute psychotic reactions include superimposed visual alterations and spatial and depth distortions. The occurrence of acute mania after LSD use is suspected but not proven. LSD-induced suicide and accidental trauma are more common than homicide. Amnesia for the events is rare.

Life-threatening reactions to LSD are rare but do occur. Death resulting from pharmacologic overdose has been reported in one case in which antemortem serum contained 14 ng/mL LSD. Death resulting from trauma experienced during hallucinations with altered perceptions is more common.

Pharmacokinetics

LSD may be self-administered orally, nasally, or by injection. However, the oral route is the most common. Absorption is rapid and complete regardless of the route of administration. Food in the stomach slows absorption when ingested. Effects are observed within 5–10 min, with psychosis evident after 15–20 min. Peak effects have been reported 30–90 min after dosing, with effects declining after 4–6 h. The duration of effects may be 8–12 h.

Pharmacokinetic studies in humans are limited, and most of the data are from the 1960s. In one study, a peak plasma LSD concentration of 5 ng/mL was observed 1 h after intravenous administration of 2 µg/kg. At 8 h, the plasma concentration had declined to 1 ng/mL.

Plasma protein binding of LSD is >80%. As the drug penetrates the CNS, it is concentrated in the visual brain areas and the limbic and reticular activating systems, correlating with perceived effects. LSD is also found in the liver, spleen, and lungs. The volume of distribution is reported to be low at 0.28 L/kg. A two-compartment open model for LSD has been described, with an elimination half-life of 3 h.

The metabolism and elimination of LSD in humans has received limited study. Animal studies demonstrated extensive biotransformation via N-demethylation, N-deethylation, and hydroxylation to inactive metabolites. In humans, demethylation and aromatic hydroxylation occur resulting in N-desmethyl-LSD and 13- and 14-hydroxy-LSD. Recent work using urine specimens from LSD users has indicated a metabolite of LSD, 2-oxo-3-hydroxy-LSD, is present in concentrations an order of magnitude above parent drug concentrations. Hydroxylated metabolites undergo glucuronidation to form water-soluble conjugates. Excretion into the bile accounts for approximately 80% of a dose. Concentrations of unchanged drug range from 1–55 ng/mL in the 24-h urine after ingestion of 200–400 µg LSD in humans. LSD or its metabolites have been detectable for 34–120 h after a 300-µg oral dose in seven human subjects. The clearance of LSD in humans is unknown.

Analysis

LSD is often difficult to analyze due to the low doses required to produce psychoactive effects. One tablet or one square of blotter paper may contain 0.1 mg LSD. In addition, LSD is relatively unstable and is sensitive to UV light and heat. LSD in biological specimens is considered stable when the samples are stored frozen. Losses during analysis may also occur due to irreversible absorptive processes, especially when using GC.

Color tests are often used to screen possible LSD samples. These include Ehrlich's test that uses p-dimethylaminobenzaldehyde to produce a purple color in the presence of LSD. TLC may also be used to analyze samples. Common mobile phases for normal-phase silica gel plates include chloroform:methanol (9:1), toluene:dimethylformamide (6:1), and acetone/ammonium hydroxide:methanol (18:1). Ergot alkaloids are highly fluorescent, and therefore fluorescence technologies are ideal for qualitative and quantitative analysis of LSD. Its fluorescence maxima are approximately 320 nm (excitation) and 400 nm (emission).

EMIT, ELISA, KIMS, and CEDIA are immunoassays available for LSD analysis. The usual screening cutoff is 0.5 ng/mL. Each immunoassay has varying cross-reactivites to LSD metabolites and congeners.

LSD may be isolated from biological specimens by liquid–liquid and solid-phase extraction procedures. Liquid–liquid methods may use methysergide as an internal standard, rendering the sample basic with ammonium carbonate and sodium hydroxide, followed by extraction into petroleum ether-dichloromethane-isoamyl alcohol (70:30:0.5). Alternative extraction methods have added 0.5 M disodium hydrogen phosphate to urine, followed by extraction with chloroform, evaporation to dryness, reconstitution in methanol, and analysis by HPLC using an RP-2 column and a methanol–water (70:30) mobile phase. A luminescence spectrometer may be used for detection. HPLC methods have detection limits similar to immunoassays, may use lysergol as the internal standard, and target LSD only, and therefore do not detect LSD metabolites often present in urine specimens.

Electron ionization and chemical ionization mass spectrometric techniques have been described for the analysis of LSD in biological samples. EI GC/MS with SIM analysis of the trimethylsilyl derivative of LSD permits detection of LSD in urine at concentrations as low as 29 pg/mL. Quantification of LSD was linear over the concentration range 50–2000 pg/mL. A negative-ion CI GC/MS assay for LSD in plasma and urine has been described using deuterium-labeled LSD as internal standard and derivatizing with trifluoroacetylimidazole to produce an N-trifluoroacetyl derivative. A linear response was achieved over the concentration range of 0.1–3.0 ng/mL. Liquid chromatographic mass spectrometric techniques, including ultra-performance technology, have been described for the analysis of LSD in biological specimens. Deuterated internal standards are utilized to measure parent drug, achieving a lower limit of quantitation < 10 pg/mL.

MESCALINE

Introduction

Mescaline (3,4,5-trimethoxyphenethylamine) is an alkaloid (Fig. 5) with hallucinogenic properties, isolated from the peyote cactus, *Lophophora williamsii*. It is controlled under Schedule I of the Controlled Substances Act and is often referred to as peyote, mescal button, or mescal. The cactus is small (3–10 cm diameter) and blue-green with well-defined ribs, pink flowers, and a large cylindrical rootstock. The dome-shaped heads are removed and dried as peyote buttons. Each button contains approximately 45 mg mescaline. Gelatin capsules may be sold on the street and contain powdered buttons with approximately 6% mescaline. Native to southern Texas and northern Mexico, peyote buttons have been found in Mexican burial caves dating back to 810–1070 B.C.

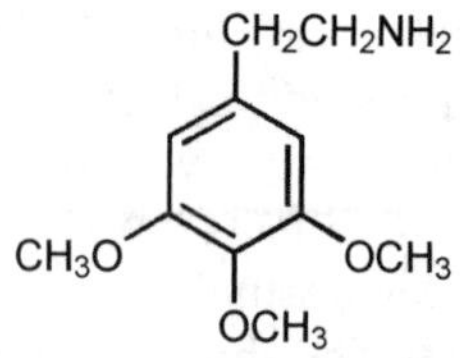

Fig. 5. Structure of mescaline.

Mescaline is commonly self-administered orally in doses of 200–500 mg as the hydrochloride or sulfate salt. It may be macerated and mixed with flavorings such as cocoa. Effects of a single administration may persist for 12 h. Mescaline may also be synthesized from 3,4,5-trimethoxybenzaldehyde by refluxing with nitromethane, ammonium acetate, and glacial acetic acid. The precipitate is reduced by refluxing with lithium aluminum hydride in ether. After drying, mescaline may be precipitated as the sulfate salt from ether by adding sulfuric acid.

Pharmacokinetics

Mescaline is rapidly absorbed after oral administration, with peak blood concentrations averaging 3.8 mg/L at 2 h in 12 subjects after a 500-mg dose. At 7 h after ingestion, the concentration had declined to 1.5 mg/L. The half-life of mescaline was estimated to be 6 h. After intravenous administration of 5 mg/kg in one study, average peak blood mescaline concentrations of 14.8 mg/L were achieved at 15 min, declining to 2.1 mg/L by 2 h. Maximum physiological effects occurred at 2 h in this study. Approximately 87% of an oral dose is excreted in the 24-h urine, with mescaline accounting for 55–60% of the excretion products. Mescaline is metabolized to four known pharmacologically inactive metabolites. The main metabolite, 3,4,5-trimethoxyphenylacetic acid, accounts for 27–30% of the urinary excretion products. The other metabolites are formed by N-acetylation, hydroxylation, and demethylation.

Effects

After oral absorption, mescaline produces a period of mild intestinal distress. This may include nausea, vomiting, and occasionally diarrhea. These effects may occur 30–60 min after eating peyote. Thereafter, sympathomimetic effects dominate with mydriasis, tachycardia, hypertension, and diaphoresis. Nystagmus and hyperreflexia may also be observed. The sensory phase of mescaline-induced effects occurs after the gastrointestinal effects subside and typically peaks 4–6 h after ingestion. Sensory effects are similar to those occurring after LSD ingestion and include visual hallucinations and perceptual distortions that may be very vivid. Emotional instability, anxiety, and panic reactions may result in accidental trauma following consumption. Sensory effects usually subside 12 h after ingestion. Mescaline doses of >20 mg/kg may result in significant bradycardia, hypotension, and respiratory depression, but death due to toxicity is rare. Violent deaths while under the influence of mescaline have been reported. One case described the death of an adult male who jumped from a height of 600 feet. Postmortem mescaline concentrations were 9.7 mg/L in the blood and 71 mg/kg in the liver.

Analysis

Mescaline may be extracted from peyote by macerating the dried buttons in a blender with absolute ethanol. The mixture should be heated over a steam bath, filtered, and dried. The dry filtrate is then dissolved in 0.1 N HCl and washed with ether. The acid is rendered alkaline and the alkaloid extracted with ether. The ether solution may be back extracted with acid and washed with chloroform. The solution is then adjusted to pH 8 with bicarbonate and hydroxide and extracted with chloroform. The chloroform layer is then evaporated to dryness, resulting in a tan-colored mescaline powder.

Mescaline may be presumptively analyzed with color tests such as Marquis reagent (orange) or Mecke's (orange to brown spots). Microcrystalline tests have also been described, such as the bismuth iodide test. Mescaline may be assayed by TLC with visualization using potassium iodoplatinate. Procedures have also been described for the analysis of mescaline in urine with GC and flame ionization detection. Fluorimetry and GC/MS of trifluoroacetyl derivatives have been used for the quantitative determination of mescaline in plasma and urine. Positive chemical ionization mode has been used for the analysis of mescaline in hair by GC/MS/MS.

PSILOCYBIN AND PSILOCIN

The use of hallucinogenic mushrooms predates the arrival of the Spaniards to the New World. The Aztecs consumed teonanácatl ("God's flesh") in religious ceremonies. Later, *Psilocybe mexicana* was discovered to be the active ingredient in teonanácatl. Indole derivatives of tryptamine, psilocybin (Fig. 6), and the less stable psilocin were isolated in 1958 from mushrooms used in Indian ceremonies in Mexico. Psilocybe is one genus of the three principal hallucinogenic mushrooms in North America. It has long, thin stalks with a conical- or bell-shaped cap and dark brown to purple-brown spores. The stalk turns blue upon handling due to bruising. It is commonly known as the liberty cap, blue legs, and magic mushroom, and is found in the Pacific Northwest, Hawaii, Texas, and Florida. Psilocybin is the primary psychoactive component of these mushrooms, with only trace amounts of psilocin found. However, psilocin is almost twice as potent as psilocybin in producing hallucinogenic effects.

Synthesis

Psilocybin may be extracted from mushrooms by repeated methanol trituration of the dried plant material for approximately 20 h. The methanol is then evaporated until the psilocybin crystallizes out. Psilocybin may be prepared in the laboratory using psilocin as the starting material. If psilocybin

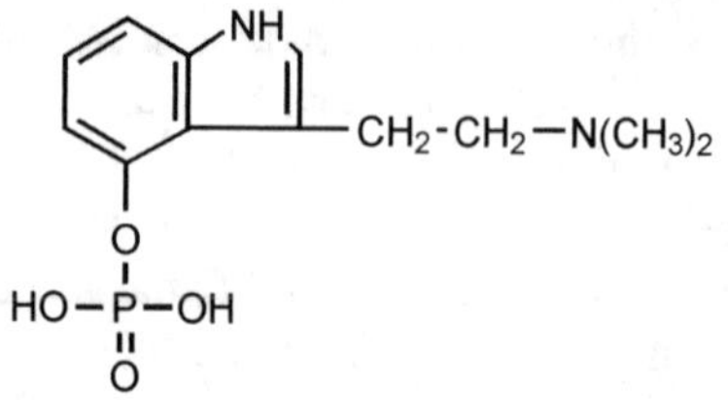

Fig. 6. Structure of psilocybin.

is synthesized completely, 4-benzoyloxyindole and oxalyl chloride are mixed and allowed to stand for 1 h. Cool dimethylamine is added and this intermediate is recrystallized, purified, and reduced with lithium aluminum hydride and then elemental palladium. Psilocin then crystallizes. Psilocybin is prepared from this by dissolving in t-amyl-alcohol and adding a solution of dibenzyl phosphorochloridate and shaking for 2 h. The residue is recrystallized in chloroform:ethanol (9:1) and then reduced with hydrogen on an aluminum oxide carrier using palladium as a catalyst.

Pharmacology

Psilocybin is usually ingested as the mushroom without prior extraction. Occasionally, brown-white psilocybin may be sold on the street, but in many instances samples turn out to be another substance, such as PCP. There is a wide variation in clinical response to mushroom ingestion. Agitation and hallucinations may occur after consuming 10 mushrooms. Typically, individuals may experience lightheadedness, muscle weakness, and anxiety approximately 30–60 min after ingestion. These symptoms may persist for about 4 h. In addition, individuals may engage in unmotivated laughter and compulsive movements. Hallucinations are usually visual, with perceptual alterations occurring in most individuals. These may involve distortion of shapes and colors. Drowsiness and dreamless sleep may follow the perceptual alterations. Other effects include mydriasis, blurred vision, dysphoria, disorientation, aggressive behavior, and antisocial behavior. Suicidal thoughts are infrequently encountered after psilocybin ingestion. The persistence of dysphoric symptoms after 12 h is rare. Persistent neurologic symptoms composed primarily of flashback phenomena do occur after use of psilocybin, but they are uncommon complications of ingestion. In some instances, flashback symptoms have been experienced for up to 4 months.

Adverse reactions after ingestion of psilocybin-containing mushrooms may occur with a frequency of 13%. Cases of serious complication have usually occurred in small children. Coma, convulsions, and a death from status epilepticus have been described. In adults, seizures have been described as a serious complication.

Analysis

Psilocybin may be detected using spot tests such as the Marquis (yellow) and Mandelin's (green). Psilocybin is thermally labile and therefore not amenable to GC analysis without derivatization. Conversion to trimethylsilyl derivatives permits accurate quantification of psilocybin and psilocin by GC. HPLC techniques have been described using UV detection at 268 nm. The detection of psilocin in urine after glucuronide hydrolysis by LC/MS and LC/MS/MS and the measurement of psilocybin in oral fluid with a limit of quantitation <5 ng/mL by LC/MS/MS have been described.

Recently, phenylethylamine was identified in the mushroom *Psilocybe semilanceata*, a wild mushroom growing in Sweden. It was present in amounts varying from 1–146 µg/g wet weight of mushroom. HPLC analysis of psilocybin was performed on mushroom extracts using reversed-phase chromatography with fluorescence detection (excitation at 270 nm and emission at 339 nm). GC and GC/MS of phenylethylamine were performed using nitrogen phosphorus detection and selected ion monitoring, respectively. The pharmacological role of this substance is unclear, but it has been reported to exert amphetamine-like activity and to have peripheral sympathomimetic effects. Therefore, its presence in mushrooms may contribute to the pharmacological effects of ingestion and may play a role in producing adverse reactions.

KETAMINE

Ketamine, 2-(2-chlorophenyl)-2-(methylamino)cyclohexanone, an analog of PCP, has a chemical formula of $C_{13}H_{16}ClNO$ and

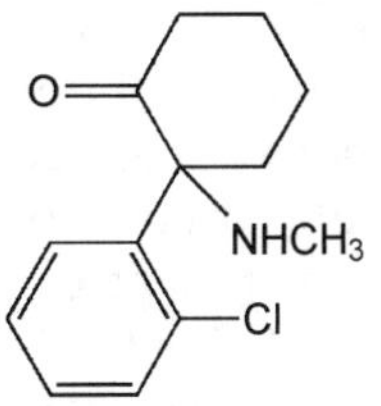

Fig. 7. Structure of ketamine.

a molecular weight of 237.7 (Fig. 7). The hydrochloride salt is available as an injectable for induction of anesthesia. It has been utilized for this purpose in human and veterinary medicine since 1972. Ketamine possesses the ability to activate bronchodilators and therefore has also been utilized in the emergency treatment of individuals in status asthmaticus. Its clinical usefulness has been limited due to incidence of hallucinations upon waking after ketamine-induced anesthesia, so called "emergence" reactions, and also due to its cardiovascular stimulating properties. At subanesthetic doses, ketamine is an effective analgesic and may have a role in the treatment of chronic neuropathic pain and ischemic pain. In addition, ketamine may have a role as an antidepressant for individuals with unipolar or bipolar depression. It is structurally and pharmacologically related to PCP (Fig. 1).

The most common licit form of ketamine is an injectable for intravenous administration. More recently, ketamine has been utilized as a drug of abuse for its hallucinogenic properties and as a drug to facilitate sexual assault. When ingested illicitly, common routes of administration include intravenous, subcutaneous, intramuscular, nasal insufflation of the powder, smoking, or oral ingestion of a tablet. When used as an agent of sexual assault, a tablet may be slipped into the victim's drink at a bar or party. Slang names for this drug include Special K, Bump, and Vitamin K.

Pharmacokinetics

Ketamine is a weakly basic compound with a pK_a of 7.5. After intravenous administration of 175 mg, peak serum concentrations average 1.0 mg/L within 12 min after injection. Continuous infusion of 41 μg/kg/min after a bolus of 2 mg/kg produced steady state plasma concentrations of 2.2 mg/L. As with PCP, blood concentrations of ketamine do not correlate with clinical findings. Blood concentrations observed in overdose are generally >3 mg/L. The plasma half-life of ketamine is 3–4 h. This basic drug has a large volume of distribution, 3–4 L/kg, with plasma protein binding of 30%.

Ketamine undergoes *N*-demethylation to form norketamine, followed by dehydrogenation to dehydronorketamine. The metabolites may reach similar blood concentrations to the parent drug and at a minimum the nor-metabolite possesses pharmacologic activity. Ketamine and metabolites undergo hydroxylation and conjugation. These conjugates comprise approximately 80% of a single dose eliminated in urine over 72 h. Urine ketamine concentrations have been reported to range from 6–7744 ng/mL, with a mean of 1083 ng/mL, (N = 33), in individuals tested by the U.S. Department of Defense. In the same individuals, metabolite concentrations ranged from 7–7986 ng/mL for norketamine and 37–23,239 ng/mL for dehydronorketamine.

Effects

Ketamine may produce hallucinations in addition to effects that include irrational behavior, gastrointestinal distress such as nausea and vomiting, and blurred vision. More severe adverse effects include cardiac arrhythmias and seizures. Effects on respiration, heart rate, and blood pressure may increase or decrease these physiological measures.

As a dissociative anesthetic, ketamine produces effects desirable as a potential drug for drug-facilitated sexual assault. Use may result in CNS depression, with impairment of speech, thought processes, and amnesia. Ketamine produces these effects by interacting with similar receptors as PCP. Ketamine possesses some μ agonist activity but most of the pharmacological effects of this compound are due to noncompetitive binding of NMDA receptors. Ketamine also binds to sigma$_1$ receptors.

Analysis

Common immunoassay procedures will not detect ketamine. The commercial thin-layer chromatography system Toxi-Lab™ system A may be used for detecting ketamine in urine. Ketamine is detected as a brown spot after exposure to formaldehyde vapors and Dragendorff's reagent with an R_f of 0.84. Following exposure to iodine vapors and a period of air drying, ketamine develops a lavender-gray appearance. The assay has a limit of detection of 1 μg/mL.

This basic drug may be easily detected using basic liquid–liquid or solid-phase extraction techniques, followed by chromatographic analysis. Gas chromatographic techniques utilizing flame ionization, nitrogen phosphorus, or electron impact mass spectrometric detection have been described. The drug may be readily detected with these techniques without derivatization. However, electron ionization GC analysis may be conducted on heptafluorobutyryl derivatives. More recently, chemical ionization techniques with deuterated internal standards have been reported that measure picogram concentrations of ketamine and norketamine in biological specimens. HPLC and LC-MS procedures have also been described. For example, one assay achieved separation with an XDB C$_8$ column at 35 °C, a mobile phase of 20 mM ammonium formate, pH 4.3 and acetonitrile at an isocratic elution of 25:75, respectively, and electrospray ionization. The limit of quantitation was 4 ng/mL.

Methoxetamine is a 3-methoxy, N-ethyl analog of ketamine, currently only marketed for research use. However, it is also a dissociative anesthetic with a similar pharmacodynamic profile to ketamine. It has a chemical formula of $C_{15}H_{21}NO_2$ and a molecular weight of 247.3. This compound may produce a false-positive result with immunoassays for PCP. Methoxetamine may be recovered from biological specimens with alkaline extraction procedures followed by GC-NPD or electron impact GC/MS detection. Prominent ions are observed at m/z 190, 219, and 134.

SUGGESTED READING

1. Annual Medical Examiner Data 1993. Data from the Drug Abuse Warning Network, Statistical Series I Number 13-B, DHHS Publication No. (SMA) 95-3019. Rockville, MD: U.S. Dept. of Health and Human Services, Substance Abuse and Mental Health Services Administration, June 1995.

2. Aronow R, Miceli JN, Done AK. Clinical observations during phencyclidine intoxication and treatment based on ion-trapping. In: Petersen RC, Stillman RC, eds. Phencyclidine (PCP) abuse: an appraisal (Research Monograph Series #21). Rockville, MD: National Institute on Drug Abuse, 1978:218–28.

3. Axelrod J, Brady RO, Witkop B, Evarts EV. Metabolism of lysergic acid diethylamide. Nature 1956;178:143–4.

4. Bailey DN, Shaw RF, Guba JJ. Phencyclidine abuse: plasma levels and clinical findings in casual users and in phencyclidine-related deaths. J Anal Toxicol 1978;2:233–8.

5. Baselt RC. Disposition of toxic drugs and chemicals in man, 7th ed. Foster City, CA: Biomedical Publications, 2004.

6. Bey T. Phencyclidine intoxication and adverse effects: a clinical and pharmacological review of an illicit drug. Cal J Emerg Med 2007;8(1):9–14.

7. Budd RD, Lindstrom DM. Characteristics of victims of PCP-related deaths in Los Angeles County. J Toxicol Clin Toxicol 1983;19:997–1004.

8. Burns RS, Lerner SE. Causes of phencyclidine-related deaths. Clin Toxicol 1978;12(4):463–81.

9. Caplan YH, Orloff KG, Thompson BC, Fisher RS. Detection of phencyclidine in medical examiner's cases. J Anal Toxicol 1979;3:47–52.

10. Cook CE, Brine DR, Jeffcoat AR, Hill JM, Wall ME. Phencyclidine disposition after intravenous and oral doses. Clin Pharmacol Ther 1982;31:625–34.

11. Cook CE, Brine DR, Quin GD, Perez-Reyes M, DiGuiseppi SR. Phencyclidine and phenylcyclohexene disposition after smoking phencyclidine. Clin Pharmacol Ther 1982;31:635–41.

12. Coppola, M, Mondola, R. Methoxetamine: from drug of abuse to rapid-acting antidepressant. Medical Hypotheses 2012;79:504–7.

13. Cravey RH, Reed D, Ragle JL. Phencyclidine-related deaths: a report of nine fatal cases. J Anal Toxicol 1979;3:199–201.

14. deRoux SJ, Sgarlato A, Marker E. Phencyclidine: a 5-year retrospective review from the New York City medical examiner's office. J Forensic Sci 2011;56(3):656–9.

15. Domino EF. History and pharmacology of PCP and PCP-related analogs. J Psychedelic Drugs 1980;12(3–4):223–7.

16. Domino SE, Domino LE, Domino EF. Comparison of two- and three-compartment models of phencyclidine in man. Subst Alcohol Actions Misuse 1982;2:205–11.

17. Done AK, Aronow R, Miceli JN. The pharmacokinetics of phencyclidine in overdosage and its treatment (Research Monograph 21). Rockville, MD: National Institute on Drug Abuse, 1978:210–17.

18. Ellenhorn MJ, Barceloux DG. Medical toxicology, diagnosis, and treatment of human poisoning. New York, NY: Elsevier Science Publishing Company, Inc., 1988.

19. Glennon RA. Classical hallucinogens an introductory overview. In: Lin GC, Glennon RA, eds. Hallucinogens: an update (Research Monograph Series, #146). National Institute on Drug Abuse, 1994:4–32.

20. Goldberger BA. Lysergic acid diethylamide. AACC Therapeutic Drug Monitoring and Toxicology 1993;14(6):99–100.

21. Brunton LL, Lazo JS, Parker KL, eds. Goodman & Gilman's The pharmacological basis of therapeutics, 11th ed. New York, NY: McGraw-Hill Co., 2006.

22. Hollister LE, Thomas CC, ed. Chemical psychoses. Springfield, IL 1968:17–8.

23. Jenkins AJ. Drug contamination of U.S. paper currency. Forensic Sci Int 2001;121:189–93.

24. Johnson K, Jones S. Neuropharmacology of phencyclidine: basic mechanisms and therapeutic potential. Am Rev Pharmacol Toxicol 1990;30:707–50.

25. Johnson LD, O'Malley PM, Bachman JG. National survey results on drug use from monitoring the future study, 1975–1994, vol. II (college students and young adults). Rockville, MD: National Institute on Drug Abuse, U.S. Department of Health and Human Services, Public Health Service, National Institutes of Health, NIH Publication #96-4027 (1996).

26. Karch, SB. Karch's pathology of drug abuse, 4th ed. Boca Raton, FL: CRC Press, 2009.

27. Kaufmann KR, Petrucha RA, Pitts FN, Weeks ME. PCP in amniotic fluid and breast milk: case report. J Clin Psychiatry 1983;44:269.

28. Kunsman GW, Levine B, Costantino A, Smith ML. Phencyclidine blood concentrations in DRE cases. J Anal Toxicol 1997;21:498–502.
29. LeBeau MA, Mozayani A, eds. Drug-facilitated sexual assault: a forensic handbook. London UK: Academic Press, 2001:27–147.
30. Liu R. Evaluation of commercial immunoassay kits for effective workplace drug testing. In: Liu R, Goldberger B, eds. Handbook of workplace drug testing. Washington, DC: AACC Press, 1995.
31. McCarron MM, Schulze BW, Thompson GA. Acute phencyclidine intoxication: clinical patterns, complications, and treatment. Ann Emerg Med 1981;10:290–7.
32. McCarron MM, Walberg CB, Soares JR, Gross SJ, Baselt RC. Detection of phencyclidine usage by radioimmunoassay of saliva. J Anal Toxicol 1984;8:197–9.
33. Moffat AC, Jackson JV, Moss MS, Widdop B, eds. Phencyclidine. In: Clarke's isolation and identification of drugs. London, UK: The Pharmaceutical Press, 1986:874–6.
34. Moore KA, Sklerov J, Levine B, Jacobs AJ. Urine concentrations of ketamine and norketamine following illegal consumption. J Anal Toxicol 2001;25:583–8.
35. Noguchi TT, Nakamura GR. Phencyclidine-related deaths in Los Angeles County, 1976. J Forensic Sci 1978;23:503–7.
36. Papac DI, Foltz R. Measurement of lysergic acid diethylamide (LSD) in human plasma by gas chromatography/negative ion chemical ionization mass spectrometry. J Anal Toxicol 1990;14:189–90.
37. Perez-Reyes M, DiGuiseppi S, Brine DR, Smith H, Cook CE. Urine pH and phencyclidine excretion. Clin Pharmacol Ther 1982;32:635–41.
38. Ropero-Miller JD, Goldberger BA. Handbook of workplace drug testing, 2nd ed. Washington, D.C.: AACC Press, 2009.
39. Preliminary Estimates from the Drug Abuse Warning Network, 1993. Preliminary estimates of drug-related emergency department episodes (Advance S Report Number 8). Rockville, MD: U.S. Dept. of Health and Human Services, Substance Abuse and Mental Health Services Administration, December 1994.
40. Substance Abuse and Mental Health Services Administration, Results from the 2010 National Survey on Drug Use and Health: summary of national findings, NSDUH Seried H-41, HHS Publication No. (SMA) 11-4658. Rockville, MD: Substance Abuse and Mental Health Services Administration, 2011.
41. Saferstein R. Phencyclidine. In: Forensic science handbook, vol. II. Englewood Cliffs, NJ: Prentice Hall, 1988:101–4.
42. Sunshine I. Phencyclidine. AACC Therapeutic Drug Monitoring and Toxicology 1989;10(7):7–13.

CHAPTER 22

Therapeutic Drugs I: Anticonvulsants and Antiarrhythmics

Barry Levine

INTRODUCTION

Therapeutic drug monitoring may be defined as the measurement of therapeutic drugs in biological specimens in an attempt to optimize the therapeutic and limit the toxic effects of the drug. The need to adjust dosage regimens according to patient response has been known for a long time. For many drug classes, these adjustments are made as a result of clinical measurements. For example, an individual with high blood pressure is treated with antihypertensive medication such as a diuretic, beta-blocker, or calcium channel blocker. To assess the effectiveness of this treatment, the patient's blood pressure is monitored. If the dosage regimen controls the blood pressure, then no changes in the treatment are necessary; if an elevated blood pressure persists, then the treating physician modifies the therapy by increasing the dose of the prescribed drug, supplementing the drug treatment with another drug, or changing the drug. The need to measure antihypertensive drugs is usually not necessary since the ultimate target of the treatment, blood pressure, can be measured.

Besides clinical measurements, drug efficacy can be monitored using clinical chemistry measurements. For instance, measuring prothrombin time may check the effectiveness of anticoagulant therapy with heparin or warfarin. Moreover, measuring serum glucose can monitor oral hyperglycemic treatment. Again, measuring the concentration of drugs in plasma would usually not be necessary.

The individualization of dosing is more difficult for drugs whose effects cannot be measured either with clinical measurements or with routine laboratory tests. For example, drugs used to prevent the onset of disease states, such as seizure disorders and cardiac arrhythmias, cannot be monitored in this way. Nevertheless, the need for optimizing treatment is still present. For these conditions, the best way to optimize drug therapy is to measure the amount of drug present in biological fluids such as serum or saliva.

Additionally, therapeutic drug monitoring may be necessary to confirm patient compliance, that is, to ensure that the patient is in fact taking the drug as prescribed. In general, a lack of compliance is not a major factor when the patient is suffering from the acute effects of an illness or a disease. However, once these symptoms dissipate and the patient is required to continue drug treatment for prophylaxis, the urgency in maintaining the prescribed dosing regimen is removed. Noncompliance may be easily detected by measuring the amount of drug in the blood; however, variable or intermittent compliance is more difficult to verify.

Assuming that the patient complies with the prescription regimen, there are other reasons why different individuals may have different blood concentrations of a drug despite taking the same dose. In Chapter 6, the pharmacokinetic factors of absorption, distribution, and elimination were discussed in great detail. Individual differences associated with all of these factors can account for differences in drug concentrations for a given dose. For example, bioavailability varies not only between individuals, but between different dosage forms of the same drug. Drug forms that have increased bioavailability can lead to increased blood concentrations and, potentially, to toxic effects. Other pharmacokinetic factors that may contribute to different blood concentrations at a given dose include first-pass effect, plasma protein binding, and regional blood flow.

Differences in drug metabolism are another significant factor in the justification of therapeutic drug monitoring. A tremendous amount of work has been done documenting polymorphism in drug metabolism. For example, procainamide, an antiarrhthymic drug, is metabolized by acetylation to N-acetyl procainamide. There are genetically determined differences whereby some individuals are slow acetylators and other individuals are rapid acetylators. Therapeutic drug monitoring can be used to monitor both parent drug and active metabolite to ascertain the individual's phenotype.

Drug interactions also play a role in causing changes in the plasma concentration of certain drugs. A number of psychoactive drugs either inhibit or induce the cytochrome P450 metabolizing system. This can either increase or decrease drug concentration, and lead to either toxic effects or reduced therapeutic efficacy, respectively.

In summary, drugs that are good candidates for therapeutic drug monitoring have some or all of the following characteristics:

1. Absence of clinical or laboratory measurements to evaluate efficacy. When possible, it is preferable to ascertain drug effectiveness by monitoring the desired effect. However, this is not desirable in disease states in which drug treatment is intended for prophylaxis.
2. Poor correlation between dose and effect. If the dose could be correlated to the effect, then there would be no need to make plasma drug measurements.

3. Good correlation between plasma concentration and effect. Unless a range of plasma concentrations has been established for drug efficacy, then measurement of drug concentrations would only be useful to identify noncompliance. A therapeutic range has been established for a large number of drugs. This range has two components: (a) a lower limit, which constitutes the minimum effective concentration for the drug, and (b) an upper limit, which represents the maximum safe concentration.
4. Narrow therapeutic index. The therapeutic index is defined as the ratio of the dose that causes toxic effects to the dose that produces the desired therapeutic effects. Drugs that have a high therapeutic index are relatively safe in that slight changes in drug concentration are unlikely to produce toxicity. These drugs do not ordinarily require therapeutic drug monitoring. Conversely, drugs with a narrow therapeutic index need therapeutic drug monitoring to make certain that the plasma concentration remains in the therapeutic range and out of the toxic range.

It is beyond the scope of this book to review all of the drugs for which therapeutic drug monitoring has become a recognized component in patient care. However, there are several classes of drugs that are routinely encountered in postmortem forensic toxicology laboratories. In general, it is the function of the postmortem forensic toxicology laboratory to measure these concentrations as it relates to one of the following:

1. Drug intoxication cases. Clearly, it is necessary to measure drug concentrations in the blood if a drug overdose or intoxication is indicated by investigation or by autopsy. All drugs will have toxicity associated with them if taken in excess. Even drugs not routinely monitored, such as antihypertensive agents, can require drug quantitation if an intoxication is suspected. The results for these drugs are usually interpreted in light of concentrations

reported in the pharmacological literature following therapeutic administration.

2. Compliance issues. Issues related to patient compliance may also be important in postmortem cases. Individuals who committed suicide may not have been taking their prescribed medication. The measurement of antidepressants, even if unrelated to the cause of death, may be a significant component to the overall case investigation. In cases where anatomic findings related to a disease state may be limited, the failure of the patient to have an adequate amount of therapeutic drugs in the body may bolster the medical examiner's final assessment that the cause of death was due to that disease state. For instance in deaths caused by a seizure disorder, a specific site of seizure activity in the brain is often not identified. The absence of therapeutic concentrations of anticonvulsant drugs supports the hypothesis that a fatal seizure had occurred.

This chapter will initially discuss the analytical methods used in therapeutic drug monitoring. Additionally, two therapeutic drug classes, the anticonvulsant drugs and the antiarrythmic drugs, will be addressed. In subsequent chapters, antidepressants, neuroleptic agents, antihistamines, and nonnarcotic analgesics will be discussed.

ANALYTICAL METHODS

Quality therapeutic drug monitoring requires appropriate and robust analytical methods. The characteristics of any method used for therapeutic drug monitoring are similar to the characteristics of methods used generally in forensic toxicology. The method should be accurate and precise. It should be free of interferences from other drugs, endogenous components and metabolites of the drug to be analyzed. Currently, immunoassay and/or chromatography can assay virtually all drugs that require therapeutic drug monitoring. Lithium is one notable exception, as this drug, which is used to treat bipolar disorder, is analyzed by atomic absorption or flame emission spectrometry.

It is beyond the scope of this chapter to discuss the theory of chromatography and immunoassay. This has been covered in great detail in Chapters 9 and 10, respectively. However, chromatography and immunoassay each have advantages and disadvantages as they pertain to therapeutic drug monitoring. For example, chromatography, either gas or liquid, has wide applications and may be used by individual laboratories to develop procedures for new drugs. Immunoassay procedures require production of kits by manufacturers; individual laboratories do not routinely possess the ability to produce their own immunoassays in-house. Nevertheless, once an immunoassay kit is available, drugs can usually be analyzed more rapidly and with less-skilled technicians than can chromatographic procedures. Immunoassays are also more amenable to emergency toxicology needs because of their faster analysis times. Chromatographic methods usually require greater specimen size than do immunoassays.

SEIZURES

A seizure is an abnormal, excessive firing of neurons in the gray matter of the brain. A seizure may cause violent, involuntary muscular contractions known as convulsions. Staring or subtle movements characterize nonconvulsive seizures, also known as absence seizures. The clinical manifestations of seizures depend on the usual function of the part of the brain where the abnormal activity is occurring. No single feature is characteristic of all forms of seizures.

Seizures may be due to natural abnormal activity in brain function. Epilepsy is a disease of the brain in which an individual experiences recurrent seizures. Seizures may also be a secondary manifestation of another disease process. Children may develop seizures as a result of a fever, referred to as febrile seizures. Alcoholics who are going through ethanol withdrawal may also develop seizures. Seizures may also develop as a result of injury to the brain. Treatment of seizures is usually based on the type of seizure experienced. The type of seizure is classified based on observed effects and electroencephalograms. Seizures are subdivided into partial, generalized, and unclassified.

Partial Seizures

As the name implies, partial seizures are focal and localized within one hemisphere of the brain. "Simple partial seizures" are usually restricted to convulsions in a single limb. Loss of consciousness is not associated with simple partial seizures. However, "complex partial seizures" are characterized by loss of consciousness and attacks of confused behavior.

Generalized Seizures

These types of seizures involve both hemispheres of the brain. There are seven subtypes of generalized seizures:

- Tonic-clonic or grand mal: major convulsions, tonic spasms followed by clonic jerking
- Tonic: loss of consciousness, notable autonomic manifestations

- Clonic: rhythmic clonic contractions of all muscles
- Myoclonic: isolated chronic jerks
- Atonic: loss of postural tone
- Absence: symmetrical motor activity such as eyelid blinking
- Atypical absence

Unclassified Seizures

These are types of seizures that do not fit into any of the above categories.

When there is no recovery between seizures, the patient is said to be in status epilepticus, which may become life-threatening if left untreated.

CLASSICAL ANTICONVULSANT DRUGS

The structures of the classical antiepileptic drugs are shown in Fig. 1.

Carbamazepine

Carbamazepine is one of the drugs used to treat generalized tonic-clonic and partial

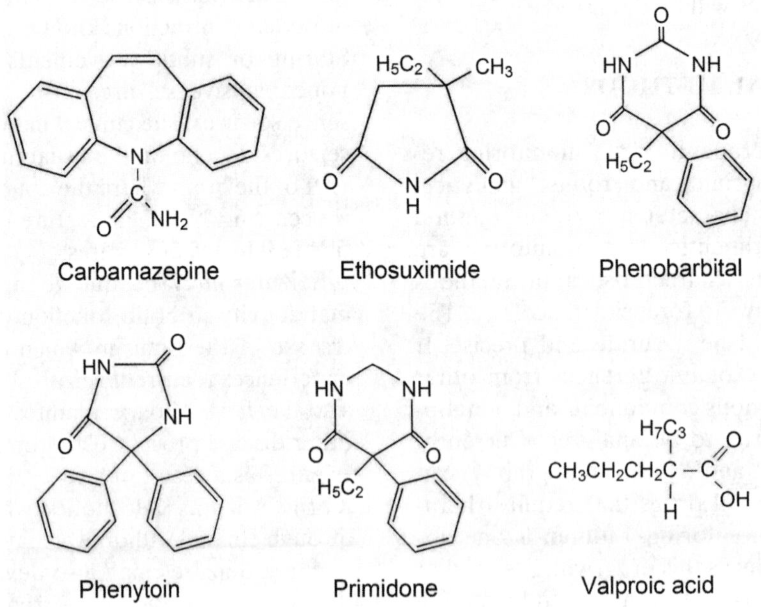

Fig. 1. Structures of classical anticonvulsant drugs.

seizures. It inhibits sodium channels and exerts a stabilizing effect on excited membranes. Carbamazepine is metabolized to carbamazepine-10,11- epoxide; this metabolism is induced by the drug itself. Therefore, the plasma half-life decreases with chronic use. The therapeutic range is 6–12 mg/L. One significant toxic effect of the drug is aplastic anemia. As a result, blood counts are recommended while on drug therapy.

Ethosuximide

Ethosuximide is used to treat absence seizures; it is not effective in the treatment of motor seizures. The plasma half-life is approximately two days, which means that fluctuations in concentration across the dosing interval are small. The drug is metabolized in the liver to a hydroxylated product. The therapeutic range is 40–100 mg/L. Use of this drug has decreased with the advent of valproic acid.

Phenobarbital

Phenobarbital was the first drug used to treat seizures, dating back to the early years of the twentieth century. Although still in use, it has become a second choice to phenytoin or carbamazepine for use in treating patients with generalized seizures. It is also used as prophylaxis for febrile seizures. Its mechanism of action involves the reduction of the excitatory effects of glutamate and the lengthening in the inhibitory effects of gamma-aminobutyric acid (GABA). After oral administration, peak plasma concentrations do not occur until several hours after a dose. It distributes throughout the whole body water and has a long plasma half-life, approximately 4 days. When phenobarbital is used as an anticonvulsant drug, the therapeutic range is 15–40 mg/L.

Phenytoin

Phenytoin is used for the prevention and treatment of generalized tonic-clonic and partial seizures. It is ineffective against absence seizures. Phenytoin inhibits voltage-gated sodium channels and reduces the spiral of excitation from epileptic foci. It is slowly absorbed after oral administration, but its bioavailability is approximately 90%. The drug is approximately 90% bound to plasma proteins. It is metabolized in the liver by the cytochrome P450 system, but its metabolism is saturable. The main metabolic product is p-hydroxyphenyl phenylhydantoin (HPPH), which is inactive. The therapeutic range is 10–20 mg/L.

Primidone

Primidone is used to treat complex partial seizures. Much of its pharmacologic activity is derived from its metabolism to two active metabolites, phenobarbital and phenylethylmalonamide (PEMA). Primidone has a much shorter plasma half-life than its metabolites: 6–8 h. Optimal therapeutic range for seizure control is 8–12 mg/L.

Valproic Acid

Valproic acid has become the drug of choice for the treatment of myoclonic seizures and generalized absence seizures. It has also been used for the prevention of febrile seizures. The mechanism of action is believed to be involved with increasing the total brain concentration of GABA, either by increasing the synthesis or reducing the breakdown of this inhibitory neurotransmitter. Valproic acid is rapidly and completely absorbed after oral administration. It is highly protein bound. A plasma half-life of 7–15 h accounts for widely fluctuating plasma concentrations. The therapeutic range is 50–100 mg/L.

NEWER ANTICONVULSANT DRUGS

The structures of the newer anticonvulsant drugs are shown in Fig. 2.

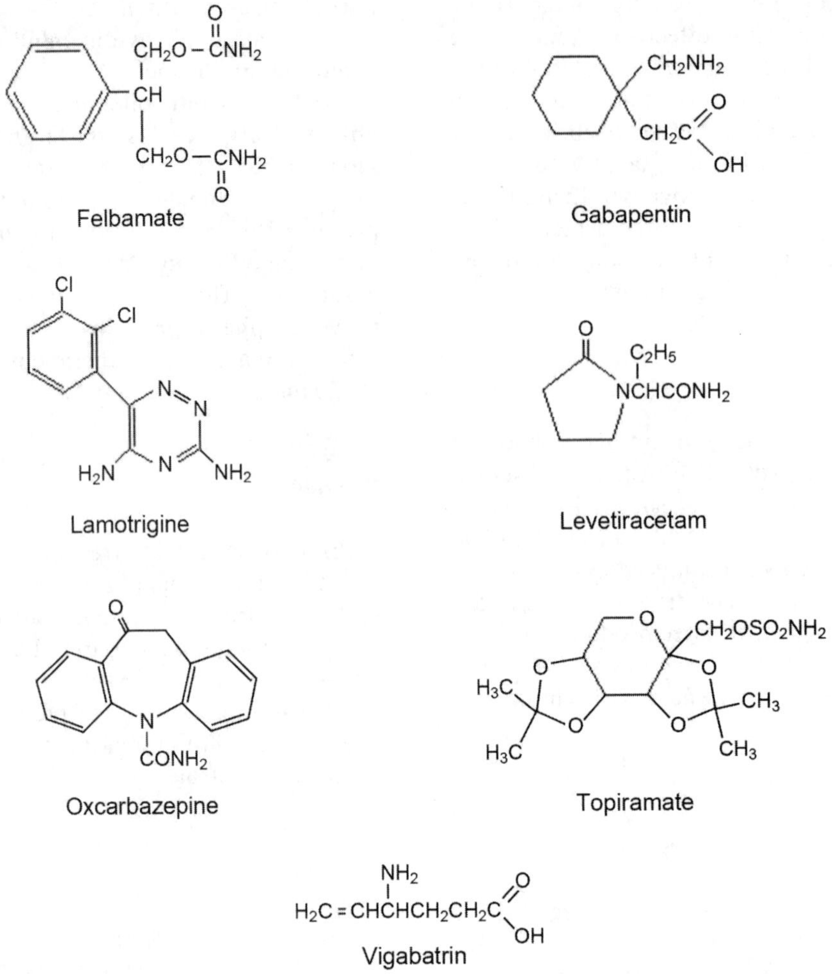

Fig. 2. Structures of newer anticonvulsant drugs.

Felbamate

Felbamate is structurally similar to meprobamate. It is used as adjunctive therapy and monotherapy to treat partial seizures with or without generalization in adults and as adjunctive therapy for the treatment of partial seizures, generalized seizures, and Lennox-Gastaut syndrome in children. Its mechanism of action is related to its ability to raise the seizure threshold and to prevent the electrical spread of seizure activity in the brain.

Felbamate is well absorbed orally. It is metabolized by the cytochrome P450 enzyme system in the liver; nevertheless, the parent drug is the major urinary metabolite. Following therapeutic usage, plasma concentrations in the range of 40–90 mg/L are observed.

Gabapentin

Gabapentin has structural similarities to GABA. Its mechanism of action is believed to be related to an effect on GABA synthesis and release. It is used as adjunct therapy for partial seizures and for partial seizures with secondary generalization in patients not controlled by other antiepileptic drugs. It is absorbed orally with the assistance of an l-amino acid active transport system. It has a short elimination half-life, approximately 5–7 h. It is not metabolized to any great extent, with mostly parent drug appearing in the urine. The effective concentration is 10–20 mg/L.

Lamotrigine

Lamotrigine is used as adjunctive therapy for partial seizures and generalized tonic-clonic seizures that are not controlled with more commonly prescribed seizure medications. Good efficacy has also been demonstrated for patients with absence, atypical absence, myoclonic, and atonic seizures, and for patients with Lennox-Gastaut syndrome. Lamotrigine has been used successfully to treat seizures in children. Its mechanism of action involves the inhibition of the release of excitatory amino acid neurotransmitters. Following oral ingestion, lamotrigine is rapidly and completely absorbed. It has an apparent volume of distribution of 1.2 L/kg. It is metabolized to a glucuronide conjugate and is excreted in the urine. Its plasma half-life is reduced by coadministration of phenytoin or carbamazepine while its plasma half-life is increased by coadministration of valproic acid. As a result, dosage regimens must be adjusted accordingly. The most common side effect associated with lamotrigine use is a rash. A therapeutic range of 4–16 mg/L is used; however, the need for therapeutic drug monitoring has not been established.

Levetiracetam

A pyrrolidine derivative, levetiracetam exists as enantiomers; the S isomer is used as the anticonvulsant drug. It is used clinically to treat partial and secondarily generalized tonic-clonic seizures. It is excreted primarily as the unchanged drug. Plasma concentrations of 10–60 mg/L are seen following therapeutic use.

Oxcarbazepine

Oxcarbazepine is a keto analog of carbamazepine and functions as a prodrug. It is rapidly converted to a 10-monohydroxy derivative, which accounts for the drug's anticonvulsant activity. Oxcarbazepine is used to treat generalized tonic-clonic and partial seizures, either alone or in combination with other drugs. Its mechanism of action is similar to that of carbamazepine but causes less enzyme induction than carbamazepine. The plasma half-life of the parent drug is 1–3 h, whereas the plasma half-life of the active metabolite is 8–15 h. Following therapeutic use, serum concentrations of hydroxycarbazepine are in the range of 8–35 mg/L.

Topiramate

Topiramate is a naturally occurring monosaccharide derived from D-fructose. The precise mechanism of action is unknown, but may be related to three factors: (1) blocking of sodium channels; (2) potentiation of GABA; or (3) blocking of a subtype of glutamate receptor. It is rapidly absorbed with peak plasma concentrations occurring approximately 2 h post dose. Topiramate is 13–17% plasma protein bound and distributes into the total body water. It is not extensively metabolized, with approximately 70% appearing in the urine as unchanged drug. No clear therapeutic range has been established, but concentrations seen after therapeutic use range from 1–30 mg/L.

Vigabatrin

Vigabatrin is used to treat seizures not controlled by more common drugs. It is a structural analog of GABA and its mechanism of action is to inhibit GABA transferase, the enzyme responsible for the metabolism of GABA. The drug exists as a racemic mixture with the S(+) isomer possessing the anticonvulsant activity. Metabolism is minimal and the major urinary product is unchanged drug. No therapeutic range has been established for vigabatrin therapy; nonetheless, plasma concentrations are related to dosage.

CARDIAC FUNCTION AND ARRHYTHMIAS

The conduction system of the heart has two basic functions. One function is to produce an electrical signal that ultimately causes the heart muscle to contract on a regular basis. The sinoatrial (SA) node provides this signal and is known as the pacemaker site. The second function of the conduction system is to facilitate the orderly propagation of the electrical signal generated by this pacemaker throughout the cells of the heart. Once the electrical signal begins in the SA node, it spreads rapidly through the atrial muscle. The atrial conduction system transports the electrical signal toward the atrio-ventricular (A-V) node. From the A-V node, it arrives at the ventricular conduction system.

The basic cell that comprises the cardiac conduction system is an electromagnetic structure that depends on the movement of ions through channels to produce an electrical signal known as an action potential. This action potential is responsible for the mechanical function of the heart. There are five phases of the action potential in the ventricular myocardium:

- Phase 0: Sodium ions rapidly move inward, leading to a rise in intracellular voltage from –90 mV to 20 mV. The primary inward current in the SA and A-V nodes is the calcium ion.
- Phase 1: After a few milliseconds, potassium ions leave the cell, causing the membrane potential to become closer to 0 mV.
- Phase 2: The membrane potential remains at 0 mV and the cell is in the refractory state.
- Phase 3: A second rapid depolarization occurs and is caused by a maximal outward potassium flux and a minimal calcium flux.

- Phase 4: Once the resting potential of –90 mV is reached, there is a slow intracellular voltage drift in the positive direction.

Cardiac arrhythmia is defined as the loss of rhythm in the heartbeat. Arrhythmias may occur due to malfunctions in the initiation and/or propagation of the cardiac action potential. Causes of arrhythmias include ischemia, heart failure, metabolic abnormalities, or drugs. Cardiac arrhythmias are treated mechanically with pacemakers or defibrillators or pharmacologically with antiarrhythmic drugs. These drugs can act in at least one of the following three ways:

- Increase the membrane potential threshold or slow the rate of diastolic depolarization
- Decrease the inward sodium current at Phase 0
- Prolong the effective refractory period

Antiarrhythmic drugs are classified according to their mechanism of action:

1) Class I: Sodium channel blockade.
   IA. Prolongs the action potential duration
   IB. Shortens the action potential duration
   IC. No effect on action potential duration
2) Class II: Beta-adrenergic blockade.
3) Class III: Prolongation of action potential duration. These agents are believed to be potassium channel blockers.
4) Class IV: Calcium channel blockade.

ANTIARRHYTHMIC DRUGS

The structures of the antiarrhythmic drugs are shown in Fig. 3.

Quinidine

Quinidine is the oldest drug still in use to treat arrhythmias. It is classified as a type IA drug; however, it also blocks potassium channels that prolong the action potential. It is administered orally with peak plasma concentrations occurring 1–5 h after ingestion, depending on the salt form. It is extensively metabolized by hydroxylation and N-oxide formation. Approximately 20% appears in urine as unchanged drug. The therapeutic range is 2–5 mg/L.

Procainamide

Procainamide is a type IA antiarrhythmic drug used in the treatment of ventricular and supraventricular arrhythmias. It may be administered orally, intramuscularly, or intravenously. It is metabolized by acetylation to N-acetylprocainamide (NAPA); NAPA has similar pharmacologic activity as the parent drug. The rate of acetylation is bimodal, with patients being classified as slow or fast acetylators. The therapeutic range for procainamide is 4–10 mg/L; the therapeutic range for procainamide plus NAPA is 5–30 mg/L.

Disopyramide

Like procainamide, disopyramide is a type IA antiarrhythmic drug. It is used to treat ventricular and supraventricular tachycardia and suppression of premature depolarizations. Disopyramide is not used as often as quinidine or procainamide. Oral bioavailability is approximately 80%, with peak plasma concentrations occurring at 2 h. It is metabolized by mono-N-dealkylation, forming nordisopyramide, which has about half of the cardiac activity as the parent drug. The therapeutic range for disopyramide is approximately 2–5 mg/L.

Lidocaine

Lidocaine is a class IB antiarrhythmic drug that shortens the action potential duration and refractoriness. In addition to its cardiac activity, lidocaine also acts as a local anesthetic. Lidocaine is one antiarrhythmic drug that is not administered orally because it has a significant first-pass effect and it also causes abdominal discomfort. Instead, lidocaine is administered intravenously for its antiarrhythmic activity and topically for its local anesthetic activity. This drug has two primary metabolites: monoethylglycinexylidide (MEGX) and glycinexylidide (GX). MEGX is eliminated hepatically with a half-life of 2 h. GX is eliminated hepatically and renally with a half-life of 10 h. Less than 10% of a dose of lidocaine is recovered in the urine as unchanged drug.

Lidocaine is the drug of choice for treating life-threatening ventricular arrhythmias and is often used in recussitative efforts. The therapeutic range of lidocaine is 1–5 mg/L. Concentrations greater than 5 mg/L are associated with central nervous system toxicity, including coma, seizures, light-headedness, disorientation, and dizziness. Cardiac toxicity including heart block and increased ventricular rate may also be observed.

Mexiletine

Mexiletine is a class IB antiarrhythmic drug that is structurally similar to lidocaine and reduces the rate of the action potential. It may be administered orally, intramuscularly, or intravenously. It has a high volume of distribution (5–12 L/kg), suggesting tissue sequestration of the drug. It is extensively metabolized in the liver to inactive hydroxymethylmexiletine, p-hydroxymexiletine, and their respective alcohols. The therapeutic range is approximately 0.7–2.0 mg/L. Concentrations above 2 mg/L are associated with side effects such as tremor, ataxia, diplopia, drowsiness, nausea, and vomiting.

Flecainide

Flecainide, classified as an IC antiarrhythmic, blocks sodium and delayed rectifier potassium currents. It is well absorbed orally

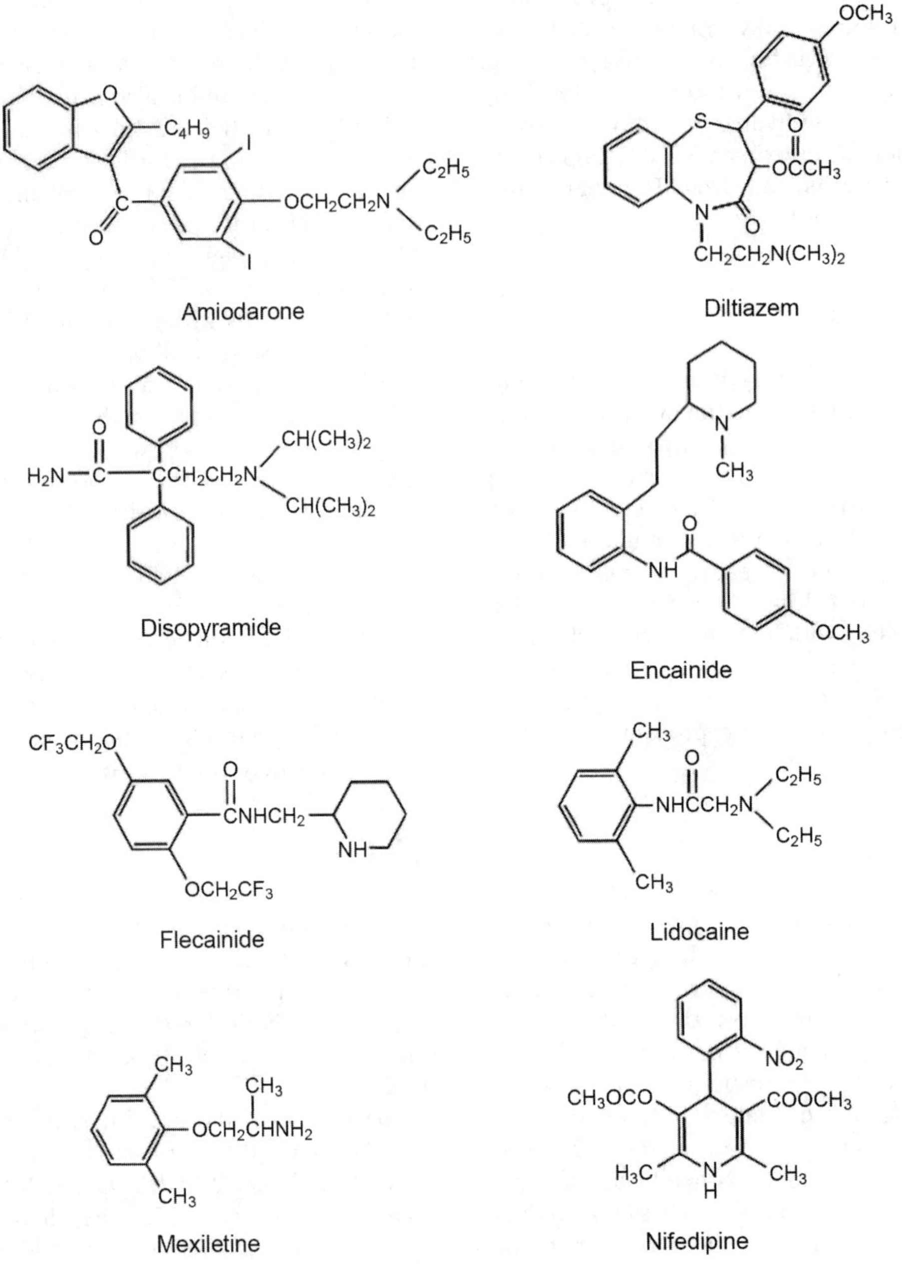

Fig. 3. Structures of antiarrhythmic drugs.

and is metabolized by CYP2D6 to m-O-de-salkylflecainide, which is pharmacologically inactive. It is further metabolized by conjugation or lactam formation. The therapeutic range is 0.2–1.0 mg/L. The drug is prescribed when other antiarrhythmic drugs have been ineffective.

Encainide

Encainide is a class IC antiarrhythmic drug used to treat life-threatening ventricular arrhythmias. It is metabolized by O- and N-demethylation, methoxylation of the terminal phenyl group, and conjugation. The two

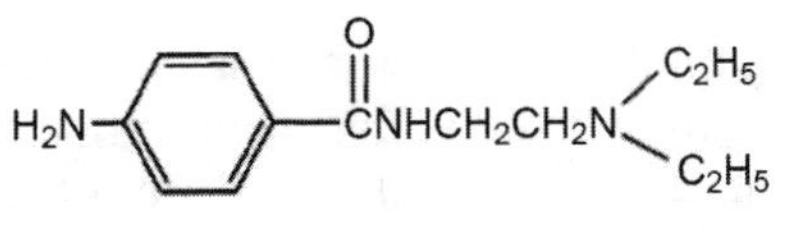

Procainamide

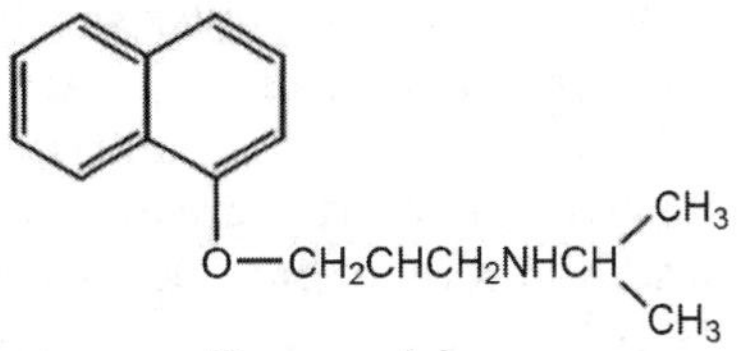

Propranolol

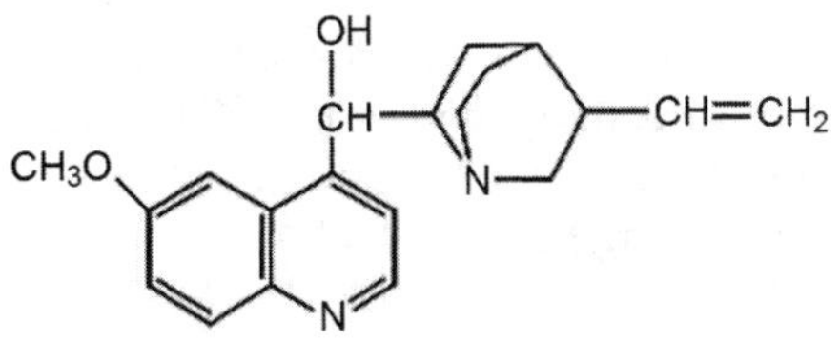

Quinidine

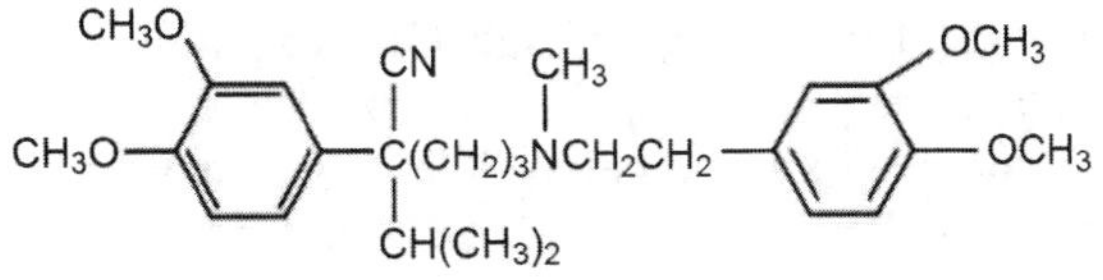

Verapamil

Fig. 3. (*Continued*)

major metabolites are O-desmethylencainide (ODE) and 3-methoxy-O-desmethylencainide (MODE), with both compounds having greater cardiac activity than the parent drug. Effective antiarrhythmic concentrations of encainide, ODE, and MODE are 0.05–0.085, 0.18–0.22, and 0.14–0.19 mg/L, respectively. Toxicity is associated with ODE concentrations >0.3 mg/L; the formation of new ventricular arrhythmias or the worsening of existing arrhythmias is the most serious toxic effect.

Propranolol

Propranolol is a nonspecific β-adrenergic receptor blocker that is classified as a group II antiarrhythmic drug. In addition to this use, propranolol is used to treat hypertension and certain coronary artery diseases. Propranolol is completely absorbed after oral administration, but undergoes significant first-pass metabolism. Approximately 80% of the dose is subjected to this effect. The drug, which is 90–95% plasma protein bound, has a plasma half-life of 4–6 h. It is metabolized by hydroxylation to 4-hydroxypropranolol, which is equipotent to the parent drug. The major urinary products are propranolol glucuronide and an oxidation product, naphthoxylactic acid. The therapeutic ranges for propranolol and

4-hydroxypropranolol are 0.05–0.1 mg/L and 0.005–0.03 mg/L, respectively.

Amiodarone

Amiodarone is a class III antiarrhythmic drug that is approved for use in the treatment of life-threatening ventricular tachyarrhythmias. It is poorly absorbed from the gastrointestinal tract, with bioavailability ranging from 31–65%. Peak serum concentrations are reached within 3 to 10 h. It is metabolized by deiodination, O-dealkylation, N-dealkylatiom, hydroxylation, and glucuronidation. Mono-N-desalkylamiodarone is the major metabolite. Amiodarone demonstrates an extremely long terminal half-life; different studies list this half-life anywhere from 26 to 107 days. An apparent therapeutic range of 0.5–2.5 mg/L has been offered for amiodarone. Use of amiodarone is restricted because of some potentially serious side effects, including alveolitis, pulmonary fibrosis, neuromuscular weakness, and tremor.

Verapamil

Verapamil is a derivative of phenylalkylamine and was the first calcium antagonist drug to receive a great deal of clinical use. It is approved for use in the prophylaxis of repetitive paroxysmal supraventricular tachycardia and the control of atrial flutter. A group IV antiarrhythmic drug, greater than 90% of a dose is absorbed, but due to substantial first-pass metabolism, bioavailability is about 30%. Verapamil is metabolized by N-dealkylation to norverapamil; it is also metabolized by O-demethylation and oxidative cleavage of the C-N-C linkage. Of these metabolites, only norverapamil has pharmacologic activity (approximately 20% of parent). Following therapeutic use, plasma concentrations of verapamil are in the 0.1–0.3 mg/L range. Therapeutic drug monitoring of verapamil is not commonly performed.

Diltiazem

Diltiazem is a benzothiazepine structurally unrelated to other calcium channel blockers available in the U.S. It is used to treat angina, supraventricular arrhythmias, and hypertension. Adult daily doses range from 60 to 420 mg. Diltiazem is deacetylated to a metabolite that is approximately one-half as potent as the parent drug as a vasodilator. It is also metabolized by N-demethylation and by O-demethylation; the N-desmethyl metabolite has about 20% of the activity of diltiazem. Steady state plasma concentrations following therapeutic use are in the range of 0.1–0.3 mg/L.

Nifedipine

Nifedipine is a calcium channel blocker used to treat angina, hypertension, and arrhythmias. It is rapidly and almost completely absorbed after oral or sublingual administration. The plasma half-life is 2–6 h. It is extensively metabolized to inactive compounds; dehydronifedipinic acid is the major serum and urinary metabolite. Peak serum concentrations after oral ingestion of 10–60 mg are <0.3 mg/L.

SUGGESTED READING

1. Baselt RC, ed. Disposition of toxic drugs and chemicals in man, 9th ed. Seal Beach, CA, Biomedical Publications, 2011.
2. Bialer M. Comparative pharmacokinetics of the newer antiepileptic drugs. Clin Pharmacokinet 1993;24:441–52.
3. Cawthon DF. Epilepsy II: diagnosis and classification. 1987;9:7–13.
4. Fraser AD, Jenkins AJ. Recent advances in drug therapy for the treatment of epilepsy. AACC Therapeutic Drug Monitoring and Toxicology 1996;17:91–103.
5. Hammett-Stabler CA, Desgupta A, eds. Therapeutic drug monitoring data: a concise guide. Washington, DC: AACC Press, 2007.
6. Jortani SA, Valdes Jr. R. Antiarrhythmics. AACC Therapeutic Drug Monitoring and Toxicology 1997;18(10):261–7.
7. Stahl AJ, Walter M. Cardiac arrhythmias. Part 1: anatomy and physiology of the cardiac conduction system. AACC Therapeutic Drug Monitoring and Toxicology 1987;8:1–6.

CHAPTER 23

Therapeutic Drugs II: Antidepressants

William H. Anderson

Depression and schizophrenia are two of the most common and most debilitating mental disorders. Depression is a mood disorder characterized by sadness, depressed mood, inactivity, loss of interest or pleasure, and a reduced ability to enjoy life. Depression in the absence of mania is referred to as unipolar disorder; in the presence of mania, it is bipolar disorder. Complete diagnostic criteria for depression has been developed and published by the American Psychiatric Association in the fifth edition of the Diagnostic and Statistical Manual (DSM-5).

Depression affects approximately 19 million Americans annually, costing the nation billions for direct care, treatment, and lost productivity. Consequently, drugs used to treat depression (antidepressants) are widely used therapeutic agents and are the focus of much research and development. They are also some of the most frequently encountered drugs in forensic and clinical toxicology. This is not surprising considering the patient population for which the drugs are designed; the frequency with which these drugs are prescribed; and their high potential for serious side effects, toxicity, and drug–drug interactions. This chapter provides an overview of the pharmacology, toxicology, and analysis of antidepressants.

PHARMACOLOGIC ACTIONS

Antidepressants, psychotherapy, and, in some circumstances, electroconvulsive therapy, are the primary treatments for clini-cal depression. Various compounds classified as antidepressants are also used in the treatment of other disorders or conditions, e.g., obsessive-compulsive disorder, chronic pain, eating disorders, panic disorders, peptic ulcer disease, and childhood enuresis.

The exact mechanism of action of the antidepressants is not entirely understood, although it has been an area of intense research for the last 30 years. A thorough discussion of the topic is beyond the scope of this chapter, but it appears that an increase in monoamine transmission, especially serotonergic transmission, is an essential element.

The earliest (first-generation) antidepressants comprised the tricyclic antidepressants (TCAs) and the monoamine oxidase inhibitors (MAOIs). The TCAs inhibit the reuptake of either norepinephrine (NE) or serotonin (5-HT) or both, and the MAOIs block their metabolism; both mechanisms produce increased amounts of neurotransmitter in the synapse. These observations led to the monoamine hypothesis of depression, which held that a deficit of either NE or 5-HT at certain sites in the brain was responsible for depression. However, it was recognized early on that the mechanism of action of antidepressant drugs had to be more complicated than merely increasing the concentration of monoamine. There is a well-recognized time delay of several weeks before the therapeutic effect of the first-generation antidepressants emerges, although the inhibition of reuptake or blockage of metabolism is acute. In addition, other compounds (e.g., cocaine) that block the reuptake of neurotransmitters do not function as antidepressants. The detection and characterization of a plethora of 5-HT receptors (5-HT$_{1A}$, 5-HT$_{1D}$, 5-HT$_{2A}$, 5-HT$_{2C}$, 5-HT$_3$, 5-HT$_4$) and NE receptors (α_1, α_2, β_1) located on pre- and postsynaptic neurons have led to many current areas of research and to the development of new antidepressant compounds. Many of the new antidepressants do not effectively block the reuptake of NE or 5-HT or hinder their metabolism. Areas under current investigation concerning the mechanism of action of antidepressants include the direct effects of neurotransmitter-binding to a variety of receptors; the subsequent downregulation of receptors; and the possibility that continued use of antidepressants produces adaptations in postreceptor signaling pathways, including regulation of neural gene expression.

Development

Antidepressants are often characterized as first-, second-, and third-generation antidepressants, depending on when they were developed. This discussion will address:

- first-generation TCAs;
- second-generation compounds amoxapine, maprotiline, trazodone, and bupropion;

- compounds that selectively block the reuptake of 5-HT, which are referred to collectively as selective serotonin reuptake inhibitors (SSRIs); and
- the newer third-generation compounds venlafaxine, nefazodone, mirtazapine, and duloxetine.

Though the definitive mechanism leading to an antidepressant effect remains elusive, the inhibition of the reuptake of 5-HT or NE is still regarded as an important action and apparently initiates the subsequent antidepressant effect for many drugs.

First-Generation Antidepressants

The structures of the TCAs are presented in Fig. 1. They obviously derive their name from the three-ring structure common to all members of this group. Most TCAs affect the reuptake of 5-HT and/or NE, but they are not equal in their action and some have substantial specificity. In general, the secondary TCAs are relatively selective inhibitors of NE reuptake, while the tertiary TCAs are less selective except for clomipramine, which is a relatively selective inhibitor of 5-HT reuptake. Trimipramine has little or no effect on reuptake of monoamine. Amitriptyline, doxepin, and nortriptyline also have high affinity for and antagonize the 5-HT$_{2A}$ receptor. The TCAs

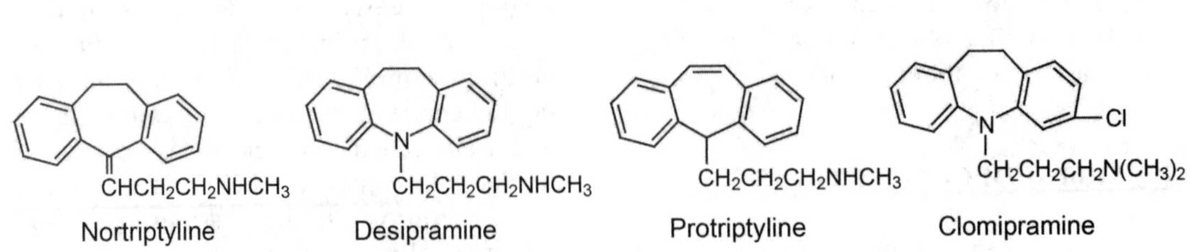

Fig. 1. Structures of the tricyclic antidepressants.

have many other pharmacologic actions that apparently do not contribute to their therapeutic effect but do contribute to the considerable side-effect profiles of these drugs. These interactions include the blockade of α_1 adrenoreceptors (hypotension, dizziness, and sedation); H_1 histamine receptors (weight gain and sedation); and M_1 muscarinic receptors (dry mouth, blurred vision, constipation, and urinary retention). Sinus tachycardia and short-term memory impairment may also be a result of M_1 blockade. TCAs are also known to lower the seizure threshold.

Second-Generation Antidepressants

The structures of specific second-generation drugs are presented in Fig. 2. Amoxapine and maprotiline have effects on reuptake of monoamines that are similar to the secondary amine TCAs. These two drugs also have antihistamine, anticholinergic, and α_1 antagonist properties similar to the TCAs. Trazodone is a weak inhibitor of 5-HT reuptake and has little effect on NE reuptake, but it is a potent antagonist of the 5-HT_{2A} and α_1 receptors. Although it is not an antihistamine, trazodone is quite sedating in vivo. Priapism has been reported to be a risk in patients taking trazodone. Bupropion is unique among the antidepressants in that it has no known effect on the serotonin system. Bupropion blocks the reuptake of NE and dopamine. This property probably contributes to the use of bupropion in attention deficit disorder and as an aid to stop smoking. The adrenergic stimulation also probably accounts for the agitation, insomnia, and nausea that have been reported with bupropion. Seizures have also been encountered with bupropion, especially in former dosage units and in doses higher than recommended.

Selective Serotonin Reuptake Inhibitors

The SSRIs have become the most widely prescribed group of antidepressants in the U.S.; their structures are presented in

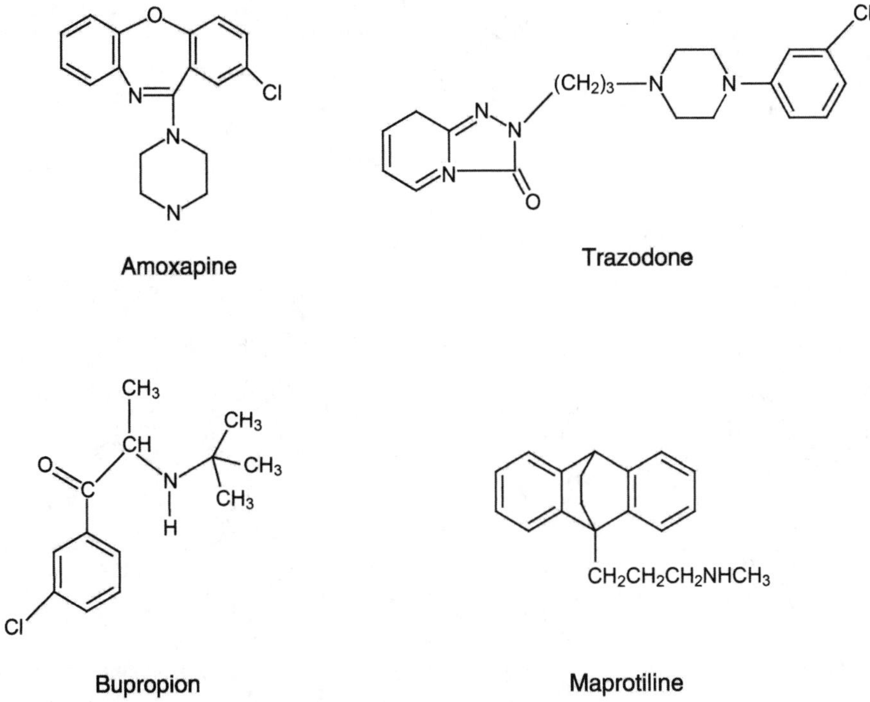

Amoxapine

Trazodone

Bupropion

Maprotiline

Fig. 2. Structures of selected second-generation antidepressants.

Fig. 3. In addition to inhibiting the reuptake of 5-HT, they interact with a variety of serotonin receptors (5-HT$_{1A}$, 5-HT$_2$, and 5-HT$_3$). The significance of these interactions is not fully understood. These drugs lack the major adrenergic, antihistaminic, and anticholinergic side effects of the TCAs; are generally much better tolerated; and are safer. However, anxiety, sleep disturbances, sexual dysfunction, and insomnia are common side effects. These drugs also have toxicity and proven drug–drug interactions that can be fatal; these topics will be discussed in a subsequent section of this chapter.

Third-Generation Antidepressants

These drugs are a chemically and pharmacologically diverse group of compounds. Their structures are presented in Fig. 4.

Venlafaxine blocks the reuptake of 5-HT and NE; it is also a weak inhibitor of dopamine. At low doses, venlafaxine may function primarily as an SSRI. It lacks affinity for H$_1$, α_1, and M$_1$ receptors. Common adverse effects include headache, nausea, somnolence, dry mouth, and sexual dysfunction. Sustained hypertension is a potentially dangerous side effect.

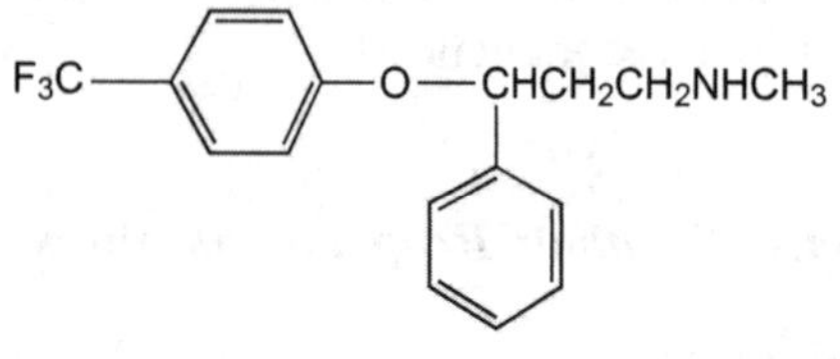

Fluoxetine

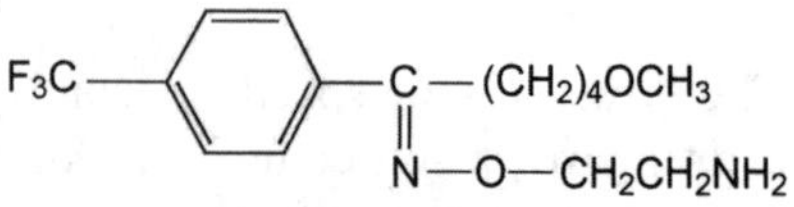

Fluvoxamine

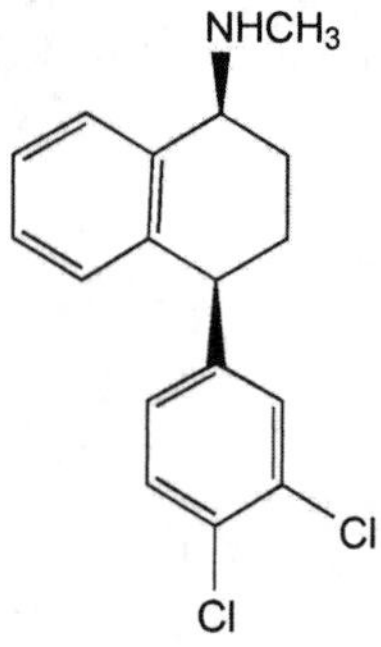

Sertraline

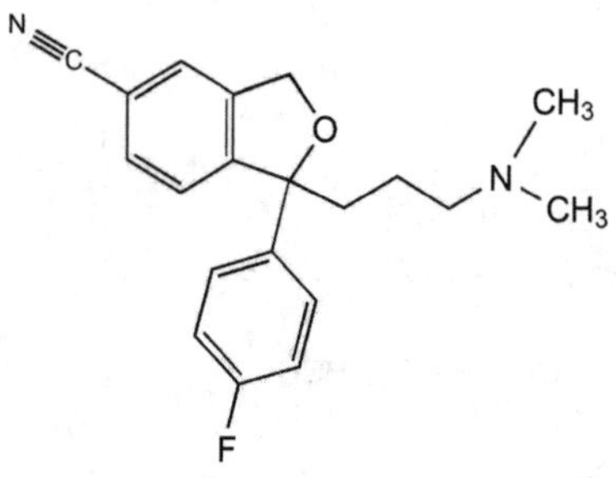

Citalopram

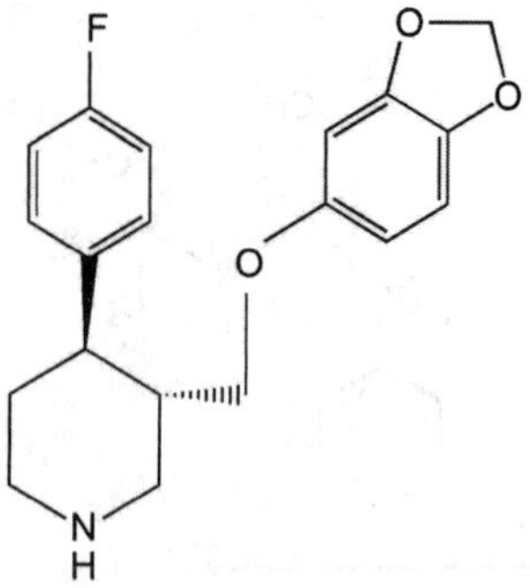

Paroxetine

Fig. 3. Structures of the selective serotonin reuptake inhibitors.

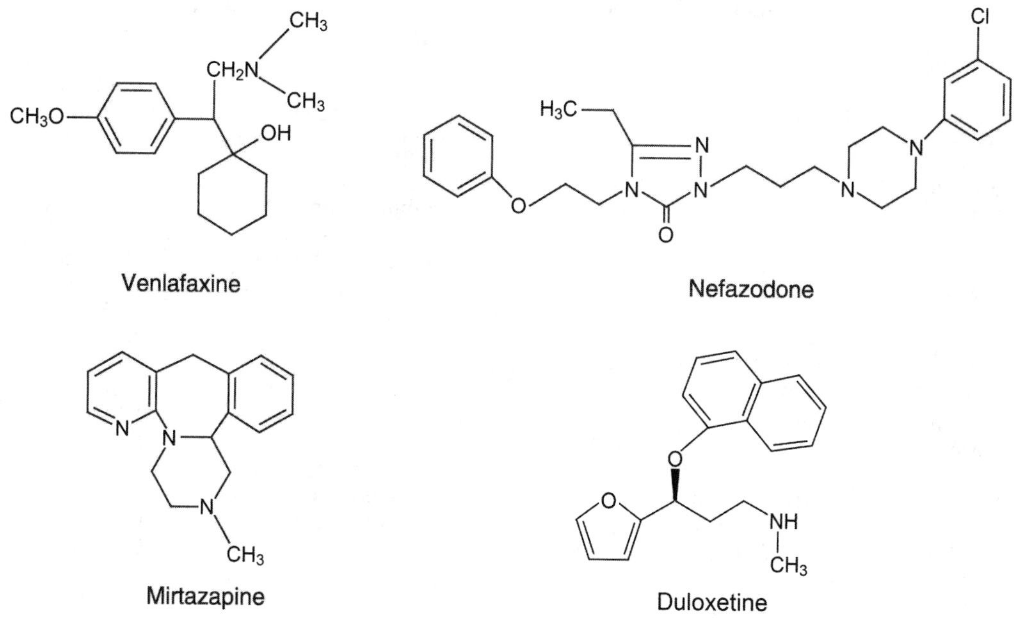

Fig. 4. Structure of selected third-generation antidepressants.

Nefazodone is similar in structure to trazodone but has a different pharmacologic profile. It is similar to the SSRIs in blockage of 5-HT reuptake, and it interacts with the 5-HT$_2$ receptors. However, the 5-HT$_2$ receptor is blocked with nefazodone and is stimulated with the SSRIs. This may explain the improved profile of nefazodone for anxiety and insomnia as compared to SSRIs, although anxiety, dizziness, and insomnia have been reported as adverse reactions. Nefazodone also interacts with α_1 receptors and weakly inhibits the reuptake of NE.

Mirtazapine has been referred to as a "designer" antidepressant. It is an α_2 antagonist, a 5-HT$_2$ antagonist, a 5-HT$_3$ antagonist, and a potent H$_1$ antagonist. Predictable side effects are weight gain and sedation.

One of the newest antidepressant approved for use in the U.S. is duloxetine. It is a potent inhibitor of both 5-HT and NE reuptake but only weakly affects dopamine reuptake. Common side effects include drowsiness, nausea, a slight increase in blood pressure, and a slight decrease in heart rate.

PHARMACOKINETICS AND METABOLISM

All of the antidepressants are well absorbed and reach peak serum concentrations within 2–12 h, but there is considerable first-pass metabolism with most of these drugs. They are rather lipophilic and have large volumes of distribution. In general, these drugs are extensively metabolized by cytochrome P450 isoenzymes to demethylated and hydroxylated metabolites, many of which are active.

Table 1 lists pharmacokinetic properties and the suggested therapeutic ranges of various antidepressants. Several caveats are associated with any such compilation of data. The half-life and volume of distribution for these drugs and their active metabolites are quite variable; average or median values may not be assumed to apply to an individual. The therapeutic ranges for many of these drugs either have not been established or are controversial. The ranges listed in Table 1 are taken from a large number of standard references that have different study designs, patient populations, and dosing regimens.

Table 1. Selected Pharmacokinetic Information for Antidepressants

Drug	Half-life (h)	Volume of Distribution (L\kg)	Active Metabolite	Therapeutic Range (mg/L)
Amitriptyline	9–46	6.4–36	Nortriptyline	0.11–0.25[a]
Amoxapine	9–14	—	8-Hydroxy amoxapine	0.20–0.60[a]
Bupropion	10–21	27–63	Hydroxy-bupropion	0.025–0.10
Citalopram	25–35	12–16	Desmethylcitalopram	0.04–0.10
Clomipramine	15–62	9–25	Desmethylclomipramine	0.20–0.80[a]
Desipramine	12–28	24–60	—	0.115–0.25
Doxepin	9–25	9–33	Nordoxepin	0.15–0.25
Duloxepine	9–19	20–24	—	0.01–0.2
Fluoxetine	26–220	12–42	Norfluoxetine	0.20–0.90[a]
Fluvoxamine	23	25	—	0.02–0.40
Imipramine	6–28	9–23	Desipramine	0.20–0.35[a]
Maprotiline	27–50	16–32	—	0.20–0.60
Mirtazapine	13.1–33.6	4.5	N-desmethyl mirtazapine	—
Nefazodone	2–5	0.51	M-chloro-phenylpiperazine hydroxynefazodone	0.30–0.50
Nortriptyline	18–56	15–23	—	0.05–0.15
Paroxetine	7–37	3–28	—	—
Protriptyline	54–198	15–31	—	0.10–0.20
Sertraline	26	25	Desmethylsertraline	—
Trazodone	6–13	0.8–1.5	M-chloro-phenylpiperazine	0.80–1.60
Trimipramine	16–40	17–48	Desmethyltrimipramine	0.10–0.30
Venlafaxine	5	7.5	O-desmethyl venlafaxine	0.25–0.50[a]

[a]Total of antidepressant and active metabolite.

However, a growing amount of evidence indicates that a curvilinear relationship exists between serum concentration and efficacy. In many cases, therapeutic effect may be enhanced by lowering the dose of antidepressant and consequently lowering the serum concentration. For the newer antidepressants, the listed "therapeutic ranges" may be more accurately considered as the concentrations observed in early clinical trials.

There is considerable debate about the necessity of performing therapeutic drug monitoring for antidepressants. Critics of routine monitoring claim that the therapeutic ranges are so ill defined that the expense and effort of determining the serum concentration are unwarranted. Proponents believe that, for many drugs, enough information concerning target concentrations is available to warrant the procedure and that toxicity due to increased serum concentration can be averted. There seems to be consensus that therapeutic ranges are well established for imipramine, desipramine, and nortriptyline.

The metabolism of the TCAs is illustrated in Fig. 5, with amitriptyline and imipramine as examples. The hydroxylated metabolites are further metabolized by glucuronidation. As is the case with amitriptyline and imipramine, the metabolism of a parent antidepressant may produce active metabolites. It is common knowledge that any therapeutic monitoring program for these two drugs should include nortriptyline and desipramine; this is also true for other, less well-understood antidepressants. There is considerable indication that the hydroxylated metabolites are also active, but these compounds are infrequently incorporated into monitoring programs. In the case of amitriptyline, the 10-hydroxy compounds exist as E and Z isomers. They are difficult to determine without special procedures.

The metabolism of amoxapine and maprotiline proceeds via demethylation and hydroxylation in a manner analogous to the TCAs (Fig. 5). The metabolism of trazodone is depicted in Fig. 6. The major active metab-

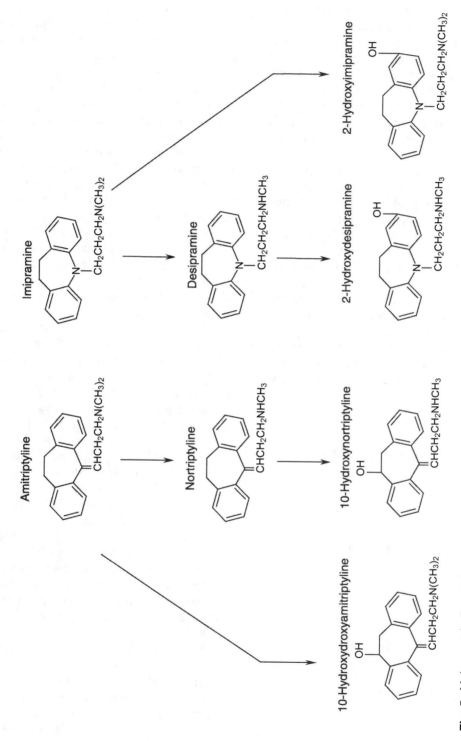

Fig. 5. Major metabolic pathways for amitriptyline and imipramine.

409

olite is m-chlorophenylpiperazine (m-CPP), which has a reported half-life of 4 h or greater. An inactive carboxylic metabolite is also produced but is not considered in most analytical schemes. The metabolites of bupropion that are usually encountered in analytical toxicology are presented in Fig. 7. Hydroxybupropion ($t_{1/2}$ = 15–22 h) and threobupropion ($t_{1/2}$ = 9–27 h) are pharmacologically active; erythrobupropion ($t_{1/2}$ = 22–43 h) is inactive. Hydroxybupropion is usually present in the highest concentration after therapeutic dosing, followed by threobupropion and bupropion. Bupropion is reported to be unstable in biological specimens. Suspected cases should be analyzed as quickly as possible, or the specimens should be frozen if immediate analysis is not possible.

The SSRIs are extensively metabolized, mostly to inactive metabolites, with very little unchanged drug excreted in the urine. The major metabolic route for the production of active metabolites is demethylation. Fluoxetine, sertraline, and citalopram are metabolized into norfluoxetine, desmethylsertraline, and desmethylcitalopram, respectively. The

metabolism of fluoxetine is illustrated in Fig. 8. Fluvoxamine and paroxetine have no demethylated or other active metabolites. The half-life of norfluoxetine is quite long: 7–15 days for short-term administration and up to 21 days for patients who have been taking the drug for extended periods. The extremely long half-life of fluoxetine and norfluoxetine is an important consideration when dose adjustments of fluoxetine are attempted, especially if fluoxetine is discontinued and another antidepressant initiated. Similarly, the half-life of desmethylsertraline is 3–10 days. Therapeutic ranges for the SSRIs have not been established with certainty. In clinical dosing, the total fluoxetine and norfluoxetine concentration is usually less than 1.0 mg/L, with a drug/metabolite ratio near unity. Sertraline concentrations are usually 0.1–0.2 mg/L, and desmethylsertraline 0.15–0.3 mg/L. Paroxetine and fluvoxamine steady state concentrations are usually less than 0.2 mg/L. Steady state citalopram concentrations range from 0.04 to 0.1 mg/L.

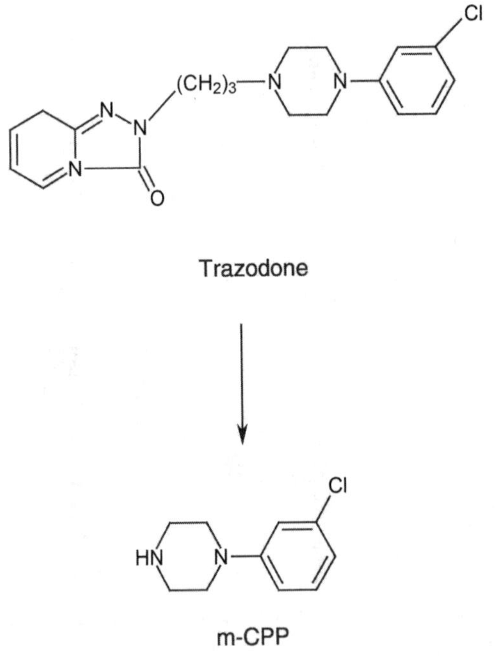

The metabolism of venlafaxine is presented in Fig. 9. O-desmethylvenlafaxine (ODV) is the major metabolite; it is active and has pharmacologic properties similar to venlafaxine. In fact, ODV has recently appeared on the market as an antidepressant drug. ODV has a half-life of 11 h and a volume of distribution of 5.7 L/kg. N-desmethylvenlafaxine may have some NE and 5-HT reuptake inhibition, but it is a minor metabolite. Concentrations of venlafaxine and ODV at steady state have been reported to be near 0.15 and 0.4 mg/L, respectively. Venlafaxine and ODV are approximately 30% bound to plasma proteins; this characteristic is unique among the antidepressants discussed in this chapter. All other antidepressants are extensively bound, usually 90% or more.

Nefazodone is metabolized to three active metabolites: hydroxynefazodone, triazoledione, and m-CPP, as illustrated by Fig. 10. The half-lives of hydroxynefazodone, triazoledione, and m-CPP are on the order of 2.5–10.5, 7–12, and 5–9 h, respectively. The concentrations after nefazodone administration are quite variable. Average maximum serum

Fig. 6. Selected metabolites of trazodone.

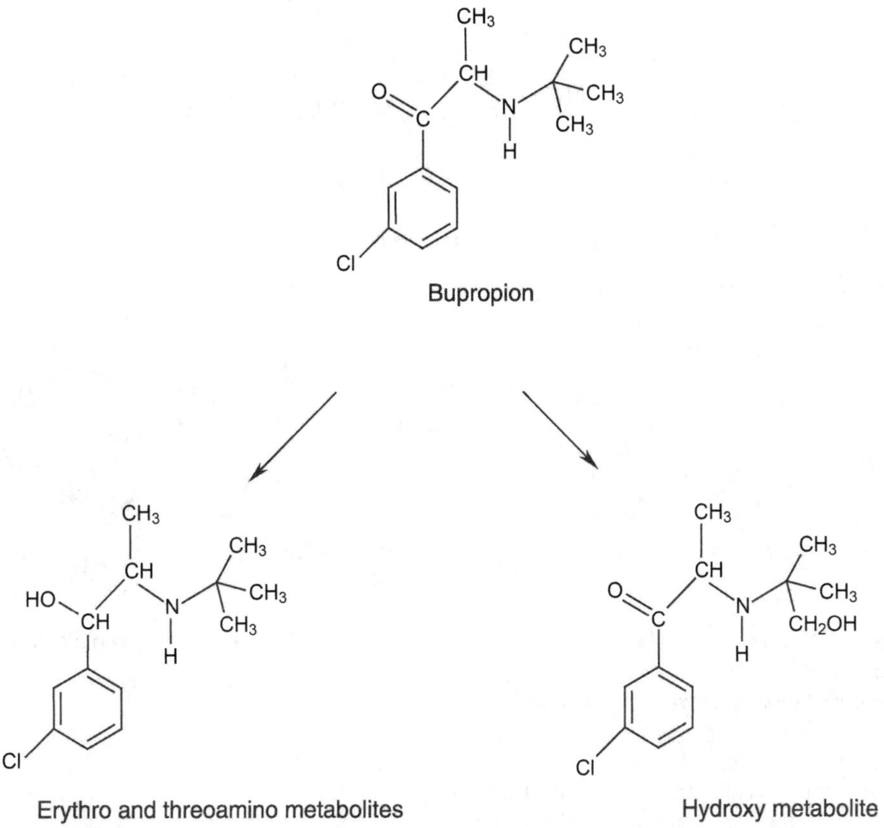

Bupropion

Erythro and threoamino metabolites

Hydroxy metabolite

Fig. 7. The metabolic pathway for bupropion.

concentrations after a single 100-mg dose have been reported within these ranges: nefazodone, 0.25–0.4 mg/L; hydroxynefazodone, 0.09–0.11 mg/L; triazoledione, 0.58–0.71 mg/L; and m-CPP, 0.01–0.025 mg/L. When two 300-mg tablets are taken daily, average maximum concentrations have been reported within these ranges: nefazodone, 2.8–3.86 mg/L; hydroxynefazodone 0.8–1.2 mg/L; and

m-CPP, 0.07–0.11 mg/L. Nefazodone exhibits nonlinear pharmacokinetics, resulting in greater than expected serum concentrations with increasing doses. Plasma concentrations per dose are greater in the elderly, especially elderly women.

Mirtazapine is metabolized to the active metabolite N-desmethylmirtazapine, as illustrated in Fig. 11. The N-desmethyl metabo-

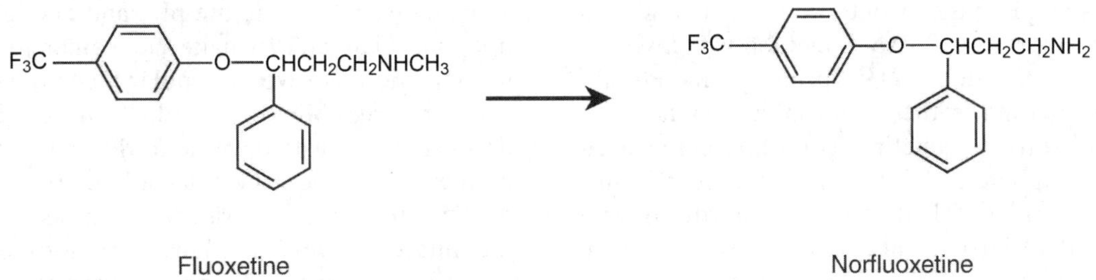

Fluoxetine

Norfluoxetine

Fig. 8. The major metabolic pathway for fluoxetine.

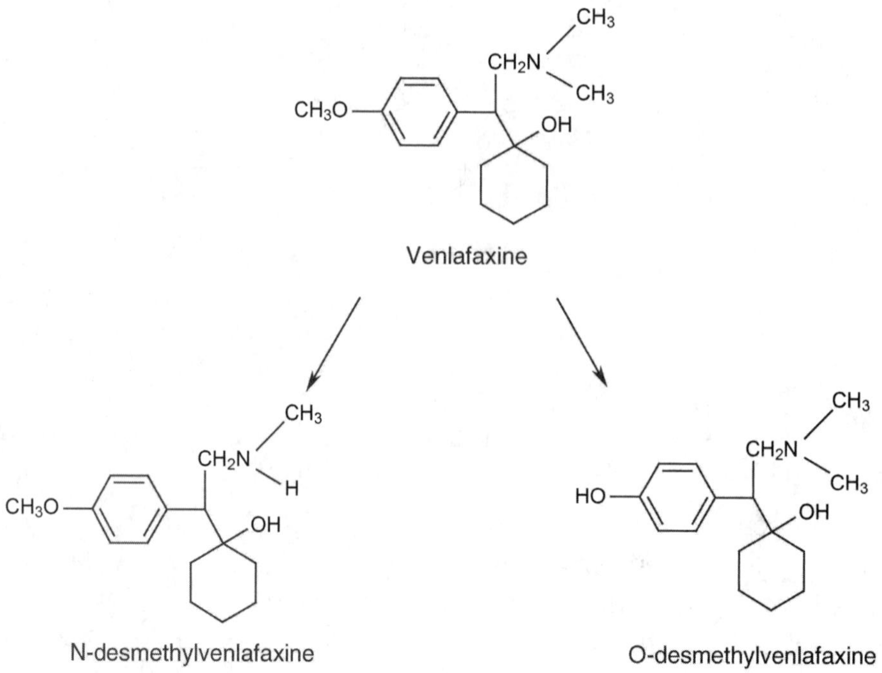

Fig. 9. The metabolic pathway for venlafaxine.

lite has pharmacologic activity of one-third to one-fourth that of mirtazapine. Inactive N-oxide and 8-hydroxy metabolites have also been reported. Little pharmacokinetic information has been published to date concerning the metabolites of mirtazapine. The drug itself displays linear kinetics over the usual therapeutic dosing range. Maximum steady state plasma concentrations are reached within 2–3 h after dose. After a once per day 15-mg dose and a once per day 75-mg dose, the concentration of mirtazapine is approximately 0.03 mg/L and 0.15 mg/L, respectively.

Duloxetine is well absorbed orally, with peak plasma concentrations occurring 6–10 h after use. Phase I metabolism involves hydroxylation. The primary metabolite in plasma is the glucuronide conjugate of 4-hydroxyduloxetine. Two other conjugated metabolites, 4,6-dihydroxyduloxetine sulfate and 6-hydroxy-5-methoxyduloxetine sulfate, have also been identified in plasma. The conjugated metabolites form rapidly and are inactive.

ANALYSIS

There are no general spot tests for the antidepressants as a group. Commercial enzyme and fluorescence polarization immunoassays are available for clinical use. Although these kit assays are useful for certain TCAs, neither is all-inclusive. Positive and negative data must be interpreted in strict accordance with the manufacturer's guidelines. Extraction and chromatographic techniques dominate the literature on the analysis of antidepressants.

An examination of the structure of the antidepressants indicates that they are organic bases with moderate pK_a and enough lipophilic character to make them amenable to extraction by several popular techniques. The large number of procedures makes it impossible to catalogue and describe all of them. However, the selected references contain numerous literature citations for the interested reader. Many variations of liquid-liquid and solid-phase extractions have been proposed. Although single-step

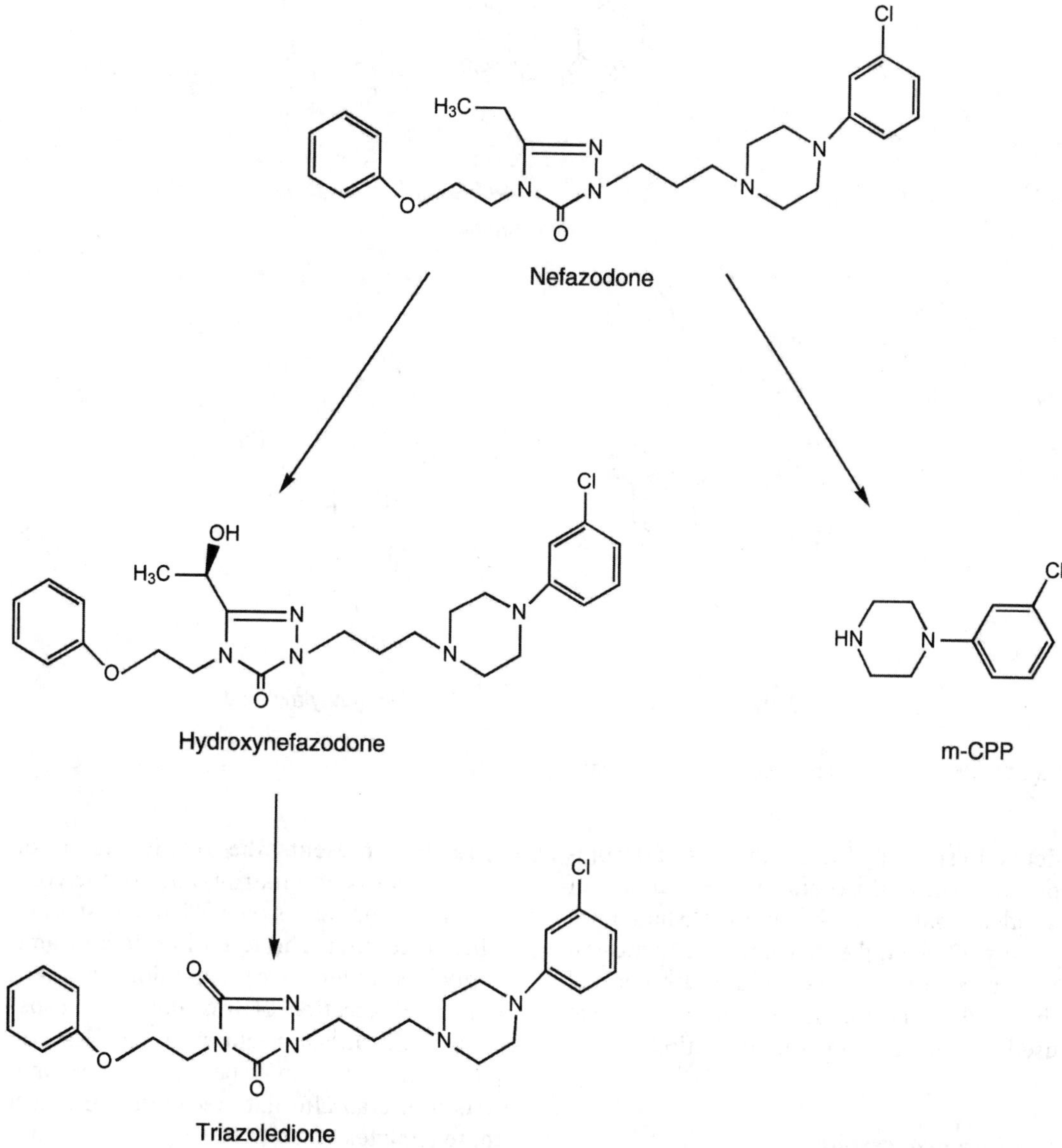

Fig. 10. The metabolic pathway for nefazodone.

extractions have been used with success, double or back extractions are more common in forensic specimens. One common procedure uses chlorobutane as the extraction solvent and is prototypical of those schemes that use back extraction. Common modifications to this procedure include addition of polar compounds to the extraction solvent and substitution of heptane/isoamyl alcohol or other nonchlorinated solvent mixtures for chlorobutane. Historically, liquid-liquid extractions have dominated the literature; however, solid-phase extraction is becoming commonplace and may well become the preferred method for extraction of biological fluids. Solid-phase sorbents include C-18, CN, and mixed-phase sorbents that are commonly used in drugs-of-abuse testing. Tissues can be successfully extracted by solid-phase schemes, but the technique is not as well

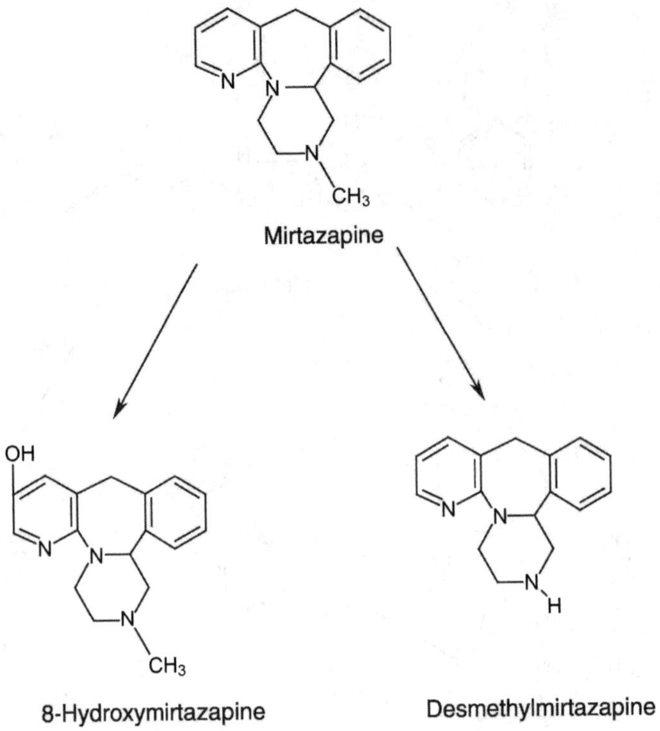

Fig. 11. The metabolic pathway for mirtazapine.

defined, especially for the analysis of decomposed tissues. In general, the extraction of antidepressants can be accomplished by a variety of techniques; the choice depends on the purpose of the assay, the preference of the analyst, and the instrumental technique used for detection and quantification.

Gas Chromatography

Gas chromatography (GC) is widely used for screening and quantifying antidepressants in biological specimens. Columns are typically fused silica capillary columns with bonded nonpolar to intermediate polarity methyl silicone liquid phases (0–50% phenyl); usual column dimensions are as follows—length 10–30 m, internal diameter 0.20–0.53 mm, and film thickness 0.25–1.5 microns. Most of the antidepressants can be detected in routine temperature programmed analyses.

Table 2 presents the relative retention times (relative to amitriptyline) of the common antidepressants on a 5% phenyl-methyl silicone column. The retention time of amitriptyline under these conditions is 10.25 min. The detection of trazodone and especially nefazodone requires a high elution temperature and may persuade some analysts to use an alternate technique to detect these analytes.

One does not usually encounter chromatographic difficulties with the antidepressant drugs in overdose quantities. However, with low concentrations or in certain chromatographic systems, the secondary amines or hydroxylated metabolites may have asymmetrical peak shapes. This can be overcome by preparing acyl, fluoracyl, or silane derivatives. The use of derivatives may also allow the separation of closely eluting pairs of antidepressants or other drugs. However, the ability to separate compounds is finite, even when many liquid phases are employed. This

Table 2. Relative Retention Time (RRT) of Antidepressants

RRT	Compound
0.43	Bupropion
0.52	Erythrobupropion
0.53	Threoaminobupropion
0.55	m-CPP
0.65	Hydroxybupropion
0.67	Norfluoxetine
0.69	Fluoxetine
0.70	Fluvoxamine
0.89	Venlafaxine
0.92	N-desmethylvenlafaxine
0.95	O-desmethylvenlafaxine
1.00	Amitriptyline (RT = 10.25 min)
1.01	cis-Doxepin
1.02	Imipramine
1.02	Nortriptyline
1.03	Trimipramine
1.03	trans-Doxepin
1.04	Mirtazapine
1.04	Desipramine
1.05	Protriptyline
1.05	Nordoxepin
1.13	Desmethylsertraline
1.14	Sertraline
1.14	Citalopram
1.14	Clomipramine
1.15	Desmethylcitalopram
1.16	Desmethylclomipramine
1.20	Duloxetine
1.30	Paroxetine
1.85	Trazodone
2.67	Nefazodone

is one reason why gas chromatography–mass spectrometry (GC/MS) is now commonly used for routine identification and quantification of antidepressants. Full spectrum acquisition and selected ion monitoring are valuable tools for the quantification and identification of antidepressants. This concept will undoubtedly gain in popularity as appropriate deuterated internal standards become readily available.

Another approach that is gaining in popularity is chemical ionization (CI) mass spectrometry. Although this technique has been advocated in forensic toxicology since the mid-1970s, it has become more accessible with the advent of less expensive benchtop CI instruments. Benchtop ion trap instruments with MS/MS capability also provide a powerful, routinely available tool.

Fig. 12 compares the electron ionization and CI mass spectra of amitriptyline. The simpler CI mass spectrum provides a much greater opportunity to obtain the selectivity and signal-to-noise ratio desired for quantification. The use of soft ionization reagents such as acetonitrile allows the formation of very prominent (M + 1) fragments that are ideal for MS/MS experiments. When multiple drugs are present or the matrix is very difficult, CI or CI/MS/MS can be very useful.

High-Performance Liquid Chromatography

High-performance liquid chromatography (HPLC) is also an attractive technique for the analysis of antidepressants. The polarity of the secondary amines and hydroxy metabolites can be overcome by the use of HPLC.

Methods have been published for all the antidepressants. For trazodone and nefazodone and their metabolites, methods are available that obviate the problems associated with their analysis by GC. The columns predominantly used in HPLC techniques are C-18, C-8, and CN. Mobile phases are typically phosphate buffers with or without ion-pairing reagents. In laboratories where an HPLC system is dedicated to the analysis of a known group of antidepressant, normal phase silica with aqueous base mobile phases are also attractive. The variety of chemistries and polarities make the quantification of all antidepressants on one column and one mobile phase difficult. As with GC, HPLC occasionally will not separate all the drugs present in a particular case. However, coupling HPLC with mass spectrometry can be used to identify and quantify all of the antidepressants.

TOXICITY AND POSTMORTEM FINDINGS

The subject of antidepressant toxicity is evolving. New compounds are being introduced at a rapid rate. As a group, the newer drugs exhibit less inherent toxicity than do

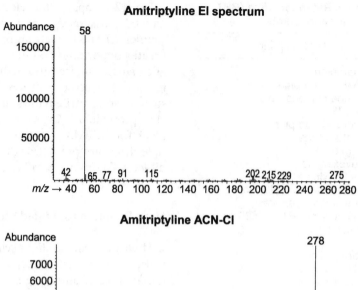

Fig. 12. The metabolic pathway for mirtazapine.

their predecessors; however, many have properties that can lead to toxic or fatal drug–drug interactions. The ability of many antidepressants to affect hepatic metabolism is an important factor in understanding the potential toxicity of this class of therapeutic agents. These concepts figure significantly in the following discussion.

The TCAs are compounds with well-known toxicity. They are among the leading causes of drug-related deaths throughout the world. There is no evidence of significant differences in toxicity among the TCAs. Amoxapine and maprotiline are so similar to TCAs in their toxicity that they are included in this discussion. The major toxicity associated with overdose of these compounds is due to anticholinergic effects, central nervous system effects, and cardiovascular effects. Effects include flushing, mydriasis, delirium, confusion, lethargy, fever, seizures, tachycardia, coma,

and, most important, cardiac arrhythmia. Hypertension can occur early in the toxicity due to an anticholinergic effect; hypotension, probably due in part to alpha-adrenergic blockade, can also occur and can be a major contributor to morbidity. Seizures and cardiac arrhythmias are the most likely conditions to cause death in TCA overdose. Although any type of arrhythmia may be observed, the prolongation of the QRS interval in the electrocardiogram is often a diagnostic tool in overdose by TCAs. In the living patient, concentrations of TCA and active metabolite above 0.45 mg/L have been associated with toxicity. Concentrations of TCAs and their active metabolite in excess of 1.0 mg/L are often associated with life-threatening toxicity. In contrast, concentrations in postmortem blood are often much higher.

Table 3 summarizes a series of 10 fatalities where amitriptyline was believed to be the single cause of death. These data typify TCA-related deaths, and several generalizations can be made. First, blood levels in postmortem specimens are much higher than expected from clinical data and in comparison to concentrations in specimens taken near or at the time of death. This is a result of the well-established concept of postmortem redistribution.

The premise of postmortem redistribution is that drug concentrations are not static after death; they tend to rise, especially for basic drugs with high volumes of distribution. It is common for TCA blood concentrations to rise by a factor of 2–8 during the postmortem interval from death to specimen collection. Typically, concentrations of TCAs rise faster and to higher concentrations in blood specimens from the central cavity as compared to more peripheral sites.

Several implications of this are obvious. The exact dose taken by an individual cannot be estimated by a pharmacokinetic calculation that depends on the concentration measured in a postmortem blood specimen, especially if obtained from the central cavity. Postmortem redistribution also plays a role in defining what constitutes a toxic concentration in postmortem specimens. A concentration of TCA plus metabolite of 1.0 mg/L in clinical specimens would be considered potentially toxic. The same concentration in postmortem specimens is often observed in cases where it is clear that the drugs played no role in the death. Postmortem blood concentrations of 2.0 mg/L are considered to be potentially toxic; however, in the absence of clear and convincing evidence of the role of a TCA in death, interpretations of concentrations in this range that are based solely upon the analysis of a blood specimen should be undertaken with extreme caution.

The analysis of peripheral blood specimens and tissues can often provide the necessary information to successfully interpret a case. A liver specimen is a most useful complement to blood specimens in the interpretation of TCA-related cases. In acute TCA overdose cases, the concentration of drug and metabolite is much higher in the liver than in the blood (see Table 3). Liver concentrations in cases related to TCA toxicity can be quite high and are typically greater than 35 mg/kg. The drug-to-metabolite ratio is typically greater than unity. For the cases in Table 3, the mean drug-to-metabolite ratio in the blood was 5.0, range 2.0–18.0. In the liver, the mean drug-to-metabolite ratio was 5.6, range 1.4–18.4. In certain situations, toxic concentrations of TCAs, and especially their active metabolites, may arise from chronic dosing because of a genetic deficiency of metabolizing enzyme or because of enzyme inhibition by coadministered medications. If the TCA in question is a tertiary amine, and a high desmethyl metabolite-to-drug ratio is observed, the toxicologist should be alerted to the possibility of a chronic poisoning. For secondary amine TCAs and other compounds, which have no routinely detected metabolites, the problem is even more vexing. If the circumstances surrounding a death are not clear, it is imperative to consider all possibilities before the manner of death is determined. Enzyme inhibition will be addressed in more detail in the discussion of toxicity of the SSRIs.

Trazodone appears to be safer in overdose situations than TCAs. Symptoms observed after trazodone overdose include drowsiness, vomiting, respiratory arrest, seizures,

Table 3. Summary of Toxicology Data in a Series of Amitriptyline-Related Deaths

Specimen	Amitriptyline			Nortriptyline		
	Mean	Range	Median	Mean	Range	Median
Blood, mg/L	11.5	2.5–43.2	7.3	2.8	0.6–7.9	2.4
Liver, mg/kg	178	42–358	148	42	19.5–112	36.3

and EKG changes. Most reported trazodone-related deaths have involved trazodone and other medications. The concentration of trazodone in reported fatal overdose cases has been 15–30 mg/L in blood and 50–80 mg/kg in liver. These blood values overlap with those reported for nonfatal outcomes; however, concentrations of this magnitude clearly indicate an overdose situation. Trazodone has been reported to be much less susceptible to postmortem redistribution than the TCAs. In contrast to therapeutic cases, significant amounts of trazodone may be detected in the urine in overdose cases.

Symptoms related to bupropion overdose include hallucinations, tachycardia, and seizures, with seizures being the most significant event. The concentrations of bupropion and metabolites in reported overdose cases have been in the ranges: bupropion, 4 mg/L or greater; hydroxybupropion, 3–5.1 mg/L; threoamino metabolite, 4.6–11.6 mg/L; and erythro metabolite, <1 mg/L. For those cases in which liver values were reported, bupropion concentrations were 1–14 mg/kg. As mentioned previously, bupropion is unstable in biological specimens; this must be taken into account not only during the analysis, but also in the interpretation of analytical results.

The SSRIs have become the most widely prescribed group of antidepressants. Their efficacy in treating other disorders such as obsessive-compulsive disorder and bulimia nervosa have added to their popularity. They exhibit fewer troublesome side effects and are better tolerated than the first-generation antidepressants. Moreover, they are safer in overdose situations, primarily because they do not demonstrate the cardiovascular toxicity associated with the TCAs. Unfortunately, their relative safety in overdoses compared to TCAs has led many to believe that there is little to no potential for a fatal outcome with these drugs. This is not the case. These drugs can cause serious toxicity, especially when taken with serotonin-enhancing drugs, and they can affect the metabolism and clearance of a variety of drugs.

All of the SSRIs exhibit similar toxicity. They have been noted to cause nausea, vomiting, mydriasis, tachycardia, tremor, seizures, and coma when taken in overdose. Serotonin syndrome, a potentially fatal condition caused by a sudden systemic excess of serotonin, has been reported after SSRI ingestion. Symptoms of serotonin syndrome include hyperthermia, diaphoresis, excitement or confusion, shivering, tremors, hypotension, and seizure. This condition can be caused by the ingestion of SSRIs alone, but occurs more often when SSRIs are ingested with other drugs that have serotonergic-enhancing properties. Serotonin syndrome is commonly seen with MAOIs, but it has been reported to occur with TCAs, tramadol, administration of more than one SSRI, lithium, dextromethorphan, and others.

The development of serotonin syndrome is often delayed as much as 12 h after ingestion. The long half-life of some of the SSRIs, such as fluoxetine, makes the development of a serotonin syndrome possible for long periods after the drug is discontinued. Another major complication of all SSRIs is their effect on the hepatic cytochrome P450 (CYP) isoenzymes. These enzymes are involved in the metabolism of many drugs. The systems primarily involved in drug metabolism are CYP 1A2, 2C, 2D6, and 3A4. The most studied of the isoenzymes is CYP2D6. This isoenzyme exhibits polymorphism; a percentage of the population (5–10% for Caucasians, other races vary) lacks it entirely or has less than normal amounts. These individuals (poor metabolizers) are in contrast to those with normally functioning CYP2D6 (extensive metabolizers). When a compound inhibits CYP2D6, an extensive metabolizer can functionally become a poor metabolizer. The CYP2D6 isoenzyme catalyzes many important hydroxylation reactions, including hydroxylation of antidepressants, antipsychotics, analgesics, and cardiovascular drugs, among others. When CYP2D6 is inhibited, it can strongly affect the concentration and clearance of any drug dependent on it for metabolism. Clinically significant interactions arising from CYP2D6 inhibition have been reported for imipramine, methadone, alprazolam, and haloperidol, among others.

The other isoenzymes primarily involved in drug metabolism do not naturally exhibit polymorphism to the degree of CYP2D6, but they can be inhibited by drugs or drug metabolites. It is not necessary for a drug to be a substrate for an isoenzyme to cause inhibition. The SSRIs vary in the isoenzymes that they inhibit and in the magnitude of their inhibition. A thorough discussion of this topic is beyond the scope of this chapter. However, it is now clear that significant drug–drug interactions can occur with the ingestion of SSRIs, and these interactions may have significance in forensic toxicology.

There are more data in the literature about fluoxetine and norfluoxetine concentrations after self-poisoning than for the other SSRIs. In one clinical study of 87 patients who had taken overdose quantities of fluoxetine, serum concentrations, when measured, were 0.23–1.39 mg/L of total fluoxetine (fluoxetine + norfluoxetine); none of the 87 patients died. A postmortem case in which fluoxetine is the only ingested agent is rare, and only a few are found in the literature. In non-fluoxetine-related postmortem cases, the total fluoxetine concentration is typically less than 2 mg/L, with a fluoxetine/norfluoxetine ratio less than or near 1.0. Liver total fluoxetine in non-fluoxetine-related cases is typically less than 20–50 mg/kg, and the fluoxetine concentration is usually less than the norfluoxetine concentration. Fluoxetine exhibits considerable postmortem redistribution.

Sertraline concentrations averaged 0.25 mg/L in a series of nonfatal overdose cases. The concentration of sertraline in non-sertraline-related deaths is generally less than 0.8 mg/L in the blood and less than 20 mg/kg in the liver. Desmethylsertraline is generally less than 1.5 mg/L in the blood and less than 50 mg/kg in the liver; a majority of the liver values are expected to be less than 20 mg/kg. One unique aspect to therapeutic sertraline use is that very low or even nondetectable concentrations of parent drug and metabolite are found in urine specimens. This is contrasted to other antidepressants where urine concentrations usually exceed blood concentrations. Therefore, blood or bile specimens are better postmortem specimens to screen for use of sertraline than is urine. In addition, several groups of investigators have reported a lack of significant differences in postmortem heart and femoral blood concentrations in sertraline cases.

Therapeutic use of paroxetine and citalopram is indicated when the postmortem heart blood concentration is <1.0 mg/L. Concentrations of these drugs in intoxication cases are generally several times higher than this. Like most other antidepressants, the liver concentration of these drugs is generally an order of magnitude higher than the blood concentration.

Of the third-generation antidepressants, venlafaxine has the most data concerning its toxicity. Overdose symptoms include tachycardia, convulsions, somnolence, and coma. The concentrations of venlafaxine in overdose deaths have varied widely. Concentrations of 6.6–89.7 mg/L have been reported for venlafaxine, and 3.44–50 mg/L for O-desmethylvenlafaxine (ODV). The ratio of venlafaxine to ODV was not consistent in these cases.

Symptoms reported as a result of nefazodone overdose include nausea, vomiting, and somnolence. Because nefazodone inhibits the reuptake of 5-HT, serotonin syndrome can be produced by the coadministration of a MAOI or another serotonin-enhancing drug. Such reactions have been reported for nefazodone and paroxetine. Nefazodone is a weak inhibitor of CYP2D6, but is a potent inhibitor of CYP3A4. It has the potential to increase the concentration of drugs metabolized by this enzyme. Very little information is available concerning the concentration of nefazodone in overdose situations. No fatal cases have been reported in which nefazodone was thought to be the sole cause of death.

Symptoms of mirtazapine toxicity include drowsiness, disorientation, tachycardia, and impaired memory. A number of postmortem studies involving mirtazapine indicate that blood concentrations <0.5 mg/L are associated with therapeutic use.

Acknowledgment

The author would like to thank Michael G. Butler for providing the chemical structures presented in this chapter.

SUGGESTED READING

1. Apter JT, Greenberg WM. New drug development in psychiatry. J Clin Res Drug Dev 1994;8:87–100.
2. Balant-Gorgia A.E., Balant LP. Therapeutic drug monitoring of antidepressants. Clin Ther 1992;14(4):612–4.
3. Cole JO, Bodkin JA. Antidepressant drug side effects. J Clin Psychiatry 1990;51[suppl]:21–6.
4. Devane CL. Monitoring cyclic antidepressants. Clin Lab Med 1987;7(3):551–66.
5. Devane CL. Pharmacokinetics of the newer antidepressants: clinical relevance. Am J Med 1994;97(6A):13S–23S.
6. Duman RS, Heninger GR, Nestler EJ. A molecular and cellular theory of depression. Arch Gen Psychiatry 1977;54(7):597–606.
7. Ereshefsky L, Riesenman C, Lam YWF. Serotonin selective reuptake inhibitor drug interactions and the cytochrome P450 system. J Clin Psychiatry 1996;57[suppl 8]:17–25.
8. Frazer A. Pharmacology of antidepressants. J Clin Psychopharmacolog 1997;17[suppl 1]:2S–8S.
9. Furlanut M, Benetello P, Spina E. Pharmacokinetic optimisation of tricyclic antidepressant therapy. Clin Pharmacokinet 1993;24(4):301–18.
10. Hebb JH, Caplan YH, Crooks CR, Mergner WJ. Blood and tissue concentrations of tricyclic antidepressant drugs in postmortem cases: literature survey and a study of forty deaths. J Anal Toxicol 1982;6:209–16.
11. Hyman SE, Nestler EJ. Initiation and adaptation: a paradigm for understanding psychotropic drug action. Am J Psychiatry 1996;153(2):151–62.
12. Jones GR, Pounder DJ. Site dependence of drug concentrations in postmortem blood—a case study. J Anal Toxicol 1987;11:184–90.
13. Joron S, Rogert H. Simultaneous determination of antidepressant drugs and metabolites by HPLC. Design and validation of a simple and reliable analytical procedure. Biomed Chromatogr 1994;8(4):158–64.
14. McIntyre IM, King CV, Skafidis S, Drummer OH. Dual ultraviolet wavelength high-performance liquid chromatographic method for the forensic or clinical analysis of seventeen antidepressants and some selected metabolites. J Chromatogr 1993;621(2):215–23.
15. Nemeroff CB, Devane CL, Pollock BG. Newer antidepressants and the cytochrome P450 system. Am J Psychiatry 1996;153(3):311–20.
16. O'Toole SM, Johnson DA. Psychobiology and psychopharmacotherapy of unipolar major depression; a review. Arch Psychiatr Nurs 1997;6:304–13.
17. Owens MJ. Molecular and cellular mechanisms of antidepressant drugs. Depression and Anxiety 1996/97;4:153–9.
18. Preskorn SH. Clinically relevant pharmacology of selective serotonin reuptake inhibitors. Clin Pharmacokinet 1997;32[suppl 1]:1–21.
19. Preskorn SH. Pharmacokinetics of antidepressants: why and how they are relevant to treatment. J Clin Psychiatry 1993;54[suppl:14-34]:55–6.
20. Prouty RW, Anderson WH. The forensic science implications of site and temporal influences on postmortem blood-drug concentrations. J Forensic Sci 1990;35(2):243–70.
21. Richelson E. Pharmacokinetic drug interactions of new antidepressants: a review of the effects on the metabolism of other drugs. Mayo Clin Proc 1997;72:835–47.
22. Stahl SM. Basic psychopharmacology of antidepressants, part 1: antidepressants have seven distinct mechanisms of action. J Clin Psychiatry 1998;59[suppl 4]:5–14.
23. Swanson JR, Jones GR, Krasselt W, Denmark LN, Ratti F. Death of two subjects due to imipramine and desipramine metabolite accumulation during chronic therapy: a review of the literature and possible mechanisms. J Forensic Sci 1997;42(2):335–9.
24. Tracqui A, Kintz P, Kreissig P, Mangin P. A simple and rapid method for toxicological screening of 25 antidepressants in blood or urine using high performance liquid chromatography with diode-array detection. Ann Biol Clin 1992;50(9):639–47.

CHAPTER 24

Therapeutic Drugs III: Neuroleptics (Antipsychotics)

Claudine Habib, Monica L. Hollowell, and James H. Nichols

INTRODUCTION

There are many indications for antipsychotic medications. Originally used for the treatment of psychotic symptoms in schizophrenia, the use of antipsychotics has been expanded to include treatment of specific aspects of bipolar disorder and has been applied with varying degrees of success for the treatment of psychosis, regardless of cause. Of note, the U.S. Food and Drug Administration (FDA) has not approved antipsychotics for dementia and should not be used in the withdrawing alcoholic. The focus of this chapter is antipsychotics for the treatment of schizophrenia.

SCHIZOPHRENIA

The Diagnostic and Statistical Manual of Mental Disorders (DSM-IV) describes schizophrenia as a disturbance lasting for at least 6 months and including at least 1 month of two or more of the following active-phase symptoms:

- Delusions
- Hallucinations
- Disorganized speech
- Grossly disorganized or catatonic behavior
- Negative symptoms

The fifth edition of the DSM is focused on revising this definition of schizophrenia and is expected in 2013.

The negative symptoms of schizophrenia include alogia (inability to speak), avolition (lack of will), anhedonia (absence of pleasure), and affective flattening (lack of emotional expression). In addition to these positive and negative symptoms, schizophrenia may also be associated with the impairment of cognition or mood, and with social or occupational dysfunction (Table 1). Schizophrenia commonly has an early age of onset (15–25 years of age) and unfolds in a chronic, relapsing course. Although less than 1% of the population develops schizophrenia at some point in their lives, schizophrenia is the most frequently occurring chronic major mental illness in people under 65 years of age.

For many patients, psychiatric drugs offer a degree of stability that enables them to remain in relationships, participate in the workplace, or tolerate insight-oriented psychotherapy. Social factors and support systems also play a role in the rehabilitation of psychiatric patients.

CHEMISTRY OF NEUROLEPTIC (ANTIPSYCHOTIC) DRUGS

Antipsychotic compounds are traditionally subdivided according to their chemical

Table 1. Clusters of Symptoms in Schizophrenia

Positive Symptoms
Delusions
Hallucinations
Disorganized speech
Catatonia

Cognitive Symptoms
Attention deficit disorder
Memory
Executive functions (such as abstractions)

Negative Symptoms
Affective flattening
Alogia
Avolition
Anhedonia

Mood Symptoms
Dysphoria
Suicidality
Hopelessness

Social and Occupational Dysfunction
Work
Interpersonal relationships
Self-care

---

structure. In this classification scheme, conventional or typical antipsychotic drugs can be divided into seven different groups (Fig. 1).

1. Phenothiazines have a tricyclic aminophenothiazine molecule with different side chains joined at the nitrogen atom of the middle ring. These side chains may be aliphatic (e.g., in chlorpromazine), piperazine (e.g., in fluphenazine), or piperidine chains (as found in thioridazine).

2. Thioxanthenes, which are chemically and pharmacologically similar to phenothiazines, have a carbon atom substituted for the nitrogen atom in the middle ring. This class of typical antipsychotics can also possess piperazine or aliphatic side chains (as chlorprothixene and thiothixene do, respectively).

3. Dibenzoxazepines are derived from phenothiazine. The only available dibenzoxazepine in the U.S. is loxapine, which has a piperazine side chain. Loxapine is structurally similar to clozapine but has different pharmacokinetic properties.

4. Dihydroindoles are structurally related to serotonin, melatonin, and indole hallucinogens. One member of this subgroup, molindone, has the unusual clinical property of not inducing weight gain and perhaps being less epileptogenic than other dopamine receptor antagonists.

5. Butyrophenones are derived from pethidine-type analgesics but lack their morphine-like activity. This group, containing haloperidol and droperidol, are potent dopamine receptor antagonists.

6. Diphenylbutylpiperidines are structurally similar to butyrophenones. The only available diphenylbutylpiperidine drug in the U.S. is pimozide.

7. Benzamides, as sulpiride and raclopride, are available in some countries outside of the U.S.

The atypical antipsychotic drugs (Fig. 2) represent a chemically diverse group of drugs.

1. Clozapine is a dibenzodiazepine derivative. Olanzapine was derived from clozapine by substitution of a thieno ring for clozapine's carbonyl ring.

2. Benzothiazepine derivatives, including quetiapine and zotepine, make up a new chemical class of antipsychotic drugs. As a group, benzothiazepines are structurally related to dibenzodiazepine. Zotepine is a substituted dibenzothiepine tricyclic agent.

3. Risperidone belongs to another new chemical class of antipsychotic drugs, the bezisoxazole derivatives. Paliperidone is the primary active metabolite of risperidone, 9-hydroxyrisperidone. Aripiprazole is also a bezisoxazole derivative.

4. Ziprasidone is a benzisothiazolyl piperazine.

5. Sertindole is an imidazolidinone derivative.

Phenothiazines

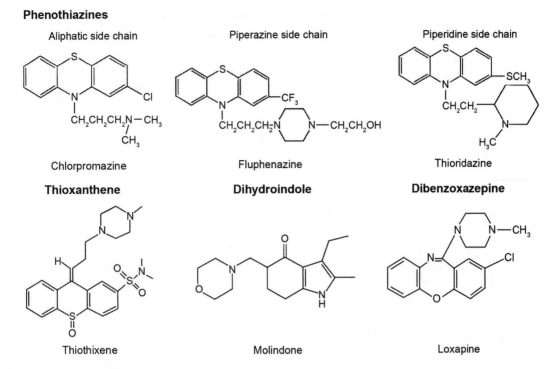

Fig. 1. Typical antipsychotic drugs.

PHARMACOKINETICS

It is beyond the scope of this chapter to completely discuss the pharmacokinetics of all antipsychotic agents. Rather, a number of drugs have been selected to illustrate aspects of the pharmacokinetics of this class of drugs.

Typical Antipsychotic Drugs

Absorption and Distribution

The drugs discussed below include chlorpromazine, fluphenazine, thioridazine, and haloperidol.

- *Chlorpromazine* is readily absorbed from the gastrointestinal tract; however, its bioavailability varies, owing to considerable first-pass metabolism by the liver. Liquid concentrates may have greater bioavailability than tablets. Food does not appear to affect bioavailability consistently. Intramuscular (IM)

administration bypasses much of the first-pass effect, and higher plasma concentrations are achieved. The onset of action usually occurs 15–30 min after IM administration and 30–60 min after oral administration. Rectally administered chlorpromazine usually takes longer to act than with oral administration. Chlorpromazine is highly bound to plasma proteins (>90%), principally albumin. It is not dialyzable. Distributed widely throughout the body, chlorpromazine crosses the blood–brain barrier and the placenta and is distributed into milk. The volume of distribution is about 20 L/kg.

- *Fluphenazine* is rapidly hydrolyzed by blood esterases with no attenuation of its antipsychotic action. The onset of action generally appears between 24 and 72 h after injection of a single dose, and the effects of the drug on psychotic symptoms become significant within 48–96 h.

- *Thioridazine* is rapidly and completely absorbed from the gastrointestinal tract.

Butyrophenones

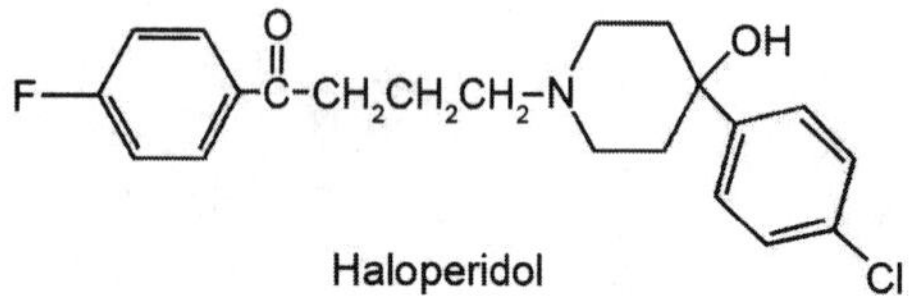

Haloperidol

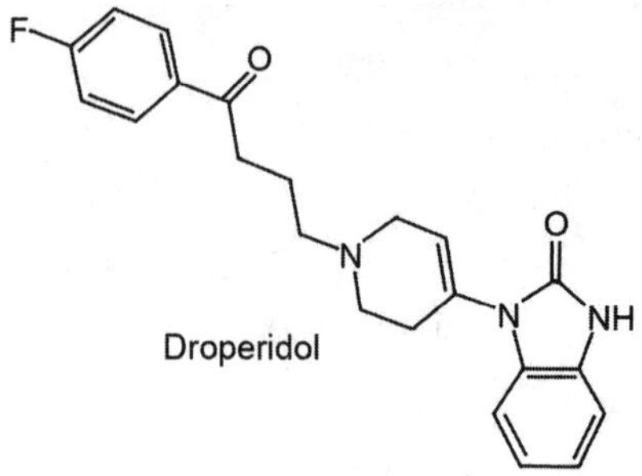

Droperidol

Diphenylbutylpiperidine

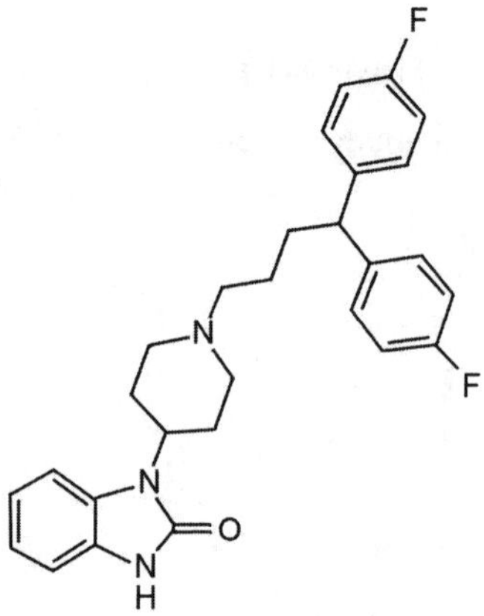

Pimozide

Benzamides

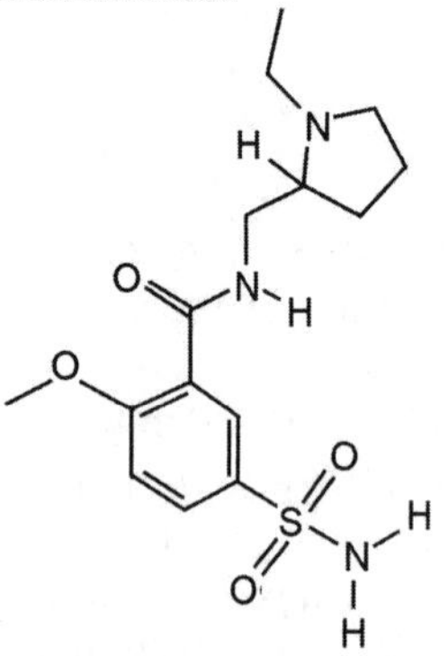

Sulpiride

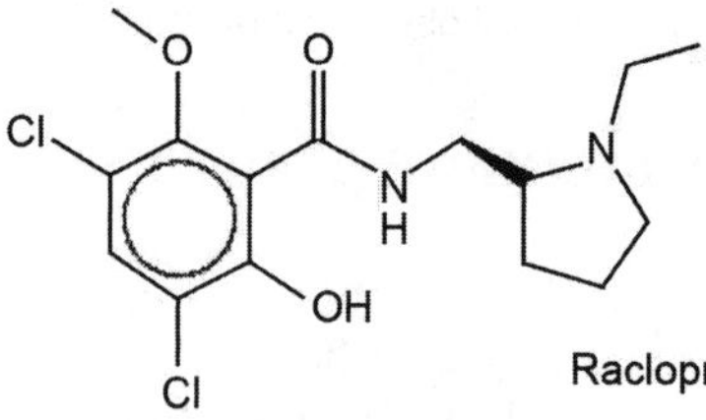

Raclopride

Fig. 1. (Continued)

Maximum plasma concentrations are reached 2–4 h after ingestion. The average systemic bioavailability is approximately 60%. The relative distribution volume is about 10 L/kg, and binding to protein is high (>95%). Thioridazine crosses the placenta and passes into breast milk.

- *Haloperidol* is the most widely used butyrophenone. Peak plasma concentrations are reached within 2–6 h after oral administration and within 20 min after IM administration. It has a half-life of approximately 20 h.

Elimination

The drugs addressed below include chlorpromazine, thioridazine, and haloperidol.

- *Chlorpromazine* is metabolized extensively, and at least 12 different metabolites are known. Less than 1% is excreted unchanged. Most metabolites are excreted in the urine as unconjugated or conjugated forms. The terminal half-life of chlorpromazine is approximately 30 h but is variable.
- *Thioridazine* is metabolized in the liver, and some of its metabolites

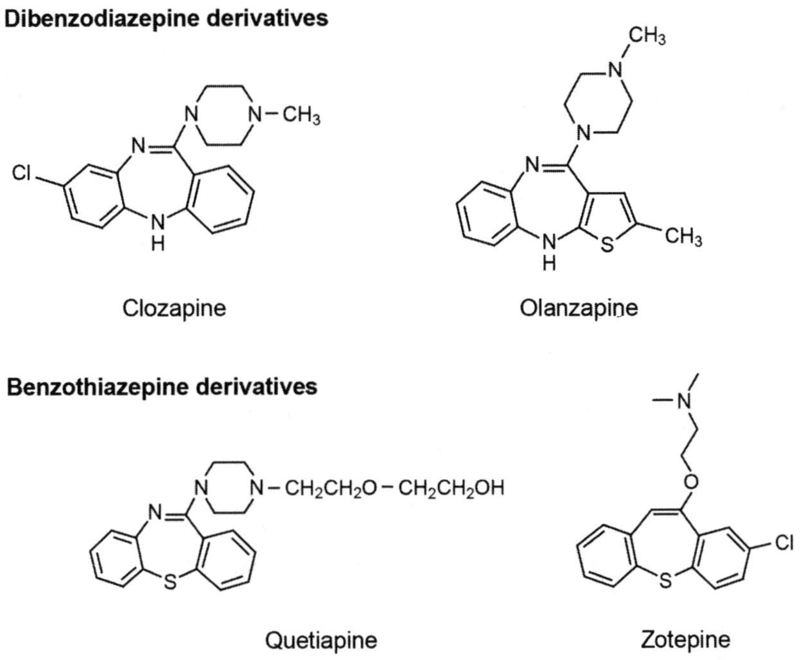

Dibenzodiazepine derivatives

Clozapine

Olanzapine

Benzothiazepine derivatives

Quetiapine

Zotepine

Fig. 2. Atypical antipsychotic drugs.

(e.g., mesoridazine, sulforidazine) possess pharmacodynamic properties similar to those of the parent compound. Excretion is mainly via the feces (50%) but also occurs via the kidney (<4% as the unchanged drug, about 30% as metabolites). The plasma elimination half-life is approximately 10 h.

- *Haloperidol* is extensively metabolized; the C-N bond is cleaved, leading to the production of two inactive acid metabolites. In addition, the ketone is reduced, forming reduced haloperidol, which possesses about one-fifth the activity of the parent drug. It has a half-life of approximately 20 h.

Atypical Antipsychotic Drugs

Absorption and Distribution

Atypical antipsychotic drugs are all available for oral administration. All of the drugs, however, are incompletely absorbed after they are administered orally. Ziprasidone and aripiprazole are also available for parenteral administration and can be given IM in short-acting injections (in emergency rooms, for example). This route of administration allows for attaining therapeutic plasma concentrations more rapidly and reliably than what is possible with oral administration. For all of the atypical antipsychotic drugs except sertindole, peak plasma concentrations are usually reached 1–5 h after oral administration. Sertindole's peak plasma concentration is reached 10 h after oral administration.

The atypical antipsychotic drugs have high binding affinity to plasma proteins (83%–99% bound). Olanzapine, sertindole, and quetiapine have higher volumes of distribution than clozapine, risperidone, ziprasidone, and aripiprazole. Most of the atypical antipsychotic drugs have relatively high solubilities in lipids.

Elimination

Atypical antipsychotic agents are metabolized in the liver and reach steady-state plasma concentrations within 2–10 days. Isoenzymes of the cytochrome P450 (CYP) system metabolize atypical agents. These enzymes are listed below and are summarized in Table 2.

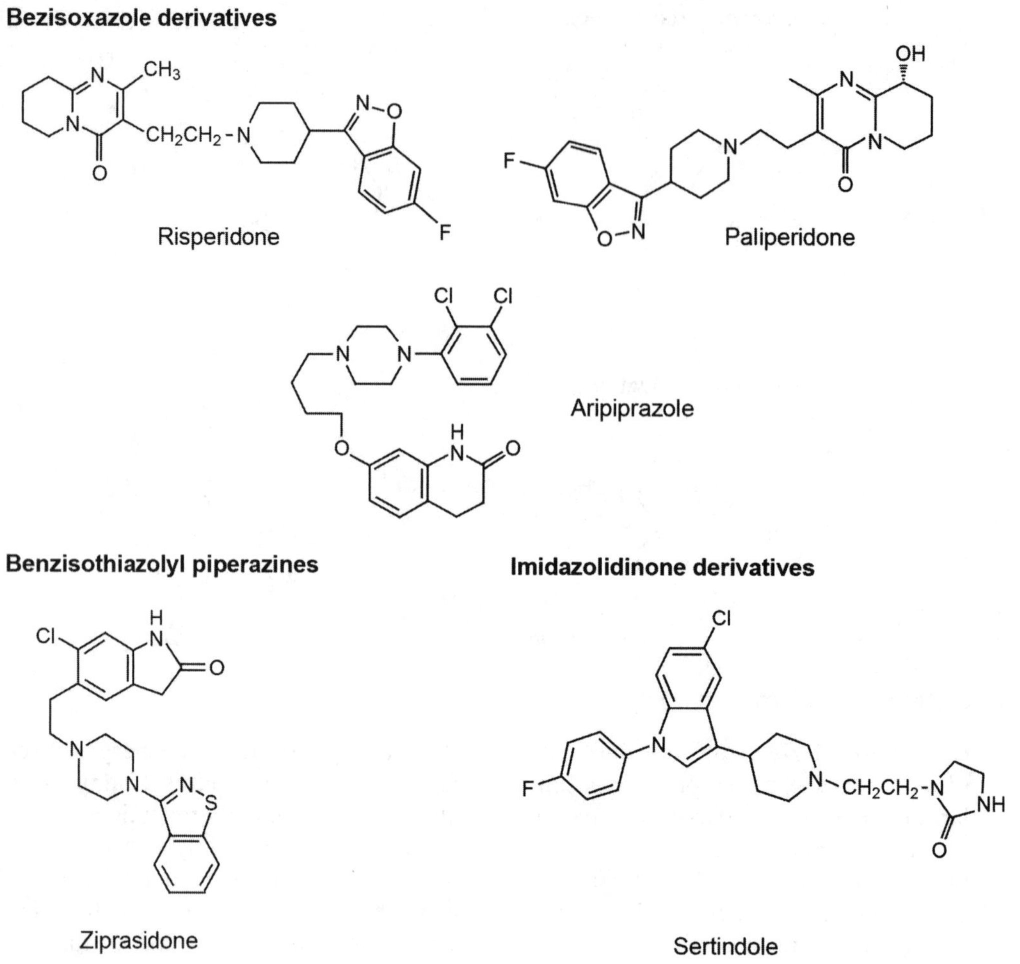

Bezisoxazole derivatives

Risperidone

Paliperidone

Aripiprazole

Benzisothiazolyl piperazines

Ziprasidone

Imidazolidinone derivatives

Sertindole

Fig. 2. *(Continued)*

- *Clozapine* appears in the urine or feces primarily (80%) as the N-desmethyl (norclozapine) and N-oxide metabolites. These metabolites have low pharmacologic activity and clear more quickly than the parent compound. Clozapine appears to be metabolized primarily by CYP1A2 and CYP3A4, with additional contributions by CYP2C19 and CYP2D6. In addition, clozapine may inhibit the activity of CYP2C9 and CYP2C19 and induce CYP1A, CYP2B, and CYP3A.

- *Risperidone* is extensively metabolized in the liver, producing 9-hydroxyrisperidone as the major active metabolite. Risperidone demonstrates metabolic changes consistent with the CYP2D6 polymorphism (there is a bimodal distribution of extensive and poor metabolizers). Because 9-hydroxyrisperidone is an active metabolite, CYP2D6 polymorphism may be of limited importance.

- *Quetiapine* is metabolized into approximately 20 inactive compounds, mainly by sulfoxidation and hydroxylation. CYP3A4 is believed to play an active role in quetiapine metabolism.

- *Olanzapine* is metabolized into multiple inactive compounds, mostly by N-glucuronidation, CYP1A2, and flavin-containing monooxygenase 3, with additional support by CYP2D6 and CYP2C19.

Table 2. Elimination of Atypical Antipsychotics by the Cytochrome P450 (CYP) System

Drug	Primary Enzyme	Other Contributors
Clozapine[a]	CYP1A2 CYP3A4	CYP2C19 CYP2D6
Risperidone	CYP2D6	
Quetiapine	CYP3A4	
Olanzapine	CYP1A2	CYP2D6 CYP2C19
Sertindole	CYP2D6 CYP3A	
Ziprasidone	CYP3A4 CYP1A2	
Zotepine	CYP3A2	CYP1A2 CYP2D6
Aripiprazole	CYP3A4 CYP2D6	
Paliperidone	CYP3A4 CYP2D6	

[a]Clozapine inhibits CYP2C9 and CYP2C19. Clozapine induces CYP1A, CYP2B, and CYP3A.

- *Sertindole* is metabolized by CYP2D6 into dehydrosertindole and by CYP3A into norsertindole. The pharmacologic activity of dehydrosertindole appears to be less than that of sertindole, possibly increasing the clinical significance of polymorphism and drug interactions at CYP2D6.
- *Ziprasidone* is metabolized primarily hepatically by aldehyde oxidase; less common pathways involve CYP3A4 and CYP1A2.
- *Zotepine* is primarily metabolized via N-demethylation by CYP3A2, producing the active metabolite norzotepin. Other minor metabolic pathways include formation of 2- and 3-hydroxyzotepine by CYP1A2 and CYP2D6, respectively.
- *Aripiprazole* is metabolized by CYP3A4 and CYP2D6 to its active metabolite, dehydroaripiprazole. N-dealkylation is catalyzed by CYP3A4.
- *Paliperidone* is also metabolized by CYP3A4 and CYP2D6.

The metabolism of atypical antipsychotic drugs can be affected by age (the elderly have decreased clearance of clozapine and olanzapine), sex (women have higher plasma concentrations of clozapine, risperidone, and sertindole), genetics (polymorphism at CYP2D6 and CYP2C19), ethnic differences, medical conditions, changes in binding proteins, and drugs that interfere with the metabolism. Inhibitors of CYP1A (furafylline, fluvoxamine) significantly increase the plasma concentrations of clozapine and olanzapine, whereas cigarette smoking induces CYP1A2 and significantly decreases the plasma concentrations of these drugs. Carbamazepine and phenytoin induce CYP3A and thereby increase the metabolism of sertindole and, to a lesser extent, clozapine and olanzapine. The inhibition of CYP3A by ketoconazole, erythromycin, and itraconazole significantly increases the plasma concentrations of clozapine and olanzapine. Ethanol decreases the plasma concentration of olanzapine by inducing CYP enzymes. CYP2D6 is induced by fluoxetine and inhibited by quinidine and paroxetine.

MECHANISM OF ACTION

The exact mechanism of action of antipsychotic drugs is not known. Typical antipsychotic drugs have been proposed to act primarily as dopamine receptor antagonists. This idea stems from studies that have shown that the ability of typical antipsychotic drugs to reduce psychotic symptoms is most closely correlated with the affinity of these drugs for dopamine D_2 receptors. The therapeutic actions of typical antipsychotic drugs are presumed to be in the limbic system, whereas extrapyramidal symptoms result from their action in the nigrostriatal region of the basal ganglia. Inhibition of the tubuloinfundibular tract is responsible for the endocrine effects of these drugs.

Clozapine and the other atypical antipsychotic drugs have a different mechanism of action that possibly involves other dopamine receptors, the serotonin 5-HT$_2$ receptors, or both. No single hypothesis can explain why a particular drug behaves as an atypical antipsychotic drug. In the case of clozapine, for example, three hypotheses have evolved to explain its potential mechanism of action.

The regional neuroanatomic specificity hypothesis postulates that clozapine's unique effects involve selective affinity for the anatomic regions that are pathologically involved in schizophrenia (the mesolimbic and mesocortical dopamine receptor neuronal system). Thus, clozapine alters dopamine receptor function where the disease is present but leaves other brain regions that dopaminergic neurons innervate (the nigrostriatal system in the basal ganglia and tuberoinfundibular system of the pituitary gland) relatively undisturbed. This pattern of action would account for clozapine's lack of unwanted side effects, such as extrapyramidal effects, galactorrhea (spontaneous flow of milk from the nipple), and oligomenorrhea (abnormal menstrual flow).

A second hypothesis postulates that the novel effects of clozapine are produced by the combined effects of the drug on the dopaminergic system and one or more additional neurotransmitter systems (including the serotoninergic, adrenergic, cholinergic, and glutaminergic systems) or on specific behaviorally active neuropeptides. Supporters of the second hypothesis put the greatest emphasis on the actions of clozapine on the serotoninergic system.

The third hypothesis postulates that clozapine exerts its effects by its selective affinity for specific dopaminergic receptor subtypes. Specifically, the hypothesis refers to the actions of clozapine on the dopamine D_1 and dopamine D_4 receptor subtypes, individually or in combination with its dopamine D_2 affinity.

At the present time, the individual significance of these three hypotheses remains unclear. Despite this uncertainty, it can be generally stated that the antipsychotic efficacy of clozapine is due to its central dopamine D_2 activity or a combination of dopamine D_1 and D_2 receptor antagonism with supplementary serotonin 5-HT$_2$ receptor antagonism and potent blockade of serotoninergic, adrenergic, and cholinergic receptors.

Like clozapine, the effects of many of the atypical antipsychotic agents can be explained by using one or a combination of the three hypotheses. Aripiprazole is different from the other atypical antipsychotics, however, because it is a partial agonist at the dopamine D_2 and serotonin 5-HT$_{1a}$ receptors and also shows serotonin 5-HT$_2$ receptor antagonism.

ADVERSE REACTIONS

The adverse effects associated with the treatment of schizophrenia vary from mild to life threatening. They are one of the major reasons for the constant search for new, better antipsychotic drugs. In general, the adverse effects of typical antipsychotic drugs are primarily nonneurologic in low doses and neurologic in high doses. Atypical antipsychotic drugs have a low risk of causing serious neurologic side effects; however, they may cause some serious nonneurologic adverse reactions. The nonneurologic and neurologic side effects are discussed below.

Nonneurologic Side Effects

Cardiac Effects

Low-potency typical antipsychotic drugs are more cardiotoxic than are high-potency drugs. Chlorpromazine prolongs QT and PR intervals, blunts T waves, and depresses the ST segment. Thioridazine, on the other hand, has marked effects on T waves and is associated with malignant arrhythmias, such as torsade de pointes. Prolonged QT intervals >0.44 milliseconds may lead to sudden death, possibly secondary to ventricular tachycardia or ventricular fibrillation. Among the atypical antipsychotic drugs, sertindole and ziprasidone have shown some prolongation of the QT interval. Patients on these drugs must have frequent electrocardiography examinations.

Orthostatic (Postural) Hypotension

Orthostatic hypotension is mediated by adrenergic blockade. It is most common with chlorpromazine, thioridazine, chlorprothixene, clozapine, and olanzapine. Orthostatic hypotension occurs within the first few days of treatment, and tolerance to its adverse effects rapidly develops. The major danger of orthostatic hypotension is injuries. The patient's blood pressure should be monitored (lying and standing) before and after the first dose and during the first few days of treatment. Patients should avoid caffeine, drink ≥2 L of fluid per day, and add salt to their food, unless they are already hypertensive. They should be instructed on how to manage possible orthostatic hypotensive attacks.

Hematologic Effects

A transient leukopenia is the most common hematologic problem. A more serious drop of leukocyte counts, agranulocytosis, is observed with chlorpromazine, thioridazine, and clozapine.

Agranulocytosis (marked leukopenia and neutropenia) is a major drawback of clozapine treatment. It occurs in 1%–2% of patients, usually within the first 6 months of treatment. Several fatalities have been attributed to agranulocytosis; however, the death rate is decreasing significantly, likely because of improved recognition, management, and treatment. The incidence of agranulocytosis is associated with an older age and female sex. Ashkenazi Jews with a specific human leukocyte antigen haplotype (B38, DR4, DQW3) appear to be at increased risk. The pathophysiology underlying clozapine-induced agranulocytosis has not been fully elucidated, but genetic factors, dose-related factors, and immunologic components may play a role. The frequent monitoring of blood counts made necessary by the risk of agranulocytosis increases the cost of treatment, reduces patient acceptance, and excludes from treatment significant numbers of patients who cannot tolerate the medication.

Peripheral Anticholinergic Effects

Anticholinergic effects of both the typical and atypical drugs usually cause dry mouth and nose, blurred vision, constipation, urinary retention, mydriasis, nausea, and vomiting.

Endocrine Effects

Blockade of dopamine receptors in the tubuloinfundibular tract may cause increased secretion of prolactin, thus leading to breast enlargement, galactorrhea, impotence in men, and inhibited orgasm in women. The vast majority of atypical antipsychotic drugs do not produce these disturbances.

Other Side Effects

Other nonneurologic side effects involve weight gain, jaundice, and dermatologic and ophthalmologic effects.

Neurologic Side Effects

The neurologic side effects are the most serious side effects associated with the typical antipsychotic drugs. This drawback contrasts with the benefits of the atypical antipsychotic agents that lack these side effects. Neurologic side effects generally correlate with the potency of the antipsychotic agent. High-potency agents (those with higher affinity for dopamine D_2 postsynaptic receptors) are usually associated with extrapyramidal effects, Parkinsonism, neuroleptic malignant syndrome, epileptogenic effects, sedation, and central anticholinergic effects. The first three effects mentioned above will be discussed in greater detail.

Extrapyramidal Effects

These effects include dystonia, tardive dyskinesia, and akathisia side effects.

- *Dystonia.* Acute dystonic reactions involve involuntary muscle contraction, especially of the head and neck. These reactions usually occur within hours to days after initiation of treatment or an increase in dose. They occur in as many as 10% of the patients treated with typical antipsychotic drugs, with young males being at greater risk for developing this syndrome. Dystonic movements result from a slow, sustained muscular contraction or spasm that can lead to involuntary movement. The symptoms can be episodic, lasting from minutes to hours, and may involve trismus (lockjaw), dystonia of the tongue, dystonia of the neck (typically arching the neck backwards), and oculgyric crisis in which extraocular muscles fix in the gaze position. Fortunately, the potentially fatal involvement of respiratory muscles is rare. Partial prophylaxis against acute dystonic reaction is achieved by the use of an anticholinergic agent with the initiation of a high-potency neuroleptic. Treatment of acute dystonic reactions consists of the administration of benztropine (1–2 mg intramuscularly), diphenhydramine (50 mg intramuscularly), or diazepam (5 mg by slow intravenous injection).

- *Tardive dyskinesia.* A late-developing extrapyramidal effect of neuroleptic therapy, tardive dyskinesia causes abnormal, involuntary, and irregular choreoathetoid muscle movements. The most common movements affected are perioral movements. The risk of tardive dyskinesia is greater in women, in patients older than 50 years, and in those with affective illness or brain injury. Management of tardive dyskinesia may include discontinuation of the neuroleptic drug, and this discontinuation may cause a transient worsening of the movements of tardive dyskinesia. Tardive dyskinesia may appear late in treatment with antipsychotic medication and is treated with the anticholinergic medication of benzodiazepines.
- *Akathisia.* This subjective feeling of muscular discomfort can cause patients to appear agitated, pace relentlessly, alternately sit and stand, and feel generally dysphoric. It may appear at any time of the treatment. Treatment of akathisia involves either reducing the dose of the antipsychotic drug or changing to a lower-potency drug, as well as pharmacologic intervention with a β-blocker (e.g., propranolol, 30–120 mg/day), a benzodiazepine (e.g., lorazepam, 0.5–1 mg three times a day), an anticholinergic agent (e.g., benztropine, 0.5–2 mg twice daily), or an α-adrenergic agonist (e.g., clonidine, 0.1 mg three times daily).

Parkinsonism

Parkinsonism, which is associated with high-potency antipsychotic medication and is dose related, usually appears within the first days to weeks after initiation of treatment. This effect occurs in approximately 15% of patients treated with dopamine receptor antagonist drugs (typical antipsychotic drugs) and is caused by the blockade of dopaminergic transmission in the nigrostriatal tract.

Symptoms of Parkinsonism include muscle stiffness (lead pipe or cogwheel rigidity), pill-rolling or coarse tremor, shuffling gait, stooped posture, drooling, mask-like faces, and akinesia. These effects are frequently seen in children receiving high-potency drugs. Women are more often affected than men. Management of Parkinsonism includes reducing the dose of the antipsychotic drug, changing to a lower-potency drug, administration of an anticholinergic drug (usually benztropine, 0.5–2 mg twice daily), and/or treatment with the dopamine agonist amantadine (100 mg, one to three times a day).

Neuroleptic Malignant Syndrome

This syndrome, the etiology of which is unknown, is the most toxic complication of neuroleptic use. It evolves over 24–72 h and presents with fluctuating levels of consciousness from agitation to stupor and autonomic disregulation, including fever, increased heart rate, labile blood pressure, sweating, and muscle rigidity. Laboratory findings consist of leukocytosis, increased creatine kinase concentrations, and myoglobinuria.

Neuroleptic malignant syndrome is seen more frequently in men and may occur at any age. The mortality rate is 10%–25%. Treatment of the syndrome consists of immediate withdrawal of neuroleptic drugs in conjunction with supportive care, including hydration and cooling.

Mortality

In 2005, the FDA issued a public health advisory stating that elderly patients taking atypical antipsychotic drugs for the treatment of dementia-related psychosis are at an increased risk of death. A second warning issued in 2008 added typical antipsychotic drugs to this advisory. The current FDA warning claims an increased mortality risk for elderly patients taking typical or atypical antipsychotic drugs for the treatment of dementia-related psychosis.

The use of typical or atypical antipsychotic drugs for dementia-related psychosis is not FDA approved. It is recommended that healthcare professionals use other treatment options; however, no other medication options are available for dementia-related psychosis.

The FDA warning does not apply to the use of antipsychotic drugs for other mental health diagnoses. In situations other than dementia-related psychosis, the mortality rate is typically higher in patients not taking any medications than in patients taking an antipsychotic drug.

ANALYSIS

Existing methods for quantifying neuroleptic concentrations include gas chromatography (GC), fluorometry, high-performance liquid chromatography (HPLC), radioimmunoassay, and the neuroleptic radioreceptor assay (NRRA).

Gas Chromatography

GC is the primary method of quantifying the neuroleptic drugs because of its high specificity and sensitivity. Sensitivity can be greatly enhanced with the nitrogen–phosphorus detector because most antipsychotic drugs contain a secondary or tertiary amine. The nitrogen–phosphorus detector is 10–100 times more sensitive than the flame-ionization detector and is as sensitive as the electron-capture detector for the neuroleptic agents.

Drugs are separated from the biological matrix by either liquid–liquid extraction after alkalinization, or by solid-phase extraction. There are several disadvantages to the use of GC for neuroleptic analysis. Some neuroleptics (e.g., fluphenazine and haloperidol) must undergo derivatization to produce symmetrical peaks. Another problem is the on-column reduction to the parent drug that occurs with some metabolites of phenothiazines, thus giving erroneously high values of the parent drug. GC coupled with mass spectrometry is the most sensitive and specific of all methods.

Fluorometry

Fluorometry is not a specific method for measuring some neuroleptic drugs because of interferences from metabolites. Butaperazine concentrations measured by fluorometry and GC are highly correlated. With another phenothiazine (thioridazine), however, fluorometry gives higher values than those obtained by GC. Mesoridazine, an active metabolite of thioridazine, has excitation and emission spectra similar to the parent compound, yielding falsely increased thioridazine levels. Fluphenazine measured by fluorometric methods has also given unexpectedly high results.

High-Performance Liquid Chromatography

HPLC is another commonly used technique for neuroleptic analysis. Both normal and reversed-phase columns have been used, the latter being more common. Peak tailing is a problem and is probably due to an interaction of these basic drugs with the column-support material in reversed-phase analysis. Interaction can be suppressed by silanization of the reversed-phase support, by use of ion-pair chromatography, or by adding alkylamines, such as triethylamine, to the mobile phase to improve resolution and decrease tailing, thereby increasing the sensitivity. With reversed-phase HPLC, metabolites are generally eluted with a shorter elution time than the parent drug, which may be beneficial with respect to the detection limits of these metabolites. Because active metabolites often contribute to the pharmacologic activity of the neuroleptic drugs, their detection in addition to the parent compound is important. A variety of detectors have been used. Most recently, tandem mass spectrometry has improved the sensitivity, specificity, and reproducibility of antipsychotic medication assays. Tandem mass spectrometry is rapidly becoming the method of choice for analysis of antipsychotic drugs.

Radioimmunoassay

With respect to detecting neuroleptic drugs, radioimmunoassay, a very sensitive procedure, offers several advantages. Because no extraction is involved, the drug in the plasma can be measured directly. In addition, sample-volume requirements are small, and a large number (e.g., hundreds) of samples can be run per batch. The disadvantage of this procedure is the unavailability of commercial kits. Furthermore, most of the assays show cross-reactivity, with different sensitivities observed for the parent compound and its metabolites.

Neuroleptic Radioreceptor Assay

NRRA is quite useful for detecting neuroleptic drugs because this procedure measures the parent compound and all pharmacologically active metabolites. The method has application for those patients for whom drug treatment has been changed before the previous neuroleptic agent has been fully eliminated. This is because the NRRA measures all neuroleptic drugs regardless of class. This assay has shown that patients may have a poor clinical response, with serum neuroleptic concentrations <50 ng/mL (expressed as chlorpromazine equivalents).

On the other hand, the NRRA has several disadvantages. The receptor assay has poor precision. Some polar metabolites of the neuroleptic drugs that are present in vitro may not cross the blood–brain barrier and reach the site of action in vivo. With the use of tritium-labeled butyrophenone standards (i.e., spiroperidol or haloperidol), the assay may not be optimal when used to measure phenothiazines. Another disadvantage is that this method requires radioactivity and a scintillation counter; clinical laboratories prefer to use nonisotopic analyses because of the regulations, physical monitoring, and disposal requirements involved in the use of radioactive reagents. One commercial kit was marketed for several years (Burroughs Wellcome Diagnostics), but the future availability of the kit is questionable.

INTERPRETATION

In general, plasma concentrations of neuroleptic agents do not correlate well with clinical signs and symptoms. Therapeutic serum reference intervals have been established for many of the typical and atypical antipsychotic medications (Table 3); however, serum reference intervals have not been established for ziprasidone, aripiprazole, and paliperidone. Therapeutic drug monitoring has been found to be appropriate in determining compliance with neuroleptic regimens, changing neuroleptic medications, documenting the concentration that is therapeutic in any given patient, and evaluating patients who exhibit signs of neuroleptic toxicity.

Table 3. Therapeutic Serum Antipsychotic Drug Concentrations[a]

Drug Name	Serum Drug Concentration, ng/mL	
	Therapeutic	Potentially Toxic
Typical antipsychotic drugs		
Haloperidol	1–40	>50
Thioridazine	250–1250	1800
Mesoridazine	150–1000	1500
Chlorpromazine	50–500	750
Thiothixene	10–30	100
Loxapine	5–30	60
Perphenazine	Low dose, 0.5–2.5	50
	High dose, 5–30	
Fluphenazine	Low dose, 0.5–2.5	40
	High dose, 5–20	
Atypical antipsychotic drugs		
Clozapine	350–1500	1800
Risperidone	10–120 (total, parent and metabolite)	NE
Quetiapine	100–1000	NE
Olanzapine	10–80	NE
Ziprasidone	NE	NE
Aripiprazole	NE	NE
Paliperidone	NE	NE

[a]Reference intervals obtained courtesy of MedTox Laboratories, St. Paul, MN. NE, not established.

One problem in the interpretation of antipsychotic drug concentrations is the significant overlap between therapeutic and toxic drug concentrations. For instance, postmortem studies have reported blood thioridazine concentrations of 0.3–8.5 mg/L and blood chlorpromazine concentrations of 1–44 mg/L in fatalities directly related to the drugs. However, because most of the signs and symptoms of neuroleptic toxicity are clinical changes in electrocardiograms and extrapyramidal symptoms, it is very difficult to determine toxic overdose of neuroleptic drugs without antemortem clinical information.

SUGGESTED READING

1. Andrès E, Maloisel F. Idiosyncratic drug-induced agranulocytosis or acute neutropenia. Curr Opin Hematol 2008;15:15–21.
2. Baselt RC, ed. Disposition of toxic drugs and chemicals in man, 7th ed, Foster City, CA: Biomedical Publications, 2004.
3. Bell J. Methods for monitoring neuroleptic drugs. AACC Therapeutic Drug Monitoring and Toxicology 1985;6:1–6.
4. Brunton LL, Lazo JD, Parker LP. Goodman and Gilman's the pharmacological basis of therapeutics, 11th ed. New York: McGraw-Hill, 2005.
5. Goldfrank LR, Lewis R, Flomenbau NE, Lewin NA, Howland MA, Hoffman RS, Nelson LS, eds. Goldfrank's toxicologic emergencies, 8th ed. New York: McGraw-Hill, 2006.
6. Klaassen CD, ed. Casarett & Doull's toxicology: the basic science of poisons, 7th ed. New York: McGraw-Hill, 2007.
7. Pierre, Joseph M. Deconstructing schizophrenia for DSM-V: challenges for clinical research and research agendas. Clin Schizophr Relat Psychoses 2008;2:166–74.
8. Vuica M, Ross AE, Nichols JH. Atypical antipsychotic drugs. AACC Therapeutic Drug Monitoring and Toxicology 2000;22:66–75.
9. Wetli CV, Mittleman RE, Rao VJ. An atlas of forensic pathology. Chicago: American Society of Clinical Pathologists Press, 1999.

CHAPTER 25

Therapeutic Drugs IV: Antihistamines

Barry Levine

HISTAMINE

Histamine (Fig. 1) consists of an imidazole ring and a chain moiety consisting of a dimethylamino group. It is synthesized by the decarboxylation of the amino acid histidine through the enzymatic activity of L-histidine decarboxylase. Histamine is metabolized by two pathways; the final products are N-methylimidazoleacetic acid and imidazoleacetic acid riboside. It is stored in basophils in the blood and in mast cells in tissues.

Histamine produces a number of physiological effects, the most prominent of which is an immediate allergic response after it is released from storage through the involvement of immunoglobulin E. The allergic response includes redness, swelling, and increased secretions. Histamine also stimulates the secretion of acid, pepsin, and intrinsic factor in the stomach. In the central nervous system, histamine acts as a neurotransmitter. This action may lead to increased wakefulness and decreased appetite, among other things. It also causes the contraction of smooth muscle cells in the lungs and the gastrointestinal tract but causes the relaxation of small blood vessels.

Four distinct histamine receptors have been classified. Therapeutic agents have been developed as antagonists to the H_1 and H_2 receptors, however, and the discussion in this chapter is limited to effects on these receptors. Bronchial constriction and gastrointestinal contraction are mediated through the H_1 receptor. Gastric secretions occur with the involvement of the H_2 receptor. Vasodilatation is mediated through both the H_1 and H_2 receptors. The edema associated with the allergic response is due primarily to interaction with the H_1 receptor. Activation of the H_2 receptor leads to increased contractile force of the heart and increased automaticity, but activation of the H_1 receptor leads to a decrease in atrial-ventricular velocity.

H_1 ANTAGONISTS

A number of different structures with H_1 antagonist activity have been developed. These compounds are subdivided into first-generation H_1 antagonists and second-generation H_1 antagonists. First-generation H_1 antagonists include the following (examples are in parentheses):

1. Alkylamines (bromopheniramine, chlorpheniramine)
2. Ethanolamines (diphenhydramine, clemastine)
3. Ethylenediamines (pyrilamine, tripelennamine)
4. Phenothiazines (promethazine)
5. Piperidines (cyproheptadine)
6. Piperazines (cyclizine, hydroxyzine, meclizine)

Fig. 2. illustrates structures of first-generation H_1 antagonists.

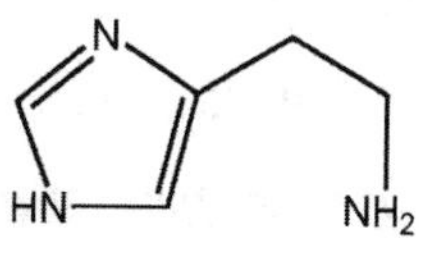

Fig. 1. Structure of histamine.

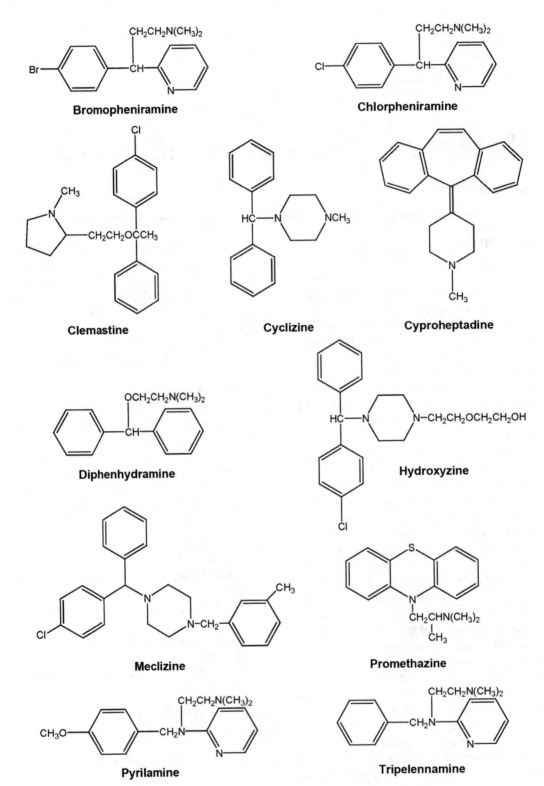

Fig. 2. Structures of first-generation H$_1$ antagonists.

Second-generation H_1 antagonists include the following:

1. Alkylamines (acrivastine)
2. Piperadines (loratadine, fexofenadine)
3. Piperazines (cetirizine)

Fig. 3 shows structures of second-generation H_1 antagonists. Most H_1 antagonists have the ethylamine chain moiety that histamine has, but most H_1 antagonists have two aromatic rings attached to this chain.

Uses

The effect of H_1 antagonists that accounts for their primary therapeutic use is their ability to mitigate hypersensitivity reactions caused by histamine. Swelling, redness, and itching are generally suppressed by these drugs. Moreover, the excess production of secretory products is also inhibited.

First-generation H_1 antagonists cause central nervous system depression, including slowed response, reduced attention, and drowsiness. In fact, some of these drugs are marketed as over-the-counter sleep aids. Conversely, second-generation H_1 antagonists do not cross the blood-brain barrier and consequently do not cause drowsiness. This major advantage allows these drugs to be used without adversely affecting regular daytime activities.

First-generation H_1 antagonists are also useful for treating vertigo, motion sickness, and postoperative vomiting. This effect occurs through their antimuscarinic cholinergic effects on the vestibular system and the brainstem. Within the vasculature, H_1 antagonists inhibit the vasoconstrictive effects of histamine.

Pharmacokinetics

Despite significant differences in structure, the H_1 antagonists share some pharmacokinetic similarities. They are well absorbed after oral administration, usually within several hours. They are highly bound to protein,

ranging from 78% to 99%. Their duration of action is generally 4–6 h, but some H_1 antagonists, such as loratadine, have activity durations of approximately 24 h.

Many H_1 antagonists are extensively metabolized by the cytochrome P450 enzyme system. Table 1 shows the major metabolic products of representative H_1 antagonists. For instance, chlorpheniramine is N-demethylated to norchlorpheniramine and dinorchlorpheniramine. Diphenhydramine undergoes an analogous demethylation process, which is followed by a deamination to produce diphenylmethoxyacetic acid. In addition to dealkylation, hydroxyzine, a first-generation H_1 antagonist, is oxidized to cetirizine, a second-generation H_1 antagonist. A less common route of metabolism is N-oxide formation; tripelennamine is converted to tripelennamine N-oxide. Fexofenadine, cetirizine, and acrivastine are excreted primarily as the unchanged drug.

Analysis

Because of their availability as over-the-counter drugs, first-generation H_1 antagonists are often encountered in forensic toxicologic analysis. These drugs are easily separated from biological samples by liquid–liquid extraction after sample alkalinization. They may also be separated by means of solid-phase extraction with an extraction system capable of separating alkaline drugs. These drugs can be resolved by a gas chromatography system equipped with a dimethyl or phenylmethyl silicone analytical column. A nitrogen–phosphorus or mass spectrometric detector provides sufficient sensitivity to detect therapeutic use of these drugs.

The analysis of second-generation H_1 antagonists is more challenging than the analysis of first-generation H_1 antagonists. Both fexofenadine and cetirizine contain carboxylic acid moieties that make gas chromatographic analysis difficult without derivatization. These drugs are more amenable to analysis by liquid chromatography and liquid chromatography–mass spectrometry.

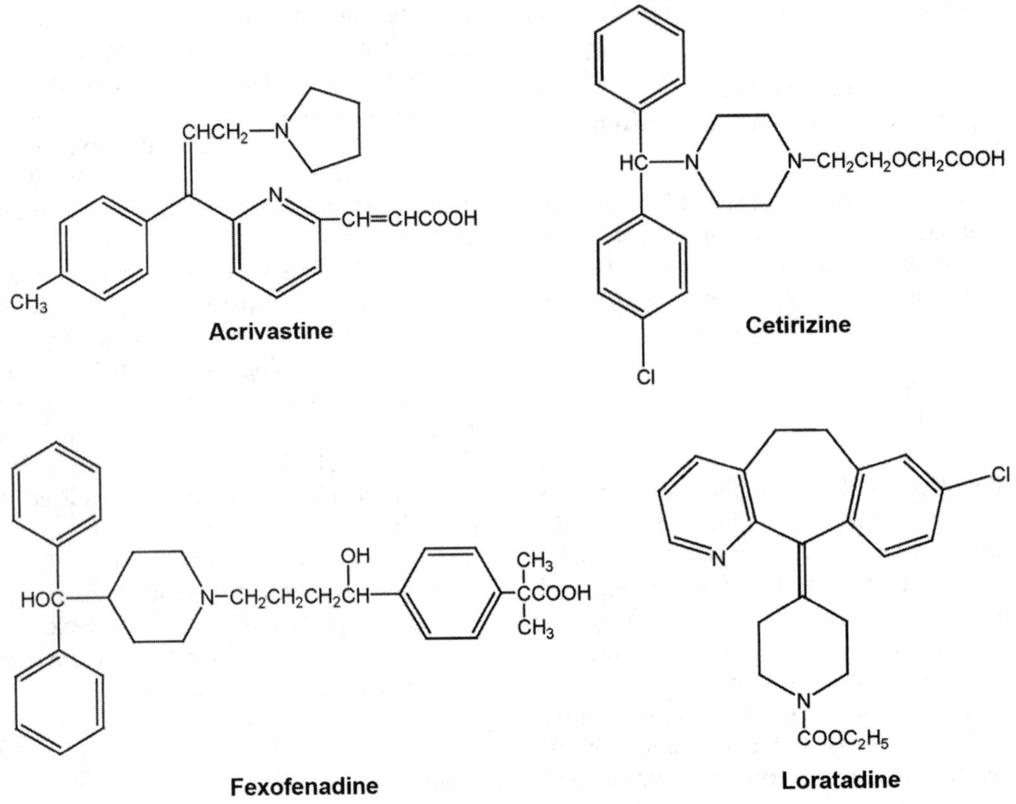

Fig. 3. Structures of second-generation H_1 antagonists.

Table 1. Metabolic Products of Selected H_1 Antagonists

Drug	Metabolites
Chlorpheniramine	Norchlorpheniramine
	Dinorchlorpheniramine
Diphenhydramine	Nordiphenhydramine
	Dinordiphenhydramine
	Diphenylmethoxyacetic acid
Hydroxyzine	Norhydroxyzine
	Cetirizine
Loratadine	Descarboethoxyloratadine
Promethazine	Desmethylpromethazine
	Promethazine sulfoxide
Tripelennamine	4-Hydroxytripelennamine
	α-Hydroxytripelennamine
	Tripelennamine-N-oxide

Furthermore, the amphoteric nature of these drugs makes them more difficult to separate from the biological specimen.

There are no commercially available immunoassays designed to detect antihistamine use.

Specimen Concentrations

The concentrations of H_1 antagonists in the serum following therapeutic use are in the range of 0.02 to 0.3 mg/L, depending on the specific drug, route of administration, and frequency of use. Urine concentrations are generally greater than blood concentrations, and urine would be the specimen of choice for identifying drug use. Diphenhydramine is the most cited H_1 antagonist in intoxication cases, with blood concentrations >8 mg/L having been reported in fatal cases. Liver concentrations will also be greater than blood concentrations. In one study, blood and liver concentrations of H_1 antagonists were summarized in cases in which the cause of death was unrelated to these drugs. The antihistamines included were diphenhydramine, chlorpheniramine, and doxylamine. From the data, heart blood concentrations <1.0 mg/L were generally associated with therapeutic use of diphenhydramine; the median blood concentration in these cases was 0.2 mg/L. The median liver concentration of diphenhydramine associated with therapeutic use was 1.2 mg/kg, and the median liver-to-blood concentration ratio was 8.0. Moreover, the median "postmortem therapeutic" heart blood and liver concentrations of chlorpheniramine were 0.3 mg/L and 2.9 mg/kg, respectively.

H_2 ANTAGONISTS

Fig. 4 illustrates the structures of H_2 antagonists available in the U.S. As stated earlier, histamine stimulates the secretion of acid in the stomach, and this action is accomplished via the H_2 receptor. The binding of histamine to the H_2 receptor activates adenylate cyclase, leading to an increase in intracellular cyclic AMP concentrations. This increase activates the proton pump in the parietal cells to secrete protons against the concentration gradient. H_2 antagonists competitively inhibit the binding of histamine to H_2 receptors, thus preventing acid secretion. H_2 antagonists are selective for the H_2 receptor and do not significantly affect activity at the H_1 receptor. Therapeutic use of H_2 antagonists is related to its effect on gastric acid secretion. They are used to promote healing of gastric and duodenal ulcers, reduce the formation of stress ulcers, and treat gastroesophageal reflux disease.

Like H_1 antagonists, H_2 antagonists are rapidly absorbed after oral ingestion, usually within several hours. Unlike their H_1 counterparts, however, H_2 antagonists are only slightly bound to proteins. They are not extensively metabolized in the liver, but routes of metabolism include hydroxylation, sulfoxide formation, and conjugation. Potential drug interactions are more significant with these drugs. For example, cimetidine inhibits cytochrome P450 enzymes CYP1A2, CYP2C9, and CYP2D6, leading to increased concentrations of coadministered drugs that are metabolized by these enzyme systems. The other drugs are much safer than cimetidine in this respect; consequently, cimetidine has seen reduced use as a therapeutic agent. Ethanol consumed while taking H_2 antagonists will produce a slight increase in blood ethanol concentration, compared with the blood ethanol concentration attained without drug use.

Although these drugs are widely used and are available without a prescription, they are not frequently encountered in forensic toxicology laboratories. These drugs have little abuse potential. Consequently, they are not tested in workplace drug screening, and no commercial immunoassays are available

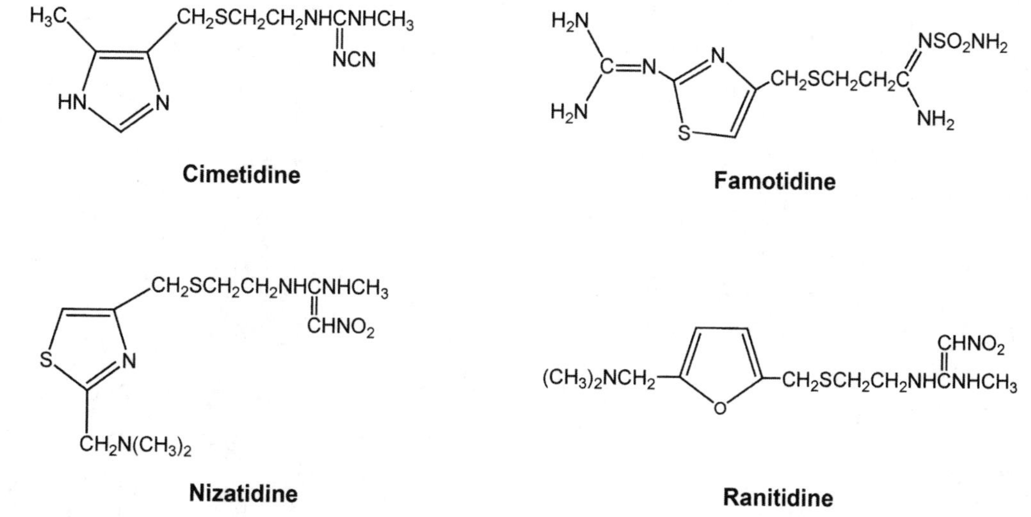

Fig. 4. Structures of H_2 antagonists.

for their detection. Furthermore, they have few central nervous system effects and are not included in drugged-driver testing. H_2 antagonists are not detected with common gas chromatographic systems. High-performance liquid chromatography is the preferred technique for detecting and quantifying these drugs. Therapeutic concentrations of these drugs in the blood range from 0.5 to 5 mg/L, with the exception of famotidine, which has a slightly lower therapeutic range of 0.1 to 1 mg/L.

SUGGESTED READING

1. Feldman M, Burton ME. Histamine$_2$-receptor antagonists. Standard therapy for acid-peptic diseases. N Engl J Med 1990;323:1672–80.

2. Krishna DR, Klotz U. Newer H_2-receptor antagonists. Clinical pharmacokinetics and drug interaction potential. Clin Pharmacokinet 1988;15:205–15.

3. Levine B, Klette K, Radentz S, Smith ML, Smialek JE. Antihistamine concentrations in postmortem blood and liver specimens. Forensic Sci Int 1996;81:73–6.

4. Paton DM, Webster DR. Clinical pharmacokinetics of the H_1 receptor antagonists (the antihistamines). Clin Pharmacokinet 1985;10:477–97.

5. Simons FER, Simons KJ. The pharmacology and use of H_1 receptor antagonists drugs. N Engl J Med 1997;330:1663–70.

6. Simons FER, Simons KJ. Clinical pharmacology of new histamine H_1 receptor antagonists. Clin Pharmacokinet 1999;36:329–52.

CHAPTER 26

Therapeutic Drugs V: Nonnarcotic Analgesics

Barry Levine

INTRODUCTION

The treatment of pain involves a number of classes of therapeutic agents. Narcotic analgesic drugs, or opioids, have been discussed in Chapter 17. Nonnarcotic analgesics are among the most widely used therapeutic agents. The agents discussed in this chapter are acetaminophen and the anti-inflammatory drugs, such as aspirin (salicylates), traditional nonsteroidal anti-inflammatory drugs (tNSAIDs), and cyclooxygenase-2 (COX-2) inhibitors. Besides their ability to treat pain, these drugs have several other uses. These drugs have antipyretic properties, and all of these drugs except acetaminophen have anti-inflammatory effects as well. Inflammation is the body's response to a potentially injurious stimulus. This stimulus may be a physical injury, an allergen, or an infection. The classic inflammatory response involves pain, redness, and swelling at the site of injury. This response is followed by the entry of white blood cells into the area, leading to tissue fibrosis.

ANTI-INFLAMMATORY DRUGS

Mechanism of Action

The mechanism by which anti-inflammatory drugs exert their pharmacologic activity has been known for decades. These drugs inhibit the synthesis of prostaglandins, a group of compounds known as eicosanoids and derived from arachidonic acid. Arachidonic acid either is ingested directly from the diet or is derived from dietary linoleic acid. Prostaglandins cause a number of effects associated with the inflammatory response. For example, prostaglandin E_2 causes vasodilation and a decrease in blood pressure. It also enhances platelet aggregation. Another prostaglandin, designated D_2, causes flushing, nasal stuffiness, and hypotension.

The first step in prostaglandin synthesis is the conversion of arachidonic acid into prostaglandin G_2 and prostaglandin H_2, two unstable intermediates. This reaction is catalyzed by the enzyme prostaglandin G/H synthase, also known as cyclooxygenase (COX). There are two main forms of this enzyme, COX-1 and COX-2. COX-1 is the primary constitutive isozyme and is found in most normal cells and tissues. COX-2 is induced by cytokines and inflammatory mediators. One significant difference between the two isoenzymes is that COX-1 is the primary isoenzyme found in gastric epithelial cells, where prostaglandins provide cytoprotective effects. Salicylates and tNSAIDs inhibit both COX isoenzymes. As a result, these drugs inhibit prostaglandin synthesis in the gastrointestinal tract, accounting for the gastrointestinal distress that these drugs produce. Conversely, COX-2 inhibitors do not affect prostaglandin synthesis in the gastrointestinal tract and do not cause the gastric upset caused by the tNSAIDs.

Aspirin/Salicylate

Aspirin is one of the most widely used nonprescription drugs in the U.S. The structure of aspirin (acetylsalicylate) and salicylate are shown in Fig. 1. It is used primarily as an analgesic and as an antipyretic. In addition, its ability to prolong bleeding time makes it a useful drug in the prevention of thromboemboli. Specifically, it prevents platelet aggregation by irreversibly acetylating platelet COX, thereby reducing the formation of thromboxane A_2 and increasing the bleeding time.

Pharmacokinetics

Aspirin serves as a prodrug. After oral ingestion, it is rapidly hydrolyzed by liver and blood esterases to salicylic acid, the drug form that accounts for aspirin's pharmacologic activity. The half-life of aspirin is approximately 15 min, whereas the half-life of salicylate is dose dependent, ranging from 3 to 20 h. In plasma, salicylate is highly bound to protein, but this binding is also concentration dependent. Ninety percent of salicylate is bound to protein at concentrations up to 100 mg/L, and binding decreases to 50% at 400 mg/L.

Salicylate concentrations up to 350 mg/L may be seen in the plasma, depending on the therapeutic use. Higher concentrations are seen in the treatment of arthritis patients than would be seen in the treatment of pain or hyperthermia. Salicylate is metabolized primarily through phase II metabolism. Approximately 80% of the dose is conjugated with glycine to form salicyluric acid. Small amounts of the acyl and phenolic glucuronide conjugates are also formed.

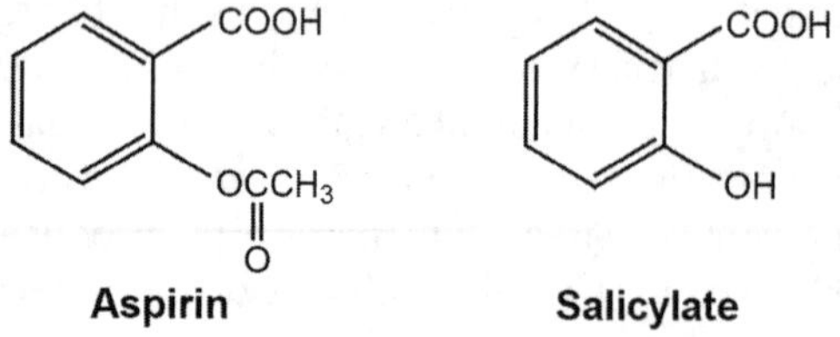

Fig. 1. Structure of aspirin and salicylate.

Toxicity

The toxic effects of salicylate generally occur at plasma concentrations >300 mg/L. Salicylate stimulates respiration by causing an uncoupling of oxidative phosphorylation, leading to increased carbon dioxide production. It also acts directly as a stimulant to the respiratory center in the medulla. The increased carbon dioxide produces a respiratory acidosis that leads to increased bicarbonate excretion as the body tries to compensate for the acidosis. On top of this compensated respiratory alkalosis is a metabolic acidosis caused by the presence of the acidic salicylate, which displaces bicarbonate, impairs the excretion of sulfuric and phosphoric acids, and inhibits various enzymes.

Salicylates produce other toxic effects beside the respiratory and pH abnormalities mentioned above. A group of these effects occurs with chronic, mild salicylate intoxication and is termed *salicylism*. Such intoxication is characterized by headache, dizziness, ringing in the ears, dimness of vision, and mental confusion. These effects subside within several days after withdrawal from the drug.

Central nervous system effects associated with high doses of salicylate include stimulation that leads to seizures, followed by central nervous system depression. Salicylates may also trigger the chemoreceptor trigger zone in the medulla, leading to nausea and vomiting. Salicylate characteristics of inhibiting platelet aggregation and prolonging bleeding time can lead to hemorrhage, especially in individuals predisposed to excess bleeding. Large doses of salicylates may also cause hyperglycemia, glycosuria, and aminoaciduria.

Analysis

There is a classic color test for the detection of salicylate in biological samples. Salicylate reacts with Trinder reagent to produce a purple color. Trinder reagent is an acidic solution of ferric chloride prepared by mixing mercuric chloride, concentrated hydrochloric acid, and ferric nitrate. For the color reaction to occur, the free carboxylic acid and the free phenolic group are required. Neither aspirin nor methyl salicylate will produce a positive test. The color test has sufficient sensitivity to measure therapeutic concentrations of salicylate. The test can be performed directly on samples, but centrifugation may be necessary to make the purple color readily apparent.

Salicylate is a strong acid and needs to be extracted from biological samples after acidification. Detection by gas chromatography requires derivatization, and trimethylsilyl derivatization has been used. Flame ionization or mass spectrometry is the primary gas chromatographic detection method. More often, liquid chromatography with ultraviolet detection is used to quantify salicylate and its metabolites. No derivatization is needed when liquid chromatography is used.

Commercially available immunoassays based on a number of technologies can also be used to measure salicylate in clinical and forensic laboratories.

Traditional Nonsteroidal Anti-Inflammatory Drugs

tNSAIDs constitute a number of different structures that have similar mechanisms of action. These drugs are subdivided as follows (examples in parentheses):

1. Acetic acid derivatives (indomethacin, sulindac)
2. Enolic acid derivatives (piroxicam, meloxicam)
3. Propionic acid derivatives (ibuprofen, naproxen)
4. Fenamates (mefenamate, meclofenamate)
5. Heteroacyl acetic acid derivatives (tolmetin, ketorolac)

Fig. 2 illustrates the structures of these drugs.

Pharmacokinetics

Despite their differences in structure, the tNSAIDs have many pharmacokinetic characteristics in common. All of these drugs are well absorbed after oral ingestion, and peak plasma concentrations are reached within 1 to 2 h after ingestion. Ketorolac is one of the few tNSAIDs that is administered parenterally. These drugs are highly bound to plasma proteins, usually >90%. This property has the potential to lead to drug interactions with coadministered drugs that are also highly bound to proteins.

The plasma half-life of these drugs is variable, even within a structurally similar group. For instance, ibuprofen has a half-life of 2–4 h, whereas naproxen has a half-life of about 14 h. The enolic acid derivatives generally have the longest plasma half-lives, 1–2 days.

Routes of phase I metabolism also vary between groups. Table 1 gives the phase I metabolic route of many of the commonly used tNSAIDs. The metabolic products are generally inactive, with the exception of sulindac, which is a prodrug (the sulfide metabolite of sulindac is a much more potent inhibitor of COX than the parent drug). The metabolites of tNSAIDs are then conjugated, usually with glucuronic acid, and are excreted in the urine.

Selective COX-2 Inhibitors

Although efficacious, the tNSAIDs have the disadvantage of causing gastrointestinal

Table 1. Phase I Metabolism of Selected Traditional Nonsteroidal Anti-Inflammatory Drugs

Drug	Route of Phase I Metabolism
Indomethacin	O-Demethylation
	N-Demethylation
Sulindac	Sulfone formation
	Sulfide formation
Mefenamic acid	3-Methyl hydroxylation
	3-Methyl carboxylation
Tolmetin	p-Methyl carboxylation
Ketorolac	None
Ibuprofen	Hydroxylation
	Carboxylation
Naproxen	6-Demethylation
Piroxicam	Pyridyl ring hydroxylation

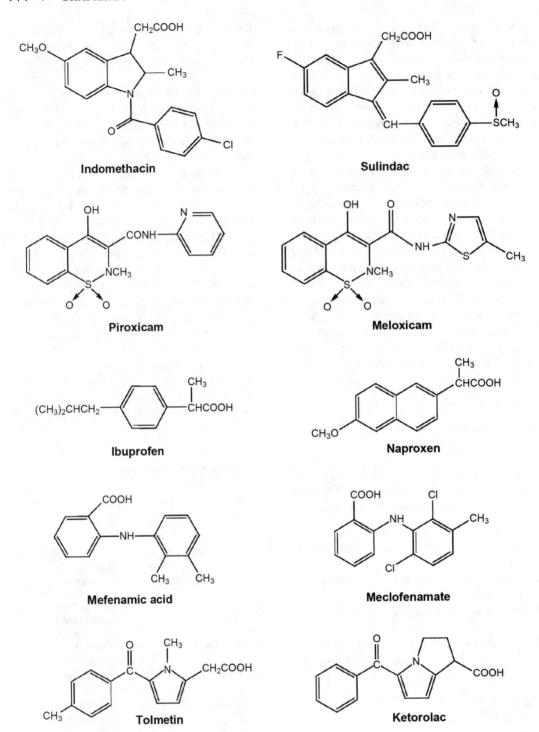

Fig. 2. Structures of traditional nonsteroidal anti-inflammatory drugs.

distress. Gene research identified a second COX enzyme, designated COX-2, that was believed to be the major cause of prostaglandin formation in inflammation. In addition, the "original" COX enzyme, designated COX-1, was the predominant enzyme in the gastrointestinal tract. Therefore, the rationale was that developing drugs that were more specific for the COX-2 enzyme could achieve the desired anti-inflammatory effect while minimizing gastrointestinal distress. The "coxibs" were the first class of drugs developed with specific COX-2 inhibition.

Three members of this class were approved for use in the U.S.: celecoxib, valdecoxib, and rofecoxib; however, concerns over cardiovascular toxicity caused the latter two drugs to be removed from the market, leaving celecoxib as the only COX-2 inhibitor available (Fig. 3). Celecoxib reaches its peak plasma concentration 2–4 h after ingestion. It is highly bound to proteins and has a plasma elimination half-life of about 11 h. Serum concentrations of approximately 0.5 mg/L are observed after therapeutic use. Celecoxib is metabolized to a hydroxymethyl compound, which is then converted to a carboxylic acid derivative. The carboxylic acid derivative is glucuronized and is excreted primarily in the feces. Celecoxib is not amenable to gas chromatographic analysis with the common analytical columns. Instead, liquid chromatography, with either ultraviolet or mass spectrometric detection, is the preferred analytical technique.

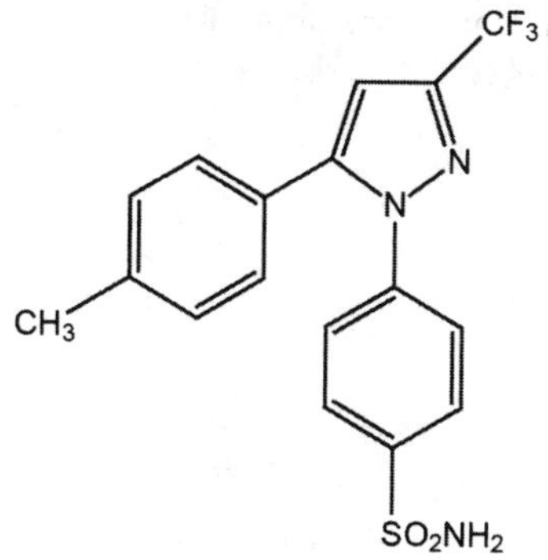

Fig. 3. Structure of celecoxib.

ACETAMINOPHEN

As stated previously, acetaminophen (Fig. 4) has analgesic and antipyretic effects similar to the anti-inflammatory drugs; however, it has minimal anti-inflammatory activity. When taken therapeutically, it also has little effect on the cardiovascular system, the respiratory system, and platelet aggregation. Moreover, gastrointestinal effects are less common than with anti-inflammatory drugs. It is well absorbed orally, reaching peak concentrations within an hour. It is less bound to plasma proteins than the anti-inflammatory drugs. It has a plasma half-life of 2 h when taken appropriately. The therapeutic range for acetaminophen is 10–20 mg/L.

Toxicity

The mechanism of acetaminophen toxicity has been extensively studied. When present in the body in therapeutic amounts, acetaminophen undergoes phase II metabolism with glucuronic acid and sulfuric acid to form conjugated products that are excreted in the urine. Acetaminophen also undergoes phase I metabolism to form N-acetyl-p-benzoquinone (NAPQI), which is eliminated by a phase II reaction with glutathione to form a mercapturic acid conjugate. When a large amount of acetaminophen is present, however, the glutathione pathway becomes saturated, and NAPQI is not detoxified. The presence of this compound leads to the production of reactive nitrogen and oxygen species that bind covalently to liver cell macromolecules, leading to hepatic necrosis.

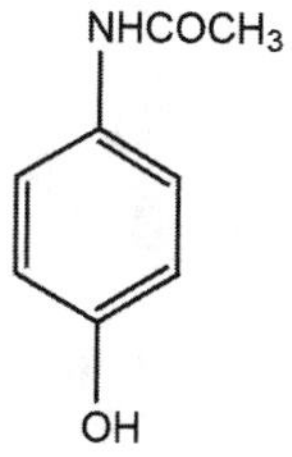

Fig. 4. Structure of acetaminophen.

This toxicity does not manifest itself immediately; signs of liver toxicity such as hepatomegaly, jaundice, and coagulopathy occur 2–4 days after ingestion.

Treatment of an acetaminophen overdose is based on the serum acetaminophen concentration and the time since ingestion. Liver damage will generally occur when the serum concentration exceeds 300 mg/L at 4 h after ingestion or 45 mg/L at 15 h after ingestion. In addition to general procedures to prevent absorption, such as the administration of activated charcoal, a specific antidote is available for treating acetaminophen overdoses. *N*-acetylcysteine replenishes the supply of glutathione for NAPQI to bind and also provides a nontoxic binding site for the reactive species.

Analysis

Similar to salicylate, a classic color test exists for detecting acetaminophen in biological samples. Trichloroacetic acid is used to prepare a protein-free precipitate. The supernatant is acidified with concentrated hydrochloric acid and heated in a boiling water bath for 10–15 min. The solution is cooled, and 1% *o*-cresol and concentrated ammonium hydroxide are added. A blue color indicates the presence of acetaminophen. Unlike many color tests, this method has the sensitivity to identify therapeutic and toxic concentrations of acetaminophen.

Acetaminophen can also be measured by gas or liquid chromatography. The drug can be extracted at neutral or slightly acid pH and can be extracted with solid-phase extraction techniques. Acetaminophen will be detected on a DB-1 or DB-5 gas chromatographic column without derivatization. Reversed-phase liquid chromatography can also be used, usually with ultraviolet detection. When liquid chromatography is used, a simple protein precipitation may be sufficient as a separation step.

A number of commercial immunoassays are available for measuring acetaminophen in biological samples. They are especially useful in emergency toxicology situations in which rapid acetaminophen quantification is necessary for more rapid treatment. Although designed primarily for serum, some of these immunoassays can also be applicable to blood and urine samples.

SUGGESTED READING

1. Brunton LL, Lazo JS, Parker KL, eds. Goodman & Gilman's the pharmacologic basis of therapeutics, 11th ed. New York: McGraw-Hill, 2006.
2. Maurer HH, Tauvel FX, Kraemer T. Screening procedure for the detection of non-steroidal anti-inflammatory drugs and their metabolites in urine as part of a systematic toxicological analysis procedure for acidic drugs and poisons by gas chromatography-mass spectrometry after extractive methylation. J Anal Toxicol 2001;25:237–44.
3. Miksa IR, Cummings MR, Poppenga RH. Multi-residue determination of anti-inflammatory analgesics in sera by liquid chromatography-mass spectrometry. J Anal Toxicol 2005;29:95–104.
4. Sunshine I. Methodology for analytical toxicology. Cleveland: CRC Press, 1975.
5. Verbeeck RK, Blackburn JL, Loewen GR. Clinical pharmacokinetics of non-steroidal anti-inflammatory drugs. Clin Pharmacokinet 1983;8:297–331.

CHAPTER 27

Carbon Monoxide/Cyanide

Gary W. Kunsman and Barry Levine

CARBON MONOXIDE

Carbon monoxide (CO) is an odorless, colorless, and tasteless gas that readily mixes with air; its density is slightly less than that of air (d = 0.968, d_{air} = 1). It is produced as a result of the incomplete combustion of organic compounds. Major sources of CO include cigarette smoke, exhaust from internal combustion engines, malfunctioning heating and ventilation systems, fires, the metabolism of dihalomethanes (e.g., dichloromethane [methylene chloride], dibromomethane, and bromochloromethane), and heme catabolism (0.4 mL/h). Exposure to 0.4% (v/v) CO in air can be fatal in <1 h. The threshold limit volume for CO is 25 ppm; however, exposure to higher concentrations can occur along expressways or in smoke-filled rooms.

Pathophysiology

CO is relatively inert chemically. Its toxic effects result from its combination with hemoglobin (Hb) in red blood cells, the means by which oxygen is transported throughout the body. Oxygen is needed by cells for respiration, the biochemical process that manufactures high-energy molecules (ATP) needed to perform the processes that sustain life. Hb contains an iron atom in the +2 valence state (ferrous ion), and CO readily binds to the ferrous ion, forming carboxyhemoglobin (COHb). When blood is exposed to a combination of CO and oxygen, binding occurs in proportion of one mole of CO or oxygen per mole of ferrous ion. However, the partial pressure required for CO binding is 1/200 to 1/300 of the partial pressure required for oxygen binding. In other words, CO has approximately 200–300 times greater affinity for Hb than oxygen does.

Binding to Hb by CO produces its toxic effect through two facets of the same mechanism. One obvious effect is that the portion of Hb that is bound to CO is no longer available to bind oxygen, thus reducing the body's oxygen-carrying capacity. This leads to a shortage of oxygen where it is needed throughout the body. This mechanism of toxicity is referred to either as anoxic anoxia or anemic hypoxia. The second, less obvious effect is the result of a leftward shift in the oxygen–Hb saturation curve due to the binding of CO to Hb. This shift means that the presence of CO causes an increase in the affinity of oxygen for Hb, thereby decreasing the release of oxygen from Hb binding sites and further exacerbating the CO-induced anoxia. Those tissues with the greatest oxygen demand (e.g., heart and brain) would therefore be the most susceptible to the toxic effects of CO.

The percentage of Hb saturated with CO (%COHb) does not completely account for all of the pathologies associated with CO exposure. For example, there is a poor correlation between the COHb saturation following exposure and the degree of neurological injury that follows many nonfatal CO exposures. There are also some studies that suggest there are physiological effects at low COHb saturations, as well as continued CO effects after COHb levels have returned to normal. In an effort to account for these and other findings, a histotoxic mechanism of CO toxicity has been proposed. This mechanism has not been completely elucidated but essentially involves the binding of CO to intracellular hemoproteins such as cytochrome c oxidase, myoglobin, catalase, and cytochrome P450, resulting in an inhibition of cellular respiration and other cellular functions. This postulation of such a mechanism does not reduce the role of anoxic anoxia in CO toxicity.

Disposition

Carbon monoxide is readily absorbed through the lungs, and its primary route of elimination is also through the lungs. There is no metabolism of absorbed CO. After absorption, CO rapidly distributes into the blood. The binding of CO to Hb is reversible, but, due to the greater affinity of CO as compared to oxygen, CO is not readily displaced at normal oxygen concentrations. This can lead to a gradual increase in the percentage of COHb with prolonged CO exposure; CO is not spontaneously displaced from Hb but is displaced by the mass action of oxygen. The half-life of carbon monoxide is 5–6 h at normal oxygen concentration (21%), 30–90 min at 100% oxygen, and 30 min under hyberbaric oxygen conditions.

Analysis

One of the early methods of CO analysis involved microdiffusion using a Conway cell. The specimen is placed in the outer well, and sulfuric acid is added to release the CO from the Hb. A solution of palladium chloride is added to the center well. The cell is sealed and incubated at room temperature for 1–2 h. As the reaction proceeds, the palladium chloride is reduced to metallic palladium, forming a black or silver mirror in the center well, and the CO is converted to carbon dioxide. This method can be made semiquantitative by measuring the amount of unreacted palladium chloride and the Hb in the blood specimen. This technique is useful for screening specimens with COHb saturation values >10%. Another qualitative technique that is effective as a preliminary screen is diluting 1 mL blood with 20 mL 0.01M ammonium hydroxide. Elevated COHb will result in a pink or bluish-red color as compared to a yellowish-red color in the absence of COHb.

Gas chromatography has been used successfully for the analysis of COHb in biological specimens. CO must first be separated from Hb to permit gas chromatographic analysis. This separation can be accomplished by adding the blood to a stoppered container and injecting a releasing agent, commonly a dilute solution of potassium ferricyanide, through the stopper. A sample of the headspace is collected with a gas syringe and injected into the gas chromatograph using a molecular sieve column to achieve the analytical separation. Two types of detectors can be used for this analysis. A thermal conductivity detector can be used to quantify the amount of CO directly. A flame ionization detector provides greater sensitivity but requires the conversion of CO to methane. This can be accomplished with a post-column nickel catalyst and hydrogen gas.

The actual calculation of %COHb may be accomplished in two ways. Blood calibrators can be prepared by saturating blood with 100% CO and subsequently making dilutions of the blood to generate a calibration curve. This necessitates the measurement of Hb in the specimen to correct for the differences in the Hb concentration between the calibration blood and the test blood. An alternative method is to saturate the test blood with 100% CO and measure the CO released from that saturated sample. The area ratio of CO in the unsaturated sample (untreated blood) to that in the saturated sample produces a ratio of CO content to CO capacity. This ratio is the percent saturation of the blood and removes the need for measuring the amount of Hb in the specimen. This Hb-independent method is very useful for determining the CO content of low-Hb specimens such as purge fluid from decomposed bodies. This technique can also be used to measure %COHb in tissue specimens such as spleen.

Spectrophotometry is commonly used to measure COHb in blood specimens. Hb, COHb, oxyhemoglobin, and methemoglobin have unique visible absorption spectra. In methemoglobin, the iron is in the +3 (ferric) valence state. In normal individuals, no more than 1–2% of total hemoglobin is in the form of methemoglobin. The simultaneous measurement of multiple species in the blood is based on the concept that at each wavelength, absorption of separate components is additive. This means that the quantification of n components in a solution can be performed by measuring n wavelengths. If the molar absorptivity of each compound at each wavelength is known, a series of n equations with n unknowns can then be solved simultaneously. Typically, the wavelengths selected are absorption maxima, minima, or isosbestic points, i.e., points where absorption spectra of two species intersect. In an ordinary blood specimen containing COHb, three Hb species would be expected to be present: Hb, COHb, and oxyhemoglobin. In postmortem specimens, a significant amount of methemoglobin is typically also present at amounts well above the normal 1–2%. The amount of methemoglobin will continue to increase in a variable manner after death. Theoretically, this would require the measurement of absorbance at four wavelengths to quantify each species. However, the addition of sodium hydrosulfite (dithionite, $Na_2S_2O_4$) reduces oxyhemoglobin and methemoglobin to Hb while leaving COHb unaffected (Fig. 1). This technique allows for the COHb measurement to be accomplished using only two wavelengths based on the

spectral differences between Hb and COHb. The Tietz method is a classic example of this technique.

Several instrument companies have developed automated spectrophotometric systems for the simultaneous analysis of multiple forms of Hb, including COHb. These instruments have a visible light source with interference filters for specific and precise wavelength selection. Whole blood is introduced into the system and is chemically hemolyzed. It then passes through a flow cell where the absorbance measurements are made. Based on these measurements and the appropriate molar extinction coefficients, the microprocessor is able to simultaneously solve the equations and either display or print out the amounts of the different Hb species present within a specimen.

Preserved whole blood, especially that preserved with EDTA (purple-top tubes), is the preferred specimen for carbon monoxide analysis in living patients. Sodium fluoride–preserved blood, spleen, and tissue fluid rich in Hb are also acceptable specimens for analysis in postmortem cases.

Poisoning and Autopsy Findings

Carbon monoxide poisoning is the leading cause of both accidental and intentional poisoning deaths in the U.S. Smoke inhalation is the most common source of CO exposure. The potentially toxic and lethal effects of the smoke from fires have been known since man first built fires in enclosed dwellings. Awareness that CO was the principal toxicant in that smoke followed much later. C. Bernard and J. B. S. Haldane were among the first scientists to thoroughly study and report on the uptake and effects of CO. Exposure to automobile exhaust is the most commonly used route of intentional CO poisoning.

The symptoms of CO toxicity are dependent upon the concentration of CO in the inspired air, the state of activity of the exposed person, the duration of exposure, and the rate of accumulation of COHb. The percentage of Hb in the COHb form is used

$$HbCO + Na_2S_2O_4 \rightarrow No\ reaction$$

$$HbO_2/MetHb + Na_2S_2O_4 \rightarrow Hb$$

Fig. 1. Dithionite reduction of hemoglobin species.

as a measure of the extent of CO exposure and the degree of CO toxicity. Because CO is produced endogenously and all individuals are exposed to some exogenously produced CO, COHb saturations of ≤3% are considered normal levels for nonsmokers and saturations of <10% are considered normal levels for smokers. In general, COHb saturations of <10% are not considered to be toxicologically significant in healthy individuals. Table 1 provides ranges of normal COHb saturation levels in selected populations.

Prolonged exposure to low levels of CO or gradually increasing levels of CO that result in a slow increase in the %COHb results in more serious long-term sequelae and lower risk of fatality than does exposure to high CO concentrations that result in a rapid increase in the %COHb.

It is suspected that many nonlethal exposures to CO are neither detected nor suspected due to the nonspecific symptomatology that develops. Exposure to CO appears to most significantly affect the blood, central nervous system (CNS), cardiovascular system, and respiratory system. The mechanism of toxic action is tissue hypoxia due to the reduced oxygen-carrying capacity of Hb, the leftward shift of the oxygen–Hb dissociation curve, and inhibition of cellular respiration. The signs and symptoms of acute CO poisoning include frontal headache, ataxia, tremor, nausea, vomiting, blurred vision, visual field constriction, mydriasis, nystagmus, dementia, atrioventricular block, arrhythmias, bradycardia, hypotension, dyspnea with hyperventilation, seizures, disorientation, hypothermia, tinnitus, drowsiness, coma, and ultimately death. Carbon monoxide exposure by a pregnant woman may result in fetal neurological abnormalities, malformations, and fetal death. Table 2 lists clinical symptoms associated with varying amounts of COHb saturation.

Nonfatal exposures to CO can be divided into three categories based on the existence and degree of residual effects:

1. Mild poisoning. The exposure to CO produces no measurable long-term effects.
2. Immediate disability. More severe exposure than mild poisoning; the patient regains consciousness after removal from the CO-containing environment, but neurological deficits are immediate (e.g., dementia, drowsiness, seizures, headache, confabulation, deafness, peripheral neuropathies, etc.). Some of the neurological deficits may improve over time.
3. Delayed neurological syndrome. A period of CO-induced unconsciousness follows removal from the environment. Upon the return to consciousness, there is a period of apparent recovery with no impairment; this may last from a few days (typically at least 5 days) to a few weeks. This period of pseudo recovery is followed by a slow deterioration resulting in long-term disabilities such as disorientation, chorea, equilibrium disturbances, cogwheel rigidity, aphasia, incontinence of urine and feces, chronic headaches, personality changes, and most frequently Parkinsonism. The mechanism(s) of this delayed toxicity may be a result of mitochondrial dysfunction, brain lipid peroxidation, direct neuronal damage leading to neuronal death, and demyelination of white matter. This syndrome occurs in approximately 10–30% of CO-poisoned patients.

There is technically no chronic CO poisoning in the sense that CO does not accumulate in the body over prolonged periods of exposure. The %COHb will eventually return to normal levels after nonfatal acute exposures. There is then no increased susceptibility to the toxic effects of CO upon subsequent exposures. Repeated anoxic

Table 1. Normal Carboxyhemoglobin Saturation

COHb (% Saturation)	Population
0.4–0.7	Endogenous production
0.4–2.6	Pregnant women
0.5–4.7	Normal infants
0–3	Nonsmokers
0–6	Hemolytic anemia
3–8	Smokers
>10	Significant toxicology

Table 2. Symptoms Associated with Various %COHb

COHb (% Saturation)	Clinical Symptoms
0–10	Normal, shortness of breath with vigorous exercise
10–20	Headache, flushed skin, shortness of breath with moderate exercise
20–30	Headache, throbbing temples, irritability, emotional instability, impaired judgment, memory impairment, rapid fatigue
30–40	Dizziness, weakness, nausea and vomiting, severe headache, visual disturbances, confusion
40–50	Intensified symptoms, hallucinations, severe ataxia, tachypnea
>50	Syncope, coma, tachycardia with weak pulse, incontinence of urine and feces, convulsions, loss of reflexes, cyanosis, respiratory paralysis, death

episodes due to CO exposure, or any other agent or event producing anoxia, can cause a gradually worsening degree of damage to the CNS, e.g., loss of sensation in the fingers, positive Romberg's sign, memory loss, persistent headache, neuropathies, and psychomotor defects.

Deaths related to CO exposure have been noted over a wide range of %COHb. Most fatalities in which CO intoxication is considered to be the ultimate cause of death are associated with %COHb >50%, with most values falling between 50% and 70%. Although death may be associated with either lower or higher %COHb, values above 50% are typically considered to be incompatible with life. Deaths due to CO may occur at lower COHb saturation levels than are normally associated with death. There are several potential explanations for this: 1) preexisting pathology (e.g., pulmonary insufficiency or cardiovascular disease), 2) administration of other CNS depressants, 3) physical exertion that would increase the body's oxygen demand, or 4) the presence of other intoxicating substances such as cyanide gas in fire-related deaths. If individuals are at rest during the time of their exposure, %COHb >70% may occur. The most significant postmortem characteristic in fatal CO intoxications is the presence of a bright cherry-red coloration of blood, fingernails, mucous membranes, and skin. This coloration, however, may also be present in cases of cyanide intoxication or exposure to cold and in the early stages of decomposition.

The specimen most frequently analyzed for COHb in the postmortem forensic toxicology laboratory is blood. Other useful postmortem specimens for CO analysis are spleen and Hb-containing fluid from within any of the solid organs. The difficulty with analysis of Hb-containing fluid is that it often has very low Hb levels that may yield unreliable results with spectrophotometric methods or other Hb-dependent methodologies. Spleen CO values do not always correlate well with blood %COHb but may be interpreted using the generalizations detailed in Table 3.

Treatment

Treatment for CO poisoning is a complicated issue due to the nonspecific symptomatology associated with CO exposure. For this reason, the diagnosis of CO intoxication is frequently missed. In cases of obvious exposure (house fire, intentional exposure to automobile exhaust, etc.), removal from the environment is the first step in treatment. Following decontamination, 100% oxygen is administered for at least 120 min ($t_{\frac{1}{2}CO}$ = 30–90 min at 100% oxygen). In cases in which the %COHb exceeds 15% in pregnant women or 30% in asymptomatic patients, hyperbaric oxygen may be considered, although there is little evidence to suggest that this treatment

Table 3. Blood/Spleen %COHb Correlation

Spleen (%COHb)	Blood (%COHb)
<10	<10
10–30	Inconclusive
>30	Toxic/lethal

is more effective than normobaric oxygen; some studies suggest hyperbaric oxygen may be effective in poisoned patients with acute neurotoxicity, metabolic acidosis, angina, or other cardiac abnormalities. Normal supportive measures should also be instituted. These include maintenance of normal vital signs, administration of mannitol or prednisolone to reduce cerebral edema, administration of diazepam in the event of seizures, administration of N-acetylcysteine and allopurinol to reduce the risk of lipid peroxidation, and administration of insulin in cases of CO-induced hyperglycemia and hypothermia. The patient should be given bed rest for at least two weeks for observation and to possibly reduce the risk of late-developing sequelae. Complete recovery is possible, but long-term disability due to CNS damage may occur if a high %COHb saturation persists for several hours. Another complicating issue in the treatment of CO poisoning is that %COHb does not correlate well with neurologic damage or the risk of late-developing effects. Therefore, rapid reduction of %COHb levels is no guarantee that a delayed neurological syndrome will not result.

Fire-Related Deaths

Carbon monoxide is one of the main products of combustion and is the most significant toxicant present in most fires. The major lethal factors in uncontrolled fires are toxic gases, heat, and oxygen depletion. The majority of fire-related deaths are due to CO exposure and injuries related to smoke inhalation as compared to thermal injuries. Fire creates a complex environment involving flame, heat, oxygen depletion, smoke, and a variety of toxic gases. Materials have different gas evolution profiles under different conditions, but CO is the predominant toxic gas generated from the incomplete combustion of wood and other cellulose materials.

Most fire-related deaths are associated with an elevated COHb saturation. Lower COHb levels (20–50%) may be associated with rapid death due to thermal injuries or trauma,

compared to more elevated levels (>50%) that are more suggestive of prolonged exposure to the fire environment resulting in CO intoxication. Ethanol intoxication has also been shown to be a significant factor in fire-related deaths. The psychomotor impairment associated with an elevated blood alcohol concentration may hinder escape from a fire environment. Escape may also be hindered by the CNS depression resulting from both ethanol and narcotic toxicants such as CO present in the fire environment.

Because a fire is a complicated environment comprising many toxicants and irritants, it is difficult to fully evaluate the role of any single component in fire-related deaths. In terms of narcotic toxicants, CO and cyanide are present in the highest concentrations in most fires (dependent on the types of materials present). Therefore, the combined exposure to these two gases may also be implicated in fire-related deaths. In a study of fire-related deaths in Maryland, more than 50% of the cases had CO levels above 30% and abnormal cyanide levels (suggestive that both gases were significant contributors in the death); approximately 10% of the cases had CO levels above 30% and normal cyanide levels (cyanide possibly enhanced the toxicity of CO or else was not significant in the death); approximately 20% of the cases had CO levels below 30% and normal cyanide levels (the gases were either not a significant factor in the death or acted in a synergistic manner to cause the death); and fewer than 10% of the cases had CO levels below 30% and abnormal cyanide levels (the low number of cases makes interpretation difficult). Animal studies have confirmed that simultaneous exposure to sublethal concentrations of both gases can cause death based on an apparent synergistic effect, possibly at cytochrome c oxidase.

Storage and Stability Considerations

One of the most significant factors affecting the measurement of %COHb and the subsequent interpretation of CO toxicity is the ability to accurately measure the CO content of the blood. Postmortem alterations in %COHb concentration have been documented in a number of studies. In general, the %COHb saturation decreases as storage time increases.

There is no evidence that CO is produced in stored blood as a result of putrefaction. Unpreserved specimens have been documented to lose up to 60% of their CO content when stored in uncapped containers at room temperature. Reduction of %COHb was dependent on the surface area of the specimen exposed to air (the greater the surface area, the greater the loss of CO); the temperature of storage (increased temperatures result in greater CO loss); and the initial %COHb saturation (higher initial %COHb results in greater and more rapid loss of CO). When containers are capped, the volume of headspace over the blood specimen is a significant factor in the amount of CO lost, because some CO will equilibrate between the blood and the headspace. The loss of CO will cease once the equilibration point has been reached; therefore, the larger the volume of headspace, the greater the loss of CO into that headspace. Storage temperature and initial %COHb also affect the rate of loss. Although loss of CO occurs in all stored specimens, this loss may be minimized by preserving blood specimens with EDTA or sodium fluoride, minimizing the headspace above the specimen, and storing specimens at reduced temperature; storage under frozen conditions minimizes CO loss more effectively than does refrigeration.

Summary

Carbon monoxide reduces the oxygen availability to tissues (anoxic anoxia) in two ways: CO binding to Hb reduces the amount of Hb available to carry oxygen to tissues and prevents the release of some of the oxygen from Hb binding sites at the low oxygen tension present in the tissues (leftward shift in the oxygen-Hb dissociation curve). The other mechanism of CO toxicity is through the binding of CO to intracellular hemoproteins inhibiting cellular respiration and other intracellular functions (a histotoxic mechanism).

CO poisoning is the leading cause of both accidental and intentional poisoning deaths in the U.S. The signs and symptoms of CO intoxication are relatively nonspecific, and for this reason a substantial percentage of poisonings are incorrectly diagnosed. Treatment of CO poisoning is primarily supportive, along with the administration of 100% oxygen. If patients survive, they may fully recover, but a substantial percentage of poisoned patients suffer from long-term neurological sequelae.

Fatalities due to CO exposure are typically characterized by %COHb >50%. Lower COHb percentages may be associated with fatalities in the presence of some preexisting pathology, physical exertion, or the administration of other CNS depressants. The presence of a bright cherry-red coloration of blood, fingernails, mucous membranes, and skin may indicate CO poisoning.

Evaluation of the extent of CO exposure is based on a determination of the percentage of Hb bound with carbon monoxide (%COHb). These determinations are typically performed using either a spectrophotometric or gas chromatographic technique. Proper storage of specimens is important to minimize the loss of CO, which could adversely affect the interpretation based upon the analytical results. Blood specimens should be preserved with EDTA or sodium fluoride and kept frozen.

CYANIDE

Cyanide is a rapidly acting and lethal poison, with death occurring within minutes after ingestion. Cyanide and cyanogenic products are used in a wide variety of ways. Hydrogen cyanide (HCN), also referred to as hydrocyanic acid or prussic acid, is used as a fumigant, for executions using the "gas chamber," and in the production of resin monomers such as acrylates and methacrylates.

HCN, a weak acid, is a colorless volatile liquid with a boiling point of 26.5 °C—and therefore presents an inhalation hazard. The density of cyanide vapor is similar to that of air and will consequently permeate an area in which it is released. The vapor has the characteristic odor of bitter almonds at an air concentration ranging from 0.2–5 ppm; beyond this concentration, olfactory fatigue occurs and the odor is no longer detectable. Cyanide gas is also released as a by-product of incomplete combustion in blast furnaces, coke ovens, cigarettes, and house fires, and also from the pyrolysis of nitrogen-containing materials such as wool, silk, acrylonitriles, polyurethane, and other polyacrylic fibers and materials. The potassium and sodium salts of cyanide readily hydrolyze in aqueous solutions, making them strong bases that can cause skin ulceration upon contact and congestion and corrosion of the gastric mucosa upon ingestion. These salts also give off the characteristic bitter almond smell associated with cyanide and are used in the processes of metal hardening, metal cleaning, electroplating, and gold and silver recovery and refining. Potassium cyanide may also be used in the illicit manufacture of phencyclidine, resulting in a final product contaminated with cyclohexane carbonitrile.

There are other forms and uses of cyanide in industry:

- Calcium cyanamide is used in the production of melamine resins that are used in laminated tabletops, dishware, shrink- and wrinkle-resistant fabrics, and high-strength paper.
- Acrylonitrile is an intermediate in the production of acrylic fibers and synthetic rubber.
- Adiponitrile is an intermediate in the manufacture of Nylon 6-6.
- Cyanoacetic acid is an intermediate in the production of pharmaceuticals (phenylbutazone and barbiturates), synthetic amino acids (methionine, glycine, and alanine), lactic acid, and antiperspirants.
- Cyanuric chlorides, the trimerization product of cyanogen chloride, are used

in the manufacture of herbicides, optical brighteners, and dyes.
- Acetonitrile and proprionitrile are used in the manufacture of pharmaceuticals.
- Nitroprussides are used in chemical synthesis and as hypotensive agents.
- Potassium ferricyanide is used in photography, blueprints, and the manufacturing of pigments.
- Finally, sodium thiocyanate is used in the printing and dyeing of textiles and in color film processing.

Several plants have also been found to contain cyanogenic glycosides. Amygdalin, the active component of laetrile, is probably the most commonly encountered cyanogenic glycoside and is found in bitter almonds; apricot, pear, and apple seeds; and peach and plum pits. (Laetrile has been purported to be an antineoplastic agent and gained popularity in the 1970s.) Enzymatic degradation of amygdalin or the other cyanogenic glycosides such as prunasin (the primary metabolite of orally administered amygdalin also found in cherry laurel) and linamarin (from cassava and some lima beans) releases hydrogen cyanide and can be a significant source of poisonings. Cyanide is found in measurable levels in most people as a result of vitamin B_{12} (cyanocobalamin) metabolism and also in smokers; cyanide levels <0.26 mg/L are generally considered to be normal levels and are nontoxic.

Pathophysiology

The molecular toxicity of cyanide is well understood. Cyanide stops cellular respiration by inhibiting electron transport at the cytochrome c oxidase step. Cytochrome c oxidase is the last step of the electron transport scheme, where molecular oxygen and two protons are converted into water, with an associated production of high-energy ATP molecules. When this process is inhibited, oxidative phosphorylation stops. This in turn stops the Kreb's cycle and leads to an accumulation of pyruvic acid, which is produced during glycolysis. Pyruvic acid is then processed anaerobically to lactic acid, causing a metabolic acidosis. Molecular oxygen, because it is not reduced, also builds up in the tissues and alters the gradient for release of oxygen from Hb. This produces hypoxia in the tissues. This inability of cells to use oxygen is referred to as histotoxic anoxia.

The binding of cyanide to cytochrome c oxidase is a two-step process. Initially, cyanide penetrates into the protein structure of the cytochrome. Once inside, it is able to bind to the heme iron. It has been demonstrated that HCN binds to both the oxidized and the reduced forms of the cytochrome a_3 component of cytochrome oxidase. However, it is believed that the kinetically relevant toxic effect of cyanide is at the reduced cytochrome a_3. The binding of cyanide produces an oxidized enzyme–cyanide complex, which is stable but can be reversed in the presence of reducing equivalents.

The primary target organ of cyanide is the brain, but there is evidence to indicate that the heart is also involved in the toxicity of cyanide. Cyanide is a very potent protoplasmic poison. It is estimated that the lethal dose of HCN is 100 mg and the lethal dose of NaCN is 200 mg. This difference is probably related to the relative ability of each to enter the brain.

Disposition

The absorption of cyanide depends on the chemical nature of the substance absorbed as well as the route of administration. HCN, being nonionized and readily diffusable, is rapidly absorbed through biological membranes and diffuses throughout the body. Therefore, absorption is more efficient through inhalation than through dermal contact. Salts of cyanide are readily absorbed after oral ingestion, but, being ionized, are absorbed at significantly lower rates. Oral ingestion of cyanide also allows entry into the portal circulation prior to its passage into the systemic circulation. The liver is capable of detoxifying a significant amount of cyanide (first-pass metabolism), meaning that less cyanide ultimately enters the circulation.

The major pathway of detoxification of cyanide is by enzymatic conversion to thiocyanate (SCN) and subsequent excretion by the kidney. Two enzymes that facilitate this transsulfuration process have been identified: rhodanese and beta-mercaptopyruvate-cyanide sulfurtransferase. The first enzyme identified was rhodanese, or thiosulfate-cyanide sulfotransferase. It is a mitochondrial enzyme that catalyzes the transfer of a sulfur atom from a donor, usually thiosulfate, to an acceptor such as cyanide. Rhodanese activity is greatest in the liver and kidney. The mechanism of action is well understood: rhodanese cleaves an S-S bond, producing a rhodanese–sulfur complex, with the subsequent regeneration of rhodanese by the transfer of the sulfur atom to cyanide, producing SCN. The second enzyme identified was beta-mercaptopyruvate-cyanide sulfurtransferase, which is present in the liver, kidney, and blood. These reactions are detailed in Fig. 2.

$$1) \ CN^- + S_2O_3{}^{2-} \xrightarrow{1} SCN^- + SO_3{}^{2-}$$

$$2) \ HSCH_2COCOO^- + CN \xrightarrow{2} SCN^- + CH_3COCOO$$

1 = Rhodanese
2 = Beta-mercaptopyruvate-cyanide sulfurtransferase

Fig. 2. Metabolic routes for cyanide.

Analysis

Many methods for the identification and quantification of cyanide in biological specimens have been published over the past 40 years. The initial step in the analysis is the separation of cyanide from the biological matrix. The most common initial step is acidification to convert cyanide to the more volatile HCN. If this reaction is performed in a sealed container at an elevated temperature, the HCN will enter the gaseous phase above the biological layer. This gas can then be sampled directly. One other technique is to perform a microdiffusion reaction using a Conway cell. A dilute base that serves as a trapping agent for the released HCN is added to the center well of the cell. In a two-reservoir cell, the blood or tissue specimen is added to the outer well, followed by a releasing agent. This releasing agent may be a dilute mineral acid such as sulfuric acid or an organic acid such as tartaric acid. The reaction is allowed to proceed at room temperature for several hours. Alternatively, a three-well cell may be used. The sample and acid are added to the middle well, while a more dilute acid is added to the outer well to serve as a sealing agent. After the reaction is complete, the center well contains the trapped cyanide and is available for detection.

A number of colorimetric reactions have been developed to detect cyanide from the trapping agent. One classical color reaction uses chloramine-T to convert cyanide to cyanogen chloride. A color reagent containing pyridine and barbituric acid is then added to produce a red color. This assay can be qualitative or quantitative using spectrophotometric measurement at 580 nm. Several fluorescent derivatives of cyanide have been produced to enhance the sensitivity of spectrophotometric methods.

Various gas chromatographic methods for the analysis of cyanide are also available. The fact that cyanide contains a nitrogen and is an electron-withdrawing group makes it amenable to both nitrogen-phosphorus and electron capture detection. One method is based on the conversion of cyanide to cyanogen chloride by chloramine-T. The cyanogen chloride is extracted with hexane, and an aliquot of the hexane layer is injected into the gas chromatograph with a Halcomid column and an electron capture detector. This method requires initial cyanide separation from the biological matrix by Conway cell microdiffusion. A simpler procedure uses headspace gas chromatography of cyanide itself. The specimen is placed in a container with a solution of acetonitrile, which serves as an internal standard. Acid is added to the headspace vial immediately prior to sealing and is heated for 10 min at 60 °C. The vapor containing HCN and acetonitrile is sampled. A Poropak column separates HCN from acetonitrile, and detection can be achieved with a nitrogen-phosphorus detector.

Microdiffusion separation has also been combined to direct potentiometric measurement of cyanide in biological specimens. An ion-specific electrode originally designed for aqueous solutions has been used. A very rapid semiquantitative screening test for cyanide uses a commercially available paper impregnated with substances that turn blue in the presence of HCN.

Poisoning and Autopsy Findings

Cyanide is an extremely fast-acting poison. The onset of symptoms is dependent on the type of exposure. HCN vapors act rapidly, with symptoms appearing in seconds and death within minutes. Cyanide salts act more slowly, with symptoms appearing in minutes and death within hours. This exposure-dependent symptomatology is the result of the rate and degree of production of histotoxic hypoxia. When the tissue cyanide concentration rises rapidly, as seen with inhalation exposure, the signs and symptoms of poisoning are more acute and the amount of cyanide required to produce toxicity is small, whereas oral or dermal exposure leads to a slower cyanide buildup in the tissue. Tissue concentrations of cyanide and the rate of increase are dependent on the cyanide compound, dose, and extent, rate, and site of absorption.

The signs and symptoms of acute cyanide exposure are relatively nonspecific and reflect cellular hypoxia due to the inability of cells to use oxygen. This cellular hypoxia generally results in cell death and also stimulates carotid and aortic bodies, causing an initial hyperpnea followed by dyspnea. Other symptoms include headache, tachypnea, and dizziness within the first few seconds following exposure. These symptoms progress toward slowed respiration, gasping breaths, lactic acidosis, bradycardia, erratic cardiac rhythms including ischemic changes on an electrocardiogram, hypotension, coma, opisthotonus, seizures, and death. Because only oxygen utilization and not oxygen saturation is affected, venous blood reaches an oxygen saturation approximating arterial blood, and cyanosis is usually not present. Cyanide poisoning should thus be considered in the differential diagnosis of patients with rapid onset of coma, metabolic acidosis, and symptoms of severe anoxia without cyanosis.

The prognosis in acute cyanide poisoning is dependent on the amount, form, and route of exposure and on the rapid support of respiration and circulation. Survival for 4 h is usually followed by recovery without sequelae, although hypoxic and hemodynamic brain damage may occur. Rapid initiation of supportive care is essential for survival. Oxygen (100%) should be used routinely, even in cases of moderate exposure or where pO$_2$ is normal. Hyperbaric oxygen has been used but does not appear to significantly contribute to recovery. Removal from a contaminated atmosphere and external decontamination should be accomplished as soon as possible to limit continued exposure to cyanide. In cases of ingested cyanide, gut decontamination should follow (not precede) antidote therapy due to the rapid onset of toxicity. Hemodialysis and hemoperfusion have been shown to be ineffective in enhancing cyanide elimination.

In some cases of cyanide poisoning, the above steps, including correction of acidosis and seizure control, can be sufficient to ensure survival without antidote therapy. In cases of severe poisonings, the primary goal of treatment after supportive measures and decontamination is to decrease the amount of cyanide available to bind to ferric iron by administering an antidote. A number of antidotes have been suggested over the years; these antidotes produce methemoglobinemia, replenish depleted stores of reducing sulfur substrates (e.g., administer thiosulfate), or chelate cyanide. One antidote combines an amyl nitrite inhalant and solutions of sodium nitrite and sodium thiosulfate. The amyl nitrite is administered by inhalation, followed by intravenous sodium nitrite. This combination results in the formation of methemoglobin, which has a greater binding affinity for cyanide than does cytochrome oxidase; a methemoglobin level of approximately 40% is most effective. The last step is administration of sodium thiosulfate, which binds the cyanomethemoglobin and, in the presence of rhodanese, forms the nontoxic compound thiocyanate. The kidneys subsequently excrete thiocyanate. Care must be taken with these types of antidotes because excessive methemoglobin formation (>70%) is life threatening, as methemoglobin cannot bind oxygen. In addition, nitrites induce vasodilation, which may drastically lower blood pressure and result in cardiovascular collapse. In some countries, dicobalt edetate (Kelocyanor) is used to chelate cyanide and facilitate its excretion.

The signs and symptoms of chronic cyanide poisoning are also diverse and pervasive. Initial signs of poisoning are CNS excitation and hyperpnea. Chronic and subchronic exposure to cyanide may result in weakness, dizziness, headache, nausea, and vomiting. Mild abnormalities of vitamin B$_{12}$, folate, and thyroid function have been noted in some cases of chronic exposure, as well as psychosis and thyroid enlargement without alteration in function. A number of disease states have been associated with chronic cyanide exposure or disordered cyanide detoxification: tobacco amblyopia (reduction of vision probably due to elevated thiocyanate levels secondary to tobacco smoking); Leber's hereditary optic atrophy; and Nigerian nutritional ataxic neuropathy (segmental demyelination leading to peripheral sensory neuropathy resulting from increased thiocyanate levels secondary to the consumption of large amounts of cassava and other nutritional factors). Smokers exhibit elevated blood cyanide levels as well as elevated blood thiocyanate levels. The actual role of cyanide and cyanide exposure in these disease states has not been well established.

Deaths from cyanide have been reported from a variety of sources. Accidental poisoning can result from occupational exposure in agriculture or in the laboratory. These exposures are usually avoidable by taking reasonable safety precautions. Accidental exposure may also occur in the home, with children being the most susceptible. The burning of nitrogen-containing materials might also provide an unexpected source of cyanide. An insidious unintentional poisoning with cyanide has occurred when medicinal products are tampered with by replacing the therapeutic agent with cyanide. This has been reported in Chicago and in the state of Washington, among other places.

Intentional ingestion of cyanide has also been well documented. The Jonestown massacre was the most extreme example of massive numbers of fatalities resulting from the known ingestion of a cyanide-containing drink. However, the worst case of mass cyanide poisoning was the use of prussic acid to exterminate millions of prisoners in Nazi concentration camps during the 1930s and 1940s. Cyanide has also been used throughout time by politicians and spies to escape the ramifications of capture. HCN has also been used to perform the judicially ordered execution of criminals.

Autopsy findings following cyanide intoxication are generally nonspecific. There are no gross or microscopic findings unique to cyanide poisoning. Findings often include visceral congestion and edema and petechial hemorrhages in the brain, pleura, lungs, and myocardium. Although the hypoxia produced by cyanide would be expected to produce a bright red color of the blood, this is not a consistent finding. The most characteristic finding that can lead the pathologist to suspect cyanide poisoning is the odor of the blood and tissues. This smell has been described as being similar to bitter almonds, but those familiar with the smell believe that it is unique to cyanide. Unfortunately, not all individuals can detect the odor of cyanide. There clearly is a genetic component to this ability, but it appears to be more complicated than simple Mendelian genetics.

The specimen most frequently analyzed for cyanide in the postmortem forensic toxicology laboratory is blood. Other useful postmortem specimens for cyanide analysis are spleen, liver, and brain. Blood cyanide concentrations <0.25 mg/L are considered normal. Blood concentrations >0.25 mg/L but <2–3 mg/L are considered elevated, but ordinarily would not cause death. Blood cyanide concentrations above 3 mg/L are consistent with death in the absence of other relevant autopsy and toxicology findings (Table 4).

Fire-Related Deaths

The presence of cyanide in fires is well established, but the role of cyanide in fire deaths is difficult to determine because it may be produced or metabolized in postmortem tissue. Fire creates a complex environment involving flame, heat, oxygen depletion, smoke, and a variety of toxic gases. The nature of that environment is dependent upon the circumstances surrounding the fire, the immediate location of the fire, the fire source, and the materials present. Materials have different gas evolution profiles under different conditions; therefore, toxic fire gas generation is not intrinsic to any one material. Large fires in buildings constitute a severe toxic threat regardless of the materials being burned.

Table 4. Interpretation of Blood Cyanide Concentrations

Range (mg/L)	Effect
≤0.25	Normal
0.25 <CN <2	Potentially toxic
>2–3	Potentially fatal

The major lethal factors in uncontrolled fires are toxic gases, heat, and oxygen depletion. CO is the predominant toxic gas that is generated from the incomplete combustion of wood and other cellulose materials. Those fires in which polymeric materials such as those used in buildings and home furnishings are consumed grow faster and generate more smoke and toxic gases than those involving more traditional building materials. These polymeric materials may produce a variety of toxic thermal decomposition gases such as CO, HCN, NO_2, NH_3, HCl, SO_2, acrolein, and isocyanates. Cyanide is generated from nitrogen-containing natural and synthetic polymers including nylon, wool, and polyurethane. This occurs at relatively low temperatures and may precede the generation of high concentrations of CO.

Storage and Stability Considerations

One factor that complicates the analysis of cyanide in biological specimens is that in vitro changes in concentration have been well documented. A recent review on the stability of cyanide in postmortem specimens indicated that the rate of change in cyanide concentrations is dependent on four criteria: (1) the initial sample concentration at the time of death; (2) the length of time the sample remains in the body after death; (3) the length of time the sample remains in storage before analysis; and (4) the conditions of sample preservation and storage (e.g., temperature, pH, sodium fluoride addition). When cyanide is present at or above toxicologically significant concentrations, a subsequent decrease in concentration occurs over periods of hours to months. The greatest rate of cyanide decrease occurs in intact bodies, and to a slightly lesser extent in blood samples, at ambient or elevated temperatures. Under conditions where cyanide decreases occur, these decreases tend to be greater with higher initial blood cyanide concentrations. When blood is frozen, a small increase tends to occur upon thawing (approximately 0.2 mg/L),

which is considered to be due to the formation of small amounts of cyanide resulting from acidification of plasma or serum thiocyanate in the presence of hemoglobin. In subsequent work by theses authors, they recommended adding sodium fluoride to a concentration of 2% to ensure cyanide stability over a longer period of time by preventing microorganism activity.

Although most studies show a decrease in cyanide concentration in postmortem specimens, there are a limited number of reports from studies of cyanide-negative transfusion blood and a small number of cases considered not to have involved cyanide exposure in which very high concentrations of cyanide have been measured in blood samples stored under room temperature, refrigerated, or frozen conditions for periods of a month or more. In several of these cases, measured cyanide concentrations were more than 30 times the lethal concentration. No obvious reasons have been identified for the very high levels of cyanide formation in these samples, although microbiological contamination is a possible consideration. The lack of reports of similar exceptionally high blood levels in several major blood cyanide studies of fire fatalities and survivors indicates that such instances are relatively uncommon.

Summary

Cyanide is a fast-acting, lethal poison, with death occurring within minutes after inhalation and more slowly following oral ingestion. Cyanide and cyanogenic compounds are abundant in a variety of applications, making the possibility of exposure or poisoning extensive. Cyanide inhibits the electron transport process of cellular respiration at the cytochrome c oxidase step, binding to the heme ion of cytochrome c oxidase. HCN is more rapidly absorbed than salts of cyanide. Detoxification of cyanide to thiocyanate occurs via two enzyme systems: rhodanese and beta-mercaptopyruvate-cyanide sulfurtransferase.

The analysis of cyanide may begin with Conway microdiffusion to separate cyanide from the biological matrix. Several reagents are available to enable spectrophotometric or spectrofluorometric analysis. Gas chromatography can also be used with either electron capture or nitrogen-phosphorus detection.

The onset of symptoms in cyanide poisoning is dependent on the type of exposure; HCN vapor acts more quickly than cyanide salts. The signs and symptoms of cyanide poisoning are relatively nonspecific, with rapid onset of coma, metabolic acidosis, and symptoms of anoxia without cyanosis as noteworthy indicators. The primary goals in treatment are supportive measures, decontamination, and administration of an antidote, e.g., Lilly Cyanide Antidote Package, to decrease the amount of cyanide available to bind ferric iron.

Cyanide deaths have occurred from both accidental and intentional exposure. The findings at autopsy are generally nonspecific. Blood cyanide concentrations of 2–3 mg/L are consistent with death in the absence of other findings. Fires in which nitrogen-containing natural and synthetic polymers are consumed can also be a source of cyanide production. The role of cyanide in fire-related deaths is difficult to interpret, but it may contribute to the incapacitation of victims, preventing their escape from the fire environment. Another complicating factor in determining the role of cyanide in death cases is that both increases and decreases in cyanide concentrations have been reported during specimen storage.

SUGGESTED READING

1. Ballantyne B, Marrs T, Turner P, eds. General and applied toxicology, 2nd ed. New York, NY: Stockton Press, 1993.
2. Baselt RC, ed. Disposition of toxic drugs and chemicals in man, 9th ed. Seal Beach, CA: Biomedical Publications, 2011.
3. Caplan YH. Pathology and pathophysiology of the systemic toxicants carbon monoxide and cyanide. In: Trump BF, Cowley RA, eds. Cell injury in shock, anoxia, and ischemia. Baltimore, MD: Williams and Wilkens Co., 1982;270–9.
4. DiPalma JR, ed. Drill's pharmacology in medicine, 4th ed. New York, NY: McGraw-Hill, 1971.
5. Dreisbach RH, Robertson WO, eds. Handbook of poisoning, 12th ed. Norwalk, CT: Appleton and Lange, 1987.
6. Ellenhorn MJ, ed. Ellenhorn's medical toxicology: diagnosis and treatment of human poisoning, 2nd ed. Baltimore, MD: Williams & Wilkins, 1997.
7. Gossel TA, Bricker JD, eds. Principles of clinical toxicology, 2nd ed. New York, NY: Raven Press, 1990.
8. Leiken JB, Paloucek FP. Poisoning and toxicology handbook, 2nd ed. Hudson, OH: Lexi-Comp Inc., 1995.
9. McAllister JL, Roby RJ, Levine B, Purser D. The effect of sodium fluoride on the stability of cyanide in postmortem blood samples from fire victims. Forensic Sci Int 2011;209:29–33.
10. McAllister JL, Roby RJ, Levine B, Purser D. Stability of cyanide in cadavers and in postmortem stored tissue specimens, a review. J Anal Tox 2008; 32:612–20.
11. Penney DG, ed. Carbon monoxide. New York, NY: CRC Press, 1996.
12. Reay DT, Insalaco SJ, Eisele JW. Postmortem methemoglobin concentrations and their significance. I Forensic Sci 1984;4:1160–3.
13. Ryan RP, Terry CE, eds. Toxicology desk reference, 4th ed. Washington, DC: Taylor and Francis, 1997.

CHAPTER 28

Inhalants

Larry A. Broussard

CLASSIFICATION AND ABUSE

Classification

The terms "inhalants" or volatile organic compounds (VOCs) are used to describe a wide range of volatile chemicals that may be inhaled accidentally or intentionally. There is no classification system based on clinical effect or chemical structure. Solids and liquids, as well as gases, contain volatile substances. The common feature is volatility, the property of existing in or being able to be converted to a form that may be inhaled. Compounds having this property include aliphatic hydrocarbons (e.g., butane, hexane, propane); aromatic hydrocarbons (e.g., benzene, toluene); mixed hydrocarbons (e.g., gasoline, lighter fluid); halogenated hydrocarbons (e.g., chloroform, carbon tetrachloride), including ozone-depleting chlorofluorocarbons (CFCs) (e.g., Freon 11, Freon 12) and alternative fluorocarbons (e.g., difluoroethane), and oxygen-containing compounds (e.g., acetone, nitrous oxide). The classification of the CFCs and their replacements is discussed later in the chapter, along with the pharmacology and effects of these compounds. With the exception of the gaseous anesthetics (e.g., halothane, isoflurane), these chemicals are not used pharmaceutically, and their use is too diverse to be discussed individually. Volatile compounds are present in many commercial products (e.g., solvents, contact adhesives, typewriter correction fluid, gasoline, lighter fluid, refrigerants, fire extinguishers) and are the propellants for virtually all aerosol products.

Abuse

The extensive availability and low cost of inhalants have contributed to an increased incidence of intentional inhalation of volatile substances (inhalant abuse, volatile-substance abuse, glue sniffing) in younger adolescents, even though legislation has been enacted to limit accessibility and to make their use by adolescents illegal. There are many more reported incidences of deaths due to inhalant abuse than deaths due to accidental exposure in the workplace or home. Worldwide, inhalants continue to be one of the most dangerous classes of abused substances because of their high prevalence in underdeveloped countries.

Products preferred by inhalant users include hair spray or aerosols, airplane glue, gasoline, paint or solvents, marker pens or correction fluid, and amyl or butyl nitrates (poppers). These products are generally relatively inexpensive and easy to obtain, and they contain volatile substances free of large quantities of toxic components. Some of the volatile substances in these products include toluene, chloroform, butane, propane, acetone, and many halogenated hydrocarbons. The development of replacements for the ozone-depleting CFCs has led to the introduction of new compounds (Freon replacements) as propellants. Abuse of many of these substances has also been reported.

Depending on the product, volatile substances may be inhaled directly from the container (snorting or sniffing), from a plastic bag ("bagging")—particularly if the

461

product is an aerosol or a viscous liquid such as glue—or from a saturated cloth ("huffing"). Of these routes of administration, bagging usually produces the highest concentration, snorting the lowest, and huffing an intermediate concentration. Products containing toxic nonrespirable compounds, such as antiperspirants containing aluminum chlorhydrate, may be bubbled through water in an attempt to separate the volatile substance from the toxic chemical. Adolescents have drowned in bath water while attempting this separation. Inhalation includes deep breathing through the mouth and nose and often involves rebreathing exhaled air when a bag is used.

Clues to inhalant abuse include chronic sore throat, cough, and runny nose; unexplained listlessness; moodiness; weight loss; bloodshot eyes or blurred vision; and chemical odors on breath, hair, bed linen, and clothes. Oral and nasal ulceration or a rash around the mouth ("glue sniffer's or huffer's rash") may be observed. Sometimes the products themselves may be discovered in the room of the abuser.

PHARMACOLOGY

Pharmacokinetics

The physical and pharmacokinetic properties of these substances are based on animal studies and are available for most inhalants. Chemicals used for anesthesia and those used in occupations leading to long-term exposure have been studied extensively. Unfortunately, most of the available data for situations of inhalant abuse are postmortem distributions and concentrations. In almost all situations (occupation, anesthesia, and abuse), exposure is chronic (repeated), although the dosage is variable. Some pharmacokinetic properties and principles apply to all inhalants.

Pulmonary uptake of a volatile substance is influenced by many factors. The individual's general health (respiratory rate, blood flow), proportion of body fat, and metabolic clearance rate are major factors. Properties of the substance, such as the partition coefficients (e.g., air–blood and blood–tissue), interaction with other inhaled compounds, and concentration in the inspired air also affect the pharmacokinetics of the inhalant. The distribution of inhaled compounds within the body generally follows a pattern of initial high concentrations in well-perfused organs such as brain, liver, heart, and kidney, followed by slow accumulation in tissues (muscle, fat) with lesser blood supply as the chronic exposure continues. When exposure ceases, the compounds are released, with those in muscle and fat being slowly released, leading to bi- or multiphasic elimination half-lives. In situations of acute fatal exposure, the inhalant may be found only in the well-perfused organs, producing a monophasic elimination pattern.

The metabolism of volatile substances includes elimination unchanged in the exhaled air and elimination as metabolites in exhaled air and urine. As with many compounds, a primary site of metabolism is the liver, with the metabolism often including oxidation or reduction followed by conjugation to produce a more polar and water-soluble compound. These more polar metabolites generally do not pass through biological membranes as easily as the parent compound. The metabolites of some volatiles are more toxic than the parent compound itself. Some examples of toxic metabolites include carbon monoxide, a metabolite of dichloromethane; phenol, a metabolite of benzene; 2,5-hexanedione, the neurotoxic metabolite of hexane; and trichloroacetic acid, the metabolite of tetrachloroethylene. Some volatiles have multiple toxic metabolites; one such volatile is carbon tetrachloride, which is metabolized to chloroform, carbon dioxide, and the hepatotoxic trichloromethyl free radical.

Effects

The abuse appeal of these inhaled substances is that they produce effects similar to those caused by ethanol, i.e., euphoria and loss of inhibition, which may be followed by hallucinations, confusion, nausea, vomiting, and ataxia. Convulsions, coma, or death may result from larger doses. Causes of death associated with inhalant abuse include asphyxiation, suffocation, dangerous high-risk behavior, and cardiac arrhythmias leading to cardiac arrest when an intoxicated subject becomes alarmed or frightened ("sudden sniffing death syndrome"). The mechanism of action for cardiac arrest has been postulated to be either sensitization of the myocardium to epinephrine by the hydrocarbon inhalants or a depressant effect on sinoatrial, atrioventricular, and ventricular conduction systems, allowing other ectopic foci to cause arrhythmias.

Problems caused by chronic inhalant abuse include central nervous system (CNS) damage characterized by loss of cognitive and other higher functions, gait disturbance, and loss of coordination. Other features of chronic abuse include nosebleed and rhinitis, halitosis, oral and nasal ulceration, conjunctivitis and bloodshot eyes, anorexia, thirst, lethargy, weight loss, and fatigue. Another frequent complication of solvent abuse is renal tubular acidosis, characterized by decreased arterial pH and serum bicarbonate, hyperchloremia, and a normal anion gap in the presence of an abnormally high urine pH. These solvents literally dissolve brain cells, as shown by the loss of brain mass and white matter degeneration detected by computed tomography and magnetic resonance imaging. Associations between specific chemicals and effects have been shown. For example, toluene abuse causes deafness and metabolic acidosis, and hexane abuse produces peripheral neuropathy.

Management of patients experiencing acute intoxication caused by volatile substances begins with the removal of the source or removal of the patient from the contaminated area. Administration of oxygen and cardiopulmonary resuscitation may be necessary. Initial laboratory support includes assessment of acid–base and electrolyte status and subsequent monitoring of treatment to correct any disturbances.

Concurrent rapid identification or confirmation of suspected inhalants by analysis for the compound or metabolite(s) is desirable. Additional laboratory testing may include screening (with conventional tests, including organ-specific profiles and complete blood count) for hematologic, hepatic, renal, and muscular complications associated with specific compounds. Treatment in general includes conventional supportive measures to stabilize potential cardiac arrhythmias and manage possible hepatic, renal, and respiratory complications, including organ system failure.

COMMON INHALANTS

According to comprehensive summary reports and individual case study reports from the U.K. and the U.S., three of the most frequently abused volatile substances or classes of substances are toluene, halogenated hydrocarbons, and butane.

Toluene

Toluene is the solvent with the most documentation of abuse, possibly because of its relative low risk of sudden death and the ease of detection in blood. It is found in many products including paint and contact adhesives. The principal metabolite of toluene is benzoic acid (approximately 80% of the dose), which is conjugated with glycine to form hippuric acid for excretion in the urine (half-life, 2–3 h). Chronic exposure to toluene causes hepatic, renal, cardiac, respiratory, and CNS problems. Toluene abuse can cause high anion gap acidosis (possibly due to accumulation of benzoic acid) and electrolyte imbalances (hypokalemia, hypophosphatemia, hypercalcemia, hypercalcuria). Renal complications include renal tubular acidosis, renal calculi formation, and glomerulonephritis, with at least one report of renal failure. Cardiorespiratory system complications of chronic toluene abuse include emphysema, reduced lung capacity, pulmonary hypertension, cardiomyopathy, and myocardial degeneration. CNS problems attributed to chronic toluene abuse include cerebellar degeneration, acute encephalopathy, cortical atrophy, peripheral neuropathy, and optic nerve atrophy. Symptoms associated with these CNS problems include tremor, amnesia, ataxia, altered mental state, hearing loss, nystagmus, convulsions, and coma. Sustained abstinence often leads to reversal of symptoms, but residual effects have been documented.

Halogenated Hydrocarbons

Halogenated hydrocarbons include not only chlorinated hydrocarbons used as solvents but also CFCs and non–ozone-depleting CFC-replacement hydrocarbons used as solvents, aerosols, refrigerants, and foams. Volatile chlorinated hydrocarbons used as solvents include chloroform, carbon tetrachloride, methylene chloride, 1,1,1-trichloroethane (correction fluid), and trichloroethylene (dry cleaning). All of these compounds may be abused, although exposure to carbon tetrachloride is usually due to ingestion or accidental exposure rather than to voluntary abuse. Chloroform inhalation has been involved in fatalities including accidents, suicides, and homicides. The primary concern associated with acute exposure is cardiac arrhythmias leading to sudden death. Trichloroethylene was formerly used as an anesthetic, and it was well known for its ability to cause cardiac arrhythmias. Signs and symptoms of chronic exposure to chlorinated hydrocarbon solvents are similar to those described for toluene. Detection and monitoring of these compounds often include analysis for the parent compound and its metabolite(s). Examples include carbon tetrachloride (metabolites: chloroform and carbon dioxide), chloroform (metabolite: carbon dioxide), and trichloroethylene (metabolites: 2,2,2-trichloroethanol and trichloroacetic acid). Ingestion of large amounts of known hepatotoxins such as carbon tetrachloride and chloroform may warrant early administration of acetylcysteine (as used for acetaminophen intoxication) as a preventive measure. The association of phosgene, the highly toxic chloroform metabolite, with hepatic glutathione depletion is the rationale for use of acetylcysteine for chloroform ingestion.

The widespread use of CFCs as propellants and components in cooling systems and fire extinguishers makes them readily available for abuse. These chemicals are identified by various nomenclatures, including the chemical name or a CFC number, which may be preceded by the words Halon or Freon. For example, trichlorofluoromethane is also identified as CFC number 11 and as Halon 11 or Freon 11. Often these chemicals are referred to as "the freons," although Freon is a DuPont trade name. Because of the ozone-depleting properties of the CFCs, replacement products have been developed, particularly for use as aerosol propellants and refrigerants. The nomenclatures for these replacement products include the chemical name or a number (HFC or HCFC). For example, difluoroethane (CH_3CHF_2) is also referred to as HFC-152a and has been referred to as Freon 152a. The names and chemical formulas of these compounds are given in Table 1. Some products contain more than one such compound as propellants, which can affect the laboratory analysis as well as possibly produce multiple/synergistic effects on the user. The distribution half-life of inhaled fluorocarbons is rapid, a mean of 13–14 s, with a plateau effect within 5–20 min. Blood clearance is rapid, usually <3 min, with tissue uptake and release inversely proportional to the fat content of the tissue. The elimination half-life for the total body is approximately 1.5 h, with most of the fluorocarbon being eliminated unchanged via the respiratory system. The primary complication of exposure is cardiovascular toxicity, including arrhythmias, myocardial depression, and reduction in peripheral vascular resistance. The treatment of exposed patients is primarily supportive to maintain cardiac stabilization.

Table 1. Chlorofluorocarbons (CFCs) and Non-Ozone-Depleting Replacements

Name	Number	Chemical Formula
Trichlorofluoromethane	CFC 11	CCl_3F
Dichlorodifluoromethane	CFC 12	CCl_2F_2
Chlorodifluoromethane	HCFC 22	$CHClF_2$
Trichlorotrifluoroethane	CFC 113	CCl_2FCClF_2
Dichlorotetrafluoroethane	CFC 114	$CClF_2CClF_2$
Chloropentafluoroethane	CFC 115	$CClF_2CF_3$
1,1,1,2-Tetrafluoroethane	HFA-134a	CF_3CH_2F
Difluoroethane	HFC-152a	CH_3CHF_2
Chlorodifluoroethane	HFC-142b	CH_3CClF_2
Bromochlorodifluoromethane (BCF)	FC12B1	$CBrClF_2$

Butane

Butane is a component of aerosol propellants and the fuel gas used in cigarette lighters, camping stoves, and small blowtorches. It consists of *n*-butane and small amounts of isobutane and propane. Small containers such as cigarette lighters may be abused by clinching the nozzle between the teeth and pressing to release the contents. This rapid release of a fluid cooled to below –20 °C may cause burning of the throat and lungs and lead to death from cardiac arrest due to vagal stimulation of the larynx. As with other inhalants, the primary concern from butane is sudden death due to cardiac arrest. Ventricular tachycardia and ventricular fibrillation have been documented in abusers of butane.

ANALYSIS

In rare instances, suspicion or detection of chronic use may result from nontoxicologic laboratory results. Chronic users may have abnormal results for aspartate aminotransferase, alanine aminotransferase, prothrombin time, and partial thromboplastin time because of an impaired liver function. Toluene abuse may produce low potassium and phosphorus concentrations and increased creatine kinase values, which help explain the symptom of muscle weakness. Abnormal electrolyte and blood gas results may also occur as the consequence of proximal and distal tubular acidosis caused by toluene abuse. Chronic

inhalation abuse may also cause bone marrow depression, causing leukopenia, anemia, thrombocytopenia, leukemia, and hemolysis.

Urine drug screens do not detect the chemicals that are commonly abused. The likelihood of detecting recent use is influenced by the dose, the length of the sampling time relative to the exposure time, and conditions of sample collection and storage. Blood is the specimen of choice, although analysis of urine for metabolites sometimes extends the time frame for detecting exposure. Proper collection techniques include the use of a glass tube with minimal headspace remaining after sample collection, an anticoagulant such as lithium heparin or EDTA, and a cap that ensures a tight seal. Soft rubber stoppers are permeable to toluene and other VOCs. Samples should be collected and stored in containers with minimal headspace, and addition of an internal standard after collection will minimize errors due to evaporation during storage or tissue homogenization. Samples should be stored, transported, and handled at temperatures between –5 °C and 4 °C. For fatalities in which inhalant abuse is suspected, tissues (brain, lung, fat, liver, heart, kidney) should be analyzed in addition to blood. The highest concentrations are typically found in blood and brain tissue. For cooperative, conscious patients, it may be possible to collect and analyze expired air. The most common method for detecting volatile substances in blood and other samples is headspace gas chromatography with flame-ionization, electron-capture, or mass spectrometer detection devices. Flame-ionization and mass spectrometer detectors have wider applicability for detecting inhalants; virtually all inhalants can be detected. Much greater sensitivity can be achieved for halogenated compounds by using an electron-capture detector (see Chapter 9). Partition coefficients and phase ratios (headspace volume relative to sample volume) affect method sensitivity as well as analyte loss. In general, the concentrations of volatile analytes in the headspace are higher when conditions are adjusted to produce the lowest values for both the partition coefficient and the phase ratio. Practical applications to achieve these results include increasing the temperature, agitation, adding inorganic salts (e.g., sodium chloride, ammonium chloride, ammonium sulfate, potassium carbonate, sodium citrate) to decrease the solubility of polar organic volatiles in aqueous matrices, and the use of sample containers with minimal headspace.

A variety of polar and nonpolar column phases have been used for the separation and quantification of volatiles. Capillary columns are more frequently used today, but packed columns can be used. The headspace capillary gas chromatographic procedures for ethanol and other volatiles used by many laboratories can often be modified for preliminary qualitative screening for particular suspected volatiles. Variations of headspace techniques used to increase sensitivity include solid-phase microextraction sampling and concentration, cryogenic focusing or cryogenic oven trapping to lower the temperature of the injection port or oven, and purge and trap dynamic analysis. Acceptable forensic practice recommends that the detection of an analyte (drug) be confirmed by a second or definitive method. For VOCs, two acceptable gas chromatographic confirmation procedures are reanalysis with a different column or use of mass spectrometry for absolute identification.

Well-documented procedures that have provided retention data for hundreds of compounds have been developed for use in screening and quantifying almost all volatile substances. These procedures have typical limits of detection of 0.1 mg/L and typical linear analytical ranges to 50 or 100 mg/L.

Table 2 provides analysis conditions and retention times for common volatiles produced by one procedure that uses dual-column elution. For the gaseous volatile substances, preparation of a standard requires determination of the partition coefficient when the substance is dissolved in a suitable solvent. The partition coefficient of the substance between the solvent and air above the solvent may be calculated from the peak areas of the two components following injection of each fraction into a gas chromatograph.

INTERPRETATION

The detection of some volatile substances in the blood does not always indicate inhalant abuse or occupational exposure. For example, acetone and other volatile compounds may be found in ketoacidotic patients, and some inborn errors of metabolism lead to the accumulation of volatile compounds. Even though many studies and case reports have described concentrations of volatile substances in the blood, definitive correlations between these blood concentrations and the clinical features of toxicity have not been demonstrated for any of these compounds. Table 3 lists concentrations of inhalants that have been published. Although these concentrations are often determined postmortem, several of the results are from exposed patients, and Table 3 should not be taken as a reflection of only postmortem (toxic) concentrations. The lack of correlation between blood concentrations and toxic effects may be illustrated by examining the reported blood concentrations of toluene. A comparison of the blood concentrations of toluene in 132 patients from one report shows concentrations ranging from 0.2 mg/L to 70 mg/L with 22 of the 25 fatalities having a toluene concentration >5 mg/L. Conversely, 13 patients with toluene concentrations >10 mg/L (suggested as the toxic concentration) were either asymptomatic or only "mildly" intoxicated, with symptoms of headache, nausea, vomiting, and drowsiness. In other studies, toluene concentrations of up to 30 mg/L have been reported

Table 2. Headspace–Gas Chromatography Retention Times for VOCs[a]

Compound	DB-1 (Run Program), min	DB-WAX (40–150 °C), min	DB-624 (40–150 °C), min
Acetaldehyde	2.33	1.55	2.20
Acetone	4.14	1.86	3.49
Acetonitrile	3.76	3.61	3.86
Amyl acetate[b]	19.96	7.17	>15
Amyl acetate, artifact	>20	10.01	>15
Benzene	13.15	2.71	7.77
Butanol, 1-	12.94	8.99	8.84
Butanol, 3-methyl-1-[c]	15.72	11.55	11.09
Butanol, 4-chloro-1-, artifact	>20	14.29	>15
Butanol, 4-chloro-1-[b]	11.31	2.10	6.76
Butanol, iso- (2-methyl-1-propanol)	11.27	6.29	7.70
Butanol, tertiary	5.45	2.43	4.25
Butyl acetate, n-	18.16	5.36	13.29
Chloral hydrate[d]	>20	>20	>15
Chlorobenzene	19.49	11.06	>15
Chlorobutane, 1-	12.51	1.96	7.32
Chloroform	10.61	3.98	6.84
Cyclohexane	13.58	1.59	7.22
Ethanol	3.39	2.75	3.02
Ethchlorvynol	>20	>20	>15
Ethyl acetate	10.44	2.27	6.42
Ethyl ether	5.04	1.46	3.15
Ethylbenzene	19.93	6.92	>15
Formaldehyde[c]	15.42	2.38	10.48
Heptane, n-	15.09	1.54	8.26
Hexane, isomer #2	9.46	1.36	4.52
Hexane, isomer #1	12.01	1.51	6.07
Hexane, n-	10.50	1.42	4.99
Hexanone, 2-	17.40	5.63	12.93
Methanol	2.33	2.36	2.31
Methyl acetate	5.60	1.93	3.94
Methyl ethyl ketone	8.88	2.36	6.28
Methyl tertiary butyl ether	8.12	1.53	4.49
Methyl-2-pentanone, 4-	15.84	3.69	10.87
Methylene chloride	5.73	2.63	4.10
Octane, n-	18.35	1.78	11.55
Octanol[d]	>20	18.25	>15
Pentane	5.07	1.38	2.92
Pentanol, 1-[b]	16.77	12.77	12.29
Pentanol, 3-	14.49	7.14	9.73
Pentanone, 4-OH-4-methyl (HMP)[d]	18.94	17.24	>15
Propanol, 2-	4.46	2.68	3.66
Propanol, n-	6.98	4.54	5.47
Toluene	17.14	4.29	11.22
Trichloroethane, 1,1,1-	12.40	2.20	7.13
Trichloroethanol, 2,2,2-	>20	>20	>15
Trichloroethylene	14.69	3.47	8.90
Trimethylpentane, 2,2,4-	14.76	1.49	7.92
Xylene, m-[b]	19.93	6.86	>15
Xylene, o-[b]	>20	7.19	>15
Xylene, p-	>20	7.20	>15

[a]DB-1 columns: 30 m × 0.32 mm (i.d.), 5.0-μm film thickness; DB-WAX columns: 30 m × 0.32 mm (i.d.), 0.25-μm film thickness; DB-624 columns: 30 m × 0.53 mm (i.d.), 3.0-μm film thickness. J&W Scientific/Agilent Technologies, Folsom, CA. Retention time entries denote compounds readily detected at 100 mg%. Modified with permission from (11).
[b]Artifact peaks detected.
[c]Split peak.
[d]Primary peak is an artifact or breakdown product.

Table 3. Blood Concentrations of Solvents/Inhalants Reported in the Literature

Solvent/Inhalant	Concentration(s)
Chlorodifluoromethane	71 mg/L
Chloropentafluoroethane	0.30 mg/L
Chloroform	252 mg/L, 60 mg/kg
Dichloromethane (methylene chloride)	510 mg/L
Diethyl ether	26-319 mg/L (n = 4)L
Enflurane (2-chloro-1,1,2-trifluoroethyl difluoromethyl ether)	130 mg/kg, 710 mg/L
Freon 11 (trichlorofluoromethane)	62.8 mg/kg, 12.0 mg/L
Freon 12 (dichlorodifluoromethane)	3.0 mg/L
Freon 22 (chlorodifluoromethane)	286 mg/kg, 538 mg/kg; 371 mg/L
Freon 152 (difluoroethane; spray paint propellant)	29-136 mg/L (n = 4)
Freon 113 (1,1,2-trichlorotrifluoroethane)	2.3 mg/L
HFA-134a (1,1,1,2-tetrafluoroethane)	0.008 mg/L, 0.46 mg/L (n = 2) <5.8 mg/L, 461 mg/L (n = 2)
MAPP (methyl acetylene and propadiene)	59.6 mg/L
Propane	2.8 mg/L, 84 mg/L
Tetrachloroethylene	4.5–66 mg/L
1,1,1-Trichloroethane (typing-correction fluid)	0.1–60 mg/L (n = 66)
1,1,1-Trichloroethane (degreasing solvent)	300 mg/L
Toluene	0.2–70 mg/L (n = 132)

in intoxicated but conscious subjects. Thus, it is almost impossible to establish definitive toluene concentrations in blood that show a direct correlation to toxicity. Determination of such definitive correlations is hampered by the volatile nature of the substances, individual variations in metabolism, and failure to collect and analyze samples in many cases of exposure.

The detection of urinary metabolites has also been used to confirm inhalation of volatile substances. Urinary metabolites that have been measured include phenol (benzene metabolite), trichloroacetic acid (tetrachloroethylene), hippuric acid (toluene), and methylhippuric acid (xylene). Results are often expressed as a ratio to the urine creatinine concentration in order to normalize results with respect to urine volume and fluid intake. These urinary metabolites may also be used to detect occupational exposure, but caution must be used when interpreting results. For example, urinary hippuric acid may be due to ingestion of benzoate preservatives in foods and not to exposure to toluene.

The toxicologist should also be aware that the presence of some volatile substances may interfere with other toxicologic analyses. The volatile substances toluene, *m*-xylene,

o-xylene, methanol, and 2-propanol have been shown to be capable of inducing false-positive readings for ethanol on the evidential infrared-based breath-testing device, the Intoxilyzer 5000.

SUGGESTED READING

1. Avella J, Wilson JC, Lehrer M. Fatal cardiac arrhythmias after repeated exposure to 1,1-difluoroethane (DFE). Am J Forensic Med Path 2006;27:58–60.
2. Baselt RC. Disposition of toxic drugs and chemicals in man, 6th ed. Seal Beach, CA: Biomedical Publications, 2011.
3. Broussard L. The role of the laboratory in detecting inhalant abuse. Clin Lab Sci 2000;13:205–9.
4. Broussard L. Chromatographic measurement of volatile organic compounds (VOCs). In: Bertholf RL, Winecker RE, eds. Chromatographic methods in clinical chemistry and toxicology. Chichester, UK: J Wiley, 2007.
5. Caldwell JP, Kim ND. The response of the Intoxilyzer 5000® to five potential interfering substances. J Forensic Sci 1997;42:1080–7.
6. Cox D, DeRienz R, Jufer-Phipps R, Levine B, Jacobs A, Fowler D. Distribution of ether in two postmortem cases. J Anal Toxicol 2006;30:635–8.
7. Dehon B, Humbert L, Devisme L, Stievenart M, Mathieu D, Houdret N, Lhermitte M.

Tetrachloroethylene and trichloroethylene fatality: case report and simple headspace SPME-capillary gas chromatographic determination in tissues. J Anal Toxicol 2000; 24:22–6.

8. Espeland K. Inhalant abuse. Lippincotts Prim Care Pract 2000;4:336–40.

9. Fonseca CA, Auerbach DS, Suarez RV. The forensic investigation of propane gas asphyxiation. Am J Forensic Med Pathol 2002; 23:167–9.

10. Jones HE, Balster RL. Inhalant abuse in pregnancy. Obstet Gynecol Clin North Am 1998;25:153–67.

11. Kurtzman TL, Otsuka KN, Wahl RA. Inhalant abuse by adolescents. J Adolesc Health 2001;28:170–80.

12. Watson WA, Litovitz TL, Rodgers GC Jr, Klein-Schwartz W, Reid N, Youniss J, et al. 2004 Annual report of the American Association of Poison Control Centers Toxic Exposure Surveillance System. Am J Emerg Med 2005;23:589–666.

13. Musshoff F, Junker H, Madea B. Rapid analysis of halothane in biological samples using headspace solid-phase microextraction and gas chromatography-mass spectrometry—a case of a double homicide. J Anal Toxicol 2000;24:372–6.

14. Sharp ME. A comprehensive screen for volatile organic compounds in biological fluids. J Anal Toxicol 2001;25:631–6.

15. Tranthim-Fryer DJ, Hansson RC, Norman KW. Headspace/solid-phase microextraction/gas chromatography-mass spectrometry: a screening technique for the recovery and identification of volatile organic compounds (VOC's) in postmortem blood and viscera samples. J Forensic Sci 2001;46:934–46.

16. Xiang Z, Avella J, Wetli CV. Sudden death caused by 1,1-difluoroethane inhalation. J Forensic Sci 2004;49:627–9.

CHAPTER 29

Metals

Joseph J. Saady

INTRODUCTION

The previous chapters in Part III have dealt primarily with organic compounds: abused drugs, therapeutic drugs, and volatile substances. This chapter deals primarily with inorganic compounds containing metals, i.e., those elements in the periodic table that, when ionized, lose electrons to form cations.

Some metals are essential for life; others are nonessential or are not known to have any biological function. Even those metals required to sustain life can produce toxic effects if present in high enough concentrations. The increased industrialization of the world has caused an increased use of metals and metallic compounds and therefore has increased the potential for human exposure to these substances. Individuals can be exposed to metals via their occupation, their living environment, or their consumption of food and beverages, including water. The following is a discussion of some of the most commonly encountered metals in forensic toxicology, as well as a brief discussion of the techniques used to assay metals in biological specimens.

ALUMINUM

Aluminum is a ubiquitous metal that presents analytical and interpretive challenges in forensic toxicology. Aluminum does not occur naturally as the metal but is found as ores of aluminum and includes oxygen, fluorine, and silicone, among others. It is the third most abundant element of the earth's crust (8%). The most important raw material for the production of aluminum is bauxite, which contains 40–60% aluminum oxide. The Romans and Greeks used alum as an astringent and also in the dyeing process. In 1761, de Morveau proposed the name "alumine" for the base in alum, and Davy proposed "aluminum" in 1807. The electrolysis method of obtaining aluminum from cryolite was used in 1886, and the Bayer process is commonly used to refine bauxite.

In the industrial setting, humans are exposed to aluminum and related compounds through dust, pyro products, welding fumes, and aluminum alkyl compounds. Portions of inhaled aluminum are retained and become bioavailable over a period of time, thus lengthening the time for excretion.

Aluminum is more readily available in the environment because of acid rain and subsequent uptake by microorganisms. Daily exposure is common because of its ubiquity in the environment and its extensive use. Small concentrations are present in drinking water, foods, dust particles, etc. Foods contain aluminum, and aluminum is leached from cooking utensils and cookware. Other consumer items that contain the metal include antiperspirants, cosmetics, internal analgesics, antiulcer and antidiarrhea medications, some vaccines, and food-packing materials. Highest exposures to the metal appear to come from antacids, phosphate-binding therapy, and certain intravenous solutions.

Absorption, Distribution, Metabolism, and Elimination

Of the approximately 5 mg in the diet, 0.015 mg is absorbed through the gastrointestinal (GI) tract, distributed by the circulation, and eventually excreted. Aluminum accumulates in bone and lung tissue with most of the body burden residing in bone. The half-life of this metal in the urine of an occupational worker can vary from 8 hours to 8 years and is directly proportional to the length of exposure years. The half-life in retired aluminum powder workers is 1–8 years.

The American Conference of Governmental Industrial Hygienists (ACGIH) has determined that aluminum oxide (Al_2O_3), containing no asbestos and <1% crystalline silica, has minimal effects on the lungs and is not a significant health risk when exposure is reasonably controlled. The kidney can eliminate 0.5 mg aluminum per 24 h, but in cases of renal insufficiency or end-stage renal disease, high concentrations accumulate in the body. The brain is the target organ in this instance. Unabsorbed aluminum is eliminated in the feces. Aluminum is distributed throughout the body, with the highest concentrations found in bone and lung tissue.

Toxicity

Aluminum phosphide, a grain fumigant, has been orally ingested in some suicides and accidents. In general, blood and tissue concentrations rise as exposure increases. Concentrations return to normal after cessation of exposure, unless kidney function is impaired or absent. The central nervous system (CNS) and bone tissue are the target organs. There is evidence of impairment of cognitive function or effects on the nervous system in aluminum workers. Patients receiving long-term dialysis are susceptible to a fatal neurological syndrome possibly caused by aluminum toxicity. This disorder affects speech and causes dementia, convulsions, and myoclonus. Because increased concentrations of aluminum have been determined in the brain of some patients with Alzheimer's disease, aluminum is suspected of causing the disease. However, brain concentrations vary considerably, and high aluminum concentrations can be found in dialysis patients without Alzheimer's disease. After decades of research, the relationship between aluminum concentrations and Alzheimer's disease is not fully understood.

ARSENIC

Arsenic is present in all living organisms, plant and animal. It can be called a semimetal because it has chemical properties of both metals and nonmetals. Forms of this substance have been known and used since ancient times for therapeutic uses and for poisonings, both overt and covert. The medicinal effects of arsenic were extolled by Hippocrates, Aristotle, and Pliny the Elder. The name was derived from the Arabic *az-zernik*. During the Middle Ages, when arsenic was used frequently as a poison to eliminate royalty, bezoar stones were used to detoxify wine and other drinks. "Bezoar" is derived from Persian words meaning "to protect" and "against poison." It was recently determined that arsenic binds to the sulfur in these stones, which are found in the alimentary tracts of mountain goats, llamas, and other ruminant animals. Arsenic is ubiquitous and can be found as a contaminant in soil, water, and air. It is the third most common element and is typically not mined but is a recoverable by-product of the smelting process of various metals such as copper, lead, zinc, and iron.

Arsenic has been used in wood preservatives, insecticides (e.g., calcium and lead arsenates), herbicides (e.g., arsenites), sheep dips, fly paper, arsenical soaps, germicides, and rat poisons. Arsenicals are also used as growth promoters in poultry and other livestock. The major source of occupational exposure to arsenic is herbicide and pesticide production. Fruits and vegetables sprayed with these substances may present another source of exposure. Lewisite is an arsenic-containing blister agent that has been used in chemical warfare.

Chromated copper arsenate and ammoniacal copper arsenate are used as wood preservatives. The metal is used in special solders and as a doping agent in silicon and germanium solid-state products; lead–antimony–arsenic alloys are used in making lead-acid storage batteries. In the computer chip industry, arsine and arsenic trioxide provide another occupational source of exposure. Gallium arsenide is used in the production of semiconductors. Arsenic can be leached from mineral-spring waters and geothermal power plant effluent coming into contact with soil and rock that contain high concentrations of the metal. Exposure to arsenic by these sources and extensive pesticide use can result in high concentrations of arsenic in runoff water, which eventually makes its way to streams, rivers, and the ocean, whereby many species of fish and seafood may be exposed.

Elemental arsenic (As^0 or As[0]) is relatively nontoxic. Common forms of arsenic exist as the arsenate (As^{+5} As[V]) and as arsenite (As^{+3} or As[III]). Arsine (AsH_3) is a gas formed when hydrogen is generated in the presence of trivalent arsenic. It is used in industrial organic synthesis, in lead-acid storage battery manufacture, and as a doping agent for solid-state electronic compounds. The relative toxicity for these species is as follows:

$$As^0 < As^{+5} < As^{+3} < arsine$$

Absorption, Distribution, Metabolism, and Elimination

Arsenic compounds are primarily absorbed via the respiratory and GI tracts. Breathing is the major route of exposure in the workplace; percutaneous exposure may occur depending on the skin permeability of the compound. Airborne arsenic is frequently deposited in the respiratory tract and, because of mucociliary clearance, is eventually swallowed and presented to the GI tract. The degree of absorption depends on the solubility of the arsenic compound, but, in general, >90% of orally consumed arsenic is absorbed. Organic arsenic compounds in seafood are readily absorbed after ingestion. Arsenic is absorbed by diffusion, enters the portal system, and circulates to the liver prior to entering the general circulation. The half-life of inorganic arsenic in blood is approximately 10 h; the half-life of methylated arsenic is 30 h. Arsenic binds the sulfhydryl groups and concentrates in hair and nails. Arsenic is excreted to a minor extent in sweat and skin. It can also be transferred to the fetus via placental transfer. The muscle tissue accumulates a large amount of this metal. Smaller amounts distribute into the liver, lungs, intestinal wall, spleen, and bone. Nails (fingernails or toenails) and hair accumulate the metal and provide another means of determining if and when exposure has occurred.

Trivalent arsenic can be oxidized in vivo to the pentavalent species, and there is evidence that pentavalent arsenic can be reduced to the trivalent species. Arsenite methyltransferase is an enzyme responsible for arsenic methylation. Urine is the major elimination pathway and accounts for approximately 60% of the amount absorbed. The metabolic pathway at low arsenic concentration is first order, with the major metabolite being dimethylarsinic acid (DMA). If oral intake exceeds 0.5 mg, then the methylation process is saturated. Organo-arsenicals are present in seafood and will not appear as inorganic arsenic or DMA.

Toxicity

Poisonings are less common than in the past, but they still occur due to the availability of arsenic-containing herbicides and pesticides. As with any poisoning, the chemical form of the arsenic compound, the age and physical condition of the individual exposed, and the dose are critical issues. Intentional poisonings frequently involve the use of arsenic-containing rodenticides or pesticides.

Arsine poisonings occur in occupational settings but do not result from the manufacture or use of the gas. Poisonings occur when arsine is formed as a by-product of a chemical reaction typically involving a base metal, an arsenic impurity, and an acid or strong base.

Acute symptoms of exposure include GI symptoms such as pain, vomiting, discomfort, diarrhea, and inflammation and can occur within minutes to hours after exposure. Rice-water and/or bloody stools can occur. Renal damage may result in proteinuria, oliguria, and hematuria. Cardiovascular effects may be evident by prolongation of the QT interval and abnormal T-wave pattern on the ECG. Complaints of skeletal muscle pain and severe thirst are common. Encephalopathy and peripheral neuropathy are common in both acute and chronic exposure. If the dose is sufficiently high, spasms, stupor, convulsions, and death will result.

Chronic arsenic poisoning can result after weeks or years of exposure. Symptoms may be subtle and mimic other conditions. Muscle weakness, hyperkeratosis (especially on the palms of the hands and soles of the feet), garlic breath, Mee's lines, and neuropathy can result. The neuropathy has sometimes been confused with Guillain-Barré syndrome. Hematological changes result in anemia and other blood abnormalities.

Arsine toxicity produces different symptoms from those listed above due to the differing mechanism of action. Arsine gas binds to hemoglobin, producing lysis of red blood cells, hemoglobinuria, anemia, and kidney damage following the severe hemolysis.

IRON

Iron has been used by humans since ancient times. There is evidence that iron from meteorites was used and formed in predynastic times in Egypt. Iron may have been smelted accidentally at first, and fragments of smelted iron date back to 2700 BC. A regular production of useful objects by smiths occurred by 1200 BC, as evidenced by the unearthing of iron hoes, sickles, plowshares, and smelting furnaces. Iron, particularly when alloyed with carbon to make steel, is perhaps the most important metal of an industrial economy. Various salts of iron are used extensively in occupational settings and in some pharmaceutics:

$FeCl_3$	Sewage and waste treatment, engraving, textiles, photography
$Fe(NO_3)_3$	Textile dyeing, tanning, weighting silt
$Fe_2(SO_4)_3$	Water treatment, textile dyeing
$FeCl_2$	Metallurgy, pharmaceutical industry, sewage treatment
$FeSO_4$	Fertilizer, food or feed additive, herbicides, process engraving, iron-deficiency anemia

Absorption, Distribution, Metabolism, and Elimination

Iron is an essential metal required by the body for routine biochemical processes. Iron is orally consumed in the normal dietary intake, but only a small portion is biologically available. Therefore, iron deficiency is more common than iron intoxication.

The largest portion of the 5–15% of absorbed iron is stored in hemoglobin, which contains two-thirds of the body burden. Approximately 25% is storage iron contained in ferritin and hemosiderin, with the remaining iron stored in myoglobin. Pathologic conditions exist where too much iron is absorbed and transferred to the liver and other organs where accumulation occurs. Stores of iron are conserved by the body, with small portions excreted in stool and urine. Only 1 mg per year is lost in males, with more losses in females due to menstruation.

Toxicity

Poisonings with this metal are rare and almost always involve children. The typical scenario involves a toddler "discovering" the mother's prenatal iron supplements or vitamins and then consuming the contents.

Acute toxicity has been divided into five phases (Table 1). The overall mortality rate from acute poisonings is about 1%. In the industrial setting, inhalation of ferric salts can cause irritation of the respiratory tract and skin. Inhalation of fumes can produce deposition of particles within the lung, sometimes determined by X-ray and termed "arc welder's lung."

MERCURY

Mercury has been used since prehistoric times; the drawings on cave walls were made with cinnabar, a red stone made of mercury sulfide. Mercury is also mined and produced as a by-product of gold and bauxite mining. Other processes involving mercury include cyanide leaching of low-grade gold and silver, which collects mercury in the ore, and amalgamation where mercury is recovered for reuse.

The metal has been used therapeutically since the 16th century for treatment of syphilis, and as a diuretic, antiseptic, skin ointment, and laxative. Mercury occurs naturally through degassing from the earth's crust and is usually produced from volcanic action and hot springs. The name and chemical symbol (Hg) are derived from the Greek "hydrargyros," meaning "water silver" and referring to the appearance of the metal, which is liquid at ambient temperature. In fact, mercury is the only metal that is liquid at room temperature. Metallic or elemental mercury (Hg^0) is the main volatile form occurring in air. Inorganic and organic mercury compounds are formed in the +1 (mercurous) and +2 (mercuric) valence states. Organic forms of mercury include methyl mercury and phenyl mercury.

Humans may be exposed to mercury from the naturally occurring amount in the environment. More commonly, humans may be close to or in contact with a site where mercury was disposed of in an industrial process. This metal is used extensively in industry because of its unique properties. Because its expansion is proportional to temperature, it is used in thermometers, manometers, barometers, gauges, and valves. It is used heavily in industries making dry-cell batteries, lamps, wiring, switching devices, and electronic equipment, as well as in the production of chlorine and caustic soda. Compounds of mercury are also used in pigments, refining, lubricating oils, heat transfer, water-based paint (as mildewcide), and paint preservative. Dental professionals use the metal in dental amalgams. Alkyl mercury compounds are used as fungicides and preservatives for wood, paper pulp, textiles, and leather.

Absorption, Distribution, Metabolism, and Elimination

Most of the mercury vapor that gets to the lungs is readily absorbed and quickly transported to other organs in the body. The kidneys are particularly susceptible; along with the brain, they receive the largest portion. Inorganic salts of mercury (e.g., mercuric chloride or mercurous chloride) that are sufficiently volatile will be similarly absorbed. Approximately 80% of the inhaled dose is absorbed into the circulation, with only 2% being absorbed percutaneously. After

Table 1. Stages of Iron Toxicity by Ingestion

Phase	Time After Ingestion	Symptoms
I	0.5–2 h	Lethargy, restlessness, bloody vomiting, diarrhea, abdominal pain (iron has a corrosive effect on the mucosa of the GI tract)
II	Variable	Apparent recovery
III	2–12 h	Shock, metabolic acidosis, cyanosis, fever
IV	2–4 days	Hepatic necrosis
V	2–4 weeks	GI obstruction secondary to gastric or pyloric scarring

Source: From Jacobs J, Green H, Grendel B. Acute iron intoxication. N Engl J Med 1965;273:1124–7.

entering the blood, the majority of the mercury is taken up by erythrocytes and then oxidized to the divalent mercuric ion (Hg^{+2}). Mercury in plasma is oxidized to Hg^{+2} and combines with sulfhydryl residues in plasma proteins. About 80% of the body burden is deposited in the proximal tubules in the kidneys. Free mercury crosses the blood–brain barrier.

Pollution of water by mine tailing is significant. Mercuric salts and organic mercury are readily absorbed by organisms in the water. Fish accumulate and retain the metal in tissue, primarily as methyl mercury. There is evidence that microorganisms cause methylation of inorganic mercury in aquatic species. Individuals who consume fish from contaminated lakes have higher than average mercury concentrations. The fetus can be exposed in utero and the newborn can be exposed via breast milk.

Routes of elimination include the feces (due to biliary excretion and intestinal secretion) and urine, which account for more than 50% of elimination. Excretion also occurs by sweat, by exhalation, and in hair. The estimated half-life approximates a two-compartment model with a rapid phase ($t_{1/2} = 3–5$ days) and a slow phase (45 days).

Toxicity

Except for dermatitis, skin contact with mercury poses little, if any, danger. Exposure to percutaneous organic mercury (e.g., dimethyl mercury) may be lethal, as shown by the death of a distinguished and knowledgeable scientist who spilled a small amount on her rubber gloves.

Orally consumed mercury poses more problems from the internal mechanical abrasions than from systemic toxicity. Most of the orally consumed mercury will be eliminated in the feces. There has been marginal effect when large quantities were released into the GI tract.

Acute toxicity can result from high vapor or dust inhalation. Flu-like symptoms and symptoms of interstitial pneumonitis, bronchitis, and metal fume fever result (e.g., chills and aching muscles with dry mouth and throat). Oral consumption of mercuric chloride can produce GI symptoms, burning mouth and throat, nausea, vomiting, severe gingivitis, and esophageal destruction.

Chronic poisoning almost always manifests itself as neurological symptoms with tremors of the arms and hands at lower concentrations, and lower limb involvement as concentration increases. Acrodynia (pink disease) can develop with erythema of the extremities, chest, and face, with photophobia, diaphoresis, anorexia, and rapid heart rate. Chronic effects lead to renal tubular injury. Classic chronic symptoms include tremor, loss of memory, excitability, gingivitis, and hallucinations (mad hatter's disease).

LITHIUM

Lithium is the lightest of metals, with an atomic number of 3, and one of the alkali metals. It was discovered in 1817 by J. Arfuedson, a Swedish chemist, and is obtained from minerals. Small amounts of the substance have been found in meteorites, soils, tobacco, grains, coffee, seaweed, and milk.

Lithium has been used therapeutically since the 19th century as an anticonvulsant, a sedative (including for manic patients), and a treatment for gout. In late 1940, its use as a table salt substitute resulted in many poisonings and deaths, and that unfortunate use was eventually discontinued. In 1949, Cade discovered that lithium carbonate (Li_2CO_3) was useful in the treatment of mania. This substance remains responsible for a significant improvement in the lives of patients with manic-depressive disorder.

Industrially, no health-related problems were reported prior to the 1950s because lithium was rarely used. Lithium hydride is used as a high-performance desiccant, a source of hydrogen, a nuclear shielding material, and a condensing agent in organic synthesis. Lithium hydride workers have the potential for dermal contact or inhalation of lithium fumes in welding and brazing operations.

Absorption, Distribution, Metabolism, and Elimination

There is rapid and nearly complete absorption of lithium from the GI tract, and almost uniform distribution to organs. The concentration in the cerebrospinal fluid is 40–50% of plasma concentration. Approximately 95% is eliminated in the urine (half-life 20–24 h). About 80% of lithium is reabsorbed in the proximal renal tubules. Less than 1% is eliminated in the feces, and 4–5% in sweat. Saliva concentrations are two times plasma concentrations, and lithium is secreted in human milk.

Toxicity

Lithium hydride is intensively corrosive and may produce skin burns. Eye injuries have developed from an explosion, and the inhalation of dust causes strictures of the larynx, bronchi, trachea, and esophagus. In atmospheres containing 0.5 mg/m^3 lithium, the skin becomes inflamed and lacrimation occurs.

Patients taking Li_2CO_3 for manic-depressive disorders sometimes develop thyroid enlargement. Acute exposure may produce polydipsia, polyuria, sedation, tremor, vomiting, diarrhea, ataxia, confusion, coma, and seizures. Other side effects include cardiac arrhythmias, hypotension, and albuminuria.

LEAD

Lead has been one of the most studied metals, and controversy still surrounds the effect of low concentrations in newborns. The most common ore of lead (galena or lead sulfide) was used as early as 4000 BC. Metallic lead objects have been discovered among ancient ruins dating to that period, and the Bible has several references to lead. The Romans used lead frequently for transporting water and for cooking. It has often been stated that the fall of the Roman Empire was due to lead poisoning because the more affluent Romans had a form of running water plumbed to their domiciles using lead pipes.

It was recognized in ancient times by Greek, Roman, and Arabic physicians that orally consumed lead would cause colic and paralysis, and that lead fumes caused the same disorder. Galena was used as an eye salve in early West African cultures and as an eye cosmetic in India. Symptoms of toxicity were later described by Hippocrates (370 BC), Nicander (second century BC), and Pliny (first century BC). Lead-contaminated products have been used for centuries for dispensing liquids and foods (e.g., ceramic pottery, clay and cooking vessels, paints, and glazes).

This metal is distributed throughout the world; there have always been "background" concentrations of lead in living creatures, caused by natural lead ores occurring worldwide. The Industrial Revolution and the use of tetraethyl lead in gasoline caused a redistribution of lead throughout the environment, thus leading to various degrees of exposure in humans and wildlife.

Many different products are produced with lead. Most water supplies in the U.S. are controlled for lead concentration. Acidic foods and beverages have a tendency to leach lead from the container or from the solder used on the can (e.g., orange juice, cider, pickles). Therefore the foods we consume contain various concentrations of lead.

Many forms of lead are used in paint pigments (e.g., lead carbonate and lead oxide), with lead composing up to 38% of the dry weight. Lead paint has been favored due to its durability, but U.S. regulations banned lead-based paints from use in residences in 1978. Leaded paint continues to be used on industrial surfaces (e.g., bridges and street surfaces). Individuals who display pica (a habitual hand-to-mouth action) are particularly vulnerable to lead poisoning from paint chips and dust.

Lead is also a major component of solder, brass, and many bronzes. It is used in lead storage batteries, glass, plastic, and ceramics, as well as smelting, refining, scrap recovery, automobile radiator repair, construction, demolition, and firing-range operations. Lead arsenate continues to be used in insecticides.

Organic lead in the form of tetraethyl lead has been used since 1923 to increase the octane rating of fuels, but this has been stopped in many industrialized countries. Tetramethyl lead has been a combustion control additive of premium gasoline and aviation fuels since 1960.

Absorption, Distribution, Metabolism, and Elimination

Ingestion of lead in food represents the major source of exposure for most individuals. In adults, typically 5–15% of ingested lead is absorbed, but up to 50% may be absorbed if the adult is fasting. Infants absorb approximately 50% of ingested lead. Iron deficiency enhances intestinal absorption of lead. Approximately 40–50% of inhaled lead is absorbed, with most of the remainder exhaled. Portions trapped in the upper respiratory tract are eventually swallowed. Of the lead that is eventually absorbed, 99% of the lead portion retained in the blood compartment is bound to hemoglobin in red blood cells, with 1–3% found in serum. Absorbed lead is gradually deposited in soft tissues, especially the tubular epithelium of the kidney and the liver. Eventually there is redistribution to bone, teeth, and hair, with 95% of the body burden in bone. Unabsorbed lead is eliminated in the feces. Absorbed lead is eliminated in the urine (76%); as GI secretions (16%); in hair, nails, and sweat (8%); and in breast milk. Lead is transferred to the fetus via placental transfer and correlates with maternal concentrations.

Lead is deposited into bone in the form of tertiary lead phosphate in the same manner that calcium is deposited into bone. The half-life of lead in bone has been estimated from 10 years to >20 years. In blood, the half-life is 1–2 months. Factors that affect distribution of calcium similarly affect lead.

Toxicity

Acute lead poisoning is an infrequent occurrence, but may occur from ingestion of acid-soluble lead salts or lead vapor inhalation. Local actions in the mouth may be apparent, with the victim having abnormal thirst and metallic taste. Nausea, vomiting, abdominal pain, and black stools from lead sulfide may occur, which is followed by shock resulting from a loss of fluid. CNS symptoms include pain, paresthesia, and muscle weakness; kidney effects include oliguria; and hematological effects due to acute hemolytic crisis may cause anemia and hemoglobinuria.

The hematological effects of lead arise from the combination with and inactivation of several enzymes in the heme system pathway. A simplified schematic representation of how lead affects enzymatic activity in the heme system pathway is shown in Fig. 1. As indicated by the sequence of steps in Fig. 1, lead poisoning eventually causes elevated urinary delta-aminolevulinic acid and coproporphyrin III concentrations, and also increases in (zinc) protoporphyrin in the blood. These blood and urine enzymes are diagnostic tests that can be used along with blood lead in assessing lead poisoning.

The resultant effect is anemia due to impaired heme synthesis and shortened erythrocyte lifespan. Red blood cells are microcytic and hypochromic, with increased basophilic stippling.

Lead neuropathy has long been recognized as an adverse health effect of lead. Kidney damage is three times more likely in lead workers than in controls. The damage is usually manifested as glomerulonephritis developing over a 20- to 30-year exposure. The kidney damage is likely to cause hypertension in lead-exposed workers. In the production of "moonshine" liquor, lead is a source of contamination in the distillation process and at times in the transport of the liquid in automobile radiators. The reversible proximal renal tubular damage may manifest itself as aminoaciduria and glycosuria.

Another manifestation of poisoning is lead palsy, characterized by muscle weakness,

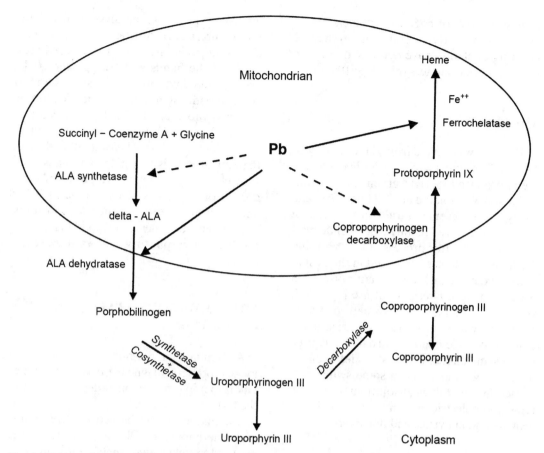

Fig. 1. Schematic representation of the effects of lead on the heme system pathway. Simplified schematic representation of lead's effects on mitochondrial and cytoplasmic enzymatic activity in the heme system pathway. Strong inhibition of enzyme activity by lead is indicated by solid arrows, with less intense inhibition indicated by dotted arrows.

fatigue, wristdrop, and footdrop. Lead encephalopathy, particularly on the developing CNS (i.e., in children), results in lethargy, ataxia, headache, irritability, loss of appetite, and projectile vomiting. Visual disturbances, delirium, and seizures follow. Metallic lead in the eye has been a cause of concern due to mechanical injury or inflammatory damage rather than lead toxicity. Other signs of plumbism include a bright color of the face, pallid lips, stooped posture, and lead line (a black or gray line along the gums due to lead sulfide).

It is necessary to mention that in children, the developing CNS is much more susceptible to the effects of lead than the adult CNS. In children, chronically elevated concentrations may cause decreased intelligence, impaired neurobehavioral development, decreased stature and growth, and impaired acuity. The interpretation of low-level lead exposure in children is made more difficult because of the sometimes controversial interpretation of neurodevelopment testing results on neonates and babies.

The Biological Exposure Indicies (BEI) of the American Conference of Governmental Hygienists establishes a maximum blood concentration of 30 µg/100 mL for workers who are exposed daily to lead. That guidance includes a note for women workers of childbearing age. If their whole blood lead concentration exceeds 10 µg/100 mL, there is a risk of delivering a child with a blood lead concentration over the current CDC guideline of 10 µg/100 mL, with warnings of possible risk of cogitative defects. Background blood lead concentrations in the U.S. general population have decreased over the past few decades to less than 5 μg/100 mL.

THALLIUM

Thallium was named from the Greek word "thallos," meaning green twig, because the metal produced a bright green spectral line. The metal was isolated in 1862 by Crooks and Lamy and is present naturally in a number of ores. It is recovered mainly from sulfide minerals in the smelting process of lead and zinc. Thallium sulfate has been used in the past as a household rodenticide and ant poison, but it was banned for residential use in 1975. It was used in the 1930s as a cosmetic depilatory cream, which unfortunately caused many cases of chronic exposure. Thallium is used in the semiconductor industry and is an alloy along with mercury in some switches. It is used in mineralogical solutions, optic systems, photoelectric cells, in the production of cement, and in pyrites and flue dusts.

Absorption, Distribution, Metabolism, and Elimination

Thallium is almost 100% absorbed from the GI tract and, like potassium, it distributes throughout the body. In the blood compartment, thallium can be found mainly in red blood cells. It also appears in brain, lung, gut, skeletal and cardiac muscle, salivary gland, spleen, pancreas, and testes, with accumulation in kidney, liver, and bone. There is some evidence for enterohepatic circulation. Thallium is secreted during glomerular filtration, with some 50% being reabsorbed in the tubule. The metal half-life of elimination in the urine is 4 weeks.

Toxicity

Thallium is regulated in many countries because of its toxicity. Acute poisoning involves GI distress, paralysis, and respiratory failure. Characteristic chronic poisoning causes alopecia and lobster-red skin. Paresthesia of the hands and feet, psychosis, delirium, and convulsions can occur. The most characteristic symptom of intoxication in patients whose death is delayed at least 20 days is alopecia. Optic cataracts and neuritis result from exposure. The oral lethal dose of thallium acetate is 12 mg/kg in humans.

In chronic poisonings, symptoms of incoordination, paralysis of extremities, hepatic and renal involvement, endocrine disorders, and psychoses may develop. Death may result from respiratory and cardiovascular collapse.

TREATMENT OF METAL POISONINGS

Assuming that poisoning by a particular metal is properly diagnosed, treatment by chelation therapy may be in order. Chelation is the formation of a complex between the metal and a charged or uncharged electron donor molecule known as a ligand. Specific ligands are used to treat a given metal poisoning.

The first clinically useful ligand was dimercaprol (2,3-dimercaptopropanol), or British Anti-Lewisite (BAL). This compound was developed during World War II to offset the toxicity of arsenic in Lewisite, an arsenic-containing war gas. Using arsenic's affinity for sulfhydryl groups, BAL's two sulfur atoms compete for arsenic with the body's sulfhydryl groups. The arsenic-BAL complex is excreted in the urine. Other chelation agents have been successfully used to treat other metal poisonings and diseases as well (e.g., transfusional iron overload in thalassemia or copper overload in Wilson's disease. These two diseases may require daily chelation therapy). Deferiprone (FDA approved in 2011), deferoxamine, and deferasirox are chelating agents used to treat thalassemia. Most recently, the need for decorporation (removal of internally deposited radionuclides from the body) has become more apparent following the Fukushima Daiichi nuclear event in Japan. Diethylnenetri-aminepentacetic acid is the only approved chelation agent for radioactive metals such as plutonium and uranium.

Table 2 lists some common chelating agents. In general, some caution is required when administering chelating agents; along with the target metal, essential metals may also be bound and removed from the body, requiring essential metal supplementation to correct the imbalance.

ANALYSIS OF METALS

The analysis of tissues for metal concentrations presents an interesting and challenging responsibility for the forensic toxicologist. Numerous techniques can be applied to metal determinations in biological tissues. By far the most commonly applied technique is graphite furnace atomic absorption spectrometry (GFAAS). Other methodologies certainly have been and are used with success, such as colorimetric procedures, inductively coupled plasma (ICP) combined with atomic emission spectroscopy, and ICP combined with mass spectrometry (ICP-MS). Several variations of each technique exist, but they are not prevalently used in forensic toxicology. The purpose of this section is to present a brief overview of methods used in metal analysis for each of the metals previously discussed.

Preanalytical Considerations

One of the main concerns of the forensic toxicologist is extraneous metal contamination of the sample. For example, there have been several instances where exhumations occur in order to collect tissue to be analyzed for possible metal poisoning. In these cases, analysis of the surrounding soil for the metal or metals of interest should be performed to exclude external contamination of the specimens. Furthermore, contamination during the analytical procedure must also be considered (specimen containers, reagents, glassware, etc.). Acid-washing containers in 10% nitric acid removes the metal contamination.

For specimens other than blood or urine, digestion of the sample by acid is required. Sometimes this requires boiling the tissue in acid and other times this can be accomplished by allowing the specimen to remain in contact with the acid overnight. The acid itself may contain excessive amounts of the metal being tested, and doubly distilled quality acid is frequently used.

Graphite Furnace Atomic Absorption Spectrometry

This technology was simplified by Massman in 1968 and is the basis of current commercial instrumentation. Other descriptors used to signify GFAAS include nonflame, flameless, electrothermal, and heated graphite furnace or atomizer AAS. The pyrolytically coated graphite tube is placed within an inert gas atmosphere, and 1 μL of sample is applied within the tube. The tube temperature is increased in a controlled fashion until atomization of the metal occurs. The absorption of the spectral line is measured by the electronics (which must be rapid); excellent

Table 2. Commonly Used Chelating Agents

Chelating Agent	Primary Target Metal
Deferoxamine, deferiprone, deferasirox	Iron
Dimercaprol (2,3-dimercaptopropanol or BAL)	Arsenic
Diethylnenetriaminepentacetic acid	Plutonium, uranium
Calcium disodium ethylenediaminetetraacetate (CaNa$_2$EDTA)	Lead
Dimercaptosuccinic acid (DMSA succimer)	Lead, arsenic, mercury
D-penicillamine	Mercury, lead

optics and background correction techniques are very necessary. This system is best automated, because pipetting μL amounts into the graphite furnace requires skill.

GFAAS supplies the sensitivity required for the analysis of metals in biological tissue, whereas the sister technique of flame AAS usually lacks the appropriate sensitivity. In addition, flame AAS is slow and only one metal can be determined at a time.

Inductively Coupled Plasma–Mass Spectrometry

This system is presently considered the state of the art in metal analysis because multiple metals can be simultaneously determined with the specificity of MS and the sensitivity of GFAAS. An inductively coupled plasma is configured to a quadrupole mass spectrometer in most instances, and the system also includes the vacuum system implicit in mass spectrometry. Other mass analyzers are also used in conjunction with ICP (e.g., magnetic sector and time-of-flight instruments).

ICP is a multielement technique that presents a large number of ionized atoms to the MS, which scans the mass range of interest. The cost of this technology has been reduced in recent years. Incorporating an MS into the ICP provides the sensitivity for biological samples that was lacking in ICP alone.

Neutron Activation Analysis (NAA)

This very sensitive and specific technique preserves the original specimen because sample destruction is unnecessary. Thermal neutrons bombard the specimen of interest, which induces radioactivity in some of the metal atoms; then the emitted radiation is measured. Thus qualitative and quantitative nondestructive analysis is possible. This nonroutine method requires a nuclear reactor, which is too large and too costly for most laboratories.

Individual Metal Determination

The uncomplicated Reinsch test methodology was developed by the German chemist Reinsch and is still used today in forensic toxicology. The Reinsch test is used as a qualitative screening test for an overdose of arsenic, antimony, bismuth, or mercury. This method involves boiling a small copper coil in an acidified solution. Arsenic (or antimony, bismuth, or mercury) replaces the copper on the coil as a dark film. This method lacks sensitivity but can usually determine an overdose. A positive test requires confirmation of the metal in question.

Arsenic can be quantitatively determined by colorimetry using the Gutzeit method or a modification thereof. It can also be determined electrochemically using anodic stripping voltammetry. When arsenic is determined using AAS, because of the metal's low volatility, arsenic is converted to arsine within a closed system, and the arsenic is then carried to the special hydrogen flame.

Mercury is another volatile metal for which the technique of cold vapor generation is needed. Typically, the specimen is digested with potassium permanganate and sulfuric acid overnight. Then the excess oxidizing agent is hydrolyzed by hydroxyl amine, and mercury is liberated with stannous chloride. The mercury vapor is measured in the flow cell.

Iron determinations are routinely included in chemistry profiles and are offered in most clinical laboratories. Some of the analyzers and commercial kits include the DuPont aca, Abbott TDx, Kodak Ektachem, etc.

Lithium is of sufficient concentration in therapeutic amounts to be measured by flame AAS, or flame emission using a flame photometer.

Thallium is generally determined with either flame or GFAAS. A colorimetric method was also developed using bromine water and sulfosalicylic acid.

Magnetic Resonance Imaging (MRI)

MRI has been used as a tool for monitoring excess iron in various organs and for monitoring the progress of chelation therapy.

Metal Speciation

Currently in metal analysis it is becoming important to determine each species of the metal in question rather than measure the total metal in a tissue. Speciation concerns the identification and quantitation of specific forms of an element. For example, as opposed to measuring total arsenic, one instead measures As(III), As(V), monomethylarsonic acid (MMA), and DMA. Similarly, one will measure Cr(III) and Cr(VI) or Hg(0), Hg(II), and methyl mercury instead of total chromium and mercury respectively. In many instances, a chemical method separates the species from one another, followed by instrumental analysis.

SUGGESTED READING

1. ACGIH. Documentation for the threshold limit values and biological exposure indices, 6th ed. Cincinnati, OH: American Conference of Governmental Industrial Hygienists, 1996.
2. ASTDR. Draft toxicological profile for aluminum, prepared by Research Triangle Institute, U.S. Department of Health and Human Services, Public Health Service. Atlanta, GA: Agency for Toxic Substances and Disease Registry, September 1997.
3. ASTDR. Draft toxicological profile for lead, prepared by Research Triangle Institute, U.S. Department of Health and Human Services, Public Health Service. Atlanta, GA: Agency for Toxic Substances and Disease Registry, September 1997.
4. ASTDR. Draft toxicological profile for mercury, prepared by Research Triangle Institute, U.S. Department of Health and Human Services, Public Health Service. Atlanta, GA: Agency for Toxic Substances and Disease Registry, September 1997.
5. Buchet J, Lauwerys R, Roels H. Urinary excretion of inorganic arsenic and its metabolites after repeated ingestion of sodium meta-arsenite by volunteers. Int Arch Occup Environ Health 1981;48:111–8.
6. Cade J. Lithium salts in the treatment of psychotic excitement. Med J Aust 1949;2:349–52.
7. Elinder C, Zenz C. Other metals and their compounds. In: Zenz C, ed., Occupational medicine, 3rd ed. St. Louis, MO: Mosby, 1994.
8. Jacobs J, Green H, Grendel B. Acute iron intoxication. N Engl J Med 1965;273:1124–7.
9. Klaassen C. Heavy metals and heavy-metal antagonists. In: Hardman T, Limbird L, eds. Goodman and Gillman's the pharmacological basis of therapeutics. New York, NY: McGraw-Hill, 1996.
10. Klaassen C. Nonmetallic environmental toxicants. In: Hardman T, Limbird L, eds. Goodman and Gillman's the pharmacological basis of therapeutics. New York, NY: McGraw-Hill, 1996.
11. Schroeder H, Balassa J. Abnormal trace metals in man: arsenic. J Chron Dis 1966;19:85–106.
12. Schutte N, Knight A, John O. Mercury and its compounds. In: Zenz C, ed. Occupational medicine, 3rd ed. St. Louis, MO: Mosby, 1994.
13. Stokinger H. The metals. In: Clayton G, Clayton F, eds. Patty's industrial hygiene and toxicology, 3rd rev. ed., vol. 2A. New York, NY: John Wiley & Sons, 1981.

PART IV

SPECIAL TOPICS

CHAPTER 30

Stability of Drugs of Abuse in Biological Specimens[*]

Barry Levine, Daniel S. Isenschmid, and Michael L. Smith

INTRODUCTION

Biological specimens are analyzed for drugs for many reasons. An analysis may be performed to indicate exposure to or use of a particular drug, to correlate the presence of a drug with physiological or behavioral effects, or to assist in the treatment of disease or other medical conditions. Analysis of postmortem specimens for drugs indicates whether drugs were responsible for or otherwise involved in the fatality.

Because toxicological tests are frequently performed a period of time after specimen acquisition, and because the results of these tests may be used in criminal or civil litigation, it is important that the test results accurately reflect the drug quantity present at the time of acquisition. Therefore, knowledge about the in vitro stability of drugs is important for the proper interpretation of test results. Much of this information has been provided in the individual chapters covering the analytes. This chapter will either summarize or expand these discussions.

BARBITURATES

Since barbiturates have been prescription drugs for approximately 100 years, a number of studies on the stability of these drugs in biological specimens have been published. Many of the earlier studies produced conflicting results on drug stability in blood and tissue specimens. However, recent studies suggest there are minimal changes in barbiturate concentrations in blood, plasma, or liver stored at room temperature or at 4 °C over a 2- to 3-month period. These small changes would not affect interpretation based on drug concentrations obtained at the time of collection or after a short period of storage.

BENZODIAZEPINES

Two functional groups appearing on the benzodiazepine backbone have been associated with in vitro instability. Chlordiazepoxide is an N-oxide compound and has been shown in numerous studies to be unstable in blood. One of the coauthors found that a blood chlordiazepoxide concentration of 5 mg/L rapidly disappeared when the blood was stored at room temperature; by day 8, no chlordiazepoxide was detected. Norchlordiazepoxide, the desmethyl metabolite of chlordiazepoxide, demonstrated similar instability. When the blood was stored at 4 °C, a substantial decrease was also observed, but the drug was still detectable after 2 months.

*Modified with permission from Levine B, Smith ML. Stability of drugs of abuse in biological fluids. In: Ropero-Miller JD, Goldberger BA, eds. Handbook of workplace drug testing, 2nd Ed. Washington, DC: AACC Press, 2009.

The presence of sodium fluoride and potassium oxalate did retard the degradation of chlordiazepoxide at room temperature to the extent that about 40% of the amount originally present was still detected after 2 months. Two breakdown products, demoxepam, and nordiazepam, were identified and accounted for some, but not all, of the lost drug.

Benzodiazepines with a nitro group, such as nitrazepam, flunitazepam, and clonazepam, also decrease in concentration during storage. These drugs are converted to their analogous amino compounds. Robertson and Drummer performed a comprehensive study on the stability of three nitrobenzodiazepines: clonazepam, nitrazepam, and flunitrazepam, and their respective amino metabolites in postmortem blood. Nitrazepam and clonazepam were stable in sterile, preserved fresh blood at 22 °C and at 4 °C over 28 days. Over the same time period, a 25% reduction in flunitrazepam was observed. In the absence of the preservative, 25–50% of the drugs were lost at 22 °C after 10 days. In nonsterile blood, all three drugs were converted to the corresponding amino compounds within 8 h at 22 °C. All three drugs were stable at –20 °C up to 2 years and for 10 months at 4 °C. Surprisingly, the amino compounds also demonstrated instability, with greater instability occurring at higher temperatures. At 22 °C, a 10–20% decrease was observed in nonpreserved blood over 45 h. At 4 °C, a 21% loss occurred after 1 month and at –20 °C, a 29% loss occurred after 2 months.

Benzodiazepines without the N-oxide or nitro groups appear to display greater stability in biological specimens. Drugs that have been studied in blood include diazepam, flurazepam, N-1 desalkylflurazepam, and temazepam. In general, these drugs have shown decreases less than 25% in blood stored at room or refrigerated temperatures over a period of several months.

CANNABINOIDS

Whole blood and plasma delta-9 tetrahydrocannabinol (THC), 11-hydroxy THC (11-OH-THC), 11-nor-delta-9 THC-9 carboxylic acid (THCCOOH), cannabidiol, cannabinol, and THC-glucuronide concentrations are stable after 4 weeks at –20 °C and 4 °C, and for at least 1 week at room temperature. THCCOOH-glucuronide was stable for 4 weeks at –20 °C, unstable at 4 °C over 4 weeks (mean whole blood decrease >–20 %; mean plasma >–66%), and very unstable at room temperature, losing more than –40% over a week for whole blood. When plasma is stored for longer periods, THC and THCCOOH concentrations can decrease, with THC showing more loss than its metabolite. One study found that THC and THCCOOH plasma concentrations stored at –20 °C decreased more than 15% by 1 year. THC and 11-OH-THC concentrations in blood at room temperature were stable for 1 month, had decreased significantly after 2 months, and at 6 months decreased 90% and 44%, respectively. Blood total THCCOOH concentrations had not changed significantly after 6 months at room temperature.

Both THC and THCCOOH have been examined in oral fluid. Earlier collection devices had problems with both analytes binding to the containers during storage, causing large decreases in concentration. This occurs due to the hydrophobic nature of THC and THCCOOH and the low concentration (pg/mL) of THCCOOH in oral fluid. Many manufacturers have designed current collection devices with buffers that minimize this loss. One study found that cannabinoids in oral fluid collected with a Quantisal™ device were much more stable than when expectorated. THC, THCCOOH, cannabidiol, and cannabinol concentrations in Quantisal™ devices were stable (i.e., within ± 20% of initial concentration) for 1 week at 4 °C. After 4 weeks at 4 °C, 4 weeks at –20 °C, and 24 weeks at –20 °C, THC was stable in 90%, 80%, and 80% of Quantisal™ samples, respectively. THCCOOH was stable in 89%, 40%, and 50% of the samples. Cannabidiol and cannabinol concentrations decreased more than 20% in over 56% of samples after 24 weeks at –20 °C.

THCCOOH concentrations are reasonably stable in urine when the method of analysis hydrolyzes the glucuronide. THCCOOH-glucuronide is stable at −20 °C for up to 10 days but at higher temperatures and longer periods of storage breaks down to form THCCOOH. When urine specimens are stored for longer periods, total THCCOOH concentration may decrease even at −20 °C in selected specimens. A number of reasons for this loss have been proposed: adsorption to the container or to solid matter, concentration of this amphipathic molecule in the foam created during mixing, or urine pH. The extent of the degradation is variable. In one study, 85 urine specimens positive for THCCOOH that were stored frozen for up to 1 year following the initial analysis were retested. The average decrease in concentration of the retested specimens was 24%. A normal bell-shaped distribution was observed, with a range of concentration changes between 30% and −80%.

COCAINE

The ester linkage on the cocaine molecule makes the drug susceptible to chemical and enzymatic hydrolysis. In fact, the two major metabolites of cocaine, benzoylecgonine (BE) and ecgonine methyl ester (EME), are hydrolytic products of cocaine. Conversion to BE occurs chemically, especially under alkaline conditions and enzymatically by a liver methyltransferase; conversion to EME occurs enzymatically by pseudocholinesterase in the plasma and by a benzoylesterase in the liver.

In unpreserved blood, in vitro stability studies have shown that cocaine is hydrolyzed almost exclusively at the phenyl ester by plasma pseudocholinesterase to yield EME. The addition of sodium fluoride, while inhibiting enzymatic hydrolysis of cocaine to EME, does not prevent spontaneous chemical hydrolysis of cocaine to BE. The rates of hydrolysis of both esters have been shown to be temperature- and pH-dependent, with higher temperatures and pH increasing the rate of hydrolysis. The loss of cocaine in unpreserved blood can be dramatic. In antemortem blood fortified with cocaine at 2000 ng/mL, cocaine concentrations decreased to 640 ng/mL after storage at room temperature for 24 h, with corresponding increases in EME concentrations. Even after the addition of 2% sodium fluoride, a 25% decrease in cocaine concentrations was observed at room and refrigerated temperatures within 5 and 80 days, respectively, with corresponding increases in BE concentrations. A small amount of EME also formed, indicating that the action of 2% sodium fluoride was not obsolete. Acidifying blood to pH 5 to inhibit chemical hydrolysis in conjunction with adding 2% sodium fluoride to inhibit enzymatic hydrolysis produced no cocaine loss after 200 days at refrigerated (4 °C) and frozen (−15 °C) temperatures and for at least 60 days at room temperature.

Both BE and EME have ester moieties and are also subject to temperature- and pH-dependent hydrolysis. BE is considerably more stable than EME in unpreserved blood (pH 7.4) at room temperature. A 50% loss of EME occurred over a 35-day period, compared with a 25% loss for BE. Little loss of either compound was observed when the blood sample was refrigerated for the same period of time.

In another study, the stability of cocaine, BE, EME, and ecgonine in blood preserved with 0.25% potassium fluoride at 4 °C and 20 °C over a 15-day period was examined. At 4 °C and 20 °C, BE and EME could be detected from cocaine 1 day after storage. Ecgonine was detectable after 2 days of storage. At 4 °C, approximately 25% of the initial cocaine concentration was still detected at day 14. The relative amount of hydrolytic products was EME > BE > ecgonine. At 20 °C, no cocaine was detected by the end of the study. BE and EME concentrations increased, but decreased after 6 and 7 days of storage, respectively. The concentration of ecgonine increased steadily. Ecgonine was stable at 4 °C and at 20 °C over the 2-week period. At 4 °C, BE was converted to ecgonine by day 3 and the concentration of ecgonine was less than 10% of the initial BE concentration. At 20 °C, about 40% of the initial BE concentration had been converted to ecgonine by day 14. At 4 °C, the EME concentration decreased by about 90% by day 14, while at 20 °C, no EME was detected by the end of the observation period. The conversion of cocaine to BE, EME, and ecgonine appeared to be stoichiometric at all time intervals at both storage temperatures.

Cocaethylene or ethylcocaine is produced in vivo following the simultaneous ingestion of alcohol and cocaine. Cocaethylene was found to break down more slowly in the blood than cocaine. About 25% of cocaethylene was still detected in blood by the third day when stored at 20–25 °C. Conversely, no cocaine was detected after the first day.

Stability studies have indicated that some hydrolysis of cocaine to EME is expected during the postmortem period, with the rate of hydrolysis decreasing as the pH of the blood sample falls. Cocaine fortified into decomposed human blood and tissues (pH 4.2–5.2) has been shown to be stable when the sample is stored at 20–37 °C for 24 h. In a study of juvenile swine, cocaine and metabolite concentrations were relatively stable in serial blood samples that had been collected from animals and allowed to decompose for 3 weeks in cool weather. The results are less predictable in humans, however. Properly collected and preserved heart and peripheral blood samples that were obtained at the scenes of suspected cocaine deaths (t_1) and at autopsy (t_2) were analyzed for cocaine, BE, and ethylcocaine. There was no consistent pattern in the magnitude or direction of change in concentration for any of the analytes with respect to the time of collection, suggesting that competing processes of hydrolysis and tissue release of the drug were occurring. The study showed a net decrease in cocaine concentrations and a net increase in BE concentrations in samples between t_1 and t_2, but the decrease in the cocaine concentration was not statistically significant and was not necessarily accompanied by increases in the BE concentration. The mean concentration of cocaine in the ventricular blood was

higher than in the femoral blood at both t_1 and t_2, but the mean differences were not statistically significant. The lack of predictability in postmortem cocaine and metabolite concentrations after death calls their usefulness into question, especially given that therapeutic, toxic, and fatal cocaine concentrations overlap.

The stability of BE in urine specimens can have significant forensic implications. Any urine testing positive under the U.S. Department of Health and Human Services guidelines must be frozen for at least 1 year. During that year, the specimen is eligible for retesting upon request. In one study of 61 retested urine specimens containing BE, an average decrease of 19% was measured. However, distribution of the percentage of change suggested a bimodal distribution, with one distribution around 10% and a second distribution around 80%. No explanation for these changes was provided. However, it has also been shown that decreases in BE concentrations can occur at neutral or alkaline pH and at room temperature. The growth of microorganisms may also be a factor.

Like BE, EME in urine has been shown to be susceptible to alkaline hydrolysis. At pH 3 to pH 5, EME is stable for up to 3 years, but at pH 9 no EME remained after 30 days of storage at 4–5 °C. Very rapid hydrolysis of EME occurs in buffers at higher pHs, but these nonphysiological conditions are not likely to be found. EME in postmortem urine is stable for at least 6 months under frozen (–20 °C) and refrigerated (4 °C) conditions. Other factors, such as microbial growth or in vitro adulteration with alkaline materials such as bleach, also affect the stability of cocaine and its metabolites in urine.

To summarize, the instability of cocaine in untreated blood or plasma is well documented. Loss of cocaine can be minimized by adding pseudocholinesterase inhibitor immediately after collection, reducing the pH to 5, and storing the sample frozen. The stability of cocaine in urine is pH dependent, similar to cocaine stability observed in aqueous solutions. BE exhibits greater stability in blood and urine, but decreases over time have been observed. EME also displays greater stability in urine, especially at neutral or slightly acidic pH.

ETHANOL

Undoubtedly, the drug most frequently studied for in vitro stability in biological specimens is ethanol. Studies have been performed using specimens from living individuals and from autopsy cases. Both increases and decreases in ethanol concentration during storage have been reported. Mechanisms of ethanol loss include evaporation, chemical oxidation to acetaldehyde, and microbial consumption. The most common source of in vitro ethanol production is microbial conversion of glucose, fatty acids, or amino acids to ethanol.

The vast majority of studies performed on ethanol stability have been on blood specimens. Autopsy specimens have been used to monitor ethanol production at room temperature. In an early study from the 1960s, 50 autopsy blood specimens were collected and stored with and without preservatives. In 34 cases, there was no significant production of ethanol after 10 days; the remaining 16 specimens showed significant ethanol production. The average increase in ethanol concentration after 2–3 days was 0.030 ± 0.028 g/dL, but the average increase after 6–10 days was 0.048 ± 0.036 g/dL. The maximum increase over 10 days was 0.13 g/dL. The presence of 1% sodium fluoride prevented in vitro ethanol formation after 10 days. In contrast, 0.1% mercuric chloride failed to prevent ethanol formation, and 1% mercuric chloride in many specimens produced a solid that precluded ethanol analysis. A subsequent study reported seven cases in which storage of the blood at room temperature produced increases greater than 0.05 g/dL. A maximum blood concentration of 0.14 g/dL was measured after 7 days in blood that initially contained no ethanol.

To ascertain whether ethanol measured in postmortem specimens is present due to alcohol consumption prior to death or due

to postmortem ethanol formation, vitreous humor is often measured for alcohol in conjunction with postmortem blood. Vitreous humor, because of its isolated location, is more resistant to the decomposition process than are other fluids and tissues in the body. One study looked at the change in alcohol concentrations in 32 paired postmortem blood and vitreous humor specimens. The blood was collected and stored in 50-mL polypropylene tubes containing sodium fluoride and potassium oxalate. The vitreous humor specimens were stored in 10-mL Vacutainer® tubes containing 25 mg of potassium oxalate and 25 mg of sodium fluoride. The specimens were stored under refrigeration and reanalyzed 5–6 years later. Decreases in ethanol concentration in both blood and vitreous humor specimens were observed. The average loss of ethanol in the blood was 0.06 g/dL, a 35% loss. The average loss of ethanol in the vitreous humor was 0.01 g/dL, a 6.1% loss. The study concluded that vitreous humor may be a more reliable specimen for reanalysis of ethanol after prolonged refrigeration.

In addition to postmortem blood ethanol analysis, testing of suspected intoxicated drivers is also commonly performed. In these cases, the integrity of the blood sample tested can be critical for successful prosecution. It is standard to collect these samples in gray top tubes that contain a preservative, sodium fluoride, and the anticoagulant potassium oxalate. Many studies have been published discussing the stability of ethanol in these samples. The general consensus is that blood collected under standard conditions into fluoride/oxalate tubes will be stable for weeks, even at room temperature. Moreover, any changes that occur in alcohol concentrations are likely to be decreases as opposed to increases.

Ethanol demonstrates greater stability in urine specimens than in blood specimens. Several studies have demonstrated that ethanol production is unlikely even when the specimens are stored at room temperature. However, under the right conditions, in vitro production of ethanol in some urine specimens can occur. In one study, 14 random urine specimens testing negative for ethanol and containing variable amounts of glucose were stored at room temperature for up to 3 weeks; of those, 5 specimens produced ethanol at concentrations ranging from 0.036–2.327 g/dL. In each case, yeast was identified in the urine specimen. Conversely, in the 6 glucose-positive specimens in which no yeast was found, no in vitro production of ethanol was observed. Ethanol production in the presence of yeast and glucose can be prevented by refrigeration or by the addition of sodium fluoride at a strength of 1% or 2% (w/v).

A large amount of literature data exists indicating that under certain storage conditions, ethanol can be produced in blood in vitro. These conditions include higher temperatures, contamination with certain microorganisms, and the absence of chemical preservatives. When blood is preserved with fluoride, the ethanol concentration remains essentially unchanged for short periods of time, regardless of the storage temperature. Long-term storage of fluoridated blood samples will usually cause decreases in ethanol concentration. Ethanol is less likely to be produced in urine specimens, except in the rare instance of high glucose concentrations and the presence of certain microorganisms. Changes in ethanol concentration in biological fluids can be minimized if the specimens are preserved with sodium fluoride and stored at as low a temperature as possible.

HEROIN AND METABOLITES

The in vitro instability of heroin in blood or plasma has been well documented; it is rapidly deacetylated to 6-acetylmorphine. However, 6-acetylmorphine and morphine display greater stability in blood and plasma. In one study, morphine was added to blood that was then stored at room temperature, refrigerated, or frozen. Aliquots of blood at each temperature were removed at 2, 4, 6, and 8 weeks and at 3, 6, 9, and 12 months. Under all conditions and times tested, more than 80% of the morphine initially present was measured. Morphine has also been shown

to be stable in postmortem blood, liver, and urine specimens over a 10-day period at temperatures ranging from 4 °C to 37 °C.

The stability of morphine-3-glucuronide (M3G) has also been examined. In general, M3G was not converted to free morphine in blood and urine specimens stored from 4 °C to 37 °C over a 10-day period. M3G was hydrolyzed completely to free morphine in liver specimens stored at 18 °C and 37 °C over 10 days, but was stable at 4 °C over the same time period.

PHENCYCLIDINE (PCP)

PCP is stable in blood and urine specimens. In one study of 41 blood specimens obtained from arrested individuals, the specimens were stored at room temperature for up to 18 months after an initial quantitation. In 30 of the 41 specimens, the difference between the original and the subsequent analysis was less than 10%; in the remaining specimens, the difference was ≤30%. The regression line correlating the original blood concentration and the reanalyzed blood concentrations had a slope of 1.00. Most of the observed differences were attributed to variations in the method. Other studies have demonstrated similar results with PCP in blood specimens for periods up to 5 years when the blood was stored in a refrigerator or freezer.

SELECTED READINGS

1. Al-Hadidi KA, Oliver JS. Stability of buprenorphine and morphine in whole blood stored at different conditions. In: Mueller RK, ed., Contribution to forensic toxicology. Leipzig: Molina Press, 1994:255.
2. Al-Hadidi KA, Oliver JS. Stability of temazepam in blood. Sci Justice 1995;35:105–8.
3. Barrett DA, Dyssegaard P, Shaw, PN. The effect of temperature and pH on the deacetylation of diamorphine in aqueous solution and in human plasma. J Pharm Pharmacol 1992;44:606–8.
4. Carroll FT, Marraccini JV, Lewis S, Wright W. Morphine-3-D-glucuronide stability in

postmortem specimens exposed to bacterial enzymatic hydrolysis. Am J Forensic Med Pathol 2000;21:323–9.

5. Christopoulos G, Kirsh ER, Gearien JE. Determination of ethanol in fresh and putrefied postmortem tissues. J Chromatogr 1073;87:454–72.

6. Clardy DO, Ragle JL. Stability of phencyclidine in stored blood. Clin Toxicol 1981; 18:929–34.

7. Isenschmid DS, Levine B, Caplan YH. A comprehensive study of the stability of cocaine and its metabolites. J Anal Toxical 1989;13:250–6.

8. Johnson JR, Jennison TA, Peat MA, Foltz RL. Stability of delta-9-tetrahydrocannabinol (THC), 11-hydroxy-THC and 11-nor-9-carboxy-THC in blood and plasma. J Anal Toxicol 1984;8:202–4.

9. Jones AW, Hylen L, Svensson E, Helander A. Storage of specimens at 4°C or addition of sodium fluoride (1%) prevents formation of ethanol in urine inoculated with *Candida albicans*. J Anal Toxicol 1999;23:333–6.

10. Lee D, Milman G, Schwope DM, Barnes AJ, Gorelick DA, Huestis MA. Cannabinoid stability in authentic oral fluid after controlled cannabis smoking. Clin Chem 2012;58:1101–9.

11. Levine B, Blanke RV, Valentour JC. Postmortem stability of barbiturates in blood and tissues. J Forensic Sci 1984;29:131–8.

12. Levine B, Blanke RV, Valentour JC. Postmortem stability of benzodiazepines in blood and tissues. J Forensic Sci 1983;28:102–15.

13. Levine B, Ramcharitat V, Smialek JE. Stability of ecgonine methyl ester in postmortem urine specimens. J Forensic Sci 1996;41: 126–8.

14. Melo P, Lourdes Bastos M, Teixeira HM. Benzodiazepine stability in postmortem samples stored at different temperatures. J Anal Toxicol 2012;36:52–60.

15. Moody DE, Monti KM, Spanbauer AC. Long-term stability of abused drugs and antiabuse chemotherapeutical agents stored at -20 degrees C. J Anal Toxicol 1999;23:535–40.

16. Moriya F, Hashimoto Y. Distribution of free and conjugated morphine in body fluids and tissues in a fatal heroin overdose: is conjugated morphine stable in postmortem specimens? J Forensic Sci 1997;42:736–40.

17. Olsen T, Hearn WL. Stability of ethanol in postmortem blood and vitreous humor in long-term refrigerated storage. J Anal Toxicol 2003;27:517–9.

18. Plueckhahn VD, Ballard B. Factors influencing the significance of alcohol concentrations in autopsy blood samples. Med J Australia 1968;1:939–43.

19. Plueckhahn VD. The significance of alcohol and sugar determinations in autopsy blood. Med J Australia 1970;1:46–51.

20. Robertson MD, Drummer OH. Stability of nitrobenzodiazepines in postmortem blood. J Forensic Sci 1998;43:5–8.

21. Romberg RW, Past MR. Reanalysis of forensic urine specimens containing benzoylecgonine and THC-COOH. J Forensic Sci 1994;39:479–85.

22. Saady JJ, Poklis A, Dalton HP. Production of urinary ethanol after sample collection. J Forensic Sci 1993;38:1467–71.

23. Schwope DM, Karschner EL, Scheidweiler KB, Gorelick DA, Huestis MA. In vitro stability of cannabinoids and cannabinoid glucuronides in authentic whole blood and plasma specimens following controlled smoked cannabis. Joint Meeting of the Society of Forensic Toxicologists & The International Association of Forensic Toxicologists, San Francisco, Abstract O 75, 25–30. Sep 2011.

24. Skopp G, Klingsmann A, Potsch L, Mattern R. In vitro stability of cocaine in whole blood and plasma including ecgonine as a target analyte. Ther Drug Monit 2001;23:174–81.

25. Skopp G, Potsch L. An investigation of the stability of free and glucuronidated 11-nor-Δ9-tetrahydrocannabinol-9-carboxylic acid in authentic urine samples. J Anal Toxicol 2004;28:35–40.

26. Skopp G, Potsch L. Stability of 11-nor-Δ9-tetrahydrocannabinol glucuronide in plasma and urine assessed by liquid chromatography-tandem mass spectrometry. Clin Chem 2002;48:301–6.

27. Skopp G, Potsch L, Mauden M, Richter B. Partition coefficient, blood to plasma ratio, protein binding and short-term stability of 11-nor-Δ9-carboxy tetrahydrocannabinol glucuronide. Forensic Sci Int 2002;126:17–23.

28. Stevens HM. The stability of some drugs and poisons in putrefying human liver tissues. J Forensic Sci Soc 1984;24:577–89.

29. Vasiliades J. Long-term stability of ecgonine methyl ester in urine. J Anal Toxicol 1993;17:253.

30. Winek CL, Paul L. Effect of short-term storage conditions on alcohol concentrations in blood from living human subjects. Clin Chem 1983;29:1959–60.

CHAPTER 31

Postmortem Redistribution of Drugs

Fred S. Apple

INTRODUCTION

The topic of postmortem redistribution (PMR) has been reviewed extensively over the past several years. Several investigators have described multiple mechanisms that can be responsible for the release of tissue-bound drugs from anatomic sites of high drug concentration to sites of lower concentration (concentration gradient), creating an artificially increased blood/fluid concentration postmortem that differs from the blood concentration that would have been present at the time of an individual's death. Therefore, for drugs or classes of drugs that have been described in the literature that demonstrate increases in blood concentrations over a postmortem (PM) interval, the degree of certainty and confidence that the autopsy (which can be hours to days after death) plasma/serum/blood concentration of a drug reflects the drug concentration at the time of death diminishes.

PMR of drugs can be defined as the physiologic process of drug release and/or mixing of drugs from one compartment (organ tissues) into another compartment (blood fluid) after death. For the past 30 years, practicing forensic toxicologists have encountered death investigation cases in which postmortem blood concentrations are inconsistent with the case history of drug or medication use. Specifically, drug concentrations were found to be substantially greater than anticipated in a decedent's blood in which the cause of death was clearly unrelated to the drug. Pharmacokinetic calculations of expected steady state concentrations by the toxicologist, based on dosing records and witnessed medication use, were found to show 5-fold to 10-fold lower concentrations than the measured PM blood level in the blood obtained at autopsy. These disparities were initially recognized in the 1970s, which led to early observational studies of site-to-site variations of drug concentrations measured at autopsy. Fig. 1 shows the findings for a representative medical examiner case involving a cancer-related death in which the patient was treated for depression with the antidepressant medication desipramine. The figure demonstrates: a) a large variation in desipramine concentrations over time between two subclavian blood specimens (10 h vs 30 h); b) a large variation in desipramine concentration by anatomic location at the same time (10 h between subclavian and heart ventricle blood); and c) variations between atrial and vitreous humor concentrations.

This chapter will address the interpretation of PM drug concentrations by forensic toxicologists and pathologists in assigning the cause of death (COD) and manner of death (MOD). Specifically, the chapter will review the following: clarification of the definition of PMR; physiologic processes that occur after death that result in PMR; drug characteristics that have been identified to suggest PMR; literature review of drugs that have been shown to result in PMR; and the role of the toxicologist in providing evidence-based literature findings to the forensic pathologist to assist in COD and MOD determinations.

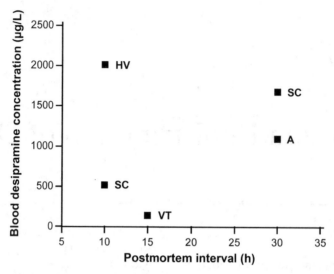

Fig. 1. Findings of tricyclic antidepressant–suspected toxicity case demonstrating serum desipramine concentrations collected at different times from varying anatomic sites. HV = heart ventricle; SC = subclavian; VT = vitreous humor; A = atrial.

DEFINITION OF PMR

The scientific fact is that PMR occurs both in central (heart) blood as well as in peripheral (femoral) blood. One misconception associated with PMR is based on the assumption that a PM heart blood to peripheral blood ratio greater than 1.0 is defined as PMR, and that the greater the heart blood to peripheral blood ratio, the greater the PMR. In reality, this ratio represents an anatomic site-to-site difference and may or may not be related to PMR. Whether the blood concentration of a drug observed at autopsy is the steady state concentration following stable, therapeutic dosing or it represents an acute toxic drug exposure resulting in death that has not distributed throughout the body will have a substantial impact on the PM heart blood to peripheral blood ratio. What has been reported frequently is that central (heart) blood is more prone to PMR compared to peripheral blood and is related to the diffusion of drugs from the stomach, liver, lungs, and heart tissues; these tissues often contain 2- to 10-fold greater drug concentrations (mg/kg of tissue) than that found in blood. However, one cannot rule out that skeletal muscle tissues are prone to drug release back into the blood. At best, all one can accurately state is that there is an anatomic site location difference between heart blood and peripheral blood drug concentration, which may or may not be an accurate representation of PMR in either location.

It is not easy to design a scientific experiment to study PMR. Ideally, blood would be drawn serially from a vessel over time without disruption of the body. Whether a blood vessel would need to be ligated or clamped is not clear. Blood drawn from a blood vessel after death may be contaminated with fluids released from surrounding tissue. Although not hampered by the sound, analytical techniques toxicologists use to quantitate drug concentrations (i.e., mass spectrometry), the inexact science of postmortem toxicology is affected by many known and unknown effects that occur postmortem. Care must be taken by scientists reporting findings in the peer-reviewed and non-peer-reviewed literature that better represent whether site-to-site differences in drug concentrations are found or if serial samples from the same blood vessel were obtained that better indicate the occurrence of PMR.

PM PHYSIOLOGICAL PROCESSES CAUSING PMR

Numerous articles have reviewed the processes that occur in the body, from the time of death to the time blood is drawn at autopsy, that cause a redistribution of drugs from an area of high concentration (e.g., tissues) to an area of low concentration (e.g., blood). PMR can result in an inaccurate representation of a blood concentration at the time of death compared to the higher blood concentration found at autopsy. The impact of PMR is that a falsely high blood concentration can lead to an inappropriate COD determination by forensic pathologists.

The general thought process has been that since PMR occurs less frequently in peripheral blood compared to heart blood, that peripheral blood drug concentrations are a reliable indication of a drug concentration at the time of death. Using fentanyl as a representative case example, the biochemical and physical mechanisms responsible for increasing fentanyl concentrations in femoral/peripheral and heart blood over the postmortem interval are complex and likely vary from case to case. Fentanyl is a lipophilic drug that is highly bound to proteins at physiological pH (7.4). A broad tissue uptake of fentanyl creates a large steady state volume of distribution. Fentanyl distribution can be described to occur in a three-compartment model: a) the circulatory system (blood) plus vessel-rich highly perfused tissue (liver, lung, heart) compartment; b) peripheral compartment comprised of skeletal muscle; and c) peripheral compartment comprised of adipose (fat) tissue. High partitioning of fentanyl into skeletal muscle occurs rapidly, with tissue concentrations 4- to 10-fold higher than in plasma. There is also a high tissue to blood concentration gradient for liver (3- to 35-fold) and heart (2- to 5.3-fold). Small decreases in plasma pH that can occur within minutes after death result in substantial decreases in protein binding of fentanyl. At death there is a decrease in plasma pH, from the physiological pH of 7.4 in the living to as low as 5.6 within 24 h postmortem. The pH decrease results in an increased permeability of tissue cell membranes, which results in a shift of drug concentrations to move along a concentration gradient (from the high tissue levels to the lower plasma levels). Postmortem fentanyl concentrations, both in the peripheral and central (heart) blood, may not remain static. Whether heart or peripheral blood is collected, it is more likely a reflection not of the blood concentration at the time of death but rather a combination of tissue-bound drug that has been released into the blood/fluid that is drawn at autopsy hours after death. Peripheral blood, such as femoral blood, is also subject to PMR influences from local tissues, skeletal muscle, and fat. Fig. 2 shows the dynamic changes that can occur in fentanyl-related death investigations. In four of the seven cases, significant increases in PB fentanyl concentrations were observed over the PM interval between blood draws.

Assessing the role of drugs in "marginally toxic" cases involves an understanding of the timing of collection, method of collection, and site of sample collection, all of which may influence the interpretation of toxicological analysis. Leading up to and following death, several physiological processes occur that lead to cell death and disintegration of cell structure and integrity. This results in release of cellular contents into surrounding blood/fluids as noted earlier. Cellular aerobic metabolism decreases and stops, energy (ATP) productivity declines, and anaerobic metabolism begins. This leads to an intracellular decrease in pH, predominantly due to lactic acid accumulation. Progressive cellular alterations occur that result in degradation of cellular integrity, with leakage of cellular contents into the extracellular space, including protein-bound drugs. Irreversible cell damage has been observed within 30 to 60 min after ischemia. The rate and extent of the movement of drugs PM varies unpredictably and can be influenced by several factors. These include the nature of the drug and the time interval between death and PM specimen collection. Typically lipophilic basic drugs concentrate in solid tissues such as liver, lung, and heart

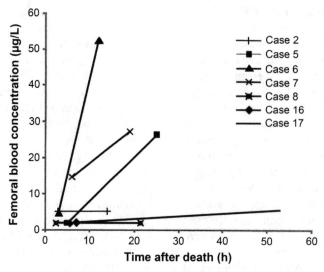

Fig. 2. Findings of postmortem redistribution of peripheral blood fentanyl concentrations in seven cases with specimens collected over two postmortem times (from Olson 2010).

muscle. These drug-enriched tissues would therefore provide a concentration gradient for passive diffusion after death, resulting in PMR. Furthermore, as cells are largely aqueous and become increasingly acidic after death, basic drugs will be more ionized in a lower pH environment, and after cell membrane lysis, basic drugs will tend to redistribute more readily.

Changes that occur in the body after death also have been attributed to the position of the body after death and subsequent movement of the body from the site of death to the site of autopsy; both may have an effect on PMR. In addition, purification of the body can also contribute to changes in blood drug concentrations after death.

DRUG CHARACTERISTICS SUGGESTING POTENTIAL PMR

Individual drug characteristics will determine the extent to which a drug undergoes PMR. The drug distribution involves the delivery of the drug by way of the circulation to the rest of the body and involves passage of the drug through cell membranes. This depends on binding of the drug to plasma protein and tissue receptors as well as drug polarity or ionization. The rate of distribution depends on the rate of tissue perfusion. For drugs that permeate membranes readily, their distribution will be perfusion limited. For example, perfusion rates can vary 500-fold between the lung (higher) compared to resting skeletal muscle or fat. The volume of distribution (V_d) measures a drug's ability to distribute throughout the body. Drug distribution is affected by protein binding since only drugs that are not bound to plasma proteins are free to cross all membranes. Other factors include lipid solubility, pK_a, tissue affinity, and energy dependant transport processes across membranes.

DRUGS DISPLAYING PMR

When a forensic pathologist or toxicologist attempts to estimate the amount of drug present at the time of death or the number of tablets consumed, the assumption is often made that the drug concentration found PM is a reliable estimate of that present at the time of death. We have learned from the evidence-based literature for many drugs that the pharmacokinetic concept that a concentration (C) equals the dose (D) of a drug divided by the volume of distribution (V_d)

does not often pertain to PM toxicology. Pounder once described PMR as a "toxicological nightmare." Examination of the postmortem to antemortem drug concentration ratio has been studied to provide information pertaining to PMR. In one study Cook examined seven drugs in peripheral blood obtained antemortem and postmortem. The PM to antemortem ratio was found to be unreliable in estimating antemortem concentrations from postmortem levels. The conclusion was that PMR is an important contributor to the substantial differences found at autopsy, with increased concentration found over the time period after death. According to Cook, PMR of drugs occurs due to drug release from the gastrointestinal tract, lungs, liver, heart, body, and skeletal muscle. Cook noted that drugs are sequestered in organs during life and act as drug reservoirs. After death, they are redistributed to the surrounding tissues and blood fluids. Table 1 proposes queries that both forensic pathologists and toxicologists should consider when interpreting drug concentrations measured in blood obtained postmortem.

As shown in Table 2, there are numerous case reports and series of cases reported for drugs that clearly demonstrate that PMR does occur in peripheral and heart blood. The following drugs have been identified as being affected by PMR: citalopram, desethylamiodarone, detropropoxyphene, digoxin, dothiepin, fentanyl, flecanide, haloperidol, MDMA/MDA, propoxyphene, quetiapene,

sotalol, tetrahydrocannabinol, thioridizine, and tricyclic antidepressants.

ROLE OF TOXICOLOGIST

PMR needs to be carefully considered in COD determinations when interpretation of PM drug concentrations is backed by literature in support of PMR. The information known by the toxicologist must be fully disclosed to forensic pathology partners to allow them to make educated COD and MOD decisions. This is especially true in death cases in which blood concentrations may be erroneously interpreted as the COD based on the assumption that the peripheral PM blood concentration is an accurate record of the perimortem blood concentration at the time of death. To assist the forensic toxicologist in interpretation of these difficult cases, some laboratories have moved to measuring PM tissue concentrations, primarily liver, that are minimally affected by PMR. For example, the history of tricyclic antidepressant (TCA) monitoring of liver concentrations, differentiating between toxic/fatal and therapeutic ingestions, has been established since 1970. Studies in postmortem cases have reported that liver TCA concentrations (total of parent drug and active metabolite) <15 mg/kg were not indicative of toxicity, while concentrations reported as >30 mg/kg were considered indicative of toxicity. A ratio of parent drug to metabolite concentration greater

---

Table 1. Questions That Should Be Asked When Interpreting Drug Concentrations Measured in Blood Obtained Postmortem

1. What blood vessel and anatomic location was the specimen drawn from?
2. If peripheral blood was obtained, was the vein ligated or clamped prior to sampling?
3. Was the blood obtained after drawing into a single tube mixed before aliquoting into multiple tubes?
4. If blood was drawn from more than one anatomic site (i.e., heart and femoral), how does one interpret differences in blood levels found between sites?
5. What was the PM interval before blood was drawn?
6. How was the body handled and stored between the time of death and blood/tissue collection?
7. Were tissue specimens (i.e., liver) obtained?
8. Was there evidence of decomposition?
9. Is there antemortem or perimortem blood available for analysis?
10. Has the literature been thoroughly reviewed to determine whether studies document PMR for the drug of interest?

Table 2. Published Studies of Drugs Demonstrating Postmortem Redistribution

Drug	Blood Source
Citalopram	Heart
Desethylamiodarone	Heart, peripheral
Detropropoxyphene	Peripheral
Digoxin	Heart, peripheral
Dothiepin	Peripheral
Fentanyl	Heart, peripheral
Flecainide	Heart
Haloperidol	Heart
MDMA/MDA	Heart, peripheral
Propoxyphene	Heart, peripheral
Quetiapine	Heart, peripheral
Sotalol	Heart, peripheral
Tetrahydrocannabinol	Heart, peripheral
Thioridizine	Heart
Tricyclic antidepressants	Heart, peripheral

than 1.0 was indicative of a recent or acute exposure to a TCA. Recently several investigators have proposed and utilized in forensic practice the measurement of fentanyl liver concentrations to differentiate therapeutic from toxic or fatal fentanyl concentrations where blood concentrations were deemed unreliable. Liver concentrations <31 µg/kg have been shown to be therapeutic or nontoxic, while concentrations >69 µg/kg were potentially toxic and fatal. Studies need to be performed to better address how and from where blood should be drawn for all drugs potentially prone to PMR. Moreover, PM blood concentrations from multiple sites should be tabulated in cases where the cause of death was not drug related, so as to develop "postmortem therapeutic" ranges for drugs. Furthermore, larger databases are needed to best optimize liver tissue cutoff concentrations. Just as important are studies that have already shown that drugs, such as cocaine and morphine, are not significantly prone to PMR; this means that either central or peripheral blood are acceptable samples for postmortem quantitation and interpretation for COD assistance.

Summarizing, the overriding goal is to provide quality and dependable forensic toxicology results that can be reliably used for interpretation by all forensic scientists and pathologists. A better understanding of PMR of drugs can go a long way in improving the field of forensic toxicology and assisting in the appropriate determination of cause of death investigations.

SUGGESTED READING

1. Anderson DT, Muto JJ. Duragesic transdermal patch: postmortem tissue distribution of fentanyl in 25 cases. J Anal Toxicol 2000;24:627–34.
2. Andresen H, Gullans A, Veselinovic M, Anders S, Schmoldt A, Iwersen-Bergmann S, Mueller A. Fentanyl: toxic or therapeutic? Postmortem and antemortem blood concentrations after transdermal fentanyl application. J Anal Toxicol 2012;36:182–94.
3. Apple FS. A better understanding of interpretation of postmortem blood drug concentrations. J Anal Tox 2011;35:381–3.
4. Apple FS, Bandt CM. Liver and blood postmortem tricyclic antidepressant concentrations. Am J Clin Pathol 1988;89:794–6.
5. Baselt RC. Disposition of toxic drugs and chemicals in man, 8th ed. Foster City, CA: Biomedical Publications, 2008.
6. Cook DS, Braithwaite RA, Hale KA. Estimating antemortem drug concentrations from postmortem blood samples, the influence of postmortem redistribution. J Clin Path 2000;53:282–5.
7. Hilborg T, Rogde S, Morland J. Postmortem drug redistribution—human cases related to results in experimental animals. J Forensic Sci 1999;44:3–9.
8. Moriya F, Hashimoto Y. Redistribution of basic drugs into cardiac blood from surrounding tissues during early-stages postmortem. J Forensic Sci 1999;44:10–6.
9. Olson K, Luckenbill K, Thompson J, Middleton O, Geiselhart R, Mills K, Kloss J, Apple F. Postmortem redistribution of fentanyl in blood. Am J Clin Path 2010;133:447–53.
10. Palmer RB. Fentanyl in postmortem forensic toxicology. Clin Tox 290;48:771–84.
11. Pelissier-Alicot AL, Gaulier JM, Champsaur P, Marquet P. Mechanisms underlying PMR of drugs: a review. J Anal Toxicol 2003;27:533–44.
12. Pounder DJ, Jones GR. Postmortem drug redistribution—a toxicological nightmare. For Sci Int 1990;45:253–63.
13. Prouty RW, Anderson MH. The forensic science implications of site and temporal influences on postmortem blood-drug concentrations. J Forensic Sci 1990;35:243–70.

CHAPTER 32

Postmortem Clinical Testing

Barry Levine

INTRODUCTION

Clinical tests to diagnose natural disease states are an important component of clinical medicine. These tests may identify both structural and functional abnormalities in the vasculature, tissues, and organs. However, after death, the performance of an autopsy, with both gross and microscopic examinations, can detect many conditions that require clinical testing for diagnosis during life. Nevertheless, there are disease states that are not identifiable without postmortem clinical testing. Since some of these conditions may account for death, the ability to perform these tests on postmortem specimens is critical to the ultimate cause-of-death ruling.

Many endogenous compounds have been studied for their potential utility in postmortem investigations. Among the more common ones used are electrolytes (sodium, potassium, and chloride), urea nitrogen, creatinine, glucose, and tryptase.

SPECIMENS

Blood

Although similar in color to a blood specimen from a living individual, a postmortem blood specimen is often quite different. The blood pH drops during the early postmortem interval, so movement of substances based on their degree of ionization may also occur. Cells lose their structural integrity rapidly after death. For example, red blood cells hemolyze, making the collection of serum or plasma more difficult. The loss of integrity allows movement of substances in and out of the cell, depending on the concentration gradient. During life, potassium is kept in the cell against a concentration gradient by an active process. After death, this active process stops and potassium leaves the cell. Similarly, blood sodium and chloride concentrations decrease rapidly after death. Due to the stress of death or cardiopulmonary resuscitation, glucose concentrations increase rapidly during the perimortem period. Attempts have been made, largely unsuccessful, to correlate these postmortem concentrations to their concentrations at death. Variables such as postmortem interval, disease state, and environmental conditions have all contributed to this failure.

Vitreous Humor

The vitreous, a chamber of the eye, is located between the lens and retina and fills the center of the eye. It constitutes 80% of the eye and has a volume of about 4 mL. The vitreous is filled with a transparent, delicate connective tissue gel called the gel vitreous, or a transparent liquid called the liquid vitreous. The gel vitreous is a water insoluble collagen gel. The liquid vitreous is present only in the adult eye. Together, they constitute the vitreous humor.

The vitreous humor weighs approximately 4 g. It consists of 99% water and has a specific gravity of 1.0050–1.0089. Its viscosity is approximately two times that of water but with an osmotic pressure close to that of aqueous humor. The pH of the vitreous humor is 7.5. The osmolality of the vitreous humor ranges from 288–323 mOsm/kg, slightly higher than the osmolality of serum, which is 275–295 mOsm/kg.

Collagen is the major structural protein of the vitreous humor. Although similar to cartilage collagen, some distinct differences exist. Another major component of the vitreous humor is hyaluronic acid (HA). HA is a glycosaminoglycan, a polysaccharide composed of repeating disaccharide units; each unit contains a hexosamine linked to uronic acid. The vitreous humor is composed of interpenetrating networks of HA molecules and collagen fibrils. In addition to collagen and HA, there are six specific noncollagenous proteins and two types of glycoproteins in the human vitreous humor.

The movement of molecules in and out of the vitreous occurs via a number of mechanisms: diffusion, hydrostatic pressure, osmotic pressure, convection, and active transport. Water movement is significant, as approximately 50% of the water is replaced every 10–15 min. High molecular weight substances and colloidal particles travel by convection. Low molecular weight substances move in and out of the vitreous primarily by diffusion; however, there is evidence that bulk flow also contributes to their movement.

A number of low molecular weight substances are found in the vitreous humor. Vitreous humor concentrations of sodium and chloride will approximate the serum concentrations of these ions in healthy adults, especially in the early postmortem period. Potassium concentrations in the vitreous humor increase rapidly after death as potassium leaves the cells and travels into nearby fluids. Urea nitrogen and creatinine are also present in concentrations similar to serum and are stable during the early postmortem period. Because of this general stability, the measurement of vitreous humor sodium, chloride, urea nitrogen, and creatinine has

become standard as indicators for serum concentrations of these substances at death.

The vitreous humor should be collected using a syringe and a 20-gauge needle. The needle is placed against the eye at the lateral aspect just above the junction between the upper and lower eyelids. The needle is inserted into the eye approximately 2 cm and the vitreous humor is gradually withdrawn. It is recommended that the vitreous humor from both eyes be collected. No preservatives need to be added to the specimen; however, it should be stored in a refrigerator until analyzed.

Other Specimens

Other fluids such as cerebrospinal fluid (CSF) or pericardial fluid have been investigated as viable specimens for postmortem clinical chemistry testing. Postmortem CSF urea nitrogen and creatinine concentrations are generally similar to antemortem serum concentrations. As with postmortem blood, CSF sodium and chloride concentrations rapidly decrease after death, while CSF potassium concentrations increase, albeit slower than in postmortem blood.

The current consensus is that vitreous humor is the specimen of choice for electrolytes, urea nitrogen, creatinine, and glucose. Normal vitreous humor concentrations for these substances are provided in Table 1.

ANAPHYLAXIS

Anaphylaxis is a serious allergic reaction that occurs rapidly and can lead to death. It results from the release of histamine from

Table 1. Normal Vitreous Humor Concentrations

Analyte	Range
Chloride	115–125 mM
Creatinine	0.6–1.3 mg/dL
Glucose	<200 mg/dL
Sodium	135–145 mM
Urea nitrogen	10–20 mg/dL

mast cells and basophils triggered by either immunologic or nonimmunologic mechanisms. In the immune response, immunoglobulin E (IgE) binds to a foreign substance that ultimately leads to the release of histamine. This increase in histamine concentration leads to a number of physiological changes, as described in Chapter 25. Life-threatening symptoms include bronchial smooth muscle cell contraction leading to difficulty in breathing, and vasodilatation, which can cause hypotension and shock.

A variety of substances can cause the immune response that culminates in anaphylaxis. Allergies to foods, notably shellfish and peanuts, can be triggers. Medications such as penicillin, cephalosporins, and narcotics have also been known to initiate an immune response. Venoms from bee or wasp stings can also cause a potentially fatal immune response.

The postmortem diagnosis of anaphylaxis has generally relied on a combination of history and autopsy findings. Known allergies to a particular substance and a report of a rapid death are initial clues that an anaphylactic death has occurred. If the allergen entered the body through an insect bite, the site of the bite may be observable during the external examination of the body. Internal examination may identify laryngeal or epiglottic swelling and mucous plugging of the airways. Microscopically, mucosal edema with mast cell infiltration and tissue eosinophilia may be observed. If the triggering substance was food or medication, examination of the stomach contents may identify the specific source.

However, none of the above findings are sufficient to make an unequivocal diagnosis of anaphylaxis. Thus, the identification of a clinical marker to support the diagnosis of anaphylaxis is important to raise the level of certainty for the ruling. Since histamine is released during the immune response, it would be the obvious choice to investigate as a clinical marker. Unfortunately, histamine has a very short half-life in the blood and its release may occur for nonallergy reasons. Moreover, IgE, the immunoglobulin that binds to the allergen and begins the process, has unknown stability postmortem.

Tryptase is a serine protease that, along with histamine, is released by mast cells during the immune response. Unlike histamine, tryptase is found only in mast cells and basophils and not in eosinophils or platelets. As a result, its detection in elevated concentrations would provide greater evidence that an immune response had occurred. In addition, it has a half-life of several hours as opposed to several minutes for histamine. There are two forms of tryptase: α and β. The β form is released as a result of a challenge by an allergen. Studies suggest that in deaths clearly unrelated to anaphylaxis, a "postmortem normal" serum concentration can exist up to 10 ng/mL. In deaths due to anaphylaxis, serum tryptase concentrations are usually several times greater than this.

Although postmortem serum tryptase concentrations are useful in making the ultimate diagnosis of anaphylaxis, they are not 100% specific for the diagnosis. Tryptase concentrations greater than 10 ng/mL have been reported in cardiac deaths and trauma deaths. One study indicated that a specificity of 90% can be attained using a threshold of 10 ng/mL. Therefore, although serum tryptase measurements are useful in supporting other facts and observations consistent with anaphylaxis, they should not be used alone for diagnosis.

DEHYDRATION

Dehydration occurs when an individual loses more water than is taken in. Physiological conditions that can lead to dehydration include vomiting, diarrhea, fever, and excessive sweating. Dehydration may also occur when an individual does not consume an adequate amount of water or fluids. The extent of dehydration is variable, but severe dehydration can be life threatening and can actually lead to death. At autopsy, observations of dried organs and sunken eyes may indicate dehydration. The diagnosis of dehydration is aided by the analysis of sodium, chloride, urea nitrogen, and creatinine in the vitreous humor. Normal vitreous humor sodium concentrations are similar to antemortem serum sodium concentrations and range from 135–145 mM. A vitreous humor sodium concentration greater than 155 mM may indicate dehydration. Similarly, normal chloride concentrations range from 115–125 mM, with a chloride concentration greater than 135 mM suggesting dehydration. Vitreous humor urea nitrogen concentrations range between 10–20 mg/dL in normal individuals; concentrations above 40 mg/dL are consistent with dehydration. A urea nitrogen-to-creatinine concentration ratio greater than 20 is typical for "prerenal" dehydration. If dehydration has occurred, all of these analytes would be elevated. If the urea nitrogen is elevated and the electrolytes are normal, kidney malfunction may explain the elevated urea nitrogen. In kidney disease, the vitreous humor creatinine would also be elevated.

DIABETES MELLITUS

Diabetes presents with elevated blood glucose concentrations. It exists in two forms: Type 1 and Type 2. Type 1 is less common and is caused by the destruction of pancreatic beta-cells, which are responsible for the production of the hormone insulin, which in turn lowers blood glucose when it becomes elevated. Type 2 diabetes is more common and occurs when the body does not produce enough insulin or is unable to utilize the insulin that is produced. Because of the imbalance of insulin with hormones that cause an increase in blood glucose concentrations, people with Type 1 diabetes break down fat to a greater degree than normal individuals, leading to increased production of free fatty acids. The subsequent metabolism of free fatty acids leads to an increased production of ketone bodies. The most prominent ketone bodies in man are beta-hydroxybutyrate (BHB), acetoacetate, and acetone. Patients with Type 2 diabetes, because there is some functioning insulin, produce hyperglycemia without the increased breakdown of fat. As a result, an increase in ketone bodies does

not occur. However, there is a hyperosmolar hyperglycemic state that leads to increased diuresis and dehydration.

Generally, there are no obvious gross or microscopic findings associated with deaths caused by diabetic ketoacidosis. Therefore, it is important to measure glucose and ketone bodies in cases in which death due to diabetes is suspected. As stated previously, because postmortem blood glucose concentrations do not reliably reflect an individual's sugar status during life, vitreous humor has become the specimen of choice for this determination. In his review of postmortem chemistries, Coe stated that a vitreous humor glucose concentration greater than 200 mg/dL will only be seen in diabetics. He further stated that even when the postmortem peripheral serum glucose concentration was greater than 500 mg/dL in nondiabetics, the corresponding vitreous humor glucose concentration was never greater than 100 mg/dL.

Unlike postmortem blood glucose concentrations, postmortem blood ketone body concentrations are a reliable indicator of ketone body concentrations at death. Of the three common ketone bodies, acetone is the easiest to measure. Acetone is detected by headspace gas chromatography at the same time that ethanol is measured (See Chapter 13). In fact, in the absence of a history of diabetes, the detection of acetone during the ethanol analysis may be the first indication that the death was caused by diabetic ketoacidosis. Subsequent measurement of glucose in the vitreous humor would indicate whether the measured acetone was caused by a diabetic ketoacidosis or alcoholic ketoacidosis. This latter condition may be seen in alcoholics and is attributed to a combination of large alcohol consumption and malnutrition. Normal vitreous glucose concentrations are observed in people with alcoholic ketoacidosis.

Although acetone is the easiest ketone body to detect, BHB is the ketone body found in highest concentrations in diabetics. BHB is the ketone body most responsible for acidosis. BHB concentrations less than 50 mg/L are considered normal, while concentrations greater than 250 mg/L are considered significant.

In addition to blood glucose, another substance used to monitor glucose control is glycated hemoglobin. In healthy adults, hemoglobin (Hb) consists of three forms: HbA1, HbA2, and HbF. HbA constitutes approximately 97% of the total hemoglobin in the blood and consists of three subgroups: HbA1a, HbA1b, and HbA1c. HbA1c comprises about 80% of HbA1. Glycated hemoglobin is produced by the nonenzymatic addition of sugars to amino acids on the protein; specifically, glucose binds to the N-terminal valine amino acids of the beta-chain of hemoglobin. The more glucose that is present in the blood, the more glycated hemoglobin. Since the life span of a red blood cell is approximately four months, the percentage of HbA1c that is glycated represents an average measure of blood glucose concentrations over this time period. In theory, this percentage would not be susceptible to the wild changes in glucose concentration that may occur around death. "Normal glycated HbA1c" is generally less than 7% in living patients, but this expected concentration has not clearly been established in postmortem cases. Several postmortem studies have indicated that glycated HbA1c is elevated in diabetic individuals, but the results have generally been used in conjunction with vitreous humor glucose and blood ketone body concentrations to conclude that death was caused by diabetes.

METABOLIC DISORDERS

Unexpected deaths in infants and children qualify for a medical-legal investigation. Since deaths due to sudden infant death syndrome (SIDS) or sudden unexpected death in infancy (SUDI) are diagnoses of exclusion, a complete investigation, autopsy, and toxicology testing are required prior to making these rulings. Deaths caused by structural abnormalities would be identified during the gross internal examination of the body. Functional abnormalities without corresponding structural deficits would not be observable and require clinical testing for a diagnosis. A number of inborn errors of metabolism have been identified, and some can lead to death:

Acute Intermittent Porphyria (AIP)

This disorder affects the production of heme, the iron-containing component of hemoglobin. The specific enzyme that is deficient is porphobilinogen deaminase, leading to an increase in porphobilinogen concentrations.

Glycogen Storage Diseases

This group of disorders results from the inability to produce or break down glycogen. Any single enzyme involved in the process of glycogen synthesis or metabolism can be the cause of these diseases.

Lysosomal Storage Diseases

These disorders have as their common characteristic a deficit in lysosome function. The lysosome breaks down unwanted material in the cell; the malfunctioning of this process leads to the buildup of these substances. A number of processes can be defective, each leading to a specific disease.

Medium-Chain Acyl-Coenzyme A Dehydrogenase (MCAD) Deficiency

This disorder in fatty acid oxidation is caused by reduced activity of this enzyme system. Fatty acids of varying lengths combine with glycerol to form triglycerides. Fatty acids with 6 to 12 carbon atoms are metabolized with this enzyme system. This condition is diagnosed by measuring elevated concentrations of medium-length acylcarnitines caused by the buildup of fatty acids. Carnitine is the molecule that transports fatty acids from the cytoplasm to the mitochondria for incorporation into triglycerides.

Organic Acidemia

This disorder disrupts normal metabolism of amino acids. One example of this disease is maple syrup urine disease; a malfunctioning branched-chain α-keto acid decarboxylase causes an increased concentration of leucine, valine, isoleucine, and alloisoleucine. Other examples of this disease are propionic acidemia and methylmalonic acidemia.

Phenylketonuria

This disorder results from a deficiency in hydroxylase, the enzyme that catalyzes the conversion of phenylalanine to tyrosine. This leads to an elevation in phenylalanine concentrations with a corresponding decrease in tyrosine concentrations.

THYROID FUNCTION

Available clinical measurements for assessing thyroid function include thyroxine (T_4), triiodothyronine (T_3), and thyroid stimulating hormone (TSH). The normal ranges for T_4, T_3, and TSH in living individuals are 9–24 pM, 3–9 pM, and 0.4–4.0 mU/L, respectively. In general, blood T_4 concentrations will decrease after death, but not in a consistent manner. It has been suggested that in the early postmortem period, T_4 is converted to T_3. Nevertheless, T_4 concentrations above 24 pM may be associated with normal histology, and an elevated T_4 concentration in the absence of other history or anatomic findings should be interpreted cautiously. T_3 concentration changes are more variable but appear to remain in the normal range when histological findings are unremarkable. T_3 is elevated in cases where focal epithelial hyperplasia is observed microscopically. T_4 and T_3 enter the vitreous humor and are generally present in much lower concentrations than blood. It appears that thyroid function tests are most properly utilized when measured in postmortem blood and combined with histological findings.

SELECTED READINGS

1. Chase DH, Kalas TA, Naylor EW. The application of tandem mass spectrometry to neonatal screening for inherited disorders of intermediary metabolism. Ann Rev Genomics Hum Genet 2002;3:17–45.
2. Coe J. Postmortem chemistry update: emphasis on forensic applications. Am J Forensic Med Pathol 1993;14:91–117.
3. Edston E, Druid H, Holmgren P, Ostrom M. Postmortem measurements of thyroid function in blood and vitreous humor combined with histology. Am J Forensic Med Pathol 2001;22:78–83.
4. Hockenhull J, Dhillo W, Andrews R, Peterson S. Investigation of markers to indicate and distinguish death due to alcoholic ketoacidosis, diabetic ketoacidosis and hyperosmolar hyperglycemic state using post-mortem samples. Forensic Sci Int 2012;214:142–7.
5. Horn KD, Halsey JF, Zumwalt RE. Utilization of serum tryptase and immunoglobulin E assay in the postmortem diagnosis of anaphylaxis. Am J Forensic Med Pathol 2004;25:37–42.
6. Palmiere C, Mangin P. Postmortem chemistry update Part I. Int J Legal Med 2012;126:187–98.
7. Palmiere C, Mangin P. Postmortem chemistry update Part II. Int J Legal Med 2012;126:199–215.
8. Randall B, Butts J, Halsey JF. Elevated postmortem tryptase in the absence of anaphylaxis. J Forensic Sci 1995;40:208–11.
9. Yunginger JW, Nelson DR, Squillace DL, Jones RT, Holley KE, Hyma BA, Biedrycki L, Sweeney KG, Sturner WQ, Schwartz LB. Laboratory investigation of deaths due to anaphylaxis. J Forensic Sci 1991;36:857–65.

CHAPTER 33

Pharmacogenomics

Thomas Kupiec

INTRODUCTION

Pharmacogenomics can be a useful tool to the forensic toxicologist. The consideration of genetic variation and its contribution to pharmacokinetics should be examined in the interpretation of drug concentrations. Understanding the potential effect of pharmacogenomics can be beneficial in evaluating postmortem drug concentrations, workplace drug testing, or drugs and driving cases. In addition to age, physical condition, diet, or coadministered drugs, genetic variation can affect drug metabolism and efficacy. Large interindividual variations can occur in drug concentration, toxicity, and drug response when given the same dosage.

Pharmacogenomics is the study of the association between an individual's genotype and the disposition of drugs in the body. The first association between adverse drug reactions and inherited variations was recognized in the 1950s, linking peripheral neuropathy with isoniazid and apnea with succinylcholine. However, genetic influence on drug disposition has existed for centuries, dating back to Pythagoras and his observation that the ingestion of fava beans triggered a potentially fatal hemolytic anemia in some but not all individuals. Variations in drug response are basically due to differences in individual genetic makeup. Genes are made of DNA sequences and if these sequences are disrupted (i.e., deletions, insertions, transpositions, etc.), it may lead to discernible differences in form or function of gene products.

An individual's phenotype corresponds to observable characteristics such as eye and hair color or rate of drug clearance. The phenotype, or external manifestation, is modulated by the individual's genotype (i.e., genetic makeup) and other factors such as age, gender, and health. Interindividual differences in phenotype are often caused by genetic polymorphisms. The most prevalent type of polymorphism involves a single base pair variant in a DNA sequence, which is referred to as a single nucleotide polymorphism (SNP). Millions of SNPs have been identified in the human genome. The effect of only one change in the base pair can change the amino acid. A change in the amino acid may result in a change in the protein folding or structure, culminating in a change in the drug-metabolizing enzyme activity (Fig. 1). Other applications of SNPs include new drug development, prediction of drug efficacy and toxicity, optimization of clinical trials, and individualization of drug therapy.

Most drug effects are determined by the interaction of several gene products (drug targets, enzymes, and transporters) that influence the pharmacokinetics and pharmacodynamics of medications. Polymorphisms have been observed in genes encoding for drug-metabolizing enzymes, drug-transport proteins, and drug targets/receptors. Polymorphic gene products can affect drug disposition, thereby causing adverse effects. For example, the enzyme thiopurine-S-methyl transferase (TPMT) metabolizes the drugs azathioprine and mercaptopurine. Individuals with the genes for reduced TPMT activity

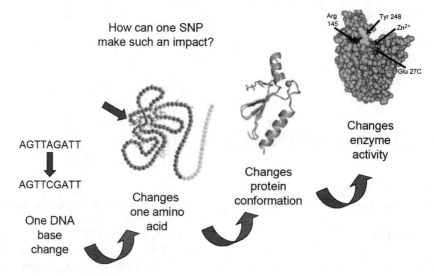

Fig. 1. Effect of base pair change on enzyme. *Source:* Reprinted with permission from *12*.

must be treated with substantially different doses of the affected drugs (e.g., about 5% to 10% of the standard dose) to prevent toxicity.

Pharmacogenomics is an additional parameter along with pharmacodynamics and pharmacokinetics, all of which influence drug response, metabolism, and toxicity (Fig. 2).

DRUG-METABOLIZING ENZYMES

The majority of drugs undergo hepatic metabolism to water-soluble compounds, which subsequently get excreted. Drug metabolism typically results in drug detoxification and elimination or, in some cases, may lead to the activation of a prodrug to the active

form. Drug-metabolizing enzymes (DMEs) may exhibit interindividual variations in protein expression or catalytic activity, thus resulting in unique drug-metabolism phenotypes. These variations can be attributed to transient causes such as enzyme inhibition and induction or to a permanent cause such as genetic mutation or gene deletion. Mutations in the cytochrome P450 (CYP) genes can lead to enzyme products with absent, reduced, or increased enzyme activity. Metabolism in the liver is primarily carried out by two groups of enzymes: phase I and phase II enzymes. Phase I enzymes, including CYP oxidative enzymes, modify functional groups on drugs via hydrolysis, oxidation, reduction, or hydroxylation. The CYP enzyme system is

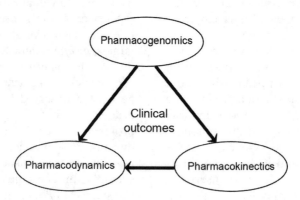

Fig. 2. Determinants of drug metabolism. *Source:* Reprinted with permission from *11*.

responsible for the metabolism of the majority of drugs and has been a major focus of pharmacogenomic research.

CYP2D6

Pharmaceutical drugs are frequently found in drug-related deaths, and some of these drugs include benzodiazepines, antidepressants, amphetamines, and opioids. CYP2D6 metabolizes a number of opioid drugs such as codeine, tramadol, oxycodone, and hydrocodone, and is one of the most widely researched cytochrome enzymes. CYP2D6 is the most polymorphic CYP enzyme, with polymorphisms resulting in the absence of enzyme, reduced enzyme, or enzyme with increased activity. Based on genetic polymorphisms of CYP2D6, three metabolizer types are currently recognized: ultraextensive metabolizers (UM), extensive metabolizers (EM), and poor metabolizers (PM).

Individuals with a UM phenotype generally have multiple copies of a gene and will metabolize drugs faster and, as a result, do not achieve therapeutic plasma drug concentrations at ordinary drug dosages. In contrast, individuals with a PM genotype may require substantial dose reduction to prevent toxicity. For instance, in the case of the tricyclic antidepressant nortriptyline, poor metabolizers have zero copies of the CYP2D6 enzyme, intermediate metabolizers have one copy, extensive metabolizers have two copies, and ultraextensive metabolizers have more than two copies. These drug metabolism profiles exhibit clinical manifestations ranging from therapeutic inefficacy to toxicity for the same dose of a drug. Thus, CYP2D6 deficiency can lead to manifestations of drug overdose and intensified drug effects when CYP2D6 is the major inactivation pathway, as with tricyclic antidepressants, or to depreciated therapeutic effect when CYP2D6 is the activator, such as in the case of the prodrug codeine. Genetic inactivity of CYP2D6 has been known to affect opioid analgesics in different ways; it renders codeine inactive, slightly decreases the clearance of methadone, and slightly reduces the efficacy of tramadol.

CYP2C9

The CYP2C9 enzyme metabolizes warfarin, phenytoin, and several nonsteroidal anti-inflammatory drugs (NSAIDs). Small variations in warfarin and phenytoin dosage may be clinically relevant because of their narrow therapeutic range. CYP2C9 polymorphisms have been associated with significant reductions in the metabolism and dosage of selected CYP2C9 substrates. Individuals with these genotypes also appear to be significantly more susceptible to adverse events during the inception of warfarin and phenytoin therapy. Subjects with reduced clearance of oral anticoagulants such as warfarin are more susceptible to adverse bleeding events. CYP2C9 polymorphisms have been reported to occur in greater frequency among individuals who experienced acute gastric-bleeding complications after NSAID use.

CYP3A

CYP3A represents a group of enzymes that are abundant in the liver and intestine. CYP3A4 is a very important enzyme in human drug metabolism and it is known to metabolize the largest number of drugs. CYP3A4 accounts for 20% to 40% of the total hepatic cytochrome enzymes in humans, and mediates the dealkylation of fentanyl to norfentanyl. Several drugs of toxicological significance, including buprenorphine, benzodiazepines, fentanyl, and methadone, are metabolized by CYP3A4. Both CYP3A4 and CYP3A5 are polymorphic, thus resulting in variable fentanyl metabolism. Although fentanyl abuse may lead to toxicity, adverse effects due to fentanyl may also be attributable in part to CYP3A4 or CYP3A5 variant alleles.

TRANSPORT PROTEINS

Transport proteins play an important role in the absorption of drugs across physiological barriers such as the blood-brain, biliary, intestinal, tubular, and renal epithelia.

Significant transporter-mediated drug interactions have been reported, and may range from inhibitory, inductive, or both. For example, the P-glycoprotein (P-gp) efflux pump belongs to the ATP-binding cassette (ABC) family transporters and is encoded by the MDR1 gene (or ABCB1). In humans, P-gp is present in several tissues that are important for drug absorption, distribution, and elimination. Due to the broad substrate specificity of P-gp, inhibitors or inducers of P-gp may produce significant drug–drug interactions. Another important group are the organic anion (protein) transporters encoded by the solute carrier gene family (SLC). These sodium ion-independent transporters partly rely on cotransport and are responsible for the transport of a wide range of endogenous compounds as well as drugs. Organic cation-transporter interactions, as well as peptide-transporter and nucleoside-transporter interactions, have also been described.

DRUG TARGETS

Most drugs exert their pharmacologic effects by interaction with specific targets (i.e., receptors, enzymes, or proteins). These targets include the β_2-adrenoceptors, insulin receptors, angiotensin-converting enzyme, etc. Polymorphisms in genes encoding these targets may influence the sensitivity to selected drugs, and these polymorphisms may be significant in cases where interindividual variations in plasma-drug concentrations are minimal but major pharmacodynamic differences are observed. For example, a greater frequency of the Gly16 polymorphism of the β_2AR gene has been identified within a patient population of asthmatics, leading to an increased risk of morbidity and mortality from asthma. Another example of a drug target polymorphism is the anticancer drug 5-fluorouracil (5-FU), which acts by the inhibition of the enzyme thymidylate synthase (TS). TS is a critical element in DNA synthesis and repair, and clinical resistance to 5-FU and other folate-based antimetabolites has been linked to overexpression of TS.

PHARMACOGENOMICS IN FORENSIC TOXICOLOGY

Forensic toxicology contributes substantially to the determination of the cause and manner of death, and provides valuable information regarding the interpretation of circumstances surrounding a fatal event. Particularly in overdose cases, it is essential to determine the drug(s) responsible for the intoxication, both for providing evidence in the particular case and for identification of drugs that could, over time, prove especially dangerous. Much effort has been put on the estimation of fatal concentrations of various drugs in postmortem material. Many fatal intoxications involve suicidal overdoses, but during recent years chronic high dosage has attracted increased interest. In order to differentiate between an acute overdose and a chronic poisoning, the distribution of the drug in different specimens can be of assistance, since in an acute overdose death the drug may not have reached high levels in less proximate samples such as vitreous humor, cerebrospinal fluid, or hair. For a number of drugs, the parent drug to metabolite ratio (higher concentrations anticipated in acute overdose cases) may provide even more convincing evidence. However, the parent drug to metabolite ratio may provide misleading information; a low ratio may be encountered in acute overdoses, preceded by a high chronic dosage of the same drug. Conversely, a high parent drug to metabolite ratio could also be due to a reduced metabolism of the parent drug, either because of interaction with other drugs or because of genetically low metabolic capacity.

The following are examples of case studies where pharmacogenomics may play an important role in the interpretation of toxicological results.

Case Study: Oxycodone

A 49-year-old Caucasian male with a history of prescription drug abuse, depression, and posttraumatic stress disorder was found dead. The decedent had been prescribed

OxyContin® and Percocet® for his chronic back pain. A postmortem oxycodone concentration of 0.437 mg/L was found in subclavian blood. Autopsy showed hepatic cirrhosis, which might have impaired his drug metabolism. CYP2D6 is the polymorphic enzyme responsible for the metabolism of oxycodone. Whereas a majority of the population exhibit high CYP2D6 activity, 5–10% of Caucasians and 1–4% of most other ethnic groups have decreased CYP2D6 activity, leading to an increased risk of toxic effects and possible fatality from routine doses of oxycodone. Molecular autopsy indicated that he was CYP2D6*4 homozygous, thus corresponding to the poor-metabolizer phenotype. This deficiency might have contributed to impaired metabolism of oxycodone, along with hepatic cirrhosis. The cause of death was ruled as oxycodone intoxication and manner of death was ruled an accident.

Case Study: Methadone

A 51-year-old Caucasian male with a history of heroin addiction was enrolled in a methadone maintenance program. He was found dead on a Monday at 0800 h. His girlfriend confirmed that he was alive at 0700 h on Sunday. The decedent had hepatitis C and hepatic cirrhosis. A postmortem iliac blood methadone concentration of 1.6 mg/L was reported. Although there is a significant overlap between quoted therapeutic methadone concentrations and the concentrations reported in fatalities, an acute ingestion was considered likely. Postmortem redistribution was assumed to be minimal since the postmortem interval was less than 24 h. However, polydrug interactions also play a role in methadone fatalities. For example, concurrent administration of CYP3A4 inhibitors such as ketoconazole and erythromycin increase the risk of methadone toxicity. Molecular autopsy showed CYP2D6*3 and *4 compound heterozygosity, corresponding to a poor metabolizer of methadone. Other drugs found included benzoylecgonine, propoxyphene, and diazepam. Autopsy findings also included end-stage alcoholic liver disease. Cause of death was ruled as mixed drug toxicity, and manner of death was ruled an accident.

Case Study: Fentanyl

A 44-year-old Caucasian female with a history of drug abuse, suicidal ideation, and psychiatric disorders was found dead. One fentanyl patch was attached to her arm, and another adhered to a blanket. Postmortem subclavian blood concentrations of 19 and 7.6 µg/L were reported for fentanyl and norfentanyl, respectively. Other drugs found included cyclobenzapine, tramadol, diphenhydramine, citalopram, and olanzapine. Pharmacogenomic testing (i.e., molecular autopsy) indicated hetereozygosity of CYP3A4*1B and CYP3A5*3. This genotype corresponded with a reduced rate of fentanyl metabolism. Therefore, the cause of death was ruled as mixed drug toxicity, and manner of death was ruled an accident.

Case Study: Fluoxetine

A 9-year-old boy diagnosed with attention deficit hyperactivity disorder, obsessive–compulsive disorder, and Tourette syndrome was treated with methylphenidate, clonidine, and fluoxetine. Over a 10-month period, he developed gastrointestinal toxicity, incoordination and disorientation, and seizures. He eventually died from cardiac arrest. Postmortem toxicology showed high fluoxetine and norfluoxetine concentrations, and pharmacogenomics analysis revealed a poor CYP2D6-metabolizer genotype resulting in fluoxetine accumulation and toxicity. Subsequently, the boy's parents were absolved from involvement in fluoxetine intoxication. (Sallee et al of the Suggested Readings)

Case Study: Doxepin

Doxepin is predominantly metabolized to the active metabolite N-desmethyldoxepin (nordoxepin) by CYP2C19. CYP2D6 appears to be involved in another important pathway catalyzing 2-hydroxylation of (E)-doxepin, but also that of (E)-nordoxepin. A case was reported of a 43-year-old male alcoholic with suicidal tendencies who was found dead; the cause of death was doxepin intoxication. The doxepin concentration was 2.4 mg/L, the concentration of nordoxepin 2.9 mg/L, and the doxepin/nordoxepin ratio 0.83, the lowest found among the 35 nordoxepin-positive postmortem cases analyzed during the same year. No alcohol or other drugs were detected in the case. The manner of death remained unclear (suicide/accident). The postmortem DNA analysis indicated a CYP2C19 genotype that was determined to be that of an extensive metabolizer. However, it also revealed two CYP2D6 alleles that were both not functional (CYP2D6*3/*4). Therefore doxepin could only be metabolized to nordoxepin but not to 2-hydroxydoxepin or 2-hydroxynordoxepin. Correspondingly high doxepin and especially high nordoxepin concentrations were found with a ratio of 0.83. In suicidal poisonings a ratio greater than one is expected; therefore an accidental chronic intoxication could be assumed. (Koski et al of the Suggested Readings)

Case Study: Codeine

Codeine is a prodrug that is metabolized to the active drug morphine by CYP2D6. A healthy male infant presented with intermittent difficulties breastfeeding and with lethargy, starting on day 7. On day 12 he presented with grey skin and decreased milk intake. The infant was deceased on day 13. The autopsy revealed no anatomical cause of death; however, a blood morphine concentration of 70 ng/mL was found. Neonates breastfed by mothers receiving codeine typically have morphine serum concentrations of 0–2.2 ng/mL. The mother received a combination preparation of codeine 30 mg and paracetamol, which she took for two weeks. She stored milk at day 10 that had a morphine concentration of 87 ng/mL (normally 1.9–20.5 ng/mL). The investigation into the reason for the intoxication (accidental/homicidal) led to genotyping that revealed that the mother was an ultrarapid metabolizer of CYPD6, thus leading to an increased formation of morphine from codeine. Thus, cause of death was ruled as accidental morphine intoxication. (Koren et al of the Suggested Readings)

SUMMARY

Emerging evidence suggests that the underlying cause of death in many postmortem cases is genetic, and that both heart and liver abnormalities can play a role. The dilemma is that death from a wide variety of genetic defects may leave no histological markers. The ability to identify these "invisible diseases" with postmortem genetic testing has become a reality far more quickly than anyone had ever imagined. In the medicolegal system, pharmacogenetic testing has the potential to significantly reduce errors and increase the accuracy of toxicological interpretations used in establishing the cause and manner of death. The cost savings and legal ramifications of this technology are vast, and will continue to grow as ongoing research supplements our understanding of individual differences in drug disposition.

Acknowledgment: I want to thank Dr. Vishnu Raj, a professional colleague, for his contribution to research and assistance with this chapter.

SUGGESTED READING

1. Carlsson B, Holmgren A, Ahlner J, Bengtsson F. Enantioselective analysis of citalopram and escitalopram in postmortem blood together with genotyping for CYP2D6 and CYP2C19. J Anal Toxicol 2009;33:65–76.
2. Druid H, Holmgren P, Carlsson B, Ahlner J. Cytochrome P450 2D6 (CYP2D6) genotyping on postmortem blood as a supplementary tool for interpretation of forensic toxicological results. Forensic Sci Int 1999;99:25–34.

3. Jannetto PJ, Wong SH, Gock SB, Laleli-Sahin E, Schur BC, Jentzen JM. Pharmacogenomics as molecular autopsy for postmortem forensic toxicology: genotyping cytochrome P450 2D6 for oxycodone cases. J Anal Toxicol 2002;26:438–47.

4. Jin M, Gock SB, Jannetto PJ, Jentzen JM, Wong SH. Pharmacogenomics as molecular autopsy for forensic toxicology: genotyping cytochrome P450 3A4*1B and 3A5*3 for 25 fentanyl cases. J Anal Toxicol 2005;29:590–8.

5. Jones AW, Holmgren A, Ahlner J. Blood methadone concentrations in living and deceased persons: variations over time, subject demographic, and relevance of coingested drugs. J Anal Toxicol 2012;36:12–8.

6. Jortani SA, Stauble E, Wong S. Pharmacogenetics in clinical and forensic toxicology: opioid overdoses and deaths. In: Mozayani A, Raumon L, eds. Handbook of drug interactions: a clinical and forensic guide. New York: Springer Science+Business Media, LLC, 2012.

7. Karch SB. Changing times: DNA resequencing and the "nearly normal autopsy." J Forensic Leg Med 2007;14:389–97.

8. Kingbäck M, Karlsson L, Zackrisson AL, Carlsson B, Josefsson M, Bengtsson F, et al. Influence of CYP2D6 genotype on the disposition of the enantiomers of venlafaxine and its major metabolites in postmortem femoral blood. Forensic Sci Int 2012;214:124–34.

9. Koren G, Cairns J, Chitayat D, Gaedigk A, Leeder SJ. Pharmacogenetics of morphine poisoning in a breastfed neonate of a codeine-prescribed mother. Lancet 2006;368:704.

10. Koski A, Ojanpera I, Sistonen J, Vuori E, Sajantila A. A fatal doxepin poisoning associated with a defective CYP2D6 genotype. Am J Forensic Med Pathol 2007;28:259–61.

11. Kupiec TC, Raj V, Vu N. Pharmacogenomics for the forensic toxicologist. J Anal Toxicol 2006;30:65–72.

12. Kupiec TC, Shimasaki C. Pharmacogenomics. In: Allen Jr LV, ed. Remington: The science and practice of pharmacy, vol. 1, 22nd ed. London: Pharmaceutical Press, 2013.

13. Musshoff F, Stamer UM, Madea B. Pharmacogenetics and forensic toxicology. Forensic Sci Int 2010;203:53–62.

14. Sajantila A, Palo JU, Ojanperä I, Davis C, Budowle B. Pharmacogenetics in medicolegal context. Forensic Sci Int 2010;203:44–52.

15. Sallee FR, DeVane CL, Ferrell RE. Fluoxetine-related death in a child with cytochrome P-450 2D6 genetic deficiency. J Child Adolesc Psychopharmacol 2000;10:27–34.

16. Shi Y, Xiang P, Li L, Shen M. Analysis of 50 SNPs in CYP2D6, CYP2C19, CYP2C9, CYP3A4 and CYP1A2 by MALDI-TOF mass spectrometry in Chinese Han population. Forensic Sci Int 2011;207:183–7.

17. van der Weide J, van Baalen-Benedek EH, Kootstra-Ros JE. Metabolic ratios of psychotropics as indication of cytochrome P450 2D6/2C19 genotype. Ther Drug Monit 2005;27:478–83.

18. Watanabe J, Suzuki Y, Fukui N, Sugai T, Ono S, Inoue Y, Someya T. Dose-dependent effect of the CYP2D6 genotype on the steady-state fluvoxamine concentration. Ther Drug Monit 2008;30:705–8.

19. Wong SH, Happy C, Blinka D, Gock S, Jentzen JM, Donald Hon J, et al. From personalized medicine to personalized justice: the promises of translational pharmacogenomics in the justice system. Pharmacogenomics 2010;11:731–7.

20. Wong SH, Wagner MA, Jentzen JM, Schur C, Bjerke J, Gock SB, Chang CC. Pharmacogenomics as an aspect of molecular autopsy for forensic pathology/toxicology: does genotyping CYP 2D6 serve as an adjunct for certifying methadone toxicity? J Forensic Sci 2003;48:1406–15.

CHAPTER 34

Hair

Michael Schaffer and Virginia Hill

INTRODUCTION

Some of the earliest papers on hair testing appeared in the literature in the years after the Vietnam War, when it was estimated that approximately 21% of military personnel in Vietnam were physically dependent on opioids. This crisis led to the development of methods for detection of opioids and other drugs in urine. In addition, some scientists were interested in finding ways to assess the severity of substance abuse. A group of scientists at the V.A. Medical Center in Los Angeles was the first to use radioimmunoassay (RIA) to test for drugs in a very small amount of hair.

Initial animal studies on the distribution of drugs in hair were performed with syngeneic mice. Mice were injected with morphine three times per week for two weeks. Hair was plucked prior to the initial injection, 1 week after the last injection, and at later times to study the time course of appearance and disappearance of the drug in the hair. For analysis, the hair was washed, pulverized with mortar and pestle, and refluxed with methanol for 2 h to extract the drug. The methanol was evaporated and the residue was reconstituted in aqueous buffer for RIA analysis. These studies showed a direct correlation between dose and drug concentrations in hair, suggesting that hair analysis could be used to indicate drug use. Hair appeared to act like a tape recorder, providing diagnostic information regarding the identity and amounts of drugs taken over a period of time. Each person could serve as their own control, and if

drug use increased or decreased, it could be followed simply by collecting multiple hair samples over time. This was a new dimension in diagnostic information, one previously unavailable to clinicians.

RIA was also utilized to test for phencyclidine (PCP) in the hair of military veterans. Hair samples were cut close to the scalp instead of plucking, and samples 0–2.5 cm (proximal to distal) and also more distal sections were collected to study the degree of use over time. This was the first time that histories of use were quantitated in terms of the length of the hair sample, which could be correlated to the time of use.

Several early studies on human hair samples from addiction subjects demonstrated the potential utility of drug testing in hair specimens. Human hair samples from heroin and cocaine addicts were collected and sectional analyses were performed. Cut hair samples from 84 heroin addicts and 30 cocaine users were extracted with 0.1 mol/L HCl for 18 h at 45 °C and analyzed by RIA. All samples were positive for the drug abused. In another early human study, hair samples from cocaine users were collected from the vertex of the scalp, where the hair was cut close to the scalp, and self-reported dose histories were taken to estimate the dose over time. Hair specimens of varying lengths were analyzed in order to ensure measurement of the drug going back into the time of use reported by the user.

Data accumulated over time has demonstrated the detection times of drugs of abuse based on studies of controlled administration

515

to volunteers or the analysis of samples from subjects who were forced to stop their use due to imprisonment or detoxification. The detection times depend on dose, route of administration, frequency of use, matrix, analyte(s) detected (parent vs metabolite), detection limits of the assay, and other parameters. Generally speaking, the detection time is longest in hair, followed by urine, sweat, oral fluid, and blood. In a very simplistic view, drug detection in blood is from minutes to hours, drug detection in urine is from hours to days, and drug detection in hair is from weeks to months.

Following the early RIA studies, more specific analytical approaches were taken to identify the individual drugs and their metabolites, including liquid chromatography/mass spectrometry (LC/MS), liquid chromatography-tandem mass spectrometry (LC-MS/MS), gas chromatography/mass spectrometry (GC/MS), and gas chromatography-tandem mass spectrometry (GC-MS/MS).

With the consensus that ingested organic compounds can be measured in hair, the next 20 years saw greater emphasis on some of the major challenges in hair testing. Two areas of concern were: (1) differentiation between drug use and external contamination; and (2) the impact of hair color effects. The European community was less concerned with external contamination and hair color effects, while in the U.S. these issues came to be the major topics of contention in the field of hair testing.

A word of warning to the reader is offered. Units of measurement in the field of hair testing are not entirely standardized at the time of writing. In reading the literature, the reader will find ng/mg hair, ng/10 mg hair, and pg/mg hair.

HAIR STRUCTURE AND INCORPORATION OF COMPOUNDS INTO HAIR

Hair is formed by matrix cells in the hair follicle that are nourished by capillary networks in the dermis of the skin. The matrix cells are 3–5 mm deep in the dermis and hypodermis beneath the surface of the scalp. A mechanism for drug deposition in hair is diffusion of drug from blood into developing hair cells, depositing the drugs in the growing hair. Researchers suggest that drugs in blood, sweat, sebum, and skin may be transferred to hair. Ingested drug is primarily deposited in the medulla whereas drugs from external sources would be on the cuticle level; with wetting and time, the drug on the cuticles can penetrate through the cuticle into the cortex. Methamphetamine may be an exception in the primary site of its deposition in hair; it has been shown in animal models that ingested labeled methamphetamine is visible in the cortex. Distinguishing the source of drug found in hair is a major challenge in hair analysis and will be discussed later in this chapter.

A cross-sectional view of the hair structure is shown in Fig. 1. Hair follicles are nourished with blood by capillary networks in the dermis of the skin. Hair in the follicle is formed by matrix cells. The cortex consists of tightly packed macrofibrils containing keratin in a microfibril network, which results in the strength of the hair structure. The human hair life cycle consists of three major phases—the anagen or growth phase, the catagen or transition phase (wherein the root of the hair becomes keratinized and begins to separate from the bulb), and the telogen or resting phase. Hair growth, as well as the proportion of the hair that is in any of the three phases, varies in different parts of the body. Head hair grows at a rate of about 0.44 mm per day, while chest, underarm, and leg hair grow at a rate of 0.4, 0.3, and 0.2 mm, respectively. The anagen phase lasts 48–72 months for head hair, 5–7 months for chest hair, 6–7 months for underarm hair, and 4–5 months for leg hair. The telogen phase lasts 4–6 months for head hair, 2.5 months for chest hair, 2.5 months for underarm hair, and 2–3 months for leg hair. Drugs remain in hair as the shaft grows outwards from the follicle (taking 5–7 days, possibly slightly longer, to emerge above the surface) at a rate of approximately 1.3 cm per month for head hair.

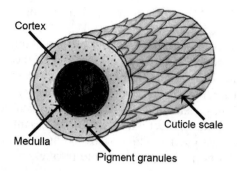

Cortex

Medulla

Cuticle scale

Pigment granules

Fig. 1. Cross-section of a hair. *Source:* Reprinted with permission from Ecobyte Pty Ltd Australia.

SOCIETY OF HAIR TESTING (SOHT) AND OTHER GUIDELINES

In its infancy, hair testing lacked the scientific consensus required for international acceptance in the scientific community. Founded in 1995, the Society of Hair Testing (SoHT) has a worldwide network of members involved in hair testing and has published several guidance documents relating to the examination of drugs and doping agents in hair. The guidance briefly addresses applications for hair testing such as drug-related death, drug-facilitated crime, child custody issues, chronic drug use, and chronic excessive ethanol consumption. Recommendations for sample collection procedures are provided, as well as comments on washing procedures and methods of extracting the drugs from hair. Screening assays are briefly mentioned, and confirmation techniques, cutoffs, and quality control are discussed. Some of the guidelines are not internationally agreed on, such as the growth rates of hair (1.0 cm/month vs 1.3 cm/month) and the techniques for washing hair to remove external drug. Guidance on validation of screening assays, mass spectrometric cutoffs, and good laboratory practice leading to better science and international standards has appeared in the peer-reviewed literature over the last 10–15 years. Many of the concerns about hair testing have been resolved over the last decade.

A separate consensus statement has been prepared by the SoHT regarding the determination of alcohol consumption by hair analysis. Another European organization, the European Workplace Drug Testing Society, has also issued a guidance document for the practice on drug and alcohol testing in hair. The statement is generally in agreement with the SoHT guidance document that is updated every several years. The College of American Pathologists has only recently accredited laboratories that perform hair testing.

Finally, in 2004 in the U.S., proposed guidelines for hair testing were issued by the Substance Abuse and Mental Health Services Administration. Because external contamination was not adequately addressed in this document, the proposed guidelines were not finalized. Instead, in the interim since its publication, much work has been invested in studying contamination methods, and these will be discussed later in this chapter. Many of the proposals in the document, however, are being followed by hair analysis practitioners in the U.S., such as recommended cutoffs, FDA approval for screening assays for workplace testing, chain of custody, and laboratory practices. Tables 1 and 2 list the

Table 1. SAMHSA Proposed Screening Cutoffs

Drug or Metabolite	Concentration (pg/mg)
Carboxy THC[a]	0.05
Cocaine	500
Benzolyecgonine	50
Morphine	200
Codeine	200
6-AM[b]	200
Phencyclidine	300
Amphetamine	300
Methamphetamine	300
MDMA[c]	300
MDA[d]	300
MDEA[e]	300

[a]11-nor-Delta-9-tetrahydrocannabinol-9-carboxylic acid
[b]6-Acetylmorphine
[c]Methylenedioxymethamphetamine
[d]Methyldioxyamphetamine
[e]Methyldioxyethamphetamine

Table 2. SAMHSA Proposed Confirmation Cutoffs

Drug or Metabolite	Concentration (pg/mg)
Carboxy THC	0.05
Cocaine	500
Benzolyecgonine	50
Morphine	200
Codeine	200
6-AM	200
Phencyclidine	300
Amphetamine	300
Methamphetamine	300
MDMA	300
MDA	300
MDEA	300

proposed screening and confirmation cutoffs for hair. Within these proposals, there were also rules about metabolite concentrations or ratios of parent to metabolite before a specimen could be called positive.

COLLECTION OF HAIR SAMPLES AND SPECIMEN ACCESSIONING

Accurate collection of the hair sample is critical. The site of hair collection should be documented. A small lock of hair visibly equal to 1 inch wide by 1–2 strands deep when held flat across your finger should be grasped and cut as close to the scalp as possible. The sample is preferably taken from an area on the head that is cosmetically undetectable to the donor. The hair sample in placed in a foil and closed. The sample is then placed on a Sample Acquisition Card (SAC) with the root ends protruding from the slanted end of the foil. The SAC is sealed by affixing the tamper-evident seal on the SAC at its open edge.

Once specimen collection has occurred, it is handled like any other forensic specimen. Hair specimens arrive at the laboratory via private courier services, the U.S. mail, or by hand delivery. The samples are accessioned and cut to the standard length for testing. For example, 3.9 cm (1½ inch) will reflect approximately a 90-day window. If a longer window is desired, a longer length of hair is collected.

The SAC, which holds the hair sample, is a part of the chain of custody. The SAC must be received into the laboratory with the tamper-evident seal intact to be tested. The face of the SAC contains information for the sample, including the date and time of the collection, the donor identification, donor initials, and the collector's signature. All samples are assigned a unique accession number that is used to identify a sample throughout the testing procedure. A sample size suitable for the screening assay is weighed and placed in a tube. The remainder of the hair is replaced in the foil and in the SAC. The samples are filed for later reweighing if determined presumptive positive by the screening assay. Most laboratories maintain negative samples for a period of 1 week to 1 month. Positive specimens are maintained for a period of 5 years or until the resolution of any litigation.

ANALYTICAL PROCESS

Specimen Preparation

Unlike biological fluids or tissues that are obtained from inside the body, hair specimens may be contaminated externally by environmental exposure to drugs either by vapor or by physical contact with the hair. For screening, a wash step is not necessary and is usually not performed. However, a wash or decontamination step is required in drug confirmation. The challenge in any wash procedure is to remove as much drug as possible that is on the external surface of the hair without removing drug that is in the hair internally. A number of wash techniques have been employed with varying degrees of success. Methanol or ethanol washes, with or without water or buffer washes, have been employed. Other solvents such as acetone and methylene chloride have also been utilized. Some procedures have used from 0.05% to 1% sodium dodecyl sulfate as a wash agent. These wash steps often occur with incubation at 37 °C for a period of time.

The authors have used an extended aqueous (polar) wash method to decontaminate the hair prior to drug extraction. This includes an isopropanol wash followed by multiple washes with 0.01 mol/L phosphate buffer, pH 6, at 37 °C. The theory behind this wash method is that hair is porous, thus a powder deposited on the hair may remain external and removable by a non-hair-swelling agent such as an organic solvent (e.g., dichloromethane, dry isopropyl alcohol). However, if this powder becomes wet, whether by sweat or humidity, the drug diffuses through the cuticular shield and into spaces of the cortex of the hair. To allow this drug to diffuse back out of the hair prior to analysis, an aqueous environment must be provided. Critics of aqueous washing contend that drugs due to ingestion may be removed by the extensive washing. This concern is mitigated for intact positive hair because a steady plateau is reached where no additional drug is removed after the initial two or three washes. However, the criticism is valid for drug-positive hair samples that have been rendered porous by various cosmetic procedures because in this case drug from ingestion could diffuse out of the hair if the hair is sufficiently damaged.

For screening, there is the additional need for speed, since the purpose is to quickly identify those samples that will need to be weighed again, washed, and confirmed for particular drugs. Unlike liquid matrices that have only to be poured and pipetted into the analytical vessel, hair samples obviously must first be liquefied prior to drug extraction. There are a number of methods in the literature. Some laboratories precede their extraction method with a pulverization step, such as with a bead beater. Pulverization does indeed increase the efficiency of the extraction process by breaking the cuticular barrier, thus permitting the penetration of solvents into the hair and diffusion of solutes out of the hair. However, pulverization is not practical for high-volume testing, so methods that recover drugs from the interior of the hair in a short time without pulverization are needed. However, pulverization does make the sample more homogeneous, thus increasing the precision of the testing.

Other methods of recovering drugs from hair for the screening process include methanol, acidic methanol, or low pH aqueous solutions at elevated temperatures and usually for 2 h or less. It is not certain how well all drugs from the interior of the hair are recovered with these methods in the usual 2 h allotted, as recovery experiments have not always been performed to demonstrate complete removal of the drug(s) from the hair. If hair washing is not performed, drugs from sweat or environmental contamination contribute to the drug in the recovered solution used for testing.

A highly effective method for complete extraction of drugs from hair is that of Baumgartner (U.S. Patent #6,350,582 B1), consisting of dithiothreitol (DTT) and proteinase K at pH 9.5, a combination that within 2 h entirely digests the hair such that the keratin matrix is dissolved, leaving only melanin granules in the resulting solution. For screening with immunoassays, this solution is then neutralized (dropping the pH to <7, where DTT is inactive) and deactivated (by addition of copper sulfate), which precipitates much of the DTT at low pH. This digestion method is particularly compatible with radioimmunoassay methods that show no interference by the residual DTT and enzyme.

A modification of this DTT-proteolytic method has recently been developed (U.S. Patent #8,329,417). This method, using DTT only, was shown to disrupt the cuticle barrier sufficiently in 2 h to allow rapid elution of drug out of the hair specimen. Again, following incubation with the DTT at high pH, the sample is deactivated with copper sulfate and acidified. While some drugs elute best at high pH, others elute rapidly upon acidification once the digestion has taken place. Thus all drugs are readily recovered with near 100% efficiencies if the proper testing conditions are optimized for extracting the drugs from the hair.

If the hair is subjected to a wash procedure, the drug still must be recovered from the samples. There are many methods in use, including aqueous, methanol, with or without pulverization and sonication. Whatever method is chosen, it must, of course, be proven to recover most of the drug from the hair without conversion of any of the analytes during the process. Once the drug has been recovered, the solution is carried through extraction or clean-up procedures tailored to remove the impurities and interferences from the extraction medium while retaining the analytes of interest.

Screening

Although RIA was the primary screening method used in the early days of hair testing, it has been replaced by microplate enzyme immunoassays (ELISA). Since hair is not an approved specimen for these commercially available assays, each laboratory that performs hair testing must validate the assay for this use. These microplates are coated with an antibody specific for a particular drug, and then horseradish peroxidase (HRP)-linked antigen and the sample are combined in the wells; after incubation the wells are washed and substrate added, usually followed by acidic stopping solution which also changes the color from blue to a higher intensity yellow. In hair testing, it is the parent compound that is present in the highest amount, similar to the composition in the subject's blood, and the antibodies for hair assays therefore need to be directed to the parent compounds unless the process of extracting the drug from the hair converts the parent to a detected product of the parent. For the cocaine group, cocaine is primarily detected, with benzoylecgoine at usually 10% or less. For heroin use detection, the antibody may be morphine specific or also react readily with 6-acetylmorphine (6-AM). In extraction of hair for opiate screening, it has been observed that morphine is more difficult than some analytes to recover from hair. Since the hair of heroin users is likely to be contaminated with 6-AM, less effective extraction procedures benefit from an assay antibody that recognizes 6-AM as well as morphine, as this will help to avoid missing low-level morphine

presence near the cutoff. For the amphetamines group, methamphetamine will be in the hair at about a 10:1 ratio with its metabolite amphetamine; MDMA and MDEA will show a similar ratio with MDA.

Antibodies for screening assays are selected to minimize unwanted cross-reactivities in some cases or, on the other hand, to exploit cross-reactivity to achieve an assay that detects a broader range of related compounds. For example, cocaine assays are primarily specific for cocaine and benzoylecgonine to different degrees. Opiate assays, however, can be designed to detect numerous opiates, including codeine, hydrocodone, hydromorphone, oxycodone, and oxymorphone in addition to morphine and 6-monoacetylmorphine. If these pain medications are not of interest in a particular setting, a more morphine-specific assay would be designed by selection of a more specific antibody. Likewise, amphetamine antibodies are usually reactive either with methamphetamine and amphetamine or with methamphetamine, MDMA, and MDEA. It is rare for a methamphetamine antibody to detect methamphetamine, amphetamine, MDMA, MDA, and MDEA, all with adequate sensitivity; therefore, to detect the range of amphetamines, two assays utilizing two different antibodies are generally required.

Marijuana use results in high levels of delta-9-tetrahydrocannabinol (THC) in the hair, but this is not conclusive evidence of use because of the abundance of THC in smoke, which could readily be on the hair of non-using occupants of a room where marijuana was being used. Thus, the definitive evidence of marijuana use is the finding of picogram levels of the metabolite 11-nor-9-carboxy-delta-9-THC in the hair extract by GC-MS/MS confirmation. The hair-screening assay, on the other hand, relies on the presence in or on the hair of multiple and even unidentified cannabinoids. Marijuana-screening antibodies tend to have a high false-positive rate, mainly because the assays are not directed at THC or carboxy THC exclusively but also other cannabinoid-like compounds. In addition, there appear to be non-cannabinoid-related cross-reacting compounds in hair that can result in false-positive screening results. The challenge in screening for marijuana-positive hair samples is to achieve sensitivity for true positives while reducing the false positives.

Screening assays for hair require orders of magnitude greater sensitivity than assays for some other matrices, especially urine. In our laboratory, assays are performed with extracted equivalents of 0.125–0.25 mg of hair. In the case of the opiate assay, for example, this equates to detection at the cutoff of 2 ng/10 mg hair of 25 pg morphine in the well of the microplate.

Confirmation

The screening assays identify negative and presumptive positive specimens for the drug classes screened. The next step is to reweigh the presumptive positive specimens and prepare them for confirmation by extensive washing, digestion (recovery of the drugs from the hair), and extraction for LC-MS/MS, GC-MS/MS, or GC/MS.

The analytes identified in the confirmation process should be based on several factors. One factor is to identify the most abundant substance found in the hair following the use of the particular drug. In hair, the parent drug is usually present in the highest concentration. This potentially complicates the interpretation of the findings as the parent drug will also be present if any external contamination of the hair has occurred. That is why it is also important to look for metabolites of these drugs, as the presence of these metabolites in the hair represents internal consumption of the drug. Table 3 lists the most abundant substances and other metabolites that may be included in confirmation testing.

As with any analytical method used in a forensic laboratory, a detailed validation must be performed in hair samples to support the use of the method for reliable identification of drugs. However, with low-level determination of drugs in hair, it is often difficult to utilize ion ratios in compound identification at the levels required for hair analysis due to the fact that the second product ion is not always available or usable. In nature one does not always know what compounds will produce the workable multiple daughter ions; not all compounds have been measured using tandem mass spectrometry, and some presently being measured also do not produce workable multiple ion profiles. The use of MS/MS technology has helped to resolve the severe matrix issue encountered in hair analysis. Other approaches such as GC-GC/MS have addressed the issue of the matrix problems but have not been able to achieve the levels of detection required for

Table 3. Targets for Confirmation Testing

Drug Used	Primary Hair Product	Metabolites Found
Amphetamines		
Amphetamine	Amphetamine	
Methamphetamine	Methamphetamine	Amphetamine
MDMA	MDMA	MDA
MDEA	MDEA	MDA
MDA	MDA	
Cocaine	Cocaine	Benzoylecgonine
		Norcocaine
		o-Hydroxycocaine
		m-Hydroxycocaine
		p-Hydroxycocaine
Heroin	6-AM	Morphine
Marijuana	Delta-9-THC	Carboxy THC
PCP	PCP	

accurate and reliable hair analysis and therefore result in increasing false-negative reporting. This is an issue of single quadrupole analysis not being sufficiently specific and sensitive for routine hair analysis, especially with the detection of carboxy THC in marijuana analysis.

ETHYL GLUCURONIDE

Ethyl glucuronide (EtG) is a specific biomarker of long-term alcohol abuse, and the sensitivity of hair EtG is better than any other long-term marker of alcohol abuse currently available. Head hair is the only appropriate sample for this test.

The proposed cutoff for EtG in hair strongly suggests chronic excessive alcohol consumption and was proposed by the World Health Organization with the SoHT. The cutoff was established at 30 pg/mg scalp hair measured in the approximate 3-month collection. The consensus, adopted in June 2009 by the SoHT and revised in March 2011, applies to the determination of chronic excessive alcohol consumption (i.e., more than 60 g of pure ethanol/day for several months). Successful participation in the EtG proficiency testing program in Europe has been the criteria for actively performing the testing commercially.

HAIR TESTING AND HAIR COLOR OR RACIAL BIAS

Claims of "race bias" have been made from time to time against hair testing as well as urine testing. These claims have not been successful in legal forums against either matrix as they are not supportable scientifically. On four separate occasions, federal courts dismissed racial bias claims made against hair testing on motions for summary judgment. Summary judgment motions are granted when all admissible evidence points to only one conclusion. There is no evidence to support a claim that people would spontaneously create cocaine in their bodies because

of their race. Likewise, there is no "genetic propensity" to produce positive results for cocaine. Variations of the claim involving the use of "products" or "environmental factors" that somehow affect only one race are equally unsupportable and without scientific merit when proper test methodology is applied.

Extensive research comparing various testing methodologies was conducted over the last decade. Several researchers using methodologies not routinely used in workplace testing claimed to see a "potential bias" in their results with hair from rats, hair soaked in cocaine, and small-scale human hair studies. However, these studies were extremely limited, inconsistent in their findings, and no actual "bias" was ever quantified, only the "potential" for bias. The methodologies used by the authors of the small human studies failed to consider or inadequately addressed the contribution of sweat and extraction efficiency on their results. In contrast, the results from large human populations were also studied using methodology commonly employed in most workplace testing, and these study results consistently demonstrated that no bias occurred when appropriate methodology was utilized.

Every large-scale population study dealing with race and/or hair color bias has concluded that hair color or race factors do not lead to any statistically important variations that would create a bias. Several studies using extended aqueous washing methodology have established that there is no systematic bias occurring with this technology. A different aspect of color effects in hair analysis is a suggestion that perhaps pigmented hair would be more prone to contamination and difficulty in identifying a contaminated hair. This too has been disproven by recent studies.

FUTURE DIRECTIONS

Compared to other biological specimens, the testing of drugs in hair is a relatively recent development. As a result, potential uses of hair testing are beginning to be explored. For example, segmental analysis of hair can provide a timeline of use over a period of months. Carrying this one step further, it may be possible to estimate the approximate dose of a drug ingested over a period of time. Obviously, a reliable wash procedure is required for these estimates to be made. Initial work in this laboratory with cannabis and opiates has yielded promising results.

SUGGESTED READING

1. Baumgartner W, Hill V. Hair analysis for organic analytes: methodology, reliability issues, and field studies. In: Kintz P, ed. Drug testing in hair. Boca Raton, FL: CRC Press, 1996:224–64.
2. Baumgartner W, Hill V. Sample preparation techniques. Forensic Sci Int 1993;63:121–35.
3. Baumgartner AM, Jones PF, Baumgartner WA, Black CT. Radioimmunoassay of hair for determining opiate abuse histories. J Nucl Med 1979;20:748–52.
4. Cairns T, Hill V, Schaffer M, Thistle W. Amphetamines in washed hair of demonstrated users and workplace subjects. Forensic Sci Int 2004;145:137–42.
5. Cairns T, Hill V, Schaffer M, Thistle W. Levels of cocaine and its metabolites in washed hair of demonstrated cocaine users and workplace subjects. Forensic Sci Int 2004;145:175–81.
6. Cairns T, Hill V, Schaffer M, Thistle W. Removing and identifying drug contamination in the analysis of human hair. Forensic Sci Int 2004;145:97–108.
7. Cone EJ. Testing human hair for drugs of abuse I. Individual dose and time profiles of morphine and codeine in plasma, saliva, urine and beard compared to drug induced effects on pupils and behavior. J Anal Toxicol 1990;14:1–7.
8. Hill V, Cairns T, Cheng CC, Schaffer M. Multiple aspects of hair analysis for opiates: methodology, clinical and workplace populations, codeine, and poppy seed ingestion. J Anal Toxicol 2005;29:696–703.
9. Kintz P. Consensus of the Society of Hair Testing on hair testing for chronic excessive alcohol consumption 2009. Forensic Sci Int 2010;196:2.
10. Mandatory Guidelines and Proposed Revisions to Mandatory Guidelines for Federal Workplace Drug Testing Programs, Federal Register, April 13, 2004, Vol. 69, No. 71.
11. Picchini S, Pacifici R, Altieri I, Pellegrini M, Zuccaro P. Determination of opiates and cocaine in hair as trimethylsilyl derivatives using gas chromatography-tandem mass spectrometry. J Anal Tox 1999;23:343–8.
12. Ropero-Miller JD, Stout PR. Analysis of cocaine analytes in human hair II. Evaluation of different hair color and ethnicity types. Research Triangle Park, NC: RTI International, 2011.
13. National Criminal Justice Reference Service. Document no. 234628. https://www.ncjrs.gov/app/topics/Topic.aspx?topicid=97 (Accessed April 10, 2013).
14. Schaffer M, Wang WL, Irving J. An evaluation of two wash procedures for the differentiation of external contamination versus ingestion in the analysis of human hair samples for cocaine. J Anal Toxicol 2002;26:485–8.
15. Society of Hair Testing. Consensus of the society of hair testing for doping agents. http://www.soht.org/html/Statements.html (Accessed April 10, 2013).
16. Society of Hair Testing. Recommendations for hair testing. Forensic Sci Int 2004;145:83–4.
17. Society of Hair Testing. Statement of the society of hair testing concerning the examination of drugs in human hair. Forensic Sci Int 1997;84:3–6.
18. Society of Hair Testing website. http://www.soht.org (Accessed April 10, 2013).
19. Verstraete AG. Detection times of drugs of abuse in blood, urine and oral fluid. Ther Drug Monit 2004;26:200–5.

CHAPTER 35

Meconium

Teresa Gray

INTRODUCTION

Alcohol, tobacco, and drug use by pregnant women is associated with adverse cognitive, physical, and psychological outcomes in their exposed children, but identifying affected children can be challenging. Maternal self-report may be unreliable due to feelings of guilt or embarrassment or fear of prosecution; therefore, toxicological testing of the mother or neonate is preferred. Meconium, the first neonatal feces, is often chosen over other maternal and/or neonatal matrices (Table 1) to provide objective evidence of prenatal drug exposure. Although meconium testing is usually initiated in a clinical setting, results can extend beyond informing diagnosis and guiding medical treatment into more traditional forensic contexts. Depending on the jurisdiction, positive meconium results could lead to maternal referral to drug treatment and/or social service programs or mandatory reporting of child abuse and neglect, potentially causing removal of the child from the mother's care, monetary fine, or imprisonment. In addition, postmortem investigations of stillborn fetuses have used meconium testing to assist cause-of-death determinations. Given the serious consequences, it is imperative that the advantages and limitations of meconium testing are understood, the chosen analytical techniques scientifically sound, and results properly interpreted.

Meconium is primarily composed of mucopolysaccharides, water, bile salts, bile acids, epithelial cells, and other lipids. Its color ranges from dark green to brown-black and its texture is highly viscous. Previously thought to be sterile, recent findings suggest bacterial colonization, yet meconium remains odorless. The complex composition and the need to aliquot by weighing make meconium analysis challenging and laborious as compared to other matrices.

Meconium is usually excreted within the first 1–3 d of life and specimens are easily and noninvasively collected from soiled diapers. Contamination by neonatal urine is possible if urine collection devices are not employed; these devices frequently irritate delicate neonatal skin and do not adhere properly. Defecation may be delayed in some infants. Decreased gestational age is associated with delayed meconium passage, as is postnatal morphine treatment, which many premature infants receive. Delayed passage hampers exposure determination and related diagnoses, such as opioid-elicited neonatal abstinence syndrome. Additionally, meconium is released into amniotic fluid prior to birth in approximately 12% of deliveries, possibly precluding meconium testing.

DRUG DISPOSITION

Drugs, metabolites, and other exogenous agents are theorized to deposit in meconium through biliary excretion following fetal hepatic metabolism and by the swallowing of contaminated amniotic fluid. Because accumulation begins around the 12th week of gestation, meconium is assumed to reflect

Table 1. Advantages, Limitations, Detection Windows, and Expected Concentration Ranges for Maternal and Neonatal Biological Fluids and Tissues Used in Gestational Drug-Exposure Monitoring

Matrix	Collection	Detection Window	Analyte Concentration	Notes
Maternal fluids and tissues				
Urine	Noninvasive; easy to adulterate	1–3 d, except for frequent cannabis use	ng - µg/mL	Standardized urine cutoff concentrations; immunoassay and chromatographic analytical procedures available
Hair	Easy, noninvasive; collected under direct observation	Months to years, depending on hair length	pg - ng/mg	Frequently requires enzymatic digestion, cutting, or pulverization before analysis; segmental analysis may reflect time of use; basic drugs preferentially bind to melanin in hair, generating a color bias; potential for external contamination
Oral fluid	Easy, noninvasive; collected under direct observation	0.5–36 h, depending on drug	pg - µg/mL	Parent drug generally more prevalent than metabolites; higher concentrations of basic drugs in oral fluid than plasma due to ion trapping; stimulation of salivary flow generally decreases drug concentrations; analyte recovery dependent on collection device
Blood/plasma	Invasive; requires trained personnel; risk of infection, pain and swelling	1–3 d	ng - µg/mL	Most closely reflects drug exposure of the fetus
Sweat	Easy, noninvasive	A few days before patch application through removal	pg - ng/patch	Results considered qualitative rather than quantitative
Neonatal fluids and tissues				
Urine	Requires special collection device that often fails to adhere or may irritate neonatal skin	1–3 d prior to delivery	ng - µg/mL	
Hair	Easy, noninvasive; however, consent may be difficult to obtain for cosmetic or cultural reasons	Third trimester	pg - ng/mg	Often insufficient quantities available; can be collected within first three months, after which time neonatal hair replaces fetal hair; may be contaminated by drug-containing amniotic fluid; basic drugs preferentially bind to melanin in hair

Specimen	Collection	Detection window	Units	Comments
Fingernails/toenails	Easy, noninvasive	Unknown	ng/mg	Few published reports specifically identifying prenatal drug exposure; pulverization required prior to extraction; all clippings over first 3 months required for adequate sensitivity
Vernix caseosa	Easily removed from a newborn's skin with gauze prior to first bath	Unknown	Qualitative assessment	Thick white lipid and cell mixture covering the fetus starting at about 24 weeks gestational age, protecting fetal skin from amniotic fluid; limited quantities available; weighing difficult; therefore, quantitative analysis not possible
Shared fluids and tissues				
Umbilical cord tissue	Easy, noninvasive	Unknown	ng/g	Available immediately after birth; little data to define detection window; analyte disposition along cord length unknown
Umbilical cord blood	Easy, noninvasive	Unknown, but presumed to be similar to maternal blood	ng - µg/mL	Available immediately after birth
Amniotic fluid	Possible, but safety risk to sample during pregnancy; may be available as excess specimen from other medical procedures; at birth, noninvasively collected if under medical observation prior to rupture of membranes	Presumed to have long window of detection, but unproven	ng/mL	Consists of a maternal blood filtrate in early pregnancy, mostly fetal urine in later gestation; fetus may be re-exposed to drug and metabolites by continuously swallowing amniotic fluid; transdermal exposure from amniotic fluid possible early in pregnancy before skin fully develops or late in pregnancy when vernix caseosa production decreases; rarely collected for prenatal drug exposure detection
Placenta	Easy, noninvasive, and adequate specimen amount; waste material after birth	Unknown	ng/g	Few published reports of placenta analysis following prenatal exposure; *in vitro* transplacental studies have analyzed placenta tissue perfused with drug-containing media

drug exposure in the second and third trimesters, representing the longest window of drug detection among neonatal matrices. However, few studies have attempted to objectively determine drug detection windows in meconium. Meconium specimens from terminated human fetuses as young as 17 weeks gestation had detectable drug concentrations. Yet other more recent human data suggest that second trimester drug exposure is poorly documented in meconium from term or near-term infants, and the time between last exposure and birth is critical for detection of prenatal exposure. Meconium testing more reliably reflected third trimester drug use, particularly if use occurred in the last few weeks of pregnancy in a population of women whose drug use was monitored by thrice-weekly urine drug screens.

Additional studies are necessary to corroborate the third-trimester drug-exposure detection window, although these results are consistent with known maternal-fetal physiology. Greater transplacental drug diffusion occurs in term placentas, as compared to preterm placentas, and the expression of P-glycoprotein, a drug efflux transporter, decreases as pregnancy progresses. Additionally, it is thought that meconium formation increases with fetal weight, thus more meconium is produced at the end of pregnancy than during the second trimester. If the window of drug detection in meconium is limited to the last trimester, earlier exposures could only be identified if the mother self-reported substance use, maternal biological specimens were positive earlier in gestation, or maternal hair was positive at birth.

DRUG ANALYSIS

Like most forensic drug testing, meconium analysis generally entails a two-stage approach. First, specimens are screened for a variety of drug classes, most often by immunoassay. If the screening result falls below a predetermined cutoff concentration, the specimen is considered negative and no further testing is required. Conversely, if the result exceeds the cutoff, a second analysis, based on a different scientific principle, is performed to confirm the identity of the reactive substance and quantify the amount present.

Screening

Urine immunoassay techniques have been modified for meconium, many times without extensive validation or confirmation. Specimens are liquefied with water or buffer prior to analysis; some assays require more involved specimen preparation, such as precipitation with organic solvent to remove particulates, in order to improve testing results. Enzyme multiplied immunoassay technique (EMIT) is historically the most commonly employed screening assay, but fluorescence polarization immunoassay (FPIA), radioimmunoassay (RIA), and enzyme-linked immunosorbent assay (ELISA) have also been utilized. Direct comparison of ELISA and EMIT for cannabinoids, amphetamines, methadone, propoxyphene, cocaine, phencyclidine, barbiturates, benzodiazepines, and opioids found fair agreement between the two screening techniques, but ELISA required half the time of EMIT. A recent publication describes a screening procedure by liquid chromatography coupled with a time-of-flight (TOF) mass spectrometer that was able to detect more than 70 compounds, including illicit drugs, local anesthetics, antidepressants, and antipsychotics.

Confirmatory Analysis

Positive immunoassay results should be confirmed by a more specific method, generally a chromatographic method such as gas chromatography/mass spectrometry (GC/MS), liquid chromatography/mass spectrometry (LC/MS), or tandem mass spectrometry (MS/MS), as false-positive immunoassay results are possible. Meconium concentrations are typically in the ng/g to mg/g range, so confirmatory techniques should be sufficiently sensitive.

Meconium preparation is more complex than traditional matrices because of its semisolid composition. Meconium is not homogenous; therefore, specimens should be mixed well before sampling. As with other solid tissues, meconium specimens are aliquoted by weighing. Specimen preparation generally includes homogenization with an aqueous buffer or solvent prior to liquid/liquid or solid-phase extraction (SPE). Homogenization with methanol or acetonitrile offers the added advantage of precipitating matrix proteins that could otherwise clog SPE columns or interfere with drug adsorption.

Often the amount of meconium is limited; therefore, prioritizing testing may be warranted. Most confirmatory analyses use a relatively large amount of meconium (0.5–1.0 g) and target a single drug class, yet many neonates are exposed to multiple drugs. As LC-MS/MS analysis gains popularity, these problems may be alleviated; newer published methods evaluate multiple drug classes (e.g., opiates, cocaine, and amphetamines) in a single method using smaller specimen amounts without sacrificing sensitivity.

Most importantly, confirmatory analyses should include appropriate drug targets to minimize false positives and maximize identification of drug-exposed children. Adult and fetal metabolism can differ and, thus, the metabolites needed in meconium testing may be different from analytes ordinarily evaluated in postmortem or workplace drug testing. For example, a large portion of cocaine-exposed neonates would not be identified if only cocaine, benzoylecgonine, and cocaethylene were included in confirmatory analyses. M-hydroxybenzoylecgonine (mOHBE), a minor urinary cocaine metabolite in adults, is the primary cocaine metabolite present in meconium. Additionally, the extent of Phase II metabolic products deposited in meconium is not well established, so hydrolysis or direct analysis of drug conjugates may be necessary to improve confirmation rates. For example, initial research indicates that cannabinoid detection improves nearly twofold following alkaline hydrolysis of 11-nor-9-carboxy-Δ^9-tetrahydrocannabinol glucuronide. Table 2 lists the most common drug biomarkers analyzed in meconium by published confirmatory methods. In addition to drugs of abuse and pharmaceuticals, meconium testing also determined exposure to selenium, phthalates, pesticides, herbicides, and other environmental agents.

Table 2. Common Drugs and Metabolites Analyzed in Meconium

Amphetamines
Amphetamine
Methamphetamine
3,4-Methylenedioxy-
  methamphetamine (MDMA)
Benzodiazepines
Alprazolam
α-Hydroxyalprazolam
Clonazepam
7-Aminoclonazepam
Diazepam
Nordiazepam
Flurazepam
Desalkylflurazepam
α-Hydroxyethylflurazepam
Lorazepam
Midazolam
Oxazepam
Temazepam
α-Hydroxytriazolam

Cannabinoids
Δ^9-Tetrahydrocannabinol (THC)
11-Hydroxy-THC
11-Nor-9-carboxy-THC
Cocaine
Cocaine
Benzoylecgonine (BE)
Cocaethylene
m-Hydroxy-BE
Opiates
Morphine
Codeine
Hydrocodone
Hydromorphone
Oxycodone
Methadone and cyclic metabolite
Buprenorphine
Norbuprenorphine

Ethanol
Fatty acid ethyl esters
  Ethyl laurate
  Ethyl myristate
  Ethyl palmitate
  Ethyl palmitoleate
  Ethyl stearate
  Ethyl oleate
  Ethyl linoleate
  Ethyl linolenate
  Ethyl arachidonate
Ethyl glucuronide
Ethyl sulfate
Other
Tobacco related
  Nicotine
  Cotinine
  3′-trans-Hydroxycotinine
PCP

INTERPRETATION OF RESULTS

Meconium testing offers objective evidence of maternal drug use. In most studies, detection rates with meconium are comparable or greater than maternal self-report or toxicological testing in other matrices. Yet, meconium's ability to reflect drug use early in pregnancy is limited by known maternal-fetal physiology, as previously described. Furthermore, women often, after discovering their pregnancy, dramatically reduce or cease drug and/or tobacco use, thus identifying early drug exposure would be dependent on maternal admission. When drug use in early pregnancy is suspected, maternal interviews must be carefully constructed to elicit more truthful and accurate recall.

Most confirmatory assays are quantitative, yet the significance of meconium concentrations is not clear. Controlled administration studies in animals demonstrate positive correlations between maternal dose and meconium concentration for some drugs of abuse; however, extrapolating animal results to humans would be imprudent. Obvious safety and ethical concerns prohibit controlled illicit drug administration to pregnant women to evaluate dose-concentration relationships. Determining maternal dose by self-report has several limitations, so for illicit drugs the dose is rarely, if ever, known. Monitoring pharmacotherapeutics, however, offers a unique opportunity to evaluate concentration dependence on maternal dose. Two studies followed women maintained on methadone or buprenorphine during pregnancy, but there was no apparent relationship between total dose during pregnancy or the third trimester and methadone, buprenorphine, or their respective metabolite concentrations in meconium.

Several factors may contribute to the lack of a dose-concentration correlation. First, maternal plasma concentrations often are not related to the dose received due to highly variable pharmacokinetic and pharmacogenetic influences. Second, placental permeability changes over pregnancy; thus, inconsistent exposure to the fetus may result in unpredictable meconium concentrations. Maternal, placental, and fetal metabolism may contribute to differing extents to the final spectrum of analytes and concentrations deposited in meconium. Also, the timing of meconium collection may influence quantitative relationships. Multiple researchers have shown decreasing concentrations in meconium passages as time from birth increases, with concentrations often falling below quantification limits within 48 h. The relative proportion of metabolites found in sequential meconium passages can differ, presumably after induction of metabolic processes at birth. Furthermore, dose-concentration relationships could be obfuscated by contributions from extracorporeal urine contaminating meconium in the diaper.

Given the state of knowledge at this time, meconium concentrations should not be employed to infer the degree of maternal drug use. Some laboratories report meconium results as positive or negative using an administratively set cutoff, likely based on analytical capability. This conservative approach appears to be reasonable, as reporting meconium concentrations may result in the requesting agency, possibly a clinician, researcher, or child protective services agent, erroneously concluding that higher concentrations indicate a higher degree of maternal substance use. The end user should also be aware of drugs administered during labor before interpreting meconium results. A recent publication screening meconium samples with TOF MS observed a high prevalence of local anesthetics and vasopressors administered intrapartum. Therefore, caution should be used when interpreting results for drugs, such as opioids, routinely used during delivery.

Although a linear dose-concentration relationship may not exist, it may be possible to differentiate active maternal use from passive exposure by defining a cutoff concentration in meconium, particularly for ethanol and tobacco. Detecting ethanol use poses a challenge, as ethanol itself is extensively metabolized and not likely to deposit unchanged in meconium. Minor nonoxidative ethanol metabolites, fatty acid ethyl esters (FAEE) (Table 2), ethyl glucuronide (EtG), and ethyl sulfate (EtS) have been investigated in meconium as evidence of maternal ethanol use. Using populations abstaining from alcohol use for cultural and/or religious reasons, several investigators have attempted to define "baseline" levels to account for endogenous ethanol or passive exposure to ethanol-containing foods or medicines. Individual FAEE, various combinations of FAEE, EtG, and EtS have been evaluated; however, to date there is no universally accepted cutoff to differentiate ethanol abstainers, moderate users, and heavy abusers.

Using meconium results to differentiate active smokers from nonsmokers and those passively exposed has been more successful. Nicotine is metabolized to cotinine, which is further metabolized to trans-3'-hydroxycotinine, the latter being the most prevalent and abundant biomarker found in meconium. Concentrations of nicotine, cotinine, or trans-3'-hydroxycotinine greater than 10 ng/g indicated active maternal smoking in two study groups, but meconium results were not able to distinguish nonsmokers from women passively exposed to tobacco smoke.

CONCLUSION

Identification of prenatal drug exposure through meconium testing or other means is important for understanding and mitigating potential consequences of exposure. Meconium is a unique analytical matrix, with many characteristics still unknown or only partially understood. Therefore, it is imperative that meconium testing results are interpreted cautiously.

RECOMMENDED READING

1. Gray T, Huestis M. Bioanalytical procedures for monitoring in utero drug exposure. Anal Bioanal Chem 2007; 388(7):1455–65.
2. Lozano J, Garcia-Algar O, Vall O, de la Torre R, Scaravelli G, Pichini S. Biological matrices for the evaluation of in utero exposure to drugs of abuse. Ther Drug Monit 2007; 29(6): 711–34.

Index

Index entries (page numbers) set in *italics* refer to figures and/or tables.

Abbott ADx® analyzer, 43, 158
Abbott Laboratories, 158–159
Absorption. *See also specific drugs*
    of alcohol, 208–210, *209*, *210*
    of cocaine, 297, *298*
    of opioids, 280
Abstinence syndrome, 276, *279*
Accidental death, drug intoxication, 4
Accuracy, 194, 195–196, 199
Acetaminophen, *445*, 445–446
    analgesics, and, 283
    dihydrocodeine and, 283
    inhalants and, 463, 464
    oxycodone and, 286
    pentazocine and, 287
    propoxyphene and, 287
Acetone, 504–505
Acidity, 102. *See also* pH
Acrivastine, *438*
Action potential, 398, 399
Acute cyanide poisoning, 457
Acute intermittent porphyria (AIP), 505
Acute pain, 62
Acute tolerance, ethanol, 222–223
Addiction, in pain management, 65
Adolescent inhalant abuse, 461, 462
Adsorbent, 128–129
Affinity, in immunology, 167
Agonist behavior, opioid, 272
Agranulocytosis, 429
Akathisia, 430
Alcohol, 205, 218–219. *See also* Ethanol
    absorption, 208–210, *209*, *210*
    behavioral effects of, 20–21
    blood analysis, 223–229
    breath analysis, 226–228

case history, 88–89
as a central nervous system depressant, 24
classification, 205–207, *206*
distribution, in the body, 210–212, *212*
driving and, 16–22
excretion, 214–215
hair specimen analysis, 517
legal and regulatory aspects, *231*, 231–235, *232*
metabolism, 212–214, *214*
performance-enhancing drug testing and, 58
pharmacokinetics, 215–217, *216*
postmortem forensic toxicology and, 3–4
production of beverages, 207–208
Widmark equation, 217–218
in the workplace, 235
Alcohol dehydrogenase (ADH), 10, 212, 217, 219, 224
Alcoholic beverage production, 207–208
Aldehyde dehydrogenase (ALDH), 212
Alprazolam, *238*, *241*, 245–246
Aluminum, 471–472
Amines. *See specific amines*
Amiodarone, *400*, 401
Amitriptyline, 268, *404*, 408, *409*, *415*
    toxicity and, 416–417, *417*
Amniotic fluid, *527*
Amoxapine, *405*, *408*
Amphetamines, 56, 353–355
    abuse, 358–360
    analysis, 362–367
    drug testing, in pain management, *67*
    effects, 355–357
    gas chromatography/mass spectrometry
        (GC/MS) and, 3
    hair specimen analysis, *521*
    interpretation, 367–370

Amphetamines (*continued*)
  metabolism, 509
  pharmacokinetics, 360–362
  postmortem forensic toxicology, 369–370
  separation, 189
  therapeutic drug conversion to, 370
  therapeutic uses, 357–358
Anabolic-androgenic steroids (AAS), *50*, 52–53, *54*. *See also* Steroids
Analgesic effect, 271, 276. *See also* Narcotic analgesics; Opiates; Opioids
Analog cyclohexamine (PCE), 380
Analyte standard, 194
Analyte, 167, 171, 175, 194. *See also* Mass spectrometry
  benzodiazepine and, 248
  separation, 7
Analytical process, 6–9
Analytical reference standard, 194
Anaphylaxis, 502–503
Anesthetic
  dissociative, 374
  topical local, 293–294, 295
Anhydroecgonine methyl ester (AEME), 46, 299, 302
Antagonist behavior, opioid, 272
Antiarrhythmics, 398–402
Antibodies, 151–155, *152, 153*, 167. *See also* Immunoassays
Anticonvulsants, *394*, 394–398, 476
Antidepressants, 4, 24, 63, *394*, 394–398, *396, 401, 405*
  analysis, 412–415, *415*
  pharmacokinetics and metabolism, 407–412, *408, 409, 410, 411, 412, 413, 414, 416*, 509
  pharmacologic actions, 403–407
  toxicity and postmortem findings, 415–419, *417*
Anti-Doping Agency (WADA), 51, 52
Antigen, 167
Antigenic determinant, 167
Antihistamines, 435–440
Anti-inflammatory drugs, 441–445
Antipsychotic drugs, 24
Antipsychotics. *See also* Neuroleptics (Antipsychotics)
  atypical, 425–427
  typical, 423–425
Anxiety, treatment, 240, 266
Anxiolytics, 242
Aqueous (polar) wash, 518–519
Arachidonic acid
Aripiprazole, *427*
Aromatic compounds: fluorescence and, 119–120
Arrhythmias, 88, 297, 416

Arsenic, 472–474
Arterial-venous (A-V) difference, 211
Aspirin, 117, *442*
Atmospheric pressure photoionization, *181*, 181–182
Atmospheric pressure chemical ionization (APCI), 179–181, *180*
Atmospheric pressure ionization (API), 176–177, *177*
Atomic emission detector, 136–137
Avidity, 167

Back-extraction techniques, 104, 106–107
Barbiturates, 24, *67*, 261–262, 266–270, *267, 268*
  analysis, 263–264
  vs benzodiazepine, 240
  interpretation, 264–266
  pharmacokinetics, 262–263
  specimen stability, 487
Baumgartner, 519
Beer-Lambert law, 113, *113*
Beer's law, 113
Behavioral effects, lysergic acid diethylamide (LSD), 382–383
Behavioral impairment. *See* Psychomotor tasks
Behavioral toxicology, 379–380. *See also* Human performance toxicology
Benzamides, 422, *424*
Benzene ring shifts, 119–120
Benzene, 104
Benzodiazepines, 24, *67*
  analysis, 248–250
  chemistry and use, 237–243, *238–239, 240*
  individual, 245–248
  metabolism, 509
  interpretation, 250–251
  metabolism, *68, 244*
  pharmacology, 243–245
  retention time, *250*
  solvents and, 103
  specimen stability, 487–488. *See also specific drugs*
Benzomorphans, 274. *See also specific drugs*
Benzothiazepine, 422
Benzoylecgonine (BE), 299, 301, 302, 305–306, 308–309, 489–490
Berson, Solomon, 149
Beta-blockers, *50, 54*, 58
Beta-hydroxybutyrate (BHB), 504–505
Beta-2-agonists, *50, 54*, 58
Bile, postmortem collection, 5
Bioavailability, 89–90. *See also* Absorption; Xenobiotic
  cocaine and, 297

neuroleptics and, 423
therapeutic drugs and, 392
Biological matrix, 194
Blank sample, 194
Blood, as a specimen, 24. *See also* Blood alcohol analysis; Blood alcohol concentration (BAC); Blood-brain barrier; Blood calibrators; Blood pressure
carbon monoxide in, 11, 448–449
cocaine and, 306–308; drug testing and, 12–13, 42
drug testing, in pain management and, 73
ethanol in, 9–10, 229–230
gamma-hydroxybutyric acid (GHB) and, 259
gestational drug-exposure, *526*
human performance toxicology and, 16
inhalants and, 465
opioids and, 289
performance-enhancing drug testing and, 51
peripheral samples, 417
postmortem analysis, 5, 417, 491, 496, 501–502, *502*
specimen stability, 490–492
supply, absorption, 78
Blood alcohol analysis, 223–229
chemical oxidation, 223–224
gas-liquid chromatography, 225–226, *226*
enzymatic oxidation, 224
Blood alcohol concentration (BAC), 16–21, 209, 210, 214, 215, 216
acute alcoholic influence and, *221*
driving under the influence (DUI) and, *231*
ethanol tolerance and, 222–223
Blood-brain barrier
amphetamine and, 362
antihistamine and, 437
cocaine and, 311
ethanol and, 220
gamma-hydroxybutyric acid (GHB) and, 257
metals and, 476
neuroleptics and, 423, 432
opioids and, 273, 280, 283, 284, 286
Blood calibrators, 448
Blood pressure
amphetamine and, 355, 356, 357, 368
anticonvulsants and, 391
antidepressants and, 407
cannabis and, 27
central nervous system (CNS) depressants and, 24
central nervous system (CNS) stimulants and, 25
cocaine and, 307
drug recognition evaluation (DRE) and, 23

hallucinogens and, 375, *377*, 388
neuroleptics and, 429
phencyclidine (PCP) and, 26
Body mass index (BMI), 211
Bonded silica sorbents, 108
Brain. *See also* Blood-brain barrier; Central nervous system (CNS)
alcohol and, 211, *212*, 220, 223
anticonvulsants and, 393, 394, 396
benzodiazepines and, 240
cannabis and, 319–320, 322, 327, 329
central nervous system (CNS) depressants and, 262, 269
cocaine and, 295, 297, 307, 308, 310–311
cyanide and, 455, 457, 458
gamma-hydroxybutyric acid (GHB), 256
hallucinogens and, 374, 375, 382, 383
inhalants and, 463
metals and, 472, 475, 480
neuroleptics and, 428, 430
opioids and, 280, 287
phentermine and, 357
Breath analysis, for alcohol, 226–228
Breathalyzer®, 227–228
British Anti-Lewisite (BAL), 480
Bromazepam, *238*
Brompheniramine, *436*
Buprenorphine, *273, 277, 281, 282,* 282–283
metabolism, 509
Bupropion, 103–104, *405,* 410, *411, 415*
overdose, 418
Buspirone, 266, *267*
Butane, 465
Butaperazine, 431
Butophanol, *273, 275, 277, 281, 282,* 283
Butyrophenones, 422

Calibration, chromatograph, 145
Calibration curve, 40, 146–148, *147,* 194
Calibrators, 168, 194
Cannabidiol, 326
Cannabis, 27, *50, 54,* 57
absorption, 327–328
administration, 328–329
chemistry, 317–319
concentration in body specimens, 332–33, 335–343, *337, 339, 342*
distribution in the body, 329
driving impairment, 322–325
drug testing, in pain management, 69
effects, 319–322, *321*
elimination, 330–332
hair specimen analysis, 520–521, *521*
last use prediction, *333,* 333–335, *334*

Cannabis (*continued*)
  metabolism, 329–330
  specimen stability, 488–489
  therapeutic uses, 326
  tolerance, 325–326
Carbamazepine, *394*, 394–395
Carbon monoxide (CO), 11
  analysis, 448–449, *449*
  disposition, 448
  fire deaths, 452
  poisoning and autopsy findings, 449–451, *451*,
    453
  storage and stabilization, 452–453
  treatment, 451–452
Carboxyhemoglobin (COHb), 447–448, *450*, 452–453
  calculation, 448–449
  toxicity, 449–451, *451*
Carboxylic acid function, 102
Cardiac arrhythmias, 416
Cardiac effects
  arrhythmias, 398
  neuroleptics, 428
Cardiovascular system, ethanol in, 220
Carisoprodol, 63, 68, 266
Carrier gas, 130–131
Carryover, 39, 195, 199
Case histories, 88–92
  pharmacogenomic, 510–511
Cathione derivatives, 359–360, 362
Cause of death (COD), postmortem
    redistribution, 499–500
CBI cannabinoid receptor, 320
Celecoxib, *445*
Central nervous system (CNS). *See also* Brain;
    Central nervous system (CNS) depressants;
    Central nervous system (CNS) stimulants
  amphetamine and, 355
  anticonvulsants and, 399
  antihistamine and, 435, 437, 449
  carbon monoxide (CO) and, 450
  inhalants and, 463, 464
  metals and, 472, 478
  narcotic analgesics and, 442
Central nervous system (CNS) depressants, 24,
    237, 253, 281–282. *See also* Antihistamines;
    Barbiturates; Benzodiazepines; Cannabis;
    Gamma-hydroxybutyric acid (GHB);
    Opioids
Central nervous system (CNS) stimulants, 25,
    294, 353, 442. *See also* Amphetamines;
    Cocaine
  ethanol effects, 220
  performance-enhancing drug testing and, *50*,
    54, 55–56

Cerebrospinal fluid (CSF), 502
Cetirizine, *438*
Charge-coupled device (CCD), 115
Chelation therapy, 480–481, *481*
Chemical Diversion and Trafficking Act
    (CDTA), 354
Chemical ionization (CI), 174–176
  antidepressants analysis, 415
  diazepam analysis, 251
  lysergic acid diethylamide (LSD), 384
Chemical oxidation, 223–224
Chiral separations, 367
Chloral hydrate, 266–267, *267*
Chlordiazepoxide, *238*, *241*, 242, 250–251
Chloroform, 104, 464
Chlorophenolred (CPR), 160
Chlorpheniramine, *436*, *438*
Chlorpromazine, 297
Chromatogram, 122–123, *123*
  ethanol analysis and, *226*
  injectors, 132–135, *133*, *134*, 140
  mass spectrometry and, *190–191*
Chromatography, 8. *See also* Chromatogram;
    specific types of chromatography
  calibration curve, 40, 146–148, *147*, 194
  column efficiency, 124–125, 129
  gas, 122, 123, 130–138
  elution, 130
  extraction techniques, 103
  fundamentals, 121–128
  high-performance liquid, 122, 123, 124,
    138–144
  liquid, 121, 122
  paper, 129
  planar, 128–130
  quantitation, 144–148
  thin-layer, 128–129
  wall-coated open tubular (WCOT) column,
    122, 126–127, *133*, 134, 136, 139
Chromatographic method validations, 197–200
Chronic cyanide poisoning, 457–458
Chronic pain, 62, 275–276, 283
Cimetidine, *439*
Citalopram, *406*, *408*, *415*
  postmortem redistribution, 499, *500*
  toxicity and, 419
Clemastine, *436*
Clobazam, *238*
Clomipramine, *404*, 408
Clonazepam, *238*, *241*, 246
Cloned enzyme donor immunoassay (CEDIA®),
    160, 160–161, 168, 195
  amphetamines, 364
  opioids, 288

Clorazepate, *238*
Clorpromazine, *423*, 424
Clozapine, 422, 426, *427*, 427–428
Coated-tube techniques, 156
Cocaine, 13, 25, 293–294
   absorption, 297
   administration variants, 297, 300–302
   benzodiazepines and, 242
   chemistry, 294–295
   direct methods of analysis, 302–303
   excretion, 302
   gas chromatography/mass spectrometry
     (GC/MS) and, 37
   hair specimen analysis, 515, 520, *521*
   indirect methods of analysis, 303–305
   metabolism, 297–300, *298*
   pharmacology, 295–297
   plasma concentrations, 300–302
   specimen stability, 489–491
   window of detection, *87*
Codeine, *273*, *274*, *275*, *277*, *281*, *282*, 283
   case study, 512
Coefficient of variance (CV), 195
Cognitive performance tests, 28
Cold on-column injection, 134
Collagen, 502
College of American Pathologists (CAP)
     Laboratory Accreditation Program, 41–42
Collision-induced dissociation (CID), 182–184
Color test
   anti-inflammatory drugs, 442–443
   lysergic acid diethylamide (LSD), 384
   postmortem toxicology, 8, 12
   spectrophotometry, 117
Column packings, 140–141
Columns, 107. *See also* Wall-coated open tubular
     (WCOT) column
   efficiency, 124–125, 129
   high-performance liquid chromatography, *141*
   homemade, 107
   liquid chromatography, 122
   on-off, 107–108
   packings, 140–141
   wall-coated open tubular (WCOT), 122,
     126–127, 133, 134, 136, 137
Commercial preparatory columns, 107
Committee on Alcohol and Other Drugs, 233
Competitive binding process, 149–151, 168
Compound identification, 188
Concentration-time curves, of ethanol, 215
Confirmation techniques, 9. *See also*
     Chromatography; Forensic drug testing;
     Immunoassays; Postmortem clinical testing
Congeners, 208

Conway cell, 448, 456
Correlation coefficient (r), *147*, 194
Covariance (r^2), 194
COX-1, 441
COX-2, 441, 443, 445
Crack, 294
Cross-reactants, in immunoassays, *154*, *155*
Cross-reactivity, 166, 168, 288
Cryofocusing, 347
Custody and control form (CCF), 35
Cutoffs, 164, 166–167, 168
   concentrations and reporting requirements, *36*
   performance-enhancing drug testing and, 52,
     55, 56
   Substance Abuse and Mental Health Services
     Administration (SAMHSA) proposed, *517*,
     518
Cyanide, 453–454, 459–460
   analysis, 456
   concentrations, *458*
   disposition, *455*
   fire-related deaths, 458–459
   in industry, 454
   pathophysiology, 454–455
   poisoning and autopsy findings, 456–458
   storage and stability, 459
Cyanide, 99
Cyclizine, *436*
Cyclobenzaprine, *267*, 268
Cyclohexanols, 274. *See also specific drugs*
Cyproheptadine, *436*
Cytochrome c oxidase, 454–455
Cytochrome P450, 81, 212, 418, 425, *427*
   antidepressants and, 418
   benzodiazepine and, 244
   mutations, 508–509
Cytochrome P450-1A2, 427
Cytochrome P450-C19, 512
Cytochrome P450-2C9, 509
Cytochrome P450-2D6, 418–419, 427, 509,
   511, 512
Cytochrome P450-2E1, 216, 222
Cytochrome P450-2SD6, 73–74
Cytochrome P450-3A, 427, 509
Cytochrome P450-3A2, 427
Cytochrome P450-3A4 (CYP3A4), 66, 212, 427,
   511
   benzodiazepine and, 245

Data set, chromatography, *148*
Data systems, gas chromatography, 137–138
DDT-proteolytic extraction method, 519
Death investigation, 4–5. *See also specific*
     toxicology types

Decongestant, 358
Dehydration, 503–504
Delirium, 305
Delta-9-tetrahydrocannabinol (THC), 317–319, 318, 329–330. *See also* Cannabis
    concentrations, 324–325, 332–333
    confirmation, 346–348
    measurement, 338–343
    mechanisms of action, 318–319
    postmortem redistribution, 499, 500
Department of Defense (DoD), 357–358
Department of Transportation (DOT), 32–33, 233–234
Depressant. *See* Central nervous system (CNS) depressants
Depression, 403. *See also* Antidepressants
Derivatization, 189
Dermal absorption, 78
Dermal exposure, cocaine, 310
Desethylamiodarone, 499, 500
Desipramine, 404, 408
Desmethylsertraline, 419
Detectors
    chromatography, 135–137
    high-performance liquid chromatography, 142, 142–144
    spectrophotometry, 114–115
Detoxification, opioid, 276–278
Detropropoxyphene, 499, 500
Diabetes mellitus, 504–505
Diabetic ketoacidosis, 504
Diazepam, 88, 239, 240, 241, 242, 246, 297
Dibenzoxazepines, 422
Digoxin, 89, 499, 500
Dihydrocodeine, 273, 274, 277, 281, 282, 283
Dihydroindoles, 422, 423
Di-hydroxy alcohol, 205. *See also* Ethylene glycol
Diltiazem, 400, 402
Dimethylamyl amine (DMAA), 196
Diode-array detector, 116, 143
Diodes, 116–117
Diphenhydramine, 436, 438
Diphenylamine, 117
Diphenylbutylpiperidines, 422
Direct-exposure probe, 172–173
Direct-insertion probe, 172
Disopyramide, 399, 400
Dissociative anesthetic, 374
Distribution
    of alcohol in the body, 210–212, 212
    of cannabis in the body, 329
    of opioids, 280
    of substances through body, 79–80
Diuretics, 50, 54, 56

Dopamine (DA), 295–296, 355
Dopamine D2 receptors, 427, 428
Dothiepin, 499, 500
Double-beam spectrophotometer, 116
Doxepin, 404, 408, 415, 511
Dragendorff's reagent, 303–304
Driving impairment, cannabis, 322–325. *See also* Driving under the influence (DUI)
Driving under the influence (DUI)
    alcohol and, 17. *See also* Alcohol, driving and
    cannabis and, 231–232, 232
    cocaine and, 312–314
Drug class effects, 24
Drug efficacy, therapeutic, 391
Drug Evaluation and Classification (DEC) program, 22
Drug interactions
    opioids, 281–282
    therapeutic, 392
Drug intoxications, postmortem forensic toxicology, 4
Drug recognition evaluation, 23
Drug recognition experts (DREs), 22
Drug screening tests, 12. *See also specific tests*
Drug targets, 510
Drug testing methodologies, 54
    in pain management, 70–71
    in the workplace, 233–234
Drug testing. *See also* Drug testing methodologies; Drug testing, in pain management; Forensic drug testing; pain; Performance-enhancing drug testing; *specific tests*
    cannabis, 343–346
    implementation, 65–66
    interpretation, 72–73
    methodology, 70–71
    in pain management, 66–69, 67, 68
    pharmacogenetic, 73–74
    point of care, 71–72
    rationale for, 64–65
    reporting, 73
    specimens, 66, 69–70
Drug use. *See also* Forensic drug testing
    cost of, 33–34
    regulation of, 32–33
Drug-facilitated sexual assault, 254–256
Drug-metabolizing enzymes, 508, 508–509. *See also specific enzymes*
Drugs. *See also* Pharmacokinetics; *specific drugs*
    acidic, 105
    alcohol and, 22–27
    basic (pH), 105
    compartmentalization of, 84–86, 85

pain management and, 63–64, 66–69, 67, 68
polar, 106
in postmortem toxicology, 12, 13–14
psychotropic, 293. See also Antidepressants;
    Neuroleptics (Antipsychotics)
Drug-use regulations, 31–33
Duloxetine, 407, 408, 412, 415
Dystonia, 429–430

Ecgonine methyl ester (EME), 299, 301, 303, 304,
    489–491
Edema, 4
Efficiency, in immunology, 168
Electrochemical detector, 143
Electrochemical oxidation, breath alcohol
    analysis, 228–229
Electromagnetic radiation, 111–112, 112
Electron Ionization (EI), 174, 183, 384
Electrospray ionization (ESI), 177–179, 178, 183
Electrospray technique, 143–144
Elimination kinetics, 84–86
Elimination. See Excretion
Elution chromatography, 130
Encainide, 400, 400–401
Endocrine effects, of neuroleptics, 429
Enzymatic oxidation, 224
Enzyme-binding, 81
Enzyme-linked immunosorbent assay (ELISA),
    162, 162–163, 168, 195
    amphetamines, 364
    cocaine analysis, 303
    hair specimen analysis, 520
    meconium, 528
Enzyme-multiplied immunoassay technique
    (EMIT®), 157–158, 158, 168, 195
    cocaine and, 310
    -dau, 362–363
    meconium, 528
    opioids and, 288
Enzymes. See Drug-metabolizing enzymes;
    specific enzymes
Ephedrine (EPH), 354–355
Epilepsy, 393
Erythropoetin (EPO), 57
Esoteric isolation techniques, 109
EtG, 213, 230, 522
Ethylene glycol, 206, 218–219
Ethanol, 9–10, 205, 206. See also Alcohol;
    Ethanol analysis
    analysis, 5, 9–11
    concentration-time curves, 215
    effects of, 219–223, 212
    functional tolerance, 223
    meconium analysis, 530–531

stability in specimens, 229–230, 491–492
as a volatile liquid, 99–100
Ethanol wash, 518
Ethchlorvynol, 267, 268–269
Ethosuximide, 394, 395
Ethyl glucuronide (EtG), 213, 230, 522
Ethyl sulfate, 213, 230
Ethylcocaine, 299–300
EtS, 230
Excretion
    of cannabis, 330–332
    of cocaine, 302, 308–309
    of cyanide, 455
    lysergic acid diethylamide (LSD), 383
    of opioids, 280
    xenobiotics, 82–84
Extraction efficiency, 195, 199
Extrapyramidal effects, of neuroleptics, 429–430

Facilitated diffusion, 77
Famotidine, 439
Fatigue, 358
Felbamate, 396
Fentanyl, 273, 275, 277, 281, 282, 283–284
    case study, 511
    metabolism, 509
    postmortem redistribution, 497, 498, 499, 500
Fermentation, 207–208
Fexofenadine, 438
Fire deaths, 11
Fire-related deaths, 452, 458–459
First-generation antidepressants, 403, 404–405.
    See also Antidepressants
First-pass effect, 82
First-pass metabolism (FPM), 217
5-HT, 296, 369
    antidepressants and, 403–404, 405–406, 407
5-HT receptors, 427–428
Flame ionization detector (FID), 135–136, 136
    chloral hydrate analysis, 268
    ethanol analysis, 225
Flecainide, 399–400, 400, 500
Flecanide, 499
4-MAX, 359, 369
Flow injection analysis (FIA), 178–179
Flumazenil, 246, 246–247
Flunitrazepam, 239, 241, 243
Fluorescence, 118, 118–120, 119
    enzyme oxidation and, 224
    meconium, 528
Fluorescence detector, 143
Fluorescence polarization immunoassay (FPIA),
    158–159, 159, 168, 195
    cocaine and, 310

Fluorometry, of neuroleptics, 431
Fluoxetine, *406*, *408*, 410
   case study, 511
   toxicity and, 419
Fluphenazine, *423*, 431
Flurazepam, *239*, *241*, 247
Fluvoxamine, *406*, *408*, 410, *411*, *415*
Forensic drug testing. *See also* Postmortem
     forensic toxicology; *specific drugs*
   accreditation/certification, 41–42
   criminal justice system, 31
   methodologies, 35–38
   military, 31
   private sector, 33
   process, 34–35, 41, 42
   public sector, 31–33
   quality control, 38–40
   review and reporting, 40–41, *36*
   specimens, 42–46
   status in the United States, 33–34
Forensic toxicology
   analytical processing, 6–9
   blood, 5
   bile, 5
   case types, 4
   death investigation, 4–5
   drug testing standards, 32–37
   drugs, 12–13
   ethanol analysis, 5, 10–11
   history, 3–4
   identification techniques, 8–9
   liver, 5–6
   organ tissue, 5–6
   pharmacokinetics, 86–92. *See also*
     Pharmacokinetics
   specimen receipt and accessioning, 6
   spectrophotometry applications, 117–118
   urine, 5
   vitreous humor, 5
Freebasing, 294
Freon, 464
Fuel cell technology, 228–229
Full-scan analysis monitor, 184
Full-scan impact mass spectra, *265*
Functional tolerance, ethanol, 223

Gabapentin, *396*, 396–397
Gamma-aminobutyric acid (GABA), 258–259,
   395, *396*, 397
Gamma-aminobutyric acid (GABA) antagonist,
   243
Gamma-aminobutyric acid (GABA) receptors,
   243
Gamma butyrolactone (GBL), 258

Gamma-hydroxybutyric acid (GHB), *253*
   analytical methods, 258
   chemical synonyms and street names, *255–256*
   drug-facilitated sexual assault, 254–256
   effects, 256–257
   interpretation, 258–260
   pharmacokinetics, 257
   synthesis and metabolism, 254, 257, *258*
   use and abuse, 253–254
Gas chromatograph, 189, *264*
Gas chromatography (GC), 130–132. *See also*
     Gas chromatography/mass spectrometry
     (GC/MS); Gas-liquid chromatography
   antidepressants, 414–415
   barbiturates and, 263
   benzodiazepines and, 248–249
   carbon monoxide (CO) and, 448
   cocaine and, 304
   cyanide and, 456
   ethanol analysis and, 8, 9, 229
   injectors, 132–135, *133*, *134*
   mass spectrometry and, 173
   method validation and, 197, 200
   opioids and, 288
   performance-enhancing drug testing and, 56
Gas chromatography/mass spectrometry
     (GC/MS), 37
   amphetamines and, 365, *366*, 366–367
   anabolic agents and, 53
   antidepressants and, 415
   cannabinoids and, 57, 341, 343, 344, 346, 347, 348
   diuretics and, 56
   phencyclidine (PCP) and, 378–379
   stimulants and, 55; 2D, 347
Gas, 98–99, 130–131
Gas-liquid chromatography, 225–226, *226*.
     See also Flame ionization detector (FID);
     Gas chromatography (GC); Liquid
     chromatography (LC)
Gas phase sampling, 98–99
Gastrointestinal (GI) tract
   alcohol effects on, 209–210, 220
   antihistamine and, 435, 439
   cocaine and, 302
   hallucinogens and, 375, 385, 388
   narcotic analgesics and, 441, 443–444, 445
   opioids and, 272, 276, *278*, 280
Gaussian distribution, *147*
Generalized seizures, 394
Genetics, 507–508. *See also* Pharmacogenomics
Gestational drug-exposure monitoring, *526–527*
Glomerular filtration rate (GFR), 83–84
Glucocoticosteroids, *50*, *54*, 58
Glutethimide, *267*, 269

Glycogen storage diseases, 505
Gradient elution, 142
Graphite furnace atomic absorption
    spectrometry (GFAAS), 481–482
Gutzeit test, 482

H₁ antagonists, 435–438, *436*
H₂ antagonists, *438*, 439, 439–440
Hair, 515–516; *517*
    cannabis testing and, 341–343
    cocaine testing and, 311
    color and racial bias, 522
    confirmation, *521*, 521–522
    drug testing and, 42, 43–44
    ethyl glucuronide, 522
    future testing direction, 522–523
    gestational drug-exposure, *526*
    opioid testing and, 290
    sample collection, 518
    structure and compound incorporation, 516
    testing guidelines, *517*, 517–518, *518*
Halazepam, *239*
Half-life, of antidepressants, 410
Hallucination. *See* Hallucinogens
Hallucinogens, 25, 371–372
    abuse, 381–382
    analysis, 383–384, 385–386, 387, 388
    effects, 382–383, 385, 388
    ketamine, *387*, 387–389
    lysergic acid diethylamide (LSD), *381*, 381–384
    mechanism of action, 382
    mescaline, *384*, 384–386
    pharmacokinetics, 383, 385, 387–388
    phencyclidine, *372*, 372–381, *373*, *377*
    psilocybin and psilocin, 386–387
Haloperidol, *424*, 425, 499, *500*
Hapten, 168
Heart
    alcohol, 210–211
    anticonvulsants and, 398
    antihistamine and, 435, 438
    cannabis and rate increase, 320, 321, 325–326
    cocaine and, 272, 297, 306, 307
    cyanide and, 455
    hallucinogens and, 380, 388
    neuroleptics and rate increase, 431
    opioids and rate increase, 276, *279*
Heart blood, 308, 439, 496, 497
Heart disease, 297, 306
Height equivalent to a theoretical plate (HETP),
    125
Helium, as a carrier gas, 130
Hematologic effects, of neuroleptics, 429
Hemoglobin (Hb), 11, 447, 505

Henderson-Hasselback equation, *78*, 79
Henry's law, 99
Hepatic excretion, 83
Hepatic metabolism, 416, *415*, 525
Heroin, 271, *273*, *274*, *281*, *282*, 284, 289
    hair specimen analysis, 515, *521*
    specimen stability, 492
Heterogeneous immunoassay, 168
High-performance liquid chromatography
    (HPLC), 8, 122, 138–144
    antidepressants and, 415
    barbiturate and, 263–264
    mass spectrometry and, 56
    neuroleptics and, 432
    phencyclidine (PCP) and, 378
    reciprocating pump, *139*
    solvents, 139
High-performance liquid chromatography/mass
    spectrometry (HPLC/MS), 56
Histamine, 435. *See also* Antihistamine
Homemade columns, 107
Homogeneous immunoassay, 168
Horizontal gaze nystagmus (HGN) test, 20
Human chorionic gonadotropin (hGH), 57–58
Human growth hormone (hGH), 57–58
Human performance toxicology
    alcohol, driving and, 16–22
    application, 16
    behavioral effects of alcohol, 20–21
    defined, 15–16
    drugs, driving and, 22–27
    history, 16–19
    laboratory testing, 27–29
    specific drugs, 24–27
    standardized field sobriety tests, 19–20
Human performance, opioid influence, *280*
Hyaluronic acid (HA), 502
Hydrochloride salts, 103, 104
Hydrocodone, 64, *273*, *274*, 277, *281*, *282*, 284
Hydrogen cyanide (HCN), 130, 453–454, 456
Hydromorphone, *273*, *274*, 277, *281*, *282*, 284–285
Hydroxyzine, *436*, 438
Hypoalbuminemia, 245

Ibuprofen, *444*
Imipramine, *404*, 408, *409*, *415*
Immunoassays (IA), 8–9, 35–36, 168. *See also* Cloned
    enzyme donor immunoassay (CEDIA®);
    Enzyme-linked immunosorbent assay
    (ELISA); Enzyme-multiplied immunoassay
    technique (EMIT®); Fluorescence
    polarization immunoassay (FPIA); Kinetic
    interaction of microparticles in solution
    (KIMS®); Radioimmunoassay (RIA)

Immunoassays (*continued*)
  amphetamines, 362–364
  antibodies, 151–155, *152, 153*
  applications, 164
  barbiturates, 264
  cannabis, 335, 344–345
  cocaine, 302–303
  competitive binding process, 149–151
  cutoffs, 164–165
  drug testing, in pain management, 70–71
  hair specimen analysis, 520
  meconium, 528
  opioids, 288
  performance-enhancing drug testing, 56, 57–58
  problems, 165–167
  quality control, 163
  specific techniques, 155–163
  spectrophotometry, 118
  therapeutic drugs, 393
Immunogen, *152*, 168
Immunoglobulin (Ig), 151
Indomethacin, *443, 444*
Inductively coupled plasma–mass spectrometry, 482
Inflammation, 441. *See also* Anti-inflammatory drugs
Infrared (IR) spectrophotometry: breath alcohol analysis and, 228
Infrared detector (IRD), 135, 137
Inhalant abuse, 461–463
Inhalants, 26–27, 461–462
  analysis, 465–466
  common, 463–465
  interpretation, 466–468
  pharmacology, 462–463
  retention time, *467*
Inhalation absorption, 77, 327–328
Injectors
  chromatography, 132–135, *133, 134*
  high-performance liquid chromatography, 140
Insomnia, treatment, 242
Instrument configuration, 115–117. *See also* Chromatograph; Mass analyzer; Mass spectrometer
  spectrophotometry, 115–117
  UV absorption and, 113–117
Inter-assay repeatability, 195
Interfaces, 194
Internal standard, 194
Intoxication
  anticonvulsants and, 392
  antidepressants and, 419
  antihistamine and, 438
  benzodiazepines and, 243, 247, 250

carbon monoxide (CO) and, 451, 452, 453
central nervous system (CNS) depressants and, 264
cyanide and, 458
inhalants and, 463
metals and, 474, 480
opioids and treatment, 272, 276–277
pharmacogenomics and, 510, 511, 512
phencyclidine (PCP) and, 376–377, 379, 380
Intra-assay repeatability, 195
Intramuscular absorption, 77
Intranasal absorption, 78
Intrathecal absorption, 78
Intravenous absorption, 77
Intravenous administration, 387–388
Ion enhancement, 195
Ion suppression, 195, 199–200
Ion trap, *185*, 185–186
Ionization, 173–184, *180, 181. See also specific methods*
  technique, 200
Ion-molecule reactions, 175
Iron, 474–475, *475*
Isopropanol, *206*, 207
Isotope ration mass spectrometry (IRMS), 55

Ketamine, *387*, 387–389
Ketorolac, *443, 444*
Kidney. *See also* Renal excretion
  alcohol and, 207, 211, *212*, 214, 219, 221
  benzodiazepines and, 245
  cannabinoids and, 57
  hallucinogens and, 374
  inhalants and, 462, 465
  metals and, 472, 474, 475–476, 478, 480
  opioids and, 280, 285, 287
Kinetic interaction of microparticles in solution (KIMS®), *161*, 161–162, 168, 195, 363

Labeled compounds, 155
Laboratory performance testing, 27–29
Lambert's law, 112–113
Lamotrigine, *396*, 397
Lead, 477–480, *479*
Least-squares straight line, 146–147, *147*
Legal and regulatory aspects, of alcohol, *231*, 231–235, *232*
Levetiracetam, *396*, 397
Levorphanol, *273, 275, 277, 281, 282*, 285
Lidocaine, 399, *400*
Limit of detection (LOD), 39, 168, 194, 198
Limit of quantitation (LOQ), 135, 194, 198
Linear range, 135
Linearity, 39, 196, 198

Liquid chromatography (LC), 121, 122. *See also* High-performance liquid chromatography (HPLC); Liquid chromatography/mass spectrometry interfaces
  amphetamines and, 366–367
  benzodiazepines and, 249
  cocaine and, 304–305
  mass spectrometry and, 173
  method validation and, 197, 199–200
Liquid chromatography/mass spectrometry interfaces, 143–144, 176, 529
Liquid-liquid extraction, 8
  of cocaine, 303
  drug distribution, 105–106; pH, 102–104
  lysergic acid diethylamide (LSD), 384
  solvent selection, 101–102
Lithium, 476–474
Liver, 508, 512. *See also specific enzymes*; Hepatic excretion
  alcohol and, 212, 213, 217, 218, 219, 222
  anticonvulsants and, 395, 396, 399
  antidepressants and, 417, 418, 419
  antihistamine and, 439
  barbiturate metabolism in, 263
  benzodiazepine metabolism in, 244
  central nervous system (CNS) depressants and, 263
  cocaine and, 299, 300, 301, 303
  gamma-hydroxybutyric acid (GHB), 257
  hallucinogens and, 374, 376, 380, 381, 383, 385
  inhalants and, 465
  narcotic analgesics and, 442, 445, 446
  neuroleptics and, 425, 426
  opioids and, 280, 284, 285, 287
  postmortem collection, 5–6
  postmortem redistribution, 497, 499, 500
Logit B/B$_0$, 168
Loratadine, *438*
Lorazepam, *239*, *241*, 247
LSD. *See* Lysergic acid diethylamide (LSD)
Lung tissue, 6
Lysergic acid diethylamide (LSD), 25, 381–384
Lysosomal storage diseases, 505

Magnetic resonance imagine (MRI), 482–483
Magnetic sector instrument, 184
Maprotiline, *405*, *408*
Marijuana. *See* Cannabis
Masking agents, *50*, *54*, 56
Mass analyzer, 184–188. *See also* Mass spectrometer
Mass spectrometer, 137, 143–144, 171–172, *172*
  application, 189–190
  direct-insertion probe, 172–173

  gas chromatography, 173
  liquid chromatography, 173
  See also Mass analyzer
Mass spectrometry (MS), 171–172. *See also* Gas chromatography/mass spectrometry (GC/MS); Mass analyzer; Mass spectrometer
  anabolic agents and, 54
  applications, 188–191
  cocaine and, 304
  drug testing, in pain management and, 71
  ionization, 173–184, *178*, *180*, *181*
  method validation and, 197, 201
  narcotic analgesics and, 57
  opioids and, 288
  stimulants and, 55
McReynolds constants, 131, 132
MDA. *See* 3,4-Methylenedioxyamphetamine (MDA)
MDMA. *See* 3,4-Methylenedioxymethamphetamine (MDMA)
Mean, 147
Meclizine, *436*
Meclofenamate, *444*
Meconium, 525, 531
  as a cocaine specimen, 312
  common drugs and metabolites analyzed, 529
  drug analysis, 528–529, *529*
  drug disposition, 525, 528
  interpretation, 530–531
Medium-chain acyl-coenzyme A dehydrogenase (MCAD) deficiency, 505–506
Mefenamic acid, *443*, *444*
Meloxicam, *444*
Memory, 320
Meperidine, *273*, *275*, *277*, *281*, *282*, 285
Meprobamate, 266
Mercury, 475–476
Mescaline, *384*, 384–386
Mesoridazine, 431
Metabolic effects, of ethanol, 219–220
Metabolism. *See also specific analytes*
  of antidepressants, 407–412, *408*, *409*, *410*, *411*, *412*
  of cannabis, 329–330
  of cocaine, 297–300, *298*
  of opioids, 280, *282*
  therapeutic drugs and, 392
  xenobiotic, 80–82, *81*, *82*
Metabolites
  parent to- ratio, *91*
  performance-enhancing drug testing and, 52, 53
  specimen stability, 492

Metals
  aluminum, 471–472
  analysis, 481–483
  arsenic, 472–474
  individual determination, 482, 483
  iron, 474–475, *475*
  lead, 477–480, *479*
  lithium, 476–474;
  mercury, 475–476
  thallium, 480
  treatment of poisoning, 480–481
Metaxalone, *267*, 269
Methadone, *273*, *275*, *277*, 277–278, *281*, *282*, 285
  case study, 511
  metabolism, 509
Methamphetamine, 353–354. *See also*
    Amphetamines
  abuse, 358
  blood concentration and, *92*
  effects, 35
  hair specimen analysis, 516, *521*
  immunoassays and, 166
  mass spectrometry and, *189*
  metabolism, *361*
  pharmacokinetics, 360
Methanol, *206*, 207, 218–219
Methanol wash, 518
Methaqualone, 268, 269
Methcathione derivatives, 360
Methemoglobin (MetHb), 11
Method validation, 193–195. *See also* Quality
    control
  chromatographic, 197–200
  immunoassays, 195–197
  mass spectrometric, 201
Methxetamine, 388–389
Methyl diethanolamine (MDEA), 520
3,4-Methylenedioxyamphetamine (MDA), 25,
    355
  abuse, 358–369
  effects of, 357
  hair specimen analysis, 521
  postmortem redistribution, 499, *500*
3,4-Methylenedioxymethamphetamine
    (MDMA), 25, 167, 355
  abuse, 358–360
  effects of, 357
  hair specimen analysis, 520
  pharmacokinetics, 362
  postmortem redistribution, 499, *500*
Methylphenidate, 56
Mexiletine, 399, *400*
M-hydroxybenzoylecgonine (mOHBE), 529
Michaelis-Menten equation, 216

Micro-diffusion screening test, 11
Micro ethanol oxidizing system (MEOS), 212
Microdiffusion separation, cyanide, 456
Midazolam, *239*, *241*, 243
Military forensic drug testing, 31
Minimum detectable quantity (MDQ), 135
Mirtazapine, *407*, *408*, 411–412, *415*, 416
  toxicity and, 419
Mixed-agonist antagonist, 64
Monoclonal antiserum, 168
Monochromatic radiation, 112
Monoclonal antibodies, *153*, 153–154
Mono-hydroxy alcohol, 205
Morphinans, 274. *See also specific drugs*
Morphine, *273*, *274*, 277, *281*, *282*, 285–286, 289, 290
  benzodiazepine and, 249–250
  pH of, 103
  gas chromatography/mass spectrometry
    (GC/MS) and, 37
  hair specimen analysis, 520
Mortality
  carbon monoxide (CO) and, 449–451, 453
  cyanide and, 458–459, 460
  neuroleptics and, 431
Motor performance tests, 28–29
MRO review, 40–41
MS/MS analysis, *186*, 186–187, 197–198. *See also*
    Mass spectrometer; Mass spectrometry
  amphetamines and, 366
Multiple mass spectrometer (MSn), 186
Multipoint calibration, 146

N-acetyl-*p*-benzoquinone (NAPQI), 445–446
NADH/NAD$^+$ ratio, 219–220
NADPH, 81
Nails, 42
Nalbuphine, 271, *273*, *274*, 277, *281*, *282*, 286
Naloxone, 277
Naproxen, *443*, *444*
Narcotic analgesics 26, 56–57, 284. *See also*
    Opiates
National Highway Traffic Safety Administration
    (NHTSA), 17, 18, 19, 22
National Institute on Drug Abuse (NIDA), 32
National Laboratory Certification Program
    (NLCP), 41
National Safety Council, 233
Natural death, 4
Nefazodone, *407*, *408*, 410–411, *413*, *415*, 419
Negative controls, 194
Negative-ion chemical ionization (NICI), 175–176
Neonatal drug exposure, *526–527*. *See also*
    Meconium
Neurodepressant, 256

Neuroleptic malignant syndrome, 430–431
Neuroleptic radioreceptor assay, 432
Neuroleptics (Antipsychotics)
    absorption, 423–424, 425
    adverse reactions, 428–431
    analysis, 431–432
    chemistry, 421–423, 423, 425–426
    concentration, 433
    distribution in the body, 423–424
    elimination, 424–425, 425–427, 427
    interpretation, 432–433
    mechanism of action, 427–428
Neurologic side effects, of neuroleptics, 429
Neutron activation analysis (NAA), 482
Nicotine adenine dinucleotide (NAD), 118, 224
Nicotine adenine dinucleotide hydrogen
        (NADH), 118, 157, 158, 224
Nicotine, 531
Nifedipine, 400, 402
Nitrazepam, 239, 241
Nitrogen-phosphorus detector, 136
Nizatidine, 439
N-methyl-D-aspartate (NMDA), 374
Nonnarcotic analgesics
    acetaminophen, 445–446
    anti-inflammatory drugs, 441–445
Nonneurologic side effects, of neuroleptics,
        428–429
Nonopioid analgesics, 63
Nonpharmacologic treatment, pain, 62–64
Nonsteroidal anti-inflammatory drugs, 443
Nordiazepam, 88
Norpropoxyphene, 103
Nortriptyline, 404, 408, 415, 419
n-Propanol, 206

Ocular absorption, 78
O-desmethylvenlafaxine (ODV), 410, 415
Olanzapine, 426, 427
11-OH-THC, 330, 332
    confirmation, 346–347
    measurement, 338, 339, 344
    specimen stability, 488
On-off columns, 107–108
Opiates, 26, 50, 54. See also Narcotic analgesics;
        Opioids; Opioid analgesics; specific drugs
    benzodiazepine and, 242
    gas chromatography/mass spectrometry
        (GC/MS) and, 37–38
    hair specimen analysis, 520
    metabolism, 68
    in pain management, 63–64, 67
Opioid abstinence syndrome, 279
Opioids. See also Opiates

analgesics, 63–64, 284
analysis, 287–289
chemistry and mechanisms of action, 271–275,
        273, 274, 275, 276
interpretation, 289–290
metabolism, 280, 282, 509
overdose treatment, 279
pharmacokinetics, 280–287, 281, 282. See also
        specific drugs
polar, 287–288
receptors, 72
use and effects, 275–280, 277, 278, 279, 280
Oral absorption, 77, 78
    amphetamines, 367–368
    cannabis, 328–329, 343
    cyanide, 455
Oral fluid
    cannabis testing and, 338–340, 339
    cocaine testing and, 311–312
    drug testing and, 45–46
    gestational drug-exposure, 526
Organ tissue, postmortem collection, 5
Organic acidemia, 506
Organic drug separation, 104
Oromucosal absorption, 329
Orthostatic (postural) hypotension, 429
Overdose, 509, 510
    antidepressant, 416, 417–419
    phencyclidine (PCP), 380
    therapeutic drug, 392–393
Oxazepam, 239, 241
Oxcarbazepine, 396, 397
Oxycodone, 64, 273, 274, 277, 281, 282, 286;
        case study, 510–511
Oxymorphone, 273, 274, 277, 281, 282, 286–287

Packed-column injectors, 133
Packing particle, 141–142
Pain, 441. See also Drug testing, in pain
        management; Nonnarcotic analgesics; Opioids
    acute, 62
    chronic, 62, 275–276, 283
    physiology, 61–62
    treatment, 62–64, 275–276, 283
Paliperidone, 427
Paper chromatography (PC), 129
Parkinsonism, of neuroleptics, 430
Paroxetine, 406, 408, 410, 411, 415, 419
Partial seizures, 394
Passive inhalation, cannabis, 343
Pathophysiology
    carbon monoxide (CO), 447–448
    cyanide, 454–455
Patient compliance: therapeutic drugs, 391, 393

PCP-abuse syndrome, 377
Pentazocine, *273, 276, 277, 281, 282,* 287
Peptide hormones, *50, 54,* 57–58
Perceptual errors, 324
Perceptual performance tasks, 28
Performance impairment, 16–27. *See also*
    Alcohol; Drugs
Performance testing, 27–29
Performance-enhancing drug testing, 49–51, 59
    drugs and drug classes, 52–59, *53, 54*
    fatality, 55
    testing approach, 51–52
Performance-enhancing drugs, 52–59, *53, 54*
Periperal anticholinergic effects, of neuroleptics,
    429
Peripheral blood, 496, 497
P-glycoprotein (P-gp), 510
pH
    absorption and, 78
    adjustment prior to extraction, 102–104
    distribution of drugs and, 79
    electrospray ionization and, 177–178
Pharmacodynamics, 77. *See also*
    Pharmacokinetics
Pharmacogenetic testing, in pain management,
    73–74
Pharmacogenomics, 507–508, 512
    drug-metabolizing enzymes, *508,* 508–509
    drug targets, 510
    CYP2C9, 509
    CYP2D6, 509, 511, 512
    CYP3A, 509
    in forensic toxicology, 510–512
    transport proteins, 509–510
Pharmacokinetics
    absorption, 77–79, *78*
    alcohol related, 215–217, *216*
    amphetamines, 360–362
    antidepressants, 407–412
    antihistamines, 437
    anti-inflammatory drugs, 442, 443
    applications to forensic toxicology, 86–92
    barbiturates, 262–263
    benzodiazepines, 243–244
    case histories, 88–92
    cocaine, 297–298
    compartmentalization of drugs, 84–86, *85*
    defined, 77
    distribution, 78–79
    elimination kinetics, 84–86
    excretion, 82–84
    gamma-hydroxybutyric acid (GHB), 257
    inhalants, 462–463
    ketamine, 387–388

lysergic acid diethylamide (LSD), 383
mescaline, 385
metabolism, 80–82, *81, 82*
opioids, 280–287
phencyclidine (PCP), 375–376, 379–380
postmortem redistribution, 495
Pharmacologic treatment, pain, 62–64
Pharmocology
    cocaine, 295–297
    psilocybin and psilocin, 386–387
Phenanthrenes, 274. *See also specific drugs*
Phenazepam, 247
Phencyclidine (PCP), 25–26, 372–381
    hair specimen analysis, 515, *521*
    intoxication, 376–377, 379, 380
    specimen stability, 492
Phenobarbital, 264–265, *394,* 395
Phenol, *276*
Phenothioazines, 422, *423*
Phenotype, 507, 509
Phenyl-2-propanone (P2P), 354
Phenylheptylamines, 274, *275. See also specific*
    drugs
Phenylketonuria, 506
Phenylpiperidines, 274, *275. See also specific drugs*
Phenylpropanolamine (PPA), 354
Phenytoin, *394,* 395
Photon transducer, 115
Photovoltaic cell, 115
Physiological effects, lysergic acid diethylamide
    (LSD), 382
Piroxicam, *443, 444*
Placenta, *527*
Planar chromatography, 128–130
Plasma cannabinoid concentrations, 332–333
Plasma concentrations, cocaine, 300–302, 306–307
Plasma protein binding, 79–80
Point-of-care testing (POCT), 71–72
Poison, 3–4, *4*
Poisoning
    carbon monoxide (CO), 449–451
    cyanide, 456–457
    historical, 3
    metal, 480–481. *See also specific metals*
Polar drugs, 106, 108, 287–288. *See also*
    Benzoylecgonine
Polar molecules, 175
Polar opioids, 287–288
Polarity, 132
Polyclonal antiserum, 153
Poly-hydroxy alcohol, 205
Polymorphisms, 510
Positive controls, 194
Positive-ion chemical ionization (PCI), 175, *183*

Postmortem clinical testing
  anaphylaxis, 502–503
  carbon monoxide (CO) poisoning, 451
  dehydration, 503–504
  diabetes mellitus, 504–505
  metabolic disorders, 505–506
  specimens, 501–502. *See also specific specimens*
  therapeutic drug concentration, 392–393
  thyroid function, 506
Postmortem redistribution
  concentrations, *496, 498*
  antidepressant, 417
  defined, 496
  drug characteristics suggesting, 498
  drugs displaying, 498–499, *500*
  physiological processes causing, 497–498
  role of toxicologists, *499,* 499–500
Prazepam, *239*
Precision, 194, 195–196, 199
Predictive methods, cannabis use, *333,* 333–335, *334*
Primidone, *394,* 395
Private sector forensic drug testing, 33, 42
Probenecid, 56
Procainamide, 399, *401*
Proficiency testing, 41
Promethazine, *436, 438*
Propoxyphene, *273, 277, 281, 282,* 287
  postmortem redistribution, 499, *500*
Propranolol, *401*
Protein precipitation, 7, 100–101
Protriptyline, *404,* 408, *415*
Prussic acid, 458
Pseudoephedrine (PE), 354, 358
Psilocybin and psilocin, 25, *386,* 386–387
Psychiatric disturbance, 296, 305
Psychiatric drugs, 421. *See also* Neuroleptics (Antipsychotics)
Psychoactive drugs, 317, 358, 392. *See also* Neuroleptics (Antipsychotics)
Psychological effects, lysergic acid diethylamide (LSD), 382
Psychomotor tasks, 27–29
Psychomotor tests, 19–20
Psychotropic drug, 293
Pulmonary congestion, 4
Pulse rate
  cannabis and, 27
  central nervous system (CNS) depressants and, 24
  central nervous system (CNS) stimulants and, 25
  hallucinogens and, 25

inhalants and, 26
  phencyclidine (PCP) and, 24
Pulverization, 519
Pupil size
  cannabis, 27
  central nervous system (CNS) depressants and, 24
  central nervous system (CNS) stimulants and, 25
  drug recognition evaluation (DRE) and, 23
  hallucinogens and, 25
  phencyclidine (PCP), 26
Pyrilamine, *436*
Pyrrolidine, 397

Quaalude. *See* Methaqualone
Quadrupole mass spectrometer, 184–186, *185*
Qualifications, 9
Quality control. *See also* Method validation
  forensic drug testing and, 38–40
  immunoassays and, 163
  performance-enhancing drug testing and, 52
Quantitation, chromatography, 144–148
Quetiapine, 426, *427,* 499, *500*
Quinidine, 389–399, *401*

Race bias, 522
Radiative energy attunement (REA), 224
Radioimmunoassay (RIA), 149–151, 156, 195
  hair specimens and, 515–516
  meconium, 528
  neuroleptics and, 432
Ranitidine, *439*
Rape, 254–256
Rayleigh limit, 177
Reaction time, 29
Real-life task, 27, 28
Recovery, 195
Rectal absorption, 78
Reinsch test, 482
Relative retention time (rrt), 127
Renal excretion, 83–84
Renal tubular acidosis, 463
Repeatability, 195, 196
Reporting, 13, 73
Resolution, 124, 125
Retention index (RI), 127
Retention time, amphetamines, 365
Risperidone, 422, 426, *427*
Roadside Testing Assessment studies (ROSITA), 338–339
Robustness, 195

Salicylate, *442*
Saliva
    cannabis testing and, 338–340, *339*
    cocaine testing and, 311–312
    drug testing and, 45–46
    opioid testing and, 290
    phencyclidine (PCP) testing and, 379
Sample Acquisition Card (SAC), 518
Sample cell, 114
Sample destructive, 135
Sample preparation, cocaine, 303
Sampling techniques, 109. *See also specific*
    techniques
Schizophrenia, 421, 422. *See also* Neuroleptics
    (Antipsychotics)
Secobarbital, 90
Second-generation antidepressants, *405. See also*
    Antidepressants
Seizures, 377–378, 393–394. *See also*
    Anticonvulsants
    overdose and, 416
    treatment, 242, 264
Selected ion monitoring (SIM), 184–185
Selective serotonin reuptake inhibitors, (SSRI),
    63, 405–406, *406*
    metabolism, 410
    toxicity, 418–419
Selectivity, 124
Self-reporting, maternal, 530
Sensitivity, 135, 169
Separation number (TZ). *See* Trennzahl
Separation. *See also* Chromatography; Columns;
    Liquid-liquid extraction; Solid phase
    extraction
    chiral, 367
    high-performance liquid chromatography,
    140–142
Serotonin-norepinephrine reuptake inhibitor
    (SNRI), 63
Serotonin syndrome, 418
Sertindole, 422, *427*
Sertraline, *406, 408, 415*, 419
Sexual assault, drug-facilitated, 254–256
Silica, 128
Single-beam spectrophotometer, *115, 116*
Single-point calibration, 146
Smoke inhalation, 452. *See also* Fire-related
    deaths
Smoked administration, 375. *See also* Carbon
    monoxide (CO); Inhalants; *specific drugs*
    amphetamine and, 358, 360, 368
    cannabis and, 318, 319–348
    cocaine, 294, 295, 297, 300, 302, 306, 307, 313
    hallucinogens and, 375, 376, 380, 387

oral administration, 46
Society of Hair Testing (SoHT), 517
Solid-phase extraction (SPE), 8, 106, 107–109
    of antidepressants, 413–414
    of cocaine, 303
Solid-phase microextraction (SPME), 109
Solubility, 78, 98
Solvent
    drug interactions, *103*, 106
    extracting utility, *102*
    in high-performance liquid chromatography,
    139
    selection, 101–102
Sotalol, 499, *500*
Specificity, 39, 195, 196
    antibody, 154
    chromatograph detector, 135
    in immunology, 169
Specimen collection, in pain management,
    69–70
Specimen validity tests, 36–37
Specimens, 487. *See also* Forensic drug testing,
    methodologies; *specific specimens*;
    Specimen collection
    acquisition, 5–6, 69–70
    adulterated, 43
    alcohol tests and, 21–22
    choice, 86–87
    chromatograph injection, 134
    cocaine detection and, 302–303, 306–312
    digestion, 101
    drug tests and, 23–24, 34–35, 42–46
    immunoassays method validation and, 197
    neonatal fluid and tissue, *526–527*
    opioid detection, 289–290
    performance-enhancing drug testing, 51
    postmortem forensic testing, 501–502
    preparation, 97–109
    receipt and accessioning, 6
Spectrophotometer, *115*, 115–117, *119. See also*
    specific spectrophotometers; Stability, in
    specimens
Spectrophotometry, 8–9. *See also* Mass
    spectrophotometry; MS/MS analysis
    carbon monoxide (CO) and, 449
    fluorescence, 118–120, *119*
    ultraviolet-visible, 111–118
Speedballing, 90–91
Spleen tissue, 6
Splitless injection, 134
Split-specimen collections, 51
Stability, 195, 107
Stability, in specimens
    barbiturates, 487

benzodiazepines, 487–488
cannabinoids, 488–489
cocaine, 489–491
ethanol, 491–492
heroin, 492
metabolites, 492
phencyclidine (PCP), 492
Standard deviation, 147
Stas-Otto method, 3
Stationary phase, chromatography, 131
Sternbach, Leo, 237
Steroid alternative, 253
Steroids, *50, 53*, 53–55, *54*
Stimulants. *See* central nervous system (CNS)
    stimulants
    storage and stability
    carbon monoxide (CO); 452–453
    cyanide, 459
Subjective tests, 29
Substance Abuse and Mental Healthy Service
    Administration (SAMHSA), 340–341, 517,
    517, 518
Succinic semi-aldehyde (SSA), 258–259
Sufentanil, 284
Sulindac, *443, 444*
Supported liquid extraction, 109
Surface area, absorption and, 78
Sweat
    cannabis testing and, 340–341, *341*
    cocaine testing and, 312
    drug testing and, 44–45
    gestational drug-exposure, *526*
    opioid testing and, 290
    phencyclidine (PCP) testing and, 379
Sympathetic nervous system, 353
Sympathomimetic amines, 353, *356*, 356–357,
    364. *See also* Amphetamines; Ephedrine
    (EPH); Phenylpropanolamine (PPA);
    Pseudoephedrine (PE)
Synthetic cannabinoids, *50, 54*, 57
System suitability check, 195
Systems suitability test, 200

T, 59. *See also* T/E ratio
T/E ratio, 54–55
Tapentadol, *273, 276, 277, 281, 282*, 287
Tardive dyskinesia, 430
Temazepam, *239*, 247
Tertiary alcohols, 207
Thallium, 480
THC. *See* Delta-9-tetrahydrocannabinol (THC)
THCCOOH, 43, 328, 329, 330, 332–336
    confirmation, 346–348
    half-lives of, 331–332

measurement, 339–343
    specimen stability, 488–489
Therapeutic drug conversion, 370
Therapeutic drug monitoring, 391–393
    analytical methods, 393
    anticonvulsants, *394*, 394–398, *396*
    antidepressants, 408
    seizures, 393–394
Therapeutic drugs. *See* Antiarrhythmics;
    Anticonvulsants; Antidepressants;
    Antihistamines; Neuroleptics
    (Antipsychotics)
Therapeutic ranges, antidepressant, 408
Therapeutic serum antipsychotic drug
    concentration, *433*
Therionic detector, 136
Thermospray (TSP), 179
Thin-layer chromatography (TLC), 128–129
    amphetamines and, 364–365
    cannabis and, 344
    cocaine and, 303–304
Thiopurine-S-methyl transferase (TPMT),
    507–508
Thioridazine, *423*, 423–424, 424–425, 499, *500*
Thioxanthenes, 422, *423*
Third-generation antidepressants, 406–407, *407.*
    See also Antidepressants
Time of flight (TOF), 187
Titer, 169
tNSAIDs, 441, 443
Tolerance. *See also specific drugs*
    cannabis, 325–326
    ethanol, 222–223
Tolmetin, *443, 444*
Toluene, 463–464
Topical local anesthetic, 293–294, 295
Topiramate, *396*, 397
Toxicology request form, 7
Traffic accidents, 205
Traffic safety legislation, 17–19
Tramadol, *273, 276, 277, 281, 282, 287*
Transport proteins, 509–510
Trazodone, *405, 408*, 410, *415*, 417
Trennzahl, 127–128
Triazolam, *239, 241*, 243
Trichloroethanol, 267
Trichloroethylene, 464
Tricyclic antidepressants (TCAs), 63, 403, 404–
    405. *See also* Antidepressants
    metabolism, *408*, 409
    postmortem redistribution of, *496*, 499–500,
    500
    toxicity, 416–418
    tri-hydroxy alcohol, 205

Trimipramine, *404*, 408
Tripelennamine, *436*, *438*
Tryptase, 503
Tswett, Michael S., 121–122
Two-dimensional gas chromatography, 138
Typical antipsychotic drugs, 423–425

Ultraviolet (UV) detector, 143
Ultraviolet (UV) spectrophotometry, 8, 111–118, 263
Umbilical cord blood and tissue, *527*
Unclassified seizures, 394
Underivatization, 191
Uniform Vehicle Code, 231–232
Upper limit of linearity (ULOL), 194, 198
Urinary albumin concentration (UAC), 214, 215
Urine, 24, 34, 36
    adulterants in, *157*
    alcohol analysis, 214–215
    barbiturates analysis, 264
    benzodiazepines analysis, 248
    cannabis analysis, 335–338
    cocaine analysis, 308–310
    drug testing, 42, 43
    drug testing, in pain management, 66
    ethanol analysis, 10, 229–230
    gamma-hydroxybutyric acid (GHB) analysis, 259
    gestational drug-exposure, *526*
    immunoassay quality control, 163
    inhalant analysis, 465, 468

opioids analysis, 289–290
performance-enhancing drug testing, 51, 52
postmortem collection, 5, 6
specimen stability, 490, 491–492

Valproic acid, *394*, 395
Van Deemter equation, 125–126
Venlafaxine, *407*, *408*, 410, *412*, *415*
Verapamil, *401*, 401–402
Vigabatrin, *396*, 397–398
Vitreous humor, 5, 501–502, *502*, 504
Vitreous urea nitrogen values, 4
Volatile liquids, 99–100
Volatile organic compounds (VOCs), 461.
    See also Inhalants

Walk and turn (WAT) test, 19–20
Wall-coated open tubular (WCOT)-column, 122, 126–127
Wavelength selectors, 114
Wet-chemical oxidation, 224
Widmark equation, 217–218
Workplace intoxication. *See* Alcohol, in the workplace

Yalow, Rosalyn, 149

Zaleplon, *268*, 269–270
Ziprasidone, 422, 425, *427*
Zolpidem, 268, *270*
Zopiclone, *268*, 270
Zotepine, *427*